VARIORUM COLLECTED STUDIES SERIES

Concord and Reform

Professor Morimichi Watanabe

Morimichi Watanabe

Concord and Reform

Nicholas of Cusa and Legal and Political Thought in the Fifteenth Century

Edited by Thomas M. Izbicki
and Gerald Christianson

Ashgate

VARIORUM

Aldershot · Burlington USA · Singapore · Sydney

Published in the Variorum Collected Studies Series by

Ashgate Publishing Limited
Gower House, Croft Road,
Aldershot, Hampshire GU11 3HR
Great Britain

Ashgate Publishing Company
131 Main Street,
Burlington, Vermont 05401–5600
USA

Ashgate website: http://www.ashgate.com

ISBN 0–86078–850–4

British Library Cataloguing-in-Publication Data
Watanabe, Morichimi
    Concord and Reform: Nicholas of Cusa and Legal and Political Thought in
    the Fifteenth Century. – (Variorum Collected Studies Series CS709).
    1. Nicholas of Cusa, Cardinal, 1401–1464. 2. Political Science – Philosophy.
    3. Law – Philosophy. I. Title. II. Izbicki, Thomas M. III. Christianson, Gerald
    320'011

US Library of Congress Cataloging-in-Publication Data
Watanabe, Morichimi, 1925–
    Concord and Reform: Nicholas of Cusa and Legal and Political Thought in
    the Fifteenth Century / Morichimi Watanabe; edited by Thomas M. Izbicki
    and Gerald Christianson.
        p.   cm. – (Variorum Collected Studies Series CS709).
    Includes bibliographical references.
    1. Nicholas of Cusa, Cardinal, 1401–1464. 2. Catholic Church – Government –
    History. I. Izbicki, Thomas M. II. Christianson, Gerald. III. Title. IV. Collected
    Studies: CS709
    BX4705.N58W38 2001
    282'.092–dc21   00–054300

Printed in Great Britain by St Edmundsbury Press Limited,
Bury St Edmunds, Suffolk

VARIORUM COLLECTED STUDIES SERIES CS709

Contents

PART THREE
CUSANUS' CONTEMPORARIES

Sources of Articles

"The Lawyer in an Age of Political and Religious Confusion" (An address delivered on the occasion of the twentieth anniversary of C.W. Post College of Long Island University, May 9, 1975).

"Humanism, Law and Reform: Reflections on Fifteenth-Century Lawyers," *Ventures in Research,* Series 8-1979 (1981): 7-35.

"The Origins of Modern Cusanus Research in Germany and the Establishment of the Heidelberg *Opera omnia,*" in *Nicholas of Cusa in Search of God and Wisdom,* ed. Gerald Christianson and Thomas M. Izbicki (Leiden, 1991): 17-42.

"Authority and Consent in Church Government: Panormitanus, Aeneas Sylvius, Cusanus," *Journal of the History of Ideas* 33 (1972): 217-236.

"The Episcopal Election of 1430 in Trier and Nicholas of Cusa," *Church History* 39 (1970): 299-316.

"Nicholas of Cusa, the Council of Florence and the *Acceptatio* of Mainz (1439)," in *The Divine Life, Light, and Love: Euntes in mundum universum: Festschrift in Honour of Petro B.T. Bilaniuk,* ed. Renate Pillinger and Erich Renhart (Graz, 1992): 137-147.

"The German Church Shortly Before the Reformation: Nicolaus Cusanus and the Veneration of the Bleeding Hosts at Wilsnack" in *Reform and Renewal in the Middle Ages and the Renaissance: Studies in Honor of Louis Pascoe,* ed. Thomas M. Izbicki and Christopher M. Bellitto (Leiden, 2000): 210-223.

"Nicholas of Cusa and the Tyrolese Monasteries: Reform and Resistance" in *The Politics of Fallen Man: Essays Presented to Herbert A. Deane* (Exeter, 1986): 53-72; also in *History of Political Thought* (1986): 53-72.

"Nicolaus Cusanus, Monastic Reform in the Tyrol and the *De visione Dei"* in *Concordia Discors: Studi su Niccolò Cusano e l'umanesimo europeo offerti a Giovanni Santinello* (Padua, 1993): 181-197.

"Nicholas of Cusa and the Reform of the Roman Curia," in *Humanity and Divinity in Renaissance and Reformation: Essays in Honor of Charles*

Trinkaus, ed. John W. O'Malley, Thomas M. Izbicki and Gerald Christianson (Leiden, 1993): 185-203.

"Nicholas of Cusa, *A General Reform of the Church"* (with Thomas M. Izbicki), in *Nicholas of Cusa on Christ and the Church: Essays in Memory of Chandler McCuskey Brooks for The American Cusanus Society,* ed. Gerald Christianson and Thomas M. Izbicki (Leiden, 1996): 175-202.

"Nicholas of Cusa and the Idea of Tolerance," in *Nicolò Cusano agli inizi del mondo moderno* (Firenze, 1970): 409-418.

"Nicholas of Cusa—Richard Fleming—Thomas Livingston," *Mitteilungen und Forschungsbeiträge der Cusanus-Gesellschaft* 6 (1967): 167-177.

"Humanism in the Tyrol: Aeneas Sylvius, Duke Sigismund and Gregor Heimburg," *Journal of Medieval and Renaissance Studies* 4 (1974): 177-202.

"Gregor Heimburg and Early Humanism in Germany," in *Philosophy and Humanism: Renaissance Essays in Honor of Paul Oskar Kristeller,* ed. Edward P. Mahoney (Leiden, 1976): 406-422.

"Duke Sigismund and Gregor Heimburg," in *Festschrift Nikolaus Grass zum 60. Geburtstag:* Vol. I, *Abendländische und deutsche Rechtsgeschichte, Geschichte und Recht der Kirche, Geschichte und Recht Österreichs,* ed. L. Carlen and F. Steinegger (Innsbruck, 1974): 559-573.

"Imperial Reform in the Mid-Fifteenth Century: Gregor Heimburg and Martin Mair," *Journal of Medieval and Renaissance Studies* 9 (1979): 209-235.

Acknowledgements

After Morimichi Watanabe recovered from a lengthy illness, including a significant period of time in the hospital, the American Cusanus Society, over which he has presided for many years and for which he has edited its remarkable *Newsletter,* met during the 34th annual Congress on Medieval Studies at Western Michigan University in Kalamazoo and enthusiastically approved two measures to celebrate the President's homecoming. First, it organized a session in his honor at the following Congress in May, 2000, for which the featured speaker was Manfred Meiner whose firm, Meiner Verlag, has had a long and distinguished career in publishing philosophical and scientific works, among them the works of Nicholas of Cusa. Watanabe himself was also asked to comment on the current state of Cusanus studies in America as a follow-up to his important paper on the origins of Cusanus research that appears in this volume.

The Society also acted to republish Watanabe's scholarly essays on Nicholas and his contemporaries in the context of late medieval legal and political thought. One might wonder why we chose such a volume rather than a *Festschrift,* but Mori already received this honor as he approached his 64th birthday when we published *Nicholas of Cusa in Search of God and Wisdom: Essays in Honor of Morimichi Watanabe by the American Cusanus Society,* ed. Gerald Christianson and Thomas M. Izbicki (Leiden: E.J. Brill, 1991).

We are especially grateful to John Smedley and Ashgate Publishing Limited for accepting our proposal for a volume that allows Mori to speak in his own voice. From our previous collaboration with Mr Smedley and Ashgate on the essays of F. Edward Cranz entitled *Nicholas of Cusa and the Renaissance,* ed. Thomas M. Izbicki and Gerald Christianson (Aldershot: Ashgate/Variorum, 2000), we have come to respect his many contributions to scholarship in general, and appreciate both his helpful suggestions and genuine good will in bringing this new project to fulfillment. We also extend our thanks to the original publishers of these essays for their kind permission to reprint them in this form.

We have depended on Kim Breighner of Gettysburg College to handle the tasks related to computer-generated, camera-ready manuscripts for so many years and through so many previous works that we have simply run out of ways to express our gratitude . . . except to say thank you!

Because Francis Oakley, former President of Williams College, remains (we say without hesitation) the dean of "silver age" conciliar thought as well as a significant contributor to sessions of the American Cusanus Society, the Introduction offers a two-fold gift, both a personal tribute to our honoree and a lively context for his contributions to the field.

Those who have worked with Mori Watanabe over the years know intimately how much his life and multifaceted career owes to the care and companionship of his wife, Kiyomi Watanabe. Because she is a distinguished scientist and scholar in her own right, she can approach her husband's work, and that of his colleagues in the Cusanus Society, with patience, encouragement, understanding, and a genial spirit.

Yet it is to the man himself—scholar, organizer, editor, and widely traveled spokesman for Cusanus studies on three continents—that we owe our deepest gratitude. He has not only moved the Society into the 21st century, but the essays contained in this volume are ready proof that he himself helped to shape the field. As a Japanese-born scholar who has done research in Germany and spent his career in the United States, he has become an extraordinary ambassador between East and West. If Cusanus himself were to write a tribute, he might say that Morimichi Watanabe is living proof of the *coincidentia oppositorum* who expresses the unfolding grace that enfolds us all. We, on the other hand, can do no better than to observe that when Mori landed on our shores and was prompted to take an interest in Nicholas of Cusa, we all became the beneficiaries of a gracious visitation from the "father of lights."

Thomas M. Izbicki
Gerald Christianson

Preface

Why study Nicholas of Cusa (1401-1464)? What are the ideas of the fifteenth-century philosopher, theologian and church statesman that are of lasting importance? To some readers, a more basic question may be: who was Nicholas of Cusa? In 2001, the year of the 600th anniversary of the birth of Cusanus, there will be commemorative congresses in several countries and many publications on his life, his thought and his time will appear. As a result, the number of people who know about Cusanus will undoubtedly increase. Probably another question in the minds of some readers might be why the author of the present book from an Asian country became interested in Cusanus and involved in the pursuit of his ideas and the promotion of Cusanus studies.

Born as the second son of a Protestant pastor in the capital of a rural province in northern Japan, I grew up through the primary and secondary educational stages without any strong religious discrimination or pressure from the outside. My father had been converted to Christianity from Buddhism by a German Reformed missionary. My maternal grandfather had become a Christian after the fall of the Tokugawa Shogunate in 1867 as a result of meeting a Dutch Reformed missionary. His three sons all became pastors, and his two daughters, the older of whom was my mother, both married pastors. Naturally, as I grew up, I was aware that all of my classmates were not Christians and that as a "yaso" (Christian), my behavior and conduct were under subtle observation.

In my father's library at home, I was able to see from childhood such classic Christian books as St. Augustine's *City of God* and his *Confessions,* Martin Luther's important works, John Calvin's *Institutes of the Christian Religion* and Bible commentaries. In addition to many Japanese books, his library also contained not only the works of Confucius, Mo Tzu, Lao Tzu and other Eastern writers, but also those of many Western writers such as Dante, Shakespeare, Pascal, Nietzsche, Tolstoy, Dostoevski, and Thomas Mann, although I began to take a serious look at some of them only in later years. Living in the region which was sometimes called "the Scotland of Japan" in the geographical and confessional sense by some Japanese Christians, my father had a fairly large number of works by Abraham Kuyper (1837-1920), Dutch Calvinist theologian; Peter Taylor Forsyth (1848-1921), Congregationalist theologian from Aberdeen whose books published after the radical change of his views from liberal theology to a "redemptionist" one in 1901 were popular among many "Calvinist" preachers in Japan; Rudolf Otto (1869-1937), author of the famous book, *The Idea of the Holy* (1917); Karl Barth (1886-1968), the noted Swiss theologian and author of *The Epistle to the Romans* (1919), and other theological writers.

Even while studying at a preparatory "higher" school in preparation for my university education, I began to have some doubts about the neat tripartite division of Western history into the exuberant Ancient Times, the dark Middle Ages, and the progressive Modern Times after the brilliant Renaissance and the revolutionary Reformation. It was not really my Protestant background and upbringing, but a strong sense of doubt about oversimplifying the complex historical processes and perhaps an intellectual curiosity about the medieval times that led me to pay an increasingly greater attention to the Middle Ages. How could there be a dark period that lasted over one thousand years? Was it true that the Catholic Church controlled everything in the Middle Ages?

There were two pieces of advice I received in the initial stages of my university education which profoundly affected my decision to choose the future direction of my life: my father's and Professor Sakae Wagatsuma's. In essence, my father's advice was that, although I had done very well academically, I would find many brighter students at the Law School of the University of Tokyo which I had entered, and that if I wanted to do something well and excel in it, I should choose an area of specialization that was not sought by many. Professor Wagatsuma, one of the most famous and distinguished professors in the Law School at that time, stated in his opening lecture: "Gentlemen, dig a well!" I do not know how some 200 students in the class, which did not include a single female student because of official restrictions, reacted to a startling remark from the mouth of the renowned authority on Civil Law. But his message was clear enough to me that, unlike wide and shallow ponds that might dry up, a deep well has a constant source of supply.

All in all, I found the procedural aspects of jurisprudence uninteresting and even boring. Discussions on Administrative Law, Civil and Criminal Procedures, and even International Law were the less attractive divisions of law to me. Instead, Legal Philosophy, Criminal Law and its philosophy and Political Theory were the areas that occupied and excited my mind. In essence, what interested me was the relationship between Law and Politics. A great regret I still have is that, since I was in the Political Science section of the Law School, I did not study Roman Law.

Even in the years after the attack on Pearl Harbor, many students at the University of Tokyo were not really captives of ultra-nationalism. Although under increasingly heavy pressure from the Right, we could talk about Beethoven, Hemingway, Voltaire and others after class. It was during this time that I read *A Study of Medieval Political Thought* (Tokyo, 1932) by Professor Toyohiko Hori. I was surprised that a book with such a theme could be written and published by a reputable scholar in contemporary Japan. It convinced me that this was a field of study I should pursue and that I should direct my academic studies towards it. Probably my father's advice was still ringing in my ears. Who among the young students in those days in Japan wanted to choose medieval political thought as a field of study? Naturally, I later took Professor Hori's Political Theory course with great profit.

Of the main medieval political thinkers whom Professor Hori discussed in his book and lectures, such as St Augustine, St Thomas Aquinas and Marsilius of Padua, I was particularly interested in and intrigued by Marsilius. It is not that I was completely familiar with the political ideas of the former two who were undoubtedly two of the greatest medieval thinkers, but that Marsilius' ideas were new, fresh and even disturbing to me. That he had been condemned as a heretic was no hindrance to my academic curiosity and pursuit.

During my two years at Princeton University as a graduate student, with Political Theory and Comparative Government as my major fields of specialization, I learned a great deal about the United States, American academic life and other related matters, but it is difficult to say that I found special stimuli to the study of Political Theory. The professor who taught Political Theory was a gracious, friendly and well-known John Locke specialist, but he provided little material for me to advance my own interest in medieval political thought. It was also difficult to take courses outside the Department of Politics because of the rather inflexible programs required of the students in the Department.

After returning to Japan, I taught for two years at a college in Tokyo. Then continuing my graduate study at Columbia University after marriage in New York, I found greater opportunities to roam around various departments and to receive support and understanding from sympathetic, supportive professors in many fields. When I registered in Latin Palaeography, Professor W.T.H. Jackson, Professor of German and History, was understandably surprised to see me in class, but encouraged and helped me a great deal. Later, when I decided to write an M.A. thesis on Marsilius of Padua, Professor Herbert A. Deane, whose graduate seminar on the *City of God* of St Augustine in the Political Science Department I had taken, told me to go to Professor Dino Bigongiari of the Italian Department who was known as one of the best scholars on St Thomas Aquinas. His knowledge and understanding of Thomas was such that there were rumors around the campus that when discussions turned to the 'Angelic Doctor' at a Columbia University Seminar, of which he was a member, he could stop the discussion by quoting directly from Thomas in Latin in response to other members' remarks about whatever Thomistic ideas were at issue at the time.

What Professor Bigongiari thought of an Asian graduate student who approached him with a proposal to write on a heretical medieval political thinker is not known to me. But he was courteous, sympathetic and very helpful. My first major academic endeavor in America to write a respectable M.A. thesis benefitted greatly from his vast knowledge about things medieval and willing-ness to support a novice in the field. The thesis on "Marsilius of Padua and Natural Law" was completed with his kind support and help. I record with gratitude that after his death in 1965 Mrs Bigongiari gave me one of his books: Thomas Aquinas' *Summa contra gentiles,* which still occupies a special place in my library.

One of the courses I had taken at the beginning of my graduate studies was "Europe in Transition, 1400-1700" taught by Professor Garrett Mattingly of the History Department. He had published *Catherine of Aragon* in 1941 and *Renaissance Diplomacy* in 1955 and was reported to be working on his next book, *The Armada* (Boston, 1959), which was, unlike in the U.S., published as *The Defeat of the Spanish Armada* in Britain. In class, he told us from time to time about his archival searches for the book and the difficulties he encountered. Discussing Machiavelli not only as a political theorist, but also as a diplomat, he surprised some of us with the statement, "Even Niccolò Machiavelli was not 'Machiavellian'," the theme which he developed in a much discussed article, under the title "Machiavelli's Prince: Political Science or Political Satire," which was published in the *American Scholar*, 27 (1958): 482-491 .

To fulfil the requirements for his course, Professor Mattingly gave us a choice: either take a long final examination at the end of the semester or submit three essays during the semester. Fearful that I should be in a far inferior position to other students in the class when taking the final examination in a language which was not my mother tongue, I opted for the second choice and worked very hard. The three papers I wrote for him were "The Development of the Reformed Church in the Palatinate under the Elector Frederick III: An Inquiry into the Influence of Calvinism in Germany," "Daniel Elzevir's Participation in the Amsterdam Branch of the Elzevir Press" and "The Influence of the Platonist Doctrines on Nicholas of Cusa," to which, to my relief, he assigned good grades. It was after the end of the semester that I went to see Professor Mattingly to seek his further comments on the papers. He had kind and encouraging words on them and pointed out especially that I should think of developing the third essay into a Ph.D. dissertation, an idea which had never occurred to me. I was grateful to him that I now had a possible direction to follow in my advanced studies.

I had come to Nicholas of Cusa by way of Marsilius of Padua. In my readings for the papers, I learned that in his early book, *De concordantia catholica,* Cusanus used some of Marsilius' ideas without indicating who their author was. No matter what the reasons were for Cusanus' failure to indicate his sources, here was a fifteenth-century philosopher, theologian and political theorist whom, with Professor Mattingly's encouragement, I could study. "Dig a well."

As my Doktorvater, Professor Deane was as demanding, but unfailingly supportive of my efforts as he had been in his graduate seminar. When the Ph.D. dissertation on "The Political Ideas of Nicholas of Cusa" was submitted to my dissertation committee, it was Professor Paul O. Kristeller of the Philosophy Department who, as second reader, read it most carefully and commented extensively on the basis of his unsurpassed understanding and knowledge of the philosophical and intellectual tradition of the West.

How have I been studying Nicholas of Cusa since that time and why? As many of the articles in the present book indicate, it is clear that because of my intellectual and academic background, I have tended to focus primarily on the political and legal ideas of Nicholas of Cusa. Cusanus as a political and legal thinker and, in this connection, his activities as reformer of the Church and the Empire have occupied my attention over the years. It is not that the philosophical ideas of Cusanus did not interest me, but that because many who studied Cusanus were studying his philosophical ideas, I tended to take a route not followed by many.

This preference was supported by a strong desire to see Cusanus' life and thought as a whole, not concentrating on some aspects of them alone, but contributing to understand his ideas as broadly as possible and his life as widely and deeply as possible. In order not to make blunders about his life and times, I have visited as many places related to him as I could, from his birthplace, Kues, to his place of death, Todi, with in between such places as Heidelberg, Padua, Rome, Mainz, Nuremberg, Deventer and, in the Tyrol, Brixen (Bressanone), Sonnenberg, Wilten, Bruneck and Castle Andraz.

To acquire geographical and historical knowledge about the places related to the events in Cusanus' life, however, was easier than to overcome a doubt or, at least, an apprehension which I had had from the beginning of my serious engagement with Cusanus and his thought: can an Asian with a Protestant background really understand the fifteenth-century Catholic thinker in Europe? I remembered and admired the expression of modesty and even humility which Sir George B. Sansom, an outstanding British authority on Japanese history and author of a three-volume *A History of Japan* (Stanford, 1958-1961) made when he delivered a series of five lectures on "Japan in World History" at the University of Tokyo in 1950. In the presence of many Japanese scholars and historians, he stated: "I have come to deliver these lectures to show that Western scholars may be able to contribute somewhat to the research carried out by Japanese scholars. . . . But no foreign scholar can acquire the same kind of (historical) knowledge and the same depth of understanding that Japanese scholars can." It was at the same time easy for me to understand why Professor Donald Keene of Columbia University, a renowned scholar in the field of Japanese literature, often expressed feelings of irritation when he was told politely by some Japanese critics and commentators that Japanese literature and culture in general are so unique that it would be difficult for non-Japanese scholars really to understand them.

Despite these forewarnings, circumspections and "disadvantages" I had decided, as a young researcher, to embark on a quest for knowledge in the complicated field of Cusanus research on the bold premise that as a human being, not as an Asian, I might be able to understand the thought and action of another human being whose background was medieval and European. But as I continued my studies and read the works of such learned Cusanus specialists as Professor Erich Meuthen and Dr Hermann Hallauer, their mastery of not only the Western religious, philosophical and intellectual tradition, but also the ecclesiastical institutions and practices of the fifteenth century became increasingly so clear that I could not help thinking whether there was any possibility at all for me to work on the same level as them. The only sensible and important question I could ask was: what can I bring as an "outsider" to Cusanus studies that is worthwhile?

Since these specialists are so much part of the whole European tradition, and since they are so familiar with the detailed facts about the development of even local history and institutions, might they not sometimes fail to note or recognize certain important features or trends which those who come from the outside may be able to detect? Without this kind of hope, perhaps wishful thinking, it would have been very difficult to continue my research on the political and legal ideas of Nicholas of Cusa. The article on the origins of modern Cusanus research in Germany, which is in the present book, is an attempt on my part to see where we stood in terms of modern Cusanus research and to find an area or areas of research that I might find worth pursuing.

One of the main reasons why I turned to the study of Gregor Heimberg (ca.1400-1472), the sharpest critic of Cusanus and sometimes called the "greatest German lawyer of the fifteenth century," was that it was important to hear Heimberg if we were to understand Cusanus well. Why not listen to the severest critic of Cusanus? After all, I have often tried to understand other writers and theorists, such as Marsilius of Padua, Panormitanus and Martin Mair, in conjunction with or in comparison with Cusanus. Since Heimberg did not leave many writings which we can pore over in order to understand his ideas, it was only possible to trace his life and examine some of the brief writings and speeches he left. Just as in the case of Nicholas of Cusa, I visited many places related to Heimberg, from Schweinfurt, his birthplace, the University of Vienna, his *alma mater,* the University of Padua, where, like Cusanus, he studied law, Mantua, where he attended the Congress of Mantua in 1459, Wehlen near Dresden, where he died in 1472, and others. A practicing lawyer for the Empire, imperial cities, Duke Sigismund of the Tyrol, Cusanus' arch-enemy, George of Podebrady, the Hussite King, and others, Heimberg had quite a different career from that of Nicholas of Cusa. Unlike Cusanus, who changed his allegiance from the conciliar to the papal party, Heimberg remained a steady supporter of the Conciliar Movement. His main goal was to defend the Empire against the Papacy, a position which was clearly demonstrated when Pope Pius II, a close friend of Cusanus, condemned him as a heretic in 1460 and again in 1461.

What brought about the differences between the two lawyers, Cusanus and Heimberg, was an important question to examine. In the course of these examinations, it was necessary or almost inevitable for me to examine the role of the lawyer or the legal profession in the fifteenth century. Some of these reflections can also be found in Part I of the present book under "Law and Society."

In his famous book, *Nikolaus Cusanus* (Munich, 1964), Karl Jaspers stated that Nicholas of Cusa was great only as a metaphysician. But despite the assertion of the distinguished philosopher, we should not neglect to study and examine other aspects of Cusanus' life and ideas. If our grasp of the entire range of Cusanus' life and thought were to become securer, we would be able to come closer to having the total and more accurate image of Cusanus the man and the thinker. Personally, it has been a gratifying and rewarding experience to attempt to make contributions to the formation of such an image.

Throughout my academic career I have been blessed to have learned teachers and scholars who showed me which way to proceed or who with their tremendous knowledge of the Western past helped and encouraged me to work hard towards the goal of understanding medieval political thought and Nicholas of Cusa. In the field of Cusanus research, special mention must be made of Professor Erich Meuthen and Dr Hermann Hallauer who, understanding my difficulties and "disadvantages" mentioned above, encouraged and helped me over the years. It is hard to describe how assuring it has been to know that the present owners of the Felix Meiner Verlag of Hamburg, Mr Richard Meiner and Mr Manfred Meiner, would do all they can to help and support me in my attempts to advance Cusanus studies.

Since the establishment of the American Cusanus Society in this country in 1983, many colleagues in the Society have supported me directly or indirectly in my endeavors to promote Cusanus studies here and abroad. Two of these colleagues, Professor Gerald Christianson as Vice President and Dr Thomas M. Izbicki as Special Advisor, have been especially helpful to me in the administration and development of the Society. The present book itself owes its origins and formation to their initiative. I am greatly indebted to them for their arduous editorial work. Professor Francis Oakley kindly wrote an Introduction to the book. I am very grateful to him. I also wish to acknowledge here that Long Island University has encouraged and supported my research activities through various ways over the years.

For his acceptance of the book as a volume in the "Variorum Collected Studies Series," I wish to thank sincerely Mr John Smedley, Publisher of Ashgate Publishing Limited. In the preparation of the final manuscript for the press, Kim S. Breighner, our computer expert, provided indispensable help and service.

Morimichi Watanabe
October 14, 2000

Introduction

Francis Oakley

Morimichi Watanabe's lifelong service on three continents to the cause of Cusanus studies has involved an enduring engagement in matters organizational and a characteristically generous encouragement of other scholars—European and Japanese as well as North American—who share his own fascination with the life, works and times of Nicholas of Cusa (1401-1464), churchman, reformer, intellectual, one of the truly great luminaries of the later Middle Ages. But his service has extended beyond that to an equally distinguished and enduring commitment to research and writing in the field. And the studies gathered together in this fine and timely collection represent the ripe fruit of that commitment.

Appropriately enough, the third of these essays affords a compelling glimpse of the power of Cusanus's attraction, and of the extent of the fascination he has held for a diverse array of prominent intellectual figures in the nineteenth and twentieth centuries. Although its primary focus is on Cusanus research in Germany and on the star-crossed history of the great Heidelberg edition of the *Opera omnia,* it succeeds in conveying a vivid sense of the ecumenicity of Cusanus's appeal. Among those touched by it in the nineteenth century, it turns out, were people of as different interests and temperament as Pierre Duhem, the great pioneering historian of science, and the activist historian-theologians Johann Adam Möhler, Lord Acton and Karl Joseph Hefele—men who did so much to shape Catholic attitudes towards papal and conciliar authority in the decades leading up to the First Vatican Council of 1870. And, in the twentieth century, philosophers of the stature of Karl Jaspers, the existentialist, and the neo-Kantian, Ernst Cassirer, as well as Raymond Klibansky, the historian of philosophy, the classicist, Ernst Hoffman, and his friend at Heidelberg, Kugai Yamamoto, conceivably the first (though clearly not the last!) Cusanus scholar to hail from Japan.

The breadth of Cusanus's appeal would appear as even more striking if one were to factor in the worlds of Italian, Francophone and Anglophone scholarship. And that is, I believe, no accident. It is grounded in the complexity of his *persona* (lawyer and mystic, professor and publicist, reformer and curialist, pastor and politician), the reach of his intellectual interests (theological as well as legal, historical and humanistic no less than philosophical, scientific and mathematical), the range and incessant nature of his travels (from the Netherlands and Germany to Austria, Italy and Constantinople). Similarly, in the people with whom he was at one time or another associated (so many of whom were themselves major actors on the historical stage)—from Eugenius IV, Cardinal Cesarini and Aeneas Sylvius Piccolomini, to the convinced conciliarists, John of Segovia and Thomas Livingston, the mystic, Denys the Carthusian, and Cardinal Bessarion, the great Byzantine churchman. Or again, in the historic movements in which he participated: the revival of humanistic studies, the conciliarist drive for constitutionalist reform in church structures, the papally-sponsored effort at reform, if not in head at least in members. Or, yet again, in the great events with which his life and career intersected: the Councils of Basel and Ferrara-Florence, the negotiations with the Hussites and with the Orthodox Church, the Ottoman conquest of Constantinople and the concomitant threat to Latin Christendom, the great legatine reform mission of 1451-52. All in all, an extraordinary track-record established by a brilliant, committed and dynamic figure who appears to have thrived on the complex intersection in his life of the *vita activa* and *vita contemplativa*.

The essays that follow touch at one point or another, directly or indirectly, on all of these topics, people, movements and events. The two essays which make up Part I dwell in wide-ranging fashion on the study of law, on its intersection in the later Middle Ages with humanistic studies, and on lawyers and the importance of the role they played in the great religio-political movements and events of the era. Cusanus himself is the topic of all ten essays gathered together in Part II, with the five remaining essays, which make up Part III, reaching out to dwell also on such contemporaries as Thomas Livingston, Gregor Heimburg and Sigismund, Duke of Austria and Count of Tyrol, with whom, for good or ill, Cusanus interacted during the course of his richly-varied career. Linking them all, however, as the central and most persistent focus of concern, is Watanabe's preoccupation with the role Cusanus played at the fifteenth-century general councils, the conciliar movement that framed so much of their agenda, and the broad complex of ideas and commitments traditionally lumped together under the rather capacious heading of "conciliarism." Councils, conciliar movement, conciliarism, then, a few general observations on these related topics may serve to set an appropriate context for what follows.

By the year 1401, when Cusanus was born, the Latin Church had already groaned in travail for almost a quarter of a century under the burden created by the disputed papal election of 1378, by the establishment of rival lines of papal claimants each with their own territorial "obediences" centering, respectively, on Rome and Avignon, and by the demoralizing failure of repeated attempts, both military and diplomatic, to bring the schism thus engendered to an end. Thrust onto center stage, as a result, was the general council, the international institution with which Cusanus's public life was to be so intimately and persistently connected. If, by the time of his maturity, Latin Christendom had finally been reunited under a single, universally recognized, papal head, that happy result had been achieved only through the efforts of the Councils of Pisa (1409) and Constance (1414-18) and their ultimately successful claim to be able to stand in judgment over the rival pontiffs and, if need be, to depose them. That claim they had grounded in the historic decree *Haec sancta synodus* (1415), which asserted the jurisdictional superiority of council to pope in matters of faith, the ending of the schism, and reform of the Church in head and members. And they had attempted to give enduring constitutional expression to that jurisdictional superiority by mandating in the decree *Frequens* (1417) the assembly of future general councils at fixed and regular intervals. In accord with the provisions of that decree, Martin V had assembled the Council of Pavia-Siena (1423-24) and subsequently convoked the Council of Basel. That council had assembled in 1431 at the start of Engenius IV's pontificate, and it was destined, having first reaffirmed *Haec sancta* and proclaimed it to be nothing less than an article of the Catholic faith, to go on to judge and depose a pope the legitimacy of whose title was uncontested (Eugenius IV) and to elect another (Felix V) to serve in his place.

It was as one of the lawyers representing the antipapal cause of Ulrich of Manderscheid, unsuccessful claimant to the archbishopric of Trier, that Cusanus in 1432 was incorporated in the Council of Basel and in 1433 presented to that assembly his *De concordantia catholica*—regarded by common consent as the greatest of all the conciliarist treatises arguing for the superiority of council to pope. Five short but turbulent years later, however, chastened by the intemperance and mounting antipapalism of the conciliar majority at Basel, Cusanus abandoned the conciliarist cause and went on to lend such vigorous support to the propapal camp as to stimulate Aeneas Sylvius Piccolomini in 1439 to proclaim him memorably as the "Hercules of all the followers of Eugenius" (*Hercules Eugeniorum*).

As Watanabe indicates below, and at more than one point, this dramatic shift in allegiance on the part of Cusanus has served over the centuries to stimulate much criticism of the man himself, as well as a good deal of speculation concerning his motives. I would suggest, however, that at least one clue to an appropriately nuanced understanding of what that shift involved and of the ease with which it occurred is to be found in the complexity of the body of ideas to which the term "conciliarism" is usually attached. That complex of ideas was susceptible of many more variations than used commonly to be assumed—too many, certainly, and too elusive to trap within the simple formula of the superiority of council to pope. Indeed, it is only by dint of a salutary measure of simplification that one can claim to discern within conciliarism (as it emerged in the fifteenth century during its age of greatest prominence) three broad but central strands. These strands were distinct both in their origins and in their subsequent careers but, during the period dominated by the Councils of Pisa, Constance and Basel-Ferrara-Florence, they were woven momentarily and fatefully into a meaningful and historic pattern. It was around these three strands and this shared pattern of belief that the various conciliar thinkers, Cusanus himself included, constructed theories of differing dimensions and textures.

The first and most prominent of the three strands in question was not, in fact, the assertion of the superiority of council to pope. Instead, it was the demand for reform of the Church in its head no less than its members, as well as the belief that this reform could best be achieved and consolidated through the periodic assembly of general councils. Rooted in the defensive reaction of the provincial churches of Europe in the thirteenth century to the diminution of their authority by the remorseless progress of papal centralization, it had taken on a tone of greater hostility to papal jurisdictional pretensions in the demand for church-wide reform elicited by the assembly of the Council of Vienne in 1311 and in William Durand the Younger's call, at that time, for the future assembly of general councils at regular, ten-yearly intervals.

A comparable advocacy of conciliar leadership in the cause of reform is to be found in the thinking of most of the leading conciliarists later on—from Heinrich von Langenstein during the early years after the disputed election of 1378, via Pierre d'Ailly, Jean Gerson, Dietrich of Niem and Francesco Zabarella during the era of Pisa and Constance, to John of Segovia, Andrew of Escobar, Panormitanus and, of course, Cusanus at the Council of Basel. And although Constance officially endorsed that position by promulgating *Frequens,* a decree closely associated in the minds of its framers with *Haec sancta,* it should be noted that *Frequens* itself did not necessarily involve any assertion of the superiority of council to pope.

Nor did the second main strand in the conciliar thinking of the classical era. Given the fact that reform was most persistently conceived as reform of the Roman curia and the restriction of its authority over the universal Church, this second strand was understandably a less prominent one. It sought to give institutional expression to the Church's corporate nature by envisaging its constitution in quasi-oligarchic terms, its government ordinarily in the hands of the curia, the pope being limited in the exercise of his power by the cardinals, with whose "advice, consent, direction, and remembrance" he was obliged to rule. This vision of the Church's constitution was grounded both in the *de facto* share in the government of the universal Church that the college of cardinals had come to enjoy in the twelfth and thirteenth centuries and in the complex theories that such canonists as Hostiensis in the thirteenth century and Johannes Monachus in the fourteenth had developed to legitimate that role. They had done so by viewing the cardinals as constituting under the pope a corporate body in the technical legal sense, by applying to the pope in relation to his cardinals the same rules of corporation law as governed a bishop in relation to his cathedral chapter, and by suggesting accordingly that the pope, as corporate head, could not legitimately act on matters touching the "state" or well-being of the corporate whole without the consent of its members.

In 1378 the dissident cardinals were moved by this point of view when they rejected the demand for a general council and took it upon themselves to pass judgment on the validity of Urban VI's election, thereby precipitating the Great Schism. Those who were not members of the Sacred College, and who were already convinced that a general council was the proper forum for deciding so important a question, were understandably unimpressed, and one would look in vain for any trace of sympathy with such oligarchic ambitions in the writings of such early conciliarists as Konrad von Gelnhausen and Heinrich von Langenstein.

Only after the immediate circumstances of the original dispute had receded into history did it become possible for conciliar theorists to harmonize what had previously seemed dissonant, and to envisage a constitutional role in the governance of the universal Church for the college of cardinals as well as for the general council. In the era of Pisa and Constance, then, it was Cardinal Pierre d'Ailly (d. 1420) and Cardinal Francesco Zabarella (d. 1417) who did so, while in that of Basel, Denys the Carthusian and Cusanus himself. And if d'Ailly's formulation of this oligarchic strand was the more influential (both Denys and Cusanus were dependent on it),[1] it was Zabarella who, in his *Tractatus de schismate*, gave it the more coherent and legally precise formulation.

Although the pope is said to possess the fullness of power (*plenitudo potestatis*), he argued, that does not mean that he alone can do everything. The expression "apostolic see" does not refer simply to the pope but, rather, to the pope and cardinals, who together form a single body of which the pope is the head and the cardinals the members, with the latter possessing under certain circumstances the right to exercise the full corporate power. Thus, for example, and as was the case with the Council of Pisa, if, under the deplorable circumstances of schism the pope were to refuse to summon a general council, then that right would devolve upon the cardinals. Or again, during a vacancy, or even a "quasi-vacancy" when the pope could not effectively rule the Church, the cardinals would succeed to the full power of the Apostolic See. For they represent, after all, the universal Church and can act in its place.

This last sentiment (which was to be one Cusanus shared) was not uncommon at the time, and it helps explain how a thinker like Zabarella, though he stressed the supreme authority of the general council in the Church, could align himself also with the quasi-oligarchic strand that others saw as being in tension with conciliarist views. For it reflects the fact that if Zabarella (and, less

---

[1] Paul E. Sigmund, *Nicholas of Cusa and Medieval Political Thought* (Cambridge, Massachusetts, 1963), pp. 103-107, notes that the *Tractatus de potestate ecclesiastica,* the work in which d'Ailly developed these ideas, is listed as no. 165 in the library at Cues and that it is possible that Cusanus himself transcribed part of it.

clearly d'Ailly) saw the (local) Roman church or Apostolic See as itself a corporate body composed of pope and cardinals—with all that this may have implied constitutionally—they saw that Apostolic See also as itself the head, in turn, of a far greater corporate body, the universal Church, from which it derived its authority and the well-being of which it existed to promote. And that points, of course, to the third and most fundamental strand in the conciliarist position which, in order to avoid confusion, I will refer to as "the strict conciliar theory."

Whatever its subsequent encapsulations in subsequent centuries might suggest, this strict conciliar theory possessed during the classical era of Pisa, Constance and Basel no monolithic unity. Instead, it took a variety of forms, conditioned by the temperament, training, calling and capacity of the individual theorists, and by the ecclesiastical, political, and diplomatic circumstances under which they made their particular conciliar pronouncements. Common to all of them, however, Cusanus himself of course included, was the belief that the pope, however divinely-instituted his office, was not an absolute monarch or incapable of doctrinal error but in some sense a constitutional ruler and susceptible to correction; that he possessed a merely ministerial authority delegated to him by the community of the faithful for the good of the whole Church, which was itself the possessor of doctrinal indefectibility; that that community had not exhausted its inherent authority by the mere act of electing its ruler, but had retained, instead, whatever residual power was necessary to preserve the truth of the Christian faith and to prevent its own subversion or destruction; that it could exercise that power through its representatives assembled in general council, could do so in certain critical cases even against the wishes of the pope, and, in such cases, could proceed if need be to judge, chastise, and even depose him.

Even though, after his break with the conciliarist majority at Basel, Cusanus was still to attribute to the universal Church some sort of emergency power over an erring pope (or one that exceeded the limits of his authority), it is clear that he had, at that point, withdrawn his adhesion to the strict conciliar theory as such. It is also clear, however, that his adhesion to the other two strands in the classical conciliarist position remained unshaken by his transference of allegiance to the papal camp. The essays reprinted below indicate on his part a firm and enduring commitment to the view that the cardinals, as representatives of the several provinces of Christendom, possessed a constitutional role in the government of the universal Church. They also make it unambiguously clear that a commitment to reform of the Church—in its head no less than its members—was probably the central, enduring motif in Cusanus's public life, extending, as it did, not only to his conciliar efforts at Basel-Ferrara-Florence, but also via his legatine mission of 1451-1452 through Germany and the Netherlands, to his frustrating (and frustrated) reforming labors as Bishop of Brixen in the Tyrol. As also, in his final years when he served as *legatus urbis* at Rome, to the stubbornness of his insistence (he has been derided, after all, as "Dickkopf") on the need for reform in the church at Rome and in the papal curia itself.

That enduring passion for reform, as well as his sympathy with the oligarchic strand in conciliarism, found expression in the celebrated and impassioned outburst (cited more than once in the essays that follow) which Pius II records in his *Commentaries* and which had elicited from him a tart reminder to Cusanus that he was merely a cardinal, not the pope. Outraged by Pius's decision to create new cardinals without the consent of a majority of the Sacred College and in contravention, therefore, of decrees of the Council of Constance, Cusanus it seems, had blurted out to his papal master and long-standing friend:

> I do not know how to flatter. I hate adulation. If you can bear to hear the truth, I like nothing which goes on in this Curia. Everything is corrupt. No one does his duty. Neither you nor the cardinals have any care for the Church. What observance of the canons is there? What reverence for laws? What assiduity in divine worship? All are bent on ambition and avarice. If I ever speak in a consistory about reform, I am laughed at. I do no good here. Allow me to withdraw. I cannot endure these ways.[2]

---

[2] *Memoirs of a Renaissance Pope: The Commentaries of Pius II. An Abridgment,* trans. Florence A. Cragg; ed. Leona C. Gabel (New York, 1959), Bk. VII, p. 228.

The Lawyer in an Age of Political and Religious Confusion: Some Fifteenth-Century Conciliarists

I appreciate more than I can express the great and undeserved honor that you have done me in selecting me to deliver this address on such an important occasion in the history of C.W. Post College. I wish sincerely that I could justify the trust.

The recent political crisis suggested the theme of this address. Are the lawyers merely "men of technical ability and moral shortsightedness," bent on defending the interest of their clients at any cost and totally oblivious of the general welfare? Or are they defenders of right causes and upholders of justice? What have they done and what are they doing in the evolution of a good society? How far are they accelerating or how far have they retarded the progress of mankind? These are some of the broad questions which must be pondered as we reflect on the meaning of recent events. In the wake of Watergate no serious discussion of the proper role and function of the legal profession would require lengthy justification. To a student of political theory and jurisprudence educated in an Asian school of law, there are two aspects of the legal profession in the West, including the United States, that seem to merit special attention: they are the great influence of the lawyers in society and politics and the widely accepted, almost classic tradition that the lawyer defends any client, however base, or any cause, however bad. The activities of the Boston trial lawyer Mr. James St. Clair on behalf of Chaplain William S. Coffin, Jr. of Yale University in 1968 and later of President Nixon dramatized the problem of legal ethics. Chaplain Coffin himself was reported as saying: "The trouble with St. Clair is that he is all case and no cause." It will be my intention this evening first to touch upon the influence and omnipresence of the lawyers in the West and then to examine, in more detail, the general reputation of the lawyer and the role which some prominent European lawyers played in the fourteenth and fifteenth centuries, a period of great political and religious confusion.

In order to understand the significance of the first question, a quick comparison of East and West may be useful. It is well known that Confucianism, which stressed the superiority of morality over legality in politics, has had great influence not only on China, but also on many other Asian countries. Confucius said: "If the ruler himself is upright, all will go well even though he does not give orders. But if he himself is not upright, even though he gives orders, they will not be obeyed." Thus Confucian political theory emphasized moral and intellectual attainments as prerequisites for good government and preferred suasive to compulsive orders. While Confucianism was the ideology of the

PART ONE

LAW AND SOCIETY

governing gentry class for over a thousand years, a rival school of legalism, advocated by Shang Yang and Han Fei Tzu, blossomed during the Ch'in period (221-207 B. C.) briefly, only to be rejected as an ideology which permitted the absolutist and cruel rule of the First Emperor of Ch'in. Lack of mercy is the charge most often brought against Han Fei Tzu and other legalists. The legalists' penchant for stratagem and harsh and ruthless treatment of the people was undoubtedly responsible for the quick downfall of the Ch'in dynasty which was strongly supported by the legalists. As the eminent French scholar Jean Escarra put it:

> In the West the law has always been revered as something more or less sacrosanct, the queen of gods and men, imposing itself on everyone like a categorical imperative, defining and regulating, in an abstract way, the effects and conditions of all social activity . . . But as one passes to the East, this picture fades away. At the other end of Asia, China has felt able to give to law and jurisprudence but an inferior place in that powerful body of spiritual and moral values which she has created . . . Though not without juridical institutions, she has been willing to recognize only the natural order, and to exalt only the rules of morality.

In his famous book, *The United States and China,* Professor John K. Fairbank summarized the Chinese attitude more succinctly: "Legality was an inferior substitute for morality. As the traditional saying put it, 'when a state is about to perish, the regulations increase in number'."

Thus the Chinese concept of law was fundamentally different from legal conceptions in the West. The idea of freedom under law has been the distinguishing feature of political life in the West ever since the days of ancient Greece and Rome. The normal Western habit has been to emphasize jurisprudence rather than morality as the core of politics. It would be quite easy to document this view of the Western tradition regardless of which period is investigated. But it becomes increasingly clear that the fourteenth and fifteenth centuries, with which we are especially concerned this evening, were no exception. As scholars have recently begun to give more serious attention to the part which the lawyers played in the evolution of modern Europe, the number of studies devoted to the lawyers of this period have increased. On the basis of his extensive research in Florentine and other archives, Professor Lauro Martines of the University of California has shown in a recent book entitled, *Lawyers and Statecraft in Renaissance Florence* (1968), how widely lawyers were employed and consulted in the most important areas of public life in Florence, the home of the Renaissance. We have also some other significant publications such as a study of the activities of lawyers in fourteenth- and fifteenth-century Bavaria by Professor Hans Lieberich of the University of Munich, a study of jurisprudence and the legal profession in the later Middle Ages in Germany by Professor Wilfried Trusen of the University of Würzburg, and recent studies of Swiss and

French humanist legal science not only by Professor Guido Kisch of the University of Basel but also by American scholars like Professors Myron Gilmore of Harvard University and Donald Kelley of the University of Rochester. No serious student of modern European society and culture can henceforth afford to ignore the results of these investigations if he is to gain a good understanding of the rise and growth of the modern nation states.

In this connection, it is important to remember that many writers and thinkers who distinguished themselves in spiritual, cultural and intellectual fields in early modern Europe had some acquaintance with law. Of those who started or completed legal studies, but who then turned to other fields, we may mention Francesco Petrarch (1304-1374), Leone Battista Alberti (1404-1472), Martin Luther (1483-1546), Jean Calvin (1509-1564), Michel E. Montaigne (1533-1592), Pierre Corneille (1606-1684), Jean Baptiste Molière (1622-1673), Jean Racine (1639-1699), Gottfried W. Leibniz (1646-1716), Giovanni Battista Vico (1668-1744), Francis Marie Arouet de Voltaire (1694-1778), Denis Diderot (1713-1784), and David Hume (1711-1776). We must also remember Thomas More (1478-1535), Francesco Guicciardini (1483-1540), Francis Bacon (1561-1626), Montesquieu (1689-1755) and others, who while actively engaged in legal work, contributed significantly to the intellectual and cultural development of modern Europe, It is worth noting that the fathers of Niccolò Machiavelli (1469-1527), Francis Bacon, Blaise Pascal (1623-1662) and Jean Racine were lawyers.

The power and influence of the American lawyer is so well known that it needs no elaboration here. It was the American lawyer who precipitated the American Revolution by his agitation for principles of liberty and equality. The Federal Constitution was primarily the work of American lawyers. Henry, Jefferson, Marshall, Hamilton, Webster, Clay, Lincoln, and others of great achievement gained much of their power as members of the American Bar. Alexis de Tocqueville devoted a special chapter in his *Democracy in America* to "Judicial Power in the United States, and Its Influence upon Political Society." The majority of American Presidents have been lawyers. In contrast with the House of Representatives of the present Japanese Diet, where only about 76 of its members are lawyers, about 60% of the members of the U. S. Congress have been trained in the law, a fact which is taken for granted in this country. It can certainly be argued that no other country in the West has placed more emphasis on the lawyer and the legal profession than the United States.

Having touched upon the question of the influence and omnipresence of lawyers in the West, we may now begin to inquire how the legal profession has been viewed in general since antiquity and more specifically how the problem of lawyer-client relationship was viewed in the fourteenth and fifteenth centuries.

Every society which has an identifiable group of professional lawyers seems to have complained about their behavior. Distrust of lawyers is a commonplace theme in ancient literature. Robert J. Bonner, in his *Lawyers and Litigants*

in Ancient Athens (1927), gave numerous examples. Complaints about lawyers
in the early Middle Ages are virtually non-existent, because there was no
organized legal profession in most regions of the West before the twelfth
century, but with the recovery of the Roman law in the late eleventh century and
the consequent growth of the canon law in the Church, the number of those who
turned to a profession which was frankly lucrative greatly increased. No wonder
that the manners, morals, and even the very existence of lawyers began to be
deplored, especially in the literature of the twelfth century. The lawyer remained
for the rest of the medieval period a particular object of parody, of satire, and
frequently of venomous attack. A famous German legal maxim read: "Juristen—
schlechte Christen (Lawyers—bad Christians)." English legal proverbs said: "A
good lawyer is a bad neighbour" and "Fools and obstinate men make lawyers
rich." The Goliardic poets were especially fond of criticizing the jurists, but the
prose writers and vernacular poets were also busy in their attack on the legal
profession.

Criticisms of lawyers were also frequently made by the Church and the
theologians. In 1219 Pope Honorius III issued a decree in which he prohibited
the study of Roman law at the University of Paris in order to promote
theological studies. The theologians were critical of the lawyers, especially of
the canonists, whom they regarded as rivals in the Church. Despite these
criticisms so many clergymen turned to the study of law that the complaints of
its critics became increasingly louder in the thirteenth century. As the noted
medievalist Martin Grabmann showed in his studies, it was often debated in the
fourteenth century whether the Church should be governed by lawyers or
theologians. It is almost ironic that the great popes of the Middle Ages, such as
Alexander III (1159-1181), Innocent III (1198-1216), Gregory IX (1227-1241),
Innocent IV (1243-1254) and Boniface VIII (1294-1303), were all canonists of
great repute. We may remember in this connection that Martin Luther showed
his sharp reaction to the concept of the Church as a legal corporation when he
burned the book of the canon law together with the bull of excommunication.

This battle between jurisprudence and theology was followed in the late
fourteenth and fifteenth centuries by yet another battle, which was waged
between humanists and lawyers. (Probably the most famous polemic against the
lawyer was that delivered against the great post-glossator Bartolus of Sassoferrato
by the young humanist Lorenzo Valla in 1433.) It is remarkable that many who
began their legal studies in their youth turned later to the study of classical
literature and poetry and became humanists. In addition to Petrarch, whom we
mentioned earlier, such famous humanists as Giovanni Boccaccio (1313-1375),
Coluccio Salutati (1331-1406), Leonardo Bruni (1370-1444), Poggio Bracciolini
(1380-1459) and Aeneas Sylvius Piccolomini (1405-1464), belong to this
category. "The greater part of our legists," wrote Petrarch,

who care nothing for knowing about the origin of law and about the founders of jurisprudence, and have no other preoccupation than to gain as much as they can from their profession, are content to learn whatever is written in the law about contracts, judgments or wills, and it never occurs to them that the knowledge of arts and of origins and of literature would be of the greatest practical use for their very profession.

One common criticism of the lawyers was that by their sophistries they managed to delay justice and to postpone judgment. They were also criticized for using prolix, incomprehensible language in order to dazzle their opponent and to hold up the process of adjudication. Furthermore, they were accused of being arrogant, perverse and presumptuous in their treatment of justice and of being excessively greedy in charging stiff fees. These are probably some of the reasons that drove idealistic youths of the time from legal to humanistic studies. But no doubt the willingness of some lawyers to argue, according to how they were paid, that White is Black or Black is White may have alienated many a youthful student of law. "To lie like a lawyer" was a proverbial phrase. But perhaps we have concentrated too much on the negative assessment of the legal profession which was partially based on erroneous impressions of law and of the lawyer. It is important to note that the popular prejudice against the lawyer arose largely from one feature of his professional life, his duties as an advocate.

We now come to the central portion of the address this evening. The question is, what was the role of the lawyer in fourteenth- and fifteenth-century Europe? What could he do, and how was he regarded? Seen from the point of view of ecclesiastical politics, the fourteenth and fifteenth centuries were a period of great religious and political confusion. Soon after the end of the exile of the papacy in Avignon, from 1309 to 1377, which is popularly called the Babylonian Captivity, the Church entered the period of the Great Schism (1378-1417), during which there were first two and later three contending popes. The moral and religious confusion which resulted from the schism was so great that a popular saying was current that no soul entered Paradise during this time. But conflict and confusion were not confined to the religious domain only. The European powers were sharply divided as to which pope to support. While England and Germany supported the Roman line, France, Scotland, and, to some extent, Spain sided with the Avignonese popes.

It is against this background that we can understand the rise of the conciliar movement which tried to heal the schism and to effect the reform of the Church "in head and members." In general, the conciliarists distinguished clearly between the Universal Church as the congregation of the faithful (*congregatio fidelium*) and the established Roman Church, understood as pope and cardinals together. According to the conciliarists, the Universal Church, which could be represented by a general council, was superior to the pope. When various ways of healing the schism failed, it was in accordance with the conciliar theory of church government that a series of general councils, such as the Council of Pisa (1409), the Council of Constance (1414-1418) and the Council of Basel (1431-1449), were held to bring about the reunification and reform of the Church. The first task was accomplished at the Council of Constance, but the councils were notoriously ineffective in carrying out the second. In reality, the strong desire for church unity was the main driving force behind the conciliar movement.

It is apparent that the conciliar movement was a great challenge to papal power. It was an audacious and, strictly speaking, illegal movement which only the grave constitutional crisis in the Church precipitated. Until recently, it was fashionable to find the origins of the conciliar movement in the heretical, anti-papal ideas of some medieval writers like Marsiglio of Padua (1275-1343) and William of Ockham (c.1290-c.1346). But the study of conciliar thought has been greatly advanced by many recent monographs dealing with the legal and canonistic background of the movement. As the late Professor E.F. Jacob of Oxford University pointed out, "it is now common to see conciliar activity against the background of law and administration." The extraordinary events in the fourteenth and fifteenth centuries which we mentioned above naturally engaged the attention of many lawyers, and a great number of them were deeply involved in ecclesiastical politics, taking their position either on the pro-papal or on the conciliar side.

In studying the activities of these lawyers, it soon becomes apparent that as a series of complicated events unfolded themselves, the number of lawyers who were forced to change sides greatly increased. Some of them reversed themselves even twice or three times in accordance with the changing position of their clients. One of the best examples of this is the case of Nicolaus de Tudeschis (1386-1445), commonly called Panormitanus, who is usually regarded as the greatest canon lawyer in the later Middle Ages.

Born in Catania, Sicily, in 1386, Panormitanus studied law at the University of Bologna under the noted scholars Franciscus Zabarella (1360-1417) and Antonius de Butrio (1338-1408). After teaching law at Bologna (1412), Parma (1412-1418), Siena (1413-1430), again at Bologna (1431-1432), and finally at Florence (1432), he was sent to the Council of Basel in 1433 by Pope Eugenius IV (1383-1447) as papal representative. In the meantime, he had published a book in support of the pro-papal conception of church government. He returned to Sicily later in 1433, but the next year he entered the service of King Alfonso V (1416-1458) of Aragon, who was then a strong supporter of the Council of Basel. Panormitanus was made Archbishop of Palermo in 1434. When he returned to Basel in 1436 as King Alfonso's representative, he fought for the council against Pope Eugenius IV until he returned to Palermo in 1439. It is not surprising that his critics quickly denounced the change of his position and accused him of disloyalty to the papacy.

Aeneas Sylvius Piccolomini, who was then a supporter of the council, described in his *Commentaries on the Proceedings of the Council of Basel* how much Panormitanus suffered as a result of changing his positions:

> It . . . became generally known that Panormitanus, when he came to his home, returned to his bedroom and after complaints to himself about his king for compelling him to fight against the truth and to endanger his reputation and his soul, in the midst of his tears he fell asleep, and through his melancholy, took no food until evening, seeing that knowingly and unknowingly he had attacked the truth.

Thus Panormitanus the lawyer had become a conciliarist despite his own pro-papal convictions. He worked for his master and client, Alfonso V, and as a result experienced a profound moral agony.

Aeneas Sylvius Piccolomini himself, who ascended the throne of St. Peter in 1458 as Pope Pius II, also made dramatic changes in his position. Born at Corsignano near Siena in 1405, of a noble but impoverished family, Aeneas went to the University of Siena to study law. But under the influence of Mariano Sozzini, he took a great interest not only in law but also in classical studies. Although it is often said that Aeneas found the study of law uninteresting, a recent study by Professor Kisch reveals that Aeneas, who later became one of the foremost humanists, was well acquainted with the legal literature of the time. Employed in 1431 as Secretary to Bishop Domenico Capranica of Fermo, he arrived in Basel in 1432 and soon became a leading figure to champion the conciliar movement. After Capranica's departure from Basel, Aeneas served a few other masters and rose so rapidly at the council that he was master of ceremonies in the conclave which elected the Anti-Pope Felix V on November 5, 1439.

In 1442, however, Aeneas decided to support Emperor Frederick III who had been taking a neutral position between pope and council. Speaking of the relations with his new master Frederick III, Aeneas said: "I shall try to stand well with the king. I shall obey him and follow him. His desire will be mine." And yet only two years later he ranged himself on the side of Pope Eugenius IV after making a dramatic appeal to the pope for understanding and forgiveness of all his previous anti-papal activities. The erstwhile conciliarist was now a papalist and had paved the way for his own eventual elevation to the papal throne. Unlike Panormitanus, who served Alfonso V faithfully as counsel regardless of what position his master took, Aeneas worked for a number of masters, thereby changing his position from conciliarism to papalism. One critic said of him: "His pen was at the service of the highest bidder, the friend or opponent of the Council, and his primary concern was the pursuit of his own career." Although the difference between Panormitanus and Aeneas must not be forgotten, it is easy to understand that contemporary critics were quick to attack both of them for their irresponsibility, expediency and lack of conscience.

These two examples which we have mentioned were by no means exceptional cases in this period of great stress and confusion. Numerous other conversions and changes are known to have taken place. Nicolaus Cusanus (1401-1464), who is known as one of the most original philosophical thinkers of the fifteenth century, was also a thoroughly trained student of law, with a doctorate in canon law from the Unviersity of Padua. After strongly supporting the cause of conciliarism at the Council of Basel, he went over to the papal side after 1437. Apparently he believed that the Council of Basel had become too anti-papal and disorderly and that the unity and harmony of the Church which he sought could be accomplished more effectively under papal auspices. Although Cusanus' transfer of allegiance has often been criticized, it seems clear that he did not act for his own personal benefit. Pope Pius II, a long-time friend of Cusanus, reported that when he created new cardinals, Cusanus remonstrated strongly against the step. The pope recorded in his *Commentaries:*

> The Cardinal of St. Peter (Cusanus) . . . finally answered as follows: ". . . Now you ignore the ordinance cf the synod and do ask the consent of the college and you wish to make me a tool of your ambition. I cannot do it. I do not know how to flatter. I hate adulation. If you can bear to hear the truth, I like nothing which goes on in this Curia. Everything is corrupt. No one does his duty. Neither you nor the cardinals have any care for the Church. What observance of the canons is there? What reverence for laws? What assiduity in divine worship? All are bent on ambition and avarice. If I ever speak in a consistory about reform, I am laughed at. I do no good here. Allow me to withdraw. I cannot endure these ways . . ." With these words he burst into tears.

Although Cusanus was on the papal side, there was still in him enough conciliar strain to make him an honest critic and reformer of the papacy.

Gregor Heimburg (1401-1470), who is often called the "greatest German lawyer in the later Middle Ages," was, like Cusanus, a graduate of the University of Padua where he studied both civil and canon law intensively and began to take a great interest in humanistic studies as well. After acquiring his doctorate in both laws in 1430, he participated in the council of Basel as representative of the Archbishop of Mainz. Although he supported conciliarism throughout his career, he later worked for numerous German princes as well as the Imperial city of Nuremberg. This was probably the reason for the persistent criticism of him that he worked for anyone as counsel so long as he was paid well. It is distressing to note that the cultivated humanist Pope Pius II, who once admired Heimburg as the most promising German humanist of the time, became a bitter critic of Heimburg as the latter pursued almost fanatically the cause of conciliarism. Heimburg was excommunicated later and denounced as a "child of the devil." But he was extolled by some modern Protestant commentators as the "Citizen-Luther before the days of Luther" because of his fight for the independence of the German Church from the papacy. He will be remembered not only for his conciliarism, but also for his advocacy of jurisprudence against its critics, such as Johannes Rot (c. 1430-1506), who had praised rhetoric and denounced the lawyers for their obscure language.

It would be rash to conclude, on the basis of some examples considered here, that all lawyers in the fourteenth and fifteenth centuries were basically indifferent to moral and ethical issues involved in the cases which they handled, that they were interested only in personal advancement and financial reward, and that they were willing to switch sides and exchange clients without scruple in order to obtain their goals. It is clear, however, that the practical questions involving the professional responsibility of lawyers was as difficult in these centuries as in our own time.

Perhaps it is significant that many of those who proposed and described utopian societies envisioned a society without lawyers and much legal restraint. As is well known, Plato, whose ideal state was governed by philosophers who were almost reminiscent of Confucian princes, did not emphasize the concept of law in his *Republic*. In the *Utopia* of Thomas More there are so few laws that everyone is a legal expert. This is probably a direct or indirect criticism of those lawyers who, desirous of defending the interests of their clients and unmindful of justice, equity and the common good, became mere technicians of the law. Is it not true to say that when the lawyers, whether they be judges, attorneys or advocates, were only concerned with the positivistic dimension of the law and neglected the ethical and moral implications of the law, they were often criticized and ridiculed?

As legal systems were stabilized and often ossified in the second half of the thirteenth century, it was the theologians rather than jurists who emphasized the importance of such concepts as equity and natural law and grappled with the problem of intricate tensions between the law on one side and ethical and moral values on the other. As the great legal historian Professor Kisch has amply shown in his *Erasmus and Jurisprudence of His Time* (*Erasmus und die Juriprudenz seiner Zeit,* 1960), the concept of equity is based on Aristotle's idea of *epieikeia,* which was developed in Book V of his *Nichomachean Ethics.* Aristotle believed that the necessarily rigid laws of the state would at time work injustice and that in such cases certain first principles must be invoked to moderate the rigor of the law. Equity is a method restoring the balance of justice when it has been tilted by the law. This concept of equity, which played a mitigating role against the rigidity of law, was first taken up by the famed medieval philosopher St. Albertus Magnus and then was developed further by his pupil St. Thomas Aquinas, the most celebrated theologian of the High Middle Ages. We must note in this connection that the British system of equity, which was evolved mainly by courts distinct from those of the common law, was presided over by the Chancellor who was known as the "keeper of the king's conscience." For the earlier Chancellors were not lawyers, but ecclesiastics. The defects of the common law could be balanced only by a tribunal whose procedure should be more or less free from technical rules. These are two interesting cases which show that in the Western tradition which emphasized legality over morality, ethical and moral considerations have also played an important role in the development of jurisprudence.

Recently a manuscript was discovered in the city archive of Lucca, Italy which contains a detailed discussion of natural law by Panormitanus. This is not the place to deal with the very complicated problem of the nature of natural law. But it may not be inaccurate to say that Panormitanus, who tried to listen to the "voice of conscience" and to follow a "higher law" while applying the positive law as skillfully as possible under orders from his king, was caught between the two dimensions of law and cried bitterly in his bedroom at night because of a great agony which he experienced.

Let us now return to our century. It is said that when Judge Learned Hand implored Justice Oliver Wendell Holmes to "do justice," Holmes replied: "That is not my job. My job is to play the games according to the rules." We can see in this exchange contrasting views of the function of the lawyer as seen by two of the most distinguished American lawyers. What is after all the proper function of the lawyer? How should he be educated? Beginning with the recent Watergate affair, we noted the omnipresence of the lawyers in Western societies and the popularity of the doctrine that the lawyer serves his clients and their causes regardless of whether they are good or bad. The record of some fifteenth-century conciliarists who switched positions and changed clients frequently was examined in order to trace the historical origin of the knotty problem and to gain a better insight into the contemporary problem of great significance. No doubt the problem of the ethics of the legal profession is likely to remain one of the difficult problems in modern society.

The *Institutes* of Emperor Justinian (527-65) boldly stated: "Jurisprudence is the knowledge of things divine and human, the science of the just and the unjust." Sir William Blackstone (1723-80), in his introduction to his famous *Commentaries on the Law of England* (1765-69), spoke of jurisprudence as:

> a science which distinguishes the criterion of right and wrong; which teaches to establish the one and prevent, punish or redress the other; which employs in its theory the noblest faculties of the soul, and exerts in its practice the cardinal virtue of the heart.

Has such an elevated conception of jurisprudence been forgotten? It is an extremely difficult task assigned to the good lawyer to aspire to vindicate, in each case he handles, high principles of protecting the interests of the client without neglecting the common good, meeting the demands of the law without completely suppressing the voice of conscience, and recognizing a "higher law" while honoring positive laws.

In the post-Watergate era, when there is a great deal of cynicism and skepticism about the legal and political institutions in general, what is the future of the profession which has traditionally been regarded as "noble"? Above all, what kind of education will be needed if the judges, attorneys and counsels are not to become mere "men of technical ability and moral shortsightedness"? The *New York Times,* in its editorial on "Lawyers' Watergate" published on June 11 last year, advocated "the development of post-graduate educational programs to help lawyers explore the multitude of complex and murky ethical questions that continually confront practitioners." Here again it would seem wise to listen to the advice of one of the greatest of American judges on the nature of education necessary for members of the legal profession. As Professor Philip B. Kurland of the University of Chicago Law School recently reminded us in the same newspaper, Judge Learned Hand once wrote:

> I venture to believe that it is as important to a judge called upon to pass on a question of constitutional law, to have at least a bowing acquaintance with Acton and Maitland, with Thucydides, Gibbon and Carlyle, with Homer, Dante, Shakespeare and Milton, with Machiavelli, Montaigne and Rabelais, with Plato, Bacon, Hume and Kant, as with the books which have been specifically written on the subject. For in such matters everything turns upon the spirit in which he approaches the questions before him.

It is abundantly clear to me that C.W. Post College, while not engaged in legal education directly, has a contribution to make in strengthening one of the most important professions in the United States.

Humanism, Law, and Reform: Reflections on Fifteenth-Century Lawyers

It is well known that one of the great contributions of Rome to Western civilization was its legal ideas and institutions. The influence of Roman law has been strongly felt in many parts of Europe. It is certainly not within the scope of this paper to discuss in detail the development of Roman law from the beginning. Our first task is rather to describe briefly how the so-called revival of Roman law occurred late in the eleventh century and how Roman law began to influence many countries of Western Europe, except England, through the law of the Church.

When the barbarian invasion began to sweep over the Roman Empire in the fifth century, Roman law had already entered a period of codification. The Theodosian Code, one of the earliest collections of Roman law, was compiled in 439 A.D. for Roman subjects of the barbarian kingdoms. But without any doubt Roman law reached an important landmark in 533 when Emperor Justinian of the East Roman Empire published the famous *Corpus iuris civilis,* which had been compiled by the famed lawyer Tribonian and his associates. The Justinian Code, consisting of the Digest, the Codex, the Institutes, and the Novels, was a remarkable work of synthesis accomplished at the end of ancient times. Although the Digest, the most important part, was introduced into Italy in 554, the Justinian Code, was never promulgated in Western Europe.[1]

During the early Middle Ages, when the barbarian invasions brought large-scale destruction to Europe, the knowledge, the teaching and the application of Roman law never disappeared completely. In the sixth century, for example, the Roman subjects of the crumbled Empire were allowed to live still under their own law as far as their relations among themselves were concerned. This certainly helped a knowledge of the Justinian Code to survive. To be sure, in the areas of Europe where the influence of Rome was weak or where Germanic institutions and customs effectively replaced those of the Romans, local and customary law began to prevail in the place of the more systematic Roman law. This was especially true after the collapse of the Empire of Charlemagne in the ninth century, when a period of local jurisdiction was inaugurated and the people of Europe began to live by local customary law. Even in Italy the study of

---

[1] On Justinian's *Corpus iuris civilis,* see, for example, Hans J. Wolff, *Roman Law: An Historical Introduction* (Norman, Oklahoma, 1951), pp. 162-74; Wolfgang Kunkel, *An Introduction to Roman Legal and Constitutional History* (Oxford, 1973), pp. 163-76; Walter Ullmann, *Law and Politics in the Middle Ages* (Cambridge, 1975), pp. 53-79.

Roman law declined to the lowest level conceivable.[2] But it would certainly be incorrect to assert that after the arrival of the Vandals and Goths in Europe, the influence of the Roman legal system disappeared until its revival in the late eleventh century.

The powerful revival of the study of Roman law in Italy was no doubt connected with the discovery of the Digest in Pisa at the end of the eleventh century.[3] It came at a time when the cities of Italy were entering a period of great economic prosperity on the eve of the Crusades. Clearly the revival was supported by a strong desire to meet the new legal needs of Italian cities which had arisen as a result of the general recovery of economic activity. The University of Bologna became the center of the intensive and systematic study of Roman law and set an example for a number of law faculties, such as Padua and Naples in Italy and Toulouse and Montpellier and Orleans in France, which appeared in the course of the thirteenth and fourteenth centuries.

The revival of the study of Roman law in Italy brought about the evolution of a new scientific jurisprudence. Irnerius (1035?-1130?), presumably a teacher of rhetoric at Bologna, began a painstaking study of the text of the Digest on his own and wrote the first glosses of the Justinian Code. The school of Bologna, which developed around 1150 as a result of Irnerius' teaching activities at the University of Bologna, is known under the name of the Glossators. It later included such eminent jurists as Placentinus, Azo and Accursius. The chief goal of the Glossators, who flourished in the twelfth and thirteenth centuries, was to establish the exact meaning of Roman law texts and to introduce pure Roman law into medieval practice. By the middle of the thirteenth century the work of the preceding generation of Glossators was compiled by the Bologna law professor Accursius in a *Glossa ordinaria* which immediately achieved canonical authority.[4]

Since the Glossators' approach did not reflect the realities of late medieval Italy, there were questions which they could not answer directly from the *Corpus iuris civilis.* Furthermore, they considered their jurisprudence universal and permanent when in fact it did not fit the needs of medieval life. This is why it proved inefficient, and the decline of the school of the Glossators set in about the middle of the thirteenth century. Obviously it was necessary to reform a declining jurisprudence, if the study of Roman law was to retain its vigor and vitality.

---

[2] Carlo Calisse, *A History of Italian Law* (Boston, 1928; reprint ed., New York, 1969), *passim;* Kunkel, *An Introduction,* p. 181.

[3] Q. Breen, "The Twelfth-Century Revival of the Roman Law," *Oregon Law Review* 24 (1944-45): 244-87; John B. Morrall, *Political Thought in Medieval Times,* 3rd ed. (London, 1971), pp. 41-58. On the so-called Vulgate text of the Digest, see Ullmann, *Law and Politics,* p. 68.

[4] Wolff, *Roman Law,* pp. 187-89; Ullmann, *Law and Politics,* pp. 83-104.

As we shall see later, chairs of Roman law began to be established in the universities, not only in Italy, but even in England, after the twelfth century. It is important to note, however, that the twelfth century witnessed the birth of another important legal system. The development of the study of Roman law in Europe cannot be understood unless it is related to that of canon law. As the medieval Church expanded and extended its sway over Europe, certain collections of Church law began to be made as early as the tenth century. But it was Gratian, a Camaldalensian monk of Bologna, who compiled the so-called *Concordia discordantium canonum* around 1140, thereby establishing what Professor Walter Ullmann called the "science of canon law" and initiating a "full-fledged canon law school at Bologna."[5] Clearly the systematic nature of the Roman law which was being studied and taught at the University of Bologna greatly influenced Gratian in his work of gathering and dovetailing previous collections of canon law. Perhaps in no other place but Bologna could this new branch of legal learning have arisen. It is also notable that just as the techniques and principles of Roman law provided the later canonists with the tools of their trade, so canon law was destined to act as the main vehicle for the dissemination of Roman law in Western Europe.

At the end of the twelfth century the Church reorganized its judicial system throughout Europe, basing its legal procedure on the new canon law system and requiring the judges of the Church courts to be graduates of university law faculties.[6] This move certainly encouraged the ecclesiastical courts in many parts of Europe to assume ever wider jurisdiction as against the secular courts. The reasons for the primacy of the ecclesiastical courts over the secular are not hard to find. Seen from the practical point of view, two reasons are especially important. First, the decisions of the ecclesiastical courts were more effectively enforced than those of the secular courts due to the ubiquitous influence and power of the Church. Second, the general populace seems to have believed that there was a greater opportunity for receiving justice in the ecclesiastical courts, which were staffed by learned, academically trained lawyers, than in the secular courts, which were administered by essentially unlearned or semi-learned local wise men. The administration of justice was strictly sacerdotal and professional in the ecclesiastical courts; by contrast, it was predominantly

[5] Ullmann, *Law and Politics,* p. 139. See also Stephan G. Kuttner, "On the Place of Canon Law in a General History of Roman Law during the Middle Ages," *Seminar,* 13 (1955), 51-55; Pierre Legendre, *La penetration du droit romain dans le droit canonique classique de Gratien a Innocent IV, 1140-1254* (Paris, 1964); Gabriel Le Bras, *Droit romain et droit canon au XIIIᵉ siècle: Comunicazione letta nella seduta ordinaria del 16 Aprile 1966* (Rome, 1967).

[6] Helmut Coing, "Römisches Recht in Deutschland," in *Ius Romanum medii aevi,* Pars V,6 (Milano, 1964), n. 12; idem, *Epochen der Rechtsgeschichte in Deutschland,* 3rd ed. (München, 1976), p. 49.

lay and non-professional in the secular courts. The Church was the first institution in Europe to adopt a judicial system which was staffed by professional, academically trained jurists.

It is not surprising, therefore, that most of those who studied canon and Roman law in the universities in the twelfth and thirteenth centuries were members of the clergy. In Italian and French universities these students came under the influence of the Glossators. But as canonistic scholarship began to attract an increasing number of laymen from the middle of the thirteenth century, the number of the lawyers who were Doctors of Both Laws (*Doctor utriusque iuris*) increased.

Having sketched an outline of the revival of the study of Roman law in Italy and the role of the Church courts in the dissemination of Roman law, I propose now to examine, as concisely as possible, certain legal developments which took place in the late Middle Ages in some of the leading European countries. Obviously we must first turn to Italy.

As we saw above, the Glossators of the twelfth and thirteenth centuries tended to limit themselves to Roman law texts and refrained from any addition or change. As a result, their approach proved restricted and inadequate, and the decline of the school of the Glossators began in the middle of the thirteenth century. The school of the Commentators, or Post-Glossators, which arose in the second half of the thirteenth century, represented a strong reaction against the teaching and method of the Glossators. The Commentators were anxious to reform the legal method of the Glossators, which was being challenged and criticized. It was, however, not in Italy, but in France, that the new method had first been developed by Jacques de Revigny, a professor at Toulouse and later at Orleans, who was followed by many disciples. The most famous of them was Pierre de Belleperche. The significant feature of the school was to apply to law the method which St. Thomas Aquinas had used in theology, the dialectics of scholasticism. The new school of legal science was introduced to Italy by Cino da Pistoia (c. 1270-c. 1337), a close friend of Dante and Petrarch. He had not only studied at Bologna, but had also familiarized himself in France with the teachings of French jurists.[7]

Dissatisfied with the essentially philological and deferential approach of the Glossators to the authoritative texts of the classical world, the Commentators emphasized the importance of adapting Roman law texts to the needs and conditions of their own time. They "resolutely introduced medieval elements into their treatment of Digest and Code,"[8] and were anxious to blend

---

[7] Wolff, *Roman Law*, pp. 189-90; Ullmann, *Law and Politics*, pp. 104-16.

[8] R.C. Van Caenegem, "The 'Reception' of Roman Law: A Meeting of Northern and Mediterranean Traditions," in *The Late Middle Ages and the Dawn of Humanism Outside Italy*, ed. M. G. Verbeke and J. Ijsewijn (The Hague, 1972), p. 199.

pure Roman law with local statutes and customary and canon law. It was "by means of the interpretative methods of formal logic, by limitations and extensions, by subtle distinctions and ingenious analogies that they succeeded in doing so."[9] The *mos italicus,* as the legal method of the new school was often called, reached its peak in the fourteenth century and continued to exert influence in and dominate the university lecture halls well into the fifteenth century. Its most famous advocates were Bartolus of Sassoferrato (1314-1357), a pupil of Cino, and Baldus de Ubaldis (1319 or 1327-1400), the pupil of Bartolus at Perugia. Their approach was so well adapted to the conditions of the time that it came to dominate the activities of the courts in Europe. Bartolus's opinions had legal force in Leon, Castile and Portugal. It was often said that no one was a jurist unless he was a Bartolist (*Nemo jurista nisi sit Bartolista*).[10]

Later, however, a period of fatigue and stagnation set in, in which there occurred a separation of practice from theory. The epigones of Bartolus and Baldus tirelessly glossed not the actual texts of Roman law, but the glosses of Accursius and other medieval jurists, thus falling into a sterile scholasticism. The original texts of Roman law were now buried beneath absurd dialectical exercises.

> . . . the eager pursuit by the commentators of their ideal to solve all problems by a painstaking and elaborate logic unquestionably led many members of the school to absurd refinements.[11]

This was the period of the decline of Roman law studies. Thus the period of reform was followed by a period of stagnation and ossification.

The gradual stagnation of Roman law studies in the fifteenth century coincided with the development of humanism in Italy. This led to a strong tension between lawyers and humanists. One distinguished historian pointed out that "the Postglossators tended to be prolix and diffuse and prone to accumulate 'authorities' which does not always make pleasurable reading for the modern student."[12] Their Latin was often barbaric in contrast to the beautiful classical Latin of the humanists, who admired and imitated Cicero. The Commentators' emphasis on procedural matters, their endless discussion on the subtle differences between various concepts used in their arguments, and their introduction of non-classical terminology, drew strong criticism from the humanists in the

---

[9] Kunkel, *An Introduction,* p. 184.

[10] H.D. Hazeltine, "Commentators," in *Encyclopedia of the Social Sciences,* III (1930), p. 680; Walter Ullmann, *The Medieval Idea of Law as Represented by Lucas de Penna* (London, 1946), p. xxv.

[11] Hazeltine, "Commentators," p. 681.

[12] Ullmann, *Law and Politics,* p. 105.

fourteenth and fifteenth centuries. Humanists like Francesco Petrarch (1304 1374) and Lorenzo Valla (d. 1437) called themselves *Antibartolistae* and ridiculed the lawyers as *homines illitterati.*[13] In 1433 Valla wrote a strong attack on Bartolus in which he described Bartolus as an "ass," "idiot," and "madman," and found Bartolus's work completely lacking in an understanding of Roman law and institutions.[14] The lawyers' predilection for regarding themselves as members of the exclusive group, *ordo jurisperitium,* and their insistence on high fees for their services were also severely criticized.

After this brief survey of the situation in Italy, we must now turn to three other countries. Seen from the point of view of the diffusion of Roman law, England was at one extreme and Germany at the other. France occupied an intermediary position.

"The problem of Roman influence on English law has received much attention and aroused much emotion."[15] The commonly accepted notion is that England was little affected by Roman law. In twelfth-century England the general legal condition was not basically different from that on the Continent. As in Italy, England came under the influence of the revival of Roman law in the twelfth century. The eminent Italian churchman Lanfranc (d. 1089), later Chancellor of England under William the Conqueror (1066-1087) and Archbishop of Canterbury, had brought the study of Roman law to England in the previous century. Master Vacarius, the Glossator of Bologna, came to England at the invitation of Archbishop Theobald in 1148 and taught Canon and Roman law at Canterbury and also at Oxford. Silenced by King Stephen (1135-1154) for some time, Vacarius later resumed his activity and exercised great influence in Oxford. His law students began to be called *pauperistae,* because his principal book was entitled *Book of Poor Scholars (Liber pauperum).*[16]

But the establishment of a centralized and close network of royal judges under Henry II (1154-1189) heralded the rise of the English Common Law in the second half of the twelfth century. The *Tractatus de legibus et consuetudinibus*

---

[13] Heinrich Mitteis, "Renaissance, Humanismus und Reception der fremden Rechte in Deutschland," in *Die Rechtsidee in der Geschichte: Gesammelte Abhandlungen und Vorträge* (Weimar, 1957), p. 556.

[14] Myron P. Gilmore, *Humanists and Jurists: Six Studies in the Renaissance* (Cambridge, Massachusetts, 1963), pp. 31-32. See also Guido Kisch, *Gestalten und Probleme aus Humanismus und Jurisprudenz* (Berlin, 1969), pp. 118-24.

[15] Peter Stein, *Roman Law and English Jurisprudence Yesterday and Today* (Cambridge, 1969), p. 4.

[16] Paul Vinogradoff, *Roman Law in Medieval Europe,* 3rd ed. (Oxford, 1929; reprint ed., Hildesheim, 1929), p. 63. For the life of Vacarius, see *The Liber pauperum of Vacarius,* ed. F. de Zulueta [Publications of the Selden Society, XLIIII] (London, 1927), xiii-xxiii.

(1189), one of the first great books of the Common Law, is generally ascribed to Ranulf de Glanvill, Henry II's trusted and capable chief justiciar, although he probably did not write it.[17] Since no part of that realm was in direct contact with Italy, the influence of Roman law began to decline and was felt by only a few jurists, of whom Henry de Bracton (d. 1268) was the most authoritative and famous. His important treatise, *De legibus et consuetudinibus Angliae,* written about 1236, exhibits a profound knowledge of Roman law, as Professor S.E. Thorne's "Introduction" to his edition of the treatise has shown.[18] According to Professor Francis de Zulueta, "England really had a glossator in Vacarius and a post-glossator in Bracton."[19] But to most practitioners of English law the systematic and abstract nature of Roman law was bewildering and not attractive.

By the end of the thirteenth century a native English legal profession had grown up, organized as a guild which rejected foreign law. As it became lay, the legal profession further drifted away from the canonists and from the universities where canon and civil law were taught. From the middle of the fourteenth century, it began to establish its own system of legal education by setting up the famous Inns of Court.[20] The concept of Roman law that influenced England was that of the Glossators. By the time the Commentators in Italy had modified Roman law to the point where it might have been acceptable to English lawyers, by meeting customary law halfway, England had consciously and successfully closed itself off from the intrusion of Roman ideas. In the fifteenth century England turned its thoughts increasingly inward and became isolated from the dissemination of Roman law on the Continent. It was only in Scotland that Roman law took root in the fifteenth century because of the long association of

---

[17] Percy H. Winfield, *The Chief Sources of English Legal History* (Cambridge, Massachusetts, 1925; reprint ed., New York, n. d.), pp. 256-58; R.C. Van Caenegem, *The Birth of the English Common Law* (Cambridge, 1973), pp. 30-33. The literature on the English Common Law is enormous. For perceptive recent discussions on the topic by foreign scholars, see the monograph by Van Caenegem mentioned above and Hans Peter, *Römisches Recht und englisches Recht* (Wiesbaden, 1969). The standard history of English law is W.S. Holdsworth, *A History of English Law,* 16 vols. (London, 1903-66).

[18] Henry de Bracton, *On the Laws and Customs of England,* trans. by S.E. Thorne, I (Cambridge, Massachusetts, 1968), pp. xxiv xlvii.

[19] William Seagle, "Reception," in *Encyclopedia of the Social Sciences,* XIII (1934), p. 154.

[20] On the Inns of Court, see, for example, D.P. Barton et al., *The Story of Our Inns of Court* (London, 1924); Anton-Hermann Chroust, "The Beginning, Flourishing and Decline of the Inns of Court: The Consolidation of the English Legal Profession after 1400," *Vanderbilt Law Review,* 10 (1956): 79-123; Walter C. Richardson, *A History of the Inns of Court, with Special Reference to the Period of the Renaissance* (Baton Rouge, 1975).

Scotland with France.[21] It is also notable that although the patronage of Duke Humfrey (1390-1447) first provided a focus and stimulus for an active interest in humanistic studies in England,[22] humanism had little influence on jurisprudence in the fifteenth century.

Examined from the point of view of the diffusion of Roman law, the situation in France in the late Middle Ages was quite different from that in England.[23] In the South, the so-called Country of Written Law (*the pays de droit ecrit*), the Roman population greatly outnumbered the Germanic population. As a result, Roman law, which was the law of the majority, was applied to everybody as the custom of the region. But southern France played practically no role in the training of its lawyers until about 1270. French students went to universities in northern Italy, notably Bologna, to study law. It was in the last third of the century that several *studia* appeared almost simultaneously, some of which succeeded in establishing themselves while others disappeared after a short time. As a result, the flow of students to Bologna decreased, and from 1270 to 1300 we see the rise of a real school of lawyers trained in southern France.[24] It can be said, therefore, that the study and the practice of Roman law were already widely accepted in southern France in the fourteenth century. There was no need to have a conscious "reception" of Roman law in the next century.

In northern France, the Country of Unwritten Law (the *pays du droit coutumier*), a somewhat different situation obtained. It is true that Roman law always had a very great authority also in this region and that the teaching of Roman law went on at the universities from their beginning. But at the University of Paris, the site of the leading school of theology in Western Europe, the clergy were forbidden to study or to teach Roman civil law in 1219 by the papal decree of Honorius III, *Super speculam*, because many of them

---

[21] See Dougas Cheape, *An Introductory Lecture on the Evil Law* (London, 1827); William M. Gloag and R.C. Henderson, *Introduction to the Law of Scotland,* 7th ed. (Edinburgh, 1968), p. 8; David M. Walker, *The Scottish Legal System: An Introduction to the Study of Scots Law,* 4th ed. (Edinburgh, 1976), pp. 51-54 ("Scotland, unlike England, 'received' the Roman law and it had great influence from the mid-sixteenth to the mid-eighteenth centuries," p. 54).

[22] *Duke Humfrey and English Humanism in the Fifteenth Century: Catalogue of an Exhibition held in the Bodleian Library, Oxford* (Oxford, 1970). See also Roberto Weiss, *Humanism in England during the Fifteenth Century,* 2nd ed. (Oxford, 1957).

[23] *A General Survey of Events, Sources, Persons and Movements in Continental Legal History,* The Continental Legal History Series, I (Boston, 1912; reprint ed., New York, 1968), pp. 203-50; Vinogradoff, *Roman Law,* pp. 71-96.

[24] Andre Gouron, "The Training of Southern French Lawyers," in *Post Scripta: Essays on Medieval Law and the Emergence of the European State in Honor of Gaines Post,* ed. J.R. Strayer and D.E. Queller (*Studia Gratiana,* 15 [1972]), pp. 219-27.

seemed ready to give up theology for the more lucrative study of law.[25] Apart from the Decretal *Super speculam,* however, the question of the authority of the Written Law was scarcely raised before the 1500's in this region.

> From the thirteenth century onwards France absorbed a good deal of Roman law under royal guidance, without any sudden break of her own tradition.[26]

It can be said in general about the role of Roman law in southern and northern France in the fifteenth century that French lawyers had slowly established legal unity through an original interpretation of native custom and Roman doctrine. Roman law did not have to be brought to France in any systematic way. It was, so to speak, already there.

The country which was at the other extreme of England from the point of view of its relations with Roman law was Germany. It was to feel the impact of Roman law more strongly than any other country. The wholesale and systematic acceptance of Roman and Canon law in fifteenth-century Germany has been exhaustively discussed by many scholars as the problem of the "reception of Roman law in Germany."[27] The reasons for this phenomenon and its relationship to the spread of humanism in Germany require more careful analysis and discussion than that given in our preceding brief examination of the development in England and France.

Broadly speaking, customary law prevailed in the secular courts in medieval Germany. The non-ecclesiastical courts were staffed generally by non-educated local laymen whose social position and legal experience had brought them to the courts. The traditional court of jurors (*Schoffen*) which was composed of laymen, used an uncodified, unrationalized customary law. Neither academically trained (*gelehrte*) jurists nor their law had penetrated into the non-ecclesiastical sphere, where, apart from various isolated instances, German customary law dominated right into the fifteenth century.

The extensive reorganization of the ecclesiastical courts, which we touched on above, was also attempted in the thirteenth and fourteenth centuries in Germany and had an enormous impact not only on the structure of the ecclesiastical judicial system, but also eventually on the nature of the entire legal

---

[25] On the decree *super speculam,* see Walter Ullmann, "Honorius III and the Prohibition of Legal Studies," *Juridical Review,* 60 (1948): 177-86; Stephan G. Kuttner, "Papst Honorius und das Studium des Zivilrechts," in *Festschrift für Martin Wolff,* ed. Ernst van Caemmerer et al. (Tübingen, 1952), pp. 79-101.

[26] Van Caenegem, "The 'Reception'," p. 201.

[27] The number of monographs and studies on the topic is very large. For recent discussions, see Franz Wiesacker, "Zum heutigen Stand der Receptionsforschung," in *Festschrift für Joseph Klein zum 70. Geburtstag,* ed. E. Fries (Göttingen, 1967), pp. 181-201; Karl Heinz Burmeister, *Das Studium der Rechte im Zeitalter des Humanismus im deutschen Rechtsbereich* (Wiesbaden, 1974), pp. 1-13.

profession. As a result, in this country, too, the ecclesiastical courts enjoyed great popularity in the Middle Ages, inasmuch as their claims to competence went far beyond the sphere of ecclesiastical law proper. The clerics trained in the law found employment not only in the ecclesiastical courts, but also as advisors and counsellors of princes and cities. Since the judges in the ecclesiastical courts were now required to be academically trained (university bred), the number of clergymen who went to law faculties increased rapidly after the thirteenth century.[28]

There were no universities in Germany in the thirteenth century. The first university in the medieval empire was established in Prague in 1348, and it was followed by the University of Vienna, which was founded in 1365. Erfurt, Heidelberg, and Cologne were the three other universities which were begun in the fourteenth century. The universities which were built in the fifteenth century and continued to exist are Würzburg (1402), Leipzig (1409), Rostock (1419), Greifswald (1456), Basel (1459), Ingolstadt (1472), Mainz (1476) and Tübingen (1476). The number of universities established reflects the vigor of intellectual activity in fifteenth-century Germany.[29]

At almost all German universities only Canon law was taught until the middle of the fifteenth century. As a result, many students from Germany went to the universities of upper Italy, such as Bologna, Pavia, Padua, Siena and Perugia, to study Roman and canon law.[30] The first German students who went to Italian law schools in the thirteenth century were for the most part members of the clergy. They came to the Italian law schools at the time of the Glossators. By this time, the University of Padua had the largest number of German students in the faculty of law. But the number of lay German students who studied law in Italy increased rapidly after about 1450. As one historian put it, "when change did come the pace was almost precipitous."[31] These sons of the nobility, the city patriciate and, increasingly in the fifteenth century and thereafter, the urban

[28] Cf. Erich Genzmer, "Kleriker als Berufsjuristen im späten Mittelalter," in *Études d'histoire du droit canoniques dediés a Gabriel Le Bras*, II (Paris, 1965), pp. 1207-36.

[29] See Heinrich Denifle, *Die Entstehung der Universitäten des Mittelalters bis 1400* (Berlin, 1885), p. 810.

[30] Gustav C. Knod, *Deutsche Studenten in Bologna (1289-1562)* (Berlin, 1899); Fritz Weigle, "Deutsche Studenten in Italien," *Quellen und Forschungen aus italienischen Archiven und Bibliotheken,* 32 (1942): 110-88; 33 (1944), 199-251; 38 (1958), 243-54; 39 (1959), 173-221. The number and the activity of German students at French universities have not been studied well. Cf. Detlef Illmer, "Die Statuten der deutschen Nation an der alten Universitat Orleans von 1378 bis 1596," *Ius Commune,* 4 (1977): 10-107.

[31] Wolfgang Kunkel, "The Reception of Roman Law in Germany: An Interpretation," in *Pre-Reformation Germany,* ed. Gerald Strauss (New York, 1972), p. 269.

bourgeoisie became chancellors and counselors of ecclesiastical or lay princes, or secretaries and advisors of large cities, after their return to Germany.

One result of the penetration of professional, academic jurisprudence from Italy into Germany was that after the middle of the fifteenth century Roman law began to be taught at many German universities as academic law. Several of the newly founded universities in the second half of the century, Basel (1459) and Tübingen (1476), for example, had chairs of Roman law from the beginning.[32] In fact, by the turn of the century the study of Roman law was beginning to force canon law very much into the background at many German universities. Another result of the rise of Roman law studies was that by the end of the nineteenth century there were a large number of learned professional jurists in the legal profession in Germany who were academically trained either abroad or at German universities. Roman law began to make inroads into the secular courts and into the legal records of the territories. With the rise of the academically trained jurists, the untrained jurors (*Schoffen*), who had played an important role in the Middle Ages, began to lose importance in the secular courts.

> In this way Germany became a stronghold of Roman law. Only in places such as Saxony where there were fairly big areas of more or less uniform character did German law hold out better.[33]

How much this important historical phenomenon called the "reception of Roman law in Germany" impressed many nineteenth-century legal historians can be seen in the famous Rede Lecture which the great English legal historian F. W. Maitland delivered at Cambridge in 1909. He expressed the view that "in the second quarter of the sixteenth century the continuity of English legal history was seriously threatened" by a reception of Roman law.[34] According to him, Roman law studies, which under the influence of humanism took a strong upward trend in sixteenth-century England, were encouraged strongly by Henry VIII, who founded chairs of civil law at Oxford and Cambridge. Professor Samuel E. Thorne of Harvard University argued convincingly in a recent paper that Maitland was unduly influenced by writings from Germany and that there was no threat or vehement attack on the Common Law under Henry VIII.[35]

---

[32] Kunkel, "The Reception," p. 269.

[33] Kunkel, *An Introduction,* p. 186.

[34] *Frederic William Maitland Reader,* ed. V.T.H. Delany (New York, 1957), p. 219; F.W. Maitland, "English Law and the Renaissance," in *Selected Historical Essays of F.W. Maitland,* ed. Helen M. Cam (Cambridge, 1957), p. 141.

[35] S. E. Thorne, "English Law and the Renaissance," *La storia del diritto nel quadro della scienze storiche.* [Atti del primo congresso internazionale della Società italiana di storia del diritto] (Firenze, 1966), pp. 437-45. See also T.F.T. Plucknett, "The Relations between Roman Law and English Common Law down to the Sixteenth Century: A General Survey," *University of Toronto Law Journal,* 3 (1939): 24-50.

What can we say about the historical developments in the fifteenth century which are called the "reception of Roman law" in various European countries? It was essentially the diffusion of a scholarly discipline, which had been flourishing in Italy since the end of the eleventh century, into many other countries in Europe. Or, as one historian put it, it was "a meeting of northern and Mediterranean traditions."[36] Especially in Germany, where a wholesale adoption of Roman law occurred in the fifteenth century, there have been heated discussions since the beginning of the Romantic movement in the nineteenth century as to its nature, its interpretation, its causes and its historical evaluation. It was regarded often as a catastrophic event which resulted in the replacement of indigenous German law by alien legal norms and institutions. In some other cases, complaints were made "more against the learned jurists and their incomprehensible methods than against the foreign law itself."[37]

In recent years, especially since the publication of Paul Koschaker's important book, *Europa und das romische Recht,*[38] in 1947, German scholars have begun to see the reception of Roman law not as a movement confined to Germany alone, but as a broader cultural and educational process which affected many European countries. The practice of Roman law had, after all, secured a foothold not only in France, Germany and Spain, but also as far afield as Bohemia, Hungary and Poland.[39] It is possible that some nationalistic German scholars who found the whole development embarrassing and distasteful have now been replaced by a new group of German historians who find it reassuring and probably consoling to learn that the reception of Roman law was in reality not an isolated event in the history of German law, but a European phenomenon. What is really remarkable is the fact that England successfully stood outside this powerful European movement which occurred in the fifteenth and sixteenth centuries.

But what caused this conscious and systematic transportation of Roman law in the fifteenth century? Why did the sudden expansion of the study of Roman law at universities in both Germany and other countries and the great success enjoyed by the popular literature on Roman law take place at the turn of

---

[36] See the title of the article in note 8.

[37] Kunkel, *An Introduction,* p. 187.

[38] Paul Koschaker, *Europa und das römische Recht* (München, 1947; 4th ed., 1966).

[39] E. Ott, *Beiträge zur Receptions-Geschichte des römisch-canonischen Prozesses in den böhmischen Ländern* (Leipzig, 1879); V. Gosovski, "Roman Law and the Polish Jurists from the Late Middle Ages to the Partition of Poland," *Seminar,* 1 (1943): 74-98; S. von Bolla, "Hergang der Rezeption in den böhmischen Ländern," in *L'Europa e il diritto romano: Studi in memoria di Paolo Koschaker,* I (Milano, 1954), pp. 375-91.

the fifteenth and sixteenth centuries? Why do we find Roman influence so much weaker in England than on the Continent? Why was Roman law so extensively and rapidly accepted in Germany?

In general, the rise of absolutism on the Continent was a development which favored the reception of Roman law. The concentration of royal power required a more rational approach to government and the administration of justice. This need could be best filled by academically trained jurists. Roman law, which was sometimes characterized as *ratio scripta,* or "written reason," was far superior to customary law because of its rationality and clarity. The triumph of Roman law was also the product of a popular movement. There existed a powerful movement from below, that is to say, from the litigants, in favor of the learned law. During the course of the reception, the litigants gradually turned from the untrained courts of jurors to the learned or semi-learned officials of their territorial sovereign, expecting a more rational verdict from them than from the traditional courts. Furthermore, the rise of a scientific, academic jurisprudence was welcome to the rising bourgeoisie because of its emphasis on persuasion rather than on the forceful solution of disputes. Judges arrived at their sentences in a scientific, rational fashion, and they judged according to their knowledge of the law, excluding ordeals by fire or water. It was increasingly realized that in an age of expanding capitalism, learned law was far more suitable than lay-centered, unsystematic, customary law. Finally, we can understand the especially rapid adoption of Roman law in fifteenth-century Germany if we remember that as a result of the political fragmentation of the country, German customary law was fissured into numerous legal systems and that these could thus not offer the same resistance to foreign law as the common law of England in the twelfth century had been able to offer.

What was the influence of humanism on jurisprudence in the fifteenth century or, to put the question more specifically, did humanism facilitate the diffusion of Roman law in central European countries? Is it true, as some have said, that humanism and the reception of Roman law were essentially contradictory in nature and had little to do with each other?[40]

Some German legal historians have distinguished between a theoretical reception of Roman law, which began in the twelfth century, and a practical reception, which started only in the fifteenth century. Obviously, the reception

---

[40] The standard works on humanistic jurisprudence are Francesco Calasso, *Medio evo del diritto* (Milano, 1954); Domenico Maffei, *Gli inizi dell' umanesimo giuridico* (Milano, 1956; 2nd ed., 1968). See also the works of Gilmore and Kisch mentioned in note 14, as well as Guido Kisch, "Humanistic Jurisprudence," *Studies in the Renaissance,* 8 (1959): 71-87; Myron P. Gilmore, "The Jurisprudence of Humanism," *Traditio,* 17 (1961): 493-501; Koschaker, *Europa,* pp. 105-245; Hans E. Troje, "Die europäische Rechtsliteratur unter dem Einfluss des Humanismus," *Ius Commune,* 3 (1970): 33-63.

of Roman law in the former sense began long before the rise of the humanist movement in the fourteenth century. Arguing on this basis, these historians assert that humanism was not the cause of the reception of Roman law.[41] But if we focus our attention on the so-called practical reception of the fifteenth century, it becomes clear that the development of humanism coincided with the spread of Italian jurisprudence, not only in Germany, but also in other central European countries. To be sure, by the fifteenth century the study of Roman law had passed the period of the Glossators in Italy and had entered the age of the Commentators. From the standpoint of the academic study of pure Roman law, it was a period of decline and stagnation. Therefore it can be said that humanism rose in Italy at a time when jurisprudence began to decline. But humanism could not arrest the decline of Italian jurisprudence because the influence and power of the Commentators were pervasive.[42]

As has been pointed out above, the fifteenth century was precisely the period in which many German students poured into Italy to attend universities, especially the University of Padua. It is quite clear that these law students became transmitters not only of Roman law but also of humanism when they returned to their home country. It must be remembered, however, that the Roman law which these students from noble and middle-class families brought home was not the Roman law of the Glossators, but that of the Commentators, and that German students of Roman law in the fifteenth century were employed more often as diplomats or counsellors to territorial or ecclesiastical princes than as university professors of Roman law. It was Bartolus's version of Roman law and not Justinian's law which was transmitted by these students. As everywhere (except in England), the jurists of fifteenth-century Germany were Bartolists.

Long before the publication of Koschaker's famous book, Roderich Stintzing had raised the question whether there would have been a reception of Roman law at all if the Glossators and Commentators had been humanists. He gave a negative answer to this question.[43] Koschaker agreed with him.[44] In reference to Germany a similar view was expressed recently by Professor Guido Kisch, one of the most distinguished legal historians of our time.[45] It seems clear that lawyers were so occupied with the practical task of the reception of Roman law in fifteenth-century Germany that the humanistic trend could not assert itself strongly.

---

[41] Mitteis, "Renaissance," pp. 558-59; Kunkel, "The Reception," p. 266.

[42] Mitteis, "Renaissance," p. 556, Kunkel, *An Introduction,* p. 188.

[43] Kisch, "Humanistic Jurisprudence," p. 73.

[44] Koschaker, *Europa,* p. 113.

[45] Kisch, "Humanistic Jurisprudence," pp. 73-75.

France was the only country on the Continent where humanism exerted any palpable influence on jurisprudence in the late Middle Ages. Already in the fourteenth century, as we have seen above, France had produced famous Roman lawyers, such as Jacques de Revigny and Pierre de Belleperche, who through Cino da Pistoia influenced the development of the school of the Commentators in Italy. But even in France it was only in the sixteenth century that humanistic jurists began to recover the real essence of Roman law by penetrating the accretions of glosses which enclosed Roman law texts in Justinian's law books. Drawing on the Romanist tradition established in the fourteenth century, French lawyers developed in the sixteenth century what is sometimes known as the school of elegant jurisprudence. It flourished especially in Bourges under such famous jurists as Andreas Alciato (1492-1540), Jacques Cujas (1522-1540), Hugo Donellus (1527-1591) and the great Guillaume Budé (1468-1540).[46] The *mos gallicus,* as the new humanistic jurisprudence was called (as opposed to the *mos italicus*), represented a new historical school of jurists which began to study the texts of Roman law simply as philological and historical documents set against their real classical background. Its task was to restore the Roman compilation to their original purity. In Germany it was Ulrich Zasius (1461-1535) of Freiburg im Breisgau who established his reputation as one of the great masters of the new jurisprudence, sharing with Alciato and Budé the credit for the development of a new science of Roman law.[47] Because of its small clientele and its antiquarian character, the new jurisprudence was sometimes ridiculed as elegant jurisprudence. It is also true that the flowering of humanistic juris-prudence did not last long. Some historians are convinced that the humanistic trend had little influence on the practice or application of the principle of Roman law, or even that humanistic jurisprudence, evaluated in its entirety, was harmful to the progressive development of the dogmatics of law.[48] But it is clear that without the foundation laid down in the fifteenth century, the humanistic jurisprudence of the sixteenth century would not have come into existence.

---

[46] On French jurists who belong to the school, see Myron P. Gilmore, *Argument from Roman Law in Political Thought 1200-1600* (Cambridge, Massachusetts, 1941), pp. 45-88; Linton C. Stevens, "The Contributions of French Jurists to the Humanism of the Renaissance," *Studies in the Renaissance,* I (1954): 92-105; Koschaker, *Europa,* pp. 105-24; Donald R. Kelley, *Foundations of Modern Historical Scholarship: Language, Law and History in the French Renaissance* (New York, 1970). Alciato, who was active in France, was by birth an Italian.

[47] Roderich Stintzing, *Ulrich Zasius: Din Beitrag zur Geschichte der Rechtswissen-schaft im Zeitalter der Reformation* (Basel, 1857); Mitteis, "Renaissance," p. 560; Kunkel, *An Introduction,* p. 188.

[48] Cf. Wolff, *Roman Law,* pp. 211-12; Kisch, "Humanistic Jurisprudence," p. 74.

Finally, we must ask what practical effects the humanist movement had in the field of jurisprudence. Did it in any way contribute to the reform of European legal systems?

The fifteenth century was a period in which the idea of reform played a very important role. After the Great Schism of the Church (1378-1417) in the fourteenth and fifteenth centuries, a series of church councils was held where not only the unity but also the reform of the Church were discussed, debated and pursued vigorously. No doubt these reform councils gave an impetus to a revitalization of the imperial reform movement, which had remained rather inactive after the adoption of the Golden Bull of 1356. The *Concordantia catholica,* which Nicholas of Cusa presented to the Council of Basel in 1432, the *Advisamentum sacrorum canonum et doctorum ecclesiae catholicae,* etc., in which an anonymous author discussed, among other topics, the problems of imperial reform, and Heinrich Toke's *Concepta* of 1430 and *Concilia* of 1442, are some of the most famous proposals for imperial reform which appeared in the fifteenth century. Many people realized at that time that the problem of imperial reform was closely related to that of church reform.[49]

Without any doubt one of the most important events in the fifteenth century which manifested the spirit of reform in the field of jurisprudence was the establishment in 1495 of the Imperial Chamber Court (*Reichskammergericht*) in Germany. Under the new system, half the assessors had to hold a doctorate, and the court was instructed to reach its verdict in accordance with the common laws of the Empire, that is to say, in accordance with Roman law. The Imperial Chamber Court later served an important role as a model for the establishment and reform of territorial high courts.[50] Another notable development occurred around 1500, especially in the individual territories and cities of southern Germany. It was the publication of comprehensive collection of laws which contained mainly Roman law, preserving Germanic customary law in only a few cases. These "reformations" of city and territorial law were the work of the learned, academically trained municipal or princely advisers and counsellors who had studied at Italian, French or German universities where Roman law was taught. These restatements and partial reforms of legal customs had far-reaching influence, especially on local legislation.

The fifteenth century was an important transitional period between the Middle Ages and the modern era in which old traditions and new developments co-existed side by side in many fields. An age of many reforms, both religious and secular, it witnessed important events whose impact on European society

[49] See my article, "Imperial Reform in the Mid-Fifteenth Century: Gregor Heimburg and Martin Mair," *Journal of Medieval and Renaissance Studies,* 9 (1979): 209-35.

[50] Kunkel, "The Reception," pp. 270-71.

was felt for many years to come. In the field of Roman law studies, the Commentators, who had, practically speaking, become the legal instructors of Europe, dominated law schools and courts. Their approach to the law was much more flexible and adaptable to medieval conditions than that of the Glossators, and they enjoyed great popularity everywhere. Another important development during this time was the reception of Roman law in many countries. The legal method and teaching of such great Commentators as Bartolus and Baldus were studied assiduously at many Italian universities by foreign students who later went home to spread the ideas and teachings of Roman law. Germany was the country where a wholesale reception of Roman law took place; France, by contrast, experienced no reception in the fifteenth century because of its closer historical and traditional connections with ancient Rome. Isolated from the Continent geographically and anxious to maintain its own legal tradition politically, England almost alone stayed outside the widespread movement which affected many other European countries.[51]

What complicated the reception of Roman law was the simultaneous spread of humanism in fifteenth century Europe. Humanism did not precipitate the reception of Roman law, nor did it successfully arrest the decline of Italian jurisprudence. Perhaps it is possible to exaggerate the significance of the conflict between the *mos italicus* and the *mos gallicus* by giving too much credit to the latter. Some scholars, on the other hand, have de-emphasized the historical significance of "elegant" jurisprudence too much.[52] Regardless of the ultimate assessment of humanistic jurisprudence, no serious student of early modern Europe can underestimate the contributions which practical, academically trained, and predominantly lay jurists of the fifteenth century made in the age of early capitalism and absolutism.

In recent years the prominence of lawyers in the formation of modern Europe has increasingly come to be recognized.[53] The nature and development of the legal profession in the fifteenth century must be further studied if we are to understand well the evolution of modern European society and culture.

The research for this article was aided by a grant from the American Philosophical Society.

[51] Kunkel, "The Reception," pp. 270-71.

[52] For a recent study which emphasizes the positive contribution of humanistic jurisprudence to modern political thought, see Quentin Skinner, *The Foundations of Modern Political Thought,* 2 vols. (Cambridge, 1978), especially pp. 1, 201-8, 211, 234, 262-69, 290-91, 310. Skinner points out that Calvin was taught by Andrea Alciato between 1529 and 1531 as a law student at the University of Bourges. On the contributions of Renaissance jurisprudence to philosophy, see Donald R. Kelley, "Vera Philosophia: The Philosophical Significance of Renaissance Jurisprudence," *Journal of the History of Philosophy,* 14 (1976): 267-79.

[53] See, for example, William J. Bouwsma, "Lawyers and Early Modern Culture," *American Historical Review,* 78 (1973): 303-27.

PART TWO

NICHOLAS OF CUSA

The Origins of Modern Cusanus Research in Germany and the Establishment of the Heidelberg *Opera Omnia*

It is apparent that in order to discuss modern Cusanus studies we must discuss publications and research activities not only in Germany but also in other European countries, especially France and Italy. In France, for example, Pierre Duhem (1861-1916), the noted historian of science, published two important studies at the beginning of the twentieth century in which he discussed Cusanus; one dealing with Cusanus and Leonardo da Vinci and another discussing Cusanus' relationship with Thierry of Chartres.[1] The most important and influential modern studies of Cusanus in French were those written by Edmond Vansteenberghe (1881-1943). Beginning with his study of *De ignota litteratura* of Johannes Wenck against Cusanus, which was published in 1910, Vansteenberghe's intensive and careful research culminated in the famous monograph, *Le cardinal Nicolas de Cues (1401-1464): L'action—la pensée* of 1920.[2]

Italian studies on Cusanus published in the late nineteenth and early twentieth centuries are much more numerous than those published in French. Giuseppe Rossi's study of Cusanus' philosophy and Enrico Constanzi's work on Cusanus as a precursor of Galileo appeared at the end of the nineteenth century.[3]

---

[1] Pierre Duhem, *Études sur Léonard de Vinci,* II (Paris, 1909): 97-279 and his "Thierry de Chartres et Nicolas de Cues," *Revue des sciences philosophiques et théologiques* 3 (1909): 525-531.

[2] Vansteenberghe's works include: *Le "De ignota litteratura" de Jean Wenck de Herrenberg contre Nicolas de Cues* [Beiträge zur Geschichte der Philosophie und Theologie des Mittelalters (=BGPhThM)] VIII, 6 (Münster, 1910); *Autour de la docte ignorance: Un controverse sur la théologie mystique au XVe siècle,* BGPhThM XIV, 2-4 (Münster, 1915); *Le cardinal Nicolas de Cues (1401-1464): L'action—la pensée* (Paris, 1920; reprint, Frankfurt a.M., 1963); "Le cardinal-légat Nicolas de Cues et le clergé de Liége," *Leodium* 15 (1922): 98-123; *La vision de Dieu,* Museum Lessianum (Paris-Louvain, 1925); "Quelques lectures de jeunesse de Nicolas de Cues," *Archives d'histoire doctrinale et littéraire du moyen âge* 3 (1928): 275-284; "Un petit traité de Nicolas de Cues sur la contemplation," *Revue des sciences religieuses* 9 (1929): 376-390.

[3] Giuseppe Rossi, *Nicolò da Cusa e la direzione monistica della filosofia nel Rinascimento* (Pisa, 1893); Enrico Costanzi, "Un precursore di Galileo nel Sec. XV: il Cardinale Niccolò da Cusa," *Rivista internazionale di scienze sociali e discipline ausiliarie* (Rome, 1898).

Remigio Sabbadini's inquiry into the manuscript studies done by conciliarists at the Council of Basel, which was published in 1910, included interesting materials on Cusanus.[4] Beginning with his *La filosofia dei valori nel pensiero di Nicolò da Cusa* of 1910, Paolo Rotta published four studies in the following decade, including his edition of *De docta ignorantia* (1913).[5] In the 1920's, Rotta continued to publish studies of Cusanus, and his translation of *De docta ignorantia* into Italian appeared in 1927. His *Il cardinal Nicolò da Cusa: La vita ed il pensiero,* which was published in Milan in 1928, can be regarded as a milestone in his research on Cusanus.[6]

Since, however, the purpose of this article is to examine the beginnings of Cusanus studies in modern Germany and show how the so-called Heidelberg edition of Cusanus' *Opera omnia* began to be published, we shall deal exclusively with studies of Cusanus published in the nineteenth and early twentieth centuries in Germany.

Perhaps it is well to remember at the outset that the first contemporary critic of Cusanus' philosophy was Johannes Wenck of Herrenberg (d. 1460), a professor at the University of Heidelberg.[7] Although there were some notable publications on Cusanus which appeared before and in the eighteenth century, such as Caspar Hartzheim's *Vita Nicolai de Cusa* and Johannes Semler's study and translation of Cusanus' *De pace fidei,*[8] it was not until the beginning of the

---

[4] See Remigio Sabbadini, "Niccolò da Cusa e i conciliari di Basilea alla ricerca dei codici," *Rendiconti della R. Accademia dei Lincei* 20 (Rome, 1911): 3-41.

[5] Paolo Rotta, "La filosofia dei valori nel pensiero di Nicolò da Cusa," *Rivista di Filosofia neo-scolastica* [=RFNs] 2 (giugno, 1910): 244-261; *De docta ignorantia* (Bari, 1913); *Il pensiero di Nicolò da Cusa nei suoi rapporti storici* (Turin, 1915).

[6] "Il Cusano e la lotta contro gli Ussiti ed i Maomettani," RFNs 18 (settembre-dicembre, 1926); "La biblioteca del Cusano," RFNs 21 (gennaio-febbraio, 1927), 22-47; Nicolò Cusano, *Della dotta ignoranzia, prima traduzione italiana* (Milan, 1927); *Il cardinal Nicolò da Cusa: la vita ed il pensiero* (Milan, 1928); "La nozione di misura nella concezione metafisico-scientifica di Nicolò da Cusa," RFNs 23 (1931): 518-524; "Un manoscritto del Cusano nell'Ambrosiana di Milano," *Rendiconti del R. Istituto Lombardo di Scienze e Lettere* 74, 2 (1941-1942): 478-480; *Nicolò Cusano* (Milan, 1942).

[7] For recent discussions of Johannes Wenck and his attack on Cusanus, see Rudolf Haubst, *Studien zu Nikolaus von Kues und Johannes Wenck,* BGPhThM 38, 1 (1955); Jasper Hopkins, *Nicholas of Cusa's Debate with John Wenck: A Translation and an Appraisal of* De Ignota Litteratura *and* Apologia Doctae Ignorantiae (Minneapolis, 1981; 3rd ed., 1988).

[8] Casparus Hartzheim, *Vita Nicolai de Cusa S.R.E. Presbyteri Cardinalis ad Vincula S. Petri* (Trier, 1730; reprint, Frankfurt a.M., 1968); Johannes Semler, *Des Kardinals Nicolaus von Cusa Dialogus von der Übereinstimmung oder Einheit des Glaubens*

nineteenth century that serious research on Cusanus' life and thought began in German-speaking countries. No doubt the Romantic movement helped revive interest in his works.[9]

How what some historians called a Cusanus Renaissance occurred at the University of Tübingen in the 1820's under the influence of Johann Adam Möhler (1796-1838) has already been discussed in detail by Jochen Köhler in his article published in the *Mitteilungen und Forschungsbeiträge der Cusanus-Gesellschaft* 10 (1973).[10] We shall touch on some of the points in the article which have a direct bearing on our main concern in this paper and comment on them with a view to clarifying the contributions of the University of Tübingen to the later development of the Heidelberg edition of Cusanus' works.

Founded in 1477 by Count Eberhard of Württemberg, the University of Tübingen initially established fifteen chairs: three in theology, five in law, two in medicine, and five in arts. When the Reformation was introduced into Württemberg in 1534, the Protestant Theological Faculty obtained the leading position at Tübingen and retained its position into the nineteenth century. In 1809 Württemberg, which included areas of heavy Catholic population, became a kingdom. As a result, the University of Tübingen created a Faculty of Catholic Theology in 1817. Here the so-called "Catholic School of Tübingen" was quickly formed, with Johann Sebastian Drey (1777-1853) as its head. The development of historical and speculative theology at the School, which occurred under the influence of German Idealism and Romanticism, was of great importance in the history of theological study in modern Germany.[11]

(Leipzig, 1787). About the influence of the philosophy of Cusanus from the fifteenth to the eighteenth century, see a recent study, Stephan Meier-Oeser, *Die Präsenz des Vergessenen: Zur Rezeption der Philosophie des Nicolaus Cusanus vom 15. bis zum 18. Jahrhundert* (Münster, 1989).

[9] For a general survey of the intellectual and theological response of Roman Catholics in Europe to the French Revolution and its aftermath, see Kenneth Scott Latourette, *Christianity in a Revolutionary Age,* vol. 1: *The Nineteenth Century in Europe—Background and the Roman Catholic Phase* (New York, 1958). See also Georg Schwaiger, ed., *Kirche und Theologie im 19. Jahrhundert* (Göttingen, 1975); Manfred Weitlauff, "Kirche und Theologie in der ersten Hälfte des 19. Jahrhundert," *Münchener Theologische Zeitschrift* 39, 3 (1988): 155-180.

[10] Jochen Köhler, "Nikolaus von Kues in der Tübinger Schule," *Mitteilungen und Forschungsbeiträge der Cusanus-Gesellschaft* [=MFCG] 10 (1976): 191-206.

[11] For a recent study of the Catholic School of Tübingen, see Thomas F. O'Meara, *Romantic Idealism and Roman Catholicism: Schelling and the Theologians* (Notre Dame, 1982). The School should not be confused with the (Protestant) Tübingen School of Historical Study. See R.W. Mackay, *The Tübingen School and Its Antecedents* (Hestford, 1869); Eduard Zeller, "Die Tübinger historische Schule," in *Vorträge und Abhandlungen,* 2nd ed., 1 (Leipzig, 1875), pp. 294-389; Peter C.

Möhler,[12] who was ordained a priest in 1819, became a *Privatdozent* in 1822 in the Catholic Theological Faculty at Tübingen and was then sent on a six-month tour of central European universities (Würzburg, Göttingen, Braunschweig, Magdeburg, Berlin, Breslau, Prague, Vienna, Munich, and others), at which he made the acquaintance of leading professors, among them some prominent Protestant scholars.[13] He was particularly impressed with the deep and precise scholarship of Johann August Wilhelm Neander (1789-1850), a professor of church history since 1813 at the University of Berlin. While speaking with Neander, Möhler said that he intended to study a great historical subject: the period of the decline of the papacy from the removal of its seat to Avignon to the Councils of Constance and Basel.[14] He was clearly one of the notable supporters of the church, but his work on the unity of the church, which he published in 1825,[15] received both enthusiastic appraisals and severe criticisms because of his ardent desire to reach an understanding with Protestants and to accomplish the reunion of the churches. In 1806 he became a full professor.

Hodgson, *The Formation of Historical Theology: A Study of Ferdinand Ch. Baur* (New York, 1966); Horton Harris, *The Tübingen School* (Oxford, 1975).

[12] There are many studies of Möhler. To mention some important ones, A. Knöpfler, *Johannes Adam Möhler: Ein Gedenkenblatt zu dessen hundertsten Geburtstag* (Munich, 1896); Edmond Vermeil, *Jean-Adam Möhler et L'École catholique de Tubingue (1815-1840)* (Paris, 1913); Josef Rupert Geiselmann, *Johann Adam Möhler: Die Einheit der Kirche und die Wiedereinigung der Konfessionen* (Vienna, 1940); J.R. Geiselmann, *Lebendiger Glaube aus geheiligter Überlieferung: Der Grundgedanke der Theologie Johann Adam Möhlers und der katholischen Tübinger Schule* (Mainz, 1942; 2nd ed., Freiburg, 1966); Hans Geisser, *Glaubenseinheit und Lehrentwicklung bei Johann Adam Möhler* (Göttingen, 1971). In commemoration of the 150th anniversary of Möhler's death, the *Münchener Theologische Zeitschrift* published a special issue [39, 3 (1988)] dedicated to Möhler and his significance. See especially Georg Schwaiger, "Vorwort: Johann Adam Möhler (1796-1889): Zum 150. Todestag," pp. 153-154, and Peter Stockmeier, "Johann Adam Möhler und der Aufbruch der wissenschaftlichen Kirchengeschichtsschreibung," pp. 181-194.

[13] Weitlauff, "Kirche," p. 177.

[14] Stockmeier, "Johann Adam Möhler," p. 183.

[15] *Die Einheit in der Kirche oder das Prinzip des Katholizismus. Dargestellt im Geiste der Kirchenväter der drei ersten Jahrhunderte* (Tübingen, 1825; critical ed., Cologne and Olten, 1957). It is perhaps worth noting that Hans Küng, who also taught in the Catholic Theological Faculty of Tübingen, cited Möhler's work, *Die Einheit,* in his *Structures of the Church,* trans. S. Attanasio (New York, 1964), pp. 318-319. Concerning the controversy that arose as a result of the book between J.A. Möhler and F.C. Baur, see Hodgson, *The Formation;* Joseph Fitzer, *Moehler and Baur in Controversy, 1832-38* (Tallahassee, Florida, 1974).

Möhler's later works, especially *Symbolik* (1832),[16] caused offense to many of his more conservative Catholic colleagues because he attempted to make a comparison between the Catholic and Protestant dogmas. His sympathy for the theses of Protestantism regarding the invisible character of the church and its mystical elements became increasingly strong. In his early academic years he had studied the period of Church Fathers intensively, but he began to take great interest in the conciliar period of the fifteenth century and first studied the philosophical and theological ideas of conciliarist writers, such as Pierre d'Ailly (1351-1420), Nicholas de Clamanges (ca. 1360-1437), and Jean Gerson (1363-1420). Although Möhler did not refer to Cusanus specifically in his lectures and writings before 1829, there is reason to believe that by 1829 he was studying the works of Cusanus.[17]

In 1829 the Catholic Theological Faculty of the University of Tübingen sponsored an essay contest. Entrants were asked to submit an essay on "A Description of the Life and the Ecclesiastical and Literary Work of Cardinal and Bishop of Brixen, Nicholas of Cusa." Judging from the extant draft of the official announcement, it is clear that the choice of Cusanus as the subject for the contest was made and supported by Professor Möhler.[18] Three major essays submitted for consideration were all written by Möhler's students, Franz Anton Scharpff (1809-1879), Karl Joseph Hefele (1809-1893), and Ludwig Schmitt (1807-1877). When the decision on the best essay was announced on November 6, 1831, Scharpff was the winner of the first prize for his essay.[19]

Scharpff published a part of the essay as *Das kirchliche und literarische Wirken des Nicolaus von Cusa* in *Theologische Quartalschrift* (1837).[20] After intensive archival research in Kues and Brixen, he was able to publish in 1843 *Der Cardinal und Bischof Nicolaus von Cusa*, I. Theil, *Das kirchliche Wirken— Ein Beitrag zur Geschichte der Reformation innerhalb der catholischen Kirche in fünfzehnten Jahrhundert* (Mainz, 1843). With the publication of this study, serious modern research on Cusanus can be said to have begun in Germany.

---

[16] *Symbolik oder Darstellung der dogmatischen Gegensätze der Katholiken und Protestanten nach ihren öffentlichen Bekenntnisschriften* (Mainz, 1832; critical ed., Cologne and Olten, 1960-61). It is interesting to note that Lord Acton, a liberal Catholic, who wrote in 1867 one of the earliest studies of Cusanus in English ["Nicholas of Cusa" in Lord Acton, *Essays on Church and State* (London, 1952), pp. 246-250], cited Möhler's *Symbolik* in his essays.

[17] Köhler, "Nikolaus von Kues," pp. 192-195.

[18] Köhler, "Nikolaus von Kues," pp. 195-198.

[19] In his *Der Cardinal und Bischof Nicolaus von Cusa* (Mainz, 1843), pp. 3-4, Scharpff cited word for word from Möhler's lectures on church history.

[20] *Theologische Quartalschrift* 9 (1837): 2-35, 201-258, 687-763.

About this time, Mathias Martini (1794-1868), rector of St. Nicholas Hospital
in Kues from 1827 to 1842, also published two articles on various documents
related to Cusanus and his life, and wrote a guide book to St. Nicholas
Hospital.[21] It is known that Martini was encouraged to study these topics and
publish his findings under Möhler's influence.[22] We must also note that in 1843
F.J. Clemens published the cosmological statements of Cusanus which he had
found in Codex Cusanus 211 in St. Nicholas Hospital.[23]

A detailed two-volume study of Cusanus and the church of his time,
published in 1847 by Johann Martin Düx (1806-1875),[24] is the only major work
on Cusanus from the first half of the nineteenth century which was not directly
inspired by Möhler. Head of the Diocesan Priestly Seminary in Würzburg, Düx
spoke of his research in the past eleven years and referred to Scharpff's book
published in 1843. But he did not mention any of Möhler's works. Köhler has
pointed out, however, that Düx was born in Simmaringen, which was close to
Möhler's hometown, Igersheim, Württemberg, and that Düx was in
correspondence with Möhler.[25]

In the second half of the nineteenth century Scharpff and many other
scholars published numerous studies of Cusanus not only dealing with his life,
but also with his philosophical and scientific ideas.[26] One of the notable writers

---

[21] Martini's publications include: "Nachträge zu Sinnachers Geschichte der
Bischöflichen Kirche Säben und Brixen, enthaltend Urkunden, den Cardinal Nicolaus
Cusanus betreffend," *Theologische Quartalschrift* 12 (1830): 171-179;
"Berechtigungen und Zusätze zu den Lebensbeschreibungen des Cardinal Cusanus,"
Theologische Quartal. 13 (1831): 386-390; *Das Hospital von Cues und dessen Stifter*
(Trier, 1841).

[22] Köhler, "Nikolaus von Kues," p. 198.

[23] Friedrich Jakob Clemens, *Giordano Bruno und Nicolaus von Cusa: Eine
philosophische Abhandlung* (Bonn, 1847).

[24] Johann Martin Düx, *Der deutsche Cardinal Nicolaus von Cusa und die Kirche seiner
Zeit,* 2 vols. (Regensburg, 1847).

[25] Köhler, "Nikolaus von Kues," p. 202.

[26] Some of the important works published in the second half of the 19th century are
listed below chronologically: Franz Anton Scharpff, *Des Cardinals und Bischofs
Nicolaus von Cusa wichtigste Schriften in deutscher Übersetzung* (Freiburg i.B.,
1862); F.X. Kraus, "Die Handschriften-Sammlung des Cardinals Nicolaus von Cusa,"
Serapeum 25, 23 (1864): 353-365; 24 (1864): 369-383; 26, 2 (1865): 24-31; 3
(1865): 33-42; 4 (1865): 49-59; 5 (1865): 65-76; 6 (1865): 81-89; 7 (1865):
97-104; Theodor Stumpf, *Die politischen Ideen des Nicolaus von Cues: Zum
Gedächtnis seines vierhundertjährigen Todestages (11. August 1464)* (Coblenz,
1864); Joseph Klein, *Über eine Handschrift des Nicolaus von Cues, nebst
ungedruckten Fragmenten Ciceronischer Reden* (Berlin, 1866); Clemens F.

in this period was Johannes Uebinger (1854-1912). Starting with his dissertation of 1880, completed at the University of Würzburg,[27] he published at least six other major studies of Cusanus, including his detailed study of Cusanus' mathematical ideas published in 1895-1897.[28] In his book, *Die Gotteslehre des Nikolaus Cusanus,* he published the text of *Tetralogus de non aliud,* which he had discovered during his archival research.[29] It is well to remember that some Cusanus scholars like Clemens, Kraus, and Uebinger had begun to realize by this time how important it was to obtain reliable, authentic texts of Cusanus'

Brockhaus, *Nicolai Cusani de Concilii Universalis Potestate Sententia explicatur* (Leipzig, 1867); F.A. Scharpff, *Der Cardinal und Bischof Nicolaus von Cusa als Reformator in Kirche, Reich und Philosophie des 15. Jahrhunderts* (Tübingen, 1871); Rudolf Eucken, "Nicolaus von Cues," *Philosophische Monatshefte* 14 (1878): 449-470; Richard Falckenberg, *Aufgabe und Wesen der Erkenntnis bei Nicolaus von Kues* (Breslau, 1880); R. Falckenberg, *Grundzüge der Philosophie des Nicolaus Cusanus, mit besonderer Berücksichtigung der Lehre vom Erkennen* (Breslau, 1880); Karl Grube, "Die Legationsreise des Cardinals Nikolaus von Cusa durch Norddeutschland im Jahre 1451," *Historisches Jahrbuch* 1 (1880): 393-412; Jacob Schaefer, *Des Nicolaus von Kues Lehre vom Kosmos* (Mainz, 1887); H. Schedel, *Die Gotteslehre des Nicolaus von Kues* (Münster, 1888); Michael Glossner, *Nikolaus von Cusa und Marius Nizolius als Vorläufer der neueren Philosophie* (Münster, 1891); Franz Falk, "Cardinal Nicolaus von Cusa in Rom und Cues an der Mosel," *Der Katholik* LXXII, 1 (1892): 88-96; H.V. Sauerland, "Notizien zur Lebensgeschichte des Kardinals Nicolaus von Cues," *Römische Quartalschrift* 9 (1893): 192; Aloys Meister, "Die humanistischen Anfänge des Nikolaus von Cues," *Annalen des Historischen Vereins für Niederrhein* 63 (1896): 1-21; Hermann Grauert, "Nicolaus von Cues als Humanist, Handschriftenforscher und Staatsphilosoph," *Literarische Beilage der Kölnischen Volkszeitung* 28, 29 (1897); Siegmund Günther, "Nikolaus von Cusa in seiner Beziehungen zur mathematischen und physikalischen Geographie," in *Abhandlungen zur Geschichte der Mathematik* (Leipzig, 1899); J. Guttmann, "Aus der Zeit der Renaissance: Nicolaus von Cusa, Jacobus Faber Stapulensis, Bonet de Lattes, Carolus Bovillus," *Monatsschrift für Geschichte und Wissenschaft des Judenthums,* N.S., 7 (Berlin, 1899): 250-266.

[27] Johannes Uebinger, *Die Philosophie des Nicolaus Cusanus* (Würzburg, 1880).

[28] "Kardinallegat Nikolaus Cusanus in Deutschland 1451 bis 1452," *Historisches Jahrbuch* 8 (1887): 629-665; *Die Gotteslehre des Nikolaus Cusanus* (Münster, 1888); "Zur Lebensgeschichte des Nikolaus Cusanus," *Historisches Jahrbuch* 14 (1893): 549-561; "Die philosophischen Schriften des Nikolaus Cusanus," *Zeitschrift für Philosophie und phil. Kritik* 103, 105, 107 (1894); "Der Begriff docta ignorantia in seiner geschichtlichen Entwicklung," *Archiv für Geschichte der Philosophie* 8 (1895): 1-32, 206-240; "Die mathematischen Schriften des Nicolaus Cusanus," *Philosophisches Jahrbuch* 8 (1895): 301-317, 403-422; 9 (1896): 54-66, 391-410; 10 (1897): 144-159; "Nikolaus Treverensis," *Philosophisches Jahrbuch* 19 (1906): 451-470.

[29] Uebinger, *Die Gotteslehre,* pp. 150-193.

writings. After all, the published editions of his works, the Strassbourg edition
of 1488 by Martin Flach, the Milan edition of 1502 by Benedictus Dolcibelli,
the Paris edition of 1514 by Jodocus Badius Ascensius, and the Basel edition of
1565 by Henricus Petri, were at least three hundred years old.

The Strassbourg edition was rare, and the Milan edition, which was a
slavish reprint of the first, was rarer still. The Paris edition by the famous
French humanist Jacques Lefèvre d'Étaples was notable for the fact that it had
important additions, the *De concordantia catholica libri tres* and the *Excitationum
libri decem*, but was not very reliable because the humanist made many
emendations of the text. The Basel edition added some mathematical treatises to
the third. As a result, the Basel edition was regarded by many as the most useful
of the printed editions.[30] Clearly there was a great need to establish an authentic,
critical modern edition of Cusanus' works.

Düx and Uebinger, two prominent Cusanus scholars of the nineteenth
century, were not members of the Catholic School of Tübingen, but members of
the Tübingen School, such as Paul Schanz (1841-1905), Johann Storz (1839-
1895), and Maximilian Birck (1841-1903), also made significant contributions
to Cusanus studies in the second half of the nineteenth century.[31] The articles
on Cusanus which were published in encyclopedias and lexica during the period
were written mostly by the members of the Catholic School of Tübingen.[32]

To summarize, modern Cusanus research in nineteenth-century Germany
was chiefly advanced by members of the Catholic School of Tübingen under the
influence of Johann Adam Möhler. Not only did they study the life,

---

[30] The edition printed at present-day Cortemaggiore is usually called the Milan
edition. About various editions, see Vansteenberghe, *Le cardinal,* pp. 465-468; Gerd
Heinz-Mohr and Willehad Paul Eckert, eds., *Das Werk des Nicolaus Cusanus: Eine
bibliophile Einführung* (Cologne, 1963; 2nd ed., 1975), pp. 164-165; W.P. Eckert,
"Der Stand der Cusanus-Edition," *Schweizer Rundschau* 63, 7/8 (1964): 443-448.

[31] Their studies are: Paul Schanz, *Der Cardinal Nicolaus von Cusa als Mathematiker*
(Rottweil, 1873); idem, *Die astronomischen Anschauungen des Nikolaus von Kues
und seiner Zeit* (Rottweil, 1873); Johann Nepomak Storz, "Die spekulative
Gotteslehre des Nicolaus Cusanus," *Theologische Quartalschrift* 55 (1873): 3-57,
220-285; Maximilian Birck, "Nikolaus von Cues' Auftreten auf dem Basler Konzil,"
Theologische Quartalschrift 73 (1891): 335-370; idem, "Hat Nikolaus von Cues seine
Ansicht über den Primat geändert?," *Theologische Quartalschrift* 74 (1892): 617-642;
idem, "Nikolaus von Cusa auf dem Konzil zu Basel," *Historisches Jahrbuch* 13
(1892): 770-782.

[32] Some of them are Carl von Prantl, "Cusanus," *Allgemeine Deutsche Biographie* 4
(Leipzig, 1876): 655-662; F.X. (von) Funk, "Nicolaus von Cusa," *Wetzer und Welte's
Kirchenlexikon,* 2nd ed., 9 (1895): 306-315; R. Schmid, "Cusanus,"
Realenzyklopädie für protestantische Theologie und Kirche, IV (Leipzig, 1898), pp.
360-364.

philosophical ideas, and influence of Cardinal Cusanus, but some of them began to pay attention to his mathematical ideas and also to the importance of discovering reliable texts.

What we must now attempt to clarify is how nineteenth-century Cusanus scholarship which was initiated and prompted by the Tübingen School was related to the Cusanus research which began at the University of Heidelberg in the late 1920's and which resulted in the publication of a modern critical edition of Cusanus' works under the auspices of the Heidelberg Academy of Sciences (*Heidelberger Akademie der Wissenschaften*).

Who were the scholars that were directly and indirectly responsible for this development? What was the philosophical and intellectual milieu that gave rise to the ambitious, enormously complicated, and still continuing academic and literary enterprise? What was the role played by Dr. Felix Meiner of the Felix Meiner Verlag in Leipzig? These are some of the important questions which we must answer as we turn to the second period of modern Cusanus studies. In the transition to this period, certain prominent leaders of Neo-Kantian schools took great interest in the ideas of Cusanus and paved the way for the launching of the Heidelberg edition of Cusanus' works. These scholars include Hermann Cohen (1842-1918), Heinrich Rickert (1863-1936), and Ernst Cassirer (1874-1945).

In 1911 Dr. Felix Meiner (1883-1965) purchased from the Dürr'sche Buchhandlung in Leipzig the *Philosophische Bibliothek,* which had been founded by Dr. Julius Hermann von Kirchmann (1802-1884) in 1868 and which had published many important German texts of prominent philosophers. The publishers of the *Philosophische Bibliothek* had changed hands many times, but the *Philosophische Bibliothek* was by 1911 a well-established library known to generations of German scholars and students.[33]

A list of forthcoming books, which Dr. Meiner received as he took over the *Philosophische Bibliothek* from the Dürr'sche Verlag, contained two volumes of Cusanus' works to be edited by Hermann Cohen, the leader of the Marburg School of Neo-Kantianism.[34] Together with Paul Natorp (1854-1924), Hermann Cohen had made Marburg a great center of Neo-Kantian studies.[35] In

---

[33] See Richard Richter, *Hundert Jahre Philosophische Bibliothek 1868-1968: Zeittafel und Gesamt-Verlagsverzeichnis* 1968 (Hamburg, 1968); *Hundert Jahre— Philosophische Bibliothek 1868-1968* (Hamburg, 1968).

[34] Type-written notes entitled "Die Cusanus-Ausgabe" kept by Dr. Felix Meiner which are dated 19 May 1945 [=*Notes*], p. 1. The author wishes to thank Mr. Richard Meiner of the Felix Meiner Verlag, Hamburg, for permission not only to use the *Notes* but also to cite passages from them in this article.

[35] There are numerous books and articles on Hermann Cohen. Interest in him seems to be growing in recent years. See, for example, Walter Kinkel, *Hermann Cohen: Eine Einführung in sein Werk* (Stuttgart, 1924); J. Ebbinghaus, "Hermann Cohen als

addition to the Marburg School of Neo-Kantianism under Hermann Cohen and
Paul Natorp, there was the South-West German School of Neo-Kantianism in
Heidelberg which had been led by Wilhelm Windelband (1848-1915) and then by
Heinrich Rickert.[36] Starting with Kant's premise that an unbridgeable gulf
separated thought from existence, the Neo-Kantians of both schools rejuvenated
the study of philosophy in the 1860's by critically re-examining Kant's works.[37]

Cohen, who had become the leader of the Marburg School of
Neo-Kantianism by 1876, developed the position which became known as the
logistic *a priori* school "because it attempted to derive its ideas of truth and of
philosophical science from mathematics and logic."[38] He defended this
mathematical perception of reality because he felt it was rooted in the nature of
reason itself. In mathematics, he believed, the work of our intellect could be
observed and studied in an unadulterated form. In many of his writings, Cohen
tried to make the infinitesimal and ordinal numbers the intellectual basis of any
comprehension of reality.[39] As Dr. Meiner himself wrote in his *Notes* of May
18, 1945, the prominent leader of the Marburg School was not himself directly
engaged in the editorial work for the projected two volumes on Cusanus.
Following the prevailing German academic practice, one of his students had
assumed the task of preparing the edition.[40] But the inclusion of the two
volumes under the editorship of the noted Marburg philosopher undoubtedly

Philosoph und Publizist," *Archiv für Philosophie* 6 (1956): 109-122; Joseph Klein,
*Die Grundlegung der Ethik in der Philosophie Hermann Cohens und Paul Natorps:
Eine Kritik des Marburger Neukantianismus* (Göttingen, 1976); Helmut Holzhey,
Cohen und Natorp, 2 vols. (Basel, 1986); William Kluback, *Hermann Cohen: The
Challenge of a Religion of Reason* (Chicago, 1984); idem, *The Idea of Humanity:
Hermann Cohen's Legacy to Philosophy and Theology* (Lanham, Maryland, 1987).
About the Marburg School, see Henri Dussort, *L'École de Marbourg* (Paris, 1963);
Bernard Tucker, *Ereignis: Wege durch die politische Philosophie des Marburger
Neukantianismus* (Frankfurt a.M., 1984).

[36] See Heinrich Rickert, *Die Heidelberger Tradition und Kants Kritizismus* (Berlin,
1934); Franz Josef Brecht, "Die Philosophie an der Universität Heidelberg seit
1803," *Ruperto Carola* 5. Jhrg. Nr. 9/10 (June 1953): 55-67; H. Rickert, *Science and
History: A Critique of Positivist Epistemology* (Princeton, 1962); Guy Oakes, *Weber
and Rickert: Concept Formation in the Cultural Sciences,* Studies in Contemporary
German Social Thought, ed. Thomas McCarthy (Cambridge, Massachusetts, 1988).

[37] On Neo-Kantianism in general, see Thomas E. Willey, *Back to Kant: The Revival
of Kantianism in German Social and Historical Thought, 1860-1914* (Detroit, 1977).

[38] David R. Lipton, *Ernst Cassirer* (Toronto, 1978), p. 21.

[39] See especially his *Das Prinzip der Infinitesimal-Methode und seine Geschichte:
Eine Kapitel zur Grundlegung der Erkenntnis Kritik* (Berlin, 1883).

[40] Meiner, *Notes,* p. 1: "Cohen hatte die textliche Arbeit einem Schüler übertragen."

reflected a deep interest which the followers of the school had taken in the thought of Cusanus.

Already in 1883, Hermann Cohen referred to Nicholas of Cusa and Giordano Bruno in his *Das Prinzip der Infinitesimal-Methode und seine Geschichte* (Berlin, 1883). [41] He tried to prove that the concept of the "infinitely small" is an indispensable and basic intellectual means for any scientific cognition of reality. In his famous book, *Logik der reinen Erkenntnis,* which was published by Bruno Cassirer in Berlin in 1902, Cohen also spoke of Cusanus' great interest in systematic philosophy, as well as in religion and ethics.[42] Since, as we saw before, there were many studies of Cusanus that had been published in the second half of the nineteenth century, it is easy to assume that Cohen was familiar with the growing literature on Cusanus. After all, one did not have to be a Neo-Kantian to take interest in Cusanus. But what is important for us to note here is that the Marburg School of Neo-Kantianism, as represented by Hermann Cohen, seems to have taken special interest in the mathematical and scientific ideas of Cusanus because of its penchant for studying philosophy in mathematical terms.

When we turn from Hermann Cohen to Ernst Cassirer, Cohen's most renowned student, it becomes clear that he also shared this preoccupation with Cusanus' mathematical and scientific ideas.[43] Born in Breslau in 1874 as the fourth child of a well-to-do merchant, Eduard Cassirer, Ernst Cassirer was studying at the University of Berlin in 1895 when in a lecture given by Georg Simmel (1858-1918) he heard the professor announce: "Undoubtedly the best books on Kant are written by Hermann Cohen, but I must confess that I do not

---

[41] *Das Prinzip,* p. 76 n. 8: "Es wäre der Vorwurf einer wichtigen und anziehenden Untersuchung, nachzuweisen, wie das theologische Interesse am Unendlichen mit diesem Grundbegriff der wissenschaftlichen Renaissance sich verbündet, um wie bei Nicolaus von Cues und Giordano Bruno die Diskussion des Infinitesimal zu fördern."

[42] Cohen, *Logik,* p. 29: "Nicolaus von Kues umfasst in seinem modernen Geiste alle Interessen der systematischen Philosophie, nicht zum mindesten auch die der Religion und der Ethik . . ."

[43] Of numerous recent studies of Cassirer, the following few may be mentioned in addition to Lipton's work cited in note 37 above. Carl H. Hamburg, *Symbol and Reality: Studies in the Philosophy of Ernst Cassirer* (The Hague, 1956); Seymour W. Itzkoff, *Ernst Cassirer: Philosopher of Culture* (Boston, 1977); John M. Krois, *Cassirer: Symbolic Forms and History* (New Haven, 1987); Massimo Ferrari, *Il giovane Cassirer e la scuola di Marburgo* (Milan, 1988). Paul A. Schlipp, ed., *The Philosophy of Ernst Cassirer* (Evanston, 1949), which is a collection of essays on Cassirer's life and ideas, as well as Cassirer's response, is a particularly useful publication.

understand them."[44] On hearing these words Cassirer made up his mind to go to Marburg and to study philosophy under Cohen's guidance. Immediately after the lecture, Cassirer went to his bookstore to purchase Cohen's books. He studied Kant's and Cohen's works thoroughly, as well as those of other philosophers essential for the understanding of Kant, such as Plato, Descartes, and Leibniz. Moreover, he devoted a considerable amount of time to the study of mathematics, mechanics, and biology which were indispensable for a clear understanding of Cohen's interpretation of Kant. Thus equipped, he arrived in Marburg in the spring of 1896 to hear Cohen's lectures.[45]

Known for his phenomenal memory and his vast knowledge on philosophical matters and admired for his kindly but somewhat aloof and unsociable attitudes because of his intensive study, Cassirer demonstrated in the first seminar under Cohen that he towered above all other Cohen's students because of his clear understanding of the most intricate problems of Kantian and Cohenian philosophy.[46] His doctoral dissertation, completed in 1899 under Cohen, was entitled *Descartes' Kritik der mathematischen und naturwissenschaftlichen Erkenntnis* and received the highest possible mark from the Philosophical Faculty of the University of Marburg.[47] In the dissertation, which was published in 1899, Cassirer spoke of Cusanus' deep understanding of the idea of the common measure of straight and curved lines.[48] The dissertation was again published in 1902 as an "Einleitung" to a larger book, *Leibniz' System in seiner wissenschaftlichen Grundlagen.*[49]

Cassirer's keen interest in Cusanus was clearly manifested in his widely acclaimed book, *Das Erkenntnisproblem in der Philosophie und Wissenschaft der neueren Zeit*, Vol. 1, which was published by his cousin Bruno Cassirer of Berlin in 1906.[50] He wrote: ". . . only in exact science—in its progress which,

[44] Schlipp, *The Philosophy*, p. 6.

[45] Schlipp, *The Philosophy*, p. 6.

[46] Schlipp, *The Philosophy*, p. 7: "'I felt at once,' said Cohen, 'that this man [Cassirer] had nothing to learn from me'."

[47] Schlipp, *The Philosophy*, p. 12. Ernst Cassirer, *Descartes' Kritik der mathematischen und naturwissenschaftlichen Erkenntnis* (Marburg, 1899).

[48] Cassirer, *Descartes' Kritik*, p. 97: "Der Gedanke des 'gemeisamen Masses' von Gerade und Krumm, den Nicolaus Cusanus bereits so tief erfasst hatte, ist hier bei Descartes also wiederum zurückgedrängt."

[49] Ernst Cassirer, *Leibniz' System in seinen wissenschaftlichen Grundlagen* (Marburg, 1902; reprint, Hildesheim, 1962).

[50] Ernst Cassirer, *Das Erkenntnisproblem in der Philosophie und Wissenschaft der neueren Zeit*, Vol. I (Berlin, 1906).

despite all vacillation, is continuous—does the harmonious concept of knowledge obtain its true accomplishment and verification; everywhere else this concept still remains a demand."[51] As one commentator put it, "[N]atural science Cassirer always looked upon as the highest and most characteristic expression of the power of the human mind."[52] In Chap. 1 of *Das Erkenntnisproblem,* which is entitled "Nikolaus Cusanus," Cassirer discusses Cusanus' concepts of God, the world, understanding, and sensitive faculty *(Sinnlichkeit),* his symbolic use of mathematics, objects, and natural philosophy, and other topics.[53] Already in this book, mostly in Chap. 2, Cassirer dealt with other notable thinkers of the fifteenth and sixteenth centuries, such as Georgius Gemistos Plethon, Pietro Pomponazzi, Lorenzo Valla, Giacomo Zabarella, Giovanni Pico della Mirandola, and Marius Nizolius.

In 1919, Cassirer accepted a call to become Professor of Philosophy at the University of Hamburg, which had been established as a result of the birth of the Weimar Republic in Germany after the end of World War I. In a book published in 1921, which dealt with Einstein's theory of relativity, Cassirer described Cusanus' contribution as follows:

> It was one of the founders of modern philosophy, Nicolas Cusanus, who, with true speculative profundity, anticipated and announced "a relative minimum of measure" as the function of the concept of the atom, which was to be actually realized only in the history of natural science. Cusanus' fundamental doctrine of the infinite and of the unity of opposites in the infinite rested entirely on this insight into the relativity in principle of all determinations of magnitude, on the coincidence of the "greatest" and the "smallest".[54]

Then, in 1927, one of Cassirer's most famous books, *Individuum und Kosmos in der Philosophie der Renaissance* (Leipzig: B.G. Teubner, 1927), was published.[55] Chap. 1, entitled "Nikolaus Cusanus," was devoted to a discussion of Cusanus' ideas, and in Chap. 2, called "Cusanus und Italien," he discussed Cusanus' influence in Italy.

It is worth noting here that the book was published as No. 10 in a series called the *Studien der Bibliothek Warburg* (Warburg Library) and was dedicated

---

[51] Schlipp, *The Philosophy,* p. 218.

[52] Schlipp, *The Philosophy,* p. 693.

[53] Cassirer, *Das Erkenntnisproblem,* 2nd. ed. (Berlin, 1911), pp. 21-72.

[54] Ernst Cassirer, *Zur Einstein'schen Relativitätstheorie: Erkenntnistheoretische Betrachtungen* (Berlin, 1921). An English translation was published as *Substance and Function, and Einstein's Theory of Relativity,* trans. William C. Swabey and Marie C. Swabey (Chicago, 1923; reprint, New York, 1953).

[55] An English translation was published as *The Individual and the Cosmos in Renaissance Philosophy,* trans. Mario Domandi (New York, 1963).

to Aby Warburg (1866-1929) on his 60th birthday, June 13, 1926. Aby Warburg was the scion of a prominent banking family in Hamburg. Independently wealthy and devoted to scholarly research, he spent most of his time traveling, writing essays on the Renaissance and Reformation, and amassing an enormous collection of books on a wide range of subjects. After his physical and mental health declined from 1918 to 1920, his collection of books, known as the Warburg Library, was entrusted to Fritz Saxl.[56] The Library had become a place where Cassirer often did his research for his books on symbolic forms.[57] *Individuum und Kosmos* was published by B.G. Teubner, the publisher in Leipzig which had published many studies sponsored by the Warburg Library.

Examining Cassirer's books, mentioned above, it is not easy to determine which printed edition or editions of Cusanus' works he used in his study of Cusanus. Judging by the quotes in the books, he seems to have used the Basel edition. We must also note that in discussing Cusanus' ideas, Cassirer cited not only Vansteenberghe, but also some German authorities, such as Uebinger and Falckenberg. The results of the studies promoted by the Catholic School of Tübingen were absorbed into his research. His reliance, however, is mostly on primary sources and not much on secondary materials.

When we turn our attention from Cusanus research done by Cohen, Cassirer, and others in the Marburg School to the project of publishing Cusanus' works under the auspices of the Heidelberg Academy, we learn that after the death of Hermann Cohen in 1918, Dr. Felix Meiner sought a successor to Cohen as editor of Cusanus' works in the *Philosophische Bibliothek.*[58] The scholar whom Meiner approached was the noted historian of medieval philosophy at the University of Munich since 1912, Clemens Baeumker (1853-1924).[59] Baeumker was very much interested in the project and emphasized the importance of studying original manuscript sources if the planned edition was to be reliable and

---

[56] On Prof. Aby Warburg and his Warburg Library, see E.H. Gombrich, *Aby Warburg: An Intellectual Biography* (London, 1970); David Farrer, *The Warburgs: The Story of a Family* (New York, 1975); Aby Warburg, *Ausgewählte Schriften und Würdigungen,* ed. Dieter Wuttke and C.G. Heil, 2nd ed. (Baden-Baden, 1980); Ulrich Raulff, "Aby M. Warburg, un inconnu," *Préfaces* 11 (Janvier-fevrier, 1989): 105-106; Salvatore Settis, "Warburg *continuatus.* Description d'une bibliothèque," *Préfaces* 11 (Janvier-fevrier, 1989): 107-122 (bibliography, p. 122).

[57] Schlipp, *The Philosophy,* p. 26.

[58] Meiner, *Notes,* p. 1.

[59] Baeumker's writings included the following: *Abhandlungen zur Geschichte der Philosophie des Mittelalters* (Münster, 1923); *Studien und Charakteristiken zur Geschichte der Philosophie, insbesondere des Mittelalters* (Münster, 1928). See also "Clemens Baeumker" in Raymund Schmidt, ed., *Die deutsche Philosophie der Gegenwart in Selbstdarstellungen,* II (Leipzig, 1927), pp. 31-60.

accurate.[60] He was anxious to undertake the task himself, but unfortunately was not able to gain access to Cusanus' library in St. Nicholas Hospital at Kues because the Hospital was at that time being used as an officers' club. The serious editorial work for the edition based on manuscripts could not be initiated until 1919 after the end of World War I.[61]

When favorable social and economic conditions returned after World War I, B.G. Teubner, the publisher of Cassirer's *Individuum und Kosmos,* approached Dr. Meiner with a proposal to publish a new edition of Cusanus' *Opera omnia.* When informed by Prof. Eugen Kühnemann (1868-1946) of the University of Breslau that Meiner had been making preparations for the edition for some time, Teubner abandoned its plan and gave free rein to Dr. Meiner.[62] Although Meiner told Kühnemann during his visit to Breslau on July 2, 1926, about the preparations he had made for the edition, he heard nothing from Kühnemann thereafter. The initiative for the edition had to be taken by others.[63]

Besides Cassirer, the two scholars who were most directly responsible for the initiation of a modern critical edition of Cusanus' works were Ernst Hoffmann (1880-1952) and Raymond Klibansky (1905-   ) of the University of Heidelberg. Born in Berlin in 1880, Ernst Hoffmann taught at the Mommsen-Gymnasium in Berlin after graduating from the University of Berlin. His field of interest was the classics. While teaching at the Gymnasium, the diligent scholar published two books on Aristotle's physics, a third one on Plato, and other studies related to classical times.[64] It was probably in 1919 or 1920 that

---

[60] Meiner, *Notes,* p. 1: "Jedoch könne eine deutsche Ausgabe in wissenschaftlich befriedigender Form erst veranstaltet werden, wenn ein zuverlässiger lateinischer Text vorläge. Die bisherigen Drucke müsstenanhand [*sic*] der Handschriften revidiert werden."

[61] Meiner, *Notes,* p. 1.

[62] Meiner, *Notes,* p. 1: "Sie (Teubner) verzichteten und träten [*sic*] zu meinen Gunsten zurück." Dr. Meiner speaks then of receiving a letter from Prof. Ludwig Baur (1871-1943), which prompted him to apply to the *Deutsche Akademie* in Munich for support, but the contents of the letter are not clearly indicated. See n. 93 below.

[63] Meiner, *Notes,* p. 2. Kühnemann had published *Grundlehren der Philosophie: Studien über Vorsokratiker, Sokrates und Platon* (Berlin, 1899). He was to visit the United States six times to teach at Harvard, the University of Wisconsin, and others. See *Festschrift für Eugen Kühnemann,* Blätter der Volkshochschule Breslau 7 (1928-1929); E. Kühnemann, *Mit unbefangener Stirn: Mein Lebensbuch* (Heilbronn, 1937).

[64] *De Aristotelis Physicorum libri septimi origine et auctoritate* (Berlin, 1905); *De Aristotelis Physicorum libri septimi duplici forma* I-II (Friedenau, 1908-1909); *Methexis und Metaxy bei Platon* (1919); *Die Sprache und die archaische Logik* (Tübingen, 1925). One of his pupils at the Gymnasium was Paul Oskar Kristeller. See

Hoffmann, who regarded himself as Cassirer's student, heard Cassirer's lecture in Berlin and learned of Cusanus.[65]

After moving to Heidelberg in 1922 as *Privatdozent,* Hoffmann pursued his study of Platonism in the Middle Ages and began to do research on Cusanus.[66] The Department of Philosophy at the University of Heidelberg was, since 1916, under the chairmanship of Heinrich Rickert, who as successor to Wilhelm Windelband had made Heidelberg ever more famous as the center of the South-West German School of Neo-Kantianism. Hoffmann's lectures at the Warburg Library on *Platonismus und Mittelalter,* which were published in 1926 as Vol. 3 of the Warburg Library series, shows how intensely he was engaged in research on medieval Platonism.[67] It was perhaps in 1926 that Ernst Cassirer told Heinrich Rickert and Ernst Hoffmann about what Felix Meiner had been doing in preparation for the critical edition of Cusanus' works.[68]

The next year, in 1927, Hoffmann taught a seminar on Cusanus at the University of Heidelberg. One of the students taking the seminar, Raymond Klibansky, was given the assignment to present a report on the works of Cusanus.[69] Thus the preparatory stage for the initiation of the project was set in 1927. As we mentioned above, Cassirer's work, *Individuum und Kosmos,* was published in 1927. It provided another occasion for advancing the publication plans. In the book, Cassirer published a text of Cusanus' *Liber de mente (Idiota de mente)* which was edited by Dr. Joachim Ritter, his student at Hamburg, and translated by his son, Heinrich Cassirer, a doctoral candidate at Heidelberg. The text of *Idiota de mente* was based on Codex Cusanus 218 in St. Nicholas

Philosophy and Humanism: Renaissance Essays in Honor of Paul Oskar Kristeller, ed. Edward P. Mahoney (Leiden, 1976), p. 1.

[65] Thea Hoffmann, "Wie die Cusanus-Ausgabe begann," MFCG 5 (1965): 164.

[66] Hoffmann, "Wie," p. 164: "Als er nun 1922 als Dozent für Philosophie nach Heidelberg berufen wurde, beschloss er, diesen unbekannten Philosophen näher zu lernen."

[67] The lecture was published as *Platonismus und Mittelalter,* Vorträge der Bibliothek Warburg 3 (Leipzig, 1926).

[68] Meiner, *Notes,* p. 2: "Von Cassirer waren inzwischen Geheimrat Rickert und Professor Ernst Hoffmann in Heidelberg von der Entwicklung der Dinge verständigt worden."

[69] "Besprechung mit Herrn Prof. Klibansky in Bernkastel-Kues am 12. August 1964," one-page document type-written by Mr. Richard Meiner on August 18, 1964. The author wishes to thank Mr. Meiner for giving him permission to use the document in this article.

Hospital Library with a few orthographical changes.[70] Klibansky, who was also a doctoral candidate in philosophy at the University of Heidelberg, told Cassirer that the publication of the text of *Idiota de mente* without appropriate scholarly apparatus did not contribute to the advancement of Cusanus research and that what was needed was a thorough study of Cusanus' texts based on extant manuscripts in and outside the Library at St. Nicholas Hospital.[71]

Critical of what he considered the non-historical approaches of two dominant intellectual schools of thought in Heidelberg at that time, that is, the South-West School of Neo-Kantianism and Karl Jaspers' *Lebensphilosophie,* Klibansky, whose main quest in Heidelberg was to answer the question *Qu'est-ce que l'homme?,*[72] had decided to study the history of philosophy.[73] He believed that despite Michelet, Burckhardt, and Huizinga, there was no "rupture" between the Middle Ages and the Renaissance, that Nicholas of Cusa, who was no radical, demonstrated the continuity of medieval ideas, and that certain Neo-Kantians who called Cusanus "the first modern philosopher" were mistaken.[74]

---

[70] R. Meiner, "Besprechung": "Einen neuen Anstoss, sich mit Cusanus innerhalb der Philosophie zu beschäftigen, gab Ernst Cassirer, als er in seinem 1927 erschienenen Buch *Individuum und Kosmos in der Philosophie der Renaissance* einen Abdruck von *Idiota de mente* nach der Pariser Ausgabe vornahm." The text of *Liber de mente* (*Idiota de mente*) is found in Cassirer, *Individuum,* pp. 204-297. Carolus Bovillus' *Liber de sapiente,* ed. R. Klibansky, follows on pp. 299-412. Hans Joachim Ritter published his dissertation at Hamburg later as *Docta ignorantia: Die Theorie des Nichtwissens bei Nicolaus Cusanus* (Leipzig, 1927). Heinrich Cassirer's dissertation was published as *Aristoteles' Schrift "Von der Seele" und ihre Stellung innerhalb der aristotelischen Philosophie* (Tübingen, 1932).

[71] R. Meiner, "Besprechung."

[72] Michèle Le Doeuff, "Raymond Klibansky—Périple d'un philosophe illustre," *Préfaces* 13 (Mai-juin, 1989): 128-129. The author is indebted to Prof. Klibansky for reference to this issue of the French publication.

[73] "Raymond Klibansky, philosophe et historien—entretien avec Yves Hersant et Alain de Libera," *Préfaces* 13 (Mai-juin, 1989): 137: "R.K.—Lorsque j'étudiais la philosophie à Heidelberg, la scène était occupée par l'affrontement d'une philosophie traditionnelle, celle de l'école kantienne du sud-ouest (*südwestdeutsche Schule*) menée par Heinrich Rickert, avec, de l'autre côté du Neckar, l'école de la Lebensphilosophie de Karl Jaspers. J'ai connu les deux intimement. Malgré leurs dissensions ils approchaient les problèmes de la même manière: ils négligeaient l'histoire. C'est cette méconnaissance qui m'a décidé à étudier l'histoire de la philosophie."

[74] "Raymond Klibansky, philosophe et historien," pp. 138-140. Perhaps one of the most famous books which shows these ideas of Prof. Klibansky is *The Continuity of the Platonic Tradition during the Middle Ages: Outlines of a Corpus Platonicum medii aevi* (London, 1939; new, expanded ed., Millwood, New York, 1982). Also worth mentioning here is his famous study, "Ein Proklos-Fund und seine Bedeutung,"

After investigating where important Cusanus manuscripts and their copies were located, Klibansky then drew up an outline for a critical edition of the works of Cusanus. Visiting Cassirer in Hamburg soon thereafter, Klibansky presented the outline to Cassirer and discussed the publication of a modern, critical edition with him.[75] The outline was then submitted to Professor Hans von Schubert (1859-1931), the famous Protestant church historian at the University of Heidelberg and President of the Heidelberg Academy of Sciences. The prestigious Academy had been founded in 1909. Although independent of the University of Heidelberg administratively, many of its members were professors at the University. Schubert found the project important and strongly supported all attempts to initiate the publication of the critical edition under the auspices of the Heidelberg Academy.[76] Meanwhile, in September, 1927, Dr. Meiner visited Professors Heinrich Rickert and Ernst Hoffmann and discussed with them how the project for publishing the edition, if accepted by the Academy, could be entrusted with them.[77] As a result of this conversation, it was decided to ask Professor Gerhard Kallen (1884-1973) of the University of Cologne to become another co-worker for the edition.[78] Kallen had already signed a contract with the Verlag Ludwig Röhrscheid in Bonn to publish a facsimile edition of Cusanus' *De concordantia catholica,* using the Paris edition of 1514 as its text.[79]

Sitzungsberichte der Heidelberger Akademie der Wissenschaften, Philosophisch-historische Klasse [=HSB], Jhrg. 1928/29, 5. Abh. (Heidelberg, 1929), which showed clearly that Cusanus was very much influenced by Proclus. Klibansky's edition of Meister Eckhart's works appeared as *Magistri Eckardi Opera Latina* (Leipzig, 1934-1935). The first volume edited by Klibansky was *Super oratione dominica* which was published in Leipzig in 1934. It carried a list of fifteen planned volumes. But the second volume published in 1935, which contained *Opus tripartitum,* seems to be the only additional one edited and published by him.

[75] R. Meiner, "Besprechung."

[76] In his letter of June 29, 1989, to the author, Prof. Klibansky wrote: "I first presented the plan of a critical edition of the *Opera omnia* to Ernst Hoffmann and Hans von Schubert; it was this plan which was submitted to the Heidelberg Academy and accepted by it. I insisted that there should be an 'Apparatus fontium' (for which, as is indicated in the Praefatio to vol. I) I alone was responsible and in which I proved (against E. Hoffmann's thesis of the rupture between Cusanus and mediaeval Platonism) the strong links between Nicolaus and the Platonists of Chartres, as well as his indebtedness to Proclus." Thea Hoffmann reports, p. 164, that Hans von Schubert and Karl Hampe, the medievalist, were interested in the study of Cusanus.

[77] Meiner, *Notes,* p. 2.

[78] Meiner, *Notes,* p. 2.

[79] *Nicolai de Cusa De concordantia catholica libri tres.* (Paris: Jodocus Badius Ascensius, 1514; reprint, Bonn, 1928).

In December, 1927, the Heidelberg Academy gave its final approval to the whole project. As a result, a Cusanus Commission was organized within the Academy. The Commission members included not only those scholars already familiar to us, Ernst Hoffmann, Raymond Klibansky, Heinrich Rickert, and Hans von Schubert, but also Heinrich Liebmann (1874-1939), who was famous for his mathematical and geometrical studies, and Friedrich Wilhelm Panzer (1870-1956), who was a noted philologist at the University of Heidelberg.[80] Klibansky was made an assistant of the Heidelberg Academy in charge of carrying out basic research for the edition.[81]

Thus began the serious preparatory work for an ambitious enterprise to publish a modern critical edition of Cusanus' works under the aegis of the Heidelberg Academy of Sciences. It was intended to supersede the defective, often distorted, Strasbourg, Milan, Paris, and Basel editions. Judging by the testimony of those familiar with the beginning phase of the project, the Commission was indeed fortunate to have as its assistant the young, bright scholar Klibansky who was sent to numerous libraries and archives to examine and copy many extant manuscripts for the edition.[82]

Completing his doctoral work in 1928 under Hoffmann, Klibansky, together with Hoffmann, published in 1929 the first study of Cusanus in the *Sitzungsberichte der Heidelberger Akademie*. It was entitled *Cusanus-Texte, I: Predigten 1: Dies Sanctificatus vom Jahre 1439* (with the text in Latin and German with commentary).[83] This was an important study which attempted to clarify the relationship between Cusanus' sermon of 1439 and his major

---

[80] Liebmann later published "Über drei neugefundene mathematische Schriften des Nikolaus von Cues und dessen Bedeutung," *Forschungen und Forschritte* 5, 22 (1929): 261.

[81] Prof. Klibansky has often emphasized that contrary to the widely held view that he became Hoffmann's assistant, he was made assistant at the Heidelberg Academy. See R. Meiner, "Besprechung."

[82] Meiner, *Notes,* p. 2: "Für die ganze Ausgabe war Klibansky ein unschätzbarer Mitarbeiter"; Hoffmann, *Wie,* 163: ". . . ein junger, hochbegabter Student, Raimund Klibansky . . . der schon nach wenigen Jahren das Amt eines Assistenten an der Cusanus-Ausgabe ausüben konnte."

[83] *Cusanus-Texte, I: Predigten 1, Dies Sanctificatus vom Jahre 1439* (HSB, Jhrg. 1928/29, 3. Abh.; Heidelberg, 1929). Another student who completed his doctoral work on Plotinus in 1928 under Hoffmann's guidance was Paul Oskar Kristeller who had followed Hoffmann from Berlin to Heidelberg in 1923. Prof. Kristeller's dissertation was published as *Der Begriff der Seele in der Ethik der Plotin* (Tübingen, 1929). See Mahoney, ed., *Philosophy and Humanism,* p. 2.

philosophical work, *De docta ignorantia,* which was completed in 1440.[84] Another study, published by Hoffmann in 1930, dealt with Cusanus' concept of the universe and was accompanied by a Latin text by Cusanus on his cosmological ideas. The Latin text was edited by Klibansky.[85] This study shows that Hoffmann and Klibansky took special interest in Cusanus' cosmological thought which had found expression especially in Bk. II, Chaps. 1 and 2 of *De docta ignorantia.* On March 16, 1932, the *Apologia doctae ignorantiae,* which had been edited by Klibansky as Vol. II of the Heidelberg edition, was published.[86] On December 24 of the same year the *De docta ignorantia,* which Hoffmann and Klibansky worked on together, followed as Vol. I in the edition.[87]

In announcing the publication of these two important works of Cusanus and appealing to prospective subscribers, a 1932 prospectus stated that the unfavorable condition of the time made it necessary, at least for the time being, to limit the scope of publication to Cusanus' philosophical and political writings. They were scheduled to appear in fourteen volumes. The prospectus went on to say, almost innocently, that these volumes would be available by 1939, the year which would mark the 500th anniversary of the completion of *De docta ignorantia.*[88] Even the editors familiar with the complexity of the task which they had assumed could not fully appreciate the enormity of their undertaking and clearly forsee what the future held for them. The task of

[84] Prof. Kugai Yamamoto (1903-   ) of Hiroshima University of Arts and Sciences in Japan, who studied in Heidelberg in 1929 and visited Hoffmann's home frequently to read books and articles together, including *Dies Sanctificatus,* stated in his special lecture delivered at the 6th Annual Meeting of the Japanese Cusanus Society on November 23, 1987, that Hoffmann was in the habit of saying "Wer hat Cusanus gelesen?", expressing his scepticism and wonder about other writers who could discuss and write about Cusanus without having read his works in their reliable, original sources. See *The Report of the Japanese Cusanus Society* 10 (1988): 35-49; "First Cusanus Scholar in Japan?," *American Cusanus Society Newsletter* V, 2 (September 1988): 15-16.

[85] Ernst Hoffmann, *Das Universum des Nikolaus von Kues* (HSB, Jhrg. 1929/30, 3. Abh.; Heidelberg, 1939), with Textbeilage, pp. 41-45, by Raymond Klibansky.

[86] Meiner, *Notes,* p. 2.

[87] Meiner, *Notes,* p. 2.

[88] The prospectus was entitled *Einladung zur Subskription: Nicolai de Cusa Opera omnia iussu et auctoritate academiae litterarum Heidelbergensis ad codicum fidem edita. Lipsiae: In aedibus Felicis Meiner 1932.* It has no page numbers. "Bis zum Jahre 1939, in welchem 500 Jahre seit der Erstveröffentlichung der *Docta ignorantia* verflossen sein werden, sollen diese Bände, auf die diese Subskription begrenzt ist, vorliegen" [(p. 7)].

determining the authentic, reliable, and accurate texts for the edition turned out to be much more difficult and complex than originally anticipated.

A detailed, very favorable review of the first two published volumes in the edition, written by a leading medievalist, Martin Grabmann, and published in the *Deutsche Literaturzeitung,* greatly encouraged both the editors and the publisher.[89] Grabmann welcomed the initiation of a monumental editorial enterprise and praised in glowing terms Klibansky's thorough, competent work and superb scholarly accomplishments. He especially emphasized the importance of the scholarly apparatus in the edition, which not only contained comparisons of manuscript variants, but also gave sources *(fontes)* used by Cusanus and information about later writers who quoted Cusanus in their writings *(testimonia).*[90]

The publisher, the Felix Meiner Verlag, considered it a great honor to publish the edition under the auspices of the Heidelberg Academy of Sciences and made every effort to produce handsome volumes with accurate texts which were worthy of an academic edition and which could be regarded as a model for modern critical editions.[91] The use of high-quality paper certainly made the volumes attractive, but the task of establishing accurate texts and the printing of three kinds of scholarly apparatus in the footnotes proved to be not only expensive but difficult and time-consuming. As a result of anti-Semitic measures adopted and various threats made on his person, Klibansky had to depart from Heidelberg in early April, 1933, to seek, as he himself put it, a *"festen Boden"* for the continuation and promotion of threatened humanistic studies in Germany.[92] It

---

[89] Review of *Nicolai de Cusa Opera omnia . . . I, De docta ignorantia,* ed. Ernst Hoffmann and Raymond Klibansky (Leipzig, 1932) and II, *Apologia doctae ignorantiae,* ed. Raymond Klibansky (Leipzig, 1932) in *Deutsche Literaturzeitung,* Heft 15 (April 9, 1933), cols. 685-692 by Martin Grabmann. See also Meiner, *Notes,* p. 4: "Für den wissenschaftlichen Erfolg der Ausgabe war entscheidend eine Besprechung durch Grabmann in der Deutschen Literatur-Zeitung."

[90] Grabmann, cols. 688-689.

[91] Meiner, *Notes,* p. 3: "Die Druckausführung wurde nach Vorschlägen von Jakob Hegner festgelegt, wobei der Verlag seinen Ehrgeitz darein setzte, ebenso Vorbildliches auf diesem Gebiete zu leisten, wie die Herausgeber im Hinblick auf die Gestaltung einer Akademie-Ausgabe."

[92] For a careful study of the exiled *Dozenten* and professors from the University of Heidelberg after 1933, see Dorothee Mussgnug, *Die vertriebenen Heidelberger Dozenten: Zur Geschichte der Ruprecht-Karls-Universität nach 1933* (Heidelberg, 1988). The author is grateful to Prof. Klibansky for reference to this book and to Mr. Richard Meiner for having a copy quickly sent to him. Mussgnug discusses Klibansky and his case on pp. 40-43, 67-68, 148, 175, 182-184, 271-280. She states on p. 184: "Klibansky empfand sich als 'Bewahrer des anderen Deutschland'." The book also discusses the fate of other members of the Cusanus Commission after

meant that the Cusanus Commission lost an indispensable worker. The pace of later publications became necessarily slow. In fact, it was not until September 27, 1937, that the Felix Meiner Verlag was able to publish a third volume (Vol. V of the *Opera*), *Idiota* (three books), which was edited by Ludwig Baur (1871-1943). Professor at the University of Tübingen since 1913, Baur became a connecting link between the initial period of modern Cusanus research in Germany as represented by the Catholic School of Tübingen and the second period of modern Cusanus scholarship which was based on the Heidelberg edition.[93]

The great care with which the publisher produced the edition was bound to attract the attention of other publishers. Dr. Meiner recalled in 1945 with pride and satisfaction that the famous Catholic publisher in Münster, the Aschendorff Verlag, approached him with the request that they be permitted to use the format of the Heidelberg edition in producing their own forthcoming edition of the works of Albertus Magnus, edited by Bernhard Geyer.[94] Father Ludger Meier, OFM, of the Duns Scotus Commission in Rome, Meiner also reported, sought advice from him about technical points in preparation for the Commission edition of the works of Duns Scotus.[95] It was clear that the Heidelberg *Opera* had established itself as a reliable, handsome edition of a medieval philosopher's works.

What happened after World War II can briefly be stated here. Of the fourteen announced volumes, only four had been published by the outbreak of World War II *(De docta ignorantia,* 1932; *Apologia doctae ignorantiae,* 1932; *Idiota,* 1937; and *De concordantia catholica,* Pt. 1, 1939). Since many subscribers to the edition were outside Germany, the war placed a heavy burden on the publisher. It also made it difficult for editors to travel to libraries and archives in and outside Germany where manuscripts were kept. Besides, in an air-raid of December 3/4, 1944, the entire establishment of the Felix Meiner Verlag in Leipzig, including the plates of the Heidelberg edition, was completely

1933: E. Hoffmann, pp. 60-70, 115-117, 129-130, 206-207, 278; F. Panzer, pp. 67-68, 116, 278; H. Liebmann, pp. 70, 90, 115. About the role which Prof. Klibansky played in the removal of the Warburg Library from Hamburg to London, see Le Doeuff, "Raymond Klibansky," pp. 125-126.

[93] Baur had published the following: "Die Lehre vom Naturrecht bei Bonaventura" in: *Festgabe zum 60. Geburtstag Clemens Baeumker* I (Münster, 1913): 217-239; "Der Einfluss des Robert Grosseteste auf die wissenschaftliche Richtung des Roger Bacon" in: A.G. Little, ed., *Roger Bacon Essays* (Oxford, 1914), pp. 35-54; *Die Philosophie des Robert Grosseteste, Bischof von Lincoln (†1253)* (Münster, 1917).

[94] Meiner, *Notes,* p. 4.

[95] Meiner, *Notes,* p. 4. See also Hans-Georg Gadamer, "Das Cusanus-Unternehmen der Heidelberger Akademie der Wissenschaften," *Ruperto Carola* 6, 15/16 (December, 1954): 78-79.

destroyed. It was a great setback for the project. Many difficulties had to be overcome to resume the work of publication. For example, Gerhard Kallen's edition of *De concordantia catholica,* which had been published before the air-raid as Vol. XIV, Pts. 1 and 2, in 1939 and 1941, had to be started all over again. Kallen was first able to bring out Pt. 3 in 1959. A new, revised edition of Pt. 1 was published in 1964. Pt. 2 appeared in its revised form in 1965 and was followed in 1968 by a register for the three parts. In the meantime, the Felix Meiner Verlag moved from Leipzig to Hamburg in 1951 for financial and political reasons, and in 1964 merged with the Richard Meiner Verlag, which had existed in Hamburg since 1948 under the leadership of Richard Meiner, Dr. Felix Meiner's son and present head of the Felix Meiner Verlag in Hamburg.[96]

Of the original fourteen volumes in the edition announced in 1932, all have thus far been published with the exception of *De visione dei* (original Vol. VI) and *De ludo globi* (original Vol. IX). A new, ambitious phase of the edition began in 1970, when *Sermones* 1, Fasc. 1, edited by Rudolf Haubst and his associates, was added as Vol. XVI, Pt. 1 of the series. Thus far Vol. XVI, Pts. 1-4 and Vol. XVII, Pt. 1 have been published in the *Sermones* series.[97] Entirely independent of the critical edition of the works of Cusanus, but in parallel with it, a new series called *Acta Cusana: Quellen zur Lebensgeschichte der Nikolaus von Kues* was launched in 1976 under the joint editorship of Erich Meuthen and Hermann Hallauer. It will include all extant deeds, documents, letters, and other materials in which Cusanus or his activities are mentioned. Two installments of Vol. 1, edited by Meuthen, have been published to date.[98] The Heidelberg edition of Cusanus' works, which began in 1932, is thus "in progress" in an expanded form.

[96] The role played by Mr. Richard Meiner in the development of the publishing house is described by many scholars in: *Ceterum censeo . . . Bemerkungen zu Aufgabe und Tätigkeit eines philosophischen Verlegers: Richard Meiner zum 8. April 1983* (Hamburg, 1983).

[97] Vol. XVI, 1: *Sermones* I (1430-1441) Fasc. 1 (Sermones 1-4), ed. R. Haubst *et al.* (Hamburg, 1970); vol. XVI, 2: *Sermones* I (1430-1441) Fasc. 2 (Sermones 5-10), ed. R. Haubst *et al.* (Hamburg, 1973); vol. XVI, 3: *Sermones* I (1430-1441) Fasc. 3 (Sermones 11-21), ed. R. Haubst and M. Bodewig (Hamburg, 1977); vol. XVI, 4: *Sermones* I (1430-1441) Fasc. 4 (Sermones 22-26), ed. R. Haubst and M. Bodewig (Hamburg, 1984); vol. XVII, 1: *Sermones* II (1443-1452) Fasc. 1 (Sermones 27-39), ed. R. Haubst and H. Schnarr (Hamburg, 1983).

[98] *Acta Cusana: Quellen zur Lebensgeschichte des Nikolaus von Kues,* vol. I, pt. 1: 1401-1437 Mai 17, ed. Erich Meuthen (Hamburg, 1976); vol. 1, pt. 2: 1437 Mai 17-1450 December 31, ed. E. Meuthen (Hamburg, 1983).

In his critical study of Cusanus and his ideas, Karl Jaspers wrote:

> An attack on him by Wenck, a professor at Heidelberg, might have led to his condemnation. . . . However, the Church paid no attention to Cusanus' ideas. In the nineteenth century, a few Catholic theologians took up the old attack again and amplified it, but the Church remained silent. . . . After 1565 (date of the Basel edition of his works), neither the Church nor any monastery arranged for a new edition. The Heidelberg *Akademieausgabe* (begun in 1932) was initiated by non- Catholics.[99]

Our previous discussion shows clearly that Jaspers gives us only a half-truth. Initiated and promoted by the Catholic School of Tübingen under the influence of religious Romanticism and under the guidance of the brilliant and controversial church historian Johann Adam Möhler, modern Cusanus research in Germany brought about what is sometimes called a "Cusanus Renaissance." It was the philosophers of the Neo-Kantian persuasion, especially Ernst Cassirer, who took special interest in Cusanus' mathematical and scientific ideas and labeled him as the "first modern philosopher."[100]

As the knowledge of Cusanus and his works became widespread and deepened, it was apparent to all serious students of Cusanus that the available editions of his works printed in the fifteenth and sixteenth centuries were often not only unreliable but also misleading. Ernst Hoffmann, a noted student of Plato and Platonism, and Raymond Klibansky, his bright and multi-lingual student, were instrumental in initiating the so-called Heidelberg edition in 1932 under the auspices of the Heidelberg Academy of Sciences and with the support of the publisher, the Felix Meiner Verlag. The edition has not been brought to an end and is likely to take some years to complete. It is perhaps significant to note that the project has been supported and carried on by scholars of various theological, philosophical, and religious backgrounds. Cusanus, who emphasized *pax* and *concordantia* so much in his writings, would probably give an approving nod to this joint enterprise for the promotion and propagation of his ideas.

---

[99] Karl Jaspers, *Nikolaus Cusanus* (Munich, 1964), p. 74; Karl Jaspers, *Anselm and Nicholas of Cusa,* ed. Hannah Arendt and trans. Ralph Manheim (New York, 1974), pp. 64-65.

[100] Cassirer, *Individuum,* p. 10; Cassirer, *The Individual,* p. 10. It is interesting to note that Cassirer, a Neo-Kantian, did use the phrase "the first modern philosopher," of which, as we saw above, Klibansky is critical. Klibansky's closeness to Cassirer is shown especially by the fact that with H.J. Paton, he edited a collection of essays dedicated to Cassirer: Raymond Klibansky and H.J. Paton, eds., *Philosophy and History—Essays Presented to Ernst Cassirer* (Oxford, 1936; reprint, New York, 1963; Gloucester, Massachusetts, 1975).

Authority and Consent in Church Government: Panormitanus, Aeneas Sylvius, Cusanus

When the Imperial Diet met in Frankfurt am Main from the end of May to the middle of August in 1442, Nicolaus de Tudeschis (1386-1445), Aeneas Sylvius Piccolomini (1405-64), and Nicolaus Cusanus (1401-64) were among those who attended the diet.[1] The former two were Italians, and the latter was a German. They had all studied law, and two of them, Tudeschis and Cusanus, had even taught it. Despite their different backgrounds and careers, they shared one thing in common: they had been greatly disturbed and influenced by a series of events which followed the famous debate in the Council of Basel (1431-49), on December 5, 1436, over the question of where a council of reunion with the Greeks should be held. The council, at its twenty-eighth session of October 1, 1437, had declared Pope Eugenius IV contumacious and proceeded to suspend him on January 24, 1438. Dissatisfied with the majority party which chose Avignon as the site for the reunion council, Cusanus had already left the council after the debate, and was representing Pope Eugenius IV at the diet. Panormitanus, as Nicolaus de Tudeschis was often called, had written many works supporting propapal doctrines, but he was in Frankfurt as an advocate of the conciliar party. As for Aeneas Sylvius, who had been an ardent supporter of the Council of Basel, he was about to change sides by going over to the neutral imperial court in Vienna.

Why did these men alter their positions and views? Were they, as has been often pointed out, essentially opportunists who sacrificed principle to self-interest?[2] What were the ecclesiastical and political conditions that affected their conduct? To what extent did their conception of church government influence their behavior? If we remember that many other noted churchmen of the day, such as Giuliano Cesarini (1398-1444), Ludovico Pontano (1409-39), Juan Cervantes (d. 1453), Andrew of Escobar (1367-1437), and Domenico Capranica (1400-58), also changed their allegiance during these ecclesiastical crises, it

---

[1] *Deutsche Reichstagsakten* (hereafter cited as *RTA*), XVI (Stuttgart/Gotha, 1928), pp. 245-49, 407-34, 439-543.

[2] J.N. Figgis, *Studies of Political Thought from Gerson to Grotius 1414-1625* (Cambridge, 1923), p. 44; Thea Buyken, *Enea Silvio Piccolominis Jugendjahre und Studienzeit* (Cologne, 1931), pp. 1-2; R.J. Mitchell, *The Laurels and the Tiara* (London, 1962), pp. 77, 95; Aeneas Sylvius Piccolominus, *De Gestis Concilii Basiliensis Commentariorum Libri II,* eds. Denys Hay and W.K. Smith (Oxford, 1967), p. xxvii.

becomes clear that the questions which we have raised can be answered only when a thorough examination is made not only of the prevailing social, political, and ecclesiastical conditions, but also of the theories and ideas of these men concerning the nature and essence of the Catholic Church.

This article will first sketch the careers of these three men under the influence of some major forces at work, then relate these factors to the development and growth of their conception of the church, and finally make some observations about the essence of the conciliar movement which rocked the Catholic Church of the fifteenth century. In studying these questions we find it convenient to organize our discussion around two focal points: the concepts of authority and consent in church government. After all, the fundamental question to which many fifteenth-century thinkers addressed themselves was: If the ultimate authority lies with the whole body of the faithful as represented in a council, what is the nature of papal authority?

Nicolaus de Tudeschis, better known as Abbas Siculus, Abbas Modernus, or Panormitanus, was born in Catania, Sicily, in 1386.[3] After entering the Benedictine Order in 1400, he went to Bologna in 1405 or 1406 to study law. The noted scholars Franciscus de Zabarella (1360-1417) and Antonius de Butrio (1338-1408) were among his teachers. Promoted to the degree of *doctor utriusque juris* by Zabarella, Panormitanus taught law at Bologna (1412), Parma (1412-1418), Siena (1418-1430), again at Bologna (1431-1432), and finally at Florence (1432). In the meantime Pope Martin V (1417-1431) named him Auditor General of the Apostolic Camera in 1421 and made him the abbot of S. Maria de Maniaco near Messina, Sicily, on January 10, 1425. In March 1433 Panormitanus was sent to the Council of Basel by Pope Eugenius IV (1431-1447) as his representative. He returned to Sicily later that year, but the next year he entered the service of King Alfonso V of Aragon (1416-1458), who supported the council because Eugenius IV preferred René of Anjou to Alfonso V as king of Naples. Panormitanus was nominated Archbishop of Palermo in February 1434 by the king, an appointment which was confirmed by Eugenius on March 9, 1435. When Panormitanus returned to Basel in 1436, he represented King Alfonso V against Eugenius IV. In this capacity he fought for the council

---

[3] On Panormitanus' life and thought: *Nomenclator literarius recentioris theologiae catholicae,* ed. H. Hurter, IV (Oeniponte, 1899), cols. 709-12; Riniero Zeno, "Niccolò Tudisco ed un nuovo contribute alla storia del Concilio di Basilea," *Archivio storico per la Sicilia Orientale,* V (1908), 258-67, 350-74; Julius Schweizer, *Nicolaus de' Tudeschi, Archiepiscopus Panormitanus et S. R. E. Cardinalis: Seine Tätigkeit am Basler Konzil* (Strassburg, 1924); C. Lefebvre, "Panormitain," in *Dictionnaire de Droit Canonique,* VI (Paris, 1957), cols. 1195-1215; Knut W. Nörr, *Kirche und Konzil bei Nicolaus de Tudeschis (Panormitanus)* (Cologne, 1964); Jean Fleury, "Le conciliarisme des canonistes au concile de Bâle d'aprés le Panormitain," in *Mèlanges Roger Secrètan* (Montreux, 1964), pp. 47-65; Aeneas Sylvius Piccolomineus, *De Viris Illustribus* (Stuttgart, 1842), pp. 2-3.

against the pope until his return to Palermo in 1439. Because of his services to the council, the antipope Felix V (1439-49) made him a cardinal on November 12, 1440, when he was on his way to Basel for the third time to attend the council. He arrived in Basel on February 9, 1441, and later participated in the Diet of Frankfurt in 1442 as a cardinal. But with the recognition of Alfonso V as king of Naples by Eugenius IV in the same year, the Aragonese king lost interest in defending the council and recalled his delegation to the council headed by Panormitanus, who left Basel on August 8, 1443, and died in Palermo on February 24, 1445.

Aeneas Sylvius Piccolomini, another Italian, had a very different career from that of Panormitanus.[4] Born at Corsignano near Siena on October 18, 1405, of a noble but impoverished family, Aeneas went to the University of Siena at the age of eighteen to study law. This was the year in which the Council of Siena (1423-24) was convened. He was particularly influenced by Mariano Sozzini not only in the field of civil law but also in that of classical studies.[5] It is possible that he attended lectures given by Panormitanus, who was teaching at Siena at that time. The famous Franciscan preacher S. Bernardino of Siena seems to have impressed the young man from Corsignano when he preached in the "City of the Virgin" in 1425. It has been said by many students that Aeneas did not find the study of law interesting.[6] However, he was employed in 1431 as secretary to Domenico Capranica, Bishop of Fermo, who was on his way to the Council of Basel to seek a red hat which had been promised by Pope Martin V, but which his successor Eugenius IV denied him. Aeneas arrived in Basel early in 1432. When Capranica left Basel after making peace with Eugenius IV on April 30, 1434, Aeneas lost his job and entered the service of Nicodemo della Scala, Bishop of Freising; Bartolomeo Visconti,

---

[4] On Aeneas' life and thought: Georg Voigt, *Enea Silvio de' Piccolomini als Papst Pius der Zweite*, 3 vols. (Berlin, 1856-63; Berlin, 1967); William Boulting, *Aeneas Silvius* (London, 1908); Cecilia M. Ady, *Pius II (Aeneas Silvius Piccolomini): The Humanist Pope* (London, 1913); *Enea Silvio Piccolomini: Papst Pius II*, ed. Berthe Widmer (Basel/Stuttgart, 1960; hereafter cited as Widmer, *Enea I*); Mitchell, *The Laurels;* Berthe Widmer, *Enea Silvio Piccolomini in der sittlichen und politischen Entscheidung* (Basel/Stuttgart, 1963; hereafter cited as Widmer, *Enea II*). Also Hermann Diener, "Enea Silvio Piccolominis Weg von Basel nach Rom," in *Adel und Kirche,* eds. J. Fleckenstein and K. Schmid (Freiburg, 1968), pp. 516-33. I have not been able to consult Heinrich G. Gengler, *Über Aeneas Sylvius und seine Bedeutung für die deutsche Rechtsgeschichte* (Erlangen, 1860) and *Enea Silvio Piccolomini— Papa Pio II: Atti del Convegno per il Quinto Centenario della Morte e altri Scritti* (Siena, 1968).

[5] Voigt, *Enea Silvio,* I, p. 10; Boulting, *Aeneas Silvius,* p. 6. For Aeneas' opinion of Sozzini, see Aeneas Sylvius, *De Viris Illustribus,* p. 27.

[6] Voigt, *Enea Silvio,* I, p. 18; Ady, *Pius II,* p. 24; Aeneas Sylvius, *De Gestis,* p. xxiv.

Bishop of Novara; and finally the saintly Carthusian Niccolò Albergati, Cardinal Presbyter of Santa Croce. Cardinal Albergati even sent Aeneas in 1438 on a secret mission to King James I (1424-37) of Scotland, a trip which Aeneas vividly described later in his *Memoirs*. His eloquent first public oration in 1436 at the Council of Basel in support of the city of Pavia as the site for the reunion council with the Greeks earned him a provostship in the Church of S. Lorenzo in Milan. It was given to him by Filippo Maria Visconti, Duke of Milan (1412-47), who had been a strong supporter of the council against Eugenius IV.

Although he was still a layman, Aeneas rose rapidly at the council, moving from *scriptor* in 1432 to *abbreviator* in 1437. He almost died during the fateful plague of 1439, which deprived the council of one of its most notable champions and Aeneas' close friend, Ludovico Pontano,[7] papal protonotary. When the council proceeded to elect a new pope after the deposition of Eugenius IV on June 25, 1439, Aeneas served as master of ceremonies in the conclave which elected on November 5, 1439 Count Amadeo of Savoy as Felix V. Aeneas' services were rewarded when Felix V made him papal secretary in 1440. Thus Aeneas went to the Diet of Frankfurt in 1442 as a defender of the conciliar position. But his high hopes for Felix V were dashed when he saw many friends of his, such as Cesarini and Cusanus, leave Basel to join Eugenius IV's side. Taking advantage of the fact that the Emperor Friedrich III had crowned him as poet laureate on July 27, 1442,[8] in Frankfurt, Aeneas decided to identify himself with the neutral policy of the empire and thereafter showed less and less enthusiasm for the conciliar cause. He left Basel on November 17, 1442, in company with the emperor, for Vienna, where he became a member of the imperial chancery under Kaspar Schlick.[9] Sent to Rome towards the end of 1444 by the emperor to confer with the pope regarding the opening of a council at a fresh place, Aeneas successfully made a dramatic appeal to Eugenius IV, who

---

[7] On Pontano, see J.F. von Schulte, *Die Geschichte der Quellen und Literatur des Canonischen Rechts von Gratian bis auf die Gegenwart*, II (Stuttgart, 1877), p. 395; Hubert Jedin, *Geschichte des Konzils von Trient*, I (Freiburg, 1949), p. 18. Pontano was buried in a Carthusian church in Klein Basel which is today an orphanage (Theodorskirchplatz Nr. 7, Basel). See E.A. Stückelberg, "Die Totenschilde der Kartäuserkirche in Basel," *Basler Zeitschrift für Geschichte und Altertumskunde*, XXIII (1925), 292-94.

[8] Joseph Chmel, *Regesta Chronologico-Diplomatica Friderici IV. Romanorum Regis (Imperatoris III.)* (Vienna, 1838; Hildesheim, 1962), p. 93; Boulting, *Aeneas Silvius*, 113; Ady, *Pius II*, p. 73.

[9] On the imperial chancery under Schlick, see Victor Bayer, *Die Historia Friderici III. Imperatoris des Enea Silvio de' Piccolomini* (Prag, 1872), p. 9; O. Hufnagel, "Caspar Schlick als Kanzler Friedrichs III," *Mitteilungen des Instituts für österreichische Geschichtsforschung*, Ergänzungsband VIII, Heft 1 (Innsbruck, 1911), pp. 253-461; Diener, "Enea Silvio," pp. 531-32.

forgave Aeneas' antipapal utterings and actions in the past. Aeneas' "conversion" to the papal party by way of neutrality was now complete, as is indicated clearly in his *De ortu et auctoritate imperii Romani* of 1446.[10] Thereafter his rise was steady. He became Bishop of Trieste in 1447 and Bishop of Siena in 1450. He was then made Cardinal of Santa Sabina in 1456 by Pope Calixtus III (1455-58) and two years later was elected pope, with the title of Pius II (1458-64). It was during his stay in Ancona to realize his dream of organizing a crusade against the Turks that he died on August 14, 1464.

The career and experience of the future cardinal Nicolaus Cusanus were somewhat unusual among those of fifteenth-century German clergymen.[11] Cusanus was born in Kues in 1401 and after a brief stay at the University of Heidelberg went to the University of Padua to study law. He was sixteen years old at that time. Graduating from the university as *decretorum doctor* in 1423, he was quickly involved in the ecclesiastical politics of his native country. It was in order to defend the antipapal cause of his patron Count Ulrich of Manderscheid that he came to the Council of Basel in February 1432.[12] His first major treatise, *De concordantia catholica,* in which he argued for the superiority of the council over the pope, was presented to the council in 1433 or 1434.[13] But deeply disturbed by the rapidly growing antipapal extremism of the Council of Basel, he went over to the papal side in 1437 and fought for the strengthening of Eugenius IV's position. In 1439 Aeneas called him the "Hercules of all the followers of Eugenius"[14] because of his propapal activities after 1437. It was in this capacity that Cusanus attended the diet in 1442. Eugenius IV named him cardinal *in petto* on December 16, 1446, but the actual elevation to the

[10] The text is in *Der Briefwechsel des Eneas Silvius Piccolomini,* ed. R. Wolkan, II (Vienna, 1912), pp. 6-24. See also Alfred Meusel, *Enea Silvio als Publicist* (Breslau, 1905); Gerhard Kallen, *Aeneas Silvius Piccolomini als Publizist* (Stuttgart, 1939); John B. Toews, "Dream and Reality in the Imperial Ideology of Pope Pius II," *Medievalia et Humanistica,* 16 (1964), 77-93; idem, "The View of Empire in Aeneas Sylvius Piccolomini (Pope Pius II)," *Traditio,* 24, (1968), 471-87.

[11] On Cusanus' life and thought, see Edmond Vansteenberghe, *Le cardinal Nicolas de Cues (1401-1464): l'action—la pensée* (Paris, 1920); Paul E. Sigmund, *Nicholas of Cusa and Medieval Political Thought* (Cambridge, Mass. 1963); Morimichi Watanabe, *The Political Ideas of Nicholas of Cusa, with Special Reference to His De Concordantia Catholica* (Geneva, 1963); Erich Meuthen, *Nikolaus von Kues 1401-1464* (Münster, 1964).

[12] Watanabe, "The Episcopal Election of 1430 in Trier and Nicholas of Cusa," *Church History,* 39 (1970), 299-316.

[13] Watanabe, *The Political Ideas,* p. 15; Gerhard Kallen, *Die handschriftliche Überlieferung der Concordantia catholica des Nikolaus von Kues* (Heidelberg, 1963).

[14] Aeneas Sylvius, *De Gestis,* pp. 14-15.

cardinalate took place on December 20, 1448, under Pope Nicholas V. With the accession of Aeneas as Pope Pius II in 1458, Cusanus became one of the most trusted friends and critics of the pope. On his way to Ancona to meet Pius II, Cusanus died at Todi in Umbria three days before the pope's death.

It is well known that one of the fundamental doctrines of the conciliar movement was the principle of common consent of the governed.[15] The conciliarists generally distinguished clearly between the Universal Church as the *congregatio fidelium* and the established Roman Church, understood as pope and cardinals together. According to them, the Universal Church, which could be represented by a general council, was superior to the pope. Of the three men with whom we are concerned, Cusanus most clearly expressed these fundamental tenets of conciliarism in his *De concordantia catholica,* said to embody "all the principles of the conciliar theory and all the demands of its adherents."[16] Cusanus argued that the general council was above the pope, that an heretical pope can be deposed by the general council, and that the consent of the governed is the basis of legislation, both civil and ecclesiastical, and of the governance of the church. "Since by nature all men are free," he said, "all government—whether based on written law or on law embodied in a ruler through whose government the subjects are restrained from evil deeds and their liberty regulated, for a good end, by fear of punishment—arises solely from agreement and consent of the subjects."[17] As J.N. Figgis describes Cusanus' position, "the consent and agreement of the Christian community is the origin of Papal authority, which is a delegation from the people, and may be removed at their will."[18] With the skillful use of various theological and canonistic doctrines which he had studied during his school years, Cusanus presented clearly what might be called a "democratic" view of church government. It is true that, as we have noted above, he was defending the cause of Ulrich of Manderscheid, who had high hopes of obtaining a favorable decision from the council against Eugenius IV, regarding the vacant archbishopric of Trier. No wonder that Cusanus, who was Ulrich's chancellor, should stress the superiority of the council over the pope and consent over papal authority in the church. We should also not forget that

---

[15] E.g., Otto Gierke, *Political Theories of the Middle Age,* trans. F.W. Maitland (Cambridge, 1951), p. 55; Ray C. Petry, "Unitive Reform Principles of the Late Medieval Conciliarists," *Church History,* 31 (June 1962), 164-81; Francis Oakley, "Figgis, Constance, and the Divines of Paris," *American Historical Review,* 75 (1969), 368-86.

[16] Hubert Jedin, *A History of the Council of Trent,* I (London, 1957), p. 23.

[17] Figgis, *Studies,* p. 52.

[18] Quoted from Francis W. Coker, *Readings in Political Philosophy* (New York, 1938), p. 262. For the text, see *Nicolai de Cusa Opera omnia:* Vol. XIV, *De concordantia catholica: Liber secundus* (Hamburg, 1965), p. 162.

Cusanus emphasized the doctrine of freedom and consent against papal authority because his patron Ulrich was strongly supported in his quest of the archbishopric of Trier by other secular princes of southern Germany who resented Eugenius IV's interference in the ecclesiastical affairs of Trier.[19]

It is very important to note, however, that while advocating these conciliar, essentially antipapal views, Cusanus does not fail to emphasize the importance of according the pope proper respect and reverence. His fundamental concern was the reform and restoration of harmony in the church which, he believed, could be accomplished through conciliar methods, without excluding the possibility that the desired goals could also be effected under a reforming pope. Unlike the period of the Great Schism (1378-1417), during which there were two, and later, three popes, the church was already united under one pope since 1417. Furthermore, the incumbent of the papal office, Eugenius IV, was making much progress in strengthening the papal power and the position of the church vis-à-vis the Greek Orthodox Church. For all his emphasis on consent and conciliar ideas, there was within the system of Cusanus a reservoir of propapal authoritarianism which could be drawn upon in later years. Small wonder that, as the Council of Basel became increasingly radical, Cusanus gradually abandoned the conciliar cause.

Unlike the Council of Constance, which was organized on the principle of "nations,"[20] the Council of Basel adopted the principle of majority rule as the rule of procedure where neither national background nor ecclesiastical position really counted. Number and arithmetic instead of ecclesiastical prestige were the guiding principles of the council.[21] It had on June 11, 1433, seven cardinals, ten patriarchs, forty-two bishops, thirty abbots, and 311 doctors, clerks, or ambassadors; and from the twelfth session in July 1433 to the twenty-first in June 1435 it proceeded "to strip the pope of his resources."[22] The rise to power of the radical party was marked by the decree of June 9, 1435, abolishing annates

---

[19] Watanabe, "The Episcopal Election," pp. 308, 312-13.

[20] For a further discussion of this problem, see J.N. Figgis, "Politics at the Council of Constance," *Transactions of the Royal Historical Society,* 13 (1899), 103-15; G.C. Powers, *Nationalism at the Council of Constance (1414-1418)* (Washington, 1927); *The Council of Constance: The Unification of the Church,* trans. Louise R. Loomis, eds. J.H. Mundy and K.M. Woody (New York, 1961).

[21] Otto Richter, *Die Organization und Geschäftsordnung des Basler Konzils* (Leipzig, 1877); Paul Lazarus, *Das Basler Konzil* (Berlin, 1912); Paul Ourliac, "La sociologie du Concile de Bale," *Revue d'Histoire Ecclésiastique,* 56 (1961), 5-32. It is to be noted that the principle of "nations" was not completely abandoned in organizing the four deputations of the Council of Basel.

[22] Denys Hay, *Europe in the Fourteenth and Fifteenth Centuries* (New York, 1966), p. 289. For the number of participants, see Ourliac, "La sociologie," pp. 13-14.

altogether. The majority of cardinals left Basel in 1435, and by 1437 there were less than one hundred mitred persons among over five hundred members of the council.[23]

When the most confusing and riotous scene during the whole history of the council took place at the twenty-fifth session on May 7, 1437,[24] Cusanus must have felt that it was not by seeking common consent, but by falling back on papal authority that the true interest of the church could best be protected. The brief but dramatic success of Eugenius IV at the Council of Ferrara-Florence in 1439 to effect a reunion of the Greeks with the Roman Church seems to have given Cusanus evidence that papal authority is a far more effective means for church union than democratic consent. As he put it in 1439 in a letter to his friend, while the Council of Basel became a center of dissensions, the Council of Ferrara-Florence was able to accomplish a reunion. *Ibi reductio et unio est, hic scisma.*[25] The process of conversion was slow, but in his writings his emphasis shifted more and more from consent to authority in the church.[26] The democratic reformer underwent changes and emerged as a defender of papal authority in church government. The Diet of Frankfurt in 1442 was then a battleground for the papal cause, as far as Cusanus was concerned. His eloquent speech on behalf of the pope which he delivered from June 21 to 23 at the residence of Cardinal Panormitanus testifies to the fact that he had accepted authority in exchange for consent as the guiding principle of church government.[27]

It is more difficult to determine clearly what Panormitanus, "one of the most distinguished canonists of the Middle Ages,"[28] believed in regard to the

---

[23] Ourliac, "La sociologie," p. 14. According to Richter, the largest number of participants was 400 in 1439: *Die Organization,* p. 11. On the membership of the council, cf. Loy Bilderback, "Proctorial Representation and the Conciliar Support at the Council of Basle," *Annuarium Historiae Conciliorum,* 1 (1969), 140-52.

[24] *Monumenta Conciliorum Generalium Saeculi XV* (hereafter cited as *MCG*), II (Vienna, 1873), Lib. XI, cap. ix, pp. 965-69.

[25] Watanabe, *The Political Ideas,* pp. 104-05.

[26] *Ibid.,* pp. 97-114.

[27] *MCG*, III, pp. 1126-52; *RTA*, XVI, pp. 245-48, 407-34. Also "Brief des Nikolaus von Cues an Rodericus Sancius de Arevalo (1442)," *Cusanus-Texte:* II. Traktate, 1. *De Auctoritate Presidendi in Concilio Generali,* ed. Gerhard Kallen (Heidelberg, 1935), pp. 106-12.

[28] Schweizer, *Nicolaus de' Tudeschi,* p. 22. J. Trithemius described Panormitanus as "ingenio subtilem et acutum, consilio promptum et firmum, sermone apertum et conspicuum, ac lucernam juris." Cited by Schweizer, *Nicolaus de' Tudeschi,* p. 194. See also Schulte, *Die Geschichte,* II, p. 312: "Nikolaus gehört unstreitig zu den bedeutendsten Canonisten des Mittelalters"; Jedin, *A History,* I, p. 25: "The greatest canonist of the period."

nature of church government. There is no doubt that he was influenced by the conciliar doctrine of his master Zabarella. But many of his writings before his first appearance at the Council of Basel in 1433 unmistakably showed his essentially propapal views concerning authority and consent in church government.[29] In his *Episcopus et quidam rector curatus* of 1426, Panormitanus gave almost unlimited power to the pope who is *dei vicarius in terris.* According to him, the pope, who recognized no superior in both spiritual and temporal matters, can never be judged by anyone.[30] It is not difficult to see why the Auditor General of the Apostolic Camera expressed these propapal views, but the question arises whether employment by Alfonso V in 1434 made it necessary for him to change his views of the church.

We must note here that even in *Episcopus et quidam rector curatus* Panormitanus carefully distinguished between the *causa fidei* and the *causa proprii delicti.* With regard to the latter, the pope cannot be judged by anyone, but he may fall into heresy concerning the former. In that case, Panormitanus asserted, the whole church has the right and duty to correct and, if necessary, to remove the pope. As head of the church Peter was entrusted and delegated with the exercise of ecclesiastical power, but this power belongs to the whole church which can therefore control its use by the pope.[31] If the pope is not sure of how to use it, he must call a general council which is a representative body of the whole church. When the pope refuses or delays to do so, a council can be called either by prelates or by the emperor, an idea which Panormitanus probably learned from Zabarella.[32] Extending his master's doctrine further, Panormitanus

---

29 Voigt, *Enea Silvio,* I, p. 200; Schweizer, *Nicolaus de' Tudeschi,* 40; Nörr, *Kirche und Konzil,* p. 7. In addition to the celebrated *Episcopus et quidam rector curatus* of 1426 (Nicolaus de Tudeschis, *Consilia, Quaestiones et Tractatus Panormitani* [n.p., 1539], 138r-43r), his writings during this period include *Ecce nunc tempus acceptabile* of 1433 (J.D. Mansi, *Sacrorum Conciliorum Nova et Amplissima Collectio,* hereafter cited as *Mansi,* XXX, cols. 498-507).

30 Nicolaus, *Consilia,* 138r, 141v. On Panormitanus' consilia, see Guido Kisch, *Consilia: Eine Bibliographie der juristischen Konsiliensammlungen* (Basel, 1970), p. 82.

31 Schweizer, *Nicolaus de' Tudeschi,* p. 27; A.J. Black, "The Political Ideas of Conciliarism and Papalism, 1430-1450," *Journal of Ecclesiastical History,* 20 (1969), 45-66.

32 Schweizer, *Nicolaus de' Tudeschi,* pp. 27-28. For a recent discussion on the ecclesiological ideas of Zabarella, see Friedrich Merzbacher, "Die ekklesiologische Konzeption des Kardinals Francesco Zabarella (1360-1417)," in *Festschrift Karl Pivec,* ed. Anton Haidacher and Hans E. Mayer (Innsbruck, 1966), pp. 279-87.

argued before the Council of Basel[33] that the council is higher than the pope, that the council is a community organized for jurisdictional purposes, and that the function of the pope is simply to execute the council's decrees. The pope cannot use his *plenitudo potestatis* to destroy the *status ecclesiae.*

When the vote was taken on April 26, 1437, on the site of a future reunion council with the Greeks, the majority, led by Cardinal Louis Aleman (1390-1450), named Basel, Avignon, or some city in Savoy as places to be chosen, while the minority, which included Cesarini, Cusanus, and Cervantes, decided that Florence or Udine should be chosen. This split in the Council of Basel also divided the Aragonese envoys. Panormitanus, together with Cardinal Aleman, supported the majority's decision, although Ludovico Pontano, another member of the Aragonese delegation, sided with the minority.[34] In a speech before the council delivered on October 6, 1437,[35] Panormitanus also protested the dissolution of the council by Eugenius IV.

Thus Panormitanus' public speeches at the council seem to indicate that he changed completely from an advocate of the papacy to a supporter of the conciliar movement. But it has been emphasized recently that we should approach his remarks on public occasions with caution because they do not necessarily express his true convictions.[36] At the council, Panormitanus, like Ludovico Pontano, was acting for his employer, Alfonso V. Regardless of his personal beliefs, he had to support conciliar or propapal ideas as chief spokesman of the Aragonese party. In this connection it is interesting to observe that when the council was faced early in 1439 with the question of whether it should proceed to depose Eugenius IV, Panormitanus did his best to prevent the deposition under orders from Alfonso V.[37] This time he was joined in his futile endeavor by Pontano, who, however, died of the plague shortly after Eugenius'

---

[33] His speeches at the council and the imperial diet include: (a) *De suprema Papae authoritate* (1437), *Mansi,* XXX, cols. 1186-88, (b) *Miratur hec sancta synodus* (1437), *Mansi,* XXXI, cols. 237-42, *MCG,* 11, pp. 1006-10, (c) *Maximum onus* (1438), *Mansi,* XXX, cols. 1123-84, *MCG,* 11, pp. 1144-93, (d) *Mecum tacitus* (1438), *RTA,* XIII, cols. 195-215, and (e) *Quoniam veritas verborum* (1442), *MCG,* 111, pp. 1022-1125, *RTA,* XVI, cols. 246-48, 439-538. On *Miratur hec sancta synodus,* see L. Buisson, *Potestas und Caritas* (Cologne, 1958), pp. 212-14.

[34] Eduard Preiswerk, *Der Einfluss Aragons auf den Prozess des Basler Konzils gegen Papst Eugen IV* (Basel, 1902), p. 21. On Alfonso V and the Council of Basel, cf. Winfried Küchler, "Alfons V. von Aragon und das Basler Konzil," *Spanische Forschungen der Görresgesellschaft,* 1. Reihe, 23 (1967), pp. 131-46.

[35] *Allegacio Panormitani archiepiscopi contra dissolucionem* in *MCG,* II, pp. 1040-41.

[36] Nörr, *Kirche und Konzil,* pp. 5-7.

[37] Schweizer, *Nicolaus de' Tudeschi,* p. 103.

deposition. Panormitanus' position was that since there were very many bishops with the pope and few against, a resolution against the pope must not be passed by a crowd of the lower clergy. In view of his conciliar ideas which he had expressed previously, this battle in 1439 against the majority of the council was a tortuous one. Cardinal Aleman, the leader of the majority party, clearly saw Panormitanus' inconsistency and attacked him: "You liked this (doctrine) on other occasions, Panormitanus, when the crowd followed you. But now you do not like it because it does not follow you."[38]

Aeneas Sylvius described, in his *Commentarii de gestis Basiliensis concilii,* the mental agony of Panormitanus. Aeneas reports that Panormitanus, when he retired to his bedroom, fell asleep in the midst of his tears after complaining about his king's orders to fight against the truth and to endanger his reputation and his soul.[39] "Panormitanus had been made leader of the conciliar party at the council not through his wish, but by necessity alone, and he was bound to obey his prince."[40] Panormitanus experienced this restless agony partly because his own ideas concerning church government were ambiguous and flexible. Small wonder that he later emphasized consent at the expense of authority when circumstances changed.

In his sermon, delivered in 1441 at the beginning of his third stay in Basel,[41] Panormitanus surprised many fathers by stating that the pope is superior to the council. But since he had returned to Basel for the third time as an envoy of Alfonso V, who was publicly committed to the support of the council, Panormitanus again began to defend the council. The fact that Alfonso had started to negotiate with Eugenius IV to effect reconciliation apparently had little impact on his views as envoy. In the famous speech *Quoniam veritas verborum,* which Panormitanus made in 1442 at the Diet of Frankfurt,[42] he strongly defended the conciliar theory. It was the views expressed in this speech which found many supporters as late as the following century. Martin Luther,

---

[38] Aeneas Sylvius, *De Gestis,* p. 109.

[39] Ibid., p. 153. Cf. Schweizer, *Nicolaus de' Tudeschi,* pp. 23-24.

[40] Aeneas Sylvius, *De Gestis,* p. 173.

[41] Schweizer, *Nicolaus de' Tudeschi,* p. 152.

[42] See above, n. 33.

who approvingly refers to Panormitanus in his writings,[43] seems to have been influenced by Panormitanus' speech in Frankfurt.

Unlike Cusanus' conversion, then, Panormitanus' case was somewhat more complex and fluctuating, partly because he was more subject to political pressure from a secular prince than was Cusanus. To a realistic lawyer like Panormitanus, inflexible and determined adherence to either consent or authority as the guiding principle of church government was perhaps untenable. Cusanus was an employee of a local prince when he acted as a conciliarist; Panormitanus defended the doctrine of conciliar supremacy or that of papal authority in accordance with the instructions which he received from a powerful king, Alfonso V of Aragon. It remains for us to see what the last of our three men advocated and said about the central problem of church government.

Aeneas Sylvius, after his initiation to the Council of Basel under the patronage of an important ecclesiastical official, Domenico Capranica, became an ardent supporter of conciliar doctrine at Basel. He then served a series of masters, two of whom were propapal in outlook. During this time his views on church government underwent subtle changes. One of the reasons why Aeneas became a conciliarist at the council was that he found it expedient as a layman to defend the council against the pope. Even when Cesarini and Cusanus deserted the council in 1437, Aeneas remained at Basel where there was clearly a better chance of advancement for the popular secretary from Siena with a facile pen. As he stated later, "Then I was a layman, and I shared in the general malice of the laity against the Church, nor was I so anxious to discover truth as to secure my own advancement."[44] He changed his status from laity to priesthood in 1445 after he had made his peace with the pope in Rome.[45]

Another reason for his support of conciliar ideas was that he was much impressed by the dynamic leader of the majority party, Louis Aleman, Cardinal

---

[43] *Tractatulus Doctor Martini Lutherii . . . De his qui ad Ecclesias confugiunt*, in D. Martin Luther, *Werke, Kritische Gesamtausgabe*, I (Weimar, 1883), pp. 1-7; *Acta F. Martini Luther Augustiniani*, in Luther, *Werke*, II (Weimar, 1884), p. 10; *Grund und ursach aller Artikel*, in Luther, *Werke*, VII (Weimar, 1897), pp. 430-31. Also *Luther's Works:* Vol. 31, *Career of the Reformer* I, ed. Harold J. Grimm (Philadelphia, 1957), pp. 265-66, and Vol. 32, *Career of the Reformer* II, ed. George W. Forell (Philadelphia, 1958), p. 81. On Luther's knowledge of Panormitanus: Ernst Schäfer, *Luther als Kirchenhistoriker* (Gütersloh, 1897), pp. 42, 61, 116, 204; Christa T. Johns, *Luthers Konzilsidee in ihrer historischen Bedingtheit und ihrem reformatorischen Neuansatz* (Berlin, 1966), pp. 28, 127, 130, 132-34.

[44] Boulting, *Aeneas Silvius*, p. 91; also Carolus Fea, *Pius II Pont. Max. a Calumniis Vindicatus* (Rome, 1823), pp. 157-58, 160; Widmer, *Enea* I, p. 32; II, p. 105.

[45] Diener, "Enea Silvio," pp. 522, 528. Cf. Ludwig Pastor, *The History of the Popes* (2nd ed., London, 1899), I, pp. 344-45.

of St. Cecilia, commonly known as the Cardinal of Arles.[46] A doctor of canon law, Aleman was noted for many virtues and in particular for his courage and steadfastness. "He was," says Aeneas, "patient of injury, not easily provoked, remarkably generous, but a bitter hater of Eugenius."[47] He had attended the councils at Pisa and Constance, and was the leader of the opponents to the pope by the end of 1435. Like the Cardinal of Lyons, he was intent on effecting the return of the papacy to Avignon. On February 14, 1438, Aleman became president of the council and demonstrated thereafter his talent as a controversialist and skillful master of procedural technique. Giuliano Cesarini had always held a special place of importance in Aeneas' mind, but Aeneas also had a profound admiration for the intrepid Cardinal of Arles.

We must note as a third reason that Aeneas was on good terms with Filippo Maria Visconti of Milan, who, as a competitor of the propapal Republics of Venice and Florence, supported the Council of Basel. It is true that Aeneas' father Silvio had tried unsuccessfully to gain recognition at the court of Gian Galeazzo Visconti (1378-1402), Filippo's father.[48] But Silvio's son was much more successful in maintaining good relations with the Duke of Milan. As we saw before, Aeneas spoke at the Council of Basel in 1436 on behalf of the city of Pavia, which was favored by Filippo Maria as the site for a reunion council. Aeneas visited Milan more than a few times to maintain favor at the ducal court.

Aeneas' dislike of law and lawyers has been commented on repeatedly since Georg Voigt's famous book on him. Ludwig Pastor said that Aeneas harbored "an increased aversion for lawyers."[49] It is possible to regard this as an expression of antipathy which many humanists had toward lawyers.[50] Like Petrarch (1304-1374) and Boccaccio (1313-1374), Aeneas no doubt preferred poetry to jurisprudence, but as Professor Kisch has pointed out in his recent study,[51] the former law student of Siena was well versed in the legal literature of his time. We may note in this connection that humanists like Coluccio Salutati (1331-1406), Leonardo Bruni (1369-1444), and Poggio Bracciolini (1380-1459) also had a legal training early in their careers. However, Aeneas' writings on the

---

[46] G. Pérouse, *Le cardinal Louis Aleman, Président du concile de Baile et la fin du grand schisme* (Paris, 1904).

[47] Fea, *Pius II,* p. 66; Boulting, *Aeneas Silvius,* p. 76.

[48] Voigt, *Enea Silvio,* I, p. 6; Widmer, *Enea II,* pp. 53-54, 104.

[49] Pastor, op. cit., I, p. 341.

[50] Myron P. Gilmore, *Humanists and Jurists* (Cambridge, Mass., 1963), pp. 63, 67; Guido Kisch, *Gestalten und Probleme aus Humanismus und Jurisprudenz* (Berlin, 1969), pp. 36-40.

[51] Guido Kisch, *Enea Silvio Piccolomini und die Jurisprudenz* (Basel, 1967).

Council of Basel and his speeches there are not so embellished with legal
terminology and citations as the writings of Cusanus or Panormitanus. But his
ideas also revolve around the two key concepts of consent and authority in the
church.

According to Aeneas,[52] the church is the body of Christ himself. As such
it cannot err. Like many other conciliarists, Aeneas states that the church is
represented by the general council. "Our interpretation is quite correct," he says,
"in defining for us the Church as the general council." The council, however, is
usually attended by the majority of ecclesiastical personages, and the whole
power of the church resides in those who come to the council. The pope is not
the head of the church, but only its vicar. The true head of the church is Christ
himself. Aeneas therefore speaks of the pope as "representative" and
"administrator" of the church. Strongly supporting one of the basic doctrines of
the conciliar theory, he attempts to prove the supremacy of the general council
over the pope. "The Church is as much superior to the Roman pontiff as the
son is inferior to his mother." If the pope does not listen to the church, he does
not listen to Christ either and should be treated like a heathen. Aeneas maintains
that where there is an inspired consensus of the prelates, the opinion of one man
ought to give way.

These ideas of Aeneas were expressed in his above-mentioned famous
book, *Commentarii de gestis Basiliensis concilii,* which was published after the
coronation of Felix V on July 24, 1440. This book, which has been called a
propaganda piece,[53] was an attempt by Aeneas to justify all the dramatic acts of
the Council of Basel, which rejected Eugenius IV, elected its own pope, and
thereby renewed a schism. In another book, *Libellus dialogorum de generalis
concilii autoritate,*[54] also published the same year, the arguments in favor of the
conciliar theory were set forth by means of a discussion between Stefano da
Caccia, an antipapal secretary, and Nicolaus Cusanus, a recent convert to the
papal party. It is perhaps true that "the arguments are perfectly familiar and
worn,"[55] and that the book is even somewhat comical. But certainly by 1440
Aeneas seemed committed to the principles of consent and conciliar supremacy
as against papal authority.

[52] Citations in the following paragraph on Aeneas' concept of the church are taken
from Aeneas Sylvius, *De Gestis, passim.* See also *Aeneae Sylvii Piccolominei
Senensis . . . Opera Quae Extant Omnia* (Basel, 1551; Frankfurt a. M., 1967), pp. 1-
61.

[53] Anton Weiss, *Aeneas Sylvius Piccolomini als Papst Pius II* (Graz, 1897), p. 4.

[54] The text is in *Analecta Monumentorum Omnis Aevi Vindobonensia,* ed. A.F.
Kollar, II (Vienna, 1761), pp. 686-790.

[55] Boulting, *Aeneas Silvius, p.* 107. Cf. Widmer, *Enea I, p.* 42.

Aeneas was, however, apparently not completely pleased with the events at Basel. They forced Cusanus to re-examine his position and to abandon conciliarism in favor of papal authoritarianism, while Panormitanus remained unaffected, at least outwardly. These same events also began to affect Aeneas slowly and gradually. It is true that Aeneas, even after these events, maintained and supported conciliar ideas because they were supported by the *maior pars* of the council, but further deterioration of the relations between pope and council, which reached its lowest point in the deposition of Eugenius IV on June 25, 1439, forced Aeneas to ponder the future of the council. He himself described well the condition which existed then at the council:

> No one among those at Basel was listened to if he defended the rights of the Apostolic See, commended the Roman Curia, or gave Eugenius a favorable word. But whoever spoke ill of the Roman See, condemned Eugenius, and detested the Curia, was held in the highest consideration.[56]

Aeneas was further troubled by the fact that Pope Felix V did not attract strong supporters around him. In contrast to him, Eugenius IV was able to announce in Florence on July 6, 1439, the *Laetentur caeli* which brought about the end of the schism between the Roman and Greek Churches that had continued since 1054. Aeneas felt the growing strength of the Eugenian party, and he probably thought that the Felician party was no longer a *maior pars* in the church. He said that quarrels "broke out again and the division arose not so much between Pope and Council as between the Fathers of the Council themselves."[57] "Among the bishops and fathers at Basel," wrote Aeneas, "we saw cooks and stablemen judging the affairs of the world; who would credit their words and acts with the authority of law?"[58] After the withdrawal of the Aragonese party from the council in August 1443, Aeneas was increasingly disturbed by the ineffectiveness of Baslean conciliarism and concerned with the maintenance of unity within the church. The Council of Ferrara-Florence, which was now aided by the former *sanior pars* of the Council of Basel as against the *maior pars,* seems to have become the *maior pars* of the church itself. "Opposition is

---

[56] Fea, *Pius II,* p. 3: "Nemo apud Basilienses audiebatur, qui Sedis Apostolicae jura defenders, qui Romanam Curiam commendaret, qui laudi Eugenium daret. Ac qui Romanae Sedis auctoritati detraxit, qui criminatus est Eugenium, et Curiam abominatus, in magnis, summisque habebatur."

[57] Fea, *Pius II,* p. 61: "Renovantur discordiae; jamque non inter papam et concilium tantum; sed inter ipsos concilii patres exoritur divisio."

[58] Ady, *Pius II,* p. 70. See J.D. Mansi, *Pii II P. M. . . . Orationes Politicae, et Ecclesiasticae,* I (Lucae, 1755), p. 231: "Inter episcopos, caeterosque patres conscriptos vidimus in Basilea coquos & stabularios orbis negotia judicantes, quis horum dicta vel facta judicaverit legis habere vigorem?"

useless," Aeneas told Kaspar Schlick later, "and will only lead to new schism."[59]
These practical questions, not theoretical speculation, apparently affected his
attitude toward the church at this time. The doctrine of consent was
deemphasized, at least in relation to the Council of Basel; authority and unity
loomed ever larger as guiding principles of church government.[60]

Although Aeneas was a representative of the Council of Basel to the
Imperial Diet of Frankfurt in 1442, he was not really committed to the principle
of consent. His coronation as poet laureate in 1442 by the Emperor Friedrich III
gave him the opportunity to start a new career as a member of the imperial
chancery in Vienna. He was now moving, as he said later,[61] into the "neutral"
area without having offended the sensitive Felix V whom he was leaving. This
move was considered infinitely better than a prompt conversion from
conciliarism to papalism[62] because he was afraid of falling into another error. In
his letter to Hartung von Kappel, written in Vienna in the spring of 1443,[63]
Aeneas still stated that the council was supreme over the pope. It is worth
noting, however, that his tone was now quite reserved and tentative. He confined
his arguments to generalities, carefully withholding any mention of the Council
of Basel.

Not only did he now realize that Eugenius IV headed the *maior pars* of the
church, but he came increasingly under the influence of imperial ideas. It is
entirely possible that the monarchical doctrine of Antonius de Rosellis,[64] under
whom Aeneas had studied civil law in Siena, began to gain ascendancy over the
mind of the Italian secretary from the Ghibelline city of Siena as he settled down
in the imperial court in Vienna. True, he found the Germans uncultured and his
life at the court boring, as he depicted it in his *De curialium miseria* (1444).[65]
But as he became a strong supporter of the empire, his concept of the church
also became more inclined towards papal monarchism. Aeneas had written to
Schlick in 1443 that unless one was in favor of schism, one could not reject

---

[59] Boulting, *Aeneas Silvius,* p. 155.

[60] In a sense Aeneas did not entirely abandon the doctrine of consent, as was indicated
by his preoccupation with the *maior pars.*

[61] Fea, *Pius II,* p. 156: "Placuit ad neutrales transire."

[62] Widmer, *Enea I,* p. 43; Diener, "Enea Silvio," p. 531.

[63] *Der Briefwechsel,* I, pp. 132-44.

[64] Widmer, *Enea II,* pp. 136-37, 150; Kisch, *Enea Silvio,* p. 34. On Rosellis' life and
thought, see Schulte, *Die Geschichte,* II, 303-05; Karla Eckermann, *Studien zur
Geschichte des monarchischen Gedankens im 15. Jahrhundert* (Berlin, 1933).

[65] *Aeneae Sylvii Opera,* pp. 720-36.

Eugenius IV.[66] No wonder that he successfully made his peace with Eugenius when he was sent to Rome in 1444 by the emperor. (See the famous speech of Aeneas.[67]) Forgiven by the pope, Aeneas was no longer a conciliarist. He became a supporter of papalism by way of imperial neutralism. As he said later, he wanted to "abandon Aeneas and accept Pius."[68]

The *De ortu et auctoritate imperii Romani,* which is actually a letter he sent to the emperor on March 1, 1446,[69] deals with the problem of the empire from the monarchical point of view. The influence of Antonius de Rosellis is quite noticeable. But the letter can also be characterized as a propapal writing because all that was said in it of the authority of the emperor applied equally to that of the pope. According to Aeneas, the pope is as supreme in the spiritual realm as the emperor is in the temporal one.

Aeneas' adherence to the doctrine of conciliar supremacy, which was asserted at Basel mostly by the French clergy under the influence and leadership of Cardinal Aleman, was gradually weakened because of his services in the imperial chancery, until he found the monarchical principle of the Italian papacy far more acceptable than the democratic principle of the Basel fathers. If the events at Basel can be interpreted as the result of the determined effort by French leaders to "recover the ascendancy over the Church which they had exercised during the Avignon period,"[70] we may construe what happened to Aeneas as a release from the spell of Gallicanism and a return to the monarchical principle of the papacy and the empire.

Once on the papal side, Aeneas did not waver. "I have great cause to hate Basel, where I spent so much time in vain," wrote Aeneas in 1445.[71] After taking holy orders in 1445, he further strengthened his position as a papalist. Rejecting the *Commentarii de gestis Basiliensis concilii* of 1440 as unacceptable, he wrote in 1450 another account of the Council of Basel from a more papalist point of view. The *De rebus Basileae gestis commentarius*[72] was an attempt to whitewash his sorry experiences at Basel. In the famous bull *Execrabilis* of 1460, which he issued two years after his accession to the papal throne as Pius II, we can see a strong assertion of the principle of authority over

---

[66] *Der Briefwechsel,* I, p. 255; Widmer, *Enea I,* p. 53.

[67] Pastor, *The History,* I, pp. 345-46.

[68] Fea, *Pius II,* p. 152: "Aeneam rejicite, Pium recipite."

[69] See above, note 10.

[70] Jedin, *A History,* I, p. 19.

[71] *Der Briefwechsel,* I, p. 542: "multa sunt, propter que Basileam odisse, deberem, in qua tam diu tempus inutiliter perdidi."

[72] The text is in Fea, *Pius II,* pp. 31-115; *Der Briefwechsel,* II, pp. 164-228.

that of consent. "An execrable, and in former ages un-heard of abuse has sprung up in our time, namely that some people, imbued with the spirit of rebellion, presume to appeal to a future council from the Roman pontiff, the Vicar of Jesus Christ."[73] This was the voice of the restored papacy. As Figgis put it, "Aeneas Sylvius Piccolomini was more than the historian of the council; he was the prophet of the Papacy."[74]

On the basis of the preceding discussions, what can we say about the general nature of the conciliar movement, the doctrinal subtleties of the three persons with whom we are concerned, and the impact of various events on their thought and the growth of their ideas?

First of all, it is obvious that the turbulent events and proceedings at the Council of Basel had a profound effect upon the thought of the three. Without fully accepting a semi-Marxist formula that ideology and thought processes in general cannot be understood adequately as long as their social origins are obscured, we may recognize that in all of these men, the ideas and concepts expressed in their speeches and writings were molded and changed by what they witnessed at the council. It is not at all surprising that the extraordinary events in the church since the beginning of the fourteenth century, such as the so-called Babylonian Captivity (1309-77), the Great Schism (1378-1417), the Council of Pisa, the Council of Constance, and the Council of Basel, had a tremendous impact on the minds of those Christians who were seriously troubled by the lack of unity in the church and who sought to understand the real meaning of the church.

Secondly, we may note a very important role which the lawyers played in the councils and diets of the fourteenth and fifteenth centuries. The study of conciliar thought has been stimulated recently by many monographs dealing with the legal background of the period. "It is now common to see conciliar activity against the background of law and administration."[75] Of those who participated in the conciliar and imperial activities, many were indeed well trained lawyers. The great controversies of the day plunged them into legal and political problems the solution of which required legal knowledge and background. It has been said recently of Renaissance Florence that wherever "we look in Florentine public affairs, we find lawyers at work; in diplomacy, in relations with the Church, in territorial government, in the formulation of policy, in administra-

---

[73] *Church and State Through the Centuries,* eds. S.Z. Ehler and J.B. Morrall (Westminster, 1954), pp. 132-33

[74] Figgis, *Studies,* p. 44.

[75] E.F. Jacob, *Essays in Later Medieval History* (Manchester, 1968), p. 124. A most notable contribution to this development was made by Professor Brian Tierney's *Foundations of the Conciliar Theory* (Cambridge, 1955, 1968).

tion and adjudication, and in the political struggle proper."[76] This can probably be applied with some modifications to fifteenth-century Europe in general. Cesarini, Panormitanus, Pontano, Aleman, and Cusanus all belong to the group of lawyers active in public affairs. Even Aeneas, who is noted for his literary and historical works, found in legal literature enough material with which to build a theory of resistance to the pope.

In examining these lawyers' conduct at various councils, it is tempting to ask whether they had a tendency to serve whomever seemed to offer the best price to them. Aeneas has especially been criticized for his opportunistic flair and lack of loyalty to his masters. "His pen was at the service of the highest bidder, the friend or opponent of the Council, and his primary concern was the pursuit of his own career."[77]   Speaking of his relations with his master Friedrich III, Aeneas said: "I shall try to stand well with the king. I shall obey him and follow him. His desire will be mine."[78] Aeneas was at his client's disposal, and he had to write as his client wished. But his attitude toward his masters was not too different from that of Panormitanus and Cusanus.[79] They served their lords and then could later change their views either moderately or almost completely as they began to work for different masters. But it would seem totally unjustifiable to conclude from the few cases which we have discussed that it was a marked trait of fifteenth-century lawyers to change their sides whenever they felt it expedient to do so.

Turning, thirdly, to the central problem of authority and consent in church government, the enthusiasm with which men like Cusanus and Aeneas accepted the doctrine of consent can be best understood and appreciated in the context of the general rise of the lower clergy and the laity in the church. Gierke wrote:

> The constitutional doctrine of the Church thus underwent violent disturbances. Nevertheless one important consequence of the principle of Popular Sovereignty remained undrawn or but partially drawn. The Conciliar Movement did not bestow any active part in the affairs of the Church upon the laity.[80]

[76] Lauro Martines, *Lawyers and Statecraft in Renaissance Florence* (Princeton, 1968), p. 3.

[77] Ady, *Pius II*, p. 54.   One of the most critical discussions on Aeneas is Johannes Haller, "Pius II, ein Papst der Renaissance," *Deutsche Rundschau*, 153 (1912), 194-220.

[78] *Der Briefwechsel*, I, p. 287: "interim me regi insinuabo, regi parebo, regem sequar, quod is volet et ego volam."

[79] Aeneas indicates that Panormitanus' change of his position was related to his corruption. See Aeneas Sylvius, *De Viris Illustribus*, p. 3. On this question, see Schweizer, *Nicolaus de' Tudeschi*, pp. 136-38; Lefebvre, "Panormitain," col. 1201. For various criticisms of Cusanus, see Watanabe, *The Political Ideas*, p. 98 n.2.

[80] Gierke, *Political Theories*, p. 57.

The Council of Basel, however, was not a council dominated by prelates, but a council consisting of lower clerks and some laymen as well as prelates. The ascendancy of the lower clergy and the laity was made possible because of the strong support which the professors and the princes gave to the conciliar movement. Alongside the noble administrators of the church sat the humbler academicians and the representatives of secular princes in the Council of Basel. It is easy to see why Cusanus, chancellor of Ulrich of Manderscheid, who was fighting Eugenius IV, appealed to the council in hopes of receiving a favorable decision; why Aeneas, the layman from Siena, preferred the council to the curia; and why Panormitanus strongly advocated the conciliar theory at the council as Alfonso V's spokesman. But the growth of radicalism at Basel convinced many fathers of the inherent danger posed by the council to the hierarchical establishment of the church. "Perhaps the most important long term consequences of Constance and Basel was the fear bred in later popes of all such meetings."[81] It was this realization which led many conciliarists to abandon their principle of consent and to become supporters of papal authoritarianism. They began to realize, like Aeneas, that the *maior pars* was not necessarily the *sanior pars*. It was authority and hierarchy which became the leading principles of church government. As Figgis has pointed out, the conciliar movement was a failure.[82] Instead the principle of authority in church government was triumphant.

But if we are to understand the decline of the conciliar movement and the victory of the papacy over it, we must finally perceive clearly the international implications of conciliar activities. Even Figgis has failed to recognize sufficiently the complexity of the diplomatic and political situation within which the councils had to operate. It would also be impossible to understand the nature of the conciliar movement without taking into account an important part which nascent nationalism played. Eugenius IV, the Venetian, was supported by England, Burgundy, Venice, and Florence; the Council of Basel was defended by France, Aragon, Milan, and Siena. Duke Philip of Burgundy supported the pope because his enemy France was on the side of the council; Duke Filippo Maria of Milan, Eugenius IV's enemy, naturally defended the council. The king of Aragon also supported the council for the same reason as the Duke of Milan. On the other hand, the Guelf towns, such as Venice and Florence, were on the papal side, while the Ghibelline city of Siena supported the council, which, in its early stages, found in the Emperor Sigismund (1410-1437) a warm supporter and friend. The German electors confirmed their neutrality in Mainz on March 17,

[81] Hay, *Europe,* p. 291.

[82] Figgis, *Studies,* p. 31.

1439[83] in the struggle between the pope and the council. This was by no means free from antipapal bias. But after the election of Felix V on November 5, 1439, a realignment of forces took place. Filippo Maria's zeal for the council cooled. Charles VII (1422-1461), king of France, who had published the Pragmatic Sanction of Bourges on July 7, 1438,[84] soon declared in favor of Eugenius IV. Scotland and Castile, as well as Aragon, also defected from the council. Aragon was won over for Eugenius IV when he confirmed Alfonso V as king of Naples in 1442. Then at the Diet of Frankfurt in September 1446, the Emperor Friedrich III and the electors decided to abandon their neutrality and to support Eugenius IV. As a result, Felix V and the fathers of Basel were left without any important supporters.

In the meantime, the papacy won the support of many because it allowed the kings and princes to conclude concordats with the papacy.[85] After long negotiations of the German ambassadors at Rome, an agreement was reached known as the Concordat of the Princes. Eugenius IV published its terms in four bulls on February 5 and 7, 1447. His successor, Nicholas V (1447-1455), confirmed the important Concordat of Vienna on March 19, 1448, in which Germany made her peace with the papacy. Thus in the end, the defeat of the fathers of Basel was decided by the actions of the princes. It is true to say that "it was the king, not the priest who came off best as the result of councils."[86] The powers of Europe desired above all to avoid another schism. Hence they supported the Roman pope who had apparently overcome the conciliar party. But when the period of conciliar activity was over, the popes were no longer figures of real political importance beyond Italy. The age of national rivalry and competition had already begun.

---

[83] Heinz Hürten, "Die Mainzer Akzeptation von 1439," *Archiv für mittelrheinische Kirchengeschichte,* 11 (1959), 42-75.

[84] Schweizer, *Nicolaus de' Tudeschi,* pp. 60, 140-41.

[85] Mandell Creighton, *A History of the Papacy from the Great Schism to the Sack of Rome,* III (London, 1897), pp. 86-89; Fred W. Neal, *The Papacy and the Nations: A Study of Concordats (1418-1516)* (University of Chicago, Ph.D. dissertation, 1944). Wilhelm Bertrams, *Der neuzeitliche Staatsgedanke und die Konkordate des ausgehenden Mittelalters* (2nd ed., "Analecta Gregoriana," XXX; Rome, 1950), esp. pp. 115-90.

[86] E.F. Jacob, "The Conciliar Movement in Recent Study," *Bulletin of the John Rylands Library,* 14 (1958), 26-53; reprinted in Jacob, *Essays,* pp. 98-123.

The Episcopal Election of 1430 in Trier and Nicholas of Cusa

Gregor Heimburg, the bitter critic of the papacy and of Nicholas of Cusa, is said to have taunted Cusanus, saying that because Cusanus was defeated in a lawsuit in Mainz, he turned from the practice of law to theology.[1] Heimburg, a *utriusque iuris doctor* who rendered his legal services to both secular and ecclesiastical princes, was certainly versed in the legal literature of his time. But, as we shall see below, history does not seem to bear out his insinuation that disappointment and failure in the field of law led Cusanus to take up theology as his career. It is probably of little importance to ask whether Cusanus would have continued to work as a lawyer had he won the case in Mainz. We must note, however, that Cusanus is so well known as a theologian, cardinal, philosopher, and even as a scientist that we are apt to forget his early career as a canon lawyer in the service of the archdiocese of Trier. It is only recently that due attention began to be paid to the legal activities of Cusanus.[2] The purpose of this paper is to throw light not only on his education and activities as a canon lawyer, but also on the role which he played in the disputed episcopal election of 1430 in the archdiocese of Trier.

When Cusanus matriculated at the University of Heidelberg in 1416 at the age of 15, he was already a cleric in the archdiocese of Trier.[3] In fifteenth-century

---

[1] Johann M. Düx, *Der deutsche Cardinal Nicolaus von Cusa und die Kirche seiner Zeit*, I (Regensburg, 1847), p. 105; Edmond Vansteenberghe, *Le cardinal Nicolas de Cues, l'action—la pensée* (Paris, 1920), p. 4. Heimburg's criticism of Cusanus is found in *Invectiva Gregorii Heimburg Vtrivsque ivris doctoris, in reverendissimum Patrem, Dominum Nicolaum de Cusa, Sanctae Romane Ecclesiae Tituli S. Petri ad Vincula Presbyterum Cardinalem, et Episcopum Brixinensem* in Marquard Freher, *Rerum germanicarum scriptores*, II (Strasbourg, 1717), pp. 255-265. On Gregor Heimburg in general, see Clemens Brockhaus, *Gregor von Heimburg: Ein Beitrag zur deutschen Geschichte des 15. Jahrhunderts* (Leipzig, 1861); Paul Joachimsohn, *Gregor Heimburg* (Bamberg, 1891).

[2] In this connection Erich Meuthen's numerous writings are of great importance. The author's indebtedness to his studies will be noted below. See also Paul E. Sigmund, *Nicholas of Cusa and Medieval Political Thought* (Cambridge, Massachusetts, 1963); Morimichi Watanabe, *The Political Ideas of Nicholas of Cusa, with Special Reference to His De concordantia catholica* (Geneva, 1963).

[3] Gustav Toepke, *Die Matrikel der Universität Heidelberg*, I (Heidelberg, 1884), p. 128. The record on Cusanus is as follows: "Nycolaus Cancer de Coesze cler(icus) Treuer(ensis) dyoc(esis) . . . d(edi)t."

Europe canon lawyers played an increasingly important role in the administration of the church, and many a young, promising boy went to law schools to prepare for a legal career. Trier, the oldest diocese in Germany, was no exception and needed many *jurisperiti* whose expert knowledge of law was indispensable in an age of numerous litigations. The future lawyers of Trier usually turned to the universities of Heidelberg, Erfurt, Paris, Bologna, or Padua after completing their preparatory work in Trier.[4] The fifteen-year-old Cusanus had not probably made up his mind to study law. The University of Heidelberg, where the famous controversy over the *via antiqua* and the *via moderna* had been going on for many years, was more under the influence of the *via moderna* while Cusanus was studying there. But it is difficult to ascertain what influence this nominalistic philosophy had on Cusanus during his three-semester stay in Heidelberg. After probably earning his *baccalaureus in artibus,* Cusanus left Heidelberg the next year to enter the famous University of Padua.[5]

While he was in Padua from October 1417 to the summer of 1423, Cusanus became interested in many subjects, such as ancient literature, mathematics, astronomy, physics, and medicine, but the study of law increasingly occupied his attention. By the beginning of the fifteenth century the canon law faculty of the University of Padua was no less famous than that of Bologna. Of the professors of Padua under whom Cusanus studied law, Prosdocimus de Comitibus apparently exercised much influence on Cusanus. It has often been maintained that Giuliano Cesarini, to whom Cusanus later dedicated his major philosophical work *De docta ignorantia* (1440), was one of the professors at Padua whose influence on the young Cusanus was indelible. The future cardinal Cesarini had among his students Domenico Capranica and Cusanus, both of whom also became cardinals. But Cesarini seems to have taught only two years as *in utroque iure doctor* and left Padua in 1422 at the

---

[4] Fritz Michel, "Jurisperiti und Advokaten zu Trier und Koblenz," in his *Zur Geschichte der geistichen Geriehtsbarkeit und Verwaltung der Trierer Erzbischöfe im Mittelalter* (Trier, 1953), pp. 128-138. On Bologna especially, see Gustav C. Knod, *Deutsche Studenten in Bologna (1289-1562)* (Berlin, 1899).

[5] On the *via antiqua* vs. *via modena* controversy, see Gerhard Ritter, "Via antiqua und via moderna auf den deutsehen Universitäten des XV. Jahrhunderts," *Sitzungsberichte der Heidelberger Akademie der Wissenschaften, Philosopisch-historische Klasse* (Heidelberg, 1922), pp. 39-144; Rudolf Haubst, "Nikolaus von Cues auf Spuren des Thomas von Aquin," *Mitteilungen und Forschungsbeiträge der Cusanus-Gesellschaft* [Hereafter cited as MFCG], V (1965): 17-19. Although there is no record to show that Cusanus received the bachelor's degree, we can probably assume that he did. See Erich Meuthen, *Nikolaus von Kues 1401-1461: Skizze einer Biographie* (Münster, 1964), p. 13.

latest.[6] His influence on Cusanus as a student of law was probably not so great as has been generally estimated. Many scholars have regarded Codex Cusanus 220, which is in the library of St. Nicholas Hospital in Kues, Germany, as a series of lectures given by Cesarini. It has been shown recently, however, that it contains notes taken of the lectures given by Prosdocimus de Comitibus with a large number of glosses in Cusanus' hand.[7] It is also important to note the influence of the great canon lawyer, Franciscus Zabarella (1360-1417), on Cusanus. The reputation of the foremost canonist of the day was such that "without proper knowledge of the cardinal's writings no man could have gained a degree in canon law."[8] Zabarella taught at Padua from 1391 to 1411. While Cusanus was at the University of Padua, Zabarella's theories were expounded by his nephew Bartholomew Zabarella, a great lawyer in his own right and later Archbishop of Florence. Apparently he was actively related to the University of Padua until about 1430.[9] Thus after six years' study Cusanus received the degree *decretorum doctor* in 1423. When he returned to his native country in 1424, Cusanus was no doubt one of the lawyers whose expert knowledge was of much help to the archdiocese of Trier.

On January 21, 1425, Cusanus was collated by Otto of Ziegenhain, Archbishop of Trier (1418-1430), to the parish church of St. Andrew at Altrich about eight miles northwest of Kues, receiving an annuity of forty florins, a cart (*plaustrum*) of wine, and four measures (*maldra*) of wheat as an income from the

[6] Joseph Gill, "Cardinal Giuliano Cesarini (1444)," in his *Personalities of the Council of Florence* (Oxford, 1964), pp. 95-103. See also Heinrich Fechner, *Giuliano Cesarini (1398-1444) bis zu seiner Ankunft in Basel am 9. September 1431* (Marburg, 1907).

[7] Alois Krchnak, "Die kanonistischen Aufzeichnungen des Nikolaus von Kues in Cod. Cus. 220 als Mitschrift einer Vorlesung seines Paduaner Lehrers Prosdocimus de Comitibus," MFCG, II (1962): 67-84. On Prosdocimus de Comitibus, see Nicolas C. Papadopoli, *Historia Gymnasii Patavini,* I (Venice, 1726), p. 216; Krchnak, *loc. cit.,* pp. 80-84.

[8] Walter Ullmann, *The Origins of the Great Schism* (London, 1948), p. 193.

[9] Papadopoli, *Historia,* I, iii, p. 216: "Bartholomaeus Zabarella, Francisci Cardinalis ex Andrea fratre nepos jus Pontificium Patavi magna cum laude publice docuit sub annum MCDXXXI floruitque deinceps. . . . " See also Jacopo Facciolati, *Fasti gymnasii Patavini,* I (Patavii, 1757), p. 30; Gasparo Zonta and Giovanni Brotto, *Acta graduum academicorum Gymnasii Patavini* (Patavii, 1922), pp. 125, 180; Erich Meuthen, *Das Trierer Schisma von 1430 auf dem Basler Konzil: Zur Lebensgeschichte des Nikolaus von Kues* (Münster, 1964), p. 91.

archbishop.[10] Otto of Ziegenhain, a man of singular personal piety and self-denial, as the fifteenth-century writer Johannes Nider (c.1380-1438) described him in *Formicarius* (c.1435), was by birth a Count of Ziegenhain and Nidda, and he attended the Council of Constance (1414-1418) to fight the spread of the Hussites and to work for the unity of the church.[11] Elected unanimously by the cathedral chapter of Trier on October 13, 1418, and accepted enthusiastically by the people of Trier, he convoked a provincial synod in 1423 to reform his archdiocese. We can see the reforming spirit of the Council of Constance at work in his endeavor. The decrees of the synod attacked the wide-spread practice of concubinage, the use of unfitting habits by the clergy, the irregular performance of the divine office, and the like.[12] But undoubtedly his attempt at reforming his archdiocese was regarded by some as contrary to the election capitulation of 1418 which he, like the other members of the cathedral chapter, had accepted before his election to the office of archbishop. The election capitulation stated clearly, among other things, that the statutes, rights, customs, and privileges of the chapter should be kept intact.[13] The cathedral chapter of Trier, which, like other cathedral chapters in Europe, had obtained independence from the archbishop by

[10] Jacob Marx, *Verzeichnis der Handschriften-Sammlung des Hospitals zu Cues bei Bernkastel a./Mosel* (Trier, 1905), p. 203. In Codex Cusanus 212 Cusanus wrote in his own hand: "Nota. 1425 die mercurii que fuit ultima dies Januarii habui graciam domini episcopi treverensis secundum quod ipse mihi deberet dare annuatim 40 florenos unum plaustrum vini 4 maldra siliginis et ecclesiam in altreya."

[11] Johannes Nider, *Formicarius,* Lib. II, cap. 2 (Augsburg, c. 1484). On Otto of Ziegenhain, see Christopher Brower and Jacob Masen, *Antiquitatum et annalium Trevirensium,* II (Leodii, 1670), pp. 267-273; J.H. Wyttenbach and M.F.J. Müller, *Gesta Trevirorum,* II (Trier, 1836), pp. 311-317; J. Christian Lager, "Aus dem Leben des Trierer Erzbischofs Otto von Ziegenhain (1418-1430)," *Pastor Bonus,* 2 (1890): 203-211, 253-265, 348-362.

[12] Wyttenbach and Müller, *Gesta,* II, pp. 311-312: ". . . dominus Otto, comes de Tzegenhayn praepositus et canonicus ecclesiae Trevirensis, per capitulum concorditer fuit electus....Qui civitatem cum magno gaudio et solemnitate introductus fuit, cum multitudine principum, cumitum, baronum, nobilium et aliorum proborum virorum." The decrees of the provincial synod of 1423 are printed in Johann Nikolaus von Hontheim, *Historia trevirensis diplomatica et pragmatica,* II (Augsburg and Würzburg, 1750), pp. 367-371; Johann F. Schannat and Joseph Hartzheim, *Concilia Germananiae,* V (Cologne, 1763), pp. 222-227.

[13] The terms of the 35-point election capitulation are printed in Wilhelm Günther, *Codex diplomaticus rheno-mosellanus,* IV (Coblenz, 1825), 199-205 as "Wahlcapitulation des Erzbischofs Otto von Trier 1419." The text given in Günther is a slightly changed version of the election capitulation of 1418 which Otto solemnly published in 1419 after his election. See Johannes Kremer, *Studien zur Geschichte der Trierer Wahlkapitulationen* (Trier, 1909), p. 12.

this time, strongly resisted the reform program of Archbishop Otto, who was supported only by Friedrich of Kröv, the provost of the chapter. In these circumstances the office of the archbishop increasingly needed legal experts who could help the archbishop to carry out his reform program and to administer the see of Trier. Cusanus' appointment to Altrich showed that a bright future was in store for him under Archbishop Otto.

It was then not surprising that Cusanus, as *doctor in iure canonico Treverensis Dyocesis,* matriculated on April 8, 1425, at the University of Cologne,[14] which was then under the 145th rector, Peter of Weller from Jülich. Cusanus' interest in theology was deepened during his stay in Cologne, as is indicated in his study of the works of Raymond Lull (c.1235-c.1315). Heimericus de Campo (or Heimeric van den Velde), who had entered the University of Cologne in 1421, was Cusanus' teacher who apparently aroused his interest in the teachings of the "Enlightened Doctor." Cusanus diligently copied and studied the works of Lull in 1427 and 1428, as the extant manuscripts in the library in Kues show.[15] It is also known that he bought a copy of Peter Lombard's *Libri sententiarum* on July 8, 1428.[16] But he seems to have developed by this time a keen interest in the study of legal history. Ulrich of Manderscheid, the son of Count Dietrich of Manderscheid and a graduate of the University of Cologne, was then dean of the cathedral chapter of Cologne. According to tradition, Dietrich sent Cusanus to the school of the Brethren of the Common Life at Deventer when he was a young boy. Although this tradition has not been indisputably confirmed, it probably indicates that Cusanus had close relations with the Manderscheid family from his childhood.[17] Of the six

---

[14] Hermann Keussen, *Die Matrikel der Universität Köln 1389 bis 1559,* 2nd ed., I (Bonn, 1928), p. 213. The entry on Cusanus is as follows: Nyc(olaus) de Cusa, d(octo)r (in) iur(e) can(onico), Trev(erensis) d(yocesis); n(on) dedit ob rev(erentiam) pers(onae), sed i(uravit) c(ompleta).

[15] Marx, *Verzeichnis,* pp. 81-90, especially Cod. Cus. 83. According to Colomer, Cusanus had 39 works of Raymond Lull. This is the largest number of works by any author in whom Cusanus was interested. See Eusebio Colomer, *Nikolaus von Kues und Raimund Llull* (Berlin, 1961), p. 1. On Heimericus de Campo, see Rudolf Haubst, "Zum Fortleben Alberts des Grossen bei Heymerich von Kamp und Nikolaus von Kues," in Heinrich Ostlender (ed.), *Studia Albertina* (Münster, 1952), pp. 420-447.

[16] Marx, *Verzeichnis,* p. 95.

[17] This tradition has been accepted in many books on Cusanus or his times. See, for example, Albert Hyma, *The Christian Renaissance: A History of the Devotio Moderna,* 2nd ed. (Hamden, Connecticut, 1965), pp. 102, 262-264, 421. But, as has been pointed out by Marx and Meuthen, there is no conclusive evidence for this tradition. Jacob Marx, *Nikolaus von Cues und seine Stiftungen zu Cues und Deventer* (Trier, 1906), p. 140; Jacob Marx, *Geschichte des Armen-Hospitals zum h. Nikolaus*

cells reserved for the nobles in Cusanus' famous hospital in Kues, one was set aside for ever (*in perpetuum*) for Count Dietrich I and his descendants probably out of gratitude to the family.[18] Thus it is possible that, thanks to Ulrich's help, Cusanus had access to the library of the cathedral in Cologne, in which he could study many old documents, manuscripts, and records for himself. The humanist Poggio Bracciolini (1380-1459) had discovered in Cologne around 1420 a manuscript of Petronius. In his letters to his friend Niccolò Niccoli (1364-1437), Poggio often spoke of Cusanus' humanistic activities with praise and expectation. Another humanist Guarino Guarini (1374-1460) wrote to Giovanni Lamola in 1426 that a certain secretary of Cardinal Orsini, called Nicolaus Treverensis, had found in a dusty library (*bibliotheca pulverunta*) in Cologne, Cicero's *De republica*. Humanists believed that the discoverer of this important find was none other than Cusanus, and in consequence his reputation as a humanist was much enhanced. The discovered book turned out to be only Macrobius' *Super Somnio Scipionis*. But it seems clear that Cusanus' research in the cathedral library continued. As he himself wrote later in the *De concordantia catholica*, he studied in the library a large volume which is believed to be *Codex Carolinus* of the Austrian National Library.[19] He was also able to read the imperial decree *Saluberrima* concerning a Roman provincial meeting of Arles from 417 to 418.[20] Thus Cusanus had much experience of documentary

zu Cues (Trier, 1907), pp. 11-13; Erich Meuthen, "Nikolaus von Kues und der Laie in der Kirche," *Historisches Jahrbuch*, LXXXI (1962): 107; Meuthen, *Nikolaus von Kues: Skizze*, pp. 10-12; Meuthen, *Das Trierer Schisma*, p. 76. Vansteenberghe, *Le cardinal*, p. 6 n. 3, says that the question is still open.

[18] Marx, *Geschichte*, pp. 12, 58-59.

[19] Gerhard Kallen (ed.), *De concordantia catholica* [hereafter cited as *DCC*], III (Hamburg, 1959), cap. iii, paragraph 316: "Ego enim Coloniae in maiori ecclesia volumen ingens omnium missivarum Hadriani I. ad Carolum et ipsius Caroli responsiones et insuper copias omnium bullarum vidi. . . . " On Guarino's letter as well as Poggio's interest in Cusanus, see Aloys Meister. "Die humanistischen Anfänge des Nikolaus von Cues," *Annalen des historischen Vereins für den Niederrhein*, LXIII (1896): 1-21; Vansteenberghe, *Le cardinal*, pp. 17-22; Klemens Löffler, *Kölnische Bibliotheksgeschichte im Umriss* (Köln, 1923), p. 16. Cf. Aloys Schmidt, "Nikolaus von Kues Sekretär des Kardinals Giordano Orsini?," in Josef Engel and Hans M. Klinkenberg, eds., *Aus Mittelalter and Neuzeit* (Bonn, 1957), pp. 137-143. Codex Carolinas, which is now Cod. Vindob. 449 of the Austrian National Library, was in Cologne till 1554. See Löffler, *Kolnische Bibliotheksgeschichte*, p. 16.

[20] *DCC*, III, cap. xxxv, paragraph 521.

research in legal history. Moreover, there is reason to believe that he taught canon law after 1425 in the University of Cologne.[21]

But his activities in Cologne were not merely academic. We find him participating in many lawsuits, giving his opinions as practicing lawyer. The faculty of law of the University of Cologne was the leading faculty of the university in the later Middle Ages, and its law professors, like professors of theology, were often consulted on various legal matters concerning the administration of the church.[22] A case in point, for which there is an interesting, valuable document, concerns the question of tax exemption on the wine which was sent by the parish church of Bacharach to the collegiate church of St. Andrew in Cologne. Winand of Steeg, parish priest of Bacharach and himself *decretorum doctor* from the University of Würzburg, had contended against Louis III, the Elector of the Palatinate (1410-1436), that the church of Bacharach could send the produce from its vineyard tax-free to the church of St. Andrew because it was related to the collegiate church in Cologne as a proprietary church (*Eigenkirche*).[23] Cusanus, along with sixty-four law professors and theologians mostly from the universities of Cologne and Heidelberg, supported Winand of Steeg's position. It is notable that many prominent professors of law and theology, such as Heinrich of Gorkum, Christian of Erpel, Johann of Spull, and Petrus of Neukirch, all of the University of Cologne; and Johann of Noet, Gerhard Brant, Otto of Stein (*de Lapide*), Nikolaus Burgmann, and Hesso Krawell, of the University of Heidelberg, were participants in the case, giving

[21] Hermann Keussen, *Die alte Universität Köln: Grundzüge ihrer Verfassung und Geschichte* (Köln, 1934), p. 452; Meuthen, *Das Trierer Schisma*, p. 79.

[22] Hermann Keussen, "Die Kölner Juristenfakultät im Mittelalter," in *XXI. Deutscher Juristentag Köln, 1891: Festschrift* (Köln, n.d.), pp. 143-156; Theodor Muther, "Kölner Rechtsgutachten über die Brüder and Schwestern von gemeinschaftlichen Leben aus dem Jahre 1398," *Zeitschrift für Rechtsgeschichte*, V (1865): 469-472; Theodor Muther, *Zur Geschichte der Rechtswissenschaft und der Universtäten in Deutschland* (Jena, 1876), pp. 245-251; Gotthold Bohne, "Die juristische Fakultät der alten Universität Köln in den beiden ersten Jahrhunderten ihres Bestehens," in *Festschrift zur Erinnerung an die Grundung der alten Universität Köln im Jahre 1388* (Köln, 1938). pp. 109-236.

[23] On Winand of Steeg, see Toepke, *Die Matrikel*, p. 57; Josef Weiss, "Winand (Ort) von Steeg," *Historisches Jahrbuch*, XXVI (1906): 470-471; Aloys Schmidt, "Zur Geschichte der älteren Universität Würzburg," *Würzburger Diözesangeschichtsblätter*, XI/XII (1949/50), 91-96; Schmidt, "Nikolaus von Kues Sekretär. . . ?" Schmidt believes that Cardinal Orsini's secretary in 1426 was not Cusanus but Winand of Steeg.

their opinions in agreement with Cusanus.[24] Meanwhile Archbishop Otto named
Cusanus, on May 29, 1426, canon of the church of St. Simeon in Trier, and
Cusanus served in July of the same year as witness for Duke Adolf of Cleve
against both Dietrich II of Mörs, Archbishop of Cologne (1414-1463), and
Elector Louis III of the Palatinate.[25] It is easy to see why Cusanus' academic
work and involvement in practical affairs during his stay in Cologne brought
him fame and prestige as a lawyer.

We must recall at this point that the see of Trier was undergoing a period
of reform which had been initiated by Archbishop Otto in 1423. In a document
published on April 9, 1426, Otto announced a reform of the office of the
chancellor. The twenty-two-point document shows clearly how extensive the
power of the chancellor was at this time. Two major consultants on the reform
of 1426 were Johannes of Berg (de Monte), a suffragan bishop (1420-1442), and
Johannes Rode, abbot of St. Matthew (1421-1439) near Trier. Johannes of Berg
was a participant in the Bacharach case, and Johannes Rode, who was a graduate
of Heidelberg and in utroque iure licentiatus, was Cusanus' close friend. Rode is
best known for his influence on the Bursfeld Congregation, the center of a most
successful Benedictine reform throughout northern and central Germany in the
fifteenth century.[26] For the reform-minded Archbishop Otto the legal services
which men like Cusanus, Johannes of Berg, and Johannes Rode could offer were
no doubt inestimably important. In the summer of 1427 Cusanus was in Rome
as Archbishop Otto's proctor, and upon his return he was named Otto's
secretary.[27] Many benefices were then bestowed upon Cusanus by Otto. The
same year Cusanus was made canon of both St. Gangolf and St. Simeon in
Trier, dean of the church of Our Lady in Oberwesel, and dean of St. Florin in
Koblenz.[28] It may seem strange that Cusanus, who later strongly criticized the

---

[24] The document is MS. No. 12 of the Geheimes Hausarchiv in Munich. On Cusanus'
role in the Bacharach case, see my article, "Nikolaus von Kues - Richard Fleming -
Thomas Livingston," MFCG, VI (1967): 167-177.

[25] Erich Meuthen, "Die Pfründen des Cusanus," MFCG, II (1962): 17; Meuthen,
"Nikolaus von Kues und der Laie," 109 n. 42.

[26] The 22-point reform document of April 9, 1426 is printed in Paul Richter, Die
Kurtrierische Kanzlei im späteren Mittelalter (Mitteilungen der K. Preusischen
Archivverwaltung, Heft 17.) (Leipzig, 1911), pp. 112-114. On Johannes Rode, see
Hontheim, Historia, II, p. 331; Wyttenbach and Müller, Gesta, II, p. 315; P. Volk,
"Abt Johannes Rode von St. Matthias-Trier und die Anfänge der Bursfelder
Kongregation," in his Fünfhundert Jahre Bursfelder Kongregation (Münster, 1950),
pp. 19-22. For a better understanding of Rode's relationship to Cusanus I am indebted
to P. Petrus Becker, O.S.B. of St. Matthew Abbey, Trier.

[27] Meuthen, "Die Pfründen," 21-22; Meuthen, Das Trierer Schisma, p. 79.

[28] Meuthen, "Die Pfründen," 19. 24.

practice of pluralism (*pluralitas beneficiorum*),[29] did not find it difficult or embarrassing to receive so many beneficies within such a short time. It has been suggested by some scholars that the clergy in the later Middle Ages were no more "corrupt" than their predecessors or successors.[30] Naturally it was those clergymen of modest means who had to rely upon the favors bestowed on them by the pope or their bishop. Cusanus, while not of a poor family, apparently found it necessary and advantageous to receive these benefices which were made available to him with the rise of his prestige and position under the patronage of the reforming archbishop.[31]

Cusanus was, then, a well-established legal expert in the see of Trier by 1427. On January 8, 1428, he appeared as mediator in a negotiation about the payment of tithes in Niederemmel and Piesport. Among other participants in the case were Friedrich of Kröv, Tilmanus of Indagine (Tilmann of Hagen), Conrad of Freiburg, and Friedrich of Dudeldorf, all of whom were *jurisperiti* of the archdiocese of Trier.[32] A graduate of the University of Cologne and *in utroque iure licentiatus*,[33] Friedrich of Dudeldorf, like Cusanus, was later to become a close advisor to Ulrich of Manderscheid. Cusanus' busy legal activities and his learning made him so famous that the University of Louvain, which had been established in 1425, extended an invitation to Cusanus on December 23, 1428, to become a professor of canon law there. But his mind was not yet set upon

[29] *DCC,* II (Hamburg, 1963), cap. xxxiii, paragraph 245: "Unde tanta pluralitas parvorum beneficiorum et subsequenter multorum sacerdotum ignarorum multum decolorat ecclesiam et facit laicos clericis infestos esse, dum tot sacerdotes conspiciunt, quos vident otio et Vitiis vacare. Sanctum etiam sacerdotale officium valde vilescit ex hoc . . ."

[30] See, for example, E.F. Jacob, *Essays in the Conciliar Epoch,* 2d ed. (Manchester, 1953), pp. 18-23; Heiko A. Oberman, *Forerunners of the Reformation: The Shape of Late Medieval Thought* (New York, 1967), pp. 4-9.

[31] Cusanus' father, Henne Krebs or Johann Cryfftz, was a fairly well-to-do winegrower and boatowner. Although not of aristocratic origin, he was closely related to the nobility of the Rhineland. See Erich Meuthen, "Obödienz- und Absolutionslisten aus dem Trierer Bistumsstreit (1430-1435)," *Quellen und Forschungen aus italienischen Archiven und Bibliotheken,* XL (1960): 58; Meuthen, "Nikolaus von Kues und der Laie, " 117. See also D.W. Chambers, "The Economic Predicament of Renaissance Cardinals," *Studies in Medieval and Renaissance History,* III (1966): 289-313.

[32] Koblenz, Staatsarchiv, Abt. 186, Nr. 319. Cf. Meuthen, "Nikolaus von Kues und der Laie," 116; Meuthen, *Das Trierer Schisma,* p. 80.

[33] Keussen, *Die Matrikel,* I, p. 171. He became rector of the University of Cologne in 1421. Michel, *Zur Geschichte,* p. 38 n. 258, seems to think that Friedrich of Dudeldorf was the same person as Friedrich of Kröv.

entering an academic life. He declined the invitation as he was to do so again in 1435.[34]

After he rejected the offer of an academic position in 1428, Cusanus continued to work as a practicing lawyer. Dietrich of Ackerbach, whom Pope Martin V (1417-1431) had provided to the canonry of St. George's church in Limburg, was not able to receive the income from his benefice because of the opposition of the dean and members of the chapter. When Martin V asked Heinrich Raiscop, provost of St. Florin in Koblenz, to intervene, Cusanus, as Heinrich's sub-executor, summoned the dean and chapter members of St. George on November 28, 1429, in behalf of Dietrich of Ackerbach.[35] On October 11, 1432 Cusanus, together with Wilhelm of Weghe, dean of St. Castor in Koblenz, served as mediator in a settlement case between the parish church and the Carmelites in Boppard over the rights of the burial place.[36] Wilhelm of Weghe, who was rector of the University of Cologne in 1424 and experienced in law as *legum doctor,*[37] was another legal expert in the archdiocese of Trier with whom Cusanus came in close contact.

We have shown above some of the cases known to us in which Cusanus played a leading role as a lawyer. A learned doctor of the University of Padua and an experienced practitioner of law since his Cologne days, Cusanus was expected to make important contributions in the administration of the archdiocese of Trier.

It was in 1430 that a disastrous, disputed election took place in the see of Trier. The Archbishops of Mainz, Cologne, and Trier had been important figures especially since the Golden Bull of 1356 not only as spiritual princes but also as electors of the empire. Their office was not hereditary like that of the secular electors, but elective like the office of the pope or the emperor. The exclusive right of the cathedral chapter to elect the next archbishop was well established by

---

[34] E. Reussens, "Documents relatifs à l'histoire de l'Université de Louvain (1425-1797)," *Analectes pour à l'histoire ecclésiastique de la Belgique,* XXX (1903): 136; Meuthen, *Das Trierer Schisma,* p. 79; Erich Meuthen, "Neue Schlaglichter auf das Leben des Nikolaus von Kues," MFCG, IV (1964): 39.

[35] W. H. Struck, *Quellen zur Geschichte der Klöster und Stifte im Gebiete der mittleren Lahn bis zum Auspang des Mittelalters,* I (Wiesbaden, 1956), p. 408 Nr. 952; Meuthen, *Das Trierer Schisma,* p. 80.

[36] Trier, Stadtbibliothek, MS. 1694/328, pp. 107-112. Cf. Meuthen, "Nikolaus von Kues und der Laie," 116.

[37] Keussen, *Die Matrikel,* I, pp. lviii, 204, 206, 218, 566; Keussen, *Die alte Universität,* pp 388, 451; Michel, *Zur Geschichte,* pp. 135, 137.

the twelfth century.[38] Because of the importance of the office, episcopal elections frequently resulted in a split, thereby causing intervention by the pope. The disputed election of 1430 in Trier was undoubtedly one of the most important turning points in the history of the archdiocese. For our purpose a short description of the course of events will suffice.[39]

Archbishop Otto of Ziegenhain died on February 13, 1430. Two weeks thereafter a majority of the cathedral chapter elected as his successor the chapter's scholastic, Jacob of Sierck, who was also provost of Würzburg and priest of St. Marien in Kreuznach. But a minority, led by the provost of the chapter, Friedrich of Kröv, supported Ulrich of Manderscheid, dean of the cathedral of Cologne and archdean of St. Mauritius in Tholey.[40] Jacob of Sierck had been most vigorously resisting Archbishop Otto's reform program since 1423. Otto himself, supported by Friedrich of Kröv, had indicated before his death his preference for Ulrich as his successor. Since neither side gave in after the election, both Jacob and Ulrich, accompanied by their advisors, proceeded to Rome in May to appeal to the pope for support. Pope Martin V, instead of choosing one of the two as Otto's successor, designated on May 22, 1430, Raban of Helmstadt, the aged Bishop of Speyer, as the next Archbishop of Trier.[41] Many popes had so often exercised the right of deciding "disputed elections" as "reserved cases" since the

---

[38] Wilhelm Kisky, *Die Domkapitel der geistlichen Kurfürsten in ihrer persönlichen Zusammensetzung im vierzehnten und fünfzehnten Jahrhundert* (Bonn, 1906), pp. 4, 8. See also Georg von Below, "Die Entstehung des ausschliesslichen Wahlrechts der Domkapitel mit besonder Rücksicht auf Deutschland," *Historische Studien,* XI (1883); Hans E. Feine, *Kirchliche Rechtsgeschichte,* 4th ed. (Köln, 1964), pp. 380-383.

[39] For further discussion on the election of 1430, see J. Christian Lager, "Raban von Helmstadt und Ulrich von Manderscheid - ihr Kampf um das Erzbistum Trier," *Historisches Jahrbuch,* XV (1894): 721-770; Richard Laufner, "Die Manderseheidsche Fehde: Eine Wende in der Geschichte Triers," *Trierisches Jahrbuch* (1953): 48-60; Richard Laufner, "Politische Korrespondenz zur Trierer Doppelwahl 1430," *Triersiches Jahrbuch* (1954): 52-59; and especially Meuthen, *Das Trierer Schisma,* pp. 55-103. See also M.F.J. Müller, "Graf Ulrich von Manderscheid: Ein Aktenstück zur trierischen Geschichte des Mittelalters," *Trierische Kronik,* IX (1824): 31-41, 49-59, 97-104.

[40] Brower and Masen, *Antiquitatum,* II, p. 273; Hontheim, *Historia,* II, p. 375 n. (a); Wyttentenbach and Müller, *Gesta,* II, p. 318.

[41] Brower and Masen, *Antiquitatum,* II, p. 273-274; Wyttenbach and Müller, *Gesta,* II, p. 319: "Dominus autem papa, nullum illorum confirmans, dedit, nescio qua de causa, tertium quendam, scilicet dominum Rabanum de Helmstet, episcopum Spirensem, virum prudentem, sed senem et canum. Qui nisi inductus maxime ducis Bavariae instinctu, ipsum coram summo pontifice promoventis, onus tantum nunquam subiisse creditur."

thirteenth century that it is difficult to regard Pope Martin V's use of his power as an unusual step. We may note here, however, that without the strong support of Count Palatine Louis III, who was anxious to extend his political and religious influence, Raban of Helmstadt might not have been selected by the pope at all.[42] Accepting the papal decision, Jacob of Sierck withdrew from the contest without much ado after reaching a financial settlement. But Ulrich of Manderscheid rejected both a papal offer to make him provost of Frankfurt and Raban's appeal to comply with the papal decision. In taking this intransigent stand, Ulrich was strongly supported not only by the minority of the cathedral chapter headed by Friedrich of Kröv, but also, as we shall see in more detail, by Count Ruprecht of Virneburg and other nobles who were much incensed at the papal intervention in the affairs of Trier.[43]

With the skillful use of threat and bribery, Ulrich succeeded in a second election held in Koblenz on July 10, 1430, to gain a unanimous support of the cathedral chapter. Since Ulrich and the chapter refused to accept the papal provision of Raban to Trier, they were excommunicated by the pope on September 15, 1430, and the see of Trier was later placed under an interdict. This interdict, which began after January 21, 1431, was to last for about four years, thereby causing many hardships in Trier.[44] Meanwhile Martin V, who had summoned the Council of Basel on February 1, 1431, died nineteen days later. Thereafter Cardinal Gabriel Condulmer, Raban's supporter in the curia, was elected pope on March 3, 1431. The new Pope Eugenius IV (1431-1447) confirmed his predecessor's convocation of the council, and the Council of Basel got off to a slow start. Ulrich of Manderscheid then decided to bring his case to the council, hoping that the council might give favorable decision for him against the pope. It was Cusanus and Johannes Rode, together with Helwig of

---

[42] On the whole question of the episcopal election and of disputed elections, see, for example, C. Eubel, "Zum päpstlichen Reservations- und Provisionswesen," *Römische Quartalschrift,* VIII (1894): 169-185; Geoffrey Barraclough, "The Making of A Bishop in the Middle Ages: The Part of the Pope in Law and Fact," *Catholic Historical Review,* XIX (1933): 275-319; Feine, *Kirochliche Rechtsgeschichte,* pp. 380-383.

[43] Wyttenbach and Müller, *Gesta,* II, p. 320: "Quapropter comes praedictus de Vyrnenburch, et ceteri nobiles indignati, de facto sedi apostolicae se opposuerunt"; Laufner, "Politische Korrespondenz," 55. On the Virneburg family in this period, see Karl Klapperich, *Die Geschichte des Grafengeschlechtes der Virneburger* (Bonn, 1921).

[44] Adam Goerz, *Regesten der Erzbischöfe zu Trier von Hetti bis Johann II 814-1503* (Trier, 1861), p. 180; Wyttenbach and Müller, *Gesta,* II, p. 320.

Boppard, who were incorporated in the council towards the end of February 1432 to represent Ulrich of Manderscheid.[45]

The Council of Basel was an important general council of the church which drew not only many prelates, but also a host of eminent canon lawyers and theologians from many countries. Cardinal Giuliano Cesarini, who was Cusanus' teacher and friend since his Paduan days, presided over many of its sessions. Nicolaus de Tudeschis (Panormitanus or Abbas Siculus), who is sometimes called the greatest canonist of the period,[46] came to Basel to represent Alfonso V of Aragon. John of Segovia, the learned Spanish theologian and author of the *Historia gestorum generalis synodi Basiliensis,* was a moderate supporter of the conciliar theory at the council.[47] Aeneas Sylvius Piccolomini, author of the *De gestis concilii Basiliensis commentariorum* and later Pope Pius II (1458-1464), must also be mentioned as one of the notable participants in the council. The University of Vienna sent the famous historian and theologian, Thomas Ebendorfer of Haselbach, and among the delegates from the University of Cologne were Christian Erpel and Heimericus de Campo. We see furthermore such familiar names as Friedrich of Dudeldorf, Wilhelm of Weghe, Johannes Nider, and Cardinal Giordano Orsini among those who attended the council.[48] For Cusanus himself, whose legal activities had been confined mostly to the ecclesiastical affairs of Trier, the council afforded a good opportunity to demonstrate his talent as a lawyer at the international level.

The Council of Basel, however, held the issue of the disputed election in Trier in abeyance for a long time. When the city of Trier declared its readiness to accept Raban of Helmstadt as Archbishop, Ulrich of Manderscheid, who had already taken possession of Pfalzel near Trier in 1432, began to attack Trier early in 1433. Destruction wrought by his troops during a siege which followed was

---

[45] Johannes Haller, *Concilium Basiliense: Studien und Quellen zur Geschichte des Concils von Basel,* II (Basel, 1897), pp. 44-45.

[46] On Panormitanus, see Papadopoli, *Historia,* II, p. 14; Jean Fleury, "Le conciliarisme des canonistes au concile de Bâle d'aprés le Panormitain," in *Mélanges Roger Secretán* (Montreux, 1964), pp. 47-65; Knut W. Nörr, *Kirche and Konzil bei Nicolaus de Tudeschis (Panormitanus)* (Köln, 1964).

[47] Uta Fromherz, *Johannes von Segovia als Geschichtsschreiber des Konzils Basel* (Basel, 1960).

[48] Hermann Bressler, *Die Stellung der deutschen Universtäten zum Baseler Konzil und ihr Anteil an der-Reformbewegung in Deutschland während des fünfzehnten Jahrhunderts* (Leipzig, 1885); Haller, *Concilium,* I-IV; Heinrich Stutt, *Die Nordwestdeutschen Diözesen und das Baseler Konzil in den Jahren 1431-1441* (Hildesheim, 1928). For a detailed study of Scottish churchmen at the Council of Basel, see J.H. Burns, *Scottish Churchmen and the Council of Basle* (Glasgow, 1962).

so heavy that its consequences were felt for many years to come.[49] Partly repelled by Ulrich's growing intransigence and partly by the great damage done to the city, the cathedral chapter also turned its back on Ulrich at the end of March 1433. Then the Council of Basel itself reached its final decision on May 15, 1434, against Cusanus' patron, upholding Raban of Helmstadt as the rightful Archbishop of Trier.[50] Meanwhile Cusanus had presented to the council in 1433 his first major work, *De concordantia catholica*. It is a book which Cusanus originally started to write in order to defend the cause of Ulrich of Manderscheid at the Council of Basel.[51] The Emperor Sigismund (1411-1437), who had not taken a clear stand between the two contending parties, accepted the decision of the council and ordered on June 12 that all the faithful in the archdiocese of Trier recognize Raban of Helmstadt as their archbishop. He also announced an imperial ban against Ulrich on August 7.[52] Excommunicated by the pope, deserted by the cathedral chapter, the city of Trier, and the Council of Basel, and now placed under the imperial ban, Ulrich still refused to retreat and intensified his effort to stop supply lines to Trier in order to force the besieged city to capitulate. A nine-man commission, made up of such men as Cusanus, Friedrich of Kröv, Professors Christian of Erpel and Otto of Stein, finally reached an agreement of peace in St. Goar on February 7, 1436, thereby bringing the so-called Manderscheid *Fehde* (1433-1436) to an end.[53] But Ulrich soon began to ignore it. Only his death, on October 18, 1438, actually terminated the long, exhausting struggle over the archbishopric of Trier. Seemingly, this was a victory for Raban of Helmstadt. But the aged Archbishop of Trier had neither the will nor the strength to solve the complicated political and economic problems which resulted from the long struggle. He resigned on April 17, 1439, and asked Pope Eugenius IV that Jacob of Sierck be named his successor. Thus nine years

---

[49] Hontheim, *Historia*, II, pp. 380-381; Laufner, "Die Manderscheidsche Fehde," 51-52; "Richard Laufner "Der Handelsbereich des Trierer Marktes im Spätmittelalter," *Rheinische Vierteljahrblätter*, XXII (1957): 194.

[50] Hontheim, *Historia*, II, p. 386; Lager, "Raban von Helmstadt," 745; Haller, *Concilium*, III, pp. 98-99.

[51] On the composition of the *DCC*, See Gerhard Kallen, "Die handschriftliche Überlieferung der *Concordantia catholica* des Nikolaus von Kues," *Sitzungsberichte der Heidelberger Akademie der Wissenschaften, Philosophisch-historische Klasse* (Heidelberg, 1963).

[52] Lager, "Raban von Helmstadt," 755.

[53] Only six of nine members signed the agreement, which was not too favorable to Ulrich. Cusanus and two other supporters of Ulrich did not accept it. See Lager, "Raban von Helmstadt," 758-760; Meuthen, *Das Trierer Schisma*, p. 250.

after his election by the majority of the cathedral chapter of Trier, Jacob of Sierck finally became Archbishop of Trier on May 19, 1439.[54]

In order to understand the real significance of the role which Cusanus played in the election of 1430 and thereafter, it is well to note, first of all, that Cusanus was made chancellor in 1430 by Ulrich of Manderscheid to represent him at the Council of Basel.[55] The chancellor was at that time a most influential official in the administration of ecclesiastical affairs in Trier.[56] The reform and reorganization program instituted by Archbishop Otto in 1426 had no doubt strengthened the office of the chancellor, although, as we noted above, the resistance of the cathedral chapter against Otto's attempt to reform the see of Trier made it difficult to accomplish the desired result fully. As chancellor of the Archbishop-elect, Ulrich of Manderscheid, who was backed by both the chapter and the see of Trier in 1430, Cusanus represented and spoke for the clergy of Trier until about the beginning of March 1433, when the city and the chapter began to turn away from Ulrich of Manderscheid. Despite his non-aristocratic origin, Cusanus was without any doubt one of the ablest and best-known lawyers in the archdiocese of Trier to defend Ulrich's case in Basel.

An examination of a document published on September 15, 1430, in Wittlich, in which Ulrich of Manderscheid strongly attacked the papal provision of Raban of Helmstadt to Trier, will indicate Cusanus' position in the administrative hierarchy of the archdiocese of Trier. Wittlich was in the Middle Ages the site of an episcopal residence which the archbishops of Trier often visited. After the decay of the residence in the fourteenth century, it was indeed Archbishop Otto of Ziegenhain who in 1422 completed the work of restoration. In September of 1430 Ulrich of Manderscheid was in Wittlich, which was hospitable to a count of the neighboring Manderscheid, and issued a protest in

---

[54] Ulrich died near Zürich. Wyttenbaeh and Müller, *Gesta*, II, pp. 324-325: "Tandem Udalricus de Manderscheit rerum suarum diffisus, dum Romam denuo proficisci niteretur, in itinere apud Thuregum morbo interiit"; Lager, "Raban von Helmstadt," 726; Meuthen, *Das Trierer Schisma*, pp. 255-256.

[55] Meuthen, *Das Trierer Schisma*, pp. 83, 89.

[56] See Hontheim, *Historia*, II, pp. 332-333 (Cancellarii Aulae Archiepiscopalis Trev.). Richter, *Die kurtrierische Kanzlei*, gives, on pp. 114-115, "Kanzleigebräuche des 14. und 15. Jahrhunderts" (Circa ordinacionem et observacionem cancellarie Treverensis, prout priscis temporibus, tempore Cunonis, Werheri et Ottonis felicis memorie in litteris expediendis tentum et observatum est). Cf. Maximilian Buchner, "Die Entstehung des trierischen Erzkanzleramtes in Theorie und Wirklichkeit," *Historisches Jahrbuch*, XXXII (1911): 1-48.

the episcopal residence "Ottenstein," which had been named after its restorer.[57] In this so-called Wittlich Appeal, Cusanus appears as witness, along with Friedrich of Dudeldorf and Hartmann of Koblenz. But, as Meuthen pointed out in his valuable study of the election of 1430,[58] the appeal was probably drawn up by Cusanus in the office of the chancellor in defense of Ulrich's demand. It reflects fairly well the views which were held at that time by many supporters of Ulrich on the state of affairs in Trier, the ideal method of administering the see of Trier, and the relationship of the papacy to the German church. Cusanus' *De concordantia catholica,* which manifests the author's conciliar theory, was mostly written in 1432 and 1433 while he was Ulrich's chancellor.[59] The similarities of ideas expressed in the *De concordantia catholica* and the Wittlich Appeal seem to confirm the view that Chancellor Cusanus was responsible, directly or indirectly, for the writing of the appeal.

According to the Wittlich Appeal, Ulrich was, of course, elected Archbishop of Trier canonically. Never in the past, the appeal says' did a pope turn down a bishop of Trier who had been legally elected by the clergy and the people of Trier.[60] In sharp contrast to this view expressed in the appeal, Martin V did not even mention the existence of a disputed election in Trier when he announced Raban's provision to the archdiocese of Trier. After consulting with Cardinal Gabriel Condulmer, he exercised the power of reservation and provision and chose Raban as Otto's successor. But the Wittlich Appeal argues, against this papal intervention, that because of the old, established rights of the Trier church, Ulrich of Manderscheid, who was elected canonically by the chapter and the people of Trier, should become Archbishop of Trier without confirmation or acceptance by the pope. Likewise Cusanus later criticized the papal power of

---

[57] The text is Bibliotheca Vaticana, Codex Ottobonianus latinus 2745, f. 218ᵛ-219ᵛ. See also Goerz, *Regesten,* p. 160; Meuthen, *Das Trierer Schisma,* pp. 11, 76, 81-85. On Wittlich as an episcopal residence, see G. Kentenich, "Das alte kurtrierische Amt Wittlich," *Trierische Chronik,* X (1914): 183-184; K. Bruckmann, "Wittlich als kurfürstliche Residenz," *Trierische Chronik,* XV (1919): 43-53.

[58] Meuthen, *Das Trierer Schisma,* p. 83. Cf. Vansteenberghe, *Le cardinal,* p. 53.

[59] Kallen, *Die handschriftlische Überlieferung,* p. 2: "Jedenfalls hat er sich das ganz Jahr 1432 und auch noch den grössten Teil von 1433 damit beschäftigt. Vor der Ankunft Sigismunds in Basel (11. Okt. 1433) lag die Concordantia catholica sicherlich nicht vor."

[60] Codex Ottob. lat. 2745, f. 218ʳ: "numquam enim sedes apostolica a clero et popolo electum pro archiepiscopo praefate sedis repulit, sed semper prefecit et confirmavit equitate suadente." The appeal is not entirely correct because the first papal provision took place in Trier with the elevation of Diether of Nassau (1300-1307) to the office of the archbishop. See Hubert Bastgen, *Die Geschichte des Trierer Domkapitels im Mittelalter* (Paderborn, 1910), p. 275.

reservation and provision in the *De concordantia catholica,* emphasizing that bishops must be elected by the consent of the chapter and of the people.[61] The Wittlich Appeal hints furthermore that Raban of Helmstadt, who was not of aristocratic origin, would not be acceptable to the see of Trier. Besides, he does not come from the archdiocese of Trier.[62]

It is well known that the German church in the Middle Ages was dominated by the nobility. This is a second factor which is to be noted in our examination of the 1430 election in Trier. According to one study, the Archbishops of Mainz, Cologne, and Trier in the fourteenth and fifteenth centuries were, with several exceptions, almost all of noble birth. The archdioceses of Mainz and Trier occasionally accepted those of lower or unfree nobility *(der niedere oder unfreie Adel; ministeriales),* that is, knights (*Ritter*) as their heads, but the archdiocese of Cologne consistently chose as archbishops only those members of the cathedral chapter who were of the higher or free nobility *(der hohe oder freie Adel),* that is, princes, counts, and barons.[63] In general, therefore, the three great sees of Germany were in the hands of the nobility in the later Middle Ages. With the decline of the health of Otto's predecessor, Werner of Falkenstein (1388-1418), the nobles in the archdiocese of Trier, especially Count Ruprecht of Virneburg, increasingly played an important role in the administration of the archdiocese. Even during the pontificate of Archbishop Otto, the influence of the nobles did not decline very much. When Otto and his entourage went to the Holy Land in 1425, it was the nobles who administered the archdiocese of Trier until Otto's return.[64] It is no exaggeration to say that Count Ulrich of Manderscheid became the Archbishop-elect after Otto's death thanks to the support given by Count Ruprecht and his aristocratic friends. Shortly after the death of Archbishop Otto, the palaces, buildings and property of the archdiocese, which had been well kept and expanded during Otto's

[61] See especially *DCC,* II, cap. XXXII. Cf. Watanabe, *The Political Ideas,* pp. 145-174.

[62] Codex Ottob. lat. 2745, f. 218[v]: "erui non poterant nisi per unum nobilem et inibi potentem, qui de illa dyocesi vel saltim de provincia Treverensi natalem duxisset originem . . ."

[63] Kisky, *Die Domkapitel.* On the nobility in the German church and especially in Trier, see Aloys Schulte, *Der Adel und die deutsche Kirche im Mittelalter,* 3rd ed. (Darmstadt, 1958); Bastgen, *Die Geschichte,* pp. 26-33; Aloys Resch, "Die Edelfreien des Erzbistums Trier im linkerheinischen deutschen Sprachgebiet," *Trierisches Archiv,* XVII/XVIII (1911): 3-8. See also Sophie-Mathilde Dohna, *Die ständischen Verhältnisse am Domkapitel von Trier vom 16. bis zum 18. Jahrhundert* (Trier, 1960), especially pp. 11-21.

[64] Wyttenbach and Müller, *Gesta,* II, pp. 312-313.

reign, were seized by Count Ruprecht of Virneburg and his troops.[65] They were no doubt anxious and ready to defend their possessions from the outsiders. It has even been suggested that the abundance of temporary goods which were left behind by Archbishop Otto was the occasion of the disputed election of 1430.[66] The nobles were convinced that the next Archbishop of Trier had to be a noble who was willing to defend their precious possessions. Obviously, then, their choice was Ulrich of Manderscheid, who was, as we have seen, of aristocratic origin and who was closely related to the Virneburg family. Reflecting the views of Ulrich's supporters, the Wittlich Appeal makes it clear that Ulrich and his supporters were ready to "secularize" the see of Trier unless some acceptable noble from Trier became its archbishop.[67] The majority of the members of the cathedral chapter, who were critical of their provost Friedrich of Kröv's support of Ulrich of Manderscheid and his friend Count Ruprecht of Virneburg, demonstrated their independence when they elected Jacob of Sierck, one of their colleagues, as Otto's successor. But, as we have seen above, they also changed their position later and supported the Manderscheider after July 10, 1430. In September 1430, therefore, Ulrich of Manderscheid had almost complete control over the see of Trier mainly through the influence of the nobility. If the church of Trier, as was traditionally said, consisted of three estates (*Stände*), i.e., clergy, knights, and burghers,[68] Ulrich was apparently supported by all of these estates in Trier against the papacy. In this sense the Wittlich Appeal may be regarded as a call for the liberties of the German church against papal interventions.

Finally, then, it is from the point of view of the relationship between papacy and German church that the significance of the disputed election of 1430 in Trier and of the role which Cusanus, the German lawyer, played can be better understood. We have noted how incensed Ulrich's supporters were at the papal provision of Raban to Trier. It was not difficult for Ulrich to pose as a champion for the independence of the German church from the papacy. It was his and also Cusanus' doctrine that a bishop can be elected by the clergy and the people of a diocese without approbation or confirmation by the pope. The good, old rights of the see of Trier must be protected against papal encroachments. The support which Ulrich received for taking this position is very impressive. A Rhenish

---

[65] Wyttenbach and Müller, *Gesta,* II, p. 318.

[66] Wyttenbach and Müller, *Gesta,* II, p. 317: "Unde abundantia temporalium, quam reliquit, facta est occasio dissensionis pro succeseoris electione."

[67] Codex Ottob. lat. 2745, f. 218ᵛ. See also Brower and Masen, *Antiquitatum,* II, p. 273; Meuthen, *Das Trierer Schisma,* pp. 56-57, 82-84.

[68] "Ecclesia Treverensis ab antiquo ex tribus statibus constituitur, quorum unus vocatur clerus Treverensis, alius milicia Treverensis, tercius incole seu populares Treverenses." Quoted in Meuthen, *Das Trierer Schisma,* pp. 56-57.

coalition which was formed in 1430 against Raban of Helmstadt included the Archbishops of Mainz and Cologne, Count Palatine Stephen of Simmern, Duke Adolf of Jülich-Berg, Landgrave Louis of Hesse, Margrave Jacob of Baden, Duke Philip the Good of Burgundy, Count Johann of Sponheim, as well as Count Ruprecht of Virneburg.[69] It is true that this coalition of princes was organized not less as a countermove against the territorial and ecclesiastical ambitions of Count Palatine Louis III, Raban's supporter,[70] than as a step toward helping Ulrich of Manderscheid in his fight against the papacy. Nevertheless, it seems clear that many members of the coalition were as much motivated as Ulrich by the desire to assert and protect their liberties and rights within their territories against what they considered unwarranted intervention in the affairs of the German church by the papacy.[71]

Opposition to growing papal encroachments on various national churches was manifested in many forms in the later Middle Ages. In England it began in earnest in the middle of the fourteenth century and resulted in the passage of the Statutes of Provisors and *Praemunire,* the earliest in 1351 and the latest in 1393.[72] The French answer to this question was the famous Pragmatic Sanction of Bourges of 1438.[73] Even in the empire, where the process of national integration was far slower than in England and France, an early attempt to limit further papal interventions was made at the Diet of Rhense on July 16, 1338.[74]

---

[69] Brower and Masen, *Antiquitatum,* II, p. 275; Hontheim, *Historia,* II, pp. 380-381; Wyttenbach and Müller, *Gesta,* II, pp. 320-321; Laufner, "Die Manderscheidsche Fehde," 49.

[70] Louis III, who was a supporter of Pope Eugenius IV, was against the Council of Basel. See Richard Lossen, *Staat und Kirche in der Pfalz im Auspang des Mittelalter* (Münster i. W., 1907).

[71] Wyttenbach and Müller, *Gesta,* II, p. 320: "Nam totius patriae comites, barones, militares, omnesque ecclesiae subjecti Trevirensi Udalrico adhaesere, summi pontificis mandata apostolica, supposito etiam ecclesiastico interdicto, floccipendentes; cuncta adverea tolerare parati. . . ."

[72] See E.B. Graves, "The Legal Significance of the Statue of Praemunire of 1353," in Charles H. Taylor (ed.), *Anniversary Essays in Medieval History by Students of Charles H. Haskins* (Boston, 1929), pp. 57-80; W.T. Waugh, "The Great Statute of Praemunire," *English Historical Review,* XXXVIII (1922): 173-205.

[73] On the so-called *Instrumentum acoeptationis* which is a somewhat mild German version of the Pragmatic Sanction, see Albert Werminghoff, Nationalkirchliche *Bestrebungen im deutschen Mittelalter* (Stuttgart, 1910), pp. 33-85; Heinz Hürten, "Die Mainzer Akzeptation von 1439," *Archiv für mittelrheinische Kirchengeschichte,* II (1959): 42-75.

[74] Earl Zeumer, *Quellensammlung zur Geschichte der deutschen Reichsverfassung im Mittelalter und Neuzeit,* I (Tübingen, 1918), p. 181.

But the Golden Bull of 1356 marked the beginning of an age of territorial principalities.[75] The empire in the later Middle Ages was not to see the growth of strong monarchical power as in England and France. Yet the *gravamina,* which were frequently raised in the Diets and the cities of the empire in later years, were remonstrances which reflected the rise of the spirit of national self-assertion in the empire.[76] Viewed in this light, the events of 1430 and thereafter in Trier can be construed as a milestone on the way to the Reformation of the sixteenth century.[77]

As chancellor of Ulrich of Manderscheid, Archbishop-elect of Trier, Cusanus, *decretorum doctor,* fought for his patron and for the German church at the Council of Basel, which had as one of its objectives the restriction of the papal jurisdiction. It is therefore easy to understand why the *De concordantia catholica,* which Cusanus submitted to the council, upheld the superiority of the general council over the pope.[78] Naturally, Ulrich of Manderscheid and his supporters hoped that the council would decide in their favor in the case of the disputed election of 1430. The ultimate failure of Ulrich of Manderscheid to become Archbishop of Trier was partly of his own making. His obstinacy and thirst for power drove the city of Trier and the cathedral chapter away from him.[79] The accession of Cardinal Gabriel Condulmer, Raban's supporter in the curia, to the papal throne as Eugenius IV augured a happy turn of events for the aged Bishop of Speyer. Although the pope was much harassed by the hostile actions of the fathers of the Council of Basel, he was able to bring diplomatic pressure to bear upon the supporters of Ulrich of Manderscheid. As a result, the Rhenish coalition of archbishops and princes gradually lost its strength and effectiveness. This was, however, a combination of historical circumstances over

[75] Geoffrey Barraclough, *The Origins of Modern Germany,* 2nd ed. (Oxford, 1947), p. 321.

[76] Bruno Gebhardt, *Die Gravamina der deutschen Nation gegen den römischen Hof,* 2nd ed. (Breslau, 1895); Anton Störmann, *Die städtischen Gravamina gegen den Klerus am Ausgange des Mittelalters und in der Reformationszeit* (Münster, 1916).

[77] It is to be noted that Caspar Olevianus (1536-1587), a Calvinist, made an attempt to reform the Trier church in 1559. See Jakob Marx, *Caspar Olevian oder der Calvinismus in Trier im Jahre 1559* (Mainz, 1846); Julius Ney, *Die Reformation in Trier 1559 und ihre Unterdrückung* (Halle, 1906), Gunther Engelbert, "Neue Arbeiten zum Trierer Reformationsversuch 1559," *Jahrbuch für Geschichte und Kultur,* XII/XIII. Jhrg. 1960/61 (1962): 150-151.

[78] Sigmund, *Nicholas of Cusa,* pp. 158-187; Watanabe, *The Political Ideas,* pp. 79-97.

[79] Wyttenbach and Müller, Gesta, II, p. 320: "licet dominus Ulricus prius, cum esset decanus Coloniae, erat pius, benignus, et quasi omnibus dilectus; hic tamen factus est consilio suorum complicum severus tyrannus."

which the chancellor of the archdiocese of Trier had little control. It is no wonder, then, that Cusanus, disappointed by the turn of events in Basel and Trier, should have gradually lost enthusiasm for the council after 1434. To be sure, he remained active in the council for a while. But by 1437 he was definitely working for the papal side which, he believed, was far more capable of maintaining unity in the church than the council.[80] With the support of Otto of Ziegenhain, Cusanus became a most successful lawyer in the archdiocese of Trier. But he was much less successful as a spokesman for Ulrich of Manderscheid and for the liberties of the German church.

It has been emphasized that the legal factors alone did not decide episcopal elections.[81] In 1450 Cusanus himself was provided to the see of Brixen by Pope Nicholas V after the the death of Bishop Johann Röttel. But the cathedral chaper of Brixen had already nominated Leonhard Wismayer, one of its members, as Bishop Röttel's successor. Afterward there followed a bitter, drawn-out conflict between Cusanus as Bishop of Brixen and Duke Sigismund of the Tyrol, who with the help of Gregor Heimburg tried to prevent the papal encroachments on the rights of the House of Austria. It was no doubt Cusanus' failure to understand clearly the extra-legal aspects of the episcopal election which led him to the protracted quarrel with the duke.[82] We may not have to accept Gregor Heimburg's taunt against Cusanus fully. But it seems that Cusanus' experiences in Basel and in Brixen reveal his weakness not only as a lawyer but also as a man of action.

---

[80] Watanabe, *The Political Ideas,* pp. 16, 97-98, 113-114.

[81] Barraclough, "The Making of a Bishop," p. 283: "The law could not do everything, and the law did not do everything: influence and money played their part;" 311.

[82] For a recent treatment of this conflict, see Pardon E. Tillinghast, "Nicholas of Cusa vs. Sigmund of Habsburg: An Attempt at Post-Conciliar Church Reform," *Church History,* XXXVI (1967): 371-390.

Nicholas of Cusa, the Council of Florence and the *Acceptatio* of Mainz (1439)

One of the most famous events in the life of Nicholas of Cusa (1401-1464) was described by himself in his letter to Cardinal Giuliano Cesarini (1398-1444) which he attached to the *De docta ignorantia* of 1440. He had gone to Constantinople as a member of the pro-papal minority party of the Council of Basel to discuss with the leaders of the Greek Church when and where the forthcoming council of union should take place.[1] Having set sail from Constantinople on November 27, 1437, Cusanus was at see with the Emperor John VIII Palaeologus (1425-1448), Patriarch Joseph II (c.1360-1439) of Constantinople and many other dignitaries of the Greek Church, when he received what he called "a supreme gift of the Father of Lights."[2] The revelation became the basis for his later work, the *De docta ignorantia*. Whether or not Cusanus's experience was an apparition, as some commentators have suggested,[3] should not detain us here in this article.

During the voyage Cusanus was in the company of "the greatest minds of the Byzantine world of that day".[4] John Bessarion (1402-1472), Metropolitan of Nicaea, Mark Eugenicus (c.1394-1444/45?), Metropolitan of Ephesus, Sylvester

---

[1] About Cusanus's voyage to Constantinople in 1437, see *Acta Cusana* 1,2, ed. Erich Meuthen (Hamburg 1983), 216-224 Nr. 323-334. About Cusanus's activities as a member of the Council of Basel and his trip to Constantinople, see also Petro B.T. Bilaniuk, "Nicholas of Cusa and the Council of Florence," in his *Studies in Eastern Christianity* 2 (München—Toronto, 1982), pp. 113-128.

[2] *Acta Cusana* 1,2,224 Nr. 334: "Accipe nunc . . ., quae iam dudum attingere variis doctrinarum viis concupivi, sed prius non potui, quousque in marl me ex Graecia redeumte, credo supemo dono a patre luminum . . . ad hoc ductus sum." See also Nicolaus Cusanus, *Of Learned Ignorance,* tr. Germain Heron (London 1954), p. 175; Jasper Hopkins, *Nicholas of Cusa on Learned Ignorance: A Tramslation and an Appraisal of De Docta Ignorantia* (Minneapolis, 1981) p. 158. About John VIII Palaeologus, see Joseph Gill, *Personalities of the Council of Florence* (Oxford, 1964), pp. 104-124. On Joseph II, Patriarch of Constantinople, see Gill, *Personalities,* pp. 15-34.

[3] Bilaniuk, *Nicholas of Cusa,* p. 118. See also Marjorie O'Rourke Boyle, "Cusanus at Sea: The Topicality of Illuminative Discourse," *Journal of Religion* 71, 2 (1991): pp. 180-201.

[4] Bilaniuk, *Nicholas of Cusa,* p. 118; Erich Meuthen, *Nikolaus von Kues 1401-1464: Skizze einer Biographie* (Münster, 1982), p. 54.

Syropoulus, the chronicler of the Council of Florence, and others were in the party.[5] Nicholas was apparently stimulated on the voyage to reflect on some of the fundamental philosophical problems. Petro B.T. Bilanink and Erich Meuthen suggested that the immense size of the ocean and the infinitesimal size of his ship may have forced him to think of a great gap between the infinite and the finite.[6] It is abundantly clear that his voyage from Constantinople to Venice, which lasted two and a half months, afforded him a good opportunity for reflection and contemplation. The fleet arrived in Venice on February 8, 1438.[7]

Traveling in advance of the main Greek delegation itself, which numbered about seven hundred, Cusanus and the Bishop of Digne arrived at Ferrara and the Bishop of Digne gave his famous report on the voyage on March 1, 1438.[8] The first session of the Council of Ferrara had been opened by Cardinal Niccolò Albergati on January 8, 1438 in the cathedral church of St. George on direct orders from Pope Eugenius IV (1431-1447). The Pope himself had arrived in Ferrara on January 24 and from then on presided in person.[9] From the papal point of view, the Council was a continuation of the Council of Basel which had been transferred in the bull *Doctoris gentium* to Ferrara by the Pope on September 18, 1437.[10] It might be well to point out here that Pope Eugenius IV, who succeeded Martin V (1368-1431) on March 3, 1431, was "well disposed towards the idea of reunion." For many years he had been a papal legate in

---

[5] About Bessarion, Eugenius amd Syropoulus, see Gill, *Personalities,* pp. 45-54, 55-64 and 178-185 respectively. Cf. Meuthen, *Nikolaus von Kues,* p. 54. About Syropoulos, see also Bilaniuk, "Nicholas of Cusa," p. 126 n. 47. Gill gives lists of those who accompanied the Emperor and the Patriarch in his *The Council of Florence* (Cambridge, 1961), p. 89 n. 2. See also Ioannes G. Leontiades, "Die griechische Delegation auf dem Konzil von Ferrara-Florenz: Eine prosopographische Skizze," *Annuarium Historiae Conciliorum* 21,2 (1989): pp. 353-369.

[6] Bilaniuk, "Nicholas of Cusa," pp. 118-119; Meuthen, *Nikolaus von Kues,* pp. 54-55.

[7] Gill, *Personalities,* pp. 4, 37; Bilaniuk, "Nicholas of Cusa," p. 119; Meuthen, *Nikolaus von Kues,* p. 53.

[8] Gill, *The Council of Florence,* pp. 91, 98; Gill, *Personalities,* p. 17.

[9] Gill, *The Council of Florence,* p. 96; Joachim W. Stieber, *Pope Eugenius IV, the Council of Basel and the Secular and Ecclesiastical Authorities in the Empire: The Conflict over Supreme Authority and Power in the Church* (Leiden, 1978), pp. 49-50; Meuthen, *Nikolaus von Kues,* p. 49.

[10] Gill, *The Coumcil of Florence,* pp. 91-93; Stieber, *Pope Eugenius IV,* pp. 38-40.

Greece, Asia Minor, Syria and Egypt.[11] But in a counter move to the Pope's transfer of the Council of Basel to Ferrara, the Council of Basel had suspended Eugenius IV from of flee on January 24, 1438.[12] As a result of these events, the Council of Ferrara was certainly expected to influence the future relations of the Pope and the Council greatly.

It was on March 4 that the main party of the Greeks finally reached Ferrara.[13] Then the combined council of union opened with a solemn session on Wednesday of the Holy Week, April 9. But since an agreement had been reached among the Pope, the Emperor and the Patriarch that there should be a delay of four months to allow time for Western princes to send their representatives, it wasn't until October 8 that the formal doctrinal discussions at Ferrara were finally begun.[14] In the northern countries, the Council of Ferrara was regarded as a papal device to waken and undermine the authority of the Council of Basel. Shortly thereafter the financial difficulties, the threat of the Milanese condottiere Niccolò Piccinino and the outbreak of the plague made it necessary for Eugenius IV to transfer the Council to Florence, where it was resumed on January 10, 1439.[15]

There is ample evidence that Cusanus, who was instrumental in the successful opening of the Council of Ferrara, was in Ferrara early in 1438. But what he did in Ferrara and if he went to Florence at all is by no means clear. Almost certainly he did not go to Florence after the transfer of the Council from Ferrara to Florence.[16] What then did he do in Ferrara, and why didn't he participate in the Council of Florence?

---

[11] Bilaniuk, "Nicholas of Cusa," p. 114 n. 9; Gill, *Personalities,* pp. 35-44; Werner Krämer, "Der Beitrag des Nikolaus von Kues zum Unionskonzil mit der Ostkirche," *Mitteilungen und Forschungsbeiträge der Cusanus-Gesellschaft* (= MFCG) 9 (1971): 51.

[12] Gill, *The Council of Florence,* p. 96; Stieber, *Pope Eugenius IV,* pp. 49-50.

[13] Gill, *Personalities,* pp. 4, 37.

[14] Gill, *The Council of Florence,* pp. 140-141; Gill, *Personalities,* pp. 4-5, 38-39; Meuthen, *Nikolaus von Kues,* p. 53.

[15] Gill, *The Council of Florence,* p. 178; Gill, *Personalities,* p. 7.

[16] Josef Koch, "Über eine aus der nächsten Umgebung des Nikolaus von Kues stammende Handschrift der Trierer Stadtbibliothek (1927/1426)," in *Aus Mittelalter und Neuzeit: Gerhard Kallen zum 70. Geburtstag dargebracht von Kollegen, Freunden und Schülern* (Bonn 1957), p. 128; Erich Meuthen, "Der Dialogus concludens Amedistarum errorem ex gestis et doctrina concilii Basiliensis," MFCG 8 (1970): 25: "In der Tat ist Nikolaus von Kues von Juni/Juli 1438 bis zum Februar 1440 nur diesseits der Alpen bezeugt"; Bilaniuk, *Nicholas of Cusa,* p. 119: "We do not know about the exact role which Nicholas played during the discussions with the Greeks in Ferrara."

Cusanus's presence at Ferrara on March 1, 1438 is clearly shown in an notarial document preserved in the Vatican Library and published by Erich Meuthen in his *Acta Cusana*.[17] Cusanus was still in Ferrara when his friend, Francesco Pizolpasso, Archbishop of Milan, sent him a letter from Basel on April 16.[18] Pizolpasso congratulated Cusanus on his successful work for the entire Church and expressed the hope that there would be peace in the Church. We also know that while at Ferrara Cusanus asked his learned friend, Ambrogio Traversari (c. 1386-1439), to translate Proclus's *Platonic Theology* which he had brought back from Constantinople with other precious Greek manuscripts.[19] Professor Raymond Klibansky, who published a famous study of Proclus and Cusanus in 1929[20] and who emphasized the importance of the ideas of Proclus in Cusanus, stated:[21]

> Nicholas of Cusa is the first philosopher in the West to draw attention to, and make use of, Proclus' *Platonic Theology*. He possessed a copy of the Greek text which, it seems most likely, he brought with him, together with other Greek manuscripts (such as Basil's *Adversus Eunomium* and the Acts of the Sixth, Seventh and Eighth Ecumenical Councils), on his return from his legation to Constantinople. At any rate, after his arrival at the Council of Ferrara, early in 1438, he left it in the hands of the General of the Camaldolese Order Ambrogio Traversari, who among the scholars of the age enjoyed a high reputation for his Latin renderings of Greek authors, above all of early Christian writers.[22]

It is recorded that Cusanus submitted a petition to Eugenius IV on May 16, asking the Pope to provide him with the deanship of the Cathedral of Liège.[23] On June 6, 1438 Eugenius IV sent him to the imperial cities in Swabia

---

[17] *Acta Cusana,* 1/2, 226, Nr. 339.

[18] *Acta Cusana,* 1/2, 229-232, Nr. 349.

[19] *Acta Cusana,* 1/2, 227, Nr. 344. See also Krämer, *Der Beitrag,* pp. 50-51; Bilaniuk, *Nicholas of Cusa,* p. 118.

[20] Raymond Klibansky, "Ein PROKLOS-Fund und seine Bedeutung," *Sitzungsberichte der Heidelberger Akademie der Wissenschaften, Philosophisch-historische Klasse* (= HSB) (Jahrgang, 1928/29), p. 5, *Abhandlung* (Heidelberg, 1929).

[21] Raymond Klibansky, *The Continuity of the Platonic Tradition during the Middle Ages* (London, 1939) (new, expanded ed. Millwood, New York, 1981).

[22] Raymond Klibansky, "Plato's Parmenides in the Middle Ages and the Renaissance: A Chapter in the History of Platonic Studies," *Medieval and Renaissance Studies* 1,2 (1943), pp. vi-vii.

[23] *Acta Cusana,* 1/2, 235, Nr. 356.

as his representative.[24] Cusanus seems to have returned to Ferrara briefly in July because there is evidence that he carried Eugenius's letter from Ferrara to Basel.[25] Then he sent another petition to Eugenius IV on July 21 from Ferrara.[26] But when the Council of Ferrara began its formal sessions on October 8, he was definitely not present at Ferrara. Because of his sojourn in Constantinople, his knowledge of Greek and his friendships with many of the Greek representatives at Ferrara, he was one of the best qualified persons to participate in the sessions from the Western side.[27]

It is true that there has been much controversy over Cusanus's ability to understand and speak Greek. Francesco Pizolpasso's letter of May 17,1437 to Pier Candido Decembrio (1392-1477) spoke of Cusanus as "a man who has been introduced to the Greek language (*vir siquidem aliquando introductus Grece lingue*)....".[28] In 1937/38 Martin Honecker argued in his study of Cusanus and the Greek language that Cusanus had a modest knowledge of the Greek language.[29] But Honecker's negative judgment is no longer accepted today. Alois Krchnak's discovery in 1964 of Cusanus's marginal notes in the Greek texts, which are preserved in the Harley Collection of the British Museum,[30] and recent studies of Martin Sicherl, Walter Berschin and others have shown that Cusanus's

---

[24] *Acta Cusana,* 1/2, 237-238, Nr.359; 1/2, 238-239, Nr.362. See also Meuthen, *Nikolaus von Kues,* p. 68.

[25] *Acta Cusana,* 1/2, 237, Nr. 359; 1/2, 240, Nr. 366.

[26] *Acta Cusana,* 1/2, 239, Nr. 363.

[27] Bilaniuk, *Nicholas of Cusa,* p. 118; Meuthen, *Nikolaus von Kues,* pp. 51-52. About two interpreters, Andreas of Rhodes and Nicholas Secundinus, who were officially employed by the papal Curia, see Deno John Geanakoplos, *Interaction of the "Sibling" Byzantine and Western Cultures in the Middle Ages and Italian Renaissance (830-1600)* (New Haven, 1976), pp. 216, 360-361, n. 16.

[28] *Acta Cusana,* 1/2, 202-203, Nr. 297. The famous book dealer of Florence, Vespasiano da Bisticci (1421-1498), wrote in his *Vite di uomini illustri del secolo XV:* "Messer Nicolo di Cusa, of Gemnan nationality, was a man of worship, a great philosopher, theologian and platonist. He was of holy life, well lettered, especially in Greek." See *Vespastano, Renaissance Princes, Popes and Prelates: The Vespasiano Memoirs: Lives of illustrious Men of the XVth Century,* tr. William George and Emily Waters; intr. Myron P. Gilmore (New York, 1963), p. 156. See also Vespasiano da Bisticci, *Le vie,* ed. Aulo Greco 1 (Firenze, 1970), p. 184.

[29] Martin Honecker, "Nikolaus von Kues und die griechische Sprache," HSB (1937/38), p. 2, *Abhandlung* (Heidelberg, 1938).

[30] Alois Krchňak, "Neue Handschriftenfunde in London und Oxford," MFCG 3 (1963): 17, 101-108.

knowledge of the Greek language was considerable.[31] As Giuliano Cesarini wrote in his letter of October 17, 1438 to Ambrogio Traversari, some of the Greek manuscripts, especially the records of the Sixth, Seventh and Eighth Councils of the Church that Cusanus had brought back from Constantinople, were of great importance in the ensuing theological debates on the questions of the *filioque* at the Council of Florence.[32] Why, then, didn't Cusanus remain in Ferrara?

Cusanus's absence from the Council of Ferrara can be understood when we turn our attention to the political and ecclesiastical situation in the Empire in 1437 and the following years. The question of the union of the Greek and Latin Churches clearly influenced not only Cusanus's attitude and activities at that time but also the relations of the Pope and the Council of Basel. Pope Eugenius IV supported Rome, Ancona and Bologna as places suitable for the negotiations with the Greeks. The Council of Basel, on the other hand, entered into separate negotiations with the Greeks and suggested Avignon, Florence and Basel itself, none of which was acceptable to the Greeks who preferred a maritime town.[33] They also insisted that the site be acceptable to the Pope. After the Council of Basel was split into a majority and a minority party at a stormy session on May 7, 1437 over the site for a union council, the relationship of the Papacy and the Council rapidly deteriorated. Eugenius IV issued on September 18,1437 the bull *Doctoris gentium,* by which he broke completely with the Council of Basel and transferred it officially to Ferrara.[34] The Council responded on October 1, 1437 by declaring the Pope contumacious and summoned him to trial. In the fall of 1437 Pope Eugenius IV sent the Bishop of Urbino to the Electors of the Empire in order to ask them to recognize the newly convened Council of Ferrara and to

[31] Martin Sicherl, "Kritisches Verzeichnis der Londoner Handschriften aus dem Besitz des Nikolaus von Kues, 3 Fortsetzung," MFCG 10 (1973): 58-93; Walter Berschin, *Griechischlateinisches Mittelalter von Hieronymus zu Nikolaus von Kues,* (Bern, 1980), pp. 314-318; Walter Berschin, *Greek Letters and Latin Middle Ages: From Jerome to Nicholas of Cusa,* rev. and expanded ed., tr. Jerold C. Frames (Washington, D. C. 1988). See also *Acta Cusana,* 1/2, 203-204, n. 8.

[32] Gill, *The Council of Florence,* p. 148; Bilaniuk, *Nicholas of Cusa,* p. 119; Meuthen, *Nicolaus von Kues,* pp. 51-52. It has been pointed out that Cusanus owned a Greek 'dictionary.' See Krämer, "Nikolaus von Kues," p. 51.

[33] Heinz Hürten, "Die Mainzer Akzeptation von 1439," *Archiv für mittelrheinische Kirchengeschichte* 2 (1959): 42-75, esp. 43; Stieber, *Pope Eugenius IV,* p. 36; Bilaniuk, "Nicholas von Cusa," pp. 62-63.

[34] Gill, *The Council of Florence,* p. 91; Bilaniuk, "Nicholas of Cusa," p. 63.

send their representatives to it. Despite his urgent invitation no German prince appeared at or sent his representative to the Council of Ferrara.[35]

In response to these developments, the Emperor Sigismund (1368-1437) broke off relations with the Council of Basel and rallied to the Pope. But at a meeting of Frankfurt between November 3 und 7, 1437 the Elector of Mainz, Dietrich Schrenk von Erbach, invited the other Electors to institute a policy of neutrality over the open break between the Pope and the Council of Basel.[36] The death of the Emperor Sigismund on December 9, 1437 meant that one of the few political figures who might have been able to heal the open break was removed from the scene.[37] At the Imperial Diet of Frankfurt, which was held on March 12-17, 1438 because of the death of the Emperor, the Electors of the Empire, after five days of secret negotiations, decided to declare their position of neutrality in the ecclesiastical conflict. The notarial instrument of German neutrality, which was entitled the *Instrumentum protestacionis electorum imperii* and is commonly referred to as the "Protestation of Neutrality," was probably drawn up by Gregor Heimburg (c. 1400-1472), Cusanus's strong critic and one of the learned legal advisers who played an important role in the ecclesiastical politics of 1438 and later.[38] The document was presented to the diet on March 17. It is important, however, not to overemphasize the significance of the Protestation of Neutrality. Professing to be utterly perplexed by the situation, the three ecclesiastical and four secular Electors, who continued to treat the Pope as a legitimate one and the Council of Basel as a legitimate general council, emphasized their unwillingness to become involved in the church conflict.[39] We must also note that they expressed no desire to deviate openly from their allegiance to the Apostolic See either through the Protestation of Neutrality or through a later step.[40]

It was very important under these circumstances for Eugenius IV to make every effort to win the German princes over to his side. As an Imperial Diet was

---

[35] Stieber, *Pope Eugenius,* IV 41, 58.

[36] *Deutsche Reichstagsakten* (= RTA) 12 (Gotha 1901), pp. 289-296, 296-325. See also Hürten, *Die Mainzer Akzeptation,* p. 46; Stieber, *Pope Eugenius IV,* pp. 131-135.

[37] Gill, *The Council of Florence,* p. 94; Stieber, *Pope Eugenius IV,* p. 39.

[38] RTA 13 (Stuttgart—Gotha, 1925), pp. 216-219. See also Paul Joachimsohn, *Gregor Heimburg* (Bamberg, 1891); (reprint Aalen 1983), pp. 52-54; Hürten, "Die Mainzer Akzeptation," p. 47; Stieber, *Pope Eugenius IV,* pp. 132, 137, 139-140.

[39] Hürten, "Die Mainzer Akzeptation," pp. 47-48; Stieber, *Pope Eugenius IV,* pp. 137-138.

[40] Hürten, "Die Mainzer Akzeptation," p. 47.

scheduled to open in Nuremberg on October 16, 1438,[41] a papal delegation was sent from Ferrara to Nuremberg on September 15. The delegation included some of the keenest minds in the papal camp, such as Cardinal Niccolò Albergati (1426-1443), Archbishop Giovanni Berardi of Taranto (1421-1444) and Juan de Turrecremata (1388-1468).[42] Included in the list of papal delegates was the only German who had already been in Nuremberg since July 9, Nicolaus Cusanus.[43]

John of Segovia reported in his *History of the Council of Basel* how Cusanus attacked the Council of Basel in his speech of October 20, 1438 and the following days at the Diet of Nuremberg.[44] Cusanus, who was once active as a supporter of the Council of Basel, was now a sharp critic of the Council who labored for the defense of Pope Eugenius IV. The years 1437 and 1438 were important in Cusanus's life not only because 1437 was the year of a great philosophical revelation at sea but also because 1438 marked the appearance of Cusanus as an important player in imperial politics.[45]

In the first half of 1439, when the Council of Florence debated at length the subtle, thorny question of the *filioque,* Cusanus was busy defending the interests of the Pope at Mainz. The congress of high secular and ecclesiastical princes of the Empire, which was opened at Mainz on March 5,1439, was attended not only by the representatives of King Albrecht II (1438-1439), the German princes and archbishops, the Papacy and the Council of Basel, but also by the representatives of the Kings of France, Castile and Portugal and of the Duke of Milan.[46] As Joachim W. Stieber put it in his careful study of the period, the congress took on "the character of a European diplomatic congress."[47]

---

[41] RTA 13² (Gotha, 1916), pp. 658-899. See also *Acta Cusana,* 1/2, 243-247, Nr. 373-376; Hürten, "Die Mainzer Akzeptation," p. 49; Stieber, *Pope Eugenius IV,* p. 146.

[42] Stieber, *Pope Eugenius IV,* p. 147; Meuthen, *Nikolaus von Kues,* p. 67. The list of participants in the Diet can be found in RTA 13², pp. 132, 693-696. Cf. RTA 13², pp. 132, 832 n. 395.

[43] *Acta Cusana,* 1/2, 239, Nr. 364. See also RTA 13², pp. 132, 781-782; Meuthen, *Nikolaus von Kues,* pp. 67-68.

[44] *Acta Cusana,* 1/2, 244, Nr. 374; Meuthen, *Nikolaus von Kues,* pp. 68-69.

[45] Stieber, *Pope Eugenius IV,* p. 156; Meuthen, *Nikolaus von Kues,* p. 66.

[46] RTA 14 (Stuttgart, 1935), p. 96; Stieber, *Pope Eugenius IV,* pp. 37, 155, 156; Meuthen, *Nikolaus von Kues,* p. 78.

[47] Stieber, *Pope Eugenius IV,* p. 157.

The only member of the papal party who was present throughout was Cusanus, although he acted as an observer.[48]

On March 26, 1439, the Congress of Mainz accepted the twenty-six reform decrees of the Council of Basel.[49] About the time of the vesper the representatives of the Roman King, the Electors of Mainz and Cologne, the representatives of the Electors of Trier, the Pfalz and Saxony, and the Archbishops of Magdeburg and Salzburg appeared before a notary in the chapter room of the Cathederal of Mainz. In the presence of many witnesses they had the royal protonotary Theodor Ebracht read the declaration concerning the acceptance of the decrees of the Council of Basel that had been presented to them by the conciliar delegation. There was no foreigner present at the meeting.[50] The notarial document drawn up on this occasion is the so-called Acceptation (*Acceptatio*) of Mainz.[51]

At first glance, the action suggests that the German princes began to lean towards the Council of Basel and to abandon the stated policy of neutrality. But the truth of the matter is far more complex. Since the anonymous publication of the original document in 1762/63[52] by Johann Baptist Horix, counselor to the Elector of Mainz, the Acceptation of Mainz has been a subject of controversy and has been discussed in detail by such learned scholars as Christoph W. Koch, Wilhelm Puckert, Albert Werminghoff and Helmut Weigel.[53] One of the questions often raised by these scholars is whether the Acceptation of Mainz was in accord with the Protestation of Neutrality. It was often compared and

---

[48] Stieber, *Pope Eugenius IV,* p. 176. Meuthen, *Nikolaus von Kues,* p. 73. Cf. *Acta Cusana,* 1/2, 252-253, Nr. 387.

[49] RTA 14, pp. 109-114. See also Hürten, "Die Mainzer Akzeptation," p. 55; Stieber, *Pope Eugenius IV,* pp. 158, 159, 163.

[50] Hürten, "Die Mainzer Akzeptation," pp. 55-56.

[51] The text is found in RTA 14, pp. 109-114, n. 56. See also Stieber, *Pope Eugenius IV,* p. 159.

[52] [Johann Baptist Horix], *Concordata Nationis Germanicae Integra* (Frankfurt-Leipzig 1762/63). See Hürten, "Die Mainzer Akzeptation," p. 42.

[53] Christoph Wilhelm Koch, *Sanctio Pragmatica Germaniorum Illustrata* (Strassburg, 1789); Wilhelm Pückert, *Die kurfürstliche Neutralitat wahrend des Baslers Konzils: Ein Beitrag zur deutschen Geschichte von 1438-1448,* (Leipzig, 1858); Albert Werminghoff, *Nationalkirchliche Bestrebungen im deutschen Mittelalter* (Stuttgart, 1910); Helmut Weigel, "Kaiser, Kurfurst und Jurist: Friedrich III, Erzbischof Jakob von Trier und Dr. Johannes von Lysura im Vorspiel zum Regensburger Reichstag vom April 1454," in: *Aus Reichstagen des 15. und 16. Jahrhunderts: Festgabe, dargebracht der Historischen Kommission der Bayerischen Akademie der Wissenschaften zur Feier ihres hundertjahrigen Bestehens* (Göttingen, 1958), pp. 80, 115.

contrasted with the Pragmatic Sanction of Bourges, which was issued by French King Charles VII (1403-1461) on July 4, 1438.[54] Issued in the name of Albrecht II, King of the Romans, and of the six archbishops, the Acceptation of Mainz was an act which was concerned mainly with the ecclesiastical affairs of the Empire. The representatives of secular Electors were associated with it only as of ficial witnesses.[55] It is also highly important to note that the Acceptation of Mainz accepted only twenty-six decrees of the Council of Basel and specifically excluded the decree on the suspension of Eugenius IV from office.[56] Of the decrees accepted, one of the most important and famous was the decree *Haec sancta* of the Council of Constance which the Council of Basel had confirmed.[57] The Acceptation of Mainz has sometimes been called the Pragmatic Sanction of the Germans, but it created no law in the Empire.[58] Albrecht II never confirmed it or issued a sanction for its enforcement. Only a few German princes appear to have taken formal steps to promulgate or to enforce the decrees which had been adopted at Mainz. Without a royal sanction, it remained little more than a statement of expectation as to how the "gravamina of the German nation by which the German nation has hitherto been miserably weighed down by the Italian nation"[59] ought to be alleviated. Stieber stated that "one cannot fail to conclude that the German archbishops and their envoys at Mainz were more concerned with reducing financial payments to Rome than with church reform as

---

[54] Stieber, *Pope Eugenius IV,* pp. 64-71, 160-166; Gill, *The Council of Florence,* pp. 125, 134-135, 339.

[55] Stieber, *Pope Eugenius IV,* p. 159.

[56] Hürten, "Die Mainzer Akzeptation," pp. 55, 61; Stieber, *Pope Eugenius IV,* pp. 159, 163.

[57] There are many studies of the famous, controversial decree. See, for example, Heinz Hürten, "Die Konstanzer Dekrete, 'Haec sancta' und 'Frequens' in ihrer Bedeutung fur Ekklesiologie und Kirchenpolitik des Nikolaus von Kues," in: *Das Konzil von Konstanz: Festgabe für H. Schäufels,* ed. Wolfgang Müller und August Franzen (Freiburg i. Br., 1964), pp. 381-396, August Franzen, *The Council of Constance: Present State of the Problem,* (Concilium: Theology in the Age of Renewal, 7; New York, 1965), pp. 29-68; Isfried H. Pichler, *Die Verbindlichkeit der Konstanzer Dekrete: Untersuchungen zur Frage der Interpretation und Verbindlichkeit der Superioritätsdekrete Haec sancta und Frequens* (Wien, 1967); Remigius Bäumer, "Die Interpretation und Verbindlichkeit der Konstanzer Dekrete," *Theologisch-praktische Quartalschrift* 116 (1968): 44-53; Walter Brandmüller, "Besitzt das Konstanzer Dekret 'Haec sancta' dogmatische Verbindlichkeit?," *Annuarium Historiae Conciliorum* 1,1 (1969): 96-113.

[58] Hürten, "Die Mainzer Akzeptation," p. 56.

[59] Stieber, *Pope Eugenius IV,* pp. 158, 170.

a matter of general principle."[60] No matter what the ultimate significance of the Acceptation of Mainz was, it strongly affected the relations of the Pope and the Council of Basel.

On June 25,1439 the Council of Basel proceeded to depose Eugenius IV for maladministration of his office and as a "stiff-necked heretic and schismatic."[61] This extreme step led a number of princes to withdraw their support for the Council of Basel. In contrast, Eugenius's position gradually improved. On July 6, 1439, only about ten days after his deposition by the Council of Basel, the union of the Latin and Greek Churches was proclaimed in Florence in the famous bull *Laetentur caeli.*[62] These events certainly put further burden on Cusanus who had to intensify his activities on behalf of the Pope. On August 4, 1439 Cusanus was on a boat sailing up the Rhine towards Frankfurt.[63] He participated in another meeting of Electors and their representatives at Mainz from August 6 to 19.[64] It is interesting to note that the envoys of the Council of Basel, John of Segovia, Thomas Livingston and Johannes von Bachenstein, all criticized the policy of neutrality which the Electors had reaffirmed.[65] Cusanus was even present at a provincial synod of Mainz which met from August 22 through August 23.[66]

When the Council of Basel elected Duke Amadeus VIII of Savoy as Pope Felix V (1439-1449) on November 8, 1439, Cusanus wrote a criticism of the supporters of Amadeus which was entitled *Dialogus concludes Amedistarum errorem ex gestis et doctrina concilii Basiliensis.* The work, which was first dicussed by Josef Koch[67] in 1957 and which was published by Erich Meuthen in 1970,[68] shows how deeply Cusanus was involved in 1439 in the defense of Pope Eugenius IV. At the end of the year he attended a meeting of the spiritual

---

[60] Stieber, *Pope Eugenius IV,* pp. 165-166.

[61] Stieber, *Pope Eugenius IV,* pp. 155, 179, 183, 190; Bilaniuk, "Nicholas of Cusa," 64; Petro B.T. Bilaniuk, "The Council of the Revolving Doors (Basle—Ferrara—Florence—Rome, 1431-1445)," in his Studies in *Eastern Christianity,* 3 (München—Toronto 1983), p. 121.

[62] Gill, *The Council of Florence,* pp. 293-294; Gill, *Personalities,* p. 10.

[63] RTA 14, p. 320; *Acta Cusana,* pp. 1, 2, 260, Nr. 397.

[64] RTA 14, pp. 325-343; Stieber, *Pope Eugenius IV,* p. 184.

[65] RTA 14, pp. 331-338; Stieber, *Pope Eugenius IV,* p. 185.

[66] RTA 14, pp. 343-394; Stieber, *Pope Eugenius IV,* pp. 184-186.

[67] Koch, "Über eine aus der nachsten Umgebung," pp. 117-135.

[68] Meuthen, "Der Dialogus," MFCG 8 (1970): 11-114, Text: 78-114. Cf. n. 16 above.

Electors of Mainz, Cologne and Trier at Lahnstein, again defending the papal interests.[69]

It is impossible in a short paper to describe in detail Cusanus's pro-papal activities in 1438 and thereafter. His defense of Eugenius IV in Germany, which began in 1438, was to continue for ten years in all. We must note at the same time that during his stay in Germany as Eugenius's proponent his advice as legal expert was sought by numerous friends and clients. A *doctor decretorum* from the University of Padua, Cusanus was deeply engaged in imperial and local politics of the time.[70] It is therefore astonishing that Cusanus was able to complete his first major philosophical work, *De docta ignorantia,* in Kues on February 12,1440.[71] His deep involvement in often petty and distracting political affairs did not completely consume his energy for reflection and contemplation. In the midst of interminable disputes and contests he was able to produce a major work of philosophical inquiry. This is a trait of his which, as is well known, he demonstrated many times in his life.

Commenting on Cusanus's labors for Eugenius IV, Aeneas Sylvius Piccolomini (1405-1464) called him the "Hercules of all the followers of the Eugenians."[72] As a reward for his almost ten-year campaign for the papacy, Pope Nicholas V elevated Cusanus to the rank of a cardinal on December 20, 1448.[73] But how was Cusanus seen in the eyes of his compatriots and others? Did his attack on the Council of Basel made at the Imperial Diet of Nuremberg in 1438 sound empty and hollow to those listeners who remembered Cusanus acting as a supporter of the Council of Basel a few years back? Didn't some Germans think of him almost as a turncoat as he endeavored to secure the support of the German princes for Eugenius IV? In 1538, one hundred years later, Johannes Kymeus expressed his displeasure and irritation at Cusanus's pro-papal activities in his famous criticism of Cusanus, *Des Babsts Hercules wider die Deutschen.*[74]

[69] RTA 15[1] (Gotha, 1912), pp. 104-110. See also Stieber, *Pope Eugenius IV,* pp. 204, 207; Meuthen, *Nikolaus von Kues,* p. 74.

[70] Meuthen, *Nikolaus von Kues,* pp. 70, 74, 87-89.

[71] *Acta Cusana,* 1/2, 281, Nr. 426; Meuthen, *Nikolaus von Kues,* p. 74.

[72] *Acta Cusana,* 1/2, 281, Nr.427a: "Hercules tamen omnium Eugenianorum Nicolaus Cusanus existimatus est."

[73] *Acta Cusana,* 1/2, 569, Nr. 777.

[74] Ottokar Menzel, "Johannes Kymeus: *Des Babsts Hercules wider die Deudschen* (Wittenberg 1538): Als Beitrag zum Nachleben des Nikolaus von Cues im 16. Jahrhundert," HSB 1940/41,6. Abhandlung (Heidelberg, 1941).

There are some questions about Cusanus's character and personality that have been raised over the years.[75] In summing up his critical study of Cusanus and his thought, Karl Jaspers tells us that "he showed himself capable of making crucial decisions: when he left home, when he dropped jurisprudence for theology, and when he went over to the papal party at the Council of Basel."[76] In a book full of criticisms, these words of Jaspers's sound almost charitable. Cusanus's activities from 1437 to 1440 demonstrate clearly that he was able to make crucial decisions, as Jaspers asserted, that, great as he was as a thinker, he was, like in other periods of his life, enmeshed in the complex political and ecclesiastical problems of the period and that somehow, to quote Jaspers again, "he succeeded in tearing himself away from mere practical action, in finding time to think quietly and to set down his ideas in writing."[77] His vision at sea on his way back from Constantinople finally gave birth to his most famous philosophical work, *De docta ignorantia.*

---

[75] See, for example, Josef Koch, "Nikolaus von Cues als Mensch nach dem Briefwechsel und personlichen Aufzeichoumgen," in: *Humanismus, Mystik und Kunst in der Welt des Mittelalters,* ed. Josef Koch (Leiden-Köln, 1959), pp. 56-75; Morimichi Watanabe, *The Political Ideas of Nicholas of Cusa, with Special Reference to His De concordantia catholica* (Geneva, 1963), p. 98, n. 2; Karl Jaspers, *Nikolaus Cusanus* (München, 1964); (new ed. München, 1987), pp. 256-262; Karl Jaspers, *Anselm and Nicholas of Cusa,* ed. Hannah Arendt; tr. Ralph Manheim (New York, 1974), pp. 177-180; James E. Biechler, "Nicholas of Cusa and the End of The Conciliar Movement: A Humanist Crisis of Identity," *Church History* 44 (1975): 5-21.

[76] Jaspers, *Anselm and Nicholas of Cusa,* p. 179; Jaspers, *Nikolaus Cusanus,* p. 259.

[77] Jaspers, *Anselm and Nicholas of Cusa,* p. 179; Jaspers, *Nikolaus Cusanus,* p. 260.

The German Church shortly before the Reformation: Nicolaus Cusanus and the Veneration of the Bleeding Hosts at Wilsnack

PREFACE

Why the Reformation started not in other European countries but in Germany is a complicated question which is still worth pondering. According to Bernd Moeller, the famous German historian of the Reformation, Germany in the Middle Ages was an "especially medieval" country.[1] If he implies that the Reformation began not in less medieval countries but in a more medieval country called Germany, his logic must be examined with great care. In his well-known article, entitled "The Essence of Late Medieval Germany," Heinrich Heimpel, one of the most famous German medievalists, characterized Germany as a "particularly medieval country."[2] Apparently, Moeller followed Heimpel's argument. But how do their interpretations relate to the beginnings and nature of the Reformation?

The purpose of this article is to examine reaction to and handling of the problem of the veneration of the bleeding hosts at Wilsnack in the archdiocese of Magdeburg by Nicolaus Cusanus (1401-1464), who went to Germany and the Low Countries from 1451 to 1452 to dispense the Jubilee indulgence and to reform the churches and monasteries in the German territories on orders from Pope Nicholas V (1447-1455). Through Cusanus we shall be able to understand better what the general and spiritual condition of the late medieval German churches was some sixty years before the Reformation and what some of the important issues were for them at that time.

I. Cusanus' Legation

Although Cusanus supported the theory of conciliar supremacy over the pope in the *De concordantia catholica,* which he submitted in 1433 or 1434 to the Council of Basel (1431-1449) as Ulrich von Manderscheid's counsel, he moved from the conciliar majority to the papal minority of the council in 1437 as the question of where to hold a reunion council of the Roman and Greek

---

[1] Bernd Moeller, "Frömmigkeit in Deutschland um 1500," *Archiv für Reformationsgeschichte* 56 (1965): 29-30.

[2] Hermann Heimpel, "Das Wesen des deutschen Spätmittelalter," *Archiv für Kulturgeschichte* 35 (1953): 38.

churches split the council into two parties.[3] Thereafter, he went to Constantinople as one of the delegates of Pope Eugenius IV (1431-1447), and in the 1440s made serious efforts at imperial and regional diets to persuade German princes, who had taken a neutral position in the conflict between the pope and the council, to return to the papal camp. As a result, his friend Aeneas Sylvius Piccolomini, who later became Pope Pius II (1459-1464), called him the "Hercules of the Eugenians."

Although Pope Eugenius IV named Cusanus a cardinal *in petto* probably on December 16, 1446, it was on December 28, 1448, that Nicholas V elevated him to the cardinalate, announcing this publicly on January 3, 1449. One year later, on March 23, 1450, the pope appointed Cusanus bishop of Brixen (Bressanone) in the Tyrol. The same year he sent Cusanus to the German lands as papal legate, not only to proclaim and distribute indulgences for the Jubilee year of 1450 but also to reform churches and monasteries in the area. At a time when Jakob von Sierck, archbishop of Trier, went to Rome in 1450 accompanied by 140 knights,[4] Cusanus left Rome on December 31, 1450 and started his wintery journey modestly on a mule, accompanied by about thirty cotravelers, including the Scotsman Thomas Livingston.[5] His great journey, which lasted 15 months from January 1451 to April 1452 and which extended about 2,800 miles from Rome to Brixen, can be called, as Josef Koch stated, the "peak in Cusanus' life."[6] In a recent lecture, Erich Meuthen, the foremost authority on

---

[3] As good, standard studies of Cusanus' life and thought, see Edmond Vansteenberghe, *Le cardinal Nicolas de Cues (1401-1464): L'action—la pensée* (Paris, 1920; reprint Frankfurt am Main, 1963); Erich Meuthen, *Nikolaus von Kues 1401-1464: Skizze einer Biographie*, 7th ed. (Münster, 1992). On his *De concordantia catholica*, see Paul E. Sigmund, *Nicholas of Cusa and Medieval Political Thought* (Cambridge, Massachusetts, 1963); Morimichi Watanabe, *The Political Ideas of Nicholas of Cusa with Special Reference to his De concordantia catholica* (Geneva, 1963); Claudia Lücking-Michel, *Konkordanz und Konsens: Zur Gesellschaftstheorie in der Schrift 'De concordantia catholica' des Nikolaus von Kues* (Würzburg, 1994).

[4] Ludwig Pastor, *The History of the Popes*, ed. Frederick Ignatius Antrobus, 7th ed., 36 vols. (London, 1949), 1-2.91.

[5] Josef Koch, *Der deutsche Kardinal in deutschen Landen: Die Legationsreise des Nikolaus von Kues (1451/52)* (Trier, 1964), p. 11. Pastor says in his *The History of the Popes*, 1-2.109, that Cusanus was accompanied "only by a few Romans." On Thomas Livingston, see Morimichi Watanabe, "Nikolaus von Kues - Richard Fleming - Thomas Livingston," *Mitteilungen und Forschungsbeiträge der Cusanus-Gesellschaft* 6 (1967): 175-177; idem, "Thomas Livingston," *American Cusanus Society Newsletter* 10/2 (1993): 6-8. Livingston was a member of Cusanus' party from the beginning to the end of December 1451; see *Acta Cusana: Quellen zur Lebensgeschichte des Nikolaus von Kues* [hereafter *Acta Cusana*], ed. Erich Meuthen (Hamburg, 1976-1996), 1/3.669, no. 963.

[6] Koch, *Der deutsche Kardinal*, p. 3.

Cusanus' legation journey, concluded that "seen from its impact and from his contemporaries' memories, the journey has always been regarded as one of the great events in the history of Germany."[7]

From Rome, Cusanus and his party reached Spittal not by way of Verona and Brixen, as was believed in the past, but, according to a recent discovery, via Treviso and across the Alps.[8] After visiting the Austrian towns such as Salzburg, Wiener Neustadt and Vienna, they entered Germany where, moving northward from Munich, they visited many historic towns, such as Freising, Regensburg, Nuremberg, Bamberg, Würzburg, Erfurt, and Halle, and then reached Magdeburg. Turning westward at Magdeburg, the party arrived at Minden on July 30, 1451, after traversing the area between the Elbe and the Weser rivers.

In the Low Countries the party went on to visit such places as Deventer, Windesheim, Zwolle, and Utrecht. Thereafter it came to Amsterdam, Leiden, Utrecht, and Roermond. Coming to the area between Belgium and Germany, it visited Maastricht, Aachen, Liège, Malmedy, Trier, Bernkastel-Kues, and Mainz. Like a football kicked back and forth, the party turned around to go to Koblenz, Cologne, Aachen, Leuven, Brussels, Frankfurt am Main, and Aschaffenburg. It was on April 7, two days before Easter, in 1452 that the party reached Brixen.[9]

During this long reforming legation to the German territories, Cusanus held and presided over provincial synods at Salzburg, Magdeburg, Mainz and Cologne, which were the sees of the archbishops, and held a diocesan synod at Bamberg. The number of churches and monasteries which he visited and reformed between a few days and two weeks each amounted to about 80. In many places, he also delivered sermons either in Latin or in German, 51 of which have been preserved.[10] It is clear, as Meuthen has pointed out, that the whole itinerary was arranged for the purpose of the reform and reconstruction of the German

---

[7] Erich Meuthen, *Nikolaus von Kues: Profile einer geschichtlichen Persönlichkeit* (Trierer Cusanus Lecture, Heft 1; Trier, 1994), p. 15.

[8] Erich Meuthen, "Das Itinerar der deutschen Legationsreise des Nikolaus von Kues 1451/1452," in *Papstgeschichte und Landesgeschichte: Festschrift für Hermann Jacobs zum 65. Geburtstag*, ed. Joachim Dalhaus et al. (Köln, 1995), p. 476.

[9] There are many studies of Cusanus' legation published since the nineteenth century. A recent, important one, in addition to the lectures cited in nn. 6 and 7 and a study in n. 8, is Erich Meuthen, "Die deutsche Legationsreise von Nikolaus von Kues 1451/52," in *Lebenslehren und Weltentwürfe* (Göttingen, 1989), pp. 421-499.

[10] Donald Sullivan, "Cusanus and Pastoral Renewal: The Reform of Popular Religion in the Germanies," in *Nicholas of Cusa on Christ and the Church: Essays in Memory of Chandler McCuskey Brooks for the American Cusanus Society,* ed. Gerald Christianson and Thomas M. Izbicki (Leiden, 1996), pp. 167-175 at pp. 169-170. In his *Praefatio generalis* in *Nicolai de Cusa opera omnia*, 19 vols. (Hamburg, 1932-), 16:xlix-l: *Sermones 1 (1430-1441)*, Rudolf Haubst lists 46 extant Latin sermons which Cusanus delivered on the legation.

church.[11] Forty years after the end of the journey Johannes Trithemius (1462-1516), the famous Benedictine abbot of Sponheim, wrote, "Nicholas of Cusa appeared in Germany as an angel of light and peace, amidst darkness and confusion, restored the unity of the Church, strengthened the authority of her Supreme Head, and sowed a precious seed of new life."[12]

Trithemius' remarks laid the foundation for very optimistic appraisals of the legation which prevailed for many years. But recent studies have revealed considerable difficulties and resistance which Cusanus experienced as he tried to accomplish his reform mission.[13] During the Provincial Synod of Cologne, for example, a Franciscan friar attempted to kill him by poison.[14] One of the reasons for the existence and rise of anti-Cusanus attitude was the perception that, although Cusanus once tried to limit the powers of the pope by championing the supremacy of the council, he became a "traitor" by later joining the papal camp. Furthermore, at a time when a German cardinal was regarded as an extraordinarily rare phenomenon, like a white crow, it was deemed anti-German for Cusanus, a German-born cardinal, to attempt to reform German churches and monasteries and to distribute indulgences on orders from the pope. This kind of critical attitude towards Cusanus among the Germans was clearly manifested in Johannes Kymeus' *Des Bapsts Herald wider die Deutschen*, which was published in 1538.[15]

It was found out several years ago that at the Provincial Synod of Salzburg, which was convened as the first synod on Cusanus' legation, he presented a comprehensive plan for ecclesiastical reform. Although it is not signed by him, it is certain, judging from its contents, that the document was a declaration issued at the beginning of the legation by Cusanus who was very anxious to accomplish the reform of the German church. This very detailed plan,

---

[11] Erich Meuthen, "Die Synode im Kirchenverständnis des Nikolaus von Kues," in *Stadt, Kultur, Politik—Beiträge zur Geschichte Bayerns und des Katholizismus: Festschrift zum 65. Geburtstag von Dieter Albrecht* (Kallmünz, 1992), p. 17.

[12] See Donald Sullivan, "Nicholas of Cusa as Reformer: The Papal Legation to the Germanies, 1451-1452," *Mediaeval Studies* 36 (1974): 383.

[13] See, for example, Koch, *Der deutsche Kardinal*, p. 14; Meuthen, *Nikolaus von Kues*, pp. 88-90; Sullivan, "Nicholas of Cusa as Reformer," pp. 404, 418 n. 116.

[14] Meuthen, *Nikolaus von Kues*, p. 89. The mendicant orders, both Franciscan and Dominican, which were directly subordinate to the pope, took Cusanus' attempts to reform them as interference with their internal affairs and often appealed to the pope during Cusanus' legation.

[15] Johannes Kymeus, *Des Babsts Hercules wider die Deutschen, Wittenberg 1538*, ed. Ottokar Menzel (Cusanus-Studien VI, Sitzungsberichte der Heidelberger Akademie der Wissenschaften, Philosophisch-historische Klasse, Jhrg. 1940/41, 6. Abh.; Heidelberg, 1941).

which was rejected by the Synod, seems to have remained unknown until recently in the library of Saint Peter's monastery in Salzburg.[16] As is well known, Cusanus wrote the *Reformatio generalis* in 1459, after moving to Rome under Pope Pius II.[17] It is clear that both during and after the legation, the reform of the Church was one of the most important concerns for Cusanus.

II. The Veneration of the Bleeding Hosts at Wilsnack

Because it is impossible, in a short article, to discuss the significance of many events that occurred during Cusanus' 456-day-long journey, we shall focus our attention especially on a controversial phenomenon, very well known at that time, but hardly remembered at present: the veneration of the bleeding hosts at a Saxon village called Wilsnack. What is its significance? How did it happen? On August 16, 1383, ten villages in the diocese of Havelberg within the archdiocese of Magdeburg, including Wilsnack, were burnt down by the noble Heinrich von Bülow and his followers. Heinrich had complaints against the bishop of Havelberg. A few days later, summoned by the repeated voice of an angel from nearby Gross Lüben, where he had spent the nights, the priest of the village church in Wilsnack, Johannes Kabuz (Cahlbuez, Calbuz) (d. 1412), began to assert that the three hosts on the altar not only remained undestroyed but had drops of blood in the center.[18] In the Prignitz region, where Wilsnack was

---

16 Concerning the description and appraisal of this manuscript (HsA 203 f. 51r-59r) which was found in the monastery of Saint Peter in Salzburg, see Meuthen, *Die Synode,* pp. 17-22; idem, "Nikolaus von Kues und die deutsche Kirche am Vorabend der Reformation," in *Nikolai von Kues, Kirche und Respublica Christiana: Konkordanz, Repräsentanz und Konsens (Mitteilungen und Forschungsbeiträge der Cusanus-Gesellschaft,* 21; Trier, 1994), pp. 56-77.

17 The text of the *Reformatio generalis* is found in Stephan Ehses, "Der Reformentwurf des Kardinals Nikolaus Cusanus," *Historisches Jahrbuch* 32 (1911): 281-299. An introduction and an English translation can be found in Morimichi Watanabe and Thomas M. Izbicki, "Nicholas of Cusa: A General Reform of the Church," in *Nicholas of Cusa on Christ and the Church,* pp. 175-202.

18 Since the sixteenth century, many studies on the veneration of the bleeding hosts at Wilsnack have been published. Some important recent studies to be mentioned are: Ludger Meier, "Wilsnack als Spiegel deutscher Vorreformation," *Zeitschrift für Religions- und Geistesgeschichte* 3 (1951): 53-69; Otto-Friedrich Gandert, "Das Heilige Blut von Wilsnack und seine Pilgerzeichen," in *Brandenburgische Jahrhunderte: Festgabe Johannes Schultze* (Berlin, 1971), pp. 72-90; Hartmut Boockmann, "Der Streit um das Wilsnacker Blut: Zur Situation des deutschen Klerus in der Mitte des 15. Jahrhunderts," *Zeitschrift für Historische Forschung* 9 (1982): 385-408; Charles Zika, "Hosts, Processions and Pilgrimages: Controlling the Sacred in Fifteenth-Century Germany," *Past and Present* 118 (1983): 24-64 at pp. 48-59. The oldest collection of important published sources is in Matteus Ludecus, *Historia von der Erfindung, Wunderwerken und Zerstörung des vermeinten heiligen Bluts zur*

located and where the natural religions of the Slavs were still strong, there had been pilgrim sites, such as Marienfliess near Stepenit (since 1231), St. Annenkirche in Alt-Krüssow, and Beelitz (1247).[19] But Wilsnack was something new; and it quickly began to draw pilgrims not only from northern Germany, but also from other European countries.

When informed about the news, Bishop Dietrich II (1370-1385) of Havelberg visited Wilsnack and confirmed the miracle. By 1384 Pope Urban VI (1378-1389) had granted the right to issue indulgences to those who visited Wilsnack.[20] Between 1384 and 1401 the construction of the mighty "Wunderblutkirche" (Wondrous-Blood Church) of Saint Nicholas was carried out by Bishops Dietrich II and Johannes II Wöpelitz (1385-1401) of Havelberg.[21] The enormous amount of money that was needed for the reconstruction of the church was raised through the sale of indulgences. By 1395 Bishop Wöpelitz, whose statute still stands in the Cathedral (Dom St. Marien) of Havelberg, made the property and possessions of the church of Wilsnack so much part of the diocese of Havelberg that all income from indulgences flowed into the treasury of the diocese.[22]

It is clear that by the end of the fourteenth century Wilsnack was certainly well established as a site of pilgrimage for the veneration of the bleeding hosts. The worship of the blood of Christ is believed to have increased considerably in late medieval Europe.[23] In Germany alone, there were over 100 pilgrimage sites, the most famous of which included those in Andechs, Waldrün, and Augsburg.[24] It is out of the scope of this paper to discuss the religious and psychological reasons why so many pious lay folks visited these sites as pilgrims. The religious and political confusion since the beginning of the Great Schism (1378-

Wilsnagk (Wittenberg, 1586); and one of the most detailed, important old studies is Ernest Breest, "Das Wunderblut von Wilsnack, 1383-1552," *Märkische Forschungen* 16 (1881): 133-301.

[19] Ulrich Woronowicz, *Ev. Kirche St. Nikolai Bad Wilsnack* (Das Christliche Denkmal, Heft 92; Regensburg, 1994), p. 4.

[20] Meier, "Wilsnack als Spiegel," p. 54; Boockmann, "Der Streit um das Wilsnacker Blut," p. 389; Zika, "Hosts, Processions and Pilgrimages," p. 50.

[21] Rita Buchholz and Klaus-Dieter Gralow, *De hystorie unde erfindinghe des hilligen Sacraments tho der wilsnagk* [Die Geschichte von der Erfindung des heiligen Sakraments zu Wilsnack] (Bad Wilsnack, 1992), p. [4].

[22] Bruno Hennig, "Kurfürst Friedrich und das Wunderblut Wilsnack," *Forschungen zur Brandenburgischen und Preussischen Geschichte* 19 (1906): 78-79.

[23] Meier, "Wilsnack als Spiegel," p. 53; Zika, "Hosts, Processions and Pilgrimages," p. 49.

[24] Boockmann, "Der Streit um das Wilsnacker Blut," p. 380; Zika, "Hosts, Processions and Pilgrimages," p. 49 n. 76.

1417) and the spread of fear and anxiety as a result of the decline of the Holy Roman Empire certainly contributed to it. It is also probable that the approach of the end of the century fostered fear in the minds of pious but simple people.[25] It can be said, however, that, as Ludger Meier argued in his perceptive article, the phenomenon of pilgrimage does have certain aspects which can be understood not from the rational points of view but only by those who actually participated in it.[26]

In the fifteenth century, Wilsnack experienced further development as a pilgrimage site. When Archbishop Sbinko of Prague noticed in 1405 that an increasing number of pilgrims went to Wilsnack from his archdiocese, he decided to establish an investigative commission to find out about the validity of this pilgrimage.[27] One of the members of the commission was Jan Hus (c.1370-1415). The results of the commission's investigation are found in a synodal decree published in 1405. It mandated all priests to preach and advise against going to Wilsnack as pilgrims.[28] The same year Hus' book *On the Blood of Christ (De sanguine Christi)*, which clearly criticized the veneration of the bleeding hosts not only at Wilsnack but elsewhere, was published.[29] Despite criticisms from the archbishop, Hus, and others, the pilgrimage to Wilsnack further expanded and flourished. Not only did it draw pilgrims from Germany and Bohemia; but it also received them from Switzerland, Holland, Belgium, and the Scandinavian countries, thus making it one of the largest pilgrimage sites after Jerusalem, Rome, Santiago de Compostela and Aachen.[30]

Many inns sprang up in Wilsnack, such as Doppelter Adler, Goldener Adler, Löwe, Bär, Neuer Mann, Weisses Ross, Roter und Schwarzer Hahn,

---

25 On the fear of the end of a century, see Norman Cohn, *The Pursuit of the Millennium* (London, 1957).

26 Meier, "Wilsnack als Spiegel," pp. 65-69.

27 Peter Browe, *Die eucharistischen Wunder des Mittelalters* (Breslau, 1938), p. 168; Meier, "Wilsnack als Spiegel," pp. 54-55; Boockmann, "Der Streit um das Wilsnacker Blut," p. 391.

28 Browe, *Die eucharistischen Wunder*, pp. 168-169; J. Fliege, "Nikolaus von Kues und der Kampf gegen das Wilsnacker Wunderblut," in *Das Buch als Quelle historischer Forschung: Fritz Juntke anlässlich seines 90. Geburtstages gewidmet* (Leipzig, 1977), p. 63; Zika, "Hosts, Processions and Pilgrimages," p. 50.

29 Meier, "Wilsnack als Spiegel," p. 55; Boockmann, "Der Streit um das Wilsnacker Blut," p. 387.

30 Browe, *Die eucharistischen Wunder*, p. 168; Boockmann, "Der Streit um das Wilsnacker Blut," p. 385.

Weisse Gans, Ochsenkopf, Pflegel, Roter Ziegel, Windmühle und Hirsch.[31] Those who came from Berlin and its environment were on the "Heiliger Blutsweg" and reached Wilsnack via Tegel, Heiligensee, Flatow, Fehrbellin, Linum, Hakenberg, Garz, Wusterhausen, Kyritz, and Gross Leppin.[32] Those who came from Scandinavia left their ships at Lübeck whence, guided by a road sign that still stands today at Roekstrasse, they headed for Wilsnack. According to one study, the number of pilgrims is said to have reached 100,000 in a few warm months between spring and early autumn. On Saint Bartholomew's Day (August 24) the crowd was especially thick.[33]

But, between 1443 and 1453, Wilsnack became an object of heated debate mainly because of the activities of Heinrich Tocke (1390-1453). After studying theology at the University of Erfurt, Tocke became a professor of theology at the university in 1418 and a member of the cathedral chapter of Magdeburg by 1426. Because of his commoner origins and theological education, he belonged to a minority of the chapter that was critical of some church policies and practices. When he attended the Council of Basel between 1432 and 1437, he participated actively in the negotiations with the Hussites and may have met Cusanus. Although the exact year of authorship is not known, his book, *Rapularius*, written in the middle of the fifteenth century, reflects, like Cusanus' *De concordantia catholica*, the author's deep learning.[34]

To Tocke, the basic questions about Wilsnack were whether the hosts really had blood drops and, if they did, how they could be shown to be Christ's blood. In the famous speech which Tocke delivered at the Provincial Synod of Magdeburg in 1451, he declared, in the presence of Cusanus, that when he examined the three hosts carefully in Wilsnack on July 10, 1443, there were no red spots on the hosts, and that even if he had found them, he would not have been able to assert that they belonged to Jesus Christ.[35] Accordingly, he went on to say that the advice given to the laity to go to Wilsnack as pilgrims is based on the clergy's deception and superstition, as well as being a clever method of

[31] Rita Buchholz and Klaus-Dieter Gralow, *Zur Geschichte der Wilsnacker Wallfahrt unter besonderer Berücksichtigung der Pilgerzeichen* (Bad Wilsnack, 1992), p. 9.

[32] Ibid., p. 16.

[33] Ibid., p. 9.

[34] Paul Lehmann, "Aus dem Rapularius des Hinricus Token," in idem, *Erforschung des Mittelalters*, 5 vols. (Stuttgart, 1959-1962), 4.187-205. For Tocke's other writings, see Hildegrund Hölzl, "Toke, Heinrich," in *Die deutsche Literatur des Mittelalters: Verfasserlexikon*, 2nd ed., 9 vols. (Berlin, 1978-1995), 9.964-971.

[35] Boockmann, "Der Streit um das Wilsnacker Blut," pp. 393-394; Zika, "Hosts, Processions and Pilgrimages," p. 55. For E. Breest's German translation of Tocke's synodal speech, see *Blättern für Handel, Gewerbe und soziales Leben* (Magdeburg, 1882), pp. 167f, 174-180.

robbing the foreigners of money by distributing indulgences.[36] It should be remembered that the theological faculties of the Universities of Prague, Erfurt, and Leipzig took a similar position about this question.[37]

It is important to realize that behind the opinions of the theologian-reformer Tocke and the theological faculties, there was the position of the Dominican and Franciscan orders about the veneration of the bleeding hosts at Wilsnack. The Dominicans essentially took a negative attitude toward Wilsnack, basing their position on the *Summa Theologiae*, 3ª, 54, 2-3 of Thomas Aquinas.[38] They concluded that, since Christ ascended to heaven with his sparkling body and full blood, it is theologically impossible to support the veneration of Christ's blood on earth. In contrast, on the strength of the theories of Bonaventure (1217/21-1274) and Johannes Duns Scotus (1265/66-1308), the Franciscans took the position that since part of Christ's blood remained on earth separate from the *unio hypostatica*, the veneration of the bleeding hosts can be affirmed.[39] Although there were few Dominicans who expressed their views on the Wilsnack affair, many Franciscans, such as Matthias Döring, Johannes Kannemann, Johannes Brewer, and Giovanni Capistrano, defended the pilgrimage to Wilsnack. Döring became famous as an opponent of Tocke; Kannemann was a theology professor at Erfurt;[40] and Capistrano was widely known as one of the greatest preachers of the fifteenth century.[41]

Another aspect of the Wilsnack controversy that must be taken into consideration is the political and ecclesiastical conditions existing in the province at that time. It is quite easy to understand that Bishop Konrad von

---

36 Lehmann, "Aus dem Rapularius," p. 55.

37 Boockmann, "Der Streit um das Wilsnacker Blut," pp. 401-402. On the standpoints of the theological faculties, see Zika, "Hosts, Processions and Pilgrimages," p. 50; Rudolf Damerau, *Das Gutachten der Theologischen Fakultät Erfurt 1452 über 'Das heilige Blut von Wilsnak'* (Marburg, 1976).

38 On Thomas Aquinas's position, see *Thomae Aquinatis Opera Omnia*, vol. 5 (Paris, 1872), pp. 278-280 [Art. 2: *Utrum Christi corpus resurrexit integrum*, pp. 278-279; Art. 3: *Utrum Christi corpus resurrexit gloriosum*, pp. 279-280]. See also Meier, "Wilsnack als Spiegel," pp. 61-62; Zika, "Hosts, Processions and Pilgrimages," pp. 52-53.

39 Boockmann, "Der Streit um das Wilsnacker Blut," p. 398; Zika, "Hosts, Processions and Pilgrimages," p. 50.

40 See Livario Oliger, "Johannes Kannemann, ein deutscher Franziskaner des 15. Jahrhunderts," *Franziskanische Studien* 5 (1918): 44-50; Ludger Meier, "Der Erfurter Franziskaner-theologe J. Bremer und der Streit um das Wilsnacker Wunderblut," in *Aus der Geisteswelt des Mittelalters: Festschrift M. Grabmann* (Münster, 1935), pp. 53-69.

41 Johannes Hofer, *Johannes von Capestrano* (Innsbruck, 1936).

Lintorff of Havelberg (1427-1450) was, as a financial beneficiary of the pilgrimage, a supporter and protector of Wilsnack. But Archbishop Friedrich von Beichlingen of Magdeburg, whose jurisdiction included the diocese of Havelberg, was reform-minded and critical of the pilgrimage to Wilsnack. Together with Tocke and other theology professors, he saw the demise of the pilgrimage as a first step towards church reform. On the other hand, the Elector of Brandenburg, Friedrich II (1440-1470), who ruled over the whole region as a secular head, was sympathetic to Wilsnack and on friendly terms with Bishop Konrad of Havelberg. In fact, Konrad was chaplain to the elector.[42] It seems also quite logical that Döring, a Franciscan, became advisor to the elector from 1443.[43] Archbishop Friedrich of Magdeburg, who was anxious to bring about church reform in his region, also was interested in controlling not only Bishop Konrad of Havelberg, who tried to be independent of him financially and politically on the strength of incomes from Wilsnack, but also the mendicant orders within his archdiocese, especially the Franciscan order. But to the Elector of Brandenburg, Archbishop Friedrich was the principal obstacle to the territorialization of the church under his domains.[44]

As stated above, in order to appreciate the significance of the Wilsnack affair, it is important to understand not only the movements of pilgrims, but also the development of theological debates and the struggle of political and ecclesiastical groups and forces. Furthermore, due attention must be paid to the reform movements within the monasteries that were spreading, as a result of the Council of Constance (1414-1418), in the Benedictine monasteries of Melk and Bursfeld and the Augustinian monastery of Windesheim.[45] The pilgrimage to

---

[42] Bruno Hennig, "Kurfürst Friedrich und das Wunderblut zu Wilsnack," *Forschungen zu Brandenburgischen und Preussischen Geschichte* 19 (1906): 83 n. 3.

[43] On the elector, see Hennig, "Kurfürst Friedrich," pp. 73-104 (391-422). Also compare Boockmann, "Der Streit um das Wilsnacker Blut," p. 399; Zika, "Hosts, Processions and Pilgrimages," p. 51.

[44] Zika, "Hosts, Processions and Pilgrimages," p. 52.

[45] On Melk and Bursfeld, see Paulus Volk, *Urkunden zur Geschichte der Bursfelder Kongregation* (Bonn, 1951); Pius Engelbert, "Die Bursfelder Benediktinerkongregation und die spätmittelalterlichen Reformbewegungen," *Historisches Jahrbuch* 103 (1983): 35-55; Klaus Schreiner, "Benediktinische Klosterreform als zeitgebundene Auslegung der Regel: Geistige, religiöse und soziale Erneuerung in spätmittelalterlichen Klöstern Süddeutschlands im Zeichen der Kastler, Melker und Bursfelder Reform," *Beiträge zur westfälischen Kirchengeschichte* 86 (1986): 105-195. Windesheim is discussed in Wilhelm Kohl, "Die Windesheimer Kongregation," in *Reformbestrebungen und Observanzbestrebungen im spätmittelalterlichen Ordenswesen*, ed. Kaspar Elm (Berlin, 1989), pp. 83-106.

Wilsnack is a good example showing clearly how religious practices could be affected by the double weight of church reform and territorial expansion.[46]

III. Cusanus and the Pilgrimage to Wilsnack

What kind of attitude then did Cusanus take toward Wilsnack? In 1446 Pope Eugenius IV approved in a bull the veneration of the bleeding hosts at Wilsnack; and the next pope, Nicholas V, declared in September 1447 that he supported his predecessor's decision. It is against this background that the problem of Cusanus' encounter with the Wilsnack affair must be considered. As has already been pointed out, Heinrich Tocke, in the famous speech at the Provincial Synod of Magdeburg, which had begun on June 18, 1451, argued clearly that the veneration of bleeding hosts at Wilsnack was a deception. How did Cusanus react to Tocke's assertion?

It was believed until recently that the same synod lasted till June 28, 1451, when Cusanus left for the next stop, Halberstadt, and that during his stay in Magdeburg Cusanus did not visit Wilsnack. But in a recent article, and then in *Acta Cusana,* Erich Meuthen, after noting the lack of any extant material or document about Cusanus between June 22 and June 24, pointed out that he found testimonies by two Dutch historians about Cusanus' visit to Wilsnack.[47] As Meuthen said, it is quite possible that Cusanus left Magdeburg on June 21 to go to Wilsnack, which was merely about 82 miles away down the Elbe river.[48] Cornelius von Zandvliet (d. ca. 1461), one of the two Dutch historians Meuthen cited, wrote in 1451 that Cusanus was in Wilsnack as papal legate.[49] Adriaan von Oudenbosch (d. ca. 1482), the other Dutch historian, also confirmed Cusanus' presence at Wilsnack.[50] But it is important to remember that the relationship between Archbishop Frederick of Magdeburg and Bishop Konrad of Havelberg was not really friendly. This is indicated by the fact that, in 1451, when the archbishop summoned all his suffragan bishops to the Provincial Synod of Magdeburg, Bishop Konrad sent only his ambassador and did not appear in person.[51] In fact, they would, as was stated earlier, excommunicate each other in 1452. Did or could Cusanus visit Wilsnack in the diocese of

---

46 Zika, "Hosts, Processions and Pilgrimages," p. 52.

47 Meuthen, "Das Itinerar," pp. 484-485; *Acta Cusana*, 1/3.944-946, nos. 1401-1403.

48 Meuthen, "Das Itinerar," pp. 484-485.

49 *Acta Cusana*, 1/3.945, no. 1402.

50 Ibid., 1/3.945-946, no. 1403.

51 Gottfried Wentz, *Das Bistum Havelberg* (Der Germania Sacra, Erste Abt., Zweiter Band; Berlin, 1933), p. 54; *Acta Cusana*, 1/3.934, no. 1384.

Havelberg under these conditions without causing political and ecclesiastical repercussions? Although in all likelihood Cusanus was at Wilsnack in 1451, it would certainly be good to have more conclusive proof about his visit.

On June 25, 1451, probably after returning from Wilsnack, Cusanus issued seven decrees in Magdeburg,[52] and on June 26 and 28 one decree each;[53] but none of them had anything to do with the veneration of the bleeding hosts at Wilsnack. It was on July 5, shortly after arriving at the next stop, Halberstadt, that he issued a general decree prohibiting the veneration of bleeding hosts without, however, specifically mentioning Wilsnack. It is quite possible that as papal legate, he did not wish to contradict directly Pope Nicholas V's approval of Wilsnack in 1447. However, his decree was addressed to all archbishops, bishops, abbots, and other ecclesiastical officials in Germany, warning them that all those who exposed the bleeding hosts would be excommunicated, and that all territories where this practice continued would automatically incur interdict.[54] The reasons he mentioned were that, although the priests not only preached but also encouraged this practice because of the money it brought them, every occasion by which the unlettered are deceived must be removed.[55] It is quite clear that he was determined to carry out this decree, because he issued similar decrees in Hildesheim on July 12, in Minden on August 4, and in Mainz on November 20.[56]

Despite Cusanus' attempt to stop the pilgrimage to Wilsnack, it continued to expand and flourish. As a result, the archbishop of Magdeburg excommunicated the bishop of Havelberg on January 8, 1452 and placed Wilsnack under interdict. But, in turn, Bishop Konrad of Havelberg took the step

---

[52] Ibid., 1/3.947-957, nos. 1409, 1410, 1412, 1414, 1415, 1417, 1418.

[53] Ibid., 1/3.960-961, no. 1423; 962-963, no. 1428.

[54] Hennig, "Kurfürst Friedrich," p. 101 (419); Meier, "Wilsnack als Spiegel," p. 51; Sullivan, "Nicholas of Cusa as Reformer," p. 403; idem, "Cusanus and Pastoral Renewal," p. 173; Meuthen, "Die deutsche Legationsreise," p. 486; *Acta Cusana*, 1/3.980-981, no. 1454. According to Koch, this decree was the thirteenth decree published by Cusanus on the legation; see *Nikolaus von Cues und seine Umwelt* (Cusanus-Texte IV, Briefe, Sitzungsberichte der Heidelberger Akademie der Wissenschaften, Philosophisch-historische Klasse, Jhrg. 1944/48, 2. Abh.; Heidelberg, 1942), pp. 112, 125.

[55] Hennig, "Kurfürst Friedrich," p. 101; Sullivan, "Nicholas of Cusa as Reformer," pp. 403-404.

[56] Fliege, "Nikolaus von Kues," p. 63; Meuthen, "Der deutsche Legationsreise," p. 486. Despite the fact that Cusanus was critical of the pilgrimage to Wilsnack and elsewhere, he made an exception for Andechs; see Zika, "Hosts, Processions and Pilgrimages," p. 61 n. 116.

of declaring the archbishop of Magdeburg excommunicated.[57] It is quite clear that the struggle that ensued between the two ecclesiastical heads was not conducive to Cusanus' reform plans. In the meantime, the Elector Friedrich of Brandenburg went to Rome in 1453 to appeal to Pope Nicholas V; and Capistrano also sent a letter to the pope urging him to support Wilsnack. The pope issued on March 6, 1453 a decree in which he re-confirmed his decree of 1447, abrogated Cusanus' decree of July 5, 1451, lifted the excommunication of the archbishop of Magdeburg and the interdict placed on Magdeburg, and officially approved the continuation of the pilgrimage to Wilsnack.[58] Although Nicholas V and Cusanus were friends as humanists, the cardinal had no choice but to retreat in regard to the question of Wilsnack.

In the second half of the fifteenth century, Wilsnack reached its peak. According to some studies, it drew the largest number of pilgrims in Christendom.[59] But, after the Reformation, Martin Luther, in his "An Open Letter to the Christian Nobility of the German Nation," published in 1520, attacked Wilsnack, saying that the forest chapels and rustic churches to which the recent pilgrimages have been directed, such as Wilsnack, Sternberg, and Trier, must be utterly destroyed.[60] In 1552, Joachim Ellefeldt, the Protestant pastor, threw the hosts of Wilsnack into fire, thereby causing the pilgrimage to come to an end.[61] In 1906 a hot spring containing ferric-oxide was found by the town forester Zimmermann outside of Wilsnack. As a result, the name of the town was changed to Bad Wilsnack in 1929. But the church of Saint Nicholas, now a Protestant one, still stands in the middle of the town, which has a population of about 2,800.

Conclusion

During a legation that lasted one year and three months Nicolaus Cusanus observed directly the actual conditions in the German church shortly before the Reformation and tried to solve many problems. One of the most difficult was the veneration of the bleeding hosts in Wilsnack which had started about seventy years before. Despite critics like Heinrich Tocke and criticisms from the

---

57 Hennig, "Kurfürst Friedrich," p. 101; Meier, "Wilsnack als Spiegel," p. 58; Sullivan, "Nicholas of Cusa as Reformer," p. 404.

58 Sullivan, "Nicholas of Cusa as Reformer," p. 404; Zika, "Hosts, Processions and Pilgrimages," p. 52.

59 Hennig, "Kurfürst Friedrich," p. 102; Meier, "Wilsnack als Spiegel," p. 59.

60 *D. Martin Luthers Werke* (Weimar, 1888), 6.447.

61 Hennig, "Kurfürst Friedrich," p. 96; Meier, "Wilsnack als Spiegel," p. 61; Boockmann, "Der Streit um das Wilsnack Blut," p. 405; Zika, "Hosts, Processions and Pilgrimages," p. 50.

theological faculties of various universities, there was no sign that the cult would wane and decline. Its prosperity was based not only on the religious ignorance of especially medieval and uncultured people, but also on the manipulation and greed of some clergymen who took advantage of the psychological anxiety that existed among the simple, pious people. Furthermore, the problem was deeply related to a power struggle among the ecclesiastical and political leaders of the province who tried to expand their territorial and economic power and influence.

It is well known that ecclesiastical reform was widely recognized as necessary in the later Middle Ages and that, as a result, there were many reform movements within the churches and monasteries. It is clear that such developments and movements were strengthened by the conciliar movement that had started as a result of the Great Schism. For Cusanus, who participated in the Council of Basel as a supporter of the doctrine of conciliar supremacy but later switched to the pro-papal camp, the problem of ecclesiastical reform was one of the most important issues and tasks, as shown in his endeavors not only during his legation as papal legate, but also in the Tyrol after reaching Brixen[62] and in Orvieto and Rome towards the end of his life.[63]

But, like the reform proposals of other late medieval reformers, Cusanus' attempts to reform the church were essentially limited in nature and scope. Cusanus' legalism and inflexibility have often been mentioned as reasons for his failure as reformer. But reform did not mean anything really radical to him. It is quite clear that he tried to accomplish it within the existing framework of the medieval church. What he criticized and tried to correct within the church was degeneration or perversion, which was based on either lack of understanding the church's teachings or widespread superstition. As one commentator pointed out, on his legation Cusanus participated faithfully and diligently in the established practices and ceremonies of the church. The thirteen decrees he issued on the legation were almost all designed to effect a return to a rigorous but simple

---

[62] On Cusanus' attempts to reform in the Tyrol, see Nikolaus Grass, *Cusanus und das Volkstum der Berge* (Innsbruck, 1972); Morimichi Watanabe, "Nicholas of Cusa and the Tyrolese Monasteries: Reform and Resistance," *History of Political Thought* 7 (Spring 1986): 53-72.

[63] On Cusanus' reform at Orvieto, see Erich Meuthen, *Die letzten Jahre des Nikolaus von Kues: Biographische Untersuchungen nach neuen Quellen* (Köln, 1958), pp. 110-125, 249-300. Cusanus' attempt to reform the Roman Curia is discussed in Morimichi Watanabe, "Nicholas of Cusa and the Reform of the Roman Curia," in *Humanity and Divinity in Renaissance and Reformation: Essays in Honor of Charles Trinkaus*, ed. John O'Malley, Thomas M. Izbicki and Gerald Christianson (Leiden, 1993), pp. 185-203; Watanabe and Izbicki, "Nicholas of Cusa: A General Reform," pp. 175-202.

spirituality in harmony with the teachings of the church. "Cusanus remained firmly rooted in the conservative hierarchical tradition of medieval renewal."[64]

When this "restorative" reform attempt was not strongly supported or even was rejected by the pope, who was reluctant to carry on his own program strongly, Cusanus certainly was not able to become "a reformer before the Reformation."[65] The Reformation required a Martin Luther who, reluctant as he was at the beginning, began to go beyond the existing institutions of the church and criticized them strongly.

---

64 Sullivan, "Cusanus and Pastoral Renewal," p. 174.

65 See Carl Ullmann, *Reformatoren vor der Reformation,* 2nd ed., 2 vols. (Gotha, 1866). The author has argued for the "restorative" nature of Cusanus' reform ideas in Watanabe, "Nicholas of Cusa and the Reform of the Roman Curia," pp. 201-203; idem, "Some Problems on the Study of Nicholas of Cusa as Church Reformer [in Japanese]," *Kuzanusu Kenkyu* [Cusanus Studies] 1 (1991): 32-50.

Nicholas of Cusa and the Tyrolese Monasteries: Reform and Resistance

Nicholas of Cusa (1401-64) is known in the history of political thought as an advocate of the conciliar movement. In his classic work, *Studies of Political Thought from Gerson to Grotius, 1414-1625,* John Neville Figgis stated that a brief account of the *De concordantia catholica,* Cusanus' major work on ecclesiastical and political thought, would give the best exposition of the ideals of the conciliar movement.[1] Among textbook writers, Charles H. McIlwain, George H. Sabine, Lee Cameron McDonald and Mulford Q. Sibley dealt with Cusanus and his political ideas.[2] His fame outside the field of political thought is even greater. To Ernst Cassirer it was clear that any "study that seeks to view the philosophy of the Renaissance as a systematic unity must take as its point of departure the doctrines of Nicholas Cusanus."[3] One of the best known modern Catholic church historians, Hubert Jedin, stated: "Nicholas's *Concordantia catholica,* completed in 1433, is the most original product of the conciliar theory in the period that concerns us."[4]

Cusanus' political thought was discussed before World War II by commentators such as K. Gottfried Hugelmann, E.F. Jacob, Andreas Posch and Gerhard Kallen.[5] The modern edition of the first book of the *De concordantia*

---

[1] John N. Figgis, *Studies of Political Thought from Gerson to Grotius, 1414-1625,* 2nd ed. (Cambridge, 1923), p. 52.

[2] Charles H. McIlwain, *The Growth of Political Thought in the West from the Greeks to the End of the Middle Ages* (New York, 1932), pp. 286, 338, 348-50; George H. Sabine, *A History of Political Theory,* 3rd ed. (New York, 1937), pp. 316, 318-19, 440; Lee C. McDonald, *Western Political Theory: From its Origins to the Present* (New York, 1968), pp. 182-7; Mulford Q. Sibley, *Political Ideas and Ideologies: A History of Political Thought* (New York, 1970), pp. 280-84.

[3] Ernst Cassirer, *The Individual and the Cosmos in Renaissance Philosophy,* trans. Mario Domandi (New York, 1963), p. 7.

[4] Hubert Jedin, *A History of the Council of Trent,* trans. Ernest Graf (London, 1957), vol. I, p. 22.

[5] K. Gottfried Hugelmann, "Der Reichsgedanke bei Nikolaus von Kues," in *Reich und Recht in der deutschen Philosophie,* ed. Karl Larenz (Stuttgart, 1943), vol. 1, pp. 1-32; E.F. Jacob, "Nicolas of Cusa," in *The Social and Political Ideas of Some Great Thinkers of the Renaissance and the Reformation,* ed. F.J.C. Hearnshaw (New York, 1925), pp. 32-60; Andreas Posch, *Die "Concordantia catholica" des Nikolaus von*

catholica was published in 1939 and its second book in 1941 by Gerhard Kallen.[6] After the complete loss of these editions due to war damage, the indefatigable editor completed Book III in 1959 and then published a revised edition of Books I and II in 1964 and 1965.[7] During the decade after the end of World War II, interest in Cusanus and his ideas steadily grew and the number of Cusanus studies increased rapidly.[8] Partly encouraged by the appearance of Kallen's editions, and partly because of the then forthcoming five-hundredth anniversary of Cusanus' death, three full-length studies of his political and ecclesiological ideas were published in the late 1950s and early 1960s.[9] Two recent, notable studies of Cusanus' political ideas are somewhat limited in scope.[10] What we need now is a comprehensive study of his political and ecclesiological thought which is solidly based on the impressive results of Cusanus studies in the last twenty years.

The present paper is intended as a modest contribution to Cusanus studies. Its purpose is to discuss how Cusanus tried to initiate church reform in the Tyrol after he took office as Bishop of Brixen in 1452, to examine his reform attempts at Neustift and Stams that have received less attention than those famous reforms

Cusa (Paderborn, 1930); Gerhard Kallen, "Der Reichsgedanke der Reformschrift *De concordantia catholica* des Nikolaus von Cues," *Neue Heidelberger Jahrbucher*, N. F. (1940), pp. 59-60; Gerhard Kallen, "Die politische Theorie im philosophischen System des Nikolaus von Cues," *Historische Zeitschrift*, CLXV (1942), pp. 246-77.

[6] *Nicolai de Cusa Opera omnia*, vol. 14, *De concordantia catholica*, ed. Gerhard Kallen, Book I (Leipzig, 1939); Book II (Leipzig, 1941).

[7] Ibid., Book I (Hamburg, 2nd ed., 1964); Book II (Hamburg, 2nd ed., 1965); Book III (Hamburg, 1959). An index to the three books, *Indices,* ed. Gerhard Kallen and Anna Berger (Hamburg, 1968), has also been published.

[8] The literature on Cusanus published since the end of World War II is extensive. For a convenient bibliography, see the *Mitteilungen and Forschungsbeiträge des Cusanus-Gesellschaft* (hereafter *MFCG*), I (1961), pp. 95-126; III (1963), pp. 223-37; VI (1967), pp. 178-202; X (1973), pp. 207-34; XV (1982), pp. 121-47.

[9] Gerd Heinz-Mohr, *Unitas Christiana: Studien zur Gesellschaftsidee des Nikolaus von Kues* (Trier, 1958); Paul E. Sigmund, *Nicholas of Cusa and Medieval Political Thought* (Cambridge, Mass., 1963); Morimichi Watanabe, *The Political Ideas of Nicholas of Cusa, with Special Reference to his De concordantia catholica* (Geneva, 1963).

[10] Arnulf Vagades, *Das Konzil über dem Papst? Die Stellungnahmen des Nikolaus von Kues und des Panormitanus zum Streit zwischen dem Konzil von Basel und Eugen IV,* 2 vol. (Paderborn, 1981); Hermann J. Sieben, "Der Konzilstraktat des Nikolaus von Kues: *De concordantia catholica,*" *Annuarium Historiae Conciliorum*, XIV (1982), pp. 171-226.

and related events at Brixen, Bruneck, Enneberg, Sonnenburg and Wilten[11] and to offer some reflections and assessments on Cusanus as theorist, administrator and reformer. Cusanus' idea of reform was clearly manifested in the *De concordantia catholica*, which he presented to the Council of Basel (1431-49) in 1433.[12] During the course of his famous legatine journey of Germany and the Low Countries in 1450-52, he put into practice his idea of church reform in many places and attempted to impose reform measures with the help of excommunications and interdicts. The journey was viewed by some of his contemporaries and later historians as a success, but recent historians' appraisals have become much more cautious and critical than earlier ones.[13]

In order to understand the nature of Cusanus' episcopate in the Tyrol, we must examine briefly how he was made Bishop of Brixen. When the news arrived in Rome that Bishop Johann Röttel of Brixen (1443-50) had died on 28 February 1450, the humanist Pope Nicholas V (1447-55), a close friend of Cusanus, decided that Cardinal Cusanus should become Röttel's successor.[14] No

[11] On Bruneck, see Albert Jäger, *Der Streit des Cardinals Nikolaus von Cusa mit dem Herzoge Sigmund von Österreich als Grafen van Tirol* (Innsbruck, 1861, reprinted Frankfurt am Main, 1968), vol. I, pp. 5-52; Hans Hörtnagl, "Der Brunecker Überfall des Herzogs Sigmund und sein Ritt an die Etsch zu Ostern 1460," *Der Schlern*, VII (1926), pp. 467-70 Erich Meuthen, *Nikolaus von Kues, 1401-1464: Skizze einer Biographie*, 3rd ed. (Münster, 1976), pp. 103-6. The events at and after Enneberg are discussed in Jäger, *Streit*, vol. II, pp. 261-96; Hermann Hallauer, *Die Schlacht in Enneberg: Neue Quellen für moralischen Wertung des Nikolaus von Kues* (Trier, 1969); Meuthen, *Nikolaus von Kues*, pp. 112-14. For the literature on events at Brixen, Sonnenburg and Wilten, see notes 22, 24 and 30 below.

[12] See Sigmund, *Nicholas of Cusa,* especially pp. 158-87; Watanabe, *The Political Ideas,* especially pp. 79-97; Meuthen, *Nikolaus von Kues,* especially pp. 39-42.

[13] On Cusanus' legatine journey, see Karl Grube, "Die Legationsreise des Cardinals Nikolaus von Cusa durch Norddeutschland im Jahre 1451," *Historisches Jahrbuch*, I (1880), pp. 393-412; Johann Uebinger, "Kardinallegat Nikolaus Cusanus in Deutschland 1451 his 1452," *Historisches Jahrbuch*, Vlll (1887), pp. 629-65; Ignaz Zibermayr, *Die Legation des Cardinals Nicolaus Cusanus und die Ordensreform in der Kirchenprovinz Salzburg* (Münster, 1914); Josef Koch, *Der deutsche Kardinal in deutschen Landen: Die Legationsreise des Nikolaus van Kues (1451/1452)* (Trier, 1964); Donald Sullivan, "Nicholas of Cusa as Reformer: The Papal Legation to the Germanies, 1451-1452," *Mediaeval Studies*, XXXVI (1974), pp. 382-428. Cf. Henry Bett, *Nicholas of Cusa* (London, 1932), pp. 41-8.

[14] On the appointment of Cusanus as Bishop of Brixen, see Pardon E. Tillinghast, "Nicholas of Cusa vs. Sigmund of Habsburg: an Attempt at Post-Conciliar Church Reform," *Church History*, XXXVI (1967), pp. 372-75; Meuthen, *Nikolaus von Kues,* pp. 94-6; Wilhelm Baum, "Nikolaus Cusanus und Leonhard Wiesmair: Der Kardinal und sein Gegenspieler: Kanzler von Tirol und Bischof von Chur," *Der Schlern*, LVII (1983), pp. 433-34.

one seemed a better choice to the pope than Cusanus because the learned German was well known and respected as an author and philosopher and also because, as a strong papalist since his defection from the conciliar movement in 1437, he would administer the diocese well and defend its independence and prerogatives from the process of secularization to which it had been subjected for over one hundred years. It is well to remember that bishops in the Empire were not merely ecclesiastical princes but were territorial rulers with full power and political rights of secular princes. As a result, most of the bishoprics were also territorial principalities. The Bishop of Brixen's domain was thus an ecclesiastical principality directly subject to the Emperor in temporal matters.

The papal provision of Cusanus to the see of Brixen on 23 March 1450 immediately encountered opposition because a three-man committee set up by the cathedral chapter of Brixen had already on 14 March 1450 elected[15] Leonhard Wismayer, one of its members and the chancellor of Sigismund, the Archduke of Austria and Count of the Tyrol (1446-96), and requested papal confirmation. The right of the cathedral canons to elect a bishop was not only based on ancient custom, but had also been confirmed in the decrees of the Councils of Constance (1414-18) and Basel and thereafter in the Concordat of Vienna, which Cusanus himself had signed on 17 February 1448 as one of its negotiators.[16] To be sure, Pope Nicholas V resorted to "an escape clause" in the Concordat of Vienna which allowed him, even after a valid election, to appoint a "more worthy and more useful" person.[17] But it was clear that the use of the pope's prerogative was not welcome to a proud Tyrolese people who cherished their independence. They were willing to challenge "a case of papal interference with German rights" by appealing to their secular ruler, Duke Sigismund.

When Cusanus entered his diocese at Easter 1452 after a two-year legation journey, he came to a duchy where the influence of the secular ruler was strong and, because of local opposition to his appointment, its cathedral chapter was by no means friendly. During his eight-year episcopate from 1452 to 1460,[18]

[15] Pope Nicholas V indicated in his bull of 31 October 1450 that the election was uncanonical because the three canons were said to have chosen Wismayer in Duke Sigismund's house which was surrounded by armed men. See Baum, "Nikolaus Cusanus," p. 434.

[16] On the Concordat of Vienna, see John B. Toews, 'Pope Eugenius IV and the Concordat of Vienna—An Interpretation," *Church History,* XXXIV (1965), pp. 178-84; Meuthen, *Nikolaus von Kues,* pp. 73-6. An English translation of the text is found in *Church and State Through the Centuries,* ed. and trans. Sidney Z. Ehler and John B. Morrall (Westminster, Maryland, 1954), pp. 126-31.

[17] Tillinghast, "Nicholas of Cusa," p. 374.

[18] Strictly speaking, Cusanus was Bishop of Brixen from 1450 to 1464. Although he was made Bishop on 23 March 1450 by Pope Nicholas V, he did not take office until

Cusanus' main interest was church reform in general and reform of the monasteries and convents in particular. He used as his model the observances of the monasteries of Windesheim, Raudnitz, Bursfeld, Tegernsee and Melk that were widely known as good examples of reformed monasteries. The chief methods he used in carrying out his objectives were diocesan synods, sermons, visitations and the threat and use of excommunications and interdicts.

While in residence in the Tyrol as Bishop of Brixen, Cusanus held diocesan synods four times—in 1453, 1454, 1455 and 1457. At these synods, he issued detailed ordinances about the dismissal of concubines, the pilgrimages to shrines, the use of a standard missal, the prohibition of card playing and consumption of dairy products during Lent and many other matters in order to reform the secular clergy of the Tyrol.[19] Wherever he went, he also preached. A contemporary recorded one hundred and thirty sermons by him during the eight-year period.[20] But his greatest attention was directed to the visitation and reform of the religious houses. He was hardly one week in Brixen, when he went to the abbey of Augustinian Canons at nearby Neustift. On 23 to 26 May he visited the Premonstratensian house in Wilten near Innsbruck, and he was guest at the wealthy Cistercian abbey of Stams on 29 to 30 May 1452. After returning from the Imperial Diet of 1454 in Regensburg,[21] which was called because of the fall of Constantinople to the Turks, he stayed on 26 to 30 August at the Collegial Stift in Innichen. Shortly thereafter, he began his efforts to reform the Franciscan convent of St. Clare in Brixen[22] and the Benedictine monastery of St.

Easter 1452. On 4 July 1457 he left the episcopal city of Brixen for Castle Andraz, never to return. Shortly after his coronation in August 1458, Pope Pius II called Cusanus to Rome. From 7 February to 27 April 1460 he was back in his diocese and then returned to Rome. Cusanus' itinerary between 1452 and 1460 is found in Georg Mutschlechner, "Itinerar des Nikolaus von Kues für den Aufenthalt in Tirol" in *Cusanus Gedächtnisschrift,* ed. Nikolaus Grass (Innsbruck/Munich, 1970) (hereafter *CG*), pp. 525-34.

[19] Anselm Sparber, "Vom Wirken des Kardinals Nikolaus von Cues als Fürstbischof von Brixen (1450-1464)," *Veröffentlichungen des Museums Ferdinandeum,* XXVII/XXIX (1947/49), p. 353; Tillinghast, "Nicholas of Cusa," p. 381; Wilhelm Baum, *Nikolaus Cusanus in Tirol: Das Wirken des Philosophen und Reformators als Fürstbischof von Brixen* (Bozen, 1983), p. 157.

[20] Jäger, *Streit,* p. 42 n. 2; Sparber, "Vom Wirken," p. 350 n. 4; Tillinghast, "Nicholas of Cusa," p. 381 n. 32.

[21] About Cusanus at the Imperial Diet of Regensburg in 1454, see Erich Meuthen, "Nikolaus von Kues auf dem Regensburger Reichstag 1454," *Festschrift für Hermann Heimpel,* ed. Mitarbeiter des Max Planck Instituts für Geschichte (Göttingen, 1972), Vol. 11, pp. 482-99.

[22] On the Clarissines in Brixen and Cusanus, see Luchesius Spätling, "Das Klarissenkloster in Brixen," *Franziskanische Studien,* XXXVII (1955), pp. 365-88;

Georgenberg.[23] The most famous, dreary and lengthy cloister reform in the Tyrol which he had already begun in 1452 was at the Benedictine convent of Sonnenburg, which has been described and discussed by many historians and commentators.[24]

In general, Cusanus' reform efforts were fairly successful when the interests of the secular ruler were not affected or challenged. The reform of the Clarissines in Brixen, the canons in Innichen and the hermits in Halltal[25] are all cases in point. But when Duke Sigismund or the Emperor Friedrich III (1452-93) was not sympathetic to Cusanus' efforts, his attempts to reform monasteries and convents resulted in opposition, defeat and failure. This is what he experienced in St. Georgenberg, Sonnenburg, Neustift, Stams and Wilten.

Cusanus' first failure to reform a Tyrolese monastery occurred at the Benedictine monastery of St. Georgenberg when in April 1454 a visitation of the monastery by Prior Bernhard von Waging and Brother Konrad von Geisenfeld of Tegernsee encountered strong opposition from Johannes II von Freiberg (1451-69), the abbot of the monastery.[26] Confronted by reluctant, resisting abbot and monks Cusanus began to use another method of reform, excommunication and interdict. In the meantime, after many futile attempts to reform the convent of Sonnenburg, Cusanus' attitude towards Abbess Verena von Stuben

Hermann Hallauer, "Nikolaus von Kues und das Brixener Klarissenkloster," *MFCG*, Vl (1967), pp. 75-103. Cusanus' attempt to reform the cathedral chapter of Brixen will not be discussed in this paper. See, for example, Baum, *Nikolaus Cusanus*, pp. 223-37.

[23] On St. Georgenberg, see Pirmin Pockstaller, *Chronik der Benediktinerabtei St. Georgenberg nun Fiecht in Tirol* (Innsbruck, 1874); Hans Bachmann, "Die Benediktinerabtei St. Georgenberg im Kulturleben des Mittelalters," *Tiroler Heimat*, XVI (1952), pp. 33-101; Maurus Kramer, *Geschichte der Benediktinerabtei St. Georgenberg*, 2nd ed. (St. Ottilien, 1977). For a recent assessment of Cusanus' reform at St. Georgenberg, see Wilhelm Baum and Karl Rauter, "Bernhard von Waging (+1472): 'Klagelieder über St. Georgenberg': Das Scheitern einer Klosterreform des Nikolaus Cusanus (1453/54)," *Der Schlern*, LVII (1983), pp. 482-94.

[24] To mention only recent studies, Hermann Hallauer, "Eine Visitation des Nikolaus von Kues im Benediktinerinnenkloster Sonnenburg," *MFCG*, IV (1964), pp. 104-25; Tillinghast, "Nicholas of Cusa," pp. 382-83; Kolumban Spahr, "Nikolaus von Cues, das adelige Frauenstift Sonnenburg OSB und die mittelalterliche Nonnenklausur," *CG*, pp. 307-26.

[25] On the hermits in Halltal, see Jäger, *Streit*, vol. 1, pp. 62-4; Gerold Fussenegger, "Nikolaus von Kues und die Waldschwestern in Halltal," *CG*, pp. 381-427. On Innichen, see Karl Wolfsgruber, "Besetzingsrecht für Propstei und Dekanat des Kollegialkapitels in Innichen bis 1785," *Der Schlern*, XLIII (1969), pp. 423-31; Karl Wolfsgruber, "Das Stift Innichen," in *Beiträge zur Geschichte Tirols* (Innsbruck, 1971), pp. 63-72.

[26] Baum, *Nikolaus Cusanus*, p. 141.

hardened. On 30 April 1455, he signed the excommunication of the Abbess in Brixen in the presence of his secretaries, Heinrich Pomert, Peter von Erkelenz and Heinrich Soetern. Sonnenburg was then placed under interdict on 4 September 1455.[27] Furthermore, on 23 March 1456, Cusanus excommunicated Prior Kaspar Aigner (1449-1467) of Neustift, with whom he had been on good terms since the beginning of his episcopate.[28] Over the question of the monastic independence from the bishop's control, Cusanus and Abbot Georg Ried (1436-1481) of Stams began to disagree, and the Abbot was finally excommunicated in May 1457.[29] The so-called Wilten Affair,[30] which took place on the night of 26 to 27 June 1457, showed that the Premonstratensian house was no haven for the Bishop of Brixen and was far more subject to the influence and might of Duke Sigismund than the religious zeal of Bishop Cusanus. Never feeling safe in his episcopal town of Brixen after the Wilten Affair, Cusanus fled in July 1457 to the castle of Andraz in Buchenstein, which was in a remote, southeastern region of the Tyrol and from which he could easily go to Venice.[31]

To appreciate the reasons for his failure to reform Tyrolese religious communities, it is important to remember that Cusanus made his unremitting efforts in an area which was by no means hostile to the idea of reform. At the Council of Constance, where the reform of the religious orders was discussed and measures for that purpose were adopted, the conciliar ideas of Heinrich von Langenstein (1325-1397), the noted theologian of Vienna, had great influence along with those of Jean Gerson (1363-1429), Chancellor of the University of Paris and prominent theologian.[32] Already in 1418 Duke Albrecht V of Austria (Albrecht II as King of the Romans, 1438-1439) carried out a reform of Melk with the support of the pope and the council.[33] It is therefore not surprising that

---

[27] Ibid., pp. 181-84.

[28] Jäger, *Streit,* vol. I, pp. 189-90, vol. II, p. 209; Baum, *Nikolaus Cusanus,* pp. 103, 443.

[29] Baum, *Nikolaus Cusanus,* p. 152.

[30] Jäger, *Streit,* vol. II, pp. 209-18; Bett, *Nicholas,* pp. 61-63; Hans Lentze, "Nikolaus von Cues und die Reform des Stiftes Wilten," *Veröffentlichungen des Museums Ferdinandeum,* XXXI (1951), pp. 501-27, reprinted in Hans (Hermann) Lentze, *Studia Wiltensia: Studien zur Geschichte des Stiftes Wilten* (Innsbruck, 1964), pp. 73-94; Tillinghast, "Nicholas of Cusa," pp. 85-86.

[31] Jäger, *Streit,* vol. II, p. 219; Nikolaus Grass, "Cusanus als Rechtshistoriker, Quellenkritiker und Jurist: Skizzen und Fragmente," *CG,* pp. 193-98; Georg Mutschlechner, "Die Burg Andraz in Buchenstein," *CG,* pp. 279-88.

[32] Tillinghast, "Nicholas of Cusa," p. 372; Baum, *Nikolaus Cusanus,* p. 59.

[33] See Gerda Koller, *Princeps in Ecclesia: Untersuchungen zur Kirchenpolitik Herzog Albrechts V. von Österreich* (Vienna, 1964).

during the Council of Basel almost the whole of Austria supported the conciliar party. The learned theologian Thomas Ebendorfer von Haselbach (1388-1464) of the University of Vienna represented the University at the council and made friends with Cusanus.[34] It was men like Ebendorfer who spread conciliar ideas and strengthened the idea of reform in the Habsburg lands. Thus Cusanus was in no way introducing a new concept or idea to the Tyrol when he embarked on his systematic programme of monastic reform. There was in fact great need for monastic reform in the region because monastic standards had fallen and laxity was widespread.

We must also remember that Cusanus was duly empowered to reform not only the secular clergy and the monks and nuns but also members of the mendicant orders. It can be said that his reform programme really began during his legatine journey when he issued a decree in Salzburg on 8 February 1451.[35] It ordered that members of all orders restore the rules of respective order within a year on pain of loss of their privileges and rights. Since the bishopric of Brixen was suffragan of the archbishopric of Salzburg, the decree was binding upon Brixen. But the decree did not extend to members of the mendicant orders, which traditionally and historically enjoyed special papal privileges and were exempt from episcopal jurisdiction.[36] When Cusanus attempted to reform the mendicant orders at the provincial synods of Mainz and Cologne in 1451 and 1452 respectively, the mendicants complained to the pope about his interference.[37]

In the Tyrol, Cusanus was better prepared than before. Having established elaborate ordinances at his first diocesan synod of 1453 in Brixen, he went to Rome in March 1453 to report on his legatine journey of 1450-1452 to Pope Nicholas V. On 12 May 1453 the friendly pope issued a bull "Inter cetera" which granted Cusanus comprehensive privileges to reform the religious houses of Wilten, Stams, Neustift, Sonnenburg, St. Georgenberg and the Clarissines in Brixen.[38] These were the religious communities in the diocese which had taken no notice of the decree of 8 February 1451, issued in Salzburg, although

---

[34] On Ebendorfer as conciliarist, see Alphons Lhotsky, *Thomas Ebendorfer, ein österreichischer Geschichtsschreiber, Theologe und Diplomat des 15. Jahrhunderts* (Stuttgart, 1957); W. Jaroschka, "Thomas Ebendorfer als Theoretiker des Konziliarismus," *Mitteilungen des Instituts für Österreichische Geschichtsforschung,* VII (1963), pp. 67-98.

[35] Baum, *Nikolaus Cusanus,* p. 92.

[36] Karl Bihlmeyer, *Church History,* ed. Hermann Tuchle, vol. II: *The Middle Ages,* trans. Victor E. Mills and Francis J. Muller (Westminster, Maryland, 1963), p. 289.

[37] Baum, *Nikolaus Cusanus,* p. 97.

[38] Jäger, *Streit,* vol. I, pp. 81-82; Baum, *Nikolaus Cusanus,* pp. 122, 155.

Cusanus had a copy posted on the doors of the cathedral in Brixen upon his entry into the diocese.

But despite the prevalence of conciliar and reform ideas in the region and the possession of ample powers by Cusanus to engage in reform activities, there were several countervailing factors which made his reform attempts difficult and unwelcome. First of all, he was seen by many people in the Tyrol as an "unwelcome outsider." Born in Kues in the Rhineland, he was after all someone who did not really belong to the Tyrol despite his high office as a cardinal and Bishop of Brixen. "In the Tyrol," one commentator wrote, "he had to deal with a stiff-necked mountain people, accustomed to their own ways and extremely suspicious of outsiders."[39] To make the matter worse, his background was merely bourgeois, the fact which made noble members of monasteries and convents reluctant to accept him as a reformer.[40] Because of his bourgeois origins and his interest in lay participation in the affairs of the Church, Cusanus encouraged laymen to take a more active part than before in the management of ecclesiastical matters.[41] But the proud sons and daughters of the Tyrolese nobility who constituted the bulk of the members of monasteries and convents in the area were not sympathetic to a bourgeois Rhinelander who attempted to reform their religious houses. It has been noted that his attempt at reform met with especially strong resistance from the aristocratic nuns of the Tyrol.[42]

If Cusanus' local origin and his social background were factors that made his reform endeavours difficult and unsuccessful, the way in which he wanted to enforce rules and ordinances strictly and rigorously and the methods which he used to counteract opposition vigorously are no doubt far more important as factors contributing to his difficulties in the Tyrol. Much has already been written about this point.[43] It cannot be denied that in responding to the reluctant,

[39] Tillinghast, "Nicholas of Cusa," p. 371; Anselm Sparber, *Die Bishofsstadt Brixen in ihrer geschichtlichen Entwicklung,* 2nd ed. (Brixen, 1962), p. 42, where Sparber calls Cusanus an "Eindringling"; Nikolaus Grass, *Cusanus und das Volkstum der Berge* (Innsbruck, 1972), pp. 100-105: "Er war landfremd, ein 'Zugereister,' wie man in Tirol abschatzig sags, und war daher der Sitten, Gebrauche und Meinungen des Landes wenig kundig" (p. 100).

[40] It is well known that the German high clergy and members of the monastic orders were often of noble background. Bihlmeyer, *Church History,* Vol. II, pp. 206, 224.

[41] On Cusanus and laymen, see Erich Meuthen, "Nikolaus von Kues und der Laie in der Kirche: Biographische Ausgangspunkte," *Historisches Jahrbuch,* LXXXI (1962), pp. 101-22; Meuthen, *Nikolaus von Kues,* pp. 69-72, 88-89.

[42] Baum, *Nikolaus Cusanus,* pp. 93, 121.

[43] Edmond Vansteenberghe, *Le cardinal Nicolas de Cues (1401-1464): L'action-la pensée* (Paris, 1920, reprinted Frankfurt am Main, 1963), pp. 140-211; Sparber, *Die Bischofsstadt,* p. 43; *Akten zur Reform des Bistums Brixen* (Cusanus-Texte, V.,

resisting and critical monks and nuns, Cusanus was often impatient and pettifogging and was willing to take the harshest measures, including excommunication and interdict, many times. His attitude seems to have been that since the channels of authority had been established, he could not brook any resistance and compromise.

A good example to illustrate his willingness to use harsh measures is the case of the abbey of Augustinian Canons at Neustift, which was briefly mentioned above. From the beginning of his episcopate in Brixen, Cusanus' relationship with the nearby monastery and with its Prior Kaspar Aigner was cordial and friendly. Cusanus had made acquaintance with the prior at the Council of Basel. He visited the monastery often, preached monastic reform there many times, invited all the canons of Neustift to Brixen for a feast on Palm Sunday in 1454 and established friendly relations between the monasteries of Tegernsee and Neustift in October 1454.[44] In no other monastery in the Tyrol did the cardinal stay more often than he did at Neustift. As a result, the friendship between the bishop and the prior deepened, and the prior strongly supported Cusanus' reform measures in the Tyrol. On 3 May 1455, for example, the bishop asked the prior to become a member of the visitation team to Wilten and later in the same year entrusted the prior with the task of examining liturgical books for the clergy in Eisacktal.[45] This seems to show that Cusanus did not see anything very objectionable in the religious life of Neustift under Prior Aigner and that the abbey was one of the most favoured Tyrolese religious communities in the eyes of the bishop.

But their differences began to show in the early months of 1456. They arose as a result of the bishop's attempt to conduct a visitation of the abbey. After the first visitation of 11 December 1454, about which we have little information, Cusanus decided to conduct a second visitation of Neustift early in 1456. When it became clear that the bishop was serious about the visitation, the prior wished to alienate neither Cusanus nor Duke Sigismund, who was the protector (*Schutzvogt*) of the abbey. When the distressed prior eventually turned to the duke for help, Cusanus was indignant. Having summoned the prior to Brixen on 23 March 1456, he accused the prior of ingratitude and treachery. The

Brixener Dokumente, 1. Sammlung), ed. Heinz Hurten (Heidelberg, 1960), p. 64: "Der erste und starkste Eindruck, den der Leser . . . von der Persönlichkeit des Kardinals und seiner Tätigkeit in Brixen empfangt, ist der einer grosser und strengen Härte, die auf strikte Einhaltung des vom Gesetz Geforderten bedacht ist."

[44] Hermann Hallauer, "Nikolaus von Kues und das Chorherrenstift Neustift," in *Festschrift Nikolaus Grass zum 60. Geburtstag dargebracht von Fachgenossen, Freunden und Schülern*, ed. Louis Carlen and Fritz Steinegger (Innsbruck/Munich, 1974), vol. I, pp. 309-23; Baum, *Nikolaus Cusanus*, p. 101.

[45] Hallauer, "Nikolaus von Kues und das Chorherrenstift," p. 310; Baum, *Nikolaus Cusanus*, p. 100.

prior, who was probably Cusanus' best friend in the Tyrol, was automatically
excommunicated the same day. But the prior did not quite understand the extent
to which the bishop was hurt and enraged. When he celebrated mass at the altar
the following day, a messenger arrived from Brixen to deliver the bishop's hand-
written letter, which warned the prior against celebrating mass because he was
under the ban of the Church. Utterly shaken, the prior attempted to seek
mediation and reconciliation with the help of Duke Sigismund, but in vain.

The relationship between Cusanus and Neustift worsened over the
ownership of the mines in Villanders, which the abbey had inherited from its
founder Reginbert van Säben (d. 1155) and Arnold van Morit (d. 1170), and also
over the mines of Fursil near Colle S. Lucia in Buchenstein, which the abbey
had leased after 1177 to Jakob Guadagnini Avoscano, lord of Buchenstein. In a
memorandum on the legal history of Buchenstein, which he composed on 16
October 1456, [46] Cusanus advanced the view, citing numerous documents in the
diocesan archives, that the German king had conferred on the Bishop of Brixen
well before 1177 prerogatives to the mines within the entire area of the
bishopric, and that as a result the Bishop of Brixen had jurisdiction over the
mines in Fursil. Prior Aigner acceded to Cusanus' demand and accepted the
suzerainty of the bishop over Fursil without any limitation. He seems to have
given way to Cusanus. But towards the end of 1456 the prior obtained from the
Paduan professors Angelo de Castro and Laurencius de Palazolis a legal opinion
which supported the abbey's claims. At the same time, in another matter, when
the Republic of Venice attempted to lessen the rights of the abbey in the region,
the prior appealed to the emperor in January 1457, a move which Cusanus also
supported. Thus Cusanus and the prior were apparently on talking terms even
early in 1457. But the visitation of Neustift finally began in May 1457 under the
supervision of Prior Nicholas of St. Dorothea in Vienna and resulted on 18 July
1457 in the adoption of the Reformcharta, which brought to the abbey a *plenam
et perfectam observanciam* and remained in effect till 1941. [47]

Cusanus' social origin and his rigorous, harsh enforcement of decrees and
ordinances were no doubt important reasons for his dismal record as a reformer in
the Tyrol. But in the last analysis there was a more decisive factor which affected
his attempts at church reform in the region: his defence of the rights of the
Church against secular rulers, especially against Duke Sigismund's encroachments on the privileges of the see. It was Cusanus' "politics of restitution"
which caused most of his troubles in the Tyrol. Cusanus wanted to restore the
rights and privileges of the bishopric and reverse the tide of secular encroach-

---

[46] Hallauer, "Nikolaus van Kues und das Chorherrenstift," p. 311; Baum, *Nikolaus
Cusanus*, p. 101.

[47] Hallauer, "Nikolaus von Kues und das Chorherrenstift," p. 315, Baum, *Nikolaus
Cusanus*, pp. 103-4.

ment. Sigismund, on his part, resented Cusanus' moves because he believed that Cusanus' diplomatic connections, especially with the papacy, were threatening the independence of his duchy.

To understand Cusanus' politics of restitution, we must at least take a brief look at the political and ecclesiastical history of the Tyrol in the fourteenth and fifteenth centuries.[48] In the Tyrol the process of secular encroachment on church privileges had been growing steadily for over a century. The Austrian duchies had been kept together by the House of Habsburg until a family quarrel in 1411 ended in the separation of Austria from the other duchies of Carinthia and the Tyrol. Albrecht V (1397-1439) ruled Austria; Ernst I (1377-1424), his cousin, ruled Styria, Carinthia and Carniola; and Friedrich IV (1382-1439), another cousin, ruled the Tyrol. Friedrich, Duke Sigismund's father, had succeeded in controlling the League of Elephants (*Elefantenbund*), to which some of the most powerful nobles, such as Counts Matsch and Wolkenstein, belonged, and the League of Falcons (*Falkenbund*), which included most of the other nobles in the land.[49]

The three Tyrolese bishoprics of Chur, Trent and Brixen had become dependent on the rulers of the Tyrol as "members of the Tyrolese Landschaft."[50] By 1451 the bishopric of Chur was administered by the Bishop of Constance, Heinrich von Höwen (1436-1462), who had become Sigismund's chancellor. The bishopric of Trent had been protected by the Duke from local risings several times early in the century. Duke Friedrich, who had forced the Bishop of Brixen and the Bishop of Trent to acknowledge his temporal sovereignty over the dioceses, arrested Bishop Georg I von Lichtenstein (1390-1419) in the cathedral of Trent and put him in prison. He also sent in troops in 1435 to occupy Trent when Bishop Alexander von Masowien (1423-1444) refused to make common cause with him against the Emperor Sigismund (1433-1437).[51] The Bishops of Brixen, who in the twelfth century had been suzerains of the counts of the Tyrol, had recognized the political rulers of the Tyrol as their rightful lords since 1348.[52] In 1418 Duke Friedrich forced the election of his chaplain Berthold von

---

[48] See, for example, Joseph Egger, *Geschichte Tirols,* vol. I (Innsbruck, 1872); Otto Stolz, *Politisch-historische Landesbeschreibung von Sudtirol* (Innsbruck, 1937); Alois Lechthaler, *Geschichte Tirols* (Innsbruck/Vienna/Munich, 1970).

[49] Lechthaler, *Geschichte,* pp. 68, 72.

[50] Anselm Sparber, *Kirchengeschichte Tirols* (Innsbruck, 1957); Tillinghast, "Nicholas of Cusa," p. 379. Cf. Jäger, *Streit,* vol. I, pp. 14-21.

[51] Baum, *Nikolaus Cusanus,* p. 44.

[52] Franz Anton Sinnacher, *Beyträge zur Geschichte der bischöflichen Kirche Säben und Brixen in Tyrol,* 9 vols. (Brixen, 1821-37); Anselm Sparber, *Die Brixner Fürstbischöfe im Mittelalter: Ihr Leben und Wirken* (Bozen, 1968), p. 116.

Buckelsburg as Bishop of Brixen (1418-1427). Thus Brixen was by 1452 an eccesiastical principality directly subject to the powers of Duke Sigismund. It seems that a complete secularization of the bishopric in the future was possible.

Entering the diocese at Easter 1452, Cardinal Cusanus certainly had no intention of being controlled and dictated by Sigismund. In the bull of appointment issued by Pope Nicholas V, it was stated clearly that his intention was to choose a virtuous man who could defend the rights of the Tyrolese Church. When Cusanus found out that the diocese carried a considerable amount of debt, he set out to rectify the situation by establishing a tight-fisted, often unpopular administration of the diocesan revenues.[53] After a careful study of the historical and financial records in the diocesan archives, he turned to the Emperor Friedrich III and was able to obtain from him on 7 December 1452 a renewal of the lucrative mining rights and privileges, which had originally been given to the Bishop of Brixen by Friedrich II (1212-1250) in 1217.[54]

Having set the coffer of the diocese in order, the economy-minded son of a Rhineland bourgeois began to plan to restore the towns, castles and properties formerly owned by the diocese which had been pawned long ago to secular authority. On 17 January 1453 Cusanus served notice to the Freundsbergs that the domains of Matrei and Steinach near the Brenner Pass, which had been in the family's possession since 1365 and 1392 respectively, be restored to the diocese.[55] As a good legal historian and lawyer, he further sought documents and records in the diocesan archives and wrote a detailed ten-point memorandum in 1456[56] in which he asserted that the great castle of Taufers be returned to the bishopric. He was able to recover the castle from Sigismund in a treaty signed by him and Sigismund in Innsbruck on 18 March 1456. On the same day he made a loan of 3,000 Gulden to the duke.[57]

Despite his nickname, which was "Rich in Coin (*Münzreiche*)," Duke Sigismund was apparently in constant need of money. As a result, although the relationship between the two had worsened by 1456, Sigismund was induced to

---

[53] Tillinghast, "Nicholas of Cusa," p. 383; Nikolaus Grass, "Cusanus und das Abgabenwesen der Brixner Diözese," *CG*, pp. 166-79; Meuthen, *Nikolaus van Kues*, pp. 124-26.

[54] Jäger, *Streit*, vol. I, p. 76; Meuthen, *Nikolaus von Kues*, p. 124; Baum, *Nikolaus Cusanus*, p. 441.

[55] Jäger, *Streit*, vol. I, pp. 76-81; Meuthen, *Nikolaus von Kues*, p. 124; Baum, *Nikolaus Cusanus*, pp. 299-306.

[56] Hermann Hallauer, "Eine Denkschrift des Nikolaus van Kues zum Kauf der Amter Taufers und Uttenheim in Südtirol," *MFCG*, I (1961), pp. 76-94. The text of the memorial is on pp. 85-94.

[57] Jäger, *Streit*, vol. I, pp. 173-9; Meuthen, *Nikolaus von Kues*, p. 126; Baum, *Nikolaus Cusanus*, p. 308.

soften his opposition to Cusanus in hopes of obtaining further loans or Cusanus' agreement not to demand repayment for the time being. On the whole, Cusanus' attempts to buy back former episcopal territories and privileges were not too successful. The only successful case was the redemption of Taufers.[58]

In order to show clearly that no real monastic reform was possible unless it was aided by the secular ruler, we can cite as a second example in this paper the case of the Cistercian abbey of Stams. As the richest and most powerful monastery in the Tyrol, the Cistercian abbey of Stams occupied a prominent position in the region.[59] Founded in 1273, it had become the burial site for the Tyrolese rulers. The Habsburgs in the Tyrol continued the tradition. Friedrich IV and Sigismund were also laid to rest at the monastery. Naturally the immensely rich monastery was on good terms with the rulers of the Tyrol. Until 1350 the imperial crown and the other imperial insignia were also kept in the monastery.[60]

The Cistercian Order was famous for its strict discipline, and each Cistercian monastery had to be visited canonically once a year by a representative of its general chapter.[61] From 1184 the Order enjoyed absolute exemption from episcopal control. Even after the Council of Constance, when the pressing need for the reform of the Order was strongly aired, Pope Eugenius IV (1431-1447) determined that no Cistercian abbot could be removed without authorization of the general chapter.[62] When Cardinal Cusanus asked the Tyrolese abbots to come to Wiener Neustadt for a conference on 25 January 1451, Abbot Georg Ried of Stams excused himself "for certain reasonable causes (*propter certas rationabiles causas*)," naming Abbot Gerhard of Viktring as his representative.[63] It was much more important for the abbot, who was entangled in political, feudal and social engagements, to obey the Tyrolese ruler and the Order than the Bishop of Brixen.

---

[58] Baum, *Nikolaus Cusanus*, p. 305.

[59] On the Cistercian abbey of Stams, see *Beiträge zur Wirtschafts- und Kulturgeschichte des Zisterzienserstiftes Stams in Tirol,* ed. Nikolaus Grass (Innsbruck, 1959); Nikolaus Grass, "Des Kloster Stams und das Land Tirol," in *Aus Österreichs Rechtsleben in Geschichte und Gegenwart: Festschrift Ernst C. Hellbing* (Berlin, 1981), pp. 509-24.

[60] Nikolaus Grass, "Stamser Mönche als Hüter der Reichskleinodien," in *Beiträge zur Geschichte Tirols* (Innsbruck, 1971), pp. 171-77. In 1950 the graves were opened and investigated. See Gustav Sauser, "Der Knochenbestand der Tiroler Fürstengräber in Stams im Jahre 1950," in *Beiträge zur Wirtschafts- und Kulturgeschichte,* pp. 221-30.

[61] Bihlmeyer, *Church History,* vol. II, p. 221.

[62] Baum, *Nikolaus Cusanus*, p. 151.

[63] Ibid., p. 152.

As noted above, Cusanus visited Stams on 29 and 30 May in 1452, probably examined the famous astronomical table at the abbey and held a conversation with Vitus von Augsburg, author of the *Calendarium Stamense*, on the reform of the calendar,[64] a topic which he had already discussed at the Council of Basel.[65] His relations with the abbot and the monks were very good at the beginning of his episcopate. It was when Cusanus obtained the papal bull in Rome on 12 May 1453 to reform Tyrolese religious houses, including Stams, that the relationship began to deteriorate. Cusanus was now determined to introduce reforms to Stams. And yet he was obliged to move slowly because Abbess Verena von Stuben of Sonnenburg, which he also wanted to reform, designated Abbot Georg of Stams as one of the acceptable visitors to her convent. When Cusanus invited Abbot Georg on 29 October 1453 to become one of the three visitors to the convent, the abbot politely declined the invitation. A second urgent invitation from the bishop went unaccepted.[66] The abbot's reluctance to involve himself in Cusanus' attempt to reform Sonnenburg is easy to understand if we remember that by this time the bishop was under attack from the duke, with whom the abbot enjoyed specially cordial relations. Early in 1454, for example, the abbot travelled to Wiener Neustadt to negotiate with the Emperor Friedrich III on behalf of the duke.

It was the question of attending the diocesan synod that brought about a breach between Cusanus and Georg. Probably because his predecessors had attended diocesan synods in the Tyrol, the abbot attended Cusanus' first diocesan synod of 6 February 1453. Although no minutes of the second diocesan synod of February 1454 are extant, it seems that the abbot was not present. When the third synod was called in November 1455 the abbot merely sent a letter of declination, without designating any representative. He also did not attend the fourth diocesan synod of 2 to 4 May 1457, but sent two vicars with an apology.[67] The synod declared at the end of its proceedings that those who were absent would be excommunicated until the next diocesan Synod unless creditable reasons were offered. When the two vicars stated that they were not the abbot's representatives, but merely his messengers, the synod declared the abbot contumacious and he was excommunicated. His ensuing attempts to justify his

---

[64] Ibid., p. 154. Regrettably, Thomas Köll, *Aus der Stamser Kulturgeschichte* (Phil. Dissertation, Innsbruck, 1971) was not accessible to me.

[65] Meuthen, *Nikolaus von Kues*, p. 38.

[66] Baum, *Nikolaus Cusanus*, p. 155. Cusanus' invitation to Abbots Kaspar von Tegernsee, Peter von St. Peter in Salzburg and Georg von Stams on 19 October 1453 is printed in *Das Brixner Briefbuch des Kardinals Nikolaus von Kues* (Cusanus-Texte, IV., *Briefwechsel des Nikolaus von Kues*, 2. Sammlung), ed. Friedrich Hausmann (Heidelberg, 1952), pp. 70-72.

[67] Baum, *Nikolaus Cusanus*, pp. 157-58.

absence on account of the monastery's exemption from episcopal control were rejected by Cusanus. Angered by the abbot's behaviour, Cusanus also took stern, vindictive measures against his vicars. They were suspended from their ecclesiastical duties and threatened with excommunication.[68] As a legal historian, Cusanus certainly knew about the traditional exemption of the Cistercian abbot from episcopal jurisdiction. But irritated and enraged by the abbot's absence from the synod, he directed his frustration and vengence not only at the abbot but also at the weak, powerless vicars of Stams. His action showed that he could be petty and vindictive.

Soon a letter, dated 6 June 1457, came to Cusanus from Duke Sigismund, in which the duke defended the abbot's absence. The Emperor Friedrich III, even though he was not on good terms with his cousin Duke Sigismund, also supported the abbot in his letter to Cusanus. The emperor specifically mentioned the fact that Stams had been for a long time the grave site for the Habsburgs. He expressed his willingness to mediate on behalf of the abbot.[69] When the abbot sent his complaint to Rome, Pope Calixtus III (1455-8), a Spaniard who, unlike Pope Nicholas V, was no friend of Cusanus, issued bulls on 12 February 1458, in which he sided with the abbot, saying that because of the privileges of the Cistercian Order the abbot was not under obligation to attend a diocesan synod.[70] It was a great blow to Cusanus, and as a result his prestige in the Tyrol sank. To Cusanus it was painful to realize that not only the secular rulers but also the pope did not fully support his reform endeavours.

In his dealings with the abbot of Stams, Cusanus went against his own principle of preserving and guarding the vested interests and rights of the Church because in this case the Church's rights were interfering with his reform plans. But it became clear that he was no match for the abbot of a powerful monastery who had deep roots in the region and close connections with powerful princes. The reform of Stams ended in failure. It is known that Cusanus had been playing with the idea of resigning his position since 1454 in favour of a Wittelsbach prince.[71] This was certainly one of the reasons for Duke Sigismund's suspicion and distrust of Cusanus. A Wittelsbach bishop in the Tyrol would have been the last choice the duke could have tolerated.

What can we say then about Cusanus' record as Bishop of Brixen? Varied and often contradictory views have been expressed by his contemporaries and

---

[68] Ibid., p. 158.

[69] Ibid., pp. 159-60.

[70] Ibid., pp. 160-61.

[71] Tillinghast, "Nicholas of Cusa," pp. 388-89; Baum, *Nikolaus Cusanus,* pp. 310, 331-43. See also Erich Meuthen, "Nikolaus von Kues und die Wittelsbacher," in *Münchener Historische Studien, Abt. Bayerische Geschichte,* vol. X: *Festschrift für Andreas Kraus zum 60. Geburtstag* (Kallmünz, 1982), pp. 95-113.

later historians about the difficulties which Cusanus experienced with the Tyrolese monasteries and convents and with Duke Sigismund. Aeneas Sylvius, Cusanus' close friend and later Pope Pius II from 19 August 1458 to 15 August 1464, thought that Cusanus was wasting his great talent imprisoned among the snows and gloomy defiles in the Tyrol, and urged him at least twice to come to Rome.[72] Ludwig Pastor (1854-1928), the noted historian of the popes, was of the opinion that Cusanus was too great for the narrow politics of the Tyrol.[73] In his famous book on Cusanus and his ideas, Edmond Vansteenberghe (1881-1943) took a very friendly and supportive attitude towards Cusanus as Bishop of Brixen.[74] By contrast, the widely used book on the topic by the Tyrol-born Benedictine Professor of History at the University of Vienna, Albert Jäger (1801-1891), essentially took the position that Cusanus was an unwanted outsider who in the name of church reform did a lot of harm and damage to the Tyrolese Church and people at large.[75]

Of more recent historians and commentators, Professor Nikolaus Grass (1913-1999), of the University of Innsbruck, has published many detailed studies of institutions and places in the Tyrol that are related to Cusanus, thereby laying the foundations for a balanced, more objective view of the conflict between the bishop and the Tyrolese Church and monasteries.[76] Professor Anselm Sparber (1883-1969) of the Priestly Seminary in Brixen generally expressed critical views on Cusanus' role in the Tyrol, although towards the end of his life his estimate of the bishop's work seems to have become more favorable and sympathetic than before.[77] While displaying a good understanding of Cusanus' life and great admiration for him as a thinker, the famous philosopher Karl Jaspers (1883-1969) offered an essentially critical estimate of Cusanus as Bishop

---

[72] Jäger, *Streit,* vol. II, pp. 230-31: "Precor igitur . . . ut jam demum in patriam redeas. Nam Cardinali sola Roma patria est . . . Veni igitur, obsecro vent; neque enim tua virtue est, quae inter nives et umbrosa clause vanes latescere debeat" (p. 231, n. 9); Meuthen, *Nikolaus von Kues,* p. 101. After sending Cusanus the letter of 27 December 1456, from which the above quote is given, Aeneas sent another letter to Cusanus on 1 August 1458.

[73] Ludwig Pastor, *History of the Popes from the Close of the Middle Ages,* ed. Frederick I. Antrobus, 2nd ed. (London, 1894), vol. III, p. 179.

[74] Vansteenberghe, *Le cardinal,* pp. 140-211.

[75] Jäger, *Streit.*

[76] See the works of Nikolaus Grass cited in notes 18, 31, 39, 59 and 60 above.

[77] In addition to Sparber's works cited in notes 19, 39, 50 and 52, see "Wie kam es zur Gefangennahme des Fürstbischofs und Kardinals Nikolaus von Cues in Bruneck," *Schlern-Schriften,* CLII (1956), pp. 97-107; "Nikolaus von Kues, Kardinal und Fürstbischof von Brixen, in seinem Leben und Wirken (1401-1464)," *Der Schlern,* XXXVIII (1964), pp. 3-16.

of Brixen, saying that the main difficulty was that Cusanus had no change of
heart which was necessary for him to be a good reformer.[78] Professor Pardon E.
Tillinghast (1921-), in the only available detailed study of the conflict in
English, has tried to understand the events critically and offered reasons for
Cusanus' failure. According to Tillinghast, Cusanus was too petty while he was
in the Tyrol.[79] The Austrian author of the most recent, substantial study of
Cusanus' episcopate in the Tyrol, Dr. Wilhelm Baum (1948-), noted that he had
been warned against undertaking the study by his colleagues because of its
controversial nature. Despite its shortcomings in organization and documentation, his study is a much more balanced and less biased piece of work than that
by Jäger.[80] It is perhaps fair to say that every scholar who studies Cusanus and
his ideas will have to decide, sooner or later, what to say about the most difficult
and controversial period of Cusanus' life. In arriving at his conclusion the
scholar must clearly remember that, despite the difficulties and frustrations he
experienced in the Tyrol, Cusanus the thinker was as productive as before and
produced a number of important philosophical and mathematical works during
this period. The philosophical works are the *De visione Dei* (1453), the *De pace
fidei* (1453), the *De beryllo* (1458), the *De principio* (1459) and the *De possest*
(1460). On mathematical topics he wrote the *De mathematicis complementis*
(1453), the *De caesarea circuli quadratura* (1457), the *De mathematica perfectione*
(1458) and the *Aurea propositio in mathematicis* (1459).[81]

When we examine Cusanus' record as Bishop of Brixen, it becomes clear
that he was sincerely and genuinely interested in the reform of the Church and
the monasteries in the Tyrol. He wanted to bring about a thorough reform of the
clergy, monks and nuns in the region. Even his critic admits that we "cannot
doubt the genuineness of his commitment."[82] As an intellectual he had a
penchant for going back to first principles and to deducing proper conclusions
from them. When applied to the Church of his time, these principles dictated to
him that the original standards of simplicity and vigour be restored in the

---

[78] Karl Jaspers, *Nikolaus Cusanus* (Munich, 1964), p. 204; cf. pp. 256-65. See also
Karl Jaspers, *The Great Philosophers,* Vol. II: *The Original Thinkers,* ed. Hannah
Arendt, trans. Ralph Manheim (New York, 1966), pp. 238, 267-72; Karl Jaspers,
Anselm and Nicholas of Cusa, ed. Hannah Arendt, trans. Ralph Manheim (New York,
1966), pp. 148, 177-82.

[79] Tillinghast, "Nicholas of Cusa," p. 390.

[80] Baum, *Nikolaus Cusanus.* For another discussion of the topic by a senior Austrian
scholar, see Andreas Posch, "Nikolaus von Cusa: Bischof von Brixen, im Kampf um
Kirchenreform und Landeshoheit in seinem Bistum," in CC, pp. 227-50.

[81] Sparber, "Vom Wirken," p. 349; Meuthen, *Nikolaus von Kues,* pp. 122-23.

[82] Jaspers, *Nikolaus,* p. 16; Jaspers, *The Great Philosophers,* vol. II, p. 116; Jaspers,
Anselm, p. 26.

religious institutions of the Tyrol. Throughout his life, Cusanus' ideal was to seek unity, harmony and concord among peoples, institutions and even religions. But the Bishop of Brixen was not able to tolerate opposition and compromise in matters of reform.

Cusanus' strong, sustained belief in church reform was clearly demonstrated in the *Reformatio generalis,* which he wrote at the invitation of Pope Pius II after his first departure from the diocese of Brixen in 1457.[83] Written probably in July 1459, the document proposes reform not only in the "members" of the Church, but also in its "head." It is well known that when Cusanus was unable to go along with Pope Pius II about the creation of a new cardinal, he expressed his disappointment and criticism in strong terms even to the pope:

> If you can bear to hear the truth, I like nothing which goes on in this Curia. Everything is corrupt. No one does his duty. Neither you nor cardinals have any care for the Church. What observance of the canons is there? What reverence for laws? What assiduity in divine worship? All are bent on ambition and avarice. If I ever speak in a consistory about reform, I am laughed at. I do no good here. Allow me to withdraw. I cannot endure these ways.[84]

What made the task of reform difficult for Cusanus was that many Tyrolese monasteries and convents of the Augustinian, Benedictine, Cistercian, Franciscan and Premonstratensian orders, which had been founded on the principle of solitude and abnegation or that of purity and austerity, were by then too wealthy in material possessions, too rigid in organization or too lax in the enforcement of the rules to respond to Cusanus' call for reform and simplicity. Their abbots and abbesses paid greater heed to the wishes of political leaders than to those of the Bishop of Brixen. The aristocratic monks and nuns of these Tyrolese religious houses had only disdain and perhaps contempt for an up-start cardinal of bourgeois origin from the Rhineland. They were too proud to change their accustomed ways.

Cusanus himself, in turn, often exhibited pettiness and rigidity when he should have treated the political leaders, monks and nuns of his diocese with warmth and patience. He displayed little uncertainty about his goals and convictions, but seemed too concerned about his personal safety to achieve

---

[83] The text is found in Stephan Ehses, "Der Reformentwurf des Nikolaus von Kues," *Historische Jahrbuch,* XXXII (1911), pp. 281- 97. On the *Reformatio generalis,* see Rudolf Haubst, "Der Reformentwurf Pius des Zweiten," *Römische Quartalschrift,* IL (1954), pp. 188-241; Erwin Iserloh, "Reform der Kirche bei Nikolaus von Kues," *MFCG,* IV (1964), pp. 54-73.

[84] *Memoirs of a Renaissance Pope: The Commentaries of Pius II,* trans. Florence A. Gragg, ed. Leona C. Gabel (New York, 1959), p. 228.

them.[85] He was not like a hero who showed the courage of the truly committed statesman. To say, however, that he was too utopian and simplistic is not to understand his role in the Tyrol. Certainly, he did not misjudge the nature of his task as Bishop of Brixen. He was not only a reforming bishop, but also a meticulous lawyer and legal historian. Historical studies always preceded his reform attempts. His research in the diocesan archives in Brixen, the monastery of Neustift and the abbey of Stams, for example, showed him what the original, pure condition of these religious institutions was and what kinds of reforms were necessary.

Because of the thorough nature of his investigation, Cusanus was well informed about the past history and the present status of an institution which he wanted to reform. But his primary concern was not innovative but "restorative." Seen from this point of view Cusanus emerges as a typical medieval prelate who was anxious to reform the Church without questioning the validity of the total structure. He was not in search of something new, but attempting to restore the old. To portray him as an almost modern political thinker because of his doctrine of consent and conciliar supremacy is, as some have pointed out,[86] to underestimate the extent to which he was a product of medieval, ecclesiastical ideas of government. In regard to church and monastic reform, too, he was no "reformer before the Reformation."

Cusanus' legal training and his experiences in ecclesiastical politics could have made his relations with Duke Sigismund or the Emperor Friedrich III more harmonious and less disruptive. As a discerning lawyer, he must have realized that no reform worthy of note was possible without the sanction and support of the secular ruler. And yet he undertook a series of reforms which provoked the secular rulers' anger and threatened their interests. It is almost tragic that he did not know that the future belonged to the secular powers against which he so sincerely fought.[87] In a contest of wills and a game of power politics, which Cusanus' attempts at church and monastic reform in the Tyrol signified, almost all participants were primarily concerned about their own reputation, jurisdiction, safety and economic gains. Cusanus' record as Bishop of Brixen is certainly not a very "pretty"[88] story to tell. But the fundamental cause of his failure to accomplish undoubtedly noble and praiseworthy goals may be found not so

---

[85] Sparber, "Wie kam," p. 105; Jaspers, *Nikolaus,* p. 257.

[86] Sigmund, *Nicholas of Cusa,* especially pp. 119-36, 304-12; Watanabe, *The Political Ideas,* especially pp. 187-91.

[87] Jaspers, *Nikolaus,* p. 221. On the rise of secular "absolutism" in the Tyrol in the sixteenth century, see Jürgen Bücking, *Frühabsolutismus und Kirchenreform in Tirol (1565-1665): Ein Beitrag zum Ringen zwischen "Staat" und "Kirche" in der Neuzeit* (Wiesbaden, 1972).

[88] Tillinghast, "Nicholas of Cusa," p. 389.

much through analyses of the political and ecclesiastical forces at work in the Tyrol at that time as by recognizing the power of the age-old, seemingly unchanging human pride, avarice and desire to exercise power, which St. Augustine called the lust for earthly desire and domination over other men.[89]

Despite his generally poor record as a reformer and administrator in the Tyrol, Cusanus demonstrated that his ability and power to think deeply and to produce philosophical and mathematical works of original value were not weakened by the frustrating events that visited him. He was not only a dedicated bishop who was anxious to reform his diocese, but also one of the most creative thinkers of the fifteenth century.

---

[89] Herbert A. Deane, *The Political and Social Ideas of St. Augustine* (New York, 1963), especially pp. 39-77. Augustine wrote: "Since we were, therefore, incapable of grasping eternal things, and the stains of sin, contracted by our love of earthly things and implanted in us, as it were, from the root of our mortality, pressed heavily upon us; it was necessary for us to be cleansed. But we could not be cleansed so as to be tempered with eternal things, except by means of the temporal things with which we had already been tempered and held fast," quoted from Saint Augustine, *The Trinity,* trans. Stephen McKenna (Washington, D.C., 1963), p. 160.

Nicolaus Cusanus, Monastic Reform in the Tyrol and the *De Visione Dei*

It is obvious that any serious study of the background of the *De visione Dei* must contain some examination of Cusanus' famous legatine journey of Germany and the Low Countries from 1451 to 1452 and an investigation of his activities as Bishop of Brixen after 1452 until 1460. The legatine journey has been studied by many scholars.[1] In preparation for the *Acta Cusana I*, III, Erich Meuthen has just published another detailed study of it.[2] The journey is important, but very complex. I shall only touch on certain aspects of it in this paper that have a direct bearing on Cusanus' episcopate in Brixen and then examine some of his reform activities as Bishop of Brixen before and shortly after the writing of the *De visione Dei* in 1453. I shall not discuss the contents of the *De visione Dei*.

This is a revised, expanded version of a paper presented at the Third Conference of the American Cusanus Society which was held at the Lutheran Theological Seminary, Gettysburg, Pennsylvania on October 19-21, 1990.

[1] On the famous legatine journey, see K. Grube, "Die Legationsreise des Cardinals Nikolaus von Cues durch Norddeutschland im Jahre 1451," *Historisches Jahrbuch,* I (1880): 393-412; J. Uebinger, "Kardinallegat Nikolaus Cusanus in Deutschland 1451 bis 1452," *Historisches Jahrbuch,* 8 (1887): 629-665; I. Zibermayr, *Die Legation des Kardinals Nikolaus Cusanus und die Ordensreform in der Kirchenprovinz Salzburg* [Reformationsgeschichtliche Studien und Texte, 29] (Münster i.W., 1914); J. Koch, *Der deutsche Kardinal in deutschen Landen: Die Legationsreise des Nikolaus von Kues* (1451/1452) (Trier, 1964); D. Sullivan, "Nicholas of Cusa as Reformer: The Papal Legation to the Germanies, 1451-1452," *Medieval Studies,* 35 (1974): 382-428. Cusanus' itinerary can be found in J. Koch, "Das Itinerar der Legationsreise 1451/52," in *Nikolaus von Cues und seine Umwelt* [Sitzungsberichte der Heidelberger Akademie der Wissenschaften, Philosophisch-historische Klasse (=HSB), Jhrg. 1944/48, 2. Abh.] (Heidelberg, 1948), pp. 111-152.

[2] E. Meuthen, "Die deutsche Legationsreise des Nikolaus von Kues, 1451/1452," in *Lebenslehren und Weltentwürfe im Übergang von Mittelalter zur Neuzeit: Politik - Bildung - Naturkunde - Theologie,* ed. H. Boockmann, B. Moeller and K. Stackmann [Abhandlungen der Akademie der Wissenschaften in Göttingen, Philologisch-historische Klasse, Dritte Folge, Nr. 179] (Göttingen, 1989), pp. 421-499.

To understand Cusanus' episcopate in the Tyrol from 1452 to 1460, it is necessary to discuss briefly how and why he was made Bishop of Brixen.[3] When the news reached Rome that Bishop Johann Röttel of Brixen (1443-50) had died on February 28, 1450, Pope Nicholas V (1447-55), a good friend of Cusanus, decided that Cusanus, whom he had elevated to the cardinalate on December 20, 1448, should become Röttel's successor because of his reputation as a scholar and author and also because of his German background. The pope undoubtedly took into account Cusanus' activities in support of the papacy since his defection from the conciliar party in 1437. In the bull of appointment issued by the pope on March 23, 1450, it was clearly stated that his intention was to choose a virtuous man who could defend the rights and privileges of the Tyrolese church.[4]

The papal provision of Cusanus to the see of Brixen immediately run into difficulties because a three-man committee set up by the cathedral chapter of Brixen had already on March 14, 1450 elected as Röttel's successor Leonhard Wiesmayer, one of its members and the chancellor of Sigismund, Archduke of Austria and Count of the Tyrol (1446-96).[5] The right of the cathedral chapter to elect a bishop was not only based on an ancient custom, but also had been confirmed in the decrees of the Councils of Constance (1414-18) and Basel (1432-49) and also in the Concordat of Vienna of February 17, 1448, of which Cusanus himself was a chief negotiator.[6] But it is difficult to say that the election of Wiesmayer was canonical; the canons chose him in the Archduke's

---

[3] On the appointment of Cusanus as Bishop of Brixen, see P.E. Tillinghast, "Nicholas of Cusa vs. Sigmund of Habsburg:An Attempt at Post-Conciliar Church Reform," *Church History,* 35 (1967), pp. 372-375; W. Baum, *Nikolaus Cusanus in Tirol: Das Wirken des Philosophen und Reformators als Fürstbischof von Brixen* [Schriftenreihe des Südtiroler Kulturinstitutes, 10] (Bozen, 1983), pp. 85-91; M. Watanabe, "Nicholas of Cusa and the Tyrolese Monasteries: Reform and Resistance," *History of Political Thought,* 7 (1986): 55. On the events that took place during Cusanus' episcopate, see A. Jäger, "Regesten und urkundliche Daten über das Verhältnis des Cardinals Nicolaus von Cusa, als Bischof von Brixen, zum Herzoge Sigmund von Oesterreich und zu dem Lande Tirol von 1450 bis 1464," *Archiv für Kunde österreichischer Geschichts-Quellen,* 4 (1850): 297-329.

[4] The bull of appointment, *Intersolicitudines varias,* can be found in *Acta Cusana: Quellen zur Lebensgeschichte des Nikolaus von Kues,* i, ii (Hamburg, 1983), p. 617 Nr. 872. Cf. Jäger, "Regesten," p. 299 no. 3.

[5] Tillinghast, "Nicholas of Cusa," p. 372. See also W. Baum, "Nikolaus Cusanus und Leonhard Wiesmair: Der Kardinal und sein Gegenspieler, Kanzler von Tirol und Bischof von Chur," *Der Schlern,* 57 (1983): 433-434.

[6] The text of the concordat is found in *Church and State Through the Centuries,* ed. and tr. S.Z. Ehler and J.B. Morrall (Westminster, Md., 1954), pp. 126-131. See also J.B. Toews, "Pope Eugenius IV and the Concordat of Vienna—an Interpretation," *Church History,* 34 (1965): 178-184.

residence which was surrounded by his armed men.[7] It is also important to note that the Concordat of Vienna itself provided that the pope could appoint another person as Bishop even when the election had been canonical, if he judged, on reasonable and manifest grounds, that his nominee was a person of greater worth.[8] Thus from the outset Cusanus' episcopate was destined to be difficultt and controversial. The cathedral chapter of Brixen and the proud Tyrolese people were willing to challenge a case of papal interference in the German rights by appealing to their secular head, Archduke Sigismund.

The conflict between Cusanus and the Tyrolese people did not come to a head immediately because Pope Nicholas V asked Cusanus on December 24, 1450 to serve as *legatus a latere* and sent him to Germany and the Low Countries for three purposes: to reform religious life, to mediate disputes and to dispense jubilee indulgences to those who could not come to Rome in the first jubilee year after the Great Schism (1378-1417).[9] It was while Cusanus was in Salzburg at the beginning of the journey that he issued a decree *Quoniam dignum* on February 8, 1451 which directed members of all religious houses to restore the rules of their orders within a year on pain of loss of their privileges and rights. The decree said bluntly: "Many among the clergy neglect the care of their souls, have bad morals and lead a dissolute life."[10] It became the basis of his later attempts to reform the religious houses in the bishopric of Brixen. Unlike some of the old descriptions of Cusanus' journey in which his reform efforts were presented as a great success, recent studies by modern historians have given us a more realistic, less flattering picture of the journey. Cusanus' entourage was often welcomed with joy, but on occasion encountered resistance and interference. Since he often tried to enforce reform measures strictly and without flexibility, they caused a great deal of anxiety and produced stiff resistance among the clergy and the monks.[11]

There is no doubt that after his arrival in Brixen on April 7, 1452, Cusanus' chief interest was in the reform of the lives of the clergy and the monks in his diocese. Upon his entry into the diocese, he posted on the doors of

---

[7] Baum, "Nikolaus Cusanus," pp. 86-87.

[8] Tillinghast, "Nicholas of Cusa," p. 374; Watanabe, *Nicholas of Cusa,* p. 36.

[9] Tillinghast, "Nicholas of Cusa," pp. 375-376; Watanabe, *Nicholas of Cusa,* p. 18; Meuthen, "Die deutsche Legationsreise," pp. 449, 495-497.

[10] The text is found in Zibermayr, *Die Legation,* pp. 106-108. See also Watanabe, *Nicholas of Cusa,* pp. 55, 60; Sullivan, "Nicholas of Cusa," p. 394.

[11] When Cusanus attempted to reform the mendicant orders at the provincial synods of Mainz and Cologne in 1451 and 1452 respectively, the mendicant orders complained to the pope about Cusanus' interference. See, for example, Koch, "Der deutsche Kardinal," pp. 12-13, 22-24.

the cathedral the decree issued at Salzburg in 1451 on the reform of the monasteries and also the ordinances concerning the strict *clausura* of nuns.[12] On April 13, in less than a week after his arrival in Brixen, Cusanus sent to Abbess Verena von Stuben of the convent of Sonnenburg in the Pustertal an invitation to make him advocate (*Vogt*) of Enneberg in relation to a long contested case between the bishopric and the convent over the rights of pasturage on the Alpe-Grunwald.[13] On April 16, he visited the abbey of Augustinian Canons at nearby Neustift (*Novacella*).[14] The conflict with Abbess Verena von Stuben became serious after Cusanus visited the convent on May 2, 1452.[15] As is well known, the convent of Sonnenburg later became a source of great difficulty for Cusanus throughout his episcopate in the Tyrol and led to all kinds of troubles that clouded his career as Bishop of Brixen. He even contemplated as early as 1454 to resign as Bishop of Brixen because of these troubles.[16]

From May 23 to 26, 1452 Cusanus visited the Premonstratensian house in Wilten near Innsbruck and went on to the wealthy Cistercian abbey of Stams on May 29-30.[17] It was when Cusanus was on his way to the *Reichstag* of Regensburg, held from June 22 to 27, 1452, that he visited the Benedictine abbey of St. Quirin at Tegernsee.[18] While staying at the abbey from May 31 to June 2, he made the acquaintance of Abbot Kaspar Ayndorffer (1402-61)[19] and

---

[12] Watanabe, *Nicholas of Cusa*, p. 57.

[13] H. Hallauer, "Eine Visitation des Nikolaus von Kues in Benediktinerinnenkloster Sonnenburg," *MFCG* 4 (1964): 105; Watanabe, *Nicholas of Cusa*, p. 57.

[14] G. Mutschlechner, "Itinerar des Nikolaus von Kues für den Aufenthalt in Tirol (1452-1460)," in *Cusanus Gedächtnisschrift* (=CG), ed. N. Grass (Innsbruck-München, 1970), p. 526; Watanabe, *Nicholas of Cusa*, p. 57.

[15] Although F.A. Sinnacher (*Beyträge zur Geschichte der bischöflichen Kirche Säben und Brixen in Tyrol*, 6, 1928, p.368) and Mutschlechner ("Itinerar," p. 526) say that Cusanus visited Sonnenburg on May 2, 1452, other authorities do not seem to support the view. See, for example, Jäger, "Regesten": 301; Baum, *Nikolaus Cusanus*, pp. 175, 348, 441. See also K. Spahr, *Nikolaus von Cues, las Frauenstift Sonnenburg OSB und die mittelalterliche Nonnenklausur* in CG, pp. 307-26.

[16] Tillinghast, "Nicholas of Cusa," pp. 388-389; Baum, *Nikolaus Cusanus*, pp. 310, 331-343; E. Meuthen, "Nikolaus von Kues und die Wittelsbacher," in *Festschrift für Andreas Kraus*, ed. P. Fried and W. Ziegler [Münchener historische Studien, Abteilung Bayerische Geschichte, 10] (Kallmünz, 1982), pp. 105, 107; Watanabe, *Nicholas of Cusa*, p. 68.

[17] Mutschlechner, "Itinerar," p. 527; Watanabe, *Nicholas of Cusa*, pp. 57, 66.

[18] Baum, "Nikolaus Cusanus," p. 132; Mutschlechner, "Itinerar," p. 527.

[19] Baum, "Nikolaus Cusanus," pp. 132, 441.

Prior Bernhard von Waging (c. 1400-1472). Cusanus' *De visione Dei* was written in response to an ardent request from the monks of Tegernsee under Ayndorffer and von Waging to explain to them his theological and philosophical ideas and was dedicated to them.

Like many fifteenth-century monasteries in Austria and southern Germany, the Benedictine monastery of Tegernsee under Abbot Hildebrand Kastner (1424-26) in the early 1420's was in poor moral condition and in great need of reform.[20] As a result of the Council of Constance (1414-18), which in its famous decree *Haec sancta* adopted the policy of "bringing about the union and reform of the Church of God in head and in members,"[21] the first visitation of the abbey by Johannes Grünwalder, General Vicar of Freising, and Petrus von Rosenheim, of the famous Benedictine abbey of Melk, took place in July 1426[22] and resulted in the appointment of Kasper Ayndorffer, the youngest member of the monastery, as its abbot. With its 24-year-old abbot at its head, Tegernsee entered a period of reform, growth and prosperity, although the young abbot, in fear of a possible assault, had to wear a coat of mail temporarily to carry out his reform measures in accordance with the instructions given by the visitors.[23] Not only did Abbot Kaspar bring about the moral reform of the abbey, but he straightened out its financial conditions, renovated the sleeping rooms, the infirmary, the guest rooms, the living quarters for the abbot and the refectory.[24] He also built and developed a good library and began to send promising young members of the abbey to the University of Vienna to elevate the cultural level of the monks.[25] He contributed so much to the rise of Tegernsee in *spiritualibus* and *temporalibus* that it would not be correct to label him merely as *Banabt*, as

---

[20] J. Angerer, *Die Bräuche der Abtei Tegernsee unter Abt Kaspar Ayndorffer, 1426-1461, verbunden mit einer textkritischen Edition der Consuetudines Tegernseenses* [Studien und Mitteilungen zur Geschichte des Benediktiner-Ordens und seiner Zweige (= SMGBOZ)], 18 (Ottobeuren, 1968): 23. On Tegernsee, see also V. Redlich, *Tegernsee und die deutsche Geistesgeschichte im 15. Jahrhundert* [Schriftenreihe zur Bayerischen Landesgeschichte, 4] (München, 1931; reprt. Aalen, Scientia-Verlag, 1974); P. Acht, *Die Traditionen des Klosters Tegernsee, 1003-1242* [Quellen und Erörterungen der bayerischen Geschichte, N.F., 9, I] (München, 1952).

[21] The text of the *Haec sancta* is printed in *Conciliorum Oecumenicorum Decreta*, ed. G. Alberigo (Bologna 1973), pp. 409-410.

[22] Angerer, *Die Bräuche*, pp. 25-26.

[23] Angerer, *Die Bräuche*, p. 18.

[24] Angerer, *Die Bräuche*, pp. 15-22.

[25] Angerer, *Die Bräuche*, p. 36. Some see the beginnings of the *studia humanitatis* at Tegernsee under the influence of Cusanus; see W. Müller, "Die Anfänge der Humanismusrezeption in Kloster Tegernsee," SMGBOZ 92 (1981): 28-90.

was often done by his contemporaries.[26] Like Subiaco in Italy and Melk in Austria, Tegernsee under Abbot Kaspar Ayndorffer became a model Benedictine monastery and a flourishing cultural center which set the tone for other monasteries in southern Germany.

Bernhard von Waging himself came to Tegernsee in 1446 from the abbey of the Augustinian Canons at Indersdorf because he thought he could find a better religious atmosphere and greater peace at Tegernsee than at Indersdorf.[27] Prior van Waging was a monk who had an unmistakably passionate yearning for inner spiritual growth and renunciation of the world. Abbot Kaspar left no written work. By contrast, Prior von Waging wrote about twenty books. They include *Laudatorium doctor ignorantiae* (1451/52), *Epistola seu tractatus contra illicitum carnium esum monachorum ordinis S. Benedicti* (1456), *De materia eucharstiae sacramenti tractatus epistolaris* (1456), *Tractatus de morte* (1458), *De cognoscendo Deum* (1459) and *Remediarius contra pusillanimes et scrupulosos* (1464/65).[28] Most of these works are still unedited and can be found in forty manuscripts in the Staatsbibliothek in Munich.[29] But it was also this often sick prior who was later engaged actively in the reform of monastic life in the Bavarian and Austrian monasteries.

By 1450 the *De docta ignorantia* (1440) of Nicholas of Cusa was known to the monks of Tegernsee. Prior Johannes Keck (1400-50), who had attended the Council of Basel and was known for his efforts to enhance the level of musical life at Tegernsee, praised Cusanus' philosophical, theological and linguistic knowledge in 1450.[30] Although he had not read the *De docta ignorantia,* he had heard about it. After reading the *De docta ignorantia,* Bernhard von Waging wrote his *Laudatorium doctae ignorantiae* in April 1452. This work was edited and

---

[26] Redlich, *Tegernsee,* p. 93.

[27] Redlich, *Tegernsee,* pp. 91-92. On Bernhard von Waging, see also M. Grabmann, "Bernhard von Waging († 1472): Prior von Tegernsee, ein bayerischer Benediktinermystiker des 15. Jahrhunderts," SMGBOZ 66 (1946): 82-96; P. Wilpert, "Bernhard von Waging, Reformator vor der Reformation," in *Festgabe für Seine Königliche Hoheit Kronprinz Rupprecht von Bayern,* ed. Walter Goetz (München 1954), pp. 260-276; *Die deutsche Literatur des Mittelalters: Verfasserlexikon,* ed. W. Stammler, cont. K. Langosch, 2nd ed., I (Berlin, 1978), pp. 779-789.

[28] *Verfasserlexikon,* I, pp. 779-789.

[29] Redlich, *Tegernsee,* p. 94.

[30] Redlich, *Tegernsee,* p. 93; Baum, "Nikolaus Cusanus," pp. 62, 131. See also H. Rossmann, "Der Tegernseer Benediktiner Johann Keck über die Mystische Theologie," *MFCG* 13 (1978): 330-352.

published by Edmond Vansteenberghe in 1915.[31] On April 14, 1452, twenty-six years after the first visitation of the abbey, the second visitation of Tegernsee was carried out by Abbot Martin of the Scottish abbey in Vienna, Abbot Laurentius of Mariazell in Wienerwald and Johann Schlitpacher of Melk.[32] The visitors found the abbey of Tegernsee in such fine condition that they wrote the following in the visitation charter:

> . . . invenimus ipsum monasterium in spirinlalibus in observantia regular) laudabiliter viguisse, in temporalibus etiam in statu fuisse commendabili . . .[33]

It was because of this monastic renewal and what Cusanus called "a zeal for God" that the monks of Tegernsee turned to Cusanus for spiritual guidance and help.

After 1452 the monks, especially Ayndorffer and von Waging, eagerly sought to maintain close contact with Cusanus and exchanged letters with him until 1458 about the essence, methods and goals of mystical theology.[34] Four hundred and fifty-four of their letters have been preserved in the famous codex Clm 19697 (Teg. 1697) of the Staatsbibliothek in Munich, which is often referred to as the Tegernsee letter-codex.[35]

Vansteenberghe published thirty-six of them in 1915,[36] and Professor Maurice de Gandillac's French translation of seventeen of the letters written by Cusanus appeared in 1985.[37] The question Abbot Ayndorffer put to Cusanus in his letter written before September 22, 1452 was "whether without intellectual knowledge *(sine intellectus),* and even without prevenient or accompanying knowledge *(sine cogitacione previa vel concomitante)* and whether only by

---

[31] The text is in E. Vansteenberghe, *Autour de la docte ignorance: une controverse sur la théologie mystique au XVe siècle* [Beiträge zur Geschichte der Philosophie des Mittelalters, XIV, 2-4] (Münster i.W. 1915), pp. 163-168.

[32] Angerer *Die Bräuche,* p. 47.

[33] Angerer, *Die Bräuche,* p. 48.

[34] M. Schmidt, "Nikolaus von Kues im Gespräch mit den Tegernseer Mönchen über Wesen und Sinn der Mystik," *MFCG* 18 (1989): 25-26.

[35] J. Koch, *Briefwechsel des Nikolaus von Cues,* Erste Sammlung [Cusanus-Texte IV, HSB, Jhrg. 1942/43, 2. Abh.] (Heidelberg, Carl Winter, 1944), pp. 107-110; Baum, "Nikolaus Cusanus," p. 142. About the codex, see C. Halm and G. Laubmann, *Catalogus Codicum latinorum Bibliothecae Regiae Monacensis,* Editio altera, Tomus IV, 3 (München 1878), p. 270.

[36] Vansteenberghe, *Autour,* pp. 107-162.

[37] Nicolas de Cues, *Lettres aux moines de Tegernsee sur la docte ignorance* (1452-1456), *Du jeu de la boule* (1463), tr. M. de Gandillac [Sagesse chéetienne] (Paris, 1985).

means of affection *(solo affectu)* or of the highest capability of the mind which many call synderesis *(per mentis apicem quam vocant synderesim)* the devout soul can attain to God."

> Est autem hec quaestio utrum anima devote sine intellectus cognicione, vel etiam sine cogitacione previa vel concomitante, solo affectu seu per mentis apicem quam vocant synderesim Deum attingere possit, et in ipsum immediate moveri aut ferri.[38]

The question dealt with the relationship between the *intellectus* and the *affectus* which is one of the fundamental questions about the nature of mystical theology. The controversy over mystical theology which developed among Cusanus, Vinzent von Aggsbach, Konrad von Geissenfeld, Johann von Weilheim and Marquard Sprenger concerning the interpretation of Jean Gerson's book, *De mystica theologia,* cannot be discussed in this paper.[39] What is especially important for us to note about the abbey of Tegernsee under Abbot Kaspar is that, as we shall see, it was later very much involved in Cusanus' attempts to reform the convent of Sonnenburg and other Tyrolese monasteries despite or because of its high level of religious fervour.

After returning from the *Reichstag* of Regensburg towards the end of June 1452, Cusanus went to Wiener Neustadt twice, in November and December 1452, to ask Emperor Friedrich III to confirm him as Bishop of Brixen.[40] He then opened in Brixen on February 6, 1453 his first diocesan synod in the Tyrol at which he issued strict decrees on the practice of simony, the dismissal of concubines, the prohibition of pilgrimages except those to Brixen, Rome, St. James of Compostella or other well-established places, and the ban on card playing.[41] Shortly thereafter he left for Rome where he stayed from March 5 to

---

[38] Vansteenberghe, *Autour,* p. 110 (Letter 3).

[39] Vansteenberghe, *Autour,* pp. 1-105; Rossmann, "Der Tegernseer Benediktiner," p. 19. See also E. Vansteenberghe, "Un écrit de Vincent d'Aggsbach contre Gerson," in *Festgabe zum 60. Geburtstag Clemens Baeumier* (Münster i.W., 1913), pp. 357-364; W. Höver, *Theologia mystica in altbairischer Übertragung: Bernhard von Clairvaux, Bonaventura, Hugo von Balma, Jean Gerson, Bernhard von Waging und andere: Studien und Übersetzungswerk eines Tegernseer Anonymous aus der Mitte des 15. Jahrhundert* [Münchener Texte und Untersuchungen zur deutschen Literatur des Mittelalters, 36] (München, 1971); H. Rossmann, "Der Magister Marquard Sprenger in München und seine Kontroversschriften zum Konzil von Basel und zur Mystischen Theologie," in *Mysterium der Gnade: Festschrift für Johann Auer,* ed. H. Rossmann and J. Ratzinger (Regensburg, 1975), pp. 350-411.

[40] Mutschlechner "Itinerar," p. 527. See also Jäger, "Regesten," pp.301 no. 39, 302 no. 42.

[41] Mutschlechner, "Itinerar," p. 527; Baum, "Nikolaus Cusanus," p. 441. Cusanus held four synods during his episcopate in Brixen from 1452 to April 27, 1460: 1453, 1454, 1455 and 1457.

May 29. [42] He reported to Nicholas V on his legatine journey and requested that he be empowered to carry out monastic reforms in the Tyrol. In his bull, *Inter cetera,* issued on May 12, 1453, Nicholas V granted Cusanus a special permission to visit and reform the religious houses of Wilten, Stams, Neustift, Sonnenburg, St. Georgenberg and the Franciscan convent of St. Clare in Brixen.[43] These were the six religious houses that had not taken any serious note of Cusanus' decree issued at Salzburg in 1451.

On May 29, 1453, Cusanus' last recorded day of stay in Rome, Constantinople was taken by the Turks. The news reached Venice on June 29. From the imperial court in Graz, Aeneas Sylvius, who was then imperial counselor, sent the news on July 21 to Cusanus,[44] but it is not known where and when Cusanus received it. After returning to Brixen on June 26 from Rome, Cusanus went to Wilten on July 11 and visited Innsbruck the next day.[45] He was back in Brixen from August 1 to August 15, on which day he preached a sermon, *Intravit Iesus in quoddam castellum,* using Luke 10:28 as his text.[46] After a brief stay at Castle Bruneck on August 24, he returned to Brixen on August 28, where he stayed until September 8.[47] On September 14, the feast day of the Exaltation of the Cross, he preached a sermon, *Ego si exaltatus fuero a terra, omnia ad me traham,* in the Church of the Holy Ghost at the Benedictine abbey of Saben near Klausen.[48] During his brief stay at Castle Branzoll near Klausen the same day, he wrote and sent a letter to Abbot Ayndorffer from the castle in which he criticized Vinzent von Aggsbach's views on mystical theology and commented on Pseudo-Dionysius' *Theologia Mystica,*[49] which his friend Ambrosius Traversari had translated for him during the Council of Basel. Clearly the question of mystical theology occupied the mind of the busy bishop at that time. We note, however, that, as he said in the same letter, he also completed at Branzoll Book I of his mathematical work, *De mathematicis complementis*

---

[42] Jäger, "Regesten," p. 302 nos. 49-50; Mutschlechner, "Itinerar," p. 527.

[43] Baum, "Nikolaus Cusanus," pp. 122, 142, 441; Watanabe, *Nicholas of Cusa,* p. 60. Cf. Jäger, "Regesten," p. 302 no. 50.

[44] Jäger, "Regesten," p. 303 no. 57; E. Meuthen, "Der Fall von Konstantinopel und der lateinische Westen," *MFCG* 16 (1984): 35.

[45] Mutschlechner, "Itinerar," p. 527.

[46] Mutschlechner, "Itinerar," p. 528.

[47] Mutschlechner, "Itinerar," p. 528.

[48] Mutschlechner, "Itinerar," p. 528.

[49] Vansteenberghe, *Autour,* pp. 113-117. See also Mutschlechner, "Itinerar," p. 528.

("Scripsi hijs diebus De mathematicis complementis libellum").[50] He returned to
Brixen on September 18 and stayed there until Septembe 28.[51] It is interesting
to note that on September 21, 1453 he completed his *De pace fidei,*[52] on which
he must also have been working seriously since receiving the shocking news
about the fall of Constantinople.

It is quite possible that the ideas expressed in the *De visione Dei* took a
long time to develop and that they did not become well formulated until just
before the writing and completion of the book. Relying on Vansteenberghe's
famous study of Cusanus, Henry Bett wrote in his book on Cusanus the
following: "The year 1453 was the most peaceful that Nicholas was to enjoy in
his episcopate. It was the period in which he wrote the *De visione Dei,* and
maintained his correspondence with the Benedictine mystics of Tegernsee."[53] But
in order to see clearly under what conditions Cusanus wrote the *De visione Dei,*
it is necessary for us to examine in some more detail what he did during the two
months before the completion of the *De visione Dei* on November 8, 1453.

On September 24, 1453, Cusanus sent a letter to Abbess Verena von
Stuben, informing her of the impending arrival of Abbot Lorenz von Ahausen
and Michael van Natz as visitors to her convent on September 27. The visitation
team arrived at Sonnenburg on the scheduled day, but it was unsuccessful
because of Verena's stiff resistance.[54] Cusanus then went to Wilten on October 3
to reform the house and bring more order.[55] After visiting Fussen on October 9
in connection with the controversy related to the bishopric of Trier, he returned
to Brixen on October 15. The extant records show that he was in his episcopal
city until October 21.[56] During this time he sent another letter on October 19 to
Abbot Kaspar Ayndorffer of Tegernsee, Abbot Peter of St. Peter in Salzburg and
Abbot Georg of Stams, asking them to participate in another visitation of

---

[50] Vansteenberghe, *Autour,* p. 116. See also Nikolaus von Kues, *Die mathematischen
Schriften,* tr. Josepha Hofmann and intr. Joseph E. Hofmann, 2nd ed.
[Philosophische Bibliothek, 231] (Hamburg, 1979), pp. 68-92.

[51] Jäger, "Regesten," p. 304 no. 63; Mutschlechner, "Itinerar," p. 528.

[52] Baum, "Nikolaus Cusanus," p. 441.

[53] H. Bett, *Nicholas of Cusa* (London, 1933), p. 59.

[54] Baum, "Nikolaus Cusanus," pp. 174, 441. Cusanus' letter of September 24, 1453 is
printed in F. Hausmann, *Briefwechsel des Nikolaus von Cues,* Zweiter Sammlung
[Cusanus-Texte, IV, HSB, *Brixner Briefbuch des Kardinals Nikolaus von Kues,* Jhrg.
1952, 2. Abh.] (Heidelberg, 1952), pp. 65-66.

[55] Mutschlechner, "Itinerar," p. 528.

[56] Jäger, "Regesten," p. 304 no. 66; Mutschlechner, "Itinerar," p. 526.

Sonnenburg on November 29.[57] On October 21, he went to Neustift where he preached a sermon which began as *Credidit ipse et tota domus eius,* using John 4:53 as the text.[58] Then from October 22 to January 1, 1454 he was back in Brixen.[59] On October 23, he sent another short letter to Abbot Kaspar Ayndorffer[60] and preached a sermon, *Gaudete et exultate, quia merces vestra copiosa est in celis,* based on Matthew 5:12.[61] Another sermon, *Qui credit in me, eciam si mortuus fuerit, vivet* (John, 2:25), dealing with Lazarus, was delivered on November 2.[62] Cusanus must also have worked on his *De visione Dei* during this stay in Brixen. According to the Giessen MS 695, the book was completed in Brixen on November 8, 1453 ("*Finivit* Brixinae 1453 8. Novembris Nicolaus Cardinalis").[63]

It is not necessary to discuss in detail all monastic reforms that were initiated by Cusanus after the completion of *De visione Dei.* I dealt with some of them in my recent article.[64] To mention only the dreary, long-lasting case of Sonnenburg again, Cusanus visited Sonnenburg, as scheduled, on November 29, 1453 accompanied by Prior Bernhard von Waging of Tegernsee, Eberhard van Wolfrathausen, Michael von Natz, Johannes Fuchs of Neustift and Johann of Westernach.[65] The dispute between Cusanus and Verena von Stuben later worsened so much that, as Hermann Hallauer described in his study of the battle of Enneberg, Cusanus' troops led by Gabriel Prack, Bishop's official at Buchenstein, attacked Verena's band of mercenaries in the Alpe-Grunwald on April 5, 1458 and killed fifty to fifty-four men and their leader Jobst von Hornstein, who had been hired by the convent of Sonnenburg.[66] Even if we do

---

[57] Hausmann, *Das Brixner Briefbuch,* p. 70.

[58] Mutschlechner, "Itinerar," p. 528.

[59] Mutschlechner, "Itinerar," p. 528.

[60] Vansteenberghe, *Autour,* p. 118.

[61] Koch, "Briefwechsel," pp. 118-119.

[62] Koch, "Briefwechsel," p. 119.

[63] Nikolaus von Kues, *Von Gottes Sehen—De Visione Dei,* tr. E. Bohnenstaedt, 2nd ed. [Philosophische Bibliothek, 219] (Leipzig, Felix Meiner, 1944), p. 222; Koch, "Briefwechsel," p. 119.

[64] Cf. Watanabe, *Nicholas of Cusa,* pp. 58-68.

[65] Baum, "Nikolaus Cusanus," p. 441. See also W. Baum, "Bernhard von Waging (†1471): Klagelieder über St. Georgenberg: Das Scheitern einer Klosterreform des Nikolaus Cusanus (1453/54)," *Der Schlern,* 57, 9 (1983): 482-494.

[66] H. Hallauer, *Die Schlacht in Enneberg: Neue Quellen zur moralischen Wertung des Nikolaus von Kues* [Kleine Schriften der Cusanus-Gesellschaft 9] (Trier, 1969). Cf. *CG,* pp. 232, 286 n. 4, 263.

not completely follow the accounts of Cusanus' episcopate in the Tyrol given by hostile historians like Albert Jäger,[67] it is clear that from 1452 to the time of his last departure from the Tyrol in 1460, Cusanus was almost continually engaged in many efforts to reform the secular clergy and the monks in the Tyrol and that his attempts were vigorously opposed not only by Abbess Verena von Stuben, but also at many monasteries and by many Tyrolese people under the guidance and protection of their secular ruler, Archduke Sigismund. It is therefore not surprising that Aeneas Sylvius sent the famous letter to Cusanus from Rome on December 27, 1456, urging him not to languish amid the snows and the dark valleys of the Tyrol and "to come to Rome which is the only home to all cardinals."[68] Another letter of appeal was sent to Cusanus on August 1, 1458. While Cusanus was visiting the Praemonstratensian house in Wilten in June, 1457, he felt that his life was threatened by Archduke Sigismund's soldiers during the night of June 24-25. After this so-called Wilten affair,[69] he never felt safe in his episcopal town of Brixen and fled in July to Castle Andraz in Buchenstein which was in the remote, southeastern region of the Tyrol and from which he could easily go to Venice.[70] Believing that he was forced by Archduke Sigismund to abandon Brixen, the bishop never returned to it thereafter.

When we think of the *De visione Dei* of 1453 as a work produced by a busy bishop engaged in difficult reform activities in his diocese, we must see it against the broader background of his writing record during his episcopate from 1452 to 1460. It is indeed remarkable that during this period of conflicts, struggles and threats, Cusanus produced not only the *De visione Dei,* but also many other writings which seemed far removed from the difficult, complicated and sometimes life-threatening situations in which he found himself. His other works in the fields of theology and philosophy written during this period were the *De pace fidei* (1453); the *De theologicis complementis* (1453); the *De beryllo* (1457); the *De aequalitate* (1459); the *De principio* (1459); the *Reformatio generalis* (1459) and the *Trialogus de possest* (1460). His books on mathematical and scientific themes published in the period were the *De mathematicis complementis,* 2 vols (1453/1454); the *Dialogus de circuli quadratura* (1457); the *De caesarea circuli quadratura* (1457); the *De mathematica*

---

[67] A. Jäger, *Der Streit des Cardinals Nicolaus von Cusa mit dem Herzoge Sigmund von Österreich als Grafen von Tirol,* 2 vols. (Innsbruck, 1861).

[68] Jäger, "Regesten," p. 308 no. 119; E. Meuthen, *Die letzten Jahre des Nikolaus von Kues: Biographische Untersuchungen nach neuen Quellen* (Köln, 1958), p. 133. Aeneas Sylvius sent another letter to Cusanus on August 1, 1457 asking him to return to Rome. Jäger, "Regesten," p. 310 no. 132; Meuthen, *Die letzten Jahre,* p. 134. See also Jäger, *Der Streit,* I, p. 231.

[69] Mutschlechner, "Itinerar," p. 531; Baum, "Nikolaus Cusanus," pp. 190, 336, 445.

[70] Mutschlechner, "Itinerar," p. 531.

perfectione (1458) and the *Aurea propositio in mathematicis* (1459). We should perhaps note that sometime in 1453 or 1454 Paolo Toscanelli (1397-1482), Cusanus' good friend since his Paduan days sent a letter to Cusanus in which he discussed mathematical problems.[71]

How could a busy reform-minded bishop produce a deeply mystical, highly meditative work such as *De visione Dei* in the midst of one of the most difficult and trying periods of his life? Karl Jaspers, who has criticised Cusanus severely stated:

> Only in occasional moments did Cusanus' life match his ideas. When he became involved in political action, he did not achieve the grand style of statesman. To an even greater extent in the course of his life, his acts were incompatible with his ideas . . . Did his philosophical pursuits become for him a sort of refuge from the cares of everyday life, an edifying distraction for his leisure moments, comparable as such to the occasional retreat of a man of the world to a monastery?[72]

These are too strong, critical words about Cusanus' motives, intentions and acts.

When one visits the isolated, forlorn Castle Andraz in the rugged, peripheral region of Buchenstein in the Tyrol which after the Wilten affair the frightened Bishop finally reached from Brixen on July 10, 1457 via Saben, the Grodner Tal, the Sella-Joch and the Pordoi-Joch and which became his abode, with some short absence, until his first departure for Rome on September 14, 1458,[73] one cannot help thinking about the anxiety, fear and perhaps agony that must have visited the Bishop of Brixen who abandoned his episcopal city. Writing in February 1458 in his notes, he said that he had arrived at Castle Andraz with the help of Archangel Raphael and that he had been "in the wilderness of the Dolomites for thirty-two weeks."[74] Even in Andraz, however, Cusanus' speculative and creative activity did not cease. His *De beryllo* and possibly *De possest* were written in the lone castle on the bank of a brook near

---

[71] Nikolaus von Kues, *Die mathematischen Schriften,* pp. 128-131 ("Magister Paulus ad Nicolaum Cusanum Cardinalem").

[72] K. Jaspers, *Anselm and Nicholas of Cusa,* ed. H. Arendt and tr. R. Manheim (New York, 1974), p. 178. See also K. Jaspers, *Nikolaus Cusanus,* new ed. [Serie Piper 60] (München-Zürich, 1987), pp. 258-259.

[73] Jäger, "Regesten," p. 316 no. 209; Mutschlechner, "Itinerar," pp. 531-532.

[74] J. Koch, *Nikolaus von Cues als Mensch nach dem Briefwechsel und persönliche Aufzeichnungen,* in *Humanismus, Mystik und Kunst in der Welt des Mittelalters,* ed. J. Koch [Studien und Texte zur Geistesgeschichte des Mittelalters, III] (Leiden-Köln, E.J. Brill, 1959), pp. 64, 75 (". . . doch so half vns sant Raphael her zu komen . . . Dijse ist die warheit vnd die sache, war umb wir also hie xxxij wochen in disser wstenien gelegen haben . . ."). See also Jäger, *Der Streit,* I. pp. 261-265; CG, pp. 284-287.

Col di Lana in Buchenstein.[75] Cusanus also completed the *De caesarea circuli quadratura* at Castle Andraz.[76] Commenting on the completion of the mathematical work at Andraz, Professor Joseph Ehrenfried Hofmann, who devoted his academic career to the study of Cusanus' mathematical works, wrote: ". . . alone, far away from all friends and even without the books he loved."[77] No matter how harrassed, troubled or burdened Cusanus was in his eventful life, he somehow managed to be active in ecclesiastical and political affairs and at the same time to be productive in religious, metaphysical and mathematical speculation. In this contrast and harmony of the *vita activa* and the *vita contemplativa* one can probably see a case of the *coincidentia oppositorum*.

[75] Nicolai de Cusa, *De beryllo (Über den Beryll)*, ed. K. Bormann [Philosophische Bibliothek, 295] (Hamburg, 1977), p. 90 ("Deo laus 1458, decima octave Augusti in Castro sancti Raphaelis."); Nicolai de Cusa, *Trialogus de possest (Dreiergespräch über das Können-Ist)*, ed. R. Steiger [Philosophische Bibliothek, 285] (Hamburg, 1973), p. viii.

[76] Nikolaus von Kues, *Die mathematischen Schriften*, p. 159.

[77] Nikolaus von Kues, *Die mathematischen Schriften*, p. 242 ("[. . .] einsam, fern von allen Freunden und sogar ohne die geliebte Bücher").

Nicholas of Cusa and the Reform of the Roman Curia

The last years of Nicholas of Cusa (1401-1464), which were spent in Rome, Orvieto, Viterbo and other places in Italy, were not well studied until recently. Even the famous monograph on Cusanus by Edmond Vansteenberghe, which is still worth consulting seventy years after its publication, was considerably weak in its handling of the period.[1] It was Erich Meuthen who felt the need for a closer study of the subject, and tried to fill the gap by seeking new sources and data in Italian archives and libraries. Meuthen's study, published in 1958,[2] has amply shown that Cusanus' later years, mostly in Rome, from 1459 to 1464, are worth investigating further, not only because they constitute a very important part of his life, but also because his religious and humanistic activities can be appreciated and evaluated on their own, and contrasted with those of others that have come to be understood better in recent years, thanks to greater attention given to what is sometimes called the "Renaissance in Rome."[3]

After the well-known legatine journey through Germany and the Low Countries in 1451-1452, during which he made many attempts to reform churches, monasteries and convents,[4] Cardinal Cusanus, who had been named

---

[1] Edmond Vansteenberghe, *Le cardinal Nicolas de Cues (1401-1464): L'action—la pensée* (Paris, 1920; reprint Frankfurt am Main, 1963).

[2] Erich Meuthen, *Die letzten Jahre des Nikolaus von Kues: Biographische Untersuchungen nach neuen Quellen,* Wissenschaftliche Abhandlungen der Arbeitsgemeinschaft für Forschung des Landes Nordheim-Westfalen, 3 (Cologne and Opladen, 1958). Meuthen's "sketch" of Cusanus' biography, which contains a great deal of information about his later years, is in its seventh, revised edition: *Nikolaus von Kues, 1401-1464: Skizze einer Biographie*, 7th ed. (Münster, 1992).

[3] On the "Renaissance in Rome" and related topics, see John W. O'Malley, "Giles of Viterbo: A Reformer's Thought on Renaissance Rome," *Renaissance Quarterly* 20 (1967): 1-11; idem, *Praise and Blame in Renaissance Rome: Rhetoric, Doctrine and Reform in the Sacred Orators of the Papal Court, c. 1450-1521* (Durham, North Carolina, 1979); John F. D'Amico, *Renaissance Humanism in Papal Rome: Humanists and Churchmen on the Eve of the Reformation* (Baltimore and London, 1983); Paolo Brezzi, *Umanesimo a Roma nel Quattrocento: Atti del convegno su umanesimo a Roma nel Quattrocento, New York, 1-4 dicembre 1981* (Rome, 1984); Charles L. Stinger, *The Renaissance in Rome* (Bloomington, Indiana, 1985).

[4] There are many studies of the legatine journey. To mention only the recent ones, Josef Koch, *Der deutsche Kardinal in deutschen Landen: Die Legationsreise des Nikolaus von Kues (1451-1452)* (Trier, 1964); Donald Sullivan, "Nicholas of Cusa as Reformer: The Papal Legation to the Germanies, 1451-1452," *Mediaeval Studies* 36 (1974): 382-428;

Bishop of Brixen by Nicholas V (1447-1455) on March 23, 1450, arrived in Brixen as its bishop at Easter in 1452. During his eight-year episcopate from 1452 to 1460,[5] Cusanus carried out church and monastic reforms in Brixen, Bruneck, Enneberg, Neustift, Sonnenburg, Wilten, and other places which often aroused local resistance and strong opposition.[6] His contest with Verena von Stuben, the abbess of the convent at Sonnenburg, is the best-studied affair in his almost tragic episcopate in the Tyrol. The situation was made worse because of the aid which Duke Sigismund of the Tyrol (1446-1490) gave to Cusanus' opponents.[7]

Concerned about Cusanus' welfare and even safety, Aeneas Sylvius Piccolomini (1405-1464), the famous humanist who had been living in Rome since his elevation to the cardinalate on December 18, 1456, urged Cusanus, in his letter of December 27, 1456, to come to Rome which was, according to him, home to all cardinals.[8] It was after the election of Aeneas Sylvius as Pope Pius II on August 16, 1458, that Cusanus began to think of following his friend's suggestion. Abandoning his see in the Tyrol on September 14, Cusanus entered the eternal city on September 30, 1458.[9]

The eighteen members of the College of Cardinals who assembled in conclave on August 16, 1458, ten days after the funeral of Calixtus III (1455-1458), had adopted on the first day an electoral capitulation which extended the rights of the college and limited the power of the new pope. The articles of the

Erich Meuthen, "Die deutsche Legationsreise des Nikolaus von Kues, 1451/1452," in *Lebenslehre und Weltentwürfe im Übergang vom Mittelalter zur Neuzeit: Politik-Bildung-Naturkunde-Theologie,* ed. Hartmut Boockmann et al. (Göttingen, 1989), pp. 421-499.

[5] Strictly speaking, Cusanus was Bishop of Brixen from 1450 to 1464. His itinerary between 1452 and 1460 is given in Georg Mutschlechner, "Itinerar des Nikolaus von Kues für den Aufenthalt in Tirol," in *Cusanus-Gedächtnisschrift,* ed. Nikolaus Grass (Innsbruck and Munich, 1970), pp. 525-534.

[6] On Cusanus' reform activities in the Tyrol, see Morimichi Watanabe, "Nicholas of Cusa and the Tyrolese Monasteries: Reform and Resistance," *History of Political Thought* 7 (1986): 53-72; also in *The Politics of Fallen Man: Essays Presented to Herbert A. Deane,* ed. M.M. Goldsmith et al. ([London], 1986), pp. 53-72. On Verena von Stuben and Cusanus, see n. 44 below.

[7] See Ludwig Pastor, *The History of the Popes from the Close of the Middle Ages,* ed. Frederick I. Antrobus (London, 1894), 3:178-192; Wilhelm Baum, *Nikolaus Cusanus in Tirol: Das Wirken des Philosophen und Reformators als Fürstbischof von Brixen* (Bozen, 1983).

[8] Meuthen, *Die letzten Jahre,* pp. 133-134. Aeneas sent another letter to Cusanus on August 1, 1458 (ibid., pp. 134-135).

[9] Vansteenberghe, *Le cardinal,* p. 187; Meuthen, *Die letzten Jahre,* p. 22.

capitulation included a promise to launch a crusade against the Turks, to reform the Roman Curia and to provide a monthly allowance to those cardinals whose stipends were inadequate.[10] Before the new pope, Pius II, left Rome on January 22, 1459, for Mantua, where he was to hold a congress to organize a crusade, he named Cusanus *vicarium generalem in temporalibus cum pleno apostolice sedis legati de latere officio*.[11] Pius II was to stay away from Rome until October 6, 1460. It was during this period that Cusanus was active as a *legatus de latere* in Rome and attempted to bring about reform in the Roman Church and the Curia.

Especially after the transfer of the Papacy to Avignon in 1378, the low administrative and moral conditions in which the Curia found itself became widely known not only in Italy but also in other European countries.[12] As the Curia continued to grow and became the place where appointments to ecclesiastical office were made, legal disputes argued, cases of conscience resolved and spiritual favors granted, critics became numerous and vociferous.[13] In his *Tractatus de modo generalis concilii celebrandi*, William Durant the Younger (d. 1328) had laid down the principle that the reform of the church must proceed from the head, that is, from the Roman Church.[14] He was among the first to use the phrase "the reform of the church in head and members (*tam in capite quam in membris*)."[15]

In the fifteenth century, the voice of criticism became more widespread, strident and persistent. It was the Gallican movement which clearly developed the notion of the *reformatio capitis*. Matthew of Cracow (d.1410) and Dietrich of Niem (1418) are considered the chief spokesmen for anti-curial reform plans of the fifteenth century. In the provocatively entitled book, *De squaloribus*

---

[10] Pastor, *History,* 3:10-11, 269. Concerning the relationship of Pius II and his cardinals, see Walter Schürmeyer, *Das Kardinalkollegium unter Pius II,* Historische Studien, 22 (Berlin, 1914). On the electoral capitulations, see J. Lulvès, "Päpstliche Wahlkapitulationen," *Quellen und Forschungen aus italienischen Archiven und Bibliotheken* 12 (1909): 212-235; Schürmeyer, *Das Kardinalkollegium,* pp. 35-36.

[11] Meuthen, *Die letzten Jahre,* pp. 143-144; Meuthen, *Nikolaus von Kues,* p. 115.

[12] The classic study of this topic is Johannes Haller, *Papsttum und Kirchenreform: Vier Kapitel zur Geschichte des ausgehenden Mittelalters,* 1 (Berlin, 1903).

[13] John A.F. Thomson, *Popes and Princes, 1417-1517: Politics and Polity in the Late Medieval Church* (London, 1980), pp. 95-113; D'Amico, *Renaissance Humanism,* p. 21; Stinger, *The Renaissance,* pp. 123-126.

[14] Hubert Jedin, *A History of the Council of Trent,* trans. Dom Ernest Graf, 2 vols. (London, 1957), 1:8-9. About William Durant the Younger's ideas, see now Constantine Fasolt, *Council and Hierarchy: The Political Thought of William Durant the Younger,* Cambridge Studies in Medieval Life and Thought, 4th Series (Cambridge, 1991).

[15] Fasolt, *Council,* p. 1, esp. n. 2.

Romanae curiae (1401), which he completed in Heidelberg, Matthew attacked the granting of benefices by the pope as contrary to the ancient canons *(priora jura).* [16] An official of the Roman Curia for many years, Dietrich argued in his famous book, *De modis uniendi ac reformandi ecclesiae* (1410), written during the Great Schism (1378-1417), that if a council intends to restore unity and to raise up the church, it must begin by limiting the papal power according to the precedent established by the Fathers.[17] Andrew Holes (d. 1470), an English canon lawyer who worked in the Roman Curia from 1431 to 1444, made it clear in his sermon of 1433 that real reformation within the church was necessary and that reform should begin with a conversion of life at the top.[18]

In *Super excellencia et dignitate curie Romane,* which was written in 1438 by the humanist Lapo da Castiglionchio the Younger (1405-1438), the author, a Florentine, seemingly defended the positive service of the pope, the attractive and secular tone of life at the Roman Curia, which was increasingly under the influence of humanism, and the splendor of worship and liturgy as conducted by high prelates in the presence of the pope, cardinals, archbishops, bishops and an infinite number of ranks.[19] There are excellent, wise, and learned men in the Curia, says Lapo, like Ambrogio Traversari, Cristoforo Garatone, Poggio Bracciolini, Flavio Biondo, Giovanni Aurispa, and Leon Battista Alberti.[20] But a closer reading of the lengthy and ironic dialogue would indicate

---

[16] On Matthew of Cracow and his ideas, see Hermann Heimpel, *Studien zur Kirchen- und Reichsreform des 15. Jahrhunderts, 2, Zu zwei Kirchenreform Traktaten des beginnenden 15. Jahrhunderts,* Sitzungsberichte der Heidelberger Akademie der Wissenschaften, Philosophisch-historische Klasse [hereafter HSB], Jahrgang 1974, 1. Abhandlung (Heidelberg, 1974), pp. 10-30; Jedin, *History,* 1:12-13; O'Malley, *Praise and Blame,* p. 225.

[17] On Niem, see Hermann Heimpel, *Dietrich von Niem, Dialog über Union und Reform der Kirche, 1410* (Leipzig and Berlin, 1933); Matthew Spinka, *Advocates of Reform from Wyclif to Erasmus,* The Library of Christian Classics, 14 (Philadelphia, 1953), pp. 149-174.

[18] Margaret Harvey, "An Englishman at the Roman Curia during the Council of Basle: Andrew Holes, His Sermon of 1433 and His Books," *Journal of Ecclesiastical History* 42 (1991): 19-38.

[19] On Lapo's dialogue, see Richard Scholz, "Eine ungedruckte Schilderung der Kurie aus dem Jahre 1438: Zugleich ein Beitrag zur Geschichte der italienischen Renaissance," *Archiv für Kulturgeschichte* 10 (1912): 399-413; idem, "Eine humanistische Schilderung der Kurie aus dem Jahre 1438," *Quellen und Forschungen aus italienischen Archiven und Bibliotheken* 16 (1914): 116-153; Renée Neu Watkins, "Mythology as Code: Lapo da Castiglionchio's View of Homosexuality and Materialism at the Curia," *Journal of the History of Ideas* 53 (1992): 138-144.

[20] Watkins, "Mythology," p. 142. See Scholz, "Eine ungedruckte Schilderung," pp. 406-407.

that Lapo was perhaps anxious to expose the dark side of the Curia which was "in miserable and abandoned times, when crimes, wicked ways, and fraud set traps for virtue, and, though the names of virtue and modesty are held dear, honorable studies and disciplines are not rewarded and are hardly to be found."[21] The Curia was dominated by ignorant, bold, dishonorable, wicked men who oppress the others who are good, temperate, and moderate.[22] There are people at the Curia who enjoy "playing, riding and hunting. You'll find zealous companions for any pursuit."[23] Nothing is more alien to the Curia than religion.[24]

Having traveled widely, no one knew better than Pius II about the evils that existed in all the countries of Christendom, as well as in Rome and Italy. Living in Rome, what did Cusanus do after 1459 to reform the church and especially the Roman Curia?

In an attempt to reform the Roman Church, he "preached four sermons in Rome to the canons of the major basilicas during his reform visitation as Pope Pius II's vicar for the city in 1459."[25] The introduction of reform into Rome by Cusanus began with his sermon *Sic currite, ut comprehendes* of January 27, 1459, in which, using I Cor. 9:24, he discussed the need for reform and visitation in the chapter of St. Peter's *(in capitulo ecclesie sancti Petri)*.[26] The second sermon *Hec sunt verba, que audivimus* was delivered at a synod of the Roman clergy held on February 10, 1459, in the papal chapel in St. Peter's *(in capella Pape apud sanctum Petrum)*.[27] It was then, on February 23, 1459, that

---

[21] Watkins, "Mythology," p. 138; Scholz, "Eine humanistische Schilderung," p. 118.

[22] Ibid.: "Imperiti, audaces, largiciosi, sordidi, flagiciosi ubique regnant ac dominantur ceteris, boni autem viri, docti, integri, abstinentes, modesti, temperati, depressi, abiecti repudiatique iacent, nec modo . . ."

[23] Watkins, "Mythology," p. 143.

[24] Scholz, "Eine ungedruckte Schilderung," p. 404; Scholz, "Eine humanistische Schilderung," p. 123: "Quid enim a curia alienius quam religio esse potest?"

[25] O'Malley, *Praise and Blame,* p. 94. These sermons are contained in Cod. Vat. lat. 1244 and Cod. Vat. lat. 1245. See Meuthen, *Die letzten Jahre,* pp. 31-32.

[26] Josef Koch, *Cusanus-Texte, 1, Predigten, 7. Untersuchungen über Datierung, Form, Sprache und Quellen. Kritisches Verzeichnis sämtlicher Predigten,* HSB, Jahrgang 1941/42, 1. Abhandlung (Heidelberg, 1942), p. 191; Meuthen, *Die letzten Jahre,* p. 145; idem, *Nikolaus von Kues,* pp. 116-117; O'Malley, *Praise and Blame,* pp. 94, 98, 99, 227, 232. On the new numbering system of Cusanus' entire sermons, different from that established by Koch in 1942, see Rudolf Haubst, "Zu den für die kritische Edition der Cusanus-Predigten noch offenen Datierungsproblemen," *Mitteilungen und Forschungsbeiträge der Cusanus-Gesellschaft* [hereafter MFCG] 17 (1986): 57-88.

[27] Koch, *Predigten,* p. 191; Meuthen, *Die letzten Jahre,* pp. 31, 45, n. 37, 145; O'Malley, *Praise and Blame,* p. 94.

Cusanus introduced a reform in St. John Lateran *(in Sancto Iohanne Lateranensi)* with the sermon *Audistis, fratres*.[28] Finally, on March 6, 1459, by giving a sermon *Sic nuper*, Cusanus introduced reform at the church of Santa Maria Maggiore *(ad sanctam Mariam maiorem)*.[29] These reform attempts in Rome reflected Cusanus' still strongly-held desire to effect reform within the Roman Church even after his transition from the tragic experiences in the Tyrol as Bishop of Brixen to the important administrative position as *legatus urbis* in Rome.

No writing of his shows more clearly his persistent devotion to the principle of reform "in head and members" than the *Reformatio generalis* of 1459. It has become clear in recent years that shortly after ascending the throne of Saint Peter on August 19, 1458, Pius II appointed a commission whose task was to deliberate on the reform of the Roman Curia.[30] The commissioners included Saint Antoninus (1389-1459), the Archbishop of Florence, Domenico de' Domenichi (1416-1478), the learned Bishop of Torcello, Nicolaus Cusanus, and other cardinals, bishops, prelates, and doctors.[31]

Of the proposals submitted to the pope, only two have been preserved. The proposal of Domenico de' Domenichi, who delivered the customary sermon addressed to the cardinals on the first day of the conclave of 1458, was the *Tractatus de reformationibus Romanae curiae,* which was written in September or October of the same year.[32] The other was the *Reformatio generalis* of

---

[28] Koch, *Predigten,* p. 192; Meuthen, *Die letzten Jahre,* p. 145; O'Malley, *Praise and Blame,* pp. 94, 237.

[29] Koch, *Predigten,* p. 192; Meuthen, *Die letzten Jahre,* p. 145; O'Malley, *Praise and Blame,* p. 94. Cf. Vansteenberghe, *Le cardinal,* p. 189, n. 1.

[30] Pastor, *History,* 3:269: "Two things are particularly near my heart," said Pius to the members of the Committee, "the war with the Turks, and the Reform of the Roman Court!" See also Denys Hay, *The Church in Italy in the Fifteenth Century* (London, 1977), p. 86.

[31] Schürmeyer, *Das Kardinalkollegium,* p. 51. On St. Antoninus, see Vespasiano da Bisticci, *Renaissance Princes, Popes and Prelates: The Vespasiano Memoires, Lives of Illustrious Men of the XV Century,* ed. W. George and E. Walters (New York, 1963), pp. 157-163. See also Raoul Morçay, *Saint Antonin, fondateur du couvent de Saint Marc, archevêque de Florence, 1389-1459* (Paris, 1914).

[32] Pastor, *History,* 3:271. A brief summary of Domenichi's book is found in ibid., 3:272-275. See also Franc Gaeta, *Domenico Domenichi: De reformationibus Romanae Curiae* (Aquila, n.d.); Herbert Jedin, *Studien über Domenico de' Domenichi (1416-1478)* (Wiesbaden, 1958); Herbert Smolinsky, ed., *Domenico de' Domenichi und seine Schrift, De potestate papae et termino eius: Edition und Kommentar* (Münster, 1976).

Nicolaus Cusanus, probably completed in the first part of July, 1459.[33] In contrast to Domenico's tract, which dealt with the reform of the Roman Curia, Cusanus' proposal, which was drafted in the form of a papal bull, was much wider in scope and presented the proposal for a general reformation of the whole church. It is known that these reform proposals exercised a great influence on the reform bull *Pastor aeternus* which Pope Pius II himself composed towards the end of his pontificate,[34] but it was never published by the pope.

Cusanus' *Reformatio generalis* consists of a theological introduction, fourteen general rules about the visitation and reform of the Roman Church and practical suggestions for the reform of the Roman Curia.[35] In his introduction, Cusanus attempts to answer the question on why created man exists. Man was created, according to him, so that he might see God in His glory. God sent Christ, who takes away ignorance, commanding that He be heard. It is necessary for us to be like Christ, who was made just for us. He is the living law and the perfect form (*forma*). The church of God is the mystical body of Christ which can be likened to the human body. All members are united together by love. It is by faith in Christ that the just man lives.[36]

---

[33] Erwin Iserloh, "Reform der Kirche bei Nikolaus von Kues," MFCG 4 (1964): 54-73, esp. p. 56. The *Reformatio generalis* has been preserved in the following three manuscripts: Cod. lat. Monacensis (Clm) 422, fol. 252-262; Cod. Vat. lat. 8090, fol. 109r-122v; and Cod. Vat. lat. 3883, fol. 1r-11r. About the manuscripts, see Vansteenberghe, *Le cardinal*, p. 474; Rudolf Haubst, *Studien zu Nikolaus von Kues und Johannes Wenck: Aus Handschriften der Vatikanischen Bibliothek* (Münster, 1955), pp. 9-11. The Latin text is found in J.M. Düx, *Der deutsche Cardinal Nicolaus von Cusa und die Kirche seiner Zeit* (Regensburg, 1847), 2:451-466. A brief summary is given in Pastor, *History*, 3:270-272.

[34] Rudolf Haubst, "Reformentwurf Pius des Zweiten," *Römische Quartalschrift* 49 (1954): 188-242. The Latin text on the chancery is published in Michael Tangl, *Die päpstlichen Kanzleiordnungen von 1200-1500* (Innsbruck, 1894; reprint Aalen, 1959), pp. 372-379. The table of contents can be found in Pastor, *History,* 3:397-403. On the bull, see also Jedin, *History*, 1:123-124; Iserloh, "Reform der Kirche," p. 56; O'Malley, *Praise and Blame,* pp. 95-96.

[35] About the *Reformatio generalis*, see also Ludwig Pastor, *Geschichte der Päpste seit dem Ausgang des Mittelalters* (Freiburg, 1889), 2:189-190; Pastor, *History,* 3:270-272; Hay, *The Church,* p. 86. The English translation used in the following is taken from the forthcoming article by Morimichi Watanabe and Thomas M. Izbicki, "Nicholas of Cusa, A General Reform of the Church." The translation was made from the Latin text published in Stephan Ehses, "Der Reformentwurf des Kardinals Nikolaus Cusanus," *Historisches Jahrbuch* 32 (1911): 281-297. The author wishes to thank Dr. Izbicki for giving him permission to use the translation in this article.

[36] Ehses, "Der Reformentwurf," p. 283. Cusanus adds later "receiving Christ by faith and works" (ibid., p. 284: ". . . fide et opere"). On the importance of Christology in Cusanus' works, see Rudolf Haubst, *Die Christologie des Nikolaus von Kues* (Freiburg, 1956).

In the latter part of the introduction Cusanus deals with the institutional dimensions of reform, basing his discussion on the well-known concept of the church as the mystical body of Christ. Cusanus' main emphasis is on the building-up of the church (*aedificatio ecclesiae*) instead of its diminution. Noting that "the body of the church in this age has declined greatly from the light and the day, becoming enveloped in the shadows,"[37] he declares that this has occurred because the eyes, which should be its light, have fallen into darkness.[38] Like the reform of individuals, the goal of ecclesiastical reform is to bring back the church of the original disciples (*ecclesia primitivorum*).[39]

In the second part of the book after the introduction, Cusanus discusses fourteen general rules for the reform of the church in terms of the visitation which will be carried out in two stages. First, the pope and the Roman Curia will be visited by three serious and mature (*graves et maturos*) men who possess knowledge, prudence, and zeal for God.[40] Then this process of visitation should be extended to the whole church.[41] None of the fourteen general rules to be used by the visitors are extraordinary or especially strict.[42] They reflect Cusanus' concern about benefices, plurality, simony, usury, indulgences, nepotism, the opposition of all secular and regular clergy to reform under pretext of papal privilege, and the like.[43] Some rules clearly reflect Cusanus' personal experiences. Rule 12, for example, which is related to the enclosure of nuns, is based on his bitter struggle with the Abbess Verena von Stuben of Sonnenburg.[44] His

---

[37] Ehses, "Der Reformentwurf," p. 285; Iserloh, "Reform der Kirche," p. 57.

[38] Ehses, "Der Reformentwurf," p. 285.

[39] Ibid., p. 291; Iserloh, "Reform der Kirche," pp. 58, 60.

[40] Ehses, "Der Reformentwurf," p. 286. He had already discussed reform *in capite* in *De concordantia catholica* II, 27 (*Opera omnia, iussu et auctoritate Academiae Litterarum Heidelbergensis ad codicum fidem edita* [Leipzig and Hamburg, 1932-   ], 14/2:254-255).

[41] Ehses, "Der Reformentwurf," p. 286; Pastor, *History,* 3:271.

[42] Iserloh, "Reform der Kirche," pp. 57-58.

[43] Pastor, *History,* 3:271-272. See also Meuthen, "Die Pfründen des Cusanus," MFCG 2 (1962): 15-66; D.S. Chambers, "The Economic Predicament of Renaissance Cardinals," *Studies in Medieval and Renaissance History* 3 (1966): 289-313; Richard B. Hilary, "The Nepotism of Pope Pius II, 1458-1464," *The Catholic Historical Review* 64 (1978): 33-35.

[44] About Verena von Stuben and Cusanus' contest with her, see Albert Jäger, *Der Streit des Cardinals Nikolaus von Cusa mit dem Herzoge Sigmund von Österreich als Grafen von Tirol* (Innsbruck, 1861; reprint Frankfurt a.M., 1968); Hermann Hallauer, "Eine Visitation des Nikolaus von Kues in Benediktinerinnenkloster Sonnenburg," MFCG 4

criticism of relics or miraculous effusion of blood from hosts in Rule 13 undoubtedly was a result of his experience at Wilsnack during the legatine journey.[45]

Cusanus states in the third section of the proposal that these fourteen rules are to be applied to the pope, the cardinals, the Curia and the divine services in Rome. He proposed a program for the visitation of the pope, the cardinals and the Curia partly in accordance with the electoral capitulations of 1458 to which Pope Pius II had agreed. "Since we should strive to be what we are called and to show in action what we profess to be," the visitors should not "fear to correct the pope," whom "they will find, like other men, sinful and infirm."[46]

In applying the rules to the cardinals, the visitors were urged to examine whether they had three things: zeal for God's house; freedom and faithfulness in counsel; and a simple, exemplary way of life.[47] Unlike the *De concordantia catholica,* in which he called the cardinals *legati provinciarum,* Cusanus likens them now to *legati nationum.*[48] The cardinals were asked to form a "daily, weighty council of the church" with the pope.[49] The visitors were then asked to reform divine worship in Rome by visiting the principal basilicas, the titular churches of the cardinals, the religious houses and the hospitals.[50] As for the curial officials, the visitors were to examine why they were in the Roman Curia and whether they were needed. Those who were in the Curia to hunt benefices

(1964): 104-115; Kolumban Spahr, "Nikolaus von Cues, das adelige Frauenstift Sonnenburg OSB und die mittelalterliche Nonnenklausur," *Cusanus-Gedächtnisschrift* (see n. 5), pp. 306-326; Watanabe, "Nicholas of Cusa and the Tyrolese Monasteries," pp. 53-72.

[45] Sullivan, "Nicholas of Cusa as Reformer," pp. 382-384; Meuthen, "Die deutsche Legationsreise," pp. 486-487.

[46] Ehses, "Der Reformentwurf," p. 292.

[47] Ibid. Cusanus recommended that a cardinal have forty members in his household, while Pius II's recommendation was sixty. See Meuthen, *Die letzten Jahre,* p. 97. Chambers, "The Economic Predicament," p. 290: "There can be little doubt that most cardinals sincerely believed it was their duty to follow a princely way of life." For a recent study of the papal bureaucracy in the fifteenth and sixteenth centuries, see Peter Partner, *The Pope's Men: The Papal Civil Service in the Renaissance* (Oxford, 1990).

[48] Ehses, "Der Reformentwurf," p. 292.

[49] Iserloh, "Reform der Kirche," p. 65.

[50] Ehses, "Der Reformentwurf," p. 292; Iserloh, "Reform der Kirche," p. 65. See also R. R. Bond, *The Efforts of Nicholas of Cusa as a Liturgical Reformer* (Salzburg, 1962); Josef A. Jungmann, "Nicolaus Cusanus als Reformator des Gottesdienstes," *Cusanus-Gedächtnisschrift,* pp. 23-31. Cusanus' great interest in liturgy can be seen in his large collection of liturgical manuscripts (Cod. Cus. 131-155); see J. Marx, *Verzeichnis der Handschriften-Sammlung des Hospitals zu Cues bei Bernkastel a. Mosel* (Trier, 1905), pp. 128-142.

should be sent back to their churches. The Curia was not an asylum for idle, greedy, and roaming prelates and priests. "Greed, which for some is like worship of idols, should not be stirred up but extinguished."[51]

Finally, the visitors were to examine most carefully the office of the Penitentiary according to the general rules. Especially since the end of the fourteenth century, the Apostolic Penitentiary had been criticized for its handling of cases related to the "internal forum," i.e., questions of conscience.[52] Cusanus is apparently concerned about its low reputation in the minds of many. The visitors were to inquire from top down "whether due gravity, zeal, knowledge, diligence, experience, cleanness of hands, vigilance, and care"[53] could be found in the head and the minor penitentiaries. If they were lacking these virtues, the visitors were to eject them.[54] The *scriptores* of the Penitentiary were to write their own documents and understand what they wrote.[55]

The brief summary given above makes it clear that Nicolaus Cusanus had a deep-seated desire for the reform of the church which he held throughout his life. The reform ideas, first enunciated in *De concordantia catholica* did not diminish despite his shift of allegiance from the conciliar to the papal party in 1437 and the bitter experiences in the Tyrol. The *Reformatio generalis* is a most evident expression in the later part of his life of his continued aspiration for reform.

It is remarkable that shortly after writing the *Reformatio generalis,* Cusanus decided to return to the Tyrol in order to carry on his reform program in the area. He arrived in Mantua on October 2, 1459, and, leaving Mantua on February 4, 1460, entered the Tyrol on February 7.[56] Only the life-threatening and humiliating defeat and arrest by Duke Sigismund at Bruneck on April 16/17,

---

[51] Ehses, "Der Reformentwurf," p. 296.

[52] About the Apostolic Penitentiary, see Emil Göller, *Die päpstliche Pönitentiarie von ihrem Ursprung bis zur ihrer Umgestaltung unter Pius V., vol. 2, Die päpstliche Pönitentiarie von Eugen IV. bis Pius V.,* pt. 1, *Darstellung* (Rome, 1911); Niccolò del Re, *La curia romana: Lineamenti storico-giuridici,* 3rd ed. Sussidi eruditi, 23 (Rome, 1970), pp. 261-272.

[53] Ehses, "Der Reformentwurf," p. 296; Pastor, *History,* 3:272.

[54] Ehses, "Der Reformentwurf," p. 296.

[55] Ibid., p. 297. Thomson, *Popes and Princes,* p. 97: "By the last quarter of the [fifteenth] century, the post of scriptor of the Penitentiary has become venal, and under Innocent VIII such a post seems to have been held by a minor."

[56] Meuthen, *Die letzten Jahre,* p. 51; Baum, *Nikolaus Cusanus,* p. 447. Nicholas' detailed itinerary in the Tyrol can be found in Mutschlechner, "Itinerar," pp. 525-534. See n. 5 above.

1460,[57] forced Cusanus finally to abandon his Bishopric of Brixen. By way of Cortina d'Ampezzo in the Dolomites and Siena, where Pius II was staying, he arrived in Rome on October 6, 1460, together with the pope and the Curia.

Although he was disappointed and disheartened by his experiences in the Tyrol, Cusanus continued his reform program at Orvieto, where he spent his summers first as guest of Cardinal Pietro Barbo in 1461 and 1462 and then in 1463 on an income from the Abbey of Santi Severo e Martirio.[58] That his attempt to reform Orvieto in 1463, like his previous attempts elsewhere,[59] was not successful must have dampened his spirit; but it certainly testifies to his strongly-held, persistent dedication to the principle of reform "in head and members." The reform of the church, as Erwin Iserloh rightly stated, was not a mere side-event or episode in Cusanus' life, but an idea that was at the center of his thought and activity throughout his life.[60]

It has been noted that, like Domenico de' Domenichi's *Tractatus de reformationibus Romanae curiae,* the *Reformatio generalis* has as its important recommendation a reform of the head (*reformatio capitis*) and that, in contrast, the *Pastor aeternus* of Pius II had no such provision.[61] Despite his express desire for reform, which was demanded by the electoral capitulation, Pius II as pope was undoubtedly reluctant to submit his office and person to the scrutiny of the visitors. When it is recalled that he supported monarchical principles in his *Epistola de ortu et auctoritate imperii romani* which was written in 1446, and that at the end of the Congress of Mantua he issued the bull *Execrabilis* (1460) which rejected any appeal from a decision of the pope to a future council as null and void, it is not difficult to understand the pope's position.[62] Unlike his friend, Cusanus was much more forthright and assertive about the need for the *reformatio capitis* as well as the *reformatio membrorum.*

---

[57] On Cusanus' defeat and arrest at Bruneck, see Jäger, *Der Streit,* 1:5-52; Hans Hörtnagl, "Der Brunecker Überfall des Herzogs Sigmund und sein Ritt an die Etsch zu Ostern 1460," *Der Schlern* 7 (1926): 467-470; Baum, *Nikolaus Cusanus,* p. 447; Meuthen, *Nikolaus von Kues,* pp. 104-106; Watanabe, "Nicholas of Cusa and the Tyrolese Monasteries," p. 54.

[58] Meuthen, *Die letzten Jahre,* pp. 43, 111.

[59] About his reforms at Orvieto and Rieti, see Meuthen, *Die letzten Jahre,* pp. 110-125; idem, *Nikolaus von Kues,* pp. 126-129.

[60] Iserloh, "Reform der Kirche," p. 54.

[61] Ibid., p. 63; O'Malley, *Praise and Blame,* p. 218.

[62] On Pius' *Epistola,* see Gerhard Kallen, *Aeneas Sylvius Piccolomini als Publizist in der Epistola de ortu et auctoritate imperii romani* (Cologne, 1939). G.B. Piccotti discussed the bull *Execrabilis* in his article, "La pubblicazione e i primi effetti della *Execrabilis* di Pio II," *Archivio R. Società romana di storia patria* 37 (1914): 5-36.

If the quest and the market for benefices and the abuse of the venality of offices were as widespread in the Roman Curia as its critics described, Cusanus' reform proposal, perhaps with the exception of the *reformatio capitis*, does not look drastic and comprehensive enough to solve the problems. It is notable that without giving a complete catalogue of abuses in the Roman Curia, the *Reformatio generalis* emphasizes the Penitentiary, whose reputation was certainly low by 1459. Hubert Jedin went so far as to say, "Nothing is said about a change in the officialdom of the Curia."[63] He suggested that the incompleteness of Cusanus' proposal was a result of his unfamiliarity with the papal bureaucracy at that time.[64] After all, Cusanus had come to Rome on September 30, 1458, only about one year before the completion of the *Reformatio generalis*. But this suggestion must be contrasted with the view advanced by Erich Meuthen that probably the *Reformatio generalis*, like some of his other reform proposals, has been only partially preserved.[65] This view gains credence when it is remembered, as Meuthen himself pointed out, that Cusanus probably wrote the *Reformatio rotae*, though it has not been handed down to us.[66]

Another notable aspect of Cusanus' treatment of the Penitentiary is that, at the time of his writing, the Penitentiary was under the guidance of Cardinal Filippo Calandrini, a "simple, moderate, and upright"[67] prelate, and that his predecessors as Major Penitentiaries in the fifteenth century—Giordano Orsini (1415-1429), Niccolò Albergati (1438-1443), Giuliano Cesarini (1443-1444), Giovanni di Tagliacozzo (1445-1449), and Domenico Capranica (1449-1458) —were all cardinals of indisputably fine character and reputation.[68] In discussing the Penitentiary, Cusanus did recommend beginning with the head (*a*

---

[63] Jedin, *History,* 1:123.

[64] Ibid., 1:124: "The reform of the various offices of the Curia takes up far more space in the Bull [*Pastor aeternus*] than in the Cardinal's draft. The Cardinal was not very familiar with these things."

[65] Erich Meuthen, "Neue Schlaglichter auf das Leben des Nikolaus von Kues," MFCG 4 (1964): 37-53 at pp. 49-50, n. 58.

[66] Meuthen, *Die letzten Jahre,* pp. 32, 183-187; idem, "Neue Schlaglichter," p. 48, n. 53.

[67] Pastor, *History,* 3:7, 276: ". . . for the simple, moderate, and upright Calandrini was appointed Grand Penitentiary." Calandrini was a half-brother of Nicholas V and Cardinal of Bologna. See also Schürmeyer, *Das Kardinalkollegium,* pp. 17, 28, 63, 81, 131.

[68] Re, *La Curia,* pp. 272-273.

capite),[69] but was probably more concerned about the *reformatio membrorum* than the *reformatio capitis*.

As the Roman Curia became the center of numerous supplications and the hunting ground for benefices and offices, it steadily and inevitably grew in size, attracting a large number of office-seekers, including ambitious lawyers and articulate humanists, and creating a morally ambivalent milieu.[70] Thus, it is easy to understand that a man like Nicolaus Cusanus, although trained in the law and influenced by humanism, became a rare soul in the Curia. In the well-known scene in 1461, where Cusanus confronted his friend Pius II after the latter's attempt to elevate the ambitious Bishop of Arras, Jean Jouffroy, and others to the cardinalate, Cusanus cried out, as the pope himself reported in his *Commentaries*:

> You are preparing to create new cardinals without any pressing reason merely at your own whim and you have no regard for the oath you swore to the sacred college in the conclave both before and after your election. . . . I do not know how to flatter. I hate adulation. If you can hear the truth, I like nothing which goes on in this Curia. Everything is corrupt. No one does his duty. Neither you nor the cardinals have any care for the Church. What observance of the canons is there? What reverence for laws? What assiduity in divine worship? All are bent on ambition and avarice. If I ever speak in a consistory about reform, I am laughed at. I do no good here. Allow me to withdraw. I cannot endure these ways.[71]

Cusanus was sincere, honest, and perhaps "old-fashioned."[72] While many others were intent on seeking their promotion, maneuvering to satisfy their

---

[69] Ehses, "Der Reformentwurf," p. 297: ". . . deinde a capite visitationem inchoent et, an debita gravitas, zelus, scientia, diligentia, experientia, mundicies manuum, vigilantia et cura tam sancto officio debita in ipso capite reperiantur." Izbicki has suggested to me that by "the head" Cusanus meant in this case the regent of the Penitentiary, but not the cardinal.

[70] Thomson, *Popes and Princes*, p. 97; Stinger, *The Renaissance*, p. 126; D'Amico, *Renaissance Humanism*, p. 21.

[71] *The Commentaries of Pius II,* bks. VI-IX, trans. Florence Aldan Gragg, notes by Leona C. Gabel, Smith College Studies in History, 25 (Northampton, Massachusetts, 1951), p. 500; see also *Memoirs of a Renaissance Pope: The Commentaries of Pius II; An Abridgement,* trans. Florence A. Gragg, ed. Leona C. Gabel (New York, 1959), p. 228. About Jouffroy, see Schürmeyer, *Das Kardinalkollegium,* pp. 67-71.

[72] Cusanus has been called *duri cervicis* and *Dickkopf*. About his personality, characteristics, uprightness, and poverty, see Josef Koch, "Nikolaus von Cues als Mensch nach dem Briefwechsel und persönlichen Aufzeichnungen," in *Humanismus, Mystik und Kunst in der Welt des Mittelalters,* ed. Josef Koch, 2nd ed. (Leiden and Cologne, 1959), pp. 56-75; Meuthen, *Die letzten Jahre,* pp. 87-109 ("Ruf und Lebensstil"); idem, *Nikolaus von Kues,* pp. 156-157.

greed, or enjoying the pleasures the Roman Curia offered, Cusanus, almost hopelessly, was concerned about the reform of the church, especially of the Curia, and engaged in his tenacious search for God and *venatio sapientiae*. A quick look at the number of philosophical and theological writings that were produced during his days in Rome indicates what he was intellectually and religiously struggling with at that time. They include *De aequalitate* (1459), *De principio* (1459), *Trialogus de possest* (1460), *Cribratio Alchorani* (1461), *De non aliud* (1461), *De venatione sapientiae* (1462), *De ludo globi* (1462/3), *Compendium* (1464), and *De apice theoriae* (1464).[73] The learned cardinal was sought after by Roman humanists, such as Giovanni Andrea de' Bussi (1417-1475), Flavio Biondo (1388-1463), and Gaspare Biondo (d.1493).[74]

Vespasiano da Bisticci (1421-1498), the keen observer of the illustrious men of the fifteenth century, clearly understood the character and essence of the man Cusanus, the only German he described in his famous book, when he wrote:

> Messer Nicolo di Cusa, of German nationality, was a man of worship, a great philosopher, theologian and platonist. He was of holy life, well lettered, especially in Greek. . . . He cared nothing for state or for possessions, and was one

---

[73] About the philosophical works of Cusanus in the later period, see F. Edward Cranz, "The Late Works of Nicholas of Cusa," in *Nicholas of Cusa in Search of God and Wisdom: Essays in Honor of Morimichi Watanabe by the American Cusanus Society,* ed. Gerald Christianson and Thomas M. Izbicki, *Studies in the History of Christian Thought,* 45 (Leiden, 1991), pp. 141-160. It should be noted that Cusanus also completed *De mathematica perfectione* at the beginning of October, 1458, and *Aurea propositio in mathematicis* on August 8, 1459, in Rome.

[74] About Bussi, who became Cusanus' secretary in 1458 and later the Librarian of the Vatican Library, see Meuthen, *Die letzten Jahre,* p. 99; idem, "Briefe des Aleriensis an die Sforza," *Römische Quartalschrift* 59 (1964): 88-99; Partner, *The Pope's Men,* p. 223. According to his famous panegyric of Cusanus which was written in 1469, Cusanus encouraged him to take interest in the recently developed method of printing. See Martin Honecker, *Cusanus-Studien,* 2, *Nikolaus von Cues und die griechische Sprache, Nebst einem Angang: Die Lobrede des Giovanni Andrea dei Bussi,* HSB, Jahrgang 1937/38, 2. Abhandlung (Heidelberg, 1938), pp. 66-76. See also Giovanni Andrea Bussi, *Prefazioni alle edizioni di Sweynheym e Pannartz,* ed. Massimo Miglio (Milan, 1978); Erich Meuthen, "Ein neues frühes Quellenzeugnis (zu Oktober 1454?) für den ältesten Bibeldruck: Enea Silvio Piccolomini am 12. März 1455 aus Wiener Neustadt an Kardinal Juan de Carvajal," *Gutenberg-Jahrbuch* (1982): 108-118. About Flavio Biondo, see Pastor, *History,* 3:90; D'Amico, *Renaissance Humanism,* passim; Partner, *The Pope's Men,* p. 220. Gaspare, Flavio's son, is described in Meuthen, *Die letzten Jahre,* p. 307 ("Cusanus' *Familiare*"); idem, *Nikolaus von Kues,* p. 127; D'Amico, *Renaissance Humanism,* passim; Partner, *The Pope's Men,* p. 220.

of the most needy of the cardinals, thus giving an excellent example in all his doings.[75]

The idea of curial reform continued to be expressed even as the bureaucratization of the papal structure and its attendant secularization under the Renaissance popes steadily continued. John O'Malley pointed out that the sacred orators of the Roman Curia in the fifteenth and early sixteenth centuries "keenly felt the need for the moral and disciplinary reform of the city of Rome and the Roman Curia" and that this "meant the transformation of institutions ridden by avarice, ambition, and luxury into institutions where virtue prevailed."[76] After Pius II's death in 1464, reform proposals continued to be published, such as the *Libellus de remediis afflictae ecclesiae* (1469) of Rodrigo Sánchez de Arévalo (1404-1470),[77] *De moribus nostrorum temporum* (1483) of Benedetto Maffei (1429-1494)[78] and *De cardinalatu* (1510) of Paolo Cortesi (1465-1510).[79] It is known that the unpromulgated text of Pius II's *Pastor aeternus* influenced the preparation of papal reform bulls—Sixtus IV's *Quoniam regnantium cura*[80] and Alexander VI's *In apostolica sedis specula.*[81] The reform program of the Fifth Lateran Council (1512-1517), as outlined in orations and documents, and Pope Leo X's two bulls, *Pastoralis officii divina providentia* of December 13, 1513 and *Supernae dispositionis arbitrio* of May 5, 1514,[82] demonstrate clearly that

---

[75] Vespasiano, *Renaissance Popes, Princes and Prelates,* p. 156. For the original, see Vespasiano da Bisticci, *Le vite,* ed. Aulo Greco (Florence, 1970), 1:185. Scholars are not in agreement on how good Cusanus' knowledge of Greek was.

[76] O'Malley, *Praise and Blame,* p. 195.

[77] Ibid., pp. 90-91, 199, 204, 226. On Arévalo, see Richard Trame, *Rodrigo Sánchez de Arévalo, 1404-1470: Spanish Diplomat and Champion of the Papacy* (Washington, D.C., 1958).

[78] D'Amico, *Renaissance Humanism,* p. 220.

[79] Ibid., pp. 227-237.

[80] Tangl, *Die päpstlichen Kanzleiordnungen,* pp. 379-385 ("Reformentwurf Sixtus IV."); Hay, *The Church,* p. 87; O'Malley, *Praise and Blame,* pp. 199-200.

[81] Tangl, *Die päpstlichen Kanzleiordnungen,* pp. 386-388 ("Bericht an die von P. Alexander VI. eingesetzte Cardinalscommission über die in der päpstlichen Kanzlei nothwendigen Reformen"), pp. 402-421 ("Reformentwurf zur einer durch P. Alexander VI. zu erlassenden Reformbulle"); Léonce Celier, "Alexandre VI et la réforme de l'Église," *Mélanges d'archéologie et d'histoire* 27 (1907): 65-124; Hay, *The Church,* p. 87; Thomson, *Popes and Princes,* pp. 108-109.

[82] About the proposal to reform the church at the Fifth Lateran Council, see Jedin, *History,* 1:128-138: "The fifth Lateran council was the last attempt at a papal reform of the Church before the break-up of Christian unity." See also Nelson Minnich, "Concepts

the desire for reform in the Curia continued to exist into the beginning of the sixteenth century.

Viewed against this background, it is important to ask what the significance of the *Reformatio generalis* was, and why Cusanus' reform efforts were not successful. There is no doubt that Cusanus sincerely desired reform, and expressed his ideas in the *Reformatio generalis*, to the extent of recommending the visitation of the pope. In this sense, the *Reformatio generalis* was a genuine attempt by an important member of the Curia and a close friend of Pope Pius II to effect change in the papal administrative structure. But, like many reformers of the period, Cusanus was no "reformer before the Reformation."[83] The ideal of reform which he had tried to apply throughout his life to all aspects of the church was essentially conservative and "restorative" in that he wanted to return to and restore the original, primitive image of the church (*ecclesia primitiva*).[84] Frustrated and disappointed especially in the later part of his life, the man from Cues in the Moselle region became increasingly pessimistic about the possibility of reform.[85] His own negative personal characteristics, such as stubbornness, inflexibility, irritability, and lack of tact and patience, may have contributed to the failure of the reform attempts.[86] The situation became worse when Pius II, who undoubtedly shared Cusanus' reform ideals especially at the beginning of his pontificate, became increasingly preoccupied with the crusade against the Turks, thereby pushing the reform program into the background.[87]

of Reform Proposed at the Fifth Lateran Council," *Archivum Historiae Pontificiae* 7 (1969): 163-251; idem, "The Participation at the Fifth Lateran Council," ibid., 12 (1974): 157-206.

[83] Carl Ullmann, *Reformatoren vor der Reformation,* 2nd ed., 2 vols. (Gotha, 1866).

[84] Iserloh, "Reform der Kirche," pp. 60, 62. It can easily be argued that Martin Luther's original intention was, like that of many medieval reformers, to restore the *ecclesia primitiva.*

[85] In his letter to Bernhard von Krayburg, chancellor of the Archdiocese of Salzburg, written in 1460, Cusanus expressed his frustration and pessimism about the possibility of reform; see Meuthen, *Nikolaus von Kues,* p. 120. Together with Cusanus himself, Bernhard von Krayburg and Giovanni Andrea de' Bussi were interlocutors in *De possest;* see ibid., p. 120.

[86] As a preacher, Cusanus was often not very successful. His sermons delivered as Bishop of Brixen were sometimes too difficult for his simple mountain people to understand. See Koch, *Predigten,* pp. 21-22; Franz Rudolf Reichert, *Prediger der Erneuerung und der Versöhnung,* Kleine Schriften der Cusanus-Gesellschaft, 10 (Trier, 1977), p. 8. On Cusanus' sermons in Rome, see also O'Malley, *Praise and Blame,* pp. 94-101, 149.

[87] Pastor, *History,* 3:275-276: ". . . in the interests of the Church, this can never be sufficiently regretted."

The political disputes that involved many of the local nobility in Rome and the possible threat from outside by the mercenary Pincinino made the implementation of reform very difficult.[88] The groups in the Curia opposed to reform were also too powerful to be curtailed.[89] Cusanus' personal sincerity, purity, and devotion to reform ideals were not enough when rapid institutional changes and swift religious upheavals were taking place.

Reformer or not, Cusanus tried hard and often alone to bring about religious renewal in an increasingly hostile environment.[90]

---

[88] About the complex, turbulent political situation in and outside Rome during the period, see Pastor, *History,* 3:102-128; Meuthen, *Nikolaus von Kues,* pp. 114, 144. A much more radical criticism is leveled at Cusanus by Karl Jaspers who says that the chief reason for Cusanus' failure to reform was his lack of inner renewal; see Jaspers, *Nikolaus Cusanus* (Munich, 1964), p. 204.

[89] Thomson, *Popes and Princes,* p. 111: "Individuals, both great and obscure, looked to Rome for privileges of many kinds, whether it were a dispensation for marriage despite the restrictions of consanguinity, commutation of a vow of pilgrimage, or a dispensation to a clerk to hold more than one incompatible benefice in plurality."

[90] On the occasion of the investiture of his namesake, a novice called Niccolò Albergati, at a Tuscan abbey of Montoliveto on June 5, 1463, Cusanus delivered a sermon *Ergo notum sit.* In a letter that he sent six days later to Albergati, which is regarded as his spiritual testament, he, after summing up his past intellectual labors, expressed his views on his approaching death. See Gerda von Bredow, *Cusanus-Texte,* 4, *Briefwechsel des Nikolaus von Kues,* pt. 3, *Das Vermächtnis des Nikolaus von Kues. Der Brief an Nikolaus Albergati nebst der Predigt in Montoliveto (1463),* HSB, Jahrgang 1955, 2. Abhandlung (Heidelberg, 1955). See also Meuthen, *Nikolaus von Kues,* p. 124. About the hospital called St. Andreas-Hospiz der Anima which Cusanus founded in Rome for ailing German officials in the Curia, see Hermann Hallauer, "Das St. Andreas-Hospiz der Anima in Rom: Ein Beitrag zur Biographie des Nikolaus von Kues," *MFCG* 19 (1991): 25-52.

Nicholas of Cusa,
A General Reform of the Church

Morimichi Watanabe and Thomas M. Izbicki

The *Reformatio generalis* is one of the most important documents written by Nicholas of Cusa,[1] or Nicolaus Cusanus, who is known as a leading creative thinker of the fifteenth century. Cusanus, for whom the problem of church reform was a central one throughout his active life, discussed the issue in this document, written in his later years, not only in general and theological terms, but also with a view to correcting current ecclesiastical practices. It is surprising that an English translation has not yet been published.[2]

Born in Bernkastel-Cues, Germany, in 1401, the son of a well-to-do boat owner (*nauta*), Cusanus studied the liberal arts at the University of Heidelberg for a year and a half before going to Italy to study canon law. He entered the University of Padua in 1417 and obtained the decree of *doctor decretorum* in 1423. With the help of an income provided by Otto von Ziegenhain, Archbishop of Trier (1418-1430), later in 1423 he matriculated at the University of Cologne, where he studied and, perhaps, taught law. Already, while in Padua, Nicholas

---

1 The most important and comprehensive work on Cusanus' life and thought is still Edmond Vansteenberghe, *Le cardinal Nicolas de Cues (1401-1464): L'action— la pensée* (Paris, 1920; reprint Frankfurt 1963). See also Erich Meuthen, *Nikolaus von Kues, 1401-1464: Skizze einer Biographie*, 6th ed. (Münster, 1989). There is no adequate study in English. Henry Bett, *Nicholas of Cusa* (London, 1923; reprint New York, 1976) depends heavily on Vansteenberghe. An ambitious attempt to publish all pertinent documents, under way since 1940, is *Acta Cusana*, edited by Erich Meuthen and Hermann Hallauer; see 1/1 and 1/2 (Hamburg, 1976-1983) [hereafter *A C*]. I/3 is almost ready for publication. An extensive bibliography of Cusanus scholarship has been published in *MFCG* since 1961.

2 The translation in the Appendix was made by Thomas M. Izbicki from the Latin text edited in Stephan Ehses, "Der Reformentwurf des Kardinals Nikolaus Cusanus", *Historisches Jahrbuch* 32 (1911): 281-297. There are three extant manuscripts of the *Reformatio generalis*: Cod. lat. Monacensis (Clm) 422, fol. 252-262 of the State Library in Munich; Cod. Vat. lat. 8090, fol. 109r-122v (used by Ehses); Cod. Vat. lat. 3883, fol. 1r-11r. For an edition from the Munich manuscript, see Johann M. Düx, *Der deutsche Cardinal Nicolaus von Cusa und die Kirche seiner Zeit* (Regensburg, 1847), 2:451-466. For a partial German translation, see ibid., 2:88-105. For a full translation, see Franz A. Scharpff, *Der Kardinal und Bischof Nicolaus von Cusa* (Mainz, 1843), 1:284-305. On the manuscripts, see Vansteenberghe, *Le cardinal*, p. 474; Rudolf Haubst, *Studien zu Nikolaus von Kues und Johannes Wenck: Aus Handschriften der vatikanischen Bibliothek* (Münster, 1955), pp. 9-11.

had begun to develop an interest in philosophy and theology; in Cologne he came under the influence of the Albertist theologian Heymericus de Campo (Heymeric van den Velde) (1395-1460), whose teaching helped interest him in the speculative currents of the age.[3]

He first attended the Council of Basel (1431-1449), beginning in February of 1431, as a counsel of an old friend, Count Ulrich von Manderscheid, who sought to become archbishop of Trier. To support Ulrich's case against the papal appointee, Jakob von Sierck, Cusanus composed his first major ecclesiological work, *De concordantia catholica*. That treatise had grown, during 1432-1433, from a short treatise for conciliar supremacy over the pope into one of the major monuments of medieval institutional thought.[4] During the debate on the presidency of the council in 1434, Cusanus tied his fortunes to those of Cardinal Giuliano Cesarini (1398-1444), the president of the council and a dedicatee of *De concordantia catholica*, with whom he sided in the later disputes over the site of a council of union with the Greeks. In 1437, Nicholas supported the minority decree naming a site in Italy; and he went to Constantinople to present that decree to the Greeks on behalf of the minority faction and Pope Eugenius IV (1430-1447).[5]

---

[3] For recent studies of Heymericus, see Eusebi Colomer, "Heimeric van den Velde entre Ramon Lull y Nicolas de Cusa," *Spanische Forschungen der Görresgesellschaft*, 1st ser., 6 (1963): 216-232; Antony Black, "Heimericus de Campo: The Council and History," *Annuarium Historiae Conciliorum* 2 (1970): 78-86; idem, "The Realist Ecclesiology of Heimerich van den Velde," in *Facultas S. Theologiae Lovaniensis 1432-1797*, ed. E.J.M. van Eijl (Louvain, 1977), pp. 273-291; Jean-Daniel Cavigioli, "Les écrits d' Heymericus de Campo (1395-1460) sur les oeuvres d'Aristote," *Freiburger Zeitschrift für Philosophie und Theologie* 28 (1981): 293-371; Pascal Ladner, *Revolutionäre Kirchenkritik am Basler Konzil?: Zum Konziliarismus des Heymericus de Campo*, Vorträge der Aeneas-Silvius-Stiftung an der Universität Basel, 19 (Basel, 1985).

[4] For an English translation, see Nicholas of Cusa, *The Catholic Concordance*, trans. Paul E. Sigmund (Cambridge, 1991). For the growth of a comparatively modest treatise into a substantial book, see Gerhard Kallen, *Die handschriftliche Überlieferung der Concordantia catholica des Nikolaus von Kues*, Cusanus-Studien, 8 (Heidelberg, 1963). For recent studies of this work, see Gerd Heinz-Mohr, *Unitas Christiana: Studien zur Gesellschaftsidee des Nikolaus von Kues* (Trier, 1958); Paul E. Sigmund, *Nicholas of Cusa and Medieval Political Thought* (Cambridge, Massachusetts, 1963); Morimichi Watanabe, *The Political Ideas of Nicholas of Cusa with Special Reference to His De concordantia catholica* (Genève, 1963); Arnulf Vagedes, *Das Konzil über dem Papst?: Die Stellungnahmen des Nikolaus von Kues und des Panormitanus zum Streit zwischen dem Konzil von Basel und Eugen IV*, 2 vols. (Paderborn, 1981); Hermann J. Sieben, "Der Konziltrakt des Nikolaus von Kues: *De concordantia catholica*," *Annuarium Historiae Conciliorum* 14 (1982): 171-226.

[5] For Cusanus and Cesarini, see, most recently, "Nicholas of Cusa: On Presidential Authority in a General Council," trans. H. Lawrence Bond, Gerald Christianson and

During his return from Constantinople, Cusanus had a mystical vision, which redirected much of his intellectual energies from institutional theory to speculative thought. Nonetheless, between 1438 and 1447, Cusanus worked so hard at imperial diets and assemblies to bring the German princes, who had taken a position of neutrality in the struggle between Basel and Pope Eugenius, back into the papal camp that Aeneas Sylvius Piccolomini, the future Pope Pius II (1458-1464), called him "the Hercules of all the Eugenians."[6] Promoted to the cardinalate in 1448 as a reward, he was appointed bishop of the Tyrolese see of Brixen in 1450. But, before assuming his episcopal responsibilities in Brixen, he went in 1451-1452 on his famous legatine journey to Germany and the Low Countries on behalf of Pope Nicholas V (1447-1455). Among his duties, whose execution often was resisted, were proclamation of the Jubilee year of 1450, reformation of religious life and mediation of disputes.[7] His ensuing eight-year episcopate in Brixen, during which he tried to reform the monastic houses of the diocese and curtail the expansion of secular power into ecclesiastical domains, aroused the powerful opposition of Duke Sigismund of the Tyrol (1446-1496). The resulting strife, no doubt, produced one of the most trying periods of

---

Thomas M. Izbicki, *Church History* 59 (1990): 19-34. For the criticism falling on Cusanus for his transfer of allegiance, see, for example, Watanabe, *Political Ideas*, pp. 97-98; James E. Biechler, "Nicholas of Cusa and the End of the Conciliar Movement: A Humanist Crisis on Identity," *Church History* 34 (1975): 5-21; Joachim Stieber, "The 'Hercules of the Eugenians' at the Crossroads: Nicholas of Cusa's Decision for the Pope and Against the Council in 1436/1437—Theological, Political and Social Aspects," *Nicholas of Cusa in Search of God and Wisdom: Essays in Honor of Morimichi Watanabe*, ed. Gerald Christianson and Thomas M. Izbicki (Leiden, 1991), pp. 221-255.

6 Aeneas Sylvius Piccolomineus, *Commentarii de gestis Basiliensis concilii* (Basel, 1571), p. 3: "Hercules tamen omnium Eugenianorum Nicolaus Cusanus existimatus est." See also idem, *De gestis concilii Basiliensis commentariorum libri II*, ed. Denys Hay and W.K. Smith (Oxford, 1967), pp. 14-15.

7 On Cusanus' legatine journey, see K. Grube, "Die Legationsreise des Cardinals Nikolaus von Cusa durch Norddeutschland im Jahre 1451," *Historisches Jahrbuch* 1 (1880): 393-412; Johannes Uebinger, "Kardinallegat Nikolaus Cusanus in Deutschland 1451 bis 1452," ibid. 7 (1887): 629-635; Ignaz Zibermayr, *Die Legationen des Kardinals Nikolaus Cusanus und die Ordensreform in der Kirchenprovinz Salzburg* (Münster, 1914); Josef Koch, *Der deutsche Kardinal in deutschen Landen: Die Legationsreise des Nikolaus von Kues (1451/1452)* (Trier, 1964); Donald Sullivan, "Nicholas of Cusa as Reformer: The Papal Legation to the Germanies, 1451-1452," *Medieval Studies* 36 (1974): 382-428. The most recent study, written in preparation for *AC* I/3, is Erich Meuthen, "Die deutsche Legationsreise des Nikolaus von Kues, 1451-1452," in *Lebenslehren und Weltentwürfe im Übergang vom Mittelalter zur Neuzeit: Politik-Bildung-Naturkunde-Theologie*, ed. Hartmut Boockmann, Bernd Moeller and Karl Stackmann (Göttingen, 1989), pp. 421-499.

Cusanus' life; but it taught him how important it was to effect ecclesiastical reforms at the various levels within Christendom.[8]

Even before ascending the throne of Saint Peter in 1458, Aeneas Sylvius, who had lived in Rome as a cardinal after December 18, 1456, urged his friend Cusanus, in his letter of December 27, 1456, to come to the Eternal City, which was the only home of cardinals, and not to waste his time and energy in the "dark valleys and snows" of the Tyrol.[9] It was on September 30, 1458, shortly after Aeneas became Pope Pius II, that Cusanus arrived in Rome, an exile from his see. No pope of the fifteenth century was as familiar with many parts of Europe as was Pius II. He knew Germany and Bohemia well, to say nothing of Italy; he even had visited Scotland via England.[10] As a result, he was naturally sensitive about the expansion of the domains of the Ottoman Turks. In his opinion, the great blemish on the pontificate of Nicholas V, a humanist like himself, was the shadow cast over Christendom by the fall of Constantinople in 1453. This concern for the borders of Christendom was heightened by the objections offered in the conclave of 1458 that Aeneas' health was too poor to permit him, if elected pope, to organize a crusade against the Turks.[11] But, alongside his famous concern with the Turkish threat to Europe, Aeneas desired to reform

---

[8] Among the numerous works on Cusanus as bishop of Brixen, see Albert Jäger, *Der Streit des Cardinals Nikolaus von Cusa mit dem Herzoge Sigmund von Österreich als Grafen von Tirol*, 2 vols. (Innsbruck, 1861; reprint Frankfurt 1968); Pardon E. Tillinghast, "Nicholas of Cusa vs. Sigmund of Habsburg: An Attempt at Post-Conciliar Church Reform," *Church History* 36 (1967): 371-390; Wilhelm Baum, *Nikolaus Cusanus in Tirol: Das Wirken des Philosophen und Reformators als Fürstbischof von Brixen* (Bozen, 1983); Morimichi Watanabe, "Nicholas of Cusa and the Tyrolese Monasteries: Reform and Resistance," *History of Political Thought* 7 (1986): 53-72.

[9] Erich Meuthen, *Die letzen Jahre des Nikolaus von Kues: Biographische Untersuchungen nach neuen Quellen* (Cologne and Opladen, 1958), pp. 133-134: "Precor igitur, si preces servitoris audiende sunt, ut iam denum in patriam redeas; nam cardinali sola Roma patria est. . . . Veni igitur, obsecro veni! Neque enim tua virtus est, que inter nives et umbrosas clausa valles languescere debeat." Aeneas sent Cusanus another letter from Rome with a similar message on August 1, 1457; see Meuthen, *Die letzen Jahre*, pp. 134-135.

[10] William Boulting, *Aeneas Silvius (Enea Silvio de' Piccolomini—Pius II.): Orator, Man of Letters, Statesman, and Pope* (London, 1908), pp. 59-64; Rosamund J. Mitchell, *The Laurels and the Tiara: Pope Pius II, 1458-1464* (London, 1962), pp. 65-73; Constance Head, "Pope Pius II (Aeneas Silvius Piccolomini) as a Student of English History," *Archivum Historiae Pontificiae* 9 (1971): 187-208.

[11] Mitchell, *The Laurels*, pp. 112-113. On Pius II and the crusade, see Ludwig Pastor, *Geschichte der Päpste seit dem Ausgang des Mittelalters* (Freiburg, 1889), 2:217-261; idem, *The History of the Popes, from the Close of the Middle Ages*, ed. Frederick I. Antrobus, 5th ed. (London, 1949), 3:311-374.

the Church. He knew the desire of many to see reform "in head and members" achieved from his years at the Council of Basel and in Germany.[12] Even the curia was not insensitive to this burning issue of the day. The electoral capitulation of 1458, which was drawn up by all the cardinals, including Aeneas, on the first day of the conclave, included promises to further the crusade and to reform the curia.[13] Although he did not regard himself as strictly bound by the capitulation, Pius acted on both of these promises. He himself summoned and attended the Congress of Mantua, which attempted to organize a crusade; but he entrusted the task of planning reform of the curia to a commission, which was to report to him on his return from Mantua. The pope told the commission that the two things closest to his heart were reform and the crusade, coupling the two issues inextricably, at least in his own mind. The appointment of the commission coincided with the nomination of Cusanus to serve as papal vicar general for Rome in the pope's absence and the cardinal's efforts, through holding a synod of the clergy of the pope's own diocese, to promote reform in the Eternal City itself.[14]

Of the proposals prepared by the commissioners only two have come down to us. One was the *Tractatus de reformationibus Romanae curiae* of the learned bishop of Torcello, Domenico de' Domenichi (1416-1478), written in September or October of 1458.[15] This was a narrowly focused tract, intended to improve the efficiency and integrity of the curia.[16] The other was the *Reformatio generalis* of Nicholas of Cusa, probably completed in the first part of July of 1459 and drafted in the form of a papal bull. This work covered not just reform

---

12 The phrase "in head and members" appeared in the famous, controversial decree *Haec sancta* of the Council of Constance, published on April 6, 1415; see C.M.D. Crowder, *Unity, Heresy and Reform 1378-1460: The Conciliar Response to the Great Schism* (London, 1977), p. 83. On the Constance reform program and its relation to *Haec sancta,* see now Phillip H. Stump, *The Reforms of the Council of Constance 1414-1418* (Leiden, 1994).

13 Pastor, *Geschichte der Päpste,* 2:188; idem, *History of the Popes,* 3:269; Mitchell, *The Laurels,* p. 217.

14 Pastor, *Geschichte der Päpste,* 2:188; idem, *History of the Popes,* 3:269. For the Congress of Mantua, see, most recently, Joycelyne G. Russell, *Diplomats at Work: Three Renaissance Studies* (Gloucestershire, 1992), pp. 51-93. For the synod held by Cusanus, see Meuthen, *Die letzen Jahre,* pp. 31-32, 145-146.

15 Pastor, *The History of the Popes,* 3:271; Hubert Jedin, *A History of the Council of Trent,* trans. Ernest Graf (London, 1957-1961), 1:247.

16 On the *Tractatus,* see Hubert Jedin, *Studien über Domenico de' Domenichi (1416-1478)* (Wiesbaden, 1958); *Domenico de' Domenichi und seine Schrift, De potestate papae et termino eius: Edition und Kommentar,* ed. Heribert Smolinsky (Münster, 1976). A brief summary is given in Pastor, *Geschichte der Päpste,* 2:190-192; idem, *The History of the Popes,* 3:272-275. Franco Gaeta, *Domenico Domenichi, De reformationibus Romanae curiae* (Aquila, s.d.) was unavailable to the authors.

of the curia but the needs of the entire church.[17] These reform tracts exercised a great influence on the drafting of the reform bull *Pastor aeternus*, which Pius II composed toward the end of his pontificate but never published.[18]

Cusanus' *Reformatio generalis* contains a theological introduction, fourteen general rules about the visitation and reform of the church and, finally, practical suggestions for the reform of the curia. Like many medieval discourses, Cusanus' proposal begins from "on high."[19] To the question of why created man exists, he replies in the introduction that man was created so that he might see God in His glory. In freedom the intellect seeks the very wisdom of God, which makes man blessed and happy. God sent Christ, who takes away ignorance, commanding that he be heard. Men should believe in him, the messenger, who built the church from those faithful to him. Whoever believes this truly and keeps his commandments does not sin and knows nothing except Christ. It is impossible for mankind to attain the kingdom of immortality unless it takes on the form (*formam*) of the Lord. It is necessary, therefore, to be like Christ, who was made just for us. He is the living law and the perfect form. Those conformed to him are the children of eternal life. The church of God is the mystical body of Christ, which can be likened to the human body. All members are united, and the diversity of the members of the body is bound together by love.[20]

One of the central concepts in this theological introduction is belief in Christ.[21] It is this faith by which the just man lives. Echoing some passages

[17] On this proposal, see Pastor, *Geschichte der Päpste*, 2:189-190; idem, *The History of the Popes*, 3:270-272; Erwin Iserloh, "Reform der Kirche bei Nikolaus von Kues," *MFCG* 4 (1964): 54-73, esp. at p. 56; Morimichi Watanabe, "Nicholas of Cusa and the Reform of the Roman Curia," in *Humanity and Divinity in Renaissance and Reformation: Essays in Honor of Charles Trinkaus*, ed. John W. O'Malley, Thomas M. Izbicki and Gerald Christianson (Leiden, 1993), pp. 185-203. See also Denys Hay, *The Church in Italy in the Fifteenth Century* (London, 1977), p. 86.

[18] For *Pastor aeternus*, see Rudolf Haubst, "Reformentwurf Pius des Zweiten," *Römische Quartalschrift* 49 (1954): 188-242. See also the Latin text in Michael Tangl, *Die päpstlichen Kanzleiordnungen von 1200-1500* (Innsbruck, 1894; reprint Aaalen, 1959), pp. 372-379. A German translation appears in Pastor, *Geschichte der Päpste*, 2:611-616; an English translation, in idem, *The History of the Popes*, 3:347-403. See also Iserloh, "Reform," p. 56.

[19] Ehses, "Der Reformentwurf," p. 281: "quaedam ex alto praemittere convenit." The translation, including the passages cited, will be found in the Appendix.

[20] Ehses, "Der Reformentwurf," pp. 281-285.

[21] Ibid., p. 283. On the importance of Christology in Cusanus' works, see Rudolf Haubst, *Die Christologie des Nikolaus von Kues* (Freiburg, 1956); H. Lawrence Bond, "Nicholas of Cusa and the Reconstruction of Theology: The Centrality of Christology in the Coincidence of Opposites," in *The Medieval Christian Tradition: Essays in Honor of Ray C. Petry*, ed. George H. Shriver (Durham, North Carolina, 1974), pp. 81-94.

in the Bible, especially Romans 1:17, Cusanus' doctrine resembles Martin Luther's evangelical doctrine of justification by faith. This has prompted the Roman Catholic historian Erwin Iserloh to discuss rather extensively Cusanus' almost "Protestant" notion of salvation.[22] But it is necessary to note that Cusanus also speaks of receiving Christ "by faith and works."[23] When Cusanus defines reform as an attempt to "bring back to the original form (*ad formam primam reducere*),"[24] he means the form of Christ, the *forma iustitiae*. This Christocentric notion of reform also is stated clearly later in the document.[25]

Turning his attention away from individuals and their faith in Christ, Cusanus deals in the later part of the introduction with the institutional dimensions of reform, basing his discussion on the well-established notion of the church as the mystical body of Christ. The organic concept of the church is essentially Pauline and reminds the reader of its secular version in the *Policraticus* of John of Salisbury and later writers.[26] Cusanus himself had dealt with the concept extensively in his *De concordantia catholica*.[27] In this section of the *Reformatio generalis*, Cusanus emphasizes again and again that the church was to be built up and that the building up of the church (*aedificatio ecclesiae*), instead of its diminution, is a key criterion in judging the performance of the diverse officers of the church.[28]

"It is notable," Cusanus writes, "that the body of the church in this age has declined greatly from the light and the day, becoming enveloped in dark shadows."[29] This has resulted because the eyes, which should be its light, have fallen into darkness. The goal of ecclesiastical reform, like the reform of individuals, should be to bring back the church of the original disciples (*ecclesiae primitivorum*).[30] It is interesting to note that the famous historian of the papacy

---

22 Ehses, "Der Reformentwurf," p. 283; Iserloh, "Reform," pp. 69-71.

23 Ehses, "Der Reformentwurf," p. 284: ". . . fide et opere . . ."

24 Ibid., p. 286. See also Iserloh, "Reform," pp. 58, 60.

25 Iserloh, "Reform," p. 69.

26 John of Salisbury, *Policraticus*, ed. C.C.J. Webb, (Oxford, 1909). The most recent English translation is John of Salisbury, *Policraticus: Of the Frivolities of Courtiers and the Footprints of the Philosophers*, trans. Cary J. Nederman (Cambridge, 1990).

27 *DCC* I,1-6 (h XIV,31-60).

28 See also Iserloh, "Reform," p. 66. For Cusanus' ideas of building up the church in the letter to Rodrigo Sánchez de Arévalo, see Thomas M. Izbicki, "The Church in the Light of Learned Ignorance," *Medieval Philosophy and Theology* 3 (1993): 196-214.

29 Ehses, "Reformentwurf," p. 285.

30 Ibid., p. 291. See also n. 24.

Ludwig Pastor criticized Georg Voigt, the author of the last major biography of Pius II in German, because he had described the preface to the *Reformatio generalis* as "a rather lengthy introduction" to, and discussion of, God, Christ and the Church in "a mystical-trifling manner."[31] Since Voigt's comment on the document was very brief and limited, Pastor may have been overly critical of him.[32] It is important to remember, however, that reform remained a crucial issue during the half century between Cusanus' death and the Reformation.[33]

In advancing his general rules for the reform of the church in the second part of the document, Cusanus framed his recommendations in terms of a visitation, the formal inspection which a superior prelate made of his subordinates to discover and correct abuses. According to Cusanus, two stages of visitation were necessary for the reform of Christendom. First, the pope and the Roman curia should submit themselves to visitation by three grave and mature men (*graves et maturos*), who combine knowledge and prudence with zeal for God.[34] Thereafter, this process of visitation was to be extended to the entire church. "We should begin in this with our Roman church and the curia; and, thereafter, we should send visitors to individual provinces."[35]

These visitors were to be given fourteen rules for the execution of their duties. In examining these rules, one finds that they contain no unusual, extraordinary or especially strict recommendations. One of the ideas advanced by Cusanus is that of "name," found in Rule Four,[36] where he wrote that everyone should be or act what his name is supposed to imply. Whoever acts differently from what the name suggests should be punished or expelled:

> How can someone be called a Christian whose life is contrary to Christ? How can [a man be called] a religious who is an apostate; a monk, if he runs around in cities; a canon, if he is irregular; a priest, if [he is] profane . . . a king, if [he is] a tyrant.[37]

In the course of his legatine journey and of his episcopate at Brixen, Cusanus apparently had found many individuals whose official designation and real manner of living were tragically at odds. He hoped that Pius II would bring them

---

31 Pastor, *Geschichte der Päpste*, 2:189 n. 1; idem, *The History of the Papacy*, 3:270.

32 Georg Voigt, *Enea Silvio de' Piccolomini* (Berlin, 1863; reprint Berlin, 1967), 2:341.

33 Jedin, *A History of the Council of Trent*, 1:30-31, 117-138.

34 Ehses, "Der Reformentwurf," p. 286.

35 Ibid., p. 286.

36 Ibid., p. 287. See also Iserloh, "Reform," pp. 58-59.

37 Ehses, "Der Reformentwurf," p. 285.

back into conformity with the names of their offices and, ultimately, with the name of Christ, from which they were called Christians.

Other rules clearly manifest Cusanus' concern about the problems involving benefices, especially pluralism, and the use of churches and convents as sinecures, as well as the opposition offered to reform by the secular and regular clergy under the pretext of papal privileges. All these rules, no doubt, were based on personal, often bitter experience. It is notable that Nicholas did not attempt a complete catalogue of abuses; but a few examples related to his experiences are mentioned. His warning to the visitors about the cloisters of nuns in Rule Twelve clearly reflects his long struggle with the Abbess Verena von Stuben about the reform of the nuns of Sonnenburg in the Tyrol.[38] His criticism of some relics or miraculous effusions of blood from hosts in Rule Thirteen resulted from his experience at Wilsnack during his legation.[39] Some readers may wonder how Cusanus, who himself obtained so many benefices in the course of his ecclesiastical career,[40] could be critical of pluralism in good conscience; but such criticisms were consistent with the theme of building up the church which runs through these rules.

In the last section of the document, Cusanus states that these fourteen rules are to be applied to the pope, the cardinals, the curia and the divine services in Rome. He especially was concerned about the office of the Penitentiary, the officials of which, who were in charge of cases of conscience, were notorious at the time for corruption.[41] Already, in *De concordantia catholica*, Cusanus had

---

38 Ehses, "Der Reformentwurf," p. 290. On Cusanus' contest with Abbess Verena, see, for example, Jäger, *Der Streit,* passim; Hermann Hallauer, "Eine Visitation des Nikolaus von Kues im Benediktinerinnenkloster Sonnenburg," *MFCG* 4 (1964): 104-125; Kolumban Spahr, "Nikolaus von Cues, das adelige Nonnenklausur," in *Cusanus-Gedächtnisschrift*, ed. Nikolaus Grass (Innsbruck, 1970), pp. 307-326; Watanabe, "Nicholas of Cusa and the Tyrolese Monasteries," pp. 53-72. For a suggestion that, since Cusanus only reached Rome on September 30, 1458, he was not as familiar with curial abuses as with those he had met elsewhere and so did not treat them at length, see Jedin, *A History of the Council of Trent*, 1:124. For a suggestion that, instead, our text of the *Reformatio generalis* simply is not complete, see Erich Meuthen, "Neue Schlaglichter auf das Leben des Nikolaus von Kues," *MFCG* 4 (1964): 37-53 at p. 50, n. 58.

39 Ehses, "Der Reformentwurf," pp. 290-291. See also Sullivan, "Nicholas of Cusa as Reformer," pp. 382-428; Meuthen, "Die deutsche Legationsreise," pp. 486-487.

40 Erich Meuthen, "Die Pfründen des Cusanus," *MFCG* 2 (1962): 15-66.

41 F.W.H. Wasserschleben, *Die Bussordnungen des abendländischen Kirche nebst einer rechtsgeschichtlichen Einleitung* (Halle, 1851); Emil Göller, *Die päpstliche Pönitentiarie von ihrem Ursprung bis zur ihrer Ungestellung unter Pius V*, vol. 2 (Roma, 1911); Walther von Hofmann, *Forschungen zur Geschichte der kurialen Behörden vom Schisma bis zur Reformation*, vol. 1 (Rome, 1914). See also Peter Partner, *The Pope's Men: The Papal Civil Service in the Renaissance* (Oxford, 1990);

emphasized that reform must start from the head and that what was needed was the execution of canons that already existed.[42] In proposing a program for the visitation of pope, cardinals and curia, Cusanus was complying with the electoral capitulations to which Pius had agreed and with the pontiff's own instructions to the commissioners. Undoubtedly, Cusanus was keenly aware that, in the opinion of many contemporaries, the sorry condition of the church was a result of the low moral state of the curia and that many had little hope for a successful reform of the curia from within. Cusanus addressed this issue on behalf of the pope, using his doctrine of conformity to one's name. Since "we should strive likewise to be what we are called and to show in action what we profess to be," the visitors should not "fear to visit the pope," whom "they will find . . . like other men, sinful and infirm."[43] "Whatever, therefore, they find in us which does not build up but rather scandalizes the church, let them show us altogether . . ."[44] It is important to note that, although the reform proposals of Cusanus and Domenichi discussed the visitation of the pope, Pius II's *Pastor aeternus* did not contain anything similar on that topic.[45]

In applying these rules to the cardinals, the visitors were supposed especially to examine whether they have three things: zeal for God's house; freedom and faithfulness in counsel; and a simple, exemplary way of life. Since they were cardinals "not for their own sakes but to cooperate with the supreme pontiff in building up the church," they, "as if legates of the nations," were to form with the pope "a daily, comprehensive council of the church."[46] This notion is reminiscent of recent discussions of collegiality in ecclesiastical government.[47] The visitors were then to proceed to reform divine worship in the city

---

idem, *The Papal State Under Martin V: The Administration and Government of the Temporal Power in the Early Fifteenth Century* (Rome, 1958), esp. pp. 131-158.

[42] Iserloh, "Reform," p. 57; Watanabe, *The Political Ideas*, pp. 110-113.

[43] Ehses, "Der Reformentwurf," p. 292.

[44] Ibid., p. 292.

[45] John W. O'Malley, *Praise and Blame in Renaissance Rome: Rhetoric, Doctrine and Reform in the Sacred Orators of the Papal Court, c. 1450-1521* (Durham, North Carolina, 1979), p. 218.

[46] Ehses, "Der Reformentwurf," p. 292: "Faciunt igitur nobiscum quotidianum compendiosum ecclesiae concilium quasi legati nationum." See also Erich Meuthen, "Die universalpolitischen Ideen des Nikolaus von Kues in seiner Erfahrung der politischen Wirklichkeit," *Quellen und Forschungen aus italienischen Archiven und Bibliotheken* 37 (1957): 215-220; idem, "Die Synode im Kirchenverständnis des Nikolaus von Kues," in *Staat, Kultur, Politik—Beiträge zur Geschichte Bayerns und des Katholizismus: Festschrift zum 65. Geburtstag von Dieter Albrecht* (Kallmünz, 1992), p. 23.

[47] See, for example, Paul E. Sigmund, "Konzilsidee und Kollegialität nach Cusanus," *MFCG* 5 (1965): 86-97; Giuseppe Alberigo, *Cardinalato e collegialità* (Florence, 1969).

of Rome by visiting the principal papal basilicas, the titular churches of the cardinals, the religious houses and the hospitals. They also were to examine the books necessary for divine worship and ensure that they were correct and conformed to the usage of Rome.[48]

Concerning curial officials, the visitors were to investigate why they dwelt in the curia and whether they were needed there. The curia was not to be an asylum for idle and roaming prelates and religious, who should not be in Rome simply "for canvassing [to obtain] greater dignities and plurality of benefices."[49] "Greed, which for some is like worship of idols, should not be stirred up but extinguished."[50] All who were detained there, for whatever reason, were to conform to the rules of the church in conduct, morals, clothing, tonsure and observance of the canonical vows. Those who were in the curia to hunt benefices were to be sent back to their churches.

Finally, the visitors were to examine carefully the office of the Penitentiary according to the general rules. After receiving testimony from three of the most experienced members of the staff about the office, its personnel, statutes, oath and servants, the visitors were to inquire from top down "whether due gravity, zeal, knowledge, diligence, experience, cleanness of hands, vigilance and care"[51] could be found in the head, possibly the senior staff member, rather than the cardinal serving as major penitentiary, who would have been visited with the other members of the Sacred College, and in the minor penitentiaries. If they were found wanting, the visitors were to eject them without difficulty. The letter writers of the Penitentiary were to write their own documents and to understand what they wrote. If they were not honest and pure, they were to be expelled.[52] Cusanus' general idea was to remove novelties which had been introduced for the sake of gain.[53]

---

48 Ehses, "Der Reformentwurf," p. 295.

49 Ibid., pp. 295-296.

50 Ibid., p. 296.

51 Ibid., p. 296.

52 Ehses, "Der Reformentwurf," p. 297. On the letter writers, see Göller, *Das päpstliche Pönitentiarie,* pp. 90-131; Brigide Schwarz, *Die Organization kurialer Schreibkollegien von ihrer Entstehung bis zur Mitte des 15. Jahrhundert* (Tübingen, 1972); idem, "Abbreviatoren unter Eugen IV: Päpstliches Reservationsrecht, Konkordanzpolitik und kuriale Ämterorganization mit zwei Anhängen," *Quellen und Forschungen aus italienischen Archiven und Bibliotheken* 60 (1980): 200-274; Thomas Frenz, "Zum Problem der Reduzierung der Zahl der päpstlichen Kanzleischreiber nach dem Konzil von Konstanz," in *Grundwissenschaften und Geschichte: Festschrift Peter Acht,* ed. Waldemar Schlögl and Peter Herde (Kallmünz, 1976), pp. 256-273.

53 Pastor, *Geschichte der Päpste,* 2:190; idem, *The History of the Popes,* 3:272.

As was mentioned above, Cusanus' *Reformatio generalis*, as well as Domenichi's tract, influenced the composition of Pius II's unpublished bull *Pastor aeternus*. Although the pope was serious about reform, he only implemented the proposals of the commissioners in an unsystematic manner.[54] The pontiff's attention increasingly was given to the defense of Christendom against the Turks and to more mundane considerations, like the struggle with Sigismondo Malatesta and the building of Pienza. Plans to reform the church inevitably were put into the background. Even the conservative historian Pastor lamented that "in the interests of the Church, this can never be sufficiently regretted."[55]

Reform of the church, especially of the curia, was much discussed in the fifteenth and early sixteenth centuries, both inside and outside Rome.[56] John O'Malley has pointed out that the sacred orators of the Roman curia in the fifteenth and early sixteenth centuries "keenly felt the need for the moral and disciplinary reform of the city of Rome and the Roman Curia" and that this "meant the transformation of institutions ridden by avarice, ambition, and luxury into institutions where virtue prevailed."[57] After Pius II's death, some notable reform tracts were published, among them the *Libellus de remediis afflictae ecclesiae* (1469) of Rodrigo Sánchez de Arévalo (1404-1470),[58] the *De moribus*

---

54 Pastor, *Geschichte der Päpste*, 2:192-197; idem, *The History of the Popes*, 3:275-282. See also John D'Amico, *Renaissance Humanism in Papal Rome: Humanists and Churchmen on the Eve of the Reformation* (Baltimore, 1983), p. 216.

55 Pastor, *Geschichte der Päpste*, 2:192-195; idem, *The History of the Popes*, 3:275. For Pastor's statement, see *Geschichte der Päpste*, 2:192: "Es kann dies im Interesse der Kirche nie genug beklagt werden"; idem, *The History of the Popes*, 3:276.

56 Johannes Haller, *Papsttum und Kirchenreform: Vier Kapitel zur Geschichte des ausgehenden Mittelalters*, vol. 1 (Berlin, 1903); Léonce Celier, "L'idée de réforme à la cour pontificale du Concile de Bâle au Concile de Lateran," *Revue des questiones historiques* 86 (n.s. 42) (1909): 418-435; Karl A. Fink, "Papsttum und Kirchenreform nach den Grossen Schisma," *Tübinger Theologische Quartalschrift* 126 (1946): 110-122; Hermann Heimpel, *Studien zur Kirchen- und Reichsreform des 15. Jahrhundert* (Heidelberg, 1974); Johannes Helmrath, "Reform als Thema der Konzilien des Spätmittelalters," in *Christian Unity: The Council of Ferrara-Florence, 1438/39-1989*, ed. Giuseppe Alberigo (Leuven, 1991), pp. 75-152.

57 O'Malley, *Praise and Blame*, p. 195.

58 Ibid., pp. 91, 199, 204, 226. On Arévalo, see Richard Trame, *Rodrigo Sánchez de Arévalo, 1404-1470: Spanish Diplomat and Champion of the Papacy* (Washington, D.C., 1958); Juan Maria Laboa, *Rodrigo Sánchez de Arévalo, alcaide de Sant' Angelo* (Madrid, 1973).

nostrorum temporum (1483) of Benedetto Maffei (1429-1494)[59] and the *De cardinalatu* (1510) of Paolo Cortesi (1465-1510).[60]

Nor were official reform proposals lacking. As the proposals of Cusanus and Domenichi influenced Pius II, the unpromulgated text of *Pastor aeternus* influenced the preparation of Sixtus IV's *Quoniam regnantium cura*[61] and Alexander VI's *In apostolica sedis specula*.[62] In addition, the reform program of the Fifth Lateran Council (1512-1517), outlined in orations and documents, as well as in two bulls of Pope Leo X (1513-1521), testifies to the continued existence of reforming sentiment in the curia.[63] But the popes of the Renaissance, surrounded by growing courts hungry for places and revenues, deeply involved in receiving appeals and supplications, pursuing political ends, bestowing patronage on artists and writers and raising the necessary revenues to support all these burdens through rampant fiscalism, found it impossible to put the reform ideals expressed by themselves and their advisers into practice.[64]

[59] D'Amico, *Renaissance Humanism*, p. 220.

[60] Ibid., pp. 227-237. See also Kathleen Weil-Carris and John D'Amico, "The Renaissance Cardinal's Ideal Palace: A Chapter from Cortesi's *De cardinalatu*," in *Studies in Italian Art and Architecture 15th through 18th Centuries*, ed. Henry A. Millon (Roma, 1980), pp. 45-123.

[61] Tangl, *Die päpstlichen Kanzleiordnungen*, pp. 379-385 [Reformentwurf Sixtus IV]; Hay, *The Church*, p. 87; O'Malley, *Praise and Blame*, pp. 199-200.

[62] Tangl, *Die päpstlichen Kanzleiordnungen*, pp. 402-421 [Reformentwurf zur einer durch P. Alexander VI. zu erlassenden Reformbulle]; Léonce Celier, "Alexandre VI et la réforme de l'Église," *Mélanges d'archéologie et d'histoire* 27 (1907): 65-124; Hay, *The Church*, p. 87. Of the surviving manuscript copies, that in Vat. lat. 3883, fol. 1r-11r was copied for the reform commission established by Alexander VI in 1496 after the murder of his favorite son, the duke of Candia; see the description in Celier's article. That in Vat. lat. 8090, fol. 109r-122v belonged to Francesco Todeschini-Piccolomini, the future Pius III, who, as a cardinal, was a member of that reform commission.

[63] D'Amico, *Renaissance Humanism*, p. 217; O'Malley, *Praise and Blame*, p. 200. See also Nelson Minnich, "Concepts of Reform Proposed at the Fifth Lateran Council," *Archivum Historiae Pontificiae* 7 (1969): 163-251; idem, "The Participation at the Fifth Lateran Council," ibid. 12 (1974): 157-206; idem, "*Incipiat judicium a domo Domini*: The Fifth Lateran Council and the Reform of Rome," in *Reform and Authority in the Medieval and Reformation Church*, ed. Guy F. Lytle (Washington, D.C., 1981), pp. 127-142.

[64] See, for example, William E. Lunt, *Papal Revenues in the Middle Ages*, 2 vols. (New York, 1934); Geoffrey Barraclough, *The Medieval Papacy* (London, 1963); J.A.F. Thomson, *Popes and Princes, 1417-1517: Politics and Policy in the Late Medieval Church* (London, 1980); Charles L. Stinger, *The Renaissance in Rome* (Bloomington, Indiana, 1985), pp. 123-140.

Even while resident in papal Rome, Nicholas of Cusa kept a reputation for upright conduct. In his *Vite di uomini illustri del secolo XV,* Vespasiano da Bisticci (1421-1498) described Cusanus as follows:

> "Messer Nicolo di Cusa, of German nationality, was a man of worship, a great philosopher, theologian and platonist. He was of a holy life, well lettered, especially in Greek. . . . He cared nothing for state or for possessions, and was one of the most needy of the cardinals, thus giving an excellent example in all his doings."[65]

Nor did Nicholas ever feel entirely at home in the curia, where his concerns were not shared by so many. Thus, when Pius II asked him his opinion on the appointment of new cardinals, especially the promotion of the learned but worldly Jean Jouffroy, Cusanus replied:

> ". . . you are preparing to create new cardinals without any pressing reason merely at your own whim and you have no regard for the oath you swore to the sacred college in conclave both before and after your election. . . . I do not know how to flatter. I hate adulation. If you can bear the truth, I like nothing which goes on in this Curia. Everything is corrupt. No one does his duty. Neither you nor the cardinals have any care for the Church. What observance of the canons is there? What reverence for laws? What assiduity in divine worship? All are bent on ambition and avarice. If I ever speak in a consistory about reform, I am laughed at. I do no good here. Allow me to withdraw. I cannot endure these ways . . .[66]

When the *Reformatio generalis* is read against the background of these statements by Bisticci and Pius II, the personal element of the document and its author's intent and desire in composing it are revealed, enriching our understanding of its historical context and theological content.

---

[65] Vespasiano da Bisticci, *Vite di uomini illustri del secolo XV* (Firenze, 1859), p. 169. See also idem, *Renaissance Princes, Popes and Prelates: The Vespasiani Memoirs, Lives of Illustrious Men of the XVth Century,* trans. William George and Emily Waters, intro. Myron P. Gilmore (New York, 1963), p. 156.

[66] *Memoirs of a Renaissance Pope: The Commentaries of Pius II—An Abridgement,* trans. Florence A. Gragg, ed. Leona C. Gabel, (New York, 1959), p. 228. See also Meuthen, *Die letzten Jahre,* pp. 80-81, 108. On Jouffroy, see Angela Lanconelli, "La biblioteca romana di Jean Jouffroy," in *Scrittura, biblioteche e stampa a Roma nel quattrocento,* ed. Concetta Bianca et al. (Città del Vaticano, 1980), pp. 275-294.

APPENDIX

Nicholas of Cusa, *A General Reform of the Church*[67]

[Preface]

The general reform conceived by Nicholas of Cusa, Cardinal of St. Peter in Chains, of holy memory.

So that this, our reform, is understood by the intellect of anyone to be just and necessary for salvation, it is fitting to begin with something from on high, that is the reason why created man exists, which the apostle Paul asserted to the Greek wise men, when he preached at the Areopagus in Athens, to be *to seek God. If they seek [him], perchance they may find [him]*.[68] This is nothing other than that mankind was created that he might see God in his glory. We see intellectual nature, participating in the goodness of God, to incline to revelation of and participation in him, just as the books of the wise, which were written because of this, teach us that anyone should display his intellect and show [himself] teachable[69] about participation in him. Thus divine goodness created intellectual nature, so that he might reveal himself to it visibly. Therefore, he created all others according to intellectual nature like a book, in which the intellect seeks the very wisdom of God, through which all things were made, having the sense of vision and the other senses like organs and instruments, so that it wonders and is spurred to seek [wisdom], and seizes it, if it can. But mankind, ignorant of the speech or Word of God, through which the book of creation was written, could not attain wisdom or creative art through its own strength, unless the Word should make itself known to him. Wherefore [anyone], even if ignorant of the speech or text of some book, still can make for himself many conjectures about the contents of the book; nevertheless, he can know nothing truly without a teacher. All men, therefore, who by nature desire to know,[70] can conjecture well that the teaching authority of creation is immortal art, wisdom and light, illuminating and leading the intellect [to be] perfect, making [it] blessed and happy, which [is] the end of desire. But God, seeing [that] ignorance, which made all men stray from knowledge of God, taking pity on many, granted, of his wisdom, his desired teacher, whom all desire exceedingly to see. [God] sent him, who takes away ignorance and

---

67 Nicolaus Cusanus, *Reformatio generalis*. Ehses' edition, on which this translation is based (see n. 2 above), must be used with caution; see Meuthen, *Die letzten Jahre*, pp. 186-187, n. 10.

68 Acts 17:27.

69 Reading Ehses' *dociles* as *docilem*.

70 Aristotle, *Metaphysics* 1:1.

illuminates all who come to him, into the world; he had to be the Word itself, the teacher, in whom are hidden all the treasures of desired knowledge.[71]

God, therefore, sent the Word made flesh, his beloved Son, *full of grace*, commanding that he be heard, giving power to all who received him, *to those who believe in his name*, to become [God's] sons.[72] And this is the only precept of God the Father, that they [should] believe in His Son and legate, who [is] his Word, that is [believe] in his name. [Whoever] receives him as such, in fact, believes in him and knows all which he announces to be true, because [he is] the Son and Word of God. Thus Christ came and chose disciples from the world; and he built from those faithful to him the church, which he invigorated and enlivened with [his] doctrine and Spirit, in which he will remain for all time. Thus the union of the faithful in him is his church, whose head [he is]. Whoever lives and moves in this faith,[73] that this Jesus Christ, veracious son of the virgin Mary, indeed is the Truth, *having the word of eternal life*.[74] This is the faith, giving all sanctity, knowledge and justice; and it beatifies anything. Whoever believes this truly keeps his commands indeed and does not sin. For he vanquishes evil, the world and its desires, knowing there is no life except in Christ's promises and that no one is justified except the one justified by the merits of his death. Here he can say with the apostle [that] he knows nothing *except Christ and him crucified*,[75] in whom is attained supreme, complete knowledge, that is faith, by which the just man lives.[76]

Since we have received responsibility for ruling the church of God, already well founded on a firm rock, we need not inquire about any other faith nor any other tenets than what we received from Christ, the holy apostles and their successors, the rulers of the church; but we are required to do such work as is given [us] to be done, with such a supernal gift, having set aside the lust of this evil world, which is not part of Christ's kingdom—the world with its lust will soon pass away, making all like unto Christ, each in his order, so that we may be heirs of God in participation in the kingdom of immortal life and coheirs with Christ himself, the unique Son of God.[77] He, however, *although he was in the form of God*,[78] who alone possesses immortality, assumed our mortal nature and

---

71 Cf. Col. 2:3.

72 Jn. 1:14, 12.

73 Cf. Acts 17:28.

74 Jn. 6:69.

75 1 Cor. 2:2.

76 Cf. Hab. 2:4; Rom. 1:17; Gal. 3:11; Heb. 10:38.

77 Cf. Rom. 8:17.

78 Phil. 2:6.

servile form, so that he could unite it to his divine nature, so that it could pass over into the form of his immortality. Wherefore, since there is one nature of humanity, that of Christ, [our] head, and ours, which shall take on itself form of God himself, it is impossible for mankind to attain the kingdom of immortality otherwise, unless it takes on the form of the lord Christ. This form is acquired by imitation. Wherefore, the apostle, who had taken on the form of Christ, says, *Be imitators of me, beloved children, as I am of Christ.*[79]

Since, therefore, we succeeded to the place of the apostles, so that we can put the form of Christ on others through imitation of us, certainly it is necessary, first of all, to be Christlike to others. Human nature has from God a teachability above all creatures of this world, which co-created humankind, so that it could be happy; therefore, *All will be teachable by God.*[80] We see, however, incorruptible virtues and One participated in by many by practice and doctrine. Christ, our king and lord of virtues, therefore also king of glory, is that living virtue, which gives that eternal rest to all participating [in him], *in whom are hidden all the treasures of wisdom and knowledge.*[81] The Teacher, therefore, calls out to all of us his disciples, who wish to change into his form, saying, *Learn from me, for I am meek and humble of heart; and you will find rest for your souls.*[82] And, elsewhere, when he wished to demonstrate humility with the work of washing the feet [of the apostles], he said, *I gave you an example, that you should do what I did.*[83] He taught them by doing, *He began to do and to teach,*[84] wishing to show not that every moral virtue can give eternal life but that [virtue] which is alive, which vanquishes this contemptible world, first possesses the victor over this world, Christ. In all the Christlike, virtue must live so that, because of virtue, which is the life of the Spirit, this sensate life is valued as nothing.

This, then, is the charity of Christ, a virtue held so dear that to give the world for it, and to die, is believed a small thing and glorious. Every divinely-inspired scripture strives to reveal to us nothing other than Christ, the form of the virtues, of eternal life and of the eternal felicity desired by all. Those receiving him as the only teacher of life by faith and works are formed so that they are capable of eternal life. Nor are they capable of it by their own effort; but [it is] necessary that Christ, who has it not just by merit of obedience, [but] so should communicate [it] and confer it on them, [not only] so that he might be

---

79 1 Cor. 4:16 and 11:1.

80 Jn. 6:45, citing Is. 54:13.

81 Col. 2:3.

82 Mt. 11:29.

83 Jn. 13:15.

84 Acts 1:1.

in the glory of the Father,[85] but even that he could make them capable of having it by his merit and claim and possess it in justice. By grace we are called to the inheritance, the utmost grade of felicity, which we cannot attain, unless we obtain [it] from the justice of the merits of Christ. Therefore, he was made justice for us, when he gave himself up to death for all; in him all the dead live eternally by God's just judgment. God the Father, the most just rewarder of all who die in Christ in order to obey, rewards them with life immortal for his sake. Therefore, all things necessary for perfect felicity, whether from grace or justice, we cannot have without him. He, therefore, is the only mediator, in whom all [is possible] and without whom it is impossible for us truly to be happy.

We, therefore, who wish to reform all Christians, at least, can put forth to them no other form on it than that which we imitate, that of Christ, from whom they receive [their] name. He is the living law and the perfect form according to which judgement is made concerning eternal life and death. Those conformed to him are the blessed children of eternal life, who are called to possess the kingdom of God. Those not conformed, however, because [they are] the children of death, are cast down into Gehenna accursed. Therefore, each entire effort ought to be directed to cleansing ourselves by penance and resuming the form of innocence, which we receive in Christ's [baptismal] bath. Thus, when Christ appears in glory on the day of God the Father, we will be like him, of his very form, which is found only in the kingdom of God, toward which we direct our course.

Since, however, the church of God is the mystical body of Christ, rightly likened by the apostle to the human body, in which, in the life-giving Spirit, all members are united, so that they might live, just as all members of Christ are given life in the whole body of the church by the Spirit of Christ, to whom all the faithful in this world adhere through faith. The diversity of members of church, however, is bound together by a certain bond of love, the glue of Christ; and diverse offices are allocated for the building up of the body.[86] And [the holders of these offices] are members like any other, each of them content to be what he is, that is as long as he is present to the life-giving Spirit. They are the eyes through which individual members are visited and adapted to their duties; and those eyes, if they are clear, enlighten the whole body,[87] for they visit the body and its individual members and they do not permit any foulness or dark ugliness to adhere to [them]. If, however, the eye were darkened, the whole body would be darkened. In the church, therefore, if the eyes, which should be the lamps of the body, are dark, then it is certain that this would make the whole body dark. It is notable, however, that the body of the church in this age has

85 Cf. Phil. 2:6.

86 Cf. 1 Cor. 12:12-20.

87 Cf. Mt. 6:22-23; Lk. 11:33-36.

declined greatly from the light and the day, becoming enveloped in dark shadows, especially because the eyes, which should be its light, have fallen into darkness. Since the eye which sees the stains of others does not see its own,[88] therefore, the eye is unable to visit itself; but it should submit itself to another visitor,[89] who will visit, correct and cleanse it, so that it can visit the members of the body.

Two things, therefore, we recommend as necessary for our proposal, that is that we, who are the eyes, should submit ourselves to those having sound vision, lest we, believing ourselves to have almost clear eyes, should be deceived to our detriment and that of the church to be visited by us. Second, that, after this, we turn clear eyes on the whole body of the church and visit the individual members skillfully by our self or through others acting for us, as we shall give back to God a strict accounting for the church entrusted [to us] and for the souls of all, unless we show all possible diligence in this. We should begin in this with our Roman church and the curia; and, thereafter, we should send visitors to individual provinces. We have decided to set down here, however, the rules which the visitors, who act on our behalf, should follow.

We wish to choose and depute three grave and mature men, in whom the form of Christ clearly shines forth, who show forth the truth to all,[90] as visitors. They should have zeal for God, knowledge and prudence; and they should expect to receive no additional honors or riches, so that they may be more free and pure in judgment, thought and work, harming no one, but being content with food and clothing according to the law's determination, and bound by oath to do these things.[91] To them we give the following fourteen rules.

[Instructions for Visitations]

First, we wish that [the visitors] should begin the visitation by celebrating devout ceremonies solemnly and publicly with fear of God and expound word of God to those[92] whom they approach, placing the form of Christ before them, so that those visited may be disposed to obey. And, after this, before [doing] anything else, they should choose three mature men from among those being visited, whom they should get to swear publicly to tell the

---

88 Cf. Lk. 6:39-42.

89 The translation interprets *visitare* in its legal sense as an inspection by a superior power to correct abuses.

90 The translation follows Ehses' emendation *cunctis*, not *cunctam* found in Vat. lat. 8090.

91 Cusanus may have had in mind the "procurations" exacted by a legate or a visitor to support his mission.

92 The translation reads *quos* for Ehses' *quid*.

truth about observances and customs. They should examine [these] individuals about these things; and a notary should write down what they hear, so that, when they have been informed about the conditions and manners then in use, they may introduce a better form if it seems necessary or praise and strengthen the good which they find. Then they may descend to examining individual persons and doing whatever is necessary for their task.

Second, we wish that these visitors should take care to bring back those being reformed to [their] original form, returning Christians generally to the form which they put on in baptism, when they became Christians. Beyond this, [they should bring] prelates [back] to the form which they received when they became prelates; kings and princes, similarly to the form they received at the time of their institution. The same [should be done] about priests, beneficed clergy, and religious, and generally about all officials and others who, beyond the form [received] in baptism, in which they bound themselves solemnly to be Christians, added another form to the previous [baptismal] one in public dignities, offices and religious orders, to which they bound themselves solemnly through a vow, an oath or some sort of promise to God. Since all things licit and honest promised to God become necessary for salvation, therefore, it is necessary that the visitors bring transgressors back to [their] form or reject [them]. [The visitors], therefore, must know those forms of oaths, vows and promises; and, therefore, they should arrange to have copies of such things in advance.

Third, we wish that, if, perhaps, the aforesaid forms are neglected in certain provinces because of bad customs and carelessness, then the visitors should impose observance of the forms they find in law; for example, religious should not profess—nor bishops and priests swear at the times of their ordinations—anything other than what the canons and papal decrees[93] contain. Because such men are no less obliged to observance of [their] rules and the canons, they should be commanded to embrace entirely the canon which commands those things which they have promised. Transgressors, since they are not absolved by bad custom from obedience to [that] canon, no less than in the preceding case, they should be brought back to the form written in the canon and pastoral instruction, or be driven out.

Fourth, beyond these oaths and vows, which should be observed entirely [and] most strictly, and [to fulfillment] of which we wish them to be driven and compelled by the visitors, anyone should live, according to the etymology of his name and the reason for it, according to the canons. Anyone's life is defined in the definition of his name. Whoever acts differently from what his name designates certainly is named thus falsely and is unworthy of that name, whose meaning his life contradicts. How can someone be called a Christian whose life is contrary to Christ? How can [a man be called] a religious who [is] an

---

[93] Literally *libri pontificales.*

apostate; a monk, if he runs around in cities; a canon, if he [is] irregular; a priest, if [he is] profane; a curate, if he flies from care [of his flock]; a ruler, if [he is] absent; a bishop, if he does not supervise the flock committed [to him]; a leader, if [he is] a betrayer; a king, if [he is] a tyrant? And [the same is true] of individuals.

Fifth, looking more particularly at beneficed clergy, we wish that the visitors should ordain that these observe the canons in [their] habit, tonsure, chastity, dealings with others, office and divine worship. Likewise, we wish that all benefices should receive their due according to their original institution, as far as possible. All unions, dispensations and trusts,[94] where the original arrangement in the foundation of the benefice is not found extinct, are to be understood; and we declare [that these things] should be understood by all and by those visitors thus: "without diminution of divine worship", as it is usual to insert the phrase in apostolic letters. The church of Christ is not entrusted to us for [its] destruction and diminution, but for [its] building up, [for its] augmentation and [that] of divine worship. Therefore, we establish that, where the visitors see in any benefice, through our dispensation or that of our predecessors,[95] through incompatibility [of benefices] or entrusting [them to absentees], neglect of divine worship, unless the right order of worship can be restored there, as it was before our dispensation, union or entrusting, that the visitors soon provide [a new occupant] to that benefice legitimately by our authority, as if it were vacated by the act [of neglect]. We wish, however, by the term "benefice" in this place to be understood generally all ecclesiastical revenues, which accrue to the one having title to the benefice by reason of [his] duty to that benefice, due from [its] foundation or otherwise by law and custom, or that it is any dignity, even an abbacy or [capitular] provostship, or some inferior rank, or a church with cure of souls, or any other dignity or a benefice requiring personal residence, of whatever condition or value.

Sixth, we wish that, if the visitors should find divine worship diminished because someone who has several compatible benefices[96] neglects to perform those services which tenure of a benefice entails, directly or through another,[97]

---

94 Union of benefices was supposed to occur only when each was too poor to support a tenant. Dispensations to hold benefices incompatible because of their conflicting pastoral responsibilities were common in the fifteenth century. The practice of entrusting or "commending" an abbacy or other dignity to an absentee prelate also was common.

95 The translation follows the variant reading *predecessorum*, not Ehses' emendation *successorum*.

96 Two benefices without pastoral responsibility or "cure of souls" or one with and one without it could be held by a cleric at the same time.

97 The tenant of a benefice was obligated to provide for its upkeep and the requisite worship services or to hire a substitute out of its revenues.

since it is wrong that someone have several compatible benefices in diminution of divine worship, they should take care then that the one having the title should do service by himself or through another; otherwise, if [the visitors] declare them vacant by the act of neglect, they can provide others [to the benefices] by our authority, since we judge them vacated by such neglect of divine worship. We wish the term "benefice" to be understood to include all those [positions and revenues] which can be obtained at the same time by custom without a papal dispensation.

Seventh, we wish any provostship, deanship, archdeaconry, [precentorship], schoolmastership, treasurership and the like, whether called dignities or offices in cathedrals or collegiate churches,[98] to be incompatible with like [offices] in any other collegiate church, since one cannot be in two places at once and give satisfaction, and divine worship and its beauty is diminished by this. Therefore, we wish that, where they find anyone holding several such [offices] in different places, [the visitors] should compel him to choose one place in which to serve; and let him give up the other to someone who will give satisfaction. Otherwise, the visitors can provide [to the other place] not withstanding any dispensation or contrary custom.

Eighth, we wish that, where the visitors find parish churches united with a cathedral, collegiate church or monastery, even if those unions were made to augment divine worship in cathedrals, collegiate [churches] or monasteries without its being neglected in the parish, should they do not find divine worship greater after the union than before or do not find the canonical hours, day and night, devoutly celebrated,[99] together with mass, let them take care that all fruits in the parish churches, as if the union never occurred, be held up and made available for augmenting divine worship. Unions are not made so that canons and religious may live in style and enjoy luxury, but so that the number of those serving God devoutly day and night should be increased.

Ninth, we wish that, if some religious do not admit the visitors or mind them, and have from the apostolic see privileges, exemptions or the like, since these were given them only so that, as if humble men, obedient and beloved by God and the apostolic see, because of observance of [their] rule, and so that they can observe it with greater peace, therefore, unless they obey presently, resume observance of the rule and continue [in it], we order the apostolic privileges revoked by the visitors in our name.

Tenth, we wish that, if the visitors find cathedrals or collegiate churches possessing apostolic exemptions, unions of churches and other apostolic and

---

[98] The configurations of cathedral chapters varied. In Italy, a provost often presided; in England, a dean.

[99] Literally *cum officio altaris*.

episcopal[100] privileges, which we do not wish to accept correction or emendation, since they do not merit any favor, on account of their rebellion and incorrigibility, therefore, all of their privileges, whether they have them from us or from the bishops, are ordered to be revoked by our authority; and the divine offices are to be forbidden them by the visitors.

Eleventh, we wish that, if the visitors find any religious or others, out of wicked audacity, holding in contempt the censures imposed by law, by us, our legates or the bishops, involved in divine worship against the prohibitions of the law or man, we wish that these irregular contemners of [the power] of the keys be deprived of their benefices and be made incapable of the ministry[101] of the altar, forbidding them entrance into any church. At the same time, let the visitors forbid all Christians, on pain of eternal damnation and automatic excommunication,[102] to support them, hear their masses or take their part. Otherwise, let them be regarded as excommunicated automatically[103] and be shunned by all Christians.

Twelfth, the visitors should take care about the reform of hospitals, that alms are given to the poor according to [their] original intent, wills and legacies, and that those in charge of them give an accounting. [The visitors] should not omit [to inquire] about the fabric of churches, so that frauds are not committed, and about alms seekers who deceive the people when they can. [The visitors] should take implement strictly reforms about the cloisters of nuns to evitate any scandals and the wrath of God, when those who dedicate themselves as brides of Christ by solemn vows draw many clerics and laymen with them into the pit by foul excess, although the law provides sufficiently for all of them. They should cause those provisions to be observed strictly in practice.

Thirteenth, we wish that the visitors, when they visit churches, sacristies, ornaments, books, chalices and the like not neglect to examine relics and to investigate, for the sake of knowledge, that they are true relics. And, where they find the same relics in diverse places, and they cannot be in both, and there is doubt where the true ones are, they should show discretion about removing scandal from the people; and it would be better to prohibit [their] display than to permit scandal. They should oppose making pilgrimages to relics or miraculous [effusions] of blood from hosts, because such things often are faked by the greedy on account of pilgrimages. Wherefore, wherever they see men running

---

100 The translation renders *ordinaria* as episcopal, since the bishop usually had ordinary or first instance jurisdiction over his diocese, except where exemptions had been granted by higher authorities.

101 The translation reads Ehses' *misterium* as *ministerium*.

102 *Latae sententiae* excommunication was incurred by commission of an act, such as striking a cleric, without the necessity of a judicial sentence.

103 Literally *absque alia declaratione*.

after the display of relics and [bleeding] hosts because of curiosity, either they should prohibit, under grave penalty, their display or the making of offerings. Thus, if anyone runs to such an image or place, as if miracles might occur there or had, let [the visitors] forbid either [pilgrims'] running there or the making of offerings. For, frequently, avarice substitutes false for true, so that it may acquire by deception what it cannot get through truth. It suffices for the Christian truly to love Christ within his church in the sacrament of the divine eucharist, in which he has all he could want for salvation. Let him venerate true relics but, much more, Christ, the head of all the saints; and let him beware lest they abuse greatly Christ and the relics for their temporal good, turning religion into pilgrimage, preying on the religious seeker, gravely offending God if they do not correct [these abuses].

Fourteenth, they should keep watch diligently, concerning extirpation of public usurers, adulterers and contemners of the church's mandates; they should condemn and eliminate partiality [in judging]. They should purge every place of divination, sorcery and all such sins through which divine majesty and Christendom are offended greatly. They should take care to make the church a pure bride, pleasing to God—just as the church of the original [disciples] was—which merits to be translated from the [church] militant to the [church] triumphant and to enjoy perpetual felicity there.

In these [fourteen instructions] the visitors will find the form, to which any sound mind will acquiesce, of reforming anything; nor will any good man be found a rebel, since no one [is good] unless he returns to [this] form, which he chooses for himself, has professed publicly, has accepted the name of his [Christian] profession and is named [by it]. Therefore, those who contradict the visitors contradict themselves and are not to be heard, but to be coerced.

[Visitation of Pope and Curia]

We who, however unworthy, hold the vicariate of Christ over his church militant, have obligated ourselves to the profession, observation and guardianship of the orthodox Christian faith, and to all the things which our predecessors obligated themselves, once [we] were assumed [to the papacy]; and we confess ourself to be bound to those things which were purposed and accepted by us when we were assumed. We know ourself to be called pope because we ought to be the ultimate father; and patriarch, because we are obligated, first of all, by all by which all the fathers were bound; also archbishop, because we hold the principate among those who superintend the [other] bishops diligently. We even call ourself bishop, because we are obligated to tend the divine flock attentively. We admit [to being called] priest, because what pertains to the priestly office we know pertains first of all to us. Because of these things, even the highest ones and those most conformable to Christ, Christians, God's servants, attribute to us, who profess ourself to be servant of those servants of God,[104] the name "holiness".

If we glory in all these names, we should strive likewise to be what we are called and to show in action what we profess to be. And, lest we should act as judge in our own case,[105] we shall ask the visitors on God's behalf to visit and judge us diligently, assuring them that we are ready to accept with grateful soul the form by which they will judge us as to our person, household, curia, and all things which pertain to the papal dignity and office. Nor should they fear to visit the pope, since they will find the vicar of Christ, minister to Christians, father of fathers and servant of the servants, most high and holy in dignity, like other men, sinful and infirm, knowing himself for such and confessing evangelical doctrine, holding the first and greatest place not for domination but for ministry to build up the church. Whatever, therefore, they find in us which does not build up but rather scandalizes the church, let them show us altogether, so that we may amend [it]. We wish, with God's help, to avoid a terrible judgment for scandalizing the church, and desire a good place with the living faithful stewards [as a reward] for our labors on earth.

Afterwards we choose to satisfy, with a whole heart, the office given us by God's gift, and we desire because of this emendation by the visitors of those who have erred. It is not unfitting that our venerable brothers, the cardinals of the holy Roman church, and every ecclesiastical order, submit themselves likewise to emendation by the visitors. Although, in the general rules given above, all things useful for the visitation are enfolded, they have to attend, nevertheless, to three things in the cardinals individually: first, that they have zeal for God's house;[106] second, that they are faithful and free in counsel; third, that they are exemplary men to whom all ecclesiastics visited may look thereafter as if a form for living.

The first thing, certainly, is necessary, since their vocation tends to this, that those who are called to the cardinalate should be firm hinges of the church,[107] in whom motion is maintained and all wavering is stabilized. In that college, after a fashion, is the consent of the whole church dispersed through the world; therefore, they choose the shepherd of the church, and the church, which is in them representatively, also consents to the one to whom they consent. They, therefore, as if legates of the nations, form with us a daily, comprehensive council of the church; and they are parts and members of our mystical body, that

---

104 The appellation "servant of the servants of God" was adopted for the papacy by Gregory the Great.

105 The inability of anyone to judge his own case was an established legal principle.

106 Cf. Ps. 69:9.

107 This is a false etymology of *cardo*, which originally referred to the schedule of clergy serving at the major Roman basilicas.

is the holy Roman, apostolic and catholic church. They are in us as the church is in the pontiff, and we are in them as the bishop in the church. For this reason, those chosen by God, ought to be agreeable and most grave men set apart from all levity. Wherefore since they are cardinals not for their own sakes but to cooperate with the supreme pontiff in building up the church, they should not have been careful to exercise their office without zeal, having which they would have taken care that buyers and sellers not be introduced into the temple.[108] (But, if [such men] are in it, they should be ejected in shame.) They should be those who are careful that the unworthy, even if kinsmen and servants, not be promoted, instead of those who can build up God's house by word and example according to canonical norms.

The second [point] is no less of the essence of a good cardinal. For how will he be a cardinal, if his counsels are not faithful in counsel; how will they be faithful, if they are not free? Those things which impede counsel, however, are: favors, hatreds, partialities and the like. If, therefore, a cardinal is protector of a nation, prince or community,[109] in so far as he is useful to any of them, his counsel is impeded. If he hopes for gifts on account of speeches to be delivered in the consistory[110] in favor of someone, he is a mercenary. It befits the perfect cardinal, therefore, to impose on himself a firm law of spurning gifts, not expecting to have more than three or four thousand florins a year, and to eschew all the blandishments of this world, which can deter him from faith and free counsel.

The third, certainly, is required for building up the church. For when the cardinals can build up the universal church more by example than by words, certainly they are obliged more than others, by priority of place, to an exemplary life. [His] life should correspond to [his] rank; [but] they should be content with maintaining an honest lifestyle, a decent household and not too many horsemen. For this reason, our predecessors decreed that in the curia a household should not exceed 40 persons and 24 animals; and likewise, [the cardinals should take care] in all things, so that they cannot be reprehended for the least pluralism in titles to benefices, nor for the ruin of churches and the diminution of worship, in places where they have benefices. Above all else which can be called praiseworthy in a cardinal, certainly [it behooves him] to be content with just

---

108 Cf. Mt. 21:12-13.

109 The office of protector of a nation, which obligated a cardinal to promote a sovereign's interests, was a comparatively new one in Cusanus' day.

110 The pope's consultations with the cardinals were modelled on the public audiences of the later Roman empire, in which the ruler remained seated, surrounded by his advisers.

his one titular church;[111] and that he give an accounting annually for whatever benefice he enjoys because of his own title, which [he receives] out of the yield of fruits according to the quality of the benefice. On its account, he incurs obligations and [may incur] blame.

Likewise, no grace more befits a cardinal than that he should show himself a servant of Christ in external dress, way of life and decency [of conduct], that he should spurn pomp, which is of the devil. There is only one college of cardinals; why are there so many types of capes? Is the religious observance of Saint Peter more lax than that of any other saint, as if it were permissible for those who do not bind themselves to the observance of any other religious order, because they are leaders and guardians of other orders, to appear in public now in red capes, now in golden ones, as they please? We believe the form of the cape is a sign of religious observance and that individual brothers of the sacred college ought to content themselves with a [cape] all of some color thought fit for priests in canon [law], although any religious who are in the college should not give up the habit which [their] order demands. Disparity of clothing seems a sign of levity and detracts from the gravity of so many men. Likewise, nothing should be found in the dress of their households which offends or suggests levity, so that those who associate with him show what sort of man their master is.

The visitors should regulate and dispose rightly all things concerning a cardinal's table, which ought to be well regulated, so that only what is necessary for refreshment is seen, without a gluttonous multitude of dishes, with reading done during meals[112] and discussion after grace. Concerning decoration of halls and chambers, eschewing all superfluity, those things which serve elegance are permitted, provided that the place of prayer and worship, where the cardinal daily should celebrate or devoutly hear mass, is ornamented most devoutly for the praise of God.

We remind the visitors, briefly, of these things, leaving the rest to them, so that they may do whatever, according to what they find, makes the universal church rejoice both in the sacred and divine college and in most worthy cardinals, who can be imitated for [their] merit as examples of the Christian religion as examples.

After this, the visitors should proceed to reforming divine worship in the city of Rome according to the aforesaid rules. First they should go to the

111 A cardinal was assigned a suburbicaran bishopric, a presbyterial church or a diaconal church, which made him a nominal member of the clergy of the province or diocese of Rome.

112 The reading of pious texts during meals was a monastic practice.

principal papal basilicas,[113] then the titular churches of the cardinals, then the religious houses; likewise they should not forget the hospitals. Nor should they add anything to the aforesaid rules when they suffice. When anyone would serve sincerely what he swore or vowed, devoutly accomplish the canonical hours at fitting times, devote himself to the divine office of the mass, fulfill vigilantly his assigned task, and wear fitting garb and a tonsure, as law and religion prescribe, even then, unless he should regard himself as a useless servant of God,[114] he has not been reformed perfectly.

The visitors should take care that God's servants are clean of all foulness of the flesh, nor should they suffer clerics who keep concubines to continue living on Christ's alms while reveling in their lusts.

Concerning care of the books necessary for divine worship, they should direct not only that they are not lacking but that they are emended and conform to the usage of Rome. The holy ornaments for celebration of the divine mysteries ought to be whole and clean; and churches, as far as possible, should be whole, well-enclosed and repaired, so that they are useful for and consecrated to divine services.

Concerning the persons who are found in our curia, the visitors should investigate whether they belong to the needed personnel, as are the cardinals and the officials, or whether they are outside of these, in which case [the visitors] should investigate why they dwell in the curia. If no just and necessary reasons are found, and [the curialists] are bishops, abbots or others with benefices, they should not permit them to waste time in our curia; but, so that they can serve God, they should send them back to their own places. It is not fitting that our curia give beneficed prelates and religious freedom for wandering and pernicious occasion for canvassing [to obtain] greater dignities and plurality of benefices. It is very indecent that a bishop or abbot, who already has taken a bride in faith,[115] should seek to annul that marriage, or to desert [his bride] by absence, or to work in the curia to have another bride than the one [he] already [has], and, so that he may fulfill his desire, wait on and flatter not only the cardinals but the lesser officials, whom he labors to make favorable to himself more by the act of fawning rather than by force, to arrange that they do not cease to vex the pope on his behalf about any vacancy of some pleasing dignity. Greed, which for some is like worship of idols,[116] should not be stirred up but extinguished. To all such prelates suspected of greed and ambition, [the visitors] should prefer in

---

[113] San Giovanni in Laterano, San Pietro in Vaticano, San Paolo fuori le Mura and Santa Maria Maggiore are the major papal basilicas.

[114] Cf. Lk. 17:10.

[115] According to ancient belief, a bishop married his church.

[116] Cf. Col. 3:5.

promotions, out of merit, those who reside in their churches like grave, just and faithful stewards pleasing to God.[117]

Those who claim that they are messengers and ambassadors of princes and who insist on hunting [benefices] in the curia under [some] pretense, after fulfilling their embassies or after a certain fitting term, should be sent back to their churches, so that they may disengage themselves [from the curia].

We confess that prelates often need the aid of the Roman pontiff; but, when, according to the oath sworn by them, they come to visit the thresholds of the apostles at Rome,[118] they can transact [their business] conveniently. Nor do we wish that beneficed [clerics visit] the curia without need; but, following greed, they [often] enjoy privileges of receiving fruits [from their benefices in their absence] and other privileges granted in the curia. It is not our intention to entice beneficed clerics and to increase the curia to God's offense and the diminution of divine worship. All, however, who remain in the curia for good reason, we wish to comport themselves in manners, life, dress, tonsure and reading of the canonical hours as the law disposes. If curialists, even lay ones, are found to be procurers, keepers of concubines, gamblers and deceivers, falling away from honesty, we command that they be expelled from our curia entirely.

The visitors, turning to the curial offices, first should examine the Penitentiary, and, calling together, in the presence of the major penitentiary, all the members of the office, according to the aforesaid rules, having said something opportune about the visitation and the preparation of souls, they should choose, as the rules [of the Penitentiary] require,[119] three of the most experienced among them, by whom testimony may be given concerning the office, staff, statutes, oath and observances. Then they shall begin with the head [of the office] and [inquire] whether due gravity, zeal, knowledge, diligence, experience, cleanness of hands, vigilance and care befitting so holy an office are found in that head. Afterwards, they should do the same with twelve of the minor penitentiaries, whom it is necessary to have out of all the nations who flock to Rome for the salvation of their souls, so that those who hear confessions understand them and are not entirely ignorant of their fatherlands. They ought to be well versed as much in Holy Scripture as in canon law; and they ought to know especially the penitential canons and the penances, solemn, public and private, designated by the holy fathers and our predecessors, so that they know [how] to weigh the conditions of those confessing [their] sins according to the assigned penances. If they find the penitentiaries flippant, ignorant and breakers of their oaths and statutes, lacking zeal for souls but

---

117 Cf. Lk. 12:42.

118 The *ad limina* visit to Rome still is required of a bishop.

119 Books of privileges and procedures for the Penitentiary were compiled during the Middle Ages.

dedicated to profiting from their office, where the receipt of gifts is abominable to all good men,[120] they are to be ejected without difficulty. [Let the visitors] enjoin that they send back to their homes pilgrims [guilty] of homicide and mutilation of the limbs of those dedicated to holy things with letters [saying] they are obliged every year publicly to repeat [their] penances with any act of humility and devotion [required], so that through this penance all may receive notice of the enormity of sin. Thus, and in other public crimes, homicide and worse, [let the penitentiaries] describe in the letter the penance, not remitting [it] entirely to the bishops, who should not dare impose harsher [penances]. It is necessary that, in public sins, public penances should contribute to building up the church. Let them beware especially lest ease of pardon should increase, rather than decrease, crime. Above all, there should not be any regard for persons among those who act on Christ's behalf.

The letter writers of the penitentiary should write their own letters and understand what they write; and, unless they are honest and pure, following their oath and not exceeding the fees set by our predecessors for their work, they are to be expelled. Should it happen that anyone, whether a procurator of the penitentiary or not, should make supplications, reach out and solicit rapid dispatch of letters for himself or anyone else, or intrudes himself into this business, deceiving and harming pilgrims, they are to be punished and expelled from the curia.

120 Pursuit of gain in such a sensitive office was a form of simony, the buying and selling of spiritual gifts.

Nicholas of Cusa and the Idea of Tolerance

It has been suggested that Nicholas of Cusa arrived at the finest expression of the idea of religious tolerance in his *De pace fidei* which he wrote in 1453.[1] Before the coming of the Reformation, the humanist movement extended all over Europe and the humanists were very much interested in the ideal of a spiritual unity amongst men. It must indeed be pointed out that their ideal was not so much tolerance as the reduction of religious differences by an attempt at conciliation.[2] But Nicholas of Cusa is sometimes characterized as an illustrious representative of the irenic humanists who, in order to unite men on the religious level, were less concerned with what separates them than with what may bring them together. It is said that this notion of tolerance, gradually severed from the religious context in which it stands in Nicholas' work, influenced later thinkers down to Lessing.[3]

In his classic work, *Individuum und Kosmos in der Philosophie der Renaissance,* first published in 1927, Ernst Cassirer discussed the emergence in Nicholas of Cusa of a new form of religion and a new religious attitude, and called his attitude a "truly grand tolerance."[4] The recent publication of an English translation of the book[5] by so eminent a student of philosophy as Cassirer may strengthen this view of Nicholas of Cusa among the English-speaking public. In discussing the direct acquaintance of fifteenth-century thinkers—Nicholas of Cusa, Marsilio Ficino, Pico della Mirandola—with the entire works of Plato and Plotinus, another noted student of Renaissance philosophy called our attention to their strong tendency to combine Platonist doctrines with Christian theology and with Aristotelian philosophy, and also to their conviction that every form of religion or of philosophy has some element of truth. This "syncretism of the

---

[1] J.P. Dolan, *Unity and Reform: Selected Writings of Nicholas de Cusa,* (Notre Dame, 1962), p. 185.

[2] J. Lecler, *Toleration and the Reformation,* I (New York, 1960), p. 105.

[3] R. Klibansky, *Nicholas of Cues,* in *Philosophy in the Mid-Century: A Survey,* IV, ed. R. Klibansky (Firenze, 1959), p. 91. See also P. Tillich, *Christianity and the Encounter of the World Religions* (New York, 1963), pp. 40-41.

[4] E. Cassirer, *Individuum und Kosmos in der Philosophie der Renaissance* (Berlin-Leipzig, 1927), p. 31.

[5] E. Cassirer, *The Individual and the Cosmos in Renaissance Philosophy,* trans. M. Domandi (New York, 1963).

Renaissance Platonists,"[6] of whom Nicholas of Cusa was one, was certainly a source of inspiration for the advocates of peaceful discussion, of moderation and tolerance, from Erasmus to Bodin.[7]

Some other students of Nicholas of Cusa, however, have argued that he was certainly a man of peace who suggested not a crusade against but discussions with the Moslems. They realize that Nicholas in his *De pace fidei* described a conference before God at which representatives of the leading religions of the world attempt to discuss problems of common concern peacefully and amicably. But they maintain that Nicholas was not really a man of the Renaissance. He was essentially a medieval thinker, and as such could not have advocated the doctrine of religious tolerance which became important in Europe only after the disintegration of the traditional concept of the Christian Commonwealth in the sixteenth century.[8]

This paper is not primarily concerned with the question whether or not Nicholas was an advocate of religious tolerance, nor does the writer wish to minimize the influence Nicholas of Cusa exercised on the later thinkers on the question of tolerance. It will rather stress the fact that in any examination of his views on religious pluralism and tolerance, not only his ideal expressed in the *De pace fidei,* but also his other writings and the ecclesiastical and political situation in which they were written must be taken into consideration.

The fourteenth and fifteenth centuries in Europe were a great period of transition. Europe was afflicted with many wars. The Holy Roman Empire was almost a nonentity, and the dominant trend of the time was toward the building of separate nation states. The strength of the Catholic Church was tested not only by the outbreak of internal troubles, but also by the growth of a foreign power whose strength was based on a militant religion. The Great Schism, which started in 1378, dealt a blow to the Church, and brought about the Conciliar Period, which ended, after a series of general councils, only in 1449 with the restoration of the papal power. The Hussite heresy, as expressed in the doctrine of communion under both kinds, was also a serious threat to unity of

---

[6] P.O. Kristeller, *Renaissance Platonism,* in *Facets of the Renaissance,* ed. W.H. Werkmeister (Los Angeles, 1959), p. 96.

[7] Ibid., p. 97.

[8] H. Grabert, *Religiöse Verständigung, Wege zur Begegnung der Religionen bei Nicolaus Cusanus, Schleiermacher, Rudolf Otto und J.W. Hauer* (Leipzig, 1932); M. Seidlmayer, "Una religio in rituum varietate: Zur Religionsauffassung des Nikolaus von Cues," *Archiv für Kulturgeschichte,* XXXVI (1954), 145-207; B. Decker, *Nikolaus von Cues und der Friede unter den Religionen,* in *Humanismus, Mystik und Kunst in der Welt des Mittelalters,* ed. J. Koch (Leiden-Köln, 1959), pp. 94-121. See also L. Mohler, *Über den Frieden im Glauben: De pace fidei* (Leipzig, 1943), pp. 5-88; E. Gilson, *Les Metamorphoses de la Cité de Dieu* (Louvain-Paris, 1952), pp. 154-181.

the Church. The rapid growth of the Ottoman Turks in eastern Europe and the resultant spread of Islam as challenger to Christianity made many Christians of Europe keenly aware of the menace of the Moslem world.

It was while he was attending the Council of Basel in 1432 that Nicholas was appointed a member of the Deputation of the Faith which was to examine the points at issue between the Hussites and the council.[9] Pope Eugenius IV in a Bull of June 1st, 1431 had proclaimed a crusade against them. But less than three months later the imperial army was defeated disastrously at Taus. Cardinal Cesarini, who had narrowly escaped, addressed a moving appeal for unity to the Hussites,[10] and the Council of Basel's invitation was sent to them on October 15, 1431 with the promise of safe-conduct. The fifteen Hussite envoys, led by Prokop the Great and John Rokycana, arrived in Basel on January 4, 1433 and were warmly welcomed. Together with three other theologians, Nicholas was given the special task of examining the first, or utraquist, article of the Four Articles which had been agreed upon at Cheb (Eger) in May 1432. His opinions are expressed in his two letters which were written in 1433 as *De communione sub utraque specie.*[11]

In reading these letters, we are at first impressed with the fact that Nicholas takes a rather friendly attitude toward the Hussites in regard to the form of worship. This seemingly "tolerant" view is also expressed in the *De concordantia catholica,* in which Nicholas wrote that although the one faith is the cable of its collectivity, sometimes a variety of opinions is compatible with the unity of the Church.[12] But a closer examination of his letters to the Hussites reveals that he allows for the variety of the forms of worship so long as unity

[9] E. Vansteenberghe, *Le cardinal Nicolas de Cues (1401-1464): L'action—la pensée* (Paris, 1920), p. 54.

[10] T. Lenfant, *Histoire de la Guerre des Hussites et du Concile de Bâle,* I (Utrecht, 1731), p. 307.

[11] Nicolaus de Cusa, *Opera,* Basileae, 1565, pp. 829-838, 838-846. On these letters, see J. Koch, "Über eine aus der nächsten Umgebung des Nikolaus von Kues stammende Handschrift der Trierer Stadtsbibliothek (1927/1946)," in *Aus Mittelalter und Neuzeit: Festschrift für Gerhard Kallen,* ed. J. Engel and H.M. Klinkenberg (Bonn, 1957), pp. 128 n. 27, 130 n. 38. On the Bohemians at Basel, see E.F. Jacob, "The Bohemians at the Council of Basel, 1433," in *Prague Essays,* ed. R.W. Seton-Watson (Oxford, 1949), pp. 81-123.

[12] Nicolai de Cusa, *Opera omnia,* I (Heidelberg, 1964), p. 48. For recent studies of the *De concordantia catholica,* see P.E. Sigmund, *Nicholas of Cusa and Medieval Political Thought* (Cambridge, Massachusetts, 1963); M. Watanabe, *The Political Ideas of Nicholas of Cusa, with Special Reference to His De concordantia catholica* (Genève, 1963).

remains in the Church.[13] It is clear that on the controversial issue of the utraquism of the Hussites Nicholas saw a parallel between the Donatist controversy of the African church in the fourth century and the difficult problem of communion the Church was confronted with in his time. Therefore, drawing upon the writings of St. Augustine, St. Jerome, and St. Cyprian, he stresses the importance of unity in matters of faith and of being united with the *sedes Romana.* The truth, says Nicholas, is found in the *cathedra Petri,* and the gift of a good life can be obtained only in the Church which was founded on the Rock.[14] Thus Nicholas attacks the Hussites not only because they diverged from the Church's custom in the use of the blessed sacrament, but also for the spirit of dissension which prompted their attitude.

He wrote these letters to the Hussites while he was an advocate of the supremacy of the general council over the pope. As is well known, he later joined the pro-papal party, and in the jubilee year 1450 Pope Nicholas V appointed him legate *a latere* to Germany to publish the indulgence of the Jubilee and to labor for the reform of the monasteries and for the reunion of the Hussites. His reform work as papal legate, which he carried out with zeal and immense energy, does not concern us here, except that in case of grave transgressions and in the event of resistance he did not hesitate to invoke the aid of the secular arm for the eradication of scandals.[15] The letters Nicholas wrote to the Hussites from Regensburg and Brixen in 1452 clearly indicate that his position vis-à-vis the Hussites had not changed.

Of these letters, the one he wrote on October 11 from Brixen[16] is especially revealing. Demonstrating his familiarity with the writings of such diverse writers as St. Augustine, St. Jerome, St. Cyprian, Dionysius, Pope Innocent III, St. Thomas Aquinas, St. Bede, and the canon lawyers Guido de Baysio and Johannes Andreae, he gives a short survey of the development of the communion in the Church, which ends with his conclusion that the Church had used over the years various forms of communion, but that it has never been found necessary for the salvation of the souls to administer communion to the laity under both kinds. Nicholas argues that the existence of a variety of forms in the administration of communion does not debase the Christian faith.[17] When the pope and the clergy, or at least its major part united with the *cathedra Petri,* change the form of worship from time to time for the building up of the Church

---

[13] *Opera,* Basil., p. 832.

[14] Ibid., pp. 832-838.

[15] L. von Pastor, *The History of the Popes from the Close of the Middle Ages,* II (St. Louis, 1912), pp. 111, 121.

[16] *Opera,* Basil., pp. 851-861. His letters written in 1452 are in ibid., pp. 846-861.

[17] Ibid., p. 857.

(*propter aedificationem ecclesiae*), they are exercising their full powers (*libera potestate*) accorded to them, and there is no deception involved there.[18] It is demonstrated conclusively, says Nicholas, that all those who deny and reject the teaching of the Holy See of Peter are in error.[19]

Is it not clear from what we have seen that Nicholas was interested not so much in a defense of the principle of religious tolerance as in the preservation of the unity of the Church? By 1452 the Conciliar Movement had clearly lost its initial momentum, and to most people it seemed that the papacy had proved stronger than the reformers. Under these circumstances Nicholas, who had been called the "Hercules of the Eugenians" by Aeneas Sylvius Piccolomini because of his successful work to increase the influence of the papacy in Germany, strongly urged the Hussites to return to the *sedes Romana* to accept its teaching, and to abandon their insistence on the administration of communion under both kinds.

But, as we noted above, a great concern for the thoughtful Christians like Nicholas was not only how to rid the Church of its internal troubles and to restore its unity, but also the question of how to maintain the unity of Christendom itself. The Christian Commonwealth, or Christendom, was the largest unit to which men in the West felt allegiance in the Middle Ages. Above all, this was the terminology which was developed during the time of the Crusades. At first, Christendom embraced all Christians and included the schismatic or irregular Christian communities of the East. It was a floating, loose concept. Yet later its meaning changed. In the fourteenth and fifteenth centuries forces were clearly at work which tended toward an identification of Europe and Christendom. They became virtually synonymous. Christendom was shrinking, and the existence of the expanding Moslem world made Europe uneasy. Thus the old notion of Christendom was weakened, and the emotional use of the word Europe significantly increased in the fourteenth and especially fifteenth centuries. The defense of Europe in face of the great external foe became a burning question of the day.[20]

The fall of Constantinople on May 29, 1453 was the end of an epoch.[21] When the news reached Venice on June 29, 1453, it sent a shudder of

---

[18] Ibid., p. 856.

[19] Ibid.

[20] M. Gilmore, *The World of Humanism* (New York, 1952), pp. 1-42; D. Hay, *Europe: The Emergence of an Idea* (Edinburgh, 1957); O. Halecki, *The Millennium of Europe* (Notre Dame, 1963).

[21] "1453-1953," in *Byzantinoslavica*, XIV (Prague, 1953); *The Fall of Constantinople: A Symposium* (London, 1955).

apprehension and pity through Christendom.[22] "It is," wrote Aeneas Sylvius Piccolimini, "a second death to Homer and to Plato. The fount of the Muses is stopped."[23] Nicholas was deeply affected by this event, because he had been to Constantinople in 1437 as a member of the papal delegation in connection with the preparations for the Council of Ferrara-Florence.[24] He was very pessimistic about the possibility of checking the advance of the Turks,[25] but in September 1453 he wrote the *De pace fidei,* which shows clearly how seriously he was concerned about the threat of the Turks and the problem of religious pluralism and unity.[26]

Much has been written about his statement in the *De pace fidei* that there is but one religion in the multiplicity of rites.[27] Whether or not this means his acceptance of the idea of religious tolerance seems to be one of the most difficult problems concerning the interpretation of the *De pace fidei.* It is true that Nicholas, like some other Christians of his time, was convinced that the issue between Christendom and the Moslem world could be solved only by peaceful means.[28] He was familiar with the writings of Raymond Lull and was under the influence of this great Majorcan who was a "firm believer in the possibility of the rational demonstration of the Christian faith to unbelievers, and hence of the need to study the language and habits of the countries surrounding Europe, and to maintain missions in them."[29]

---

[22] L. von Pastor, *op. cit.,* pp. 272-273.

[23] M. Creighton, *A History of the Papacy from the Great Schism to the Sack of Rome,* III (London, 1911), p. 140.

[24] Vansteenberghe, *op. cit.,* pp. 61-63.

[25] Watanabe, *op. cit.,* p. 22 n. 11; E. Meuthen, "Die universalpolitischen Ideen des Nikolaus von Kues in seiner Erfahrung der politischen Wirksamkeit," *Quellen und Forschungen aus italienischen Archiven und Bibliotheken,* XXXVII (1957), 208.

[26] R. Klibansky and H. Bascour (eds.), "Nicolai de Cusa De pace fidei," in *Mediaeval and Renaissance Studies,* Supplement III (London, 1956).

[27] In addition to the works cited above in notes 1, 2, and 8, see B. Decker, "Die Toleranzidee bei Nikolaus von Kues und in der Neuzeit," in *Nicolò da Cusa: Relazioni tenute al Convegno Interuniversitario di Bressanone* (Firenze 1962), pp. 5-24; K. Jaspers, *Nikolaus Cusanus* (München, 1964), pp. 179-181, 188, 217-221.

[28] R.W. Southern, *Western Views of Islam in the Middle Ages* (Cambridge, Massachusetts, 1962). For a fuller treatment of the topic up to the middle of the fourteenth century, see N. Daniel, *Islam and the West: The Making of an Image* (Edinburgh, 1960).

[29] R.W. Southern, *op. cit.,* p. 72 n. 12. See also Vansteenberghe, *op. cit.,* pp. 417-420; E. Colomer, *Nikolaus von Kues und Raimund Llull* (Berlin, 1961).

We must further note that in his *De docta ignorantia,* completed in 1440, Nicholas had developed the principle of *docta ignorantia* which held that there is no relationship between the finite and the infinite; that the truth can be attained in its "otherness"; and that it can only be approached by a series of approximations and conjectures which will come closer and closer to it.[30] These ideas may certainly "steer towards the admission that in every religious system there is a relative truth, a more or less distant partaking of the one truth." Thus his view may be interpreted as presenting Judaism, Christianity, and Islam as different aspects of one and the same way toward God.[31]

But if we examine the text of the *De pace fidei* carefully and listen to the Logos, the archangel, St. Peter, and St. Paul who together seem to speak for Nicholas himself, it becomes clear that Nicholas does not really admit the equal status of Christianity with other religions. He says that it is not by works but rather by faith that the salvation of the soul is gained. Once this is admitted, one should not be disturbed by a variety of rites.[32] Concerning the use and rite of the sacrament of the Eucharist, for example, the Church authorities should be able to arrange what seems most expedient according to circumstances.[33] If this multiplicity of rites cannot be done away with, or if it is not desirable to give it up, let there at least be one religion and one cult of worship, even as God is one.[34] The truth is but one, and every diversity of religion can be reduced to the one orthodox faith.[35] The various nations may be permitted to use their own devotions and ceremonies, provided that faith and peace are preserved.[36] Toleration in matters of ritual should be allowed, but there must be unanimity in matters of belief.[37] Thus his position seems to be that so long as the orthodox faith is preserved, a concession in secondary matters can be made. But he emphasizes that a diversity of rites can exist only when the peace and faith of the Church is maintained.[38]

[30] *Opera,* Heidel., I, 1932.

[31] Lecler, *op. cit.,* p. 108. See also E. Hoffmann, *Nikolaus von Cues: Zwei Vorträge* (Heidelberg, 1947), pp. 30-32.

[32] Klibansky and Bascour, *op. cit.,* pp. 51-52.

[33] Ibid., p. 61.

[34] Ibid., p. 7.

[35] Ibid., p. 10.

[36] Ibid., p. 62.

[37] Ibid., p. 56.

[38] Ibid., pp. 61, 62.

As has been noted by some students,[39] Nicholas nowhere in this book discusses the problem of church government in detail. Although he touches upon the Church authorities and ecclesiastical offices,[40] his discussion is brief. But his allowance for a variety of rites and his failure to discuss church government at length in the *De pace fidei* do not in any degree indicate that Nicholas rejected the superiority of Christianity over other religions and the importance of the *cathedra Petri* within Christendom. This interpretation of his position seems to be corroborated not only by his consistent position on religious pluralism and unity over the years, but also by the fact that in his letter of December 29, 1454 to John of Segovia, Nicholas, although he was afraid that the worst might happen, expressed hope that the Turks could be convinced of the truth of the Christian faith by peaceful means. The threat of the Turks to Christendom was real and great. But Nicholas was still hopeful that the unity of Christendom could be preserved.

From his election in 1458 Pope Pius II made the launching of a crusade against the Turks the chief object of his policy. In October 1458 he summoned the princes of Europe to meet at Mantua to organize such an expedition, and in June 1459 he opened the Congress of Mantua in person. The response to his appeal was disappointing, and he himself was toying with the idea that the conqueror of Constantinople, Mohammed II, might be converted.[41] By 1461, however, the Turks were penetrating into Europe. The defense of Europe was an ever more urgent problem.

The *Cribratio Alchorani*,[42] which Pius II asked Nicholas to write probably late in 1460 or early in 1461 to refute the errors of Islam, is notable for the fact that its tone is less conciliatory than that of the *De pace fidei*. With the aid of the works of Ricoldo of Montecroce, Thomas Aquinas' *De ratione fidei*, and John of Torquemada's *Contra principales errores perfidi Mahometis,* and using the method of textual criticism which he had used so successfully in his demonstration of the unauthenticity of the Donation of Constantine, Nicholas attempted to sift out the truth which is found in the Koran, and then to demonstrate the truth of Christianity.[43] In Chapter XVII of Book II Nicholas

---

[39] Seidlmayer, *op. cit.,* p. 182; Dolan, *op. cit.,* p. 193; Sigmund, *op. cit.,* p. 294.

[40] Klibansky and Bascour, *op. cit.,* pp. 61, 62.

[41] J.G. Rowe, "The Tragedy of Aeneas Sylvius Piccolomini (Pope Pius II): An Interpretation," *Church History,* XXX (1961), 228-313.

[42] *Opera,* Basil., pp. 879-932.

[43] P. Naumann, *Sichtung des Alkorans: Cribratio Alkoran,* I (Leipzig, 1948), pp. 5-76; G. Hölscher, "Nikolaus von Cues und der Islam," *Zeitschrift für Philosophische Forschung,* II (1948), 259-274; J.W. Sweetman, *Islam and Christian Theology,* Part II, Vol. 1 (London, 1955), pp. 159-170.

addresses himself directly to Mohammed II, whom he calls the Sultan of the Babylonians. It was in 1461 that Pius II sent a famous letter to Mohammed II.[44] Whether or not Nicholas had any influence on this letter is difficult to establish, but the letter begins with a magnificient account of the power of the "Christian people":

> We cannot believe that you are unaware of the resources of the Christian people—how strong in Spain, how warlike France, how numerous are the people of Germany, how powerful Britain, how bold Poland, how vigorous Hungary, how rich, spirited and skilled in warfare is Italy.[45]

In these statements Pius II clearly reflects the pride and confidence of the people living in Christendom. Both Nicholas' appeal to Mohammed II to accept Christianity and Pius II's letter to him went unheeded. In the end, it was not through the work of either Nicholas or Pius II that the Turkish problem was solved. It was gradually solved by a series of events. Meanwhile the idea of Christendom, to which Nicholas clung, lingered on. The *Cribratio Alchorani* shows that in face of the imminent threat to Christendom, Nicholas still thought that its unity could be maintained.

The fifteenth century has elicited different interpretations partly because of the coexistence, and sometimes overlapping, of old and new. There has been much controversy over the interpretation of the ideas of Nicholas of Cusa, who is undoubtedly one of the most important thinkers of the fifteenth century. In reading his writings and examining the circumstances under which he wrote, we are strongly impressed with the fact that his primary concern was the maintenance of unity and peace not only in the Church, but also in the Christian Commonwealth itself. To be sure, Nicholas, who as a student of law, geography, comparative religion, and church history was very much interested in different ritualistic forms and national customs, found it necessary and desirable to accept a diversity of customs and rites, but this is possible only so long as the peace and unity of the Church and Christendom can be preserved.

The unity of Christendom, which was in his time almost identical with Europe, was being threatened not only internally, but also from outside. It was this unity which Nicholas, like his friends Pius II and John of Segovia, wanted to maintain. It has been said that "the very intolerance of Christianity . . . came from this overwhelming sense of human unity, in which it was thought that all men should have, and deserved to have, the one true saving religion."[46] The word tolerance, which came into vogue especially in the sixteenth century, is said to

---

[44] G. Toffanin, *Lettera a Maometto II (Epistola ad Mahumetem)* (Napoli, 1953). See also Southern, *op. cit.,* pp. 99-103.

[45] The translation used here is found in Hay, *op. cit.,* pp. 83-84.

[46] R.R. Palmer, *A History of the Modern World,* 2nd ed. (New York, 1956), p. 11.

have a passive meaning of endurance.[47] Was Nicholas prepared to endure the coexistence of largely incompatible and hostile systems of belief? Christendom was caught in the grip of an internal and an even more formidable external enemy, and some were afraid that the final dissolution of Christendom as an organic unity was near. In all the writings we have examined, however, Nicholas overtly or covertly supports the primacy of the *sedes Romana* within the Church and superiority of Christianity over other religions.[48]

[47] Lecler, *op. cit.,* p. X.

[48] I am grateful to the American Philosophical Society for a grant which helped me to attend the International Cusanus Congress at Bressanone (Brixen), Italy in 1964 to read this paper.

PART THREE

CUSANUS' CONTEMPORARIES

Nicholas of Cusa—Richard Fleming— Thomas Livingston

As Professor Klibansky pointed out, "the full history of Cusanus' influence remains to be written."[1] Thus far, only tentative or partial attempts have been made.[2] Nicholas of Cusa was influenced by many predecessors and absorbed many of their ideas, and he, in turn, influenced later thinkers and generations. A well-investigated history of his influence would be very fascinating and illuminating to those of us who are interested in the development of European culture. There are, however, many areas which must be studied carefully before the full history of his influence can be written. Take, for example, the case of his influence in England and Scotland.

It is known that on August 13, 1451, Nicholas of Cusa was asked to go to England as papal legate in order to establish peace between England and France which had been engaged in the One Hundred Years' War. Pope Nicholas V had been urged to this by the Duke of Burgundy. But Nicholas never went to England, and the Cardinal d'Estouteville was sent instead.[3] If Nicholas had gone to England, would he have also visited Scotland like his friend Aeneas Silvius Piccolomini who as ambassador from the Council of Basel went to the court of James I of Scotland? This is a question which we cannot discuss here. But a quick look at later developments in England shows that Nicholas' books were published and read in that country.

We note that in 1534 an English translation of Nicholas' attack on the Donation of Constantine was published in London.[4] This shows perhaps that in

---

[1] Raymond Klibansky, "Nicholas of Cues," in *Philosophy in the Mid-Century,* vol. 4 (Florence, 1959), p. 92.

[2] See Morimichi Watanabe, *The Political Ideas of Nicholas of Cusa, with Special Reference to His De concordantia catholica* (Geneva, 1963), p. 191-194.

[3] Johannes Krudewig, *Übersicht über Inhalt der kleineren Archive der Rheinprovinz* vol. 4 (Bonn, 1915), p. 261; Edmond Vansteenberghe, *Le Cardinal Nicolas de Cues* (Paris, 1920), p. 138; Erich Meuthen, *Nikolaus von Kues: Skizze einer Biographie* (Münster, 1964), p. 93.

[4] Nicholas de Cusa, *A treatyse of the donation of gyfte and endowmèt of possessyons gyuen and grainted unto Syluester pope of Rhome by Constantyne emperour of Rome* (London, 1534). See also P.A. Sawada, "Two Anonymous Tudor Treatises on the General Council," *Journal of Ecclesiastical History* 2 (1961): 203, n. 3, where he reports that Cutbert Tunstal, Bishop of Durham, places reference to Cusanus' *De*

the beginning of the English Reformation the ideas of Nicholas were known to those Englishmen who were anxious to criticize the Roman Church and its doctrine of the Donation of Constantine. It is also interesting to find that the "judicious" Richard Hooker, the author of the influential *Of the Laws of Ecclesiastical Polity,* published in 1594-1597, cites in Book I a passage from the *Compendium* of Nicholas of Cusa.[5] In fact, Nicholas' ideas were more widely spread later in England where after 1600 English translations of older, continental mystical writings began to appear rather extensively. Giles Randall, a Puritan mystic, published in 1646 a translation of *De visione Dei* under the title *The Single Eye, Entituled the Vision of God.*[6] This may have been based on the translation done by John Everard, who also translated *Theologia Germanica,* Sebastian Franck's *The Tree of Knowledge of Good and Evil,* and selections from Hermes Trismegistus, Dionysius the Areopagite, Hans Denck and Johann Tauler.[7] In 1650 an English translation of the *Idiota* appeared in London.[8] These facts lead us to ask: What is the relationship between Nicholas of Cusa and England? Furthermore, did he have any influence at all in Scotland?

The purpose of this article is to examine briefly Nicholas' relationship to an Englishman and a Scotsman. The former's relation to Nicholas is by no means clear, but there is no doubt that the latter worked closely with him. By examining his relationship to these men, we may be able to point to certain problems which need more study and await further clarification. This is, then, only a tentative sketch which is drawn in order to emphasize the importance of research along these lines. It may make a small contribution to a future history of Nicholas' influence on later generations.

concordantia catholica in his letter of 3 July 1536 to Reginald Pole, Archbishop of Canterbury.

[5] *The Works of That Learned and Judicious Divine Mr. Richard Hooker, Containing Eight Books of the Laws of Ecclesiastical Polity, and Several Other Treatises,* vol. 1 (Oxford, 1807), p. 226.

[6] Nicolaus Khrypffs, Οφθαλμος 'Απλους, *Or The single Eye, Entituled the Vision of God Wherein is infolded the Mistery of Divine presence, So to be in one place finitely in appearance, as yet in every place no less present, and whilst Hee is here, Hee is universally every where infinitely himself. Penned by that Learned Dr. Cusanus and Published for the good of the Saints* (London, 1646).

[7] William Haller, *The Rise of Puritanism* (New York, 1938), pp. 207-208.

[8] *The idiot in four books: The first and second of wisdom, the third of the minde, the fourth of statick experiments, or experiments of the balance. By the famous and learned C. Cusanus. Printed for William Leake* (London, 1650).

We first come to Richard Fleming who is said to have been born about 1378 at Crofton, England.[9] He studied at University College, Oxford, and became junior proctor in 1407. After receiving the degrees of M.A., B.Th. and D.Th., he attended later sessions of the Council of Constance and preached four sermons there.[10] Pope Martin V made him a papal chamberlain, and sent him as his envoy to England on January 31, 1417.[11] The reward for his services was that on November 21, 1419, he received his bull of provision to the see of Lincoln.[12] He was consecrated at Florence on April 28, 1420.[13]

The Treaty of Canterbury, which had been concluded in 1416 between Henry V of England and Sigismund, King of the Romans, did not lead to the defeat of France envisaged by the signatories.[14] To remind Sigismund of the duties which he had assumed but had not fulfilled, Henry V empowered Richard Fleming, in the royal instructions dated December 18, 1421, to seek armed support from Sigismund.[15] Crossing the Channel soon after February 23, 1422, Bishop Fleming arrived in Regensburg in May, where he was to meet

[9] On the biography of Richard Fleming (or Flemyng, Flemming), see Reginald L. Poole, "Fleming, Richard" (d. 1431) in *Dictionary of National Biography*, vol. 7 (1921), pp. 282-284; Alfred B. Emden, *A Biographical Register of the University of Oxford to A.D. 1500* vol. 2 (Oxford, 1958), pp. 697-699; John Le Neve, *Fasti Ecclesiae Angelicanae 1300-1541*, vol. 1 (Diocese of Lincoln), ed. H.P.F. King (London, 1962), p. 2.

[10] These four sermons were delivered actually on 6 January, 21 June, 9 September and 2 October 1417. See Emden, *A Biographical Register*, vol. 2, p. 698. See C.M.D. Crowder, "Constance Acta in English Libraries" in August Franzen und Wolfgang Müller, *Das Konzil von Konstanz: Beiträge zu seiner Geschichte und Theologie* (Freiburg, 1964), p. 514.

[11] *Calendar of Entries in the Papal Registers Relating to Great Britain and Ireland, Papal Letters* (hereafter cited as CPR Let.), vol. 7 (London, 1906), p. 5.

[12] CPR Let., vol. 7, pp. 116, 134.

[13] Conrad Eubel, *Hierarchia Catholica Medii Aevi*, vol. 1 (Münster, 1913), p. 306. For an example of the nomination of bishops in this time, see Lita-Rose Betcherman, "The Making of Bishops in the Lancastrian Period," *Speculum* 41 (1966): 397-419.

[14] Text in *Deutsche Reichstagsakten* (hereafter cited as RTA) vol. 7, pp. 332-337 (Nr. 224). I am obligated for my knowledge of this to the following study by V. Murdoch, "John Wyclyf and Richard Flemyng, Bishop of Lincoln: Gleanings from German Sources," *Bulletin of the Institute of Historical Research* 37 (1964): 239-245. See also Caro, *Das Bündnis von Canterbury: Eine Episode aus der Geschichte des Constanzer Concils*, Gotha 1880.

[15] Emden, *A Biographical Register*, vol. 2, p. 698.

Sigismund.[16] But the available records do not indicate whether he ever had an opportunity to discuss Sigismund's obligations to the English king. He returned to England probably in October, 1422, without the soldiers he was supposed to recruit.[17]

At the end of March, 1423, he again left England. The purpose of this journey was to represent the English nation at the council which opened its meeting at Pavia on April 23.[18] The poorly attended council was transferred to Siena owing to an outbreak of plague, and was re-opened there on July 2, 1423.[19] Pope Martin V had written to Fleming, asking him to promote the peace and concord of the faithful in the council, and to send him information not only of what was actually done there, but of what was attempted to be done.[20] Flemyng preached before the council on July 21, 1423, and made an eloquent speech championing the papacy on January 23, 1424. The council, split into rival parties and weakened by papal opposition, was finally broken up on March 7, 1424.[21] But on February 14, 1424 Fleming's support of the papacy had been rewarded by a bull providing him to the See of York, which fell vacant at the death of Archbishop Henry Bowet on October 30, 1423.[22] The chapter, however, had already elected Philip Morgan, Bishop of Worcester, and the crown had given its assent on January 1.[23] Fleming was thus in danger of incurring the penalties of the Statute of *Praemunire*.[24] After a long dispute, the matter was

---

[16] RTA, vol. 8, p. 220 (Nr. 182). See also RTA, vol. 8, pp. 132, 137, 225, 230.

[17] Cf. Emden, *A Biographical Register,* vol. 2, p. 698. S. Léon Mirot and E. Deprez, "Les ambassades anglaises pendant la guerre de Cent ans: Catalogue chronologique (1327-1450)," *Bibliothèque de l'Ecole des Chartes* 61 (1900), 30.

[18] *Monumenta Conciliorum Generalium, Seculi Decimi Quinti,* vol. 1 (Vienna, 1857), p. 11. Charles-Joseph Hefele, *Histoire des Conciles,* vol. 7 (Paris, 1916), p. 614, n. 3.

[19] We find an account of the journey of John Whethamstede, Abbot of St. Albans, to Siena in E.F. Jacob, *Essays in the Conciliar Epoch* (Manchester², 1953), pp. 44-46.

[20] CPR Let., vol. 7, p. 27; A.H. Thompson, *Visitations of Religious Houses in the Diocese of Lincoln* (1420-1449), vol. 1 (Horncastle, 1914), p. XV.

[21] *Monumenta Conciliorum Generalium, Seculi Decimi Quinti,* vol. 1, pp. 12, 64.

[22] Eubel, *Hierarchia,* vol. 1, p. 233.

[23] E.F. Jacob, *The Fifteenth Century, 1399-1485* (Oxford, 1961), p. 269.

[24] On the Statute of Praemunire see E.B. Graves, "The Legal Significance of the Statute of Praemunire of 1353," *Haskins Anniversary Essays in Medieval History,* ed.

compromised by his re-translation to Lincoln and the translation of John Kempe, Bishop of London, to York on July 20, 1425.[25]

It was this Richard Fleming who, together with the young canon lawyer Nicholas of Cusa and about sixty other professors of law and theology, submitted his advisory opinion sometime between 1424 and 1426 to Cardinal Giordano Orsini, the papal legate in Germany,[26] on a case concerning the exemption of taxes from the vineyard which belonged to a parish church in Bacharach.[27] The priest of the church was Winand of Steeg, who was not only a learned humanist and *doctor decretorum,* but also Sigismund's secretary.[28] As a member of the chapter of St. Andreas in Cologne, he brought the suit to Cardinal Orsini against the Elector of the Palatinate, Ludwig III, who claimed to lay taxes on the produce from the vineyard. The richly illustrated notarial instrument (MS 12) in the Königliches Geheimes Hausarchiv in Munich has been studied and commented on by Josef Weiss, Hermann Grauert, Karl Voll, Erich König, Karl Christ and recently Aloys Schmidt.[29] The picture of the young canon lawyer Nicholas writing his opinion has also been reproduced more

Charles H. Taylor (Boston, 1929), pp. 57-80; W.T. Waugh, "The Great Statute of Praemunire," *English Historical Review* 38 (1922): 173-205.

[25] Eubel, *Hierarchia,* vol. 1, pp. 233, 306, n. 10. See also Jacob, *The Fifteenth Century,* pp. 234-235, 269, 434; Betcherman, *The Making of Bishops,* pp. 408-409.

[26] RTA, vol. 8, pp. 455, 482.

[27] *Vita S. Vernheri,* Stadtbibliothek Trier, Hs. 1139/65. On this Manuscript see Erwin Iserloh, "Werner von Oberwesel: Zur Tilgung seines Festes im Trierer Kalender," *Trierer Theologische Zeitschrift* 72 (1963): 270-285; Ferdinand Pauly, "Zue Vita des Werner von Oberwesel," *Archiv für mittelrheinische Kirchengeschichte* 16 (1964): 94-109.

[28] On Winand von Steeg see Josef Weiss, "Winand (Ort) von Steeg," *Historisches Jahrbuch* 26 (1906): 470-471; Aloys Schmidt, "Zur Geschichte der älteren Universität Würsburg," *Würsburger Diözesangeschichtsblätter* ii./12. Jahrg. (1949/50): 91-96; Aloys Schmidt, "Nikolaus von Kues Sekretär des Kardinals Giordano Orsini?," in *Aus Mittelalter und Neuzeit: Festschrift für Gerhard Kallen* (Bonn, 1957), pp. 137-143.

[29] Josef Weiss, "Von den Beziehungen der pfälzischen Kurfürsten zum Geistesleben am Mittelrhein," *Jahresbericht der Görresgesellschaft* (1905): 25-34; Hermann Grauert, "Petrarka und die Renaissance," *Hochland* I. Jahrg., vol. 2 (Kempten u. München, April 1904 bis September 1904), 583; Karl Voll, "Ein Beitrag zur Geschichte der deutschen Porträtsmalerei," *Beilage zur Allgemeinen Zeitung,* Jahrg. 1905, Nr. 215 Sonntag 17. September, München; Erich König, *Kardinal Giordano Orsini* (Freiburg, 1906); Karl Christ, "Werner von Bacharach: eine mittelrheinische Legende in Reimen," in *Otto Glauning zum 60. Geburtstag,* vol. 2 (Leipzig, 1938), pp. 1-17; A. Schmidt, "Nikolaus von Kues Sekretär des Kardinals Giordano Orsini?"

than a few times.[30] But thus far little attention has been given to *Richardus electus in Archiepiscopum Eboracensis Anglie primatem,* whose picture and opinion appear on folio 9r of the manuscript.[31]

Not much is known about the activities of Fleming between February 14, 1424, and 1427, when he founded Lincoln College at Oxford primarily to educate opponents of Wycliffite teaching with which he was suspected of sympathy while teaching at Oxford.[32] But how did it happen that this Archibishop-elect of York wrote his opinion on the tax problem concerning the vineyard in Bacharach?[33] Did he know any of such eminent professors as Johann von Noet, Otto von Stein, Nikolaus Burgmann, and Hesso Kravell of Heidelberg University and Heinrich von Gorkum, Christian von Erpel, Johannes von Spull, and Petrus von Neukirch of Cologne University, all of whom submitted their opinions on the case to the cardinal? Is it possible that Fleming, who was once called *sacre theologie professor,*[34] has some connection with the Faculty of Theology in Cologne? It is known that the eminent theologian Heinrich von Gorkum, whose opinion Richard approvingly adduces, became Vice Chancellor of Cologne University in 1424.[35] Since Heinrich is referred to as Vice Chancellor in Fleming's opinion, it is safe to assume that it was written after 1423. But what was his relation to Heinrich von Gorkum and Cologne University? As was noted above, Flemyng was provided by Pope Martin V to the see of York on February 14, 1424. Strictly speaking, he was not *Richardus electus.* It is, however, not surprising that the designation was used in the manuscript

[30] Max Jansen, *Kaiser Maximilian,* vol. 1 (München, 1905), p. 28; Gerhard Kallen, "Der Reichsgedanke in der Reformschrift, De concordantia catholica des Nikolaus von Cues," *Neue Heidelberger Jahrbücher* N.F. (1940), 58; Ernst Hoffmann, "Nikolaus von Cues," *Zwei Vorträge* (Heidelberg, 1947), p. 7; Gerd Heinz-Mohr und Willehad P. Eckert, *Das Werk des Nicolaus Cusanus* (Köln, 1963), p. 2.

[31] Only Kurt Voll designates Richard as "Archbishop Richard of York" in the article mentioned above (p. 532). I wish to express my thanks to Professor Dr. Hans Rall

(Munich) and Mr. Otto Mutzbauer for their assistance in obtaining permission from his highness Duke Albrecht of Bavaria to reproduce Tables IV and V.

[32] Jacob, *The Fifteenth Century,* p. 672.

[33] Hermann Keussen, *Die Matrikel der Universität Köln 1389 bis 1559,* vol. 1 (Bonn, 1928), p. 277.

[34] Thompson, *Visitations,* I, p. xiv. See also Franzen und Müller, *Das Konzil von Konstanz,* p. 514.

[35] A.G. Weiler, *Heinrich von Gorkum: Seine Stellung in der Philosophie und der Theologie des Spätmittelalters* (Hilversum, 1962), pp. 48-49. We find a short form of Nikolaus von Gorkum's opinion in Manuscript 2 at pp. 46-47.

made between 1424 and 1426. This may be due to the lack of precise information on the Continent about what took place in England. Flemyng's "election" to York was apparently known in February of 1424 among the participants of the Council of Siena.[36] But we find that Fleming is still referred to as *Richardus archiepiscopus electus Eboracensis* by John of Segovia in his *Historia Gestorum Generalis Synodi Basiliensis,* which was written after 1440.[37]

Let us next turn to a Scotsman who was a friend of Nicholas of Cusa for many years. Thomas Livingston was one of the first graduates of the University of St. Andrews in Scotland,[38] and seems to have taught there for a while, becoming *temptator* in Spring, 1419.[39] Entering the Cistercian order, he became a monk, and for a time, in 1422, abbot-elect of Newbattle.[40] In 1423, he entered the University of Cologne to study theology.[41] This was two years before Nicholas of Cusa came to Cologne. It is possible that Livingston made acquaintance with Nicholas there. Livingston was a Bachelor of Systematic Theology when he matriculated at the University of Cologne, and he became later a Doctor of Theology.[42] Sometime in the 1420's he became Abbot of Dundrennan.[43]

---

[36] Wladimir J. Koudelka, "Eine neue Quelle zur Generalsynode von Siena 1423-1424," *Zeitschrift für Kirchengeschichte* 74 (1963): 256, 262.

[37] Joannes de Segovia, *Historia Gestorum Generalis Synodi Basiliensis in Monumenta Conciliorum Generalium, Seculi Decimi Quinti,* vol. 4, p. 284. See Uta Fromherz, *Johannes von Segovia als Geschichtsschreiber des Konzils von Basel* (Basel and Stuttgart, 1960), p. 72.

[38] James M. Anderson, *Early Records of the University of St. Andrews* (Edinburgh, 1926), pp. 1-2.

[39] J.H. Burns, *Scottish Churchmen and the Council of Basle* (Glasgow, 1962), p. 12.

[40] A.I. Cameron and E.R. Lindsay, *Calendar of Scottish Supplications to Rome 1423-1428,* vol. 2 (Edinburgh, 1934), pp. 8-9; Burns, *Scottish Churchmen,* p. 12.

[41] Keussen, *Die Matrikel,* vol. 1, p. 253.

[42] See James H. Burns, "The Conciliar Tradition in Scotland," *Scottish Historical Review* 42 (1963): 94. The connection with Cologne University is especially important at this stage: of thirteen Scots who can be said to have adhered, or to have persisted in adherence, to the Council of Basle after the breach with Eugenius IV, no fewer than ten had some connection with Cologne.

[43] Burns, *Scottish Churchmen,* p. 12. Cf. Keussen, *Die Matrikel,* vol. 1, p. 253, note to 137.

In 1432 he was incorporated in the Council of Basel.[44] No Scotsman was present before his arrival at the council. He may have been encouraged to go there by Nicholas of Cusa.[45] The most distinguished Scotsman at the council, Livingston remained its active and devoted adherent until its final dissolution in 1449.[46] In August, 1439, for example, he was appointed to an embassy directed to Frankfurt[47] and to the forthcoming provincial Diet at Mainz.[48] On August 3[49] he addressed the latter body,[50] and a week later he delivered a still longer exposition of the council's position to the Diet.[51] When the council proceeded to elect a new pope after the deposition of Eugenius IV, Livingston became one of the electors to choose a pope.[52] The choice fell upon Amadeus, Duke of Savoy, who was elected on November 5, 1439. History knows him as the antipope Felix V. Hereafter Livingston's position in the council seems to have been strengthened. At the end of September, 1440, he was appointed by the council as a member of the embassy to Cologne.[53] He was then provided to the See of Dunkeld by Felix V on November 29, 1440.[54]

This provision, however, never took effect, and on April 10, 1441 Eugenius IV deprived him of the Abbey of Dundrennan.[55] Despite these difficulties, he seems to have kept an important position in the council. We find that on March 20, 1447, Livingston was appointed Felix V's legate to

---

[44] RTA, vol. 15, pt. 2, 939. See also J.H. Baxter, "Four 'New' Medieval Scottish Authors," *Scottish Historical Review* 25 (1928): 96; J.H. Baxter, *Copiale Prioratus Sanctiandree: The Letter-Book of James Haldenstone, Prior of St. Andrews, 1418-1443* (London, 1930), pp. 432, 490.

[45] RTA, vol. 13, p. 570 ("abbas de Scocia tunc presidens nationis Germanice").

[46] RTA, vol. 13, p. 784.

[47] RTA, vol. 14, p. 317.

[48] RTA, vol. 14, p. 331.

[49] RTA, vol. 14, p. 143. On the activity of Nicholas of Cusa in Mainz, see Anton Ph. Brück, "Nikolaus von Cues in Mainz," *Mainzer Almanach* (Mainz, 1965): 36-60.

[50] RTA, vol. 14, pp. 331-338.

[51] RTA, vol. 14, pp. 344-346.

[52] *Monumenta Conciliorum Generalium, Seculi Decimi Quinti*, vol. 3, pp. 406, 36.

[53] RTA, vol. 15, pt. 1, p. 454. Cf. RTA, vol. 15, pt. 1, pp. 473-475.

[54] Burns, *Scottish Churchmen*, p. 68.

[55] CPR Let., vol. 9, p. 226; Burns, *Scottish Churchmen*, pp. 12, 73.

Scotland.[56] As is known, however, the council came to an end in 1449. It is interesting to note that even after the final collapse of the Council of Basel, Livingston retained his standing in ecclesiastical affairs. He was still styled "Bishop in the Universal Church."[57]

Nicholas of Cusa was once an adherent to the cause of the Council of Basel. Like Cesarini, Pizolpassus, Capranica and Andrew of Escobar, however, he began to change his position towards the council around 1437, until he became a champion of the papacy. Did his attitude change towards Livingston who remained an advocate of the council till its end? What was exactly Livingston's relationship to Nicholas of Cusa? It is very interesting to note that during 1449 Nicholas delivered three sermons in German at Hildesheim to the people of the town while Livingston preached two sermons in Latin to the monks and other clergymen in the monastery church there.[58] It is also recorded that in June, 1449, Pope Nicholas V granted him the church of Kirkinner *in commendam*.[59] Our Cistercian "bishop" was probably with Nicholas when he returned to Rome on January 11, 1450, and he might have been present at his consecration as Bishop of Brixen by the pope on March 23.[60]

When Nicholas and his retinue began the famous reform trip to Germany and the Low Countries on the last day of 1450, Livingston was probably with them.[61] He was one of the delegation chosen by the cardinal to carry out reforms in the Benedictine houses in Germany in 1451. Among other duties he was entrusted with the examination of the Ordinary at Bursfeld after the provincial council at Mainz in November, 1451.[62] After his return to Scotland, he is said

---

[56] Burns, *Scottish Churchmen,* p. 83.

[57] Burns, *Scottish Churchmen,* p. 12. See also Erich Meuthen, *Die letzten Jahre des Nikolaus von Kues* (Köln and Opladen, 1958), p. 136, n. 2.

[58] Richard Doebner, "Annalen und Akten der Brüder des gemeinsamen Lebens im Lüchtenhofe zu Hildesheim," in *Quellen und Darstellungen zur Geschichte Niedersachsens,* vol. 9 (Hannover and Leipzig, 1903), p. 22: "Ipse fecit adminus tres sermones solempnes ad populum, qui undique confluebant ad civitatem Hildensem, in vulgari, quia Teutonicus erat genera, quia de Chusa. Habuit idem cardinalis secum episcopum pro cancellario puto doctorem ordinis Cistercienses domui nostre faventem, qui et duos sermones fecit in ecclesia nostra pro fratribus et clero concurrente in Latino."

[59] CPR Let. vol. 10, p. 196. See Duncan Shaw, "Thomas Livingston, a Conciliarist," *Records of the Scottish Church History Society* 12 (1955): 134.

[60] Shaw, "Thomas Livingston," p. 132.

[61] Shaw, "Thomas Livingston," p. 129.

[62] Baxter, *Copiale,* p. 490: "Ordinariumque . . . coram nobis exhibitum per rev. patrem Thomam, in ecclesia universali episcopum, regule s. Benedicti et sacre

to have become confessor and counselor of James II, sustained by benefices granted him by Nicholas V.[63] He died before April 8, 1460, in Scotland.[64]

It has been pointed out that Thomas Livingston[65] is the most notable among the Scottish exponents of conciliar opinions, and that as such he forms a direct and essential link in the chain which connects George Buchanan and John Major back to Pierre d'Ailly and Jean Gerson.[66] If the Scottish humanist George Buchanan and other advocates of constitutional doctrines in the sixteenth and seventeenth centuries exhibit familiarity with conciliar ideas, it may partly be due to Thomas Livingston's activities as a conciliarist and his friendship with Nicholas of Cusa.[67]

Harold J. Laski wrote in 1936: "The road from Constance to 1688 is a direct one. Nicholas of Cusa, Gerson, and Zabarella are the ancestors, through pamphlets like the *Vindiciae Contra Tyrannos,* of Sidney and Locke."[68] But he did not explain fully how his statement could be substantiated. We have tried to show the existence of certain relations between the Conciliar Movement on the Continent and the followers of conciliar ideas and constitutionalism in England

theologie professorem eximium et expertum, denuo studiosius examinari fecimus." See also Paulus Volk, *Fünfhundert Jahre Bursfelder Kongregation* (Regensburg-Münster, 1950), p. 129. Father Volk, like Professor Koch (Cusanus-Texte, I. *Predigten* (Heidelberg, 1942), p. 10 n. 2; *Nikolaus von Cues und seine Umwelt* (Heidelberg, 1948), p. 106, Anm. I), identifies Bishop Thomas as Thomas Lauder O.S.B., Bishop of Dunkeld. But Erich Meuthen (*Die letzten Jahre,* p. 136, n. 2) says that Thomas Lauder became Bishop of Dunkeld on 28 April 1452 (Eubel, *Hierarchia,* vol. 2, p. 147).

[63] Burns, *The Conciliar Tradition,* p. 97.

[64] Burns, *Scottish Churchmen,* pp. 13, 85.

[65] Burns, *Scottish Churchmen,* p. 9.

[66] Baxter, "Four 'New'," p. 96. See also Francis Oakley's following writings: "On the Road from Constance to 1688: The Political Thought of John Major and George Buchman," *Journal of British Studies* (1962): 1-31; *The Political Thought of Pierre d'Ailly* (New Haven, 1964); "Almain and Major: Conciliar Theory on the Eve of Reformation," *American Historical Review* 70 (1965): 673-690; "From Constance to 1688 Revisited," *Journal of the History of Ideas* 27 (1966): 429-432. Zofia Rueger, "Gerson, the Conciliar Movement and the Right of Resistance (1642-1644)," *Journal of the History of Ideas* 25 (1964): 467-486 provides very interesting material for our discussion.

[67] Burns, *Scottish Churchmen,* p. 77. See also Rueger, "Gerson," pp. 483-484.

[68] Harold J. Laski, "Political Theory in the Later Middle Ages," *Cambridge Medieval History,* vol. 8 (1936), p. 638.

and Scotland,[69] using Richard Fleming and Thomas Livingston as two case studies. The case of Richard Fleming, who was in no sense a conciliarist, especially needs further study. It is clear, however, that although Nicholas of Cusa never went to England or Scotland in person, his ideas and books began to exert influence in these countries.

---

[69] See A.N.E.D. Schofield, "England, the Pope, and the Council of Basel," *Church History* 33 (1964): 248-278.

Humanism in the Tyrol: Aeneas Sylvius, Duke Sigismund, Gregor Heimburg

Many students of humanism have traced the diffusion of Italian humanism into the countries north of the Alps. It has been pointed out that the channels through which Italian humanism spread abroad were the exchange of persons and students, the presence of Italian scholars, bankers, and businessmen in other countries, the foreign correspondence of the Italian humanists, and the distribution of Italian humanist books and vernacular translations.[1] Contacts between south and north Europe increased greatly during the second half of the fourteenth and the first half of the fifteenth centuries, facilitating the European diffusion of Italian humanism. Although no adequate general account of the reception of Italian humanism in the North exists, Geiger, Hay, Kristeller, and Weiss, to mention only some, have shed much light on the subject.[2]

With regard to Germany in general, it is known that the Councils of Constance (1414-1417) and Basel (1431-1449), where Italian humanists met learned colleagues from Germany and sought in their spare time classical manuscripts in nearby monasteries, played an important role in spreading humanist ideas.[3] Studies of humanism in Bohemia, Erfurt, Heidelberg, Leipzig,

---

[1] Roberto Weiss, "Italian Humanism in Western Europe: 1460-1520," in *Italian Renaissance Studies,* ed. E.F. Jacob (London, 1960), pp. 69-70; Denys Hay, *The Italian Renaissance in Its Historical Background* (Cambridge, 1966), pp. 190-91. In this article the term humanism is interpreted to mean a cultural and educational movement which was chiefly concerned with rhetoric, scholarship and literature. For the various interpretations of humanism, see, for example, William J. Bouwsma, *The Interpretation of Renaissance Humanism* (Washington, 1959); Paul O. Kristeller, "Studies on Renaissance Humanism during the Last Twenty Years," *Studies in the Renaissance,* 9 (1962): 7-30; Donald Weinstein, "In Whose Image and Likeness? Interpretations of Renaissance Humanism," *Journal of the History of Ideas,* 33 (1972): 165-68.

[2] Ludwig Geiger, *Renaissance und Humanismus in Italien und Deutschland* (Berlin, 1882); Hay, *The Italian Renaissance;* Paul O. Kristeller, "The European Diffusion of Italian Humanism," *Italica,* 39 (1962): 1-20, reprinted in his *Renaissance Thought II: Papers on Humanism and the Arts* (New York, 1965), pp. 69-88; Weiss, "Italian Humanism"; Roberto Weiss, "Learning and Education in Western Europe from 1470 to 1520," in *The New Cambridge Modern History,* I (Cambridge, 1957), pp. 95-126; idem, *The Spread of Italian Humanism* (London, 1964).

[3] Paul Lehmann, "Konstanz und Basel als Büchermarkte während der grosser Kirchenversammlungen," *Zeitschrift des deutschen Vereins für Buchwesen und*

Nuremberg, Augsburg, Ingolstadt, Wittenberg, and Mainz are available.[4] A
number of studies on the reception of humanism in the University of Vienna
have also been published.[5] It is notable, however, that outside the Tyrol little
attention has been paid to the development of humanism in the Tyrol, which
constituted the threshold of the Empire.[6] Did the Tyrol play any important part

Schrifttum, 4 (1921): 6-11, 17-27; reprinted in his *Erforschung des Mittelalters,* I
(Leipzig, 1959), pp. 1253-80.

[4] Important studies of humanism in these places include F.W. Kampschulte, *Die
Universität Erfurt in ihrem Verhaltnis zu dem Humanismus und der Reformation* (Trier,
1858); Karl Hartfelder, "Heidelberg und der Humanismus," *Zeitschrift für allgemeine
Geschichte,* 2 (1885), 177-95, 671-96; Max Herrmann, *Die Reception des
Humanismus in Nürnberg* (Berlin, 1898); Gustav Bauch, *Geschichte des Leipziger
Frühhumanimus mit besonderer Rücksicht auf die Streitigkeiten zwischen Konrad
Wimpina und Martin Hellerstadt* (Leipzig, 1899); G. Bauch, *Die Anfange des
Humanismus in Ingolstadt* (Munich and Leipzig, 1901) G. Bauch, *Die Universität
Erfurt im Zeitalter des Frühhumanismus* (Breslau, 1904); G. Bauch, "Aus der
Geschichte des Mainzer Humanismus," *Archiv für hessische Geschichte und
Altertumskunde,* N.F., 5 (1907), 3-86; Eduard Winter, "Die europaische Bedeutung des
Frühhumanimus in Bohmen," *Zeitschrift fur deutsche Geistesgeschichte,* 1 (1935):
233-42; Hans Rupprich, *Humanismus und Renaissance in den deutschen Städten und
Universitäten* (Leipzig, 1935); Karl Schadle, *Sigmund Gossenbrot, ein Augsburger
Kaufmann, Patrizier und Frühhumanist* (Augsburg, 1938); H. Rupprich, *Die Frühzeit
des Humanismus und der Renaissance in Deutschland* (Leipzig, 1938; Darmstadt,
1964); Friedrich Zoepfl, "Der Humanismus am Hof der Fürstbischöfe von Augsburg,"
Historisches Jahrbuch, 62/69,2 (1949): 671-708; E. Winter, *Frühhumanimus: seine
Entwicklung in Bohmen und deren europaische Bedeutung für die Kirchenreform-
bestrebungen im 14. Jahrhundert* (Berlin, 1964); Hans-Heinrich Fleischer, *Dietrich
Gresemund der jüngere: ein Beitrag zur Geschichte des Humanismus in Mainz*
(Wiesbaden, 1967).

[5] J. Aschbach, *Geschichte der Wiener Universität,* 3 vols. (Vienna, 1865; Farn-
borough, 1967); G. Bauch, *Die Reception des Humanismus in Wien* (Breslau, 1903);
Karl Grossmann, "Die Frühzeit des Humanismus in Wien bis zu Celtis Berufung
1497," *Jahrbuch für Landeskunde von Niederösterreich,* 22 (1929): 150-325;
Alphons Lhotsky, *Quellenkunde zur mittelalterlichen Geschichte Österreichs,* MIÖG
Erganzungsband 19 (Graz, 1963), pp. 437-41.

[6] Studies of humanism in the Tyrol by Tyrolese historians are David von Schonherr,
"Die Kunstbestrebungen Erzherzog Sigmunds von Tirol," *Jahrbuch der
kunsthistorischen Sammlungen des a. h. Kaiserhauses,* I (1883): 182-212, reprinted
in David von Schonherr, *Gesammelte Schriften,* ed. M. Mayr, I (Innsbruck, 1900),
pp. 58-92; Anton Zingerle, "Der Humanismus in Tirol unter Erzherzog Sigmund dem
Münzreichen," *Fest-Gruss aus Innsbruck an die XLII. Versammlung deutscher
Philologen und Schulmänner in Wien* (Innsbruck, 1893), pp. 21-42, reprinted in his
Tirolensia: Beiträge zur Volks- und Landeskunde Tirols (Innsbruck, 1898), pp. 138-
62; Heinrich Hammer, "Literarische Beziehungen und musikalisches Leben des Hofes
Herzog Siegmunds von Tirol," *Zeitschrift des Ferdinandeums für Tirol und Vorarlberg,*

in the diffusion of Italian humanism in the North? Were there conditions favorable to a rapid development of humanism in the area? Who were chiefly responsible for the growth of humanism in the Tyrol? Were there distinctive features of Tyrolese humanism? These are some of the questions which must be studied carefully if we are to understand more clearly the general diffusion of Italian humanism in the North. These questions assume a greater significance when we realize that large numbers of scholars, students, and other persons passed through the Tyrol on their way to or from Italy.

In the Tyrol there was no university in the fifteenth and sixteenth centuries where humanist studies could be promoted on a continuing basis. The university with which the Tyrol was in closest touch was the University of Freiburg im Breisgau. Although a bull was granted by Pope Calixtus III (1455-1458) on April 20, 1455, authorizing the founding of a university at Freiburg, the lectures were not begun until April 27, 1460.[7] Thus the most natural places where the new learning could be promoted were the princely courts in the Tyrol, especially the ducal court in Innsbruck. Although there was little trace of humanist activities during the reign of Duke Friedrich IV (1407-1439), much progress was made under his son Sigismund (or Sigmund) "der Münzreiche" (1439-1496). It should also be remembered that the Emperor Maximilian I (1493-1519), who was himself a humanist of no small pretensions and a patron of the arts, held court frequently in Innsbruck as Sigismund's successor.

The purpose of this article is to discuss the development of humanism in the Tyrol, especially in relation to some of its contributors, and to assess its significance in the history of the diffusion of Italian humanism in the North.

It may be said in general that the cultural developments in Renaissance Italy had three stages: there was first a period in the fourteenth century,

---

3. Folge, 43 (1899): 69-124; Hans Kramer, *Das Zeitalter des Humanimus in Tirol, Ewiger Humanismus-Schriften der österreichischen humanistischen Gesellschaft in Innsbruck,* 13. Heft (Innsbruck, 1947). Johannes von Allesch, "Die geistesgeschichtliche Lage Tirols im XV. Jahrhundert," *Deutsche Vierteljahrsschrift für Literaturwissenschaft und Geistesgeschichte,* 9 (1931): 711-44, is of little value because it lacks documentation.

[7] Heinrich Schreiber, *Geschichte der Stadt und Universität Freiburg im Breisgau,* new ed. (Freiburg, 1868), pp. 7-9, 19; Peter P. Albert, "Gründung und Gründer der Universität Freiburg im Breisgau," *Zeitschrift der Gesellschaft für Beförderung der Geschichts-, Alterthums- und Volkskunde von Freiburg,* 37 (1923): 19-62; Hastings Rashdall, *The Universities of Europe in the Middle Ages,* ed. F.M. Powicke and A.B. Emden, II (London, 1936), p. 273; H. Ott and J.M. Fletcher, *The Mediaeval Statutes of the Faculty of Arts of the University of Freiburg im Breisgau,* Texts and Studies in the History of Mediaeval Education, No. 10 (Notre Dame, 1964), p. 11. It is to be noted that the University of Florence played a very small role in the development of humanism. See Gene A. Brucker, "Florence and Its University, 1348-1434," in *Action and Conviction in Early Modern Europe: Essays in Memory of E.H. Harbison,* ed. T.K. Rabb and J.E. Seigel (Princeton, 1969), pp. 220-36.

culminating about 1370, in which a few men of genius speculated afresh on the moral and literary problems that faced them; this was followed by nearly a century when many of the leaders in ideas and art were Florentines; and finally we come to the century from about 1450 to 1550 when Renaissance style in literature, art, and morality was adopted by other courts of Italy.[8] An almost parallel development can be seen in German humanism. First, there was a brief period of blossoming humanist interest in Prague under the Emperor Charles IV (1346-1378), who founded the University of Prague in 1348 and reformed the imperial chancery under Johann von Neumarkt (ca. 1310-1380). Then there was the phase of frankly avowed inspiration from the Italian Renaissance, a phase which lasted to the end of the third quarter of the fifteenth century. In the last quarter of the century there was a greater development of emphasis on religious reform and a growing feeling of romantic patriotism.[9]

It was toward the end of the second period that Aeneas Sylvius Piccolomini, whom Paul Joachimsohn called the "apostle of German humanism,"[10] left the Council of Basel, where he had been active since 1432. A graduate of the University of Siena, where he studied classics as well as law, Aeneas had moved quickly at the council from scriptor to abbreviator and played an important role as a defender of the council in the election of Anti-Pope Felix V in 1439. But disappointed by the increasing ineffectiveness of the conciliar party and desirous of a release from heightening tensions between pope and council, Aeneas decided, as he himself put it later, to move into the neutral ground of King Friedrich III's chancery. He joined the chancery early in 1443 after taking an oath of allegiance to Friedrich III at Brixen in the Tyrol.[11]

To the cultured young Italian humanist, the imperial courts at Graz, Wiener Neustadt, and Vienna must have looked quite drab and dull. Friedrich III, who became emperor in 1452, was himself no humanist either by inclination or

---

[8] Hay, *The Italian Renaissance,* pp. 185-86.

[9] Lewis W. Spitz, *The Religious Renaissance of the German Humanists* (Cambridge, Massachusetts, 1963), pp. 5-6.

[10] Paul Joachimsohn, *Gregor Heimburg,* Historische Abhandlungen aus dem Münchener Seminar, I. Heft (Bamberg, 1891), p. 103. Cf. Paul Joachimsen (=Joachimsohn), *Geschichtsauffassung und Geschichtschreibung in Deutschland unter dem Einfluss des Humanismus* (Leipzig, 1910; Aalen, 1968), p. 27; Grossmann, "Die Frühzeit," p. 195; Alphons Lhotsky, *Aeneas Silvius und Österreich,* Vorträge der Aeneas-Silvius-Stiftung an der Universität Basel, 5 (Basel and Stuttgart, 1965).

[11] *The Commentaries of Pius II,* trans. Florence A. Gragg, introd. Leona C. Gabel, in Smith College Studies in History, 22 (Oct. 1936/Jan. 1937), p. 30. For Aeneas' life and thought, see, for example, Georg Voigt, *Enea Silvio de' Piccolomini als Papst Pius der Zweite und sein Zeitalter,* 3 vols. (Berlin, 1856-63; Berlin, 1967); Berthe Widmer, *Enea Silvio Piccolomini in der sittlichen und politischen Entscheidung,* Basler Beiträge zur Geschichtswissenschaft, Band 88 (Basel and Stuttgart, 1963).

by education, and the constantly depleted condition of his treasury prevented any considerable patronage of learning.[12] Aeneas wrote and dedicated to Friedrich III a tract called the *Pentalogus*[13] soon after entering the chancery. In the tract, which purported to be conversations between him and four other persons, including Friedrich III, Aeneas discussed, among other things, the relative merits of force of arms and humanist education, but Friedrich III seems to have taken little note of it. No wonder that Aeneas once characterized Friedrich III as almost stupid (*pene stupidum*).[14]

As for Aeneas' life as a member of the imperial chancery, he seems to have exchanged his unhappy life toward the end of his stay at Basel for something even less enjoyable. The presence of a thirty-seven-year-old foreigner in the chancery created resentment among his colleagues. Describing the working conditions in the chancery, Aeneas wrote: "All of us in the chancery have to work in one office and we also have to eat and drink in one room; ants are not crowded in their quarters as we are. Bees are at least separated into individual cells; we crowd together like sheep in a corral."[15] He also seems to have suffered real hardships from the coarse food and the slovenly manners of his colleagues. His letter to Johann von Eich, bishop of Eichstatt since 1445, on the *Miseries of Courtiers*[16] has much in it that is autobiographical.

Aeneas' meeting with Duke Sigismund of the Tyrol at the imperial court in Graz in 1443 was an important event in the history of humanism in the Tyrol. Upon the death of Sigismund's father Friedrich IV ("the Old") on June 24,

---

[12] Cf. Alphons Lhotsky, "Die Bibliothek Kaiser Friedrichs III.," *Mitteilungen des Instituts fur österreichische Geschichtsforschung,* 58 (1950): 124-35. On why Friedrich III crowned Aeneas as poet laureate on July 27, 1442, see Grossmann, "Die Frühzeit," 187-89. For recent reappraisals of Friedrich III, see Brigitte Haller, *Kaiser Friedrich III. im Urteil der Zeitgenossen* (Vienna, 1965); *Ausstellung-Friedrich III.: Kaiserresidenz Wiener Neustadt* (Vienna, [1966]), pp. 13-230.

[13] *Pentalogus de rebus ecclesiae et imperii in Thesaurus anecdotorum novissimus,* ed. B. Pez, IV, iii (Augsburg, 1723), cols. 637-744. Cf. Lhotsky, *Quellenkunde,* pp.397-98.

[14] Lhotsky, *Aeneas Silvius,* p. 25.

[15] *Der Briefwechsel des Aeneas Silvius Piccolomini,* ed. Rudolf Wolkan, in *Fontes Rerum Austriacarum,* 2. Abt., 61. Band (Vienna, 1909), p. 236. The translation is from *Selected Letters of Aeneas Silvius Piccolomini,* trans. Albert R. Baca, San Fernando Valley State College Renaissance Editions, No. 2 (Northridge, California, 1969), p. 19.

[16] *Aeneae Sylvii Piccolominei Senensis . . . opera* (Basel, 1551; Frankfurt am Main, 1967), cols. 720-36; Wolkan, *Der Briefwechsel,* 61, 453-87; *Aeneae Silvii de curialium miseriis epistola,* ed. Wilfred P. Mustard (Baltimore, 1928). Cf. Grossmann, "Die Frühzeit," pp. 189-90.

1439, Sigismund's cousin Friedrich III ("the Young") had taken the eleven-year-old boy to Graz in violation of an agreement between himself and Sigismund's advisors.[17] In Graz, and after 1443 in Wiener Neustadt, King Friedrich III gave a proper education and training not only to his cousin Sigismund but also to the future Bohemian King Ladislas Posthumus, who was kept in his charge until 1452. Although the theory that Aeneas was Sigismund's teacher the imperial court has not been proved beyond doubt,[18] it would seem clear that Aeneas and Sigismund came to know each other well.

Sufficiently impressed by the good reputation which the young prince of the Tyrol enjoyed at the imperial court, Aeneas wrote a letter on December 5, 1443,[19] in which he praised Sigismund's modest bearing and his use of pure Latin. "Nothing can help you in guiding your life," wrote Aeneas, "more than the study of literature, a study in which you have already been initiated." Noting that Sigismund had "thrown off studies like some yoke," Aeneas went on to admonish the prince saying: "We ought to study literature because it offers us models of behavior after which we can pattern our lives; knowing these will be helpful. And one must know literature deeply, not superficially, if real progress is to be made. Contemporary rulers are happy with a smattering of knowledge and leave detailed study to philosophers and jurisconsultants, just as if it were less important for them to know the principles of a good life. I entreat you not to fall into this pattern of thinking which will block your developing into a good man and famous ruler."[20] In strongly urging Sigismund to emulate both ancient and contemporary literate princes, Aeneas told Sigismund to read Quintilian, Cicero, Vegetius, Livy, Quintus Curtius, Justinus, Suetonius, Aristotle, Seneca, Plutarch, Virgil, Pliny, Plautus, Terence, Horace, Juvenal,

---

[17] On Sigmund's wardship, see Joseph Chmel, *Geschichte Kaiser Friedrichs IV. und seines Sohnes Maximilian I.,* I (Hamburg, 1840), pp. 414-42; Justinian Ladurner, "Über Herzog Sigmund's Vormundschaft 1439-1446," *Archiv für Geschichte und Alterthumskunde Tirols,* 3 (1866), 23-140; Josef Egger, *Geschichte Tirols von den ältesten Zeiten in die Neuzeit,* I (Innsbruck, 1872), pp. 533-35; Albert Jäger, *Geschichte der landständisch Verfassung Tirols,* II, 2 (Innsbruck, 1885; Aalen, 1970), pp. 3-69.

[18] Some writers, such as Schanherr, Zingerle, and Hegi, held that Aeneas was Sigismund's teacher. Schanherr, *Gesammelte Schriften,* I, p. 182; Zingerle, "Der Humanismt pp. 22-23; Friedrich Hegi, *Die geächteten Räte des Erzherzogs Sigmund von Österreich und ihre Beziehungen zur Schweiz 1487-1499* (Innsbruck, 1910), p. 1. Others, including Voigt, Ladurner, and Hammer, rejected the view. Voigt, *Enea,* I (1856), p. 343; Ladurner "Über Herzog," pp. 49-50; Hammer, "Literarische," p. 73.

[19] Wolkan, *Der Briefwechsel,* 61, pp. 222-36; Baca, *Selected Letters,* pp. 1-19. Cf. G. Voigt, "Die Briefe des Aeneas Silvius vor seiner Erhebung auf den päpstlichen Stuhl," *Archiv für Kunde österreichischen Geschichts-Quellen,* 16 (1856), 348.

[20] Wolkan, *Der Briefwechsel,* 61, p. 226; Baca, *Selected Letters,* p. 5.

and Ovid, as well as religious writers such as Jerome, Augustine, Ambrose, Gregory, Lactantius, Cyprian, and Leo. It should be noted in this connection that Aeneas' essay on the education of children (*De liberorum educatione*),[21] which he wrote in 1450 for the eleven-year-old Ladislas Posthumus, contains a similar list of classical writers whom Aeneas recommended.

When Duke Sigismund asked Aeneas on December 12, 1443, to compose a model love letter for him to use in his efforts to win over his lady love, Aeneas, after some hesitation, produced next day a letter in humanistic style which took the form of Hannibal's letter to his lady Lucretia, the daughter of the king of Epirus.[22] Although this famous letter became a source of embarrassment to Aeneas in his later life as pope, it showed unmistakably that Aeneas was anxious at that time to remain on friendly terms with the young prince of the Tyrol. It is possible that Duke Sigismund came under the influence of Aeneas, one of the foremost leaders of humanist learning of the fifteenth century. In 1446, when Aeneas paid another visit to the Tyrol to receive from Friedrich III the parish church of Sarantanerthal, the humanist spent a day off to go stag hunting with Duke Sigismund, thus renewing their friendship.[23] In 1456 Sigismund, together with King Ladislas of Hungary and Bohemia and other German princes, recommended his humanist friend to Pope Calixtus III as a cardinal.[24]

It is perhaps true, as has been asserted by some commentators,[25] that the young Duke Sigismund was not very seriously interested in the study of

---

[21] *Aeneae . . . opera,* cols. 965-92; Wolkan, *Der Briefwechsel* in *Fontes Rerum Austriacarum,* 2. Abt., 67. Band (Vienna, 1912), 103-58. An English translation is in William H. Woodward, *Vittorio da Feltre and Other Humanist Educators,* Classics in Education, No. 18 (New York, 1963), pp. 136-58, and *De liberorum educatione: A Translation with an Introduction,* ed. J. St. Nelson (Washington, 1940); a German translation is in Rupprich, *Die Frühzeit,* pp. 215-34. Cf. Lhotsky, *Quellenkunde,* pp. 396-97.

[22] Wolkan, *Der Briefwechsel,* 61, pp. 245-47; Baca, *Selected Letters,* pp. 20-22. Cf. Voigt, "Die Briefe," 351.

[23] Gragg-Gabel, *The Commentaries,* pp. 32, 39. The church of Sarantanerthal, which stood high in the Alps between Italy and Germany, brought Aeneas an annual stipend of sixty florins.

[24] Cf. Gragg-Gabel, *The Commentaries,* pp. 76-77.

[25] Voigt, *Enea,* II, p. 343; Ludwig Pastor, *Geschichte der Päpste im Zeitalter der Renaissance,* 3d ed., II (Freiburg im Breisgau, 1904), p. 140; Kramer, *Das Zeitalter,* p. 5. A more sympathetic view of Sigismund is expressed by Albert Jäger, *Der Streit des Cardinals Niholaus von Cusa mit dem Herzoge Sigmund von Österreich als Grafen von Tirol,* 2 vols. (Innsbruck, 1861; Frankfurt am Main, 1968); Karl Kirchlechner, *Aus den Tagen Herzog Sigmunds des Müncreichen und Kaiser Maximilians I.* (Linz, 1884), p. 23; Joachimsohn, *Heimburg,* p. 173.

humanism. Greatly fond of hunting and of the pursuit of beautiful women, he did not have enough time to develop a good understanding of humanist ideals personally. But Sigismund was clearly in favor of promoting humanist learning in the Tyrol. He did not forget Aeneas' advice to him that he should support scholars as well soldiers.[26]

There was already some basis in the Tyrol for the development o humanist studies. The writing of history, one branch of humanist literature, found its practitioners early in the fifteenth century in the Tyrol, which had not made any notable contribution in previous times. As in other parts of Germany, monks who were in contact with what might be called monastic humanists in Italy were in the forefront of "monastic humanism." During the period after the death of Duke Friedrich IV in 1439 their attempts reached the highest point in the Tyrol.[27] The Benedictine Goswin von Marienberg wrote his *Registrum monasterii Montis sancte Marie,* discussing the years from 1101 to 1427.[28] The Cistercian Burchard Gamorett produced a chronicle of the Cistercian monastery at Stams in 1414.[29] Johann Spies, prior of the Augustinian cloister at Rattenberg, expanded in 1441 the *Flores temporum.*[30] It is also to be noted that in the

---

[26] Wolkan, *Der Briefwechsel,* 61, p. 228: "sicut enim milites pascis ita et doctrinarun institutores nutrire posses." For a detailed discussion of Sigismund's court in Innsbruck see Margarete Ortwein, "Der Innsbrucker Hof zur Zeit Erzherzog Sigmunds des Münzreichen" (Diss., Innsbruck, 1936).

[27] Lhotsky, *Quellenkunde,* p. 358. On the contribution of monasteries to humanism see Joachimsen, *Geschichtsauffassung,* pp. 40-60; Richard Newald, "Beiträge zur Geschichte des Humanismus in Oberösterreich," *Jahrbuch des oberösterreichischen Musealvereins,* 81 (1926), 155-223, reprinted in his *Probleme und Gestalten des deutschen Humanismus* (Berlin, 1963), pp. 67-112; Rudolph Arbesmann, *Der Augustiner-Ermitenorden und der Beginn der humanistischen Bewegung* (Würzburg, 1965); Paul O. Kristeller, "The Contribution of Religious Orders to Renaissance Thought and Learning," *American Benedictine Review,* 21 (1970): 1-55.

[28] The text is in *Chronik des Stiftes Marienberg verfasst von P. Goswin, Prior und Hofcaplan,* ed. Basilius Schwitzer, Tirolische Geschichtsquellen, 2 (Innsbruck, 1880). A partial German translation is Joseph Röggl, "Goswins Chronik von Marienberg: Aus dem Lateinischen in das Deutsche frei übersetzt," *Beiträge zur Geschichte, Statistik Naturkunde und Kunst von Tirol und Vorarlberg,* I (1825), 67-165. I have not been able to consult Josef Egger, "Die ältesten Geschichtschreiber Tirols," *Jahresbericht der Oberrealschule in Innsbruck* (1866/67). See also Lhotsky, *Quellenkunde,* pp. 358-59.

[29] Lhotsky, *Quellenkunde,* p. 359.

[30] The text is in *Monumenta Germaniae historica: scriptores,* XXIV (Hanover, 1879) 230-50. See also Lhotsky, *Quellenkunde,* p. 360; J. Riedmann, *Die Fortsetzung des Flores temporum durch Johannes Spies, Prior der Augustiner-Eremiten in Rattenberg* (Vienna/Cologne/Graz, 1970).

middle of the fifteenth century Berchtold Pötzer, an alderman of the city of Hall, published a chronicle of his city, which has unfortunately been lost.[31] Although these mostly monastic contributions to historiography in the Tyrol were not too impressive, they laid the foundations for the development of humanist learning.

In promoting humanism in the Tyrol, Duke Sigismund may also have been anxious to gain the reputation of being a patron of the new learning. A good customer of the bookdealers Preumair and Kaestlin of Augsburg, he expanded the court library considerably by purchasing manuscripts and books from them.[32] He was in touch with famous learned men of the time, such as the astronomer Hans Volkart and the humanists Francis Niger, Johannes Mathias Tiburinus, Petrus Bonomus, and Peter Luder.[33] Because of his interest in manuscripts, Sigismund also employed a large number of scribes to copy manuscripts. Georg Costenzer (1463), Jorg Walther (1465), Oswald Haring (1479), Sigmund Paumann (1495), and Sigmund Priefenschalk are known to have been engaged by the duke between 1463 and 1495.[34] Regrettably there is no record about what manuscripts were copied by these scribes. The so-called Reckenbuch, which Nicolaus Schupf copied in 1463, is the only exception.[35] Gratified with Duke Sigismund's support of humanist studies, Johannes Mathias Tiburinus praised him highly, calling him "dux Teutonicae decus et spes inclitae linguae."[36] In 1475 the famous translator and humanist Heinrich Steinhöwel (1412-1482) dedicated to him a German translation of Aesop's life and fables from the Latin version.[37] Heinrich Gundelfingen also dedicated to him in 1476

31 Lhotsky, *Quellenbunde,* p. 359.

32 Schönherr, *Gesammelte Schriften,* I, 90. Although Schönherr mentions Preumair as one of the bookdealers of Augsburg from whom Sigismund bought books, I have not been able to find any reference to Preumair in the standard works on printing, printers, and bookdealers by Konrad Burger, Ferdinand Geldner, Konrad Haebler, L. Hain, Albrecht Kirchhoff, K. Löffler and J. Kirchner, and Ernst H. Voulliéme.

33 Schönherr, *Gesammelte Schriften,* I, 90; Kirchlechner, *Aus den Tagen,* p. 18; Grossmann, "Die Frühzeit," 198, 287; Margarete Köfler, "Eleonore von Schottland: Versuch einer Biographie" (Diss., Innsbruck, 1968), p. 191.

34 Schönherr, *Gesammelte Schriften,* I, p. 91; Kirchlechner, *Aus den Tagen,* p. 18.

35 Schönherr, *Gesammelte Schriften,* I, p. 91; Kirchlechner, *Aus den Tagen,* p. 18; Konrad Fischnaler, *Innsbrucker Chronik mit Bildschmuck nach alten Originalen und Rekonstraktions-Zeichnungen:* III. Wissenschafts- und Literatur-Chronik (Innsbruck, 1930), p. 8.

36 Anton Zingerle, *De carminibus latinis saeculi XV. et XVI. ineditis* (Innsbruck, 1880), p. 128.

37 Paul Joachimsohn,"Frühhumanismus in Schwaben," *Württembergische Viertel-jahrshefte für Landesgeschichte,* N.F., 5 (1896): 116; Kramer, *Das Zeitalter,* p. 5. The

his *Austrie principum chronici epitome triplex* with a preface full of flattery and praise.[38]

Duke Sigismund's wife Eleanor was another contributor to the development of humanist learning in the Tyrol. In 1449, three years after his return to the Tyrol, Sigismund married Eleanor (1433-1480), the sixth child of James I (king, 1406-1437) of Scotland.[39] Known in the history of English literature as an imitator of Chaucer through his poem *The Kingis Quair,* James I held court in Perth, where Aeneas Sylvius was received in 1435. Eleanor apparently became interested in literature as she grew up in the court of her father, whose own interest in letters had been aroused during his boyhood by Bishop Henry Wardlaw, the founder of the University of St. Andrews, and then strengthened during his captivity in England between 1406 and 1424.[40] Judging from the fact that some Irish missionaries, such as St. Gall, had come to Switzerland and Salzburg, it is possible that some inhabitants of the British Isles had already visited the Tyrol before the marriage of the sixteen-year-old Scottish princess to the twenty-two-year-old Tyrolese prince. However that may be, the marriage marked the beginning of a fairly close relationship over the years

text is in *Steinhöwels Äsop,* ed. Hermann Österley, Bibliothek des litterarischen Vereins in Stuttgart, CXVII (Tübingen, 1873). Cf. *Gesamtkatalog der Wiegendrucke,* I (Leipzig, 1925), cols. 153-63; Rupprich, *Die Frühzeit,* pp. 256-63. On the significance of the vernacular translations of Italian humanist writings, see Kristeller, *Renaissance Thought II,* pp. 84-86.

[38] The partial text is in Adam Kollar, *Analecta monumentorum omnis aevi Vindobonensia,* I (Vienna, 1761), cols. 728-824. See also Joachimsohn, "Frühhumanismus," 71; Lhotsky, *Quellenkunde,* pp. 92, 421-22. Dr. Conrad Wenger dedicated his *De bello inter Venetos et Sigismundum Austriae archiducem commentarius* to Duke Sigismund. See Marquard Freher, *Rerum Germanicarum scriptores,* ed. B.G. Struve, II (Strasbourg, 1717), pp. 445-58. Dr. Wenger was Duke Sigismund's advisor after 1473.

[39] For Eleanor's life, see J. Ladurner, "Was that man am Hofe der Erzherzogin Eleonora," *Archiv für Geschichte und Alterthumskunde Tirols,* 1 (1864), 320; Jäger, *Geschichte,* III (1885), pp. 80-86; Paul Würst, *Die deutschen Prosaromane von Pontus und Sidonia* (Marburg, 1903), pp. 12-21; Köfler, "Elenore von Schottland."

[40] For James I's life and literary interest, see, for example, Patrick F. Tytler, *The History of Scotland,* III (Edinburgh, 1866), pp. 171-275; Wust, *Die deutschen Prosaromane,* p. 12; Rashdall, *The Universities,* II, pp. 302-7; Gordon Donaldson, *Scottish Kings* (New York, 1967), pp. 63-82.

between the two areas.[41] The young couple first took up residence in a castle in Meran, which has been preserved to this day as Landesfürstliche Burg.[42]

Living in a land far from her home country and married to an often unfaithful husband, Eleanor, whose only child died young, seems to have found consolation and enjoyment in poetry and literature. She was in close touch with Countess Mechthild (1418-1482) of the Palatinate, another princess of learning. Mechthild married Duke Albrecht VI (1418-1463) of Austria, Sigismund's cousin, two years after the death of her first husband, Count Ludwig of Württemburg, in 1450. It was on her petition that the University of Freiburg im Breisgau was founded in 1455.[43] Eleanor also exchanged books frequently with Duke Albrecht IV of Bavaria. The duke wrote from Munich on April 20, 1478, for example, that he had sent Eleanor the *buoch des Lancilets* of Ulrich Füterer as a new publication.[44] Her own translation of the French chivalric romance *Ponthus et Sidoine* into German, done between 1449 and 1456, was one of the good examples of her literary activities. It was first published in 1483 by Hans Schönsperger of Augsburg.[45] Since Eleanor knew no Latin, Steinhöwel dedicated to her his translation of Boccaccio's *De claris mulieribus* which had been published by Johann Zainer of Ulm in 1473.[46] In his preface Steinhöwel called

---

[41] Anton M. Pirkhofer, *England-Tyrol, vom Bild Tirols im englischen Schrifttum: ein 500-jährigen Spiegel der tirolisch-englischen Beziehungen* (Innsbruck, 1950), pp. 19-20.

[42] Otto R. von Lutterotti, *Schloss Tirol und landesfürstliche Burg zu Meran,* 3d ed. (Innsbruck, 1967), pp. 23-24. Cf. Pirkhofer, *England-Tyrol,* Pl. II and pp. 20-21.

[43] On Mechthild of the Palatinate, see Ernst Martin, "Erzherzogin Mechthild," *Zeitschrift der Gesellschaft für Beförderung der Geschichts-, Alterthums- und Volkskunde von Freiburg,* 2 (1870/72): 146-270; Philipp Strauch, *Pfalzgraefin Mechthild in ihren litterarischen Beziehungen* (Tübingen, 1883); *Die deutsche Literatur des Mittelalters: Verfasserlexikon,* ed. Wolfgang Stammler, I (Berlin, 1933), p. 94.

[44] Kirchlechner, *Aus den Tagen,* p. 17; Wüst, *Die deutschen Prosaromane,* p. 16; Stammler, *Verfasserlexikon,* I, p. 543.

[45] Wüst, *Die deutschen Prosaromane,* pp. 6-7, 19, 21-23, 72; Stammler, *Verfasserlexikon,* II (1936), p. 770. According to Georg W. Zapf, *Augsburgs Buchdruckergeschichte nebst den Jahrbüchern derselben,* I (1786), pp. 11-12, there is a 1471 edition of the translation. Whether or not Eleanor consulted the first English translation of 1450 is not clear.

[46] Joachimsohn, "Frühhumanismus," 116-25; Wüst, *Die deutschen Prosaromane,* p. 16; Stammler, *Verfasserlexikon,* I, p. 544; Rupprich, *Die Frühzeit,* pp. 39, 249-56. The text is in Boccaccio, *De claris mulieribus: deutsch übersetzt von Stainhöwel,* ed. Karl Drescher, Bibliothek des litterarischen Vereins in Stuttgart, CCV (Tübingen, 1895). Cf. *Gesamtkatalog der Wiegendrucke,* IV (1930), cols. 283-85.

Eleanor "ain liebhaberin aller guter künst und künster."[47] During her husband's
frequent absences from Innsbruck, Eleanor as his regent showed a great respect
for Nicolaus Cusanus, the learned humanist bishop of Brixen, despite the fact
that the bishop had been in serious conflict with her husband since his arrival in
Brixen in 1452 over the question of the convent at Sonnenburg.[48] Cusanus sent
letters to Eleanor, whom the monk Felix Fabri of Ulm described as "mulier
deuotissima et sancta."[49] It might be argued that Eleanor's literary interests were
pre-humanist and chivalric and that in this sense she was not different from many
other ladies in German princely courts of her time. But it would seem clear that
by her activities or encouragement Eleanor succeeded in creating in the ducal
court in Innsbruck an atmosphere conducive to the development of humanist
activities.

In order to understand the growth of humanism in the Tyrol, we must also
examine the contributions made by Duke Sigismund's officials and advisors in
and out of his court. According to the court regulation of 1488, there were in the
ducal household a Court Master (*Hofmeister*), a Court Marshal (*Hofmarschall*),
four Chamberlains (*Kämmerer*), eight Lord High Stewards (*Truchsesse*), four
Butlers (*Schenken*), four Doctors, two Chaplains (*Kapläne*), as well as many
other servants.[50] Sigismund's court was a fairly large one by contemporary
standards.

---

[47] Drescher, *De claris mulieribus,* p. 16: ". . . hab ich dich, durchlüchtigiste fürstin,
usz gemainem rum ain solliche erkennet und ain liebhaberin aller guter kunst vnd
künster."

[48] The standard work on the Sonnenburg affair is still Albert Jäger's study cited in n.
25 above. See Jäger, *Der Streit,* I, pp. 147-48, 185, 302-16, II, p. 152; Köfler,
"Eleonore von Schottand," pp. 38-39; Georg Mutschlechner, "Nikolaus Cusanus und
Eleonore von Schottland," *Cusanus Gedächtnisschrift,* ed. Nikolaus Grass (Innsbruck
and Munich, 1970), pp. 251-70.

[49] F. Fabri, *Historiae Sueuorum,* I, p. xvi: "Verum vnam habuit vxorem Dominam
Helienoram filiam Regis Scotiae sibi matrimonio innctam, quae erat mulier
denotissima et sancta, quee nunquam credere voluit dicentibus Principem adulterum, et
sine prole defuncta est." Quoted by Wüst, *Die deutschen Prosaromane,* p. 19. For
Cusanus' letters to Eleanor, see Friedrich Hausmann, *Das Brixner Brieibuch des
Kardinals Nikolaus von Kues,* Cusanus-Texte, IV. Briefwechsel des Nikolaus von
Kues, *Sitzungsberichte der Heidelherger Akademie der Wissenschaften, Philos.-hist.
Klasse,* Jg. 1952, 2. Abh., pp. 96-97, 121-22, 132-33, 141-42, 145, 165-66. See
also *Fontes rerum Austriacarum,* 2. Abt., 2. Band (Vienna, 1850), pp. 289-91, 321-
22, 337-40 for her other letters.

[50] Ivan Ritter von Zolgar, *Der Hofstaut des Hauses Österreich,* Wiener staatswissen-
schafdichen Studien, 14 (Vienna and Leipzig, 1917), pp. 22, 26. Cf. Kirchlechner,
Aus den Tagen, pp. 13-17; Ortwein, "Der Innsbrucker Hof," pp. 13-23; Otto Stolz,
Geschichte der Stadt Innsbruck (Innsbruck, 1959), pp. 55-56.

After his return to Innsbruck in 1446, Duke Sigismund surrounded himself with advisors, such as Ulrich von Matsch, Wolfgang von Freundsberg, Ludwig von Landsee, Parcival von Annenberg, Heinrich von Mörsberg and Oswald Sebner von Reifenstein, all of whom were local nobles.[51] The Gradner brothers, Vigilius and Bernhard Gradner, whom Sigismund brought in on his return to Innsbruck, became so powerful that Sigismund could exile them in 1456 only with great difficulty.[52] In addition to these political advisors, some scholars became Sigismund's advisors at the Innsbruck court. Jakob Puterich advised the duke in 1466.[53] Anton von Pforr, Mechthild's court chaplain, came to Innsbruck in 1467 as Sigismund's advisor.[54] Dr. Georg von Absberg, a friend of the humanist Niklas von Wyle (d. 1478), became advisor and chancellor of the duke from 1476.[55] Of Sigismund's advisors, a relatively small number resided in the ducal palace in Innsbruck and served him daily. Dr. Lorenz Blumenau and Dr. Gregor Heimburg, as we shall see later, can be mentioned as two important examples of advisors in residence. The other advisors were either in Innsbruck or scattered all over the duke's lands. Dr. Johannes Hinderbach, bishop of Trent, Abbot Caspar Augsburger of St. Georgenberg (Fiecht) near Schwaz, Dr. Johann Fuchsmagen of Hall were among the foremost of these nonresident advisors.

Of the three learned nonresident advisors we have mentioned, the most famous was no doubt Dr. Johannes Hinderbach (1418-1486), Aeneas Sylvius' close friend and a relative of the famous theologian Heinrich von Langenstein.[56] Born in Rauschenberg near Kassel in 1418, Hinderbach entered the University of

51 Egger, *Geschichte,* I, p. 545; Karl Mosser and Fritz Dworschak, *Die grosse Münzre- form unter Erzherozg Sigmund von Tirol* (Munich, 1936), p. 16; Ortwein, "Der Inns- brucker Hof," pp. 13-14.

52 See Albert Jäger, *Die Fehde der Brüder Vigilius und Bernhard Gradner gegen den Herzog Sigmund von Tirol,* Denkschriften der kaiserlichen Akademie der Wissenschaften, Philos.-hist. Classe, IX (Vienna, 1859); Jäger, *Geschichte,* III, pp. 100-133.

53 Wüst, *Die deutschen Prosaromane,* p. 16; Stammler, *Verfasserlexikon,* I, p. 544.

54 Strauch, *Pfalzgraefin,* p. 5; Wüst, *Die deutschen Prosaromane,* p. 16; Stammler, *Verfasserlexikon,* I, p. 544; Köfler, "Eleonore von Schottland," p. 189.

55 Joachimsohn, "Frühhumanismus," p. 96; Köfler, "Elenore von Schottland," p. 189.

56 For Hinderbach's life and work, see, for example, Aschbach, *Geschichte,* I, pp. 561-67; Zingerle, "Der Humanismus," pp. 25-31; Victor Hofmann-Wellenhof, "Leben und Schrifien des Doctor Johannes Hinderbach: Bishop von Trient (1465-1486)," *Zs. d. Ferd.,* 37 (1893), 203-62; Grossmann, "Die Frühzeit," pp. 214-18; Lhotsky, *Quellen- kunde,* pp. 403-5; Alfred A. Strnad, "Johannes Hinderbachs Obedienz-Ansprache vor Papst Pius II: Papstliche und kaiserliche Politik in der Mitte des Quattrocento," *Römische Historische Mitteilungen,* 10 (1966/67): 43-183.

Vienna in 1434, receiving the baccalaureate in 1436. He taught Latin grammar from 1438 to 1441 as *magister artium* in the law faculty of the university. Pursuing his studies in Roman and canon law at the University of Padua after 1441 under such famous teachers as Angelus de Castro, Antonius de Rosellis, Jacobus de Zochis, and Leonardus de Baziolis, he received the degree of *doctor decretorum* on January 14, 1452, in the presence of Friedrich III and many dignitaries from the empire. Employed by the emperor and later also by the Empress Eleanor, Hinderbach came in contact with Aeneas Sylvius in the imperial court. Aeneas called Hinderbach "secretarius caesaris, pontificii iuris egregie peritus ac facundia nobilis."[57] The emperor sent him on many diplomatic missions. In 1455 Hinderbach accompanied Aeneas on a mission to pay homage to the newly elected Pope Calixtus III on behalf of the emperor. As Aeneas was elected pope on August 19, 1458, Hinderbach was sent to Siena next year by the emperor to deliver a long speech in which he praised and paid homage to the new pope. At the Congress of Mantua, which Pope Pius II (1458-1464) called in 1459, Hinderbach made a learned and elegant speech full of sympathy for and flattery to the pope.[58] Thus the relationship between Aeneas and Hinderbach was so close that his rapid rise in the ecclesiastical hierarchy was perhaps partially attributable to this friendship. He became priest of Mödling near Vienna in 1449, provost of the cathedral chapter in Trent in 1455, and finally bishop of Trent in 1465.

As bishop of Trent, Hinderbach promoted the arts, restored the cathedral library, which had been impoverished by Duke Friedrich IV of the Tyrol in 1410, and called the printer Albrecht Kunne of Duderst I to Trent in 1475 to establish the first press.[59] His most important literary production was in the field of historiography. The *Hystoria eiusdem (Friderici) expeditionis et belli,*[60] which has often been regarded as a continuation of Aeneas' work on Friedrich III, is a series of tentative notes written by the humanist on the life and deeds of the emperor. It is clear, from what Hinderbach says, that he was prompted to write this history by Aeneas Sylvius. Although it is not known clearly what kind of

---

[57] Hofmann-Wellenhof, "Leben," 216.

[58] Strnad, "Johannes Hinderbachs"; cf. Hofmann-Wellenhof, "Leben," 228.

[59] F. Waldner, "Quellenstudie zur Geschichte der Typographie in Tirol bis zum Beginn des 17. Jahrhundert," *Zs. d. Ferd.,* 32 (1888): 22-23; Hofmann-Wellenhof, "Leben," pp. 243-54; *Bibliographie der österreichischen Drucke des XV. und XVI. Jahrhunderts,* ed. Eduard Langer, I, i (Vienna, 1913), pp. 1-7; Grossmann, "Die Frühzeit," p. 215; Stammler, *Verfasserlexikon,* II (Berlin, 1936), p. 461; Lhotsky, *Quellenkunde,* p. 404.

[60] The text is in Kollar, *Analecta,* II (Vienna, 1762), cols. 555-666. See Hofmann-Wellenhof, "Leben," pp. 244-52; Grossmann, "Die Frühzeit," 216-217; Kramer, *Das Zeitalter,* pp. 13-14; Lhotsky, *Quellenkunde,* pp. 404-5; Lhotsky, *Aeneas Silvius,* p. 23.

assistance Hinderbach gave to Duke Sigismund, he was no doubt one of the most important advisors to the duke.

The less famous of Sigismund's nonresident advisors were Abbot Caspar Augsburger of St. Georgenberg (1469-1491) and Dr. Johann Fuchsmagen or Fusemanus (ca. 1450-1510). The *Benedictine* abbot,[61] who shortly after his election in 1469 was made Duke Sigismund's advisor, was on good terms with the duke. Born in Freiburg im Breisgau, he studied at Italian universities before coming to the Tyrol in May 1469 as abbot. The duke dispatched him to many places for negotiations, such as Rome, Cologne, Milan, and Pavia, and often sought his advice on important matters of state. As the right-hand man of the duke, the abbot's influence at the Innsbruck court was considerable. His own writings have been lost, but undoubtedly he influenced the duke to promote humanist studies in the court.

A patron of the learned men and a leading humanist in the Tyrol, the abbot was highly regarded by Aeneas Sylvius. With great zeal he acquired for the library of his cloister many manuscripts and books, which included a fifteenth-century manuscript with notes on Francesco Filelfo, a manuscript on the Roman satirist Persius, and many writings of Italian humanists, including Petrarch's *De vita solitaria*.[62] Not only did he run his cloister well for twenty-two years, but he was a strong supporter of the University of Freiburg im Breisgau.

More important and widely known as a humanist than Abbot Caspar Augsburger was Dr. Johann Fuchsmagen[63] of Hall, where his father Sigismund

---

61 Kirchlechner, *Aus den Tagen,* p. 26; Zingerle, "Der Humanismus," p. 25; Stammler, *Verfasserlexikon,* II, p. 767; Kramer, *Das Zeitalter,* p. 15; Lhotsky, *Quellenkunde,* pp. 433-34, 436.

62 See Anton Zingerle, *Zu den Persius-Scholien, Sitzungsberichte der philos.-hist. Classe der kaiserlichen Akademie der Wissenschaften,* 97 (Jg. 1880; Vienna, 1881), 731-60; Kirchlechner, *Aus den Tagen,* p. 25; Anton Zingerle, "Übersicht über veröffentlichte oder besprochene philologische Handschriften und Handschriftenreste aus Tirolischen Bibliotheken," *Commentationes Aenipontanae,* IV (Innsbruck, 1908), 2; Stammler, *Verfasserlexikon,* II, 768-69; Lhotsky, *Quellenbunde,* p. 436. For a discussion of the cultural role played by the abbey, see Hans Bachmann, "Die Benediktinerabtei St. Georgenberg im Kulturleben des Mittelalters," *Tiroler Heimat,* 16 (1952): 33-101. According to Anton Zingerle, *Dom- und Stiftsschulen Tirols im Mittelalter mit besonderer Berückszchtigung ihrer Lehrmittel* (Innsbruck, 1896), pp. 21-22, the works of such humanist writers as Aeneas Sylvlus, Prancesco Filelfo, Lorenzo Valla, Angelo Poliziano, Marsilio Ficino, and Pietro Bembo could be found in the libraries of the monasteries at Marienberg Stams, Neushft Wilten, and Schnals.

63 For the life of Fuchsmagen, see Aschbach, *Geschichte,* II, pp. 72-73; Sebastian Ruf, "Doctor Johannes Fuchsmagen . . . 1469-1510." *Zs. d. Ferd.,* 21 (1877), 95-119; Grossmann, "Die Frühzeit," pp. 273-279; Hans Kramer, "Dr. Johannes Fuchsmagen—ein berühmter Haller," in *Haller Buch,* Schlern-Schriften, 106 (Innsbruck, 1953), pp. 430-33; *Die deutsche literatur des Mittelalters: Verfasserlexikon,* ed. Karl Langosch, V (Berlin, 1955), pp. 246-47; Lhotsky,

was mayor and guardian of Hasegg Castle. Matriculating on October 25, 1469, Fuchsmagen studied at the University of Freiburg as a fellow student of Johann Reuchlin (1455-1522) and received the degrees of master of arts and licentiate in canon law. He became Duke Sigismund's secretary in 1482 and served from 1484 on as his advisor until he went on to become the Emperor Friedrich III's diplomat in 1485. Fuchsmagen's contribution to the development of humanism during his comparatively short period of service in the Tyrol was limited. In later years, however, he played an important role at the imperial court in Vienna as the leading advisor and diplomat of both Friedrich III and Maximilian I. At his invitation Conrad Celtis (1459-1508) came to Vienna in 1497 to teach at the University of Vienna. Fuchsmagen was also responsible, as curator of the University of Vienna, for the establishment of the Collegium Poetarum et Mathematicorum, which was opened on February 1, 1502, Celtis' forty-third birthday.[64] Together with Florian von Waldauf, who once worked as a scribe in Sigismund's chancery,[65] he founded the Stubengesellschaft at Hall in 1508, which was not only a place of conviviality but also the Tyrolese counterpart of the humanistic societies in Vienna.[66]

In assessing the nonresident advisors' humanistic contributions in the Tyrol, it would seem difficult to say that they helped the new learning to grow rapidly during their period of service. This is perhaps due either to their involvement in local affairs or to their comparatively short stay in the Tyrol. All were learned and well-trained men by contemporary standards, but they seem not to have played a really significant role in promoting humanistic ideals in the Tyrol.

In comparison with the nonresident advisors, the resident advisors could obviously exercise a more powerful influence in the ducal court. Did they promote humanistic studies in cooperation with Duke Sigismund and Duchess Eleanor? Dr. Lorenz Blumenau (ca. 1415-1484), as we have noted above, was

---

Quellenkunde, pp. 434-36. For many songs dedicated to Fuchsmagen, see Zingerle, *De carminibus.*

[64] Grossmann, "Die Frühzeit," pp. 274-75; Ruf, "Doctor Johannes Fuchsmagen," pp. 104-12; Langosch, *Verfasserlexikon,* V, pp. 246-47; Lewis W. Spitz, *Conrad Celtis: The German Arch-Humanist* (Cambridge, Massachusetts, 1957), pp. 55-57; Karl Jordak, *Die Universität Wien 1365-1965* (Vienna, 1965), pp. 120-21.

[65] Ernst Verdross-Drossberg, *Florian Waldauf von Waldenstein: Festschrift zur 450-Jahr-Feier der Haller Stubengesellschaft,* Schlern-Schriften, 184 (Innsbruck, 1958), p. 11.

[66] Ernst Verdross, "Die Haller Stubengesellschaft," in *Haller Buch,* pp. 490-91; Verdross-Drossberg, *Florian,* p. 45; Lhotsky, *Quellenkunde,* p. 434. The Stubengesellschaft was a place "allwo Herren von Adel, Salzbeamte, Bürgermeister, Räte, Honoratiores zusammenkommen, damit sie von den Wirtshäusern und vom gemeinen Pövel abgesondert sein können." Verdross-Drossberg, *Florian,* p. 45.

one of such advisors.[67] A graduate of the Universities of Leipzig, Padua, and Bologna, he began to serve Duke Sigismund toward the end of 1457, assuming an increasingly important position among the duke's advisors. Before coming to the Tyrol this native of Prussia had served as advisor to the Teutonic Knights from 1446. As the famous feud between Duke Sigismund and Cardinal Cusanus as bishop of Brixen over the convent of Sonnenburg intensified, Blumenau actively engaged in a campaign in support of the duke both in the Tyrol and in Rome. His imprisonment as a heretic in 1460 because of antipapal activities and his dramatic escape from Siena[68] indicate how deeply Blumenau was involved in Duke Sigismund's fight against Cardinal Cusanus and Pope Pius II, who despite his past relationship with the duke increasingly assumed a major role as Sigismund's critic in support of his friend the cardinal.

It is notable, however, that important as Blumenau was as Sigismund's advisor, his contribution to the literary development at the Innsbruck court and in the Tyrol in general seems very limited. As a humanist, Blumenau was interested in collecting manuscripts and had a large library of his own.[69] He corresponded with the humanist Hermann Schedel (1410-1485) of Augsburg between 1457 and 1468, and his letters manifest a deep interest in ancient historians such as Sallust, Cornelius Nepos, Tacitus, Suetonius, Justinus and Orosius.[70] But we have no clear reference to his humanistic activities in the

---

[67] For Blumenau's life and work, see Georg Voigt, " Laurentius Blumenau, Geschäfts-träger und Geschichtschreiber des Deutschen Ritterordens: eine biographische Skizze aus dem 15. Jahrhundert," *Neue Preussische Provinzial-Blätter*, 3. Folge, 4 (1859): 242-64; Hartmut Boockmann, *Laurentius Blumenau: Fürstlicher Rat-Jurist-Humanist (ca. 1415-1484)*, Göttinger Bausteine zur Geschichtswissenschaft, 37 (Göttingen, 1965). See numerous references to "Doctor Lorentzen" in *Landesregierungsarchiv Innsbruck,* Raitbuch, Band I (1460/61), ff. 58^V, 61^r, 9I^v and others.

[68] When the process against Duke Sigismund began in Siena on August 4, 1460, Blumenau appeared before Pope Pius II and pleaded Sigismund's case. Four days later, however, a bull was issued which banned Sigismund and his followers, and the Tyrol was placed under an interdict. Although imprisoned as a heretic, Blumenau managed to escape later, reaching Innsbruck shortly before September 9, 1460. See E. M. Lichnowsky, *Geschichte des Hauses Habsburg: 7. Theil, Kaiser Friedrich III. und sein Sohn Maximilian* (Vienna, 1843), pp. cccxiii-cccxiv; Albert Jäger, "Regesten und urkundliche Daten über das Verhältnis des Cardinals Nicolaus von Cusa, als Bischof von Brixen, zum Herzoge Sigismund von Österreich und zu dem Lande Tirol von 1450 bis 1464," *Archiv für Kunde österreichischer Geschichts-Quellen*, 4 (1850): 325; Voigt, *Enea*, III (1863), pp. 370-72; Hammer, "Literarische Beziehungen," p. 78; Fischnaler, *Innsbrucker Chronik*, I (1929), 22.

[69] Kramer, *Das Zeitalter*, p. 10; Boockmann, *Blumenau*, pp. 208-25.

[70] Boockmann, *Blumenau*, p. 232. For his letters sent to Schedel, see *Hermann Schedels Briefwechsel (1452-1478)*, ed. Paul Joachimsohn, Bibliothek des Litterarischen Vereins in Stuttgart, 196 (Tübingen, 1893), pp. 8, 84, 177. Cf. Richard Stauber, *Die Schedelsche Bibliothek* (Freiburg im Breisgau, 1908); Paul Ruf,

Innsbruck court during his service for Sigismund. To be sure, his unfinished chronicle of the Teutonic Knights in Prussia,[71] which he compiled before coming to the Tyrol, can hardly be said to be humanistic in orientation. But judging from a great interest in classical writers which he showed during his stay in the Tyrol from 1457 to 1465, it would seem difficult to say that he did not have any desire to contribute to the development of humanism. It is possible that his busy life as legal advisor and diplomat prevented him from participating in the literary activities in the ducal court.

Duke Sigismund's most important resident advisor was no doubt Gregor Heimburg (ca. 1400-1472).[72] Born in the Franconian city of Schweinfurt around 1400 as the son of the burgher Hans Heimburg, Gregor was in all probability educated at a Latin school which was attached to the Church of St. Johannis in Schweinfurt. This is the school where the humanists Conrad Celtis and Johann Cuspinian (1473-1529) studied in later years.[73] Heimburg matriculated in the faculty of arts at the University of Vienna on October 13, 1413, as "pauper."[74] After studying at some other German universities, he crossed the Alps in 1421 to study at the University of Padua, where he received the degree of *doctor in jure canonico* on February 7, 1430.[75] The famous teachers under whom he studied

Mittelalterliche Bibliothekskataloge Deutschlands und der Schweiz, III (Munich, 1932-39), pp. 798-802.

[71] Voigt, "Blumenau," p. 254; Boockmann, *Blumenau,* pp. 208-25. The text of *Historia de inicio ordinis beate marie theotonicorum hierosolomitanorum in prusia ac eorum regimine ac gestis* is in Bayerische Steatsbibliothek München, Clm 529 and Clm 902. Cf. *Catalogus codicum latinorum Bibliothecae Regiae Monacensis,* ed. Carolus Halm and Georgius Laubmann, III, I (Munich, 1892), p. 322.

[72] The best study of Heimburg's life and activities is still Paul Joachimsohn's book mentioned in n. 10 above. See also Johann A. Ballensted, *Vitae Gregorii de Heimburg . . . Brevis Narratio* (Helmstedt, 1737); Clemens Brockhaus, *Gregor von Heimburg* (Leipzig, 1861).

[73] On the Latin school in Schweinfurt, see V. Völcker, *Geschichte der Studienanstalt Schweinfurt,* I (Schweinfurt, 1882); Karl Ziegler, *Geschichte des humanistischen Gymnasiums in Schweinfurt (1634-1934) und der Lateinische Schule daselbst* (Schweinfurt, 1934); Friedrich Beyschlag, "Die älteste Geschichte der lateinischen Schule in Schweinfurt (bis 1554)," *Schweinfurter Tagblatt,* No. 113, 15 Mai 1905 and No. 114, 16 Mai 1905. Joachimsohn, *Heimburg,* p. 2, states: "gab es damals wohl noch keine städtische Schule."

[74] *Die Matrikel der Universität Wien,* I (Graz and Cologne, 1956), p. 99; Albin F. Scherhaufer, "Jung-Schweinfurt auf hohen Schulen," *Schweinfurter Heimatblätter,* 26 (1957): 55-56. Cf. Joachimsohn, *Heimburg,* p. 2, n. 10, where it is said: "Eine deutsche Universität hat Heimburg, soweit wir sehen, nicht besucht."

[75] Arnold Luschin von Ebengreuth, *Quellen zur Geschichte deutschen Rechtshörer in Italien, Sitzungsberichte der philos.-hist. Klasse der kaiserlichen Akademie der Wissenschaften,* 124, Jg. 1890 (Vienna, 1891), p. 23; *Acta graduum academicorum*

both canon and civil law included Prosdocimus de Comitibus, Henricus de Alano, Paulus de Dotis, and Jacobus de Zochis.[76]

After attending the Council of Basel in 1432 as general vicar in ecclesiastical affairs of the archbishop of Mainz,[77] Heimburg became legal advisor to the city of Nuremberg in 1435, and continued to serve in this capacity almost without interruption until 1461, although his services were not confined to Nuremberg during the period.[78] In 1444, when he began his second term as legal advisor, Heimburg gathered around him a small circle of friends of humanist studies which included Heinrich Leubing (d. 1472), Niklas von Wyle (d. 1478), and Martin Mair (ca. 1420-1480).[79] When Heimburg discussed

gymnasii Patavini ab anno MCCCCVI ad annum MCCCCL, ed. C. Zonta and I. Brotto (Padua 1922), pp. 166-67. It is not known what other German universities Heimburg attended before coming to Padua. In a speech which he made in 1430 to accept the doctorate Heimburg spoke of many transalpine universities which he had attended. The speech, *Oratio pro petendis insigniis doctoratus canonici arengata,* is in Bayerische Staatsbibliothek München, Clm 504, ff. 313^v-314^r and has been printed in Joachimsohn, Heimburg pp. 302-3. His compatriot Matthaus Niethart's doctoral speech, which is in Clm 504 ff. 314^r-315^r, has been published in Agostino Sottili, *Studenti tedeschie Umanesimo italiano nell'Università di Padova durante il Quattrocento,* Contributi alla storia dell'Università di Padova, 7 (Padua, 1971), pp. 61-63. I am indebted to Professor Paul O. Kristeller for this reference. Sottili states on p. 2 that Heimburg was a doctor of arts and medicine before obtaining the doctorate in canon law from the University of Padua. The second editor (1970) of Zonta-Brotto, *Acta graduum,* which seems to be Sottili's source, has not been accessible to me.

[76] Joachimsohn, *Heimburg,* p. 303. For the list of professors of law at Padua during this period, see Jacopo Facciolati, *Fasti gymnasii Patavini,* I (Padua, 1757), p. 23.

[77] For his speech "Memoria repetente" which he delivered as Vicarius Maguntinus at the Council of Basel on November 29, 1432, see *Deutsche Reichstagsakten,* X, 2 (Gottingen, 1957), pp. 651-56. Cf. Joachimsohn, *Heimburg,* pp. 19-22.

[78] Herrmann, *Die Reception,* pp. 5-20; Friedrich W. Ellinger, "Die Juristen der Reichsstadt Nürnberg vom 15. bis 17. Jahrhundert," in *Genealogica, Heraldica, Juridica: Reichsstadt Nürnberg, Altdorf und Hersbruck,* Freie Schriftenfolge der Gesellschaft für Familienforschung in Franken, 6 (Nuremberg, 1954), p. 162. His letters of commission issued, respectively, on February 4, 1435, January 28, 1444, December 20, 1450, January 20, 1455 and May 19, 1457, have been preserved as Bayer. Staatsarchiv Nürnberg, 35 neue Laden, Urk. 1575, 1576, 1579, 1577, and 1578. Cf. Joachimsohn, *Heimburg,* pp. 42-45.

[79] On Leubing, see Georg A. Will, *Nürnbergisches Gelehrten-Lexicon,* II (Nuremberg, 1756), p. 432; Joachimsohn, *Heimburg,* pp. 108, 129, 195, 251; Herrmann, *Die Reception,* pp. 9, 26; Hans Lieberich, "Die gelehrten Räte: Stadt und Juristen in Bayern in der Frühzeit der Rezeption," *Zeitschrift für bayerische Landes-Geschichte,* 27 (1964): 170. Niklas van Wyle's humanistic activities are discussed in Joachimsohn, "Frühhumanismus," pp. 74-126; Bruno Strauss, *Der Übersetzer Nicolaus von Wyle* (Berlin, 1912). For Mair's life and work, see Gustav Freiherr von

humanist studies at the imperial court in Wiener Neustadt in 1449, Aeneas Sylvius, bishop of Trieste since 1447, was so impressed by Heimburg's speech that he wrote a letter to Heimburg the same day, praising him as the most promising German humanist of the day.[80]

On January 20, 1458, Heimburg acquired a position under Duke Albrecht VI of Austria. It was apparently in Albrecht's court in Vienna that Heimburg first met Duke Sigismund of the Tyrol on May 11, 1458.[81] At the Congress of Mantua next year, Heimburg made a speech on behalf of Duke Sigismund, who was by then deeply involved in the prolonged and bitter feud between himself and Cardinal Cusanus as bishop of Brixen.[82] Heimburg may have renewed his friendship with Niklas von Wyle, who was sojourning at the court of the marquis of Mantua, Lodovico Gonzaga, and his wife, Barbara of Hohenzollern, at

Hasselholdt-Stockheim, *Herzog Albrecht IV. von Bayern und seine Zeit: Archivalischer Beitrag zur deutschen Reichsgeschichte in der zweiten Hälfte des 15. Jahrhunderts,* I. Band, I. Abt. (Leipzig, 1865), pp. 317-32; *Allgemeine Deutsche Biographie,* XX (Leipzig, 1884), pp. 113-20; Lieberich, "Die gelehrte Räte," p. 176. I have not been able to consult G. Schrötter, *Dr. Martin Mair, ein biographischer Beitrag zur Geschichte der Reformation des XV. Jahrhunderts* (Munich, 1896).

[80] The letter is printed in *Aeneae . . . opera,* col. 647; Wolkan, *Der Briefwechsel,* 67, pp. 79-81.

[81] Jäger, "Regesten," IV, p. 315; Jäger, *Der Streit,* I, p. 300; Joachimsohn, *Heimburg,* p. 158. His declaration of service for Albrecht VI, dated January 20, 1458, is printed in Joseph Chmel, *Materialien zur österreichischen Geschichte aus Archiven und Bibliotheken,* II (Vienna, 1838), pp. 143-44. For his speech in defense of the duke which he delivered in 1458 at the University of Vienna, see "Excusacio contra communem wulgi opinionem contra Albertum ducem Austrie in captiuitate Udalrici Eyezingeri in oppido Wiennensi, etc.," *Archiv für österreichische Geschichte,* 58 (1879): 169-70. Cf. Joachimsohn, *Heimburg,* pp. 229, 239, 258.

[82] Heimburg's three speeches in Mantua—(1) October 29, 1449, for Duke Albrecht of Austria, (2) November 12, 1449, for Duke Wilhelm of Saxony, and (3) November 21, 1449, for Duke Sigismund—have been preserved in Bayer. Staatsbibliothek München, Clm 522 ff. 150^r-163^v: (1), ff. 156^r - 160^v; (2), ff. 150^r-155^r; (3), ff. 161^v-163^v. See also Clm 3786 ff. 173^r-174^r for a portion of the speech (1) and Clm 4016 ff. 15^v-18^r and 13^r-15^v for speeches (1) and (2). The Cod. Cent. V. App. 15, of the Stadtbibliothek Nürnberg also contains these three speeches on ff. 247^r-253^v. On the Congress of Mantua see Voigt, *Enea,* III, 54-110; Giovanni B. Picotti, *La dieta di Mantova e la politica de' Veneziani,* Miscellanea di storia Veneta, 3, iv (Venice, 1912).

that time.[83] In 1460, when the feud worsened, Duke Sigismund took Heimburg into his service on a permanent basis.[84]

Heimburg's participation in Duke Sigismund's advisory group seems to have affected the duke's moves almost immediately. Many radical appeals and manifestoes which poured from the ducal court in Innsbruck had Heimburg as their author. The famous appeals of August 13, 1460,[85] September 9, 1460,[86] and January 1461,[87] for example, clearly showed Heimburg's antipapal, conciliar position. It was probably Heimburg himself who translated the appeal of January 1461 into German in order to assure wide circulation for it.[88] Thus Heimburg was by then Duke Sigismund's most important advisor in his fight against Pope Pius II and Cardinal Cusanus.

[83] Strauch, *Pfalzgraefin*, pp. 15-16; Wüst, *Die deutschen Prosaromane*, p. 15. Cf. Paul Kristeller, "Barbara von Brandenburg, Markgräfin von Mantua," *Hohenzollern-Jahrbuch*, 3 (1899): 66-85.

[84] Jäger, *Der Streit*, II, p. 90; Joachimsohn, *Heimburg*, p. 188. Heimburg's name first appears on folio 123[r] of the Raitbuch, Band I (Jahr 1460/61) of the Landesregierungs-archiv in Innsbruck.

[85] The text is in Freher-Struve, *Rerum Germanicarum*, II, pp. 203-6. See also Jäger, "Regesten," IV, 325; Joachimsohn, *Heimberg*, pp. 188-89.

[86] Bayerische Staatsbibliothek München, Cgm 975 ff. 12[v]-25[v]; Landesregierungs-archiv Innsbruck, Codex "Handlung," ff. 323[r]-332[v]. The Codex "Handlung," which Jäger used extensively in his *Der Streit*, has been missing since before World War II. I am indebted to Dr. Hermann Hallauer of Bad Godesberg, Germany, for sending me photoprints of certain folios from the microfilm of the Codex in his possession. There is some doubt about Heimburg's authorship of the appeal. See Jäger, "Regesten," IV, 326, n. 330; Jäger, *Der Streit*, II, p. 117; Voigt, *Enea*, III, pp. 380-81; Joachimsohn, *Heimburg*, p. 189.

[87] The Latin text of Heimburg's most famous appeal, which is found in Bayerische Staatsbibliothek München, Cgm 975 ff. 228[v]-234[r], is printed in Melchior Goldast, *Monarchia S. Romana Imperii . . .*, II (Frankfurt a.M., 1614; Graz, 1960), pp. 1292-95; Freher-Struve, *Rerum*, II, pp. 211-14. The appeal is also found in the following manuscripts: Universitäts-Bibliothek Leipzig, Cod. 1092 ff. 33-36; Stadtarchiv Mainz, Nr. 26, Sammelkasten II, 436; Clm 215 ff. 226[r]-228[r]; Cod. Cent. V. App. 15 ff. 239[r]-241[r]; Biblioteca Apostolica Vaticana, Cod. Palat. 362 f. 87[v], Cod. Reg. 557 ff. 77[r]-78[v]; Bibliotheca Palat. Vindobonensis, Cod. 3244 ff. 129[r]-132[v]; Herzogliche Bibliothek Wolfenbüttel, Cod. Wolfenb. 332 ff. 16[r]-17[v]; Universitäts-Bibliothek Würzburg, Cod. M. ch. f. 47 ff. 232[v]-233[v]. Professor Paul O. Kristeller has kindly provided me with the following information: Sevilla, Colombina, cod. 5-5-19. misc. ms. from Germany. f. 310-310[v]. Greg. Hanburg [*sic*], appellatio. See also Jäger, "Regesten," VII, 175; Jäger, *Der Streit*, II, p. 184; Voigt, *Enea*, III, pp. 385-87.

[88] The translation is in Cgm 975 ff. 298[r]-306[v]. Joachimsohn printed it with some emendation in his *Heimburg*, pp. 197-204, on which is based Rupprich, *Die Frühzeit*, pp. 290-97.

In assessing Heimburg's contribution to humanism in the Tyrol, it is important to remember that he came to a court which, as we have seen above, was favorably inclined to the promotion of humanist studies. We must also recognize that unlike Pope Pius II and Cardinal Cusanus, who had already abandoned the conciliar doctrine, Heimburg was still deeply committed to the cause when he took up his duties as legal advisor to Duke Sigismund. The result was that although Heimburg's humanist learning is clearly discernible in his writings, these radical, often militant appeals and manifestoes were not merely literary exercises by the humanist, but effective weapons in the fight between Pope Pius II and Cardinal Cusanus on the one hand and Duke Sigismund and Heimburg himself on the other. In the heat of the Sonnenburg affair Heimburg the humanist was placed at the disposal of Heimburg the legal advisor who strongly supported conciliarism.

As examples of his writings during this time, we may mention, in addition to those appeals already referred to, his famous apology to Teodoro Laelio,[89] auditor of the Rota and bishop of Feltre, and an exchange of invectives between Cusanus and Heimburg in 1461.[90] In most of his writings, Heimburg's familiarity with classical writers is so clearly demonstrated that some readers might think that they were reading literary works rather than polemical pieces. In the apology to Laelio, for example, Heimburg refers not only to the Bible and Church Fathers but also to such classical figures as Homer, Solon, Thales, Zeno, Herodotus, Plato, Aristotle, Diogenes, Terence, Sallust, Virgil, Horace, Livy, Seneca, Quintilian, Plutarch, Lactantius, and above all, Cicero. It is clear to any careful reader of Heimburg's writings in this period that they are all polemical pieces occasioned by the Sonnenburg, affair. Because of antipapal views expressed in them, they were roundly criticized, and Heimburg, like his master Duke Sigismund, was excommunicated by Pope Pius II.[91]

When Heimburg led a ducal delegation to Venice in November 1461 for peace negotiations between the two feuding parties, he is reported to have made a

---

[89] Clm 232 ff. 154^r-174^r; Goldast, *Monarchia,* II, pp. 1604-25; Freher-Struve, *Rerum,* II, pp. 228-55. On the exchange between Heimburg and Laelio, see *Defensorium obedientiae apostolicae et alia documenta,* ed. and trans. Heiko A. Oberman et al. (Cambridge, Massachusetts, 1968), pp. 46-55, 282-347.

[90] Goldast, *Monarchia,* II, pp. 1626-31; Freher-Struve, *Rerum,* II, pp. 255-65; Jäger, "Regesten," VII, 178. See also Clm 215 ff. 324^r-327^r; Clm 3550 ff. 369^r-378^v; Cod. Reg. 557 ff. 79^r-85^v.

[91] Heimburg was first excommunicated by Pope Pius II in his brief of October 18, 1460, sent to the City Councils of Nürnberg and of Würzburg. Goldast, *Monarchia,* II, p. 1591; Freher-Struve, *Rerum,* II, pp. 208-9. See also Cgm 975 ff. 227^r-228^v; Cod. Reg. 557 f. 76^v; Cod. Cent. V. App. 15. ff. 238^v-239^r. On this breve, see Jäger, "Regesten," IV, 329; Joachimsohn, *Heimburg,* p. 194; Lhotsky, *Quellenkunde,* pp. 431-32. The excommunication of the duke and his followers was announced on November 2, 1460.

brilliant speech in the presence of the Doge Pasquale Malipiero and the Venetian Senate.[92] It is not difficult to understand that Heimburg the humanist could rise to the occasion and carry out his mission well. As a member of the second ducal embassy to Venice, which included Dr. Blumenau and five others Heimburg delivered eloquent speeches in November 1462 and August 1463.[93]

So long as Duke Sigismund was in conflict with Cusanus and Pope Pius II, Heimburg's humanist learning and his talent as orator were used by the Tyrolese prince. But as Sigismund began to seek reconciliation with the pope after the second excommunication of Sigismund and Heimburg on Maundy Thursday (April 2) in 1461[94] Heimburg as well as Blumenau, began to lose his position as an important advisor because of his strong proconciliar and antipapal views. The period of fighting by appeals and manifestoes was coming to an end. Although there is evidence that Heimburg was on the payroll of the duke until 1465,[95] he played a far less important role after 1464. Pope Pius II had issued the famous bull *Execrabilis* in 1460,[96] condemning in strong terms the practice of appealing to a future council from the Roman pontiff. The conciliar theory was under attack, the papacy was regaining its strength, and Duke Sigismund was seeking readmission to the Church through the good offices of his cousin, the Emperor Friedrich III. The only course of action open to the learned humanist-lawyer after the absolution of Duke Sigismund in 1464 was to enter the service of George of Podebrady, "King of Heretics," who had been in conflict with Pius II since the repeal of the Compacts of Prague in 1462.[97]

---

[92] Jäger, *Der Streit,* II, pp. 257-59; Joachimsohn, *Heimburg,* pp. 212, 240, 242; [Hans Hörtnagl], "Eine tirolische Gesandtschaft in Venedig," *Innsbrucker Nachrichten,* Samstag 4. Sept. 1926, No. 203, p. 7. For the text of the speech, see Cgm 975 ff. 318r-319v.

[93] Jäger, "Regesten," VII, p. 183; Jager, *Der Streit,* II, pp. 374-77; Voigt, *Enea,* II, p. 417 Joachimsohn, *Heimburg,* pp. 243-44.

[94] Heimburg was again condemned as a heretic on April 1, 1461, and the following day, Maundy Thursday, Duke Sigismund and his followers were placed under a general ban and excommunication. Freher-Struve, *Rerum,* II, pp. 191-93. See Jäger, "Regesten," VII, p. 177; Jäger, *Der Streit,* II, pp. 198-201; Joachimsohn, *Heimburg,* p. 218; Boockmann, *Blumenau,* p. 179.

[95] Landesregierungsarchiv Innsbruck, Raitbuch, Band 3 (Jahr 1463/65), f. 270r. See also Joachimsohn, *Heimburg,* p. 247; Boockmann, *Blumenau,* p. 185, n. 886.

[96] For the text of the bull, see Carl Mirbt, *Quellen zur Geschichte des Papsttums und des römischen Katholizismus,* 4th ed. (Tübingen, 1924), pp. 242-43. The exact dating of the bull has been a matter of controversy. It was probably issued on January 18, 1460, four days after the solemn closing of the Congress of Mantua. See Voigt, *Enea,* III, pp. 101-3; Joachimsohn, *Heimburg,* p. 179; Picotti, *La dieta,* pp. 11-12.

[97] See Joachimsohn, *Heimburg,* pp. 250-87; Frederick G. Heymann, *George of Bohemia: King of Heretics* (Princeton, 1965). Although Duke Sigismund and his

When we consider the contribution of Duke Sigismund's two important resident advisors, Blumenau and Heimburg, to the development of humanism in the Tyrol, it seems clear that because of their involvement in political affairs, they could not devote much of their time to fostering the growth of the new learning at Duke Sigismund's court in Innsbruck. Compared with Heimburg's five-year stay in the Tyrol, Blumenau had a longer service with Duke Sigismund. Yet, aside from his personal interest in collecting manuscripts and his correspondence with Hermann Schedel, there is no clear evidence that the advisor and diplomat Blumenau was also active as humanist at the ducal court. This is also true of the relations between Heimburg and the growth of humanism in the Tyrol. The appeals and manifestoes which were authored by this humanist as legal advisor to Duke Sigismund were not enough to leave a deep impression on the Innsbruck court and Tyrolese friends of humanism. Though in Nuremberg Heimburg had organized a group of friends to promote humanist studies, he does not seem to have started any group for similar purposes in the Tyrol. It is possible that both Blumenau and Heimburg were anxious to distinguish between their busy careers as legal advisors and their scholarly pursuit of learning as humanists.

It has been pointed out by many that as humanism spread from Italy to the countries north of the Alps, local circumstances influenced its nature. What emerged in a northern country was a national humanism which had its own characteristics. In general, transalpine humanism tended to be more religiously oriented than its southern counterpart. It has indeed been argued that humanism did not take root in the native soil in the North until, toward the end of the fifteenth century, it became allied to religious interests.[98] Because of wide first-hand knowledge of Italy, the response to Italian humanism was no less rapid in Germany than anywhere else in the North.[99] In common with humanism in other northern countries, German humanism manifested its religious orientation. It is also notable that the purely literary version of early German humanism flourished more in schools and universities than in princely courts and public

---

other followers were absolved on September 2, 1464, in Wiener Neustadt, Heimburg alone remained condemned and was not absolved until March 19, 1472, five months before his death. See Joachimsohn, *Heimburg,* pp. 286-87. For Heimburg's last years, see Gustav Sommerfeldt, "Aus Doktor Gregor Heimburgs letzten Lebensjahren," *Mitteilungen des Vereins für Geschichte der Deutschen in Böhmen,* 69 (1931): 46-56.

[98] Hans Baron, "Fifteenth-Century Civilisation and the Renaissance," in *The New Cambridge Modern History:* I, *The Renaissance* (Cambridge, 1967), pp. 55, 68.

[99] For the spread of humanism to England, see Roberto Weiss, *Humanism in England During the Fifteenth Century* (Oxford, 1941); for France, Franco Simone, *Il rinascimento francese* (Turin, 1961), which has been translated as *The French Renaissance* (London 1969). See also n. 2 above.

life, and that toward the end of the fifteenth century, it increasingly developed
what some historians called its "romantic," "antiquarian," or "patriotic" traits.[100]

Located in an advantageous place geographically, the Tyrol was exposed
to the new learning no later than many other regions of the Continent. Duke
Sigismund and his wife were favorably disposed to humanist studies, and
scholars, scribes, and poets were welcomed by them at the court in Innsbruck.
Some of the duke's advisors made direct contributions to humanist studies by
writing books, collecting manuscripts, or encouraging others to pursue humanist
ideals. Yet it would seem difficult to maintain that the Tyrolese contribution to
the growth of humanism was very significant in the fifteenth and early sixteenth
centuries. Understandably, local historians—David von Schönherr, Anton
Zingerle, Heinrich Hammer, Hans Kramer and others[101]—have emphasized the
Tyrol's contribution to humanism, but it is necessary to assess the situation in
the general context of the humanist movement.

Aeneas Sylvius, Duke Sigismund, Gregor Heimburg, and others in
various ways helped Tyrolese humanism to grow. But several factors seem to
have worked against a rapid growth of humanism in the Tyrol. There was no
university in the Tyrol where humanist studies could be maintained on a
continuing basis. Advisors of Duke Sigismund who could have contributed more
to the growth of the new learning were either too far from Innsbruck to be able
to exercise great influence on the ducal court or anxious to distinguish between
their active public life as lawyer-advisor and their scholarly private life as
humanist. The Sonnenburg affair, which embroiled the whole of the Tyrol in a
state of insecurity and confusion for over a decade, could not but have negative
effects on the humanist movement in the Tyrol. Although Duke Sigismund
could secure the services of men like Blumenau and Heimburg for his defense,
the affair caused the Tyrol to be placed under an interdict, which resulted in the
isolation of the Tyrol from the rest of Europe.[102] But probably a more important
reason was that, unlike Florence, for example, where there was a fairly large
number of merchants, bankers, officials, and lawyers who were strongly attracted

---

[100] See, for example, Weiss, "Italian Humanism," p. 88; Weiss, *The Spread,* p. 94
Spitz, *The Religious Renaissance,* p. 2.

[101] See n. 6 above.

[102] The deleterious effect which Cardinal Cusanus' reform activities had and the
resultant rise of anticlericalism in the Tyrol are emphasized by Hermann Wopfner,
Die Lage Tirols zu Ausgang des Mittelalters und die Ursachen des Bauernkrieges,
Abhandlungen zur Mittleren und Neueren Geschichte, 4 (Berlin and Leipzig, 1908),
pp. 86-94; Franz Kolb, *Die Wiedertäufer im Wipttal,* Schlern-Schriften, 74
(Innsbruck, 1951), p. 9.

to humanism,[103] the Tyrol lacked an aristocratic ruling class which might steadily sustain the humanist movement. Although the Fugger family of Augsburg, which had business dealings with Duke Sigismund through its expanding Tyrolese mining industry in Hall,[104] helped the new learning in Augsburg to grow, its contribution to Tyrolese humanism was negligible.

At the beginning of the sixteenth century the influence of humanism was still felt, especially in the Latin schools in the Tyrol.[105] But the political, economic, and religious conditions of the following period were certainly not conducive to the growth of humanist studies. The dreary war against the Venetians (1508-1516) exhausted the people of the Tyrol and paved the way for the rise of discontent and radicalism in later years. The penetration of Lutheran ideas into the region four years after the beginning of the Reformation marked the opening of a new era in Tyrolese history. The common people, who had never really been influenced by the humanists in the ducal and ecclesiastical courts or monasteries, were stirred by the anticlerical preaching of Jakob Strauss, the first preacher of Lutheran persuasion in the Tyrol.[106] The Peasant Rebellion of 1525 and the ensuing advent and spread of anabaptism in the Tyrol under the leadership of Michael Gaismair ushered in a long period of confusion and destruction[107] which further weakened whatever basis there was in the Tyrol for the development of humanist studies.[108]

[103] See Lauro Martines, *The Social World of the Florentine Humanists 1390-1460* (Princeton, 1963); Lauro Martines, *Lawyers and Statecraft in Renaissance Florence* (Princeton, 1968).

[104] Friedrich Dobel, " Über den Bergbau und Handel des Jacob und Anton Fugger in Kärnten und Tirol (1495-1560)," *Zeitschrift des Historischen Vereins für Schwaben und Neuburg,* 9 (1882): 193-213; Richard Ehrenberg, *Capital and Finance in the Age of the Renaissance* (New York, 1928; rpr. 1963), pp. 65-67, 133; Eike E. Unger, *Die Fugger in Hall i. T.,* Studien zur Fuggergeschichte, 19 (Tübingen, 1967).

[105] Cf. Fr. Waldner, "Petrus Tritonius Athesinus, recte Peter Treibenraiff, als Humanist, Musiker und Schulmann," *Zs. d. Ferd.,* 47 (1903): 185-230.

[106] Fr. Waldner, " Dr. Jakob Strauss in Hall und seine Predigt vom grünen Donnerstag (17. April 1522)," *Zs. d. Ferd.,* 26 (1882): 3-39; Wopfner, *Die Lage,* pp. 94-96; *Haller Buch,* pp. 180-82.

[107] On the Peasant Rebellion and anabaptism in the Tyrol, see, for example, Egger, *Geschichte,* II (1876), pp. 69-120; Johann Loserth, "Der Anabaptismus in Tirol von seinen Anfängen bis zum Tode Jakob Huters (1526-1536)," *Archiv für österreichische Geschichte,* 78 (1893): 427-604; Wopfner, *Die Lage,* pp. 192-204; Kolb, *Die Wiedertäufer; Haller Buch,* pp. 184-89; Josef Macek, *Der Tiroler Bauernkrieg und Michael Gaismair,* trans. Eduard Ullmann (Berlin, 1965).

[108] The present article is a revised version of a paper read at a meeting of the University Seminar on the Renaissance, Columbia University, on May 16, 1972. It is based on the research in Europe which was made possible by a grant from the American Philosophical Society.

Gregor Heimburg and Early Humanism in Germany

Gregor Heimburg (c. 1400-1472) is best known as a jurist and politician who strongly criticized the Church in the fifteenth century.[1] But in order to understand the full range of his religious, intellectual, and political ideas it is important to recognize the influence of humanism on the growth of this controversialist and the role which he played in the development of early humanism in Germany. It is sometimes said that German humanism originated in the universities at Erfurt, Heidelberg, Leipzig, and Vienna.[2] But we must note that many lawyers who worked as advisors to secular or ecclesiastical princes in the fifteenth and sixteenth centuries were educated in Italy and contributed a great deal to the growth of humanism after returning to their own country.[3] Heimburg was one of the fifteenth-century German lawyers whose career and thought deserve a close study for our understanding of the diffusion of humanism in general and of its early manifestation in Germany in particular. Joachimsohn's impressive work on Heimburg, which appeared in 1891,[4] must be corrected and brought up to date on some aspects of Heimburg's life.

---

[1] C. Ullmann, *Reformers & Before the Reformation,* trans. R. Menzies, I (Edinburgh, 1855), 195-208; Kamil Krofta, "Bohemia in the Fifteenth Century," *Cambridge Medieval History,* VIII (New York, 1936), p. 99; Frederick G. Heymann, *George of Bohemia: King of Heretics* (Princeton, 1965).

[2] See, for example, Roberto Weiss, *The Spread of Italian Humanism* (London, 1964), p. 94.

[3] See Paul Lehmann, "Grundzüge des Humanismus deutscher Lande zumal im Spiegel deutscher Bibliotheken des 15. und 16. Jahrhunderts," *Aevum* 31 (1957): 253-268; reprinted in his *Erforschung des Mittelalters,* V (Stuttgart, 1962), 481-496; Hans Lieberich, "Die gelehrten Rate: Stadt und Juristen in Bayern in der Frühzeit der Rezeption," *Zeitschrift für bayerische Landes-Geschichte* 27 (1964): 120-189; Franz Wisacker, "Einflüsse des Humanismus auf die Rezeption," *Zeitschrift für die gesamte Staatswissenschaft* 100 (1940): 423-25; Lewis W. Spitz, "German Humanism," *Renaissance Quarterly* 21 (1968): 126-131.

[4] Paul Joachimsohn, *Gregor Heimburg,* Historische Abhandlungen aus dem Münchener Seminar, I (Bamberg, 1891). The other main biographies of Heimburg are Joannes A. Ballenstadius, *Vitae Gregorii de Heimburg . . . brevis narratio* (Helmstedt, 1737); Clemens Brookhaus, *Gregor von Heimburg: Ein Beitrag zur deutschen Geschichte des 15. Jahrhunderts* (Leipzig, 1861, repr. Wiesbaden, 1969).

It is not within the scope of this paper to deal in detail with the complex history of early humanism in the German Empire and to discuss how humanism grew in Bohemia, the Netherlands, Austria, Swabia, the Palatinate, and Franconia.[5] We note in reviewing these developments that early humanism in Germany was fostered in the first instance by Italian humanists who came to the North, secondly by German students who after studying in Italian universities became advisors to princes and prelates, doctors for towns or cities, or teachers in universities, and finally by those Germans who contributed to its growth although, or precisely because, they did not visit Italy. The most famous of the first group was, no doubt, Aeneas Sylvius Piccolomini (1405-1464), whom Joachimsohn called "the apostle of humanism in Germany."[6] Pier Paolo Vergerio, Benedetto da Piglio, Jacopo Publicio, and Poggio Bracciolini may also be mentioned in this connection. The second group includes a large number of Germans who were influenced by humanism, such as Gregor Heimburg, Heinrich Steinhowel (1412-1482), Thomas Pirckheimer (d. 1473), Laurentius Blumenau (c. 1415-1484), Niklas von Wyle (d. 1478), Sigismund Gossembrot (1417-1493), Albrecht von Eyb (1420-1475), Peter Luder (d. 1474), Hermann Schedel (1410-1485), Samuel Karoch, Rudolf Agricola (1444-1484), and Sigismund Meisterlin (d. after 1491). The significance of the last group as a whole is not to be neglected, but with the exception of such famous ones as Martin Mair (Mayr, Mayer, Meyer) (c. 1420-1480), most of them remain unknown or forgotten.

[5] To mention some of the important works on this topic: Franz W. Kampschulte, *Die Universität Erfurt in ihrem Verhältnisse zu dem Humanismus und der Reformation,* 2 vols. (Trier, 1858-1860, repr. Aalen, 1970); Ludwig Geiger, *Renaissance und Humanismus in Italien und Deutschland* (Berlin, 1882); Georg Voigt, *Die Wiederbelebung des classischen Alterthums oder das erste Jahrhundert des Humanismus,* 2nd ed., 2 vols. (Berlin, 1880-1881); Paul Joachimsohn, "Frühhumanismus in Schwaben," *Württembergische Vierteljahrshefte für Landesgeschichte,* n.s. 5 (1896), 63-126, 257-291; Max Herrmann *Die Reception des Humanismus in Nürnberg* (Berlin, 1898); Gustav Bauch, *Die Reception des Humanismus in Wien* (Breslau, 1903); Gustav Bauch, *Die Universität Erfurt im Zeitalter des Frühhumanismus* (Breslau, 1904); Karl Grossmann, "Die Frühzeit des Humanismus in Wien bis zu Celtis Berufung 1497," *Jahrbuch für Landeskunde von Niederösterreich* 22 (1929), 150-325; Hans Rupprich, *Die Frühzeit des Humanismus und die Renaissance in Deutschland* (Lepzig, 1938, repr. Darmstadt, 1964); Eduard Winter, *Frühhumanismus: Seine Entwicklung in Böhmen und deren europäische Bedeutung für die Kirchenreformbestrebungen im 14. Jahrhundert* (Berlin, 1964). See also Paul O. Kristeller, "The European Diffusion of Italian Humanism," *Italica* 39 (1962): 1-12; reprinted in his *Renaissance Thought II: Papers on Humanism and the Arts* (New York, 1965), pp. 69-88.

[6] Joachimsohn, *Heimburg,* p. 103.

What then was the educational, intellectual, and political background of Gregor Heimburg? How did he contribute to the spread of humanism in Germany? Born in the Franconian city of Schweinfurt near Würzburg around 1400 as the son of the burgher Hans Heimburg, mayor of Schweinfurt four times, Gregor was, as we shall see in more detail, educated in local schools and studied at German universities. Crossing the Alps like many aspiring youths of his time, he went to Italy to study at the University of Padua and received the degree of Doctor of Laws from the university in 1430.[7] In Nuremberg, to which he came after graduation, Heimburg met Konrad III of Daun, Archbishop of Mainz, who appointed him on June 21, 1430, his general vicar in ecclesiastical affairs despite the fact that Heimburg was a layman. In this capacity he went to the Council of Basel in 1432 which had begun the previous year. After serving as representative of the Emperor Sigismund in 1434 at the council, he became legal advisor to the city of Nuremberg next year and continued to serve almost continuously until 1461, in spite of the fact that there were occasional frictions between the city council and Heimburg.[8] During this time his services were not confined to Nuremberg. His legal counsel was sought by many prelates and princes, such as the Duke of Saxony, the Margrave of Brandenburg, the Archduke of Austria, the Kings of Hungary and Bohemia, the Archbishops of Mainz and of Trier, and the Bishops of Wurzburg. He was also involved in the famous struggle between Cardinal Nicolaus Cusanus, Bishop of Brixen, and Sigismund, Duke of Austria and Count of the Tyrol (1446-1490). In 1459 he appeared at the Congress of Mantua as Sigismund's representative not only to defend Sigismund's cause, but also to oppose Pope Pius II's crusade program.[9]

---

[7] See below, n. 26.

[8] On legal advisors in Nuremberg, see Georg Freiherr von Kress, *Gelehrte Bildung im alten Nürnberg und das Studium der Nürnberger an italienischen Hochschulen* (Nürnberg, 1877), 10-11; Friedrich W. Ellinger, "Die Juristen der Reichsstadt Nürnberg vom 15. bis 17. Jahrhundert," in *Genealogica, Heraldica, Juridica: Reichsstadt Nürnberg, Altdorf und Hersbruck,* Freie Sohriftenfolge der Gesellschaft für Familienforschung in Franken, VI (Nürnberg, 1954).

[9] Heimburg made three speeches in Mantua: (1) October 29, 1459, for Duke Albrecht of Austria; (2) November 12, 1459, for Duke Wilhelm of Saxony; and (3) November 21, 1459, for Duke Sigismund of Austria. They have been preserved in Munich, Bayerische Staatsbibliothek, Cod. lat. mon. 522 ff. 150 160^v [(1), ff. 150-160^v; (2), ff. 150-155; (3), ff. 161^v-163^v] and are in the legible hand of Hartmann Schedel. Cod. Cent. V. App. 15. of the Stadtbibliothek in Nuremberg also contains these three speeches on ff. 247-253^v. On the Congress of Mantua in general and Heimburg's role in it, see Georg Voigt, *Enea Silvio de' Piccolomini als Papst Pius der Zweite,* III (Berlin, 1863), pp. 59-110; Joachimsohn, *Heimburg,* pp. 144-180; Giovanni B. Picotti, *La dieta di Mantova e la politica de' Veneziani,* Miscellanea di storia Veneta, 3rd ser., IV (Venice, 1912).

Excommunicated by the pope in 1461 because of his support of Sigismund against Cusanus,[10] Heimburg spent most of his later years in Bohemia in the service of King George of Podebrady (1458-1471).[11] He was not reconciled with the Church until March 19 in 1472, the year of his death which occurred in Dresden in August.[12]

To understand the relations between Heimburg and early humanism, it would be helpful to know clearly what kind of education he received in his youth. Unfortunately, what we know about it is very fragmentary because almost all documents relative to the history of Schweinfurt during this period were destroyed in the Margrave War of 1554 and the Thirty Years' War.[13] In all probability, Heimburg first went to a Latin school in Schweinfurt whose origins went back to the thirteenth century. The Church of St. Johannis, which maintained the school,[14] had been paying tithes since the Middle Ages to the Stift Haug in Wurzburg, the tithe-owner of the whole district of Schweinfurt.[15] The scholastic of the Stift Haug was therefore responsible for the supervision of

---

[10] Albert Jäger, *Der Streit des Cardinals Nicolaus von Cusa mit dem Herzoge Sigmund von Österreich als Grafen von Tirol*, II (Innsbruck, 1861), p. 198.

[11] Heymann, *George of Bohemia*, pp. 408-620.

[12] Joachimsohn, *Heimburg, p.* 287, was incorrect in stating that Heimburg was buried in the Kreuzkirche in Dresden. It was in the Sophienkirche that he found his resting place. See Cornelius Gurlitt, *Stadt Dresden,* Beschreibende Darstellung der älteren Bauund Kunstdenkmäler des Königreichs Sachsen, XXI-XXIV (Dresden, 1903), p. 96; Gustav Sommerfeldt, "Aus Doktor Gregor Heimburgs letzten Lebensjahren," *Mitteilungen des Vereins für Geschichte der Deutschen in Böhmen* 69 (1931): 46-56.

[13] Erich Saffert, "Die Schule in der Stadtrechnung: Bemerkungen zu einer Kirchenund Schulamtsrechnung des 16. Jahrhunderts," in *325 Jahre Gymnasium Schweinfurt 1634-1959* (Schweinfurt, 1959), pp. 13-23; Erich Saffert, "Die Stadiarchiv Schweinfurt im Friedrich-Rückert-Bau," *Archivalische Zeitschrift* 59 (1963): 177.

[14] On the Latin school in Schweinfurt, where the humanists Conrad Celtis and Johann Cuspinian also studied, see V. Völcker, *Geschichte der Studienanstalt Schweinfurt,* I (Schweinfurt, 1882); Karl Ziegler, *Geschichte des humanistischen Gymnasiums in Schweinfurt (1634-1934) und der Lateinischen Schule daselbst* (Schweinfurt, 1934); Friedrich Beyschlag, "Die älteste Gesehichte der lateinischen Schule in Schweinfurt (bis 1554)," *Schweinfurter Tagblatt,* Nr. 113, 15 Mai 1905 and Nr. 114, 16 Mai 1905. Joachimsohn (*Heimburg,* p. 2) says: ". . . gab es damals wohl noch keine städtische Schule."

[15] Friedrich Schneider, "Neuer Beitrag zur richtigen Erkenntnis des früheren Verhältnisses des Chorherrenstiftes zu Haug in Würzburg zur St. Johanniskirche in Schweinfurt," *Archiv für Stadt and Bezirksamt Schweinfurt* 5 (1907): 46-49; Erich Saffert, "Schweinfurt—Würzburg: Die gegenseitigen historischen Beziehungen," *Veröffentlichungen des Historischen Vereins und des Stadlarchivs Schweinfurt,* Sonderreihe, II (Schweinfurt, 1957).

education in the district. As Schweinfurt became the seat of an archdeaconry in the fourteenth century, the Church of St. Johannis and, as a result, its Latin school acquired more importance in the area.[16] But as far as the educational program of the school is concerned, it must have been traditional in nature and under the influence of scholasticism at the time of Heimburg's entry. The school was probably a "trivial" school where only the elements of the trivium were taught. We know little about its teaching staff in the fifteenth century. Master Friedrich Marquard, who was apparently a supporter of scholasticism, was the head of the school from 1430 to 1440, and among the teachers at the school toward the end of the century, Masters Petrus Popon, Konrad Scheffer and Johann May were more inclined toward humanistic education than Konrad Haug who clung to the traditional approach.[17] By that time there was even in Schweinfurt a controversy between scholasticism and humanism which had first started at the Universities of Heidelberg and Vienna and later spread to many universities in Germany. But Heimburg, who must have entered the Latin school at the beginning of the century, could not have been much influenced by this controversy.

Did Heimburg then go on to the Cathedral school in Würzburg which was so important in the ecclesiastical and cultural development of Schweinfurt? There is no conclusive evidence that he did despite the assertions of many writers in the past.[18] Because of the close relationship between the Latin school in Schweinfurt and the Stift Haug, the young boy could have been sent to either the Cathedral school or the school of the Newminster (Neumünster) in Würzburg where advanced education not available in Schweinfurt could be obtained. It is known that Master Popon, who moved from Schweinfurt to Würzburg toward

---

[16] Erich Saffert, *Im Dienst der Humanitas: Aus der Geschichte des Schweinfurter Gymnasiums* (Schweinfurt, 1959) [Sonderdruck aus dem Schweinfurter Tagblatt vom 5., 6., und 9. Mai 1959].

[17] On Petrus Popon, see *Magistri Petri Poponis colloquia de scholis Herbipolensibus: Ein Beitrag zur Vorgeschichte der Würzburger Hochshule als Festgabe zu deren dreihundert-Jährigen Jubiläum,* ed. Georg Schepes (Würzburg, 1882), pp. 5-15; [Georg] Schepss, "Die Gedichte des Magisters Petrus Popon: Ein Beitrag zur frankischen Gelehrtengeschichte des 15. Jahrhunderts," *Archiv des Historischen Vereins von Unterfranken und Aschaffenburg* 27 (1884): 277-300. The former article discusses the *Dictum Magistri Petri Popon contra Herbipolensium scolasticum in Novo Monasterio Herbipolensi,* which is found in Cod. lat. mon. 18910 ff. 26-32. Popon, who taught Cuspinian in Schweinfurt, compiled *Rudimenta Grammaticae ad pueros de Remigio, Donato, Alexeandroque studiosissime lecta* (Nürnberg, 1499). See Georg W. Panzer, *Annales Typographici,* II (Nürnberg, 1794), 227; Ludwig F.T. Hain, *Repertorium bibliographicum,* II² (Milan, 1948), p. 235, nos. 14022-14026.

[18] Ballenstadius, *Vitae,* p. 6; Ullmann, *Reformers,* I, p. 195; Joachimsohn, *Heimburg,* p. 2.

the end of the century to teach at the Cathedral school, criticized the scholastic curriculum which was in use at the Newminster school.[19] The Cathedral school of Würzburg, which had a long history of education going back to St. Burkard (741-791), the first Bishop of Würzburg, had such high reputation in the tenth century and thereafter that it was no doubt the best cathedral school in Franconia.[20] An examination of the curriculum at the schools of the Cathedral and the Newminster in the fifteenth century shows that while the Newminster school took a rather conservative and cautious attitude toward humanist learning, the Cathedral school was decidedly humanist in orientation and emphasized disputation and reading of poetry.[21] But all these changes took place long after Heimburg left Würzburg even if he actually attended one of the schools there. For we know that he matriculated in the Faculty of Arts of the University of Vienna (founded 1365) on October 13, 1413, as "pauper."[22]

Like the Universities of Erfurt (1392) and Leipzig (1409), the University of Vienna attracted many students from Franconia in the fifteenth century partly because it was by that time a well established school and partly because it was relatively close to Franconia. Konrad von Ebrach from Franconia was active in Vienna as the famous professor of theology after 1384, and Konrad von Rothenburg, another Franconian, had been teaching in the Faculty of Arts probably since 1388.[23] But the dominant trend at the University of Vienna was still scholastic, and it was Aeneas Sylvius Piccolomini who was to become instrumental in fostering humanistic studies in Vienna after he became a member

[19] Ziegler, *Geochichte,* p. 5; Schepss, "Die Gedichte," p. 278.

[20] Christian Bönicke, *Grundriss einer Geochichte von der Universität zu Würzburg,* I (Würzburg, 1782), p. 7; Georg J. Keller, *Die Gründung des Gymnasiums zu Würzburg durch den Fürstbisohof Friedrich von Wirsberg* (Würzburg, 1850).

[21] *Magistri Poponis,* p. 15; Schepss, "Die Gedichte," p. 279.

[22] *Die Matrikel der Univeristät Wien,* I (Graz and Cologne, 1956), p. 99; Albin F. Seherhaufer, "Jung-Schweinfurt auf hohen Sohulen," *Schweinfurter Heimatblätter* 26 (1957), 55-56. Joachimsohn, *Heimburg,* p. 2, n. 10 states: "Eine deutsche Universität hat Heimburg, soweit wir schen, nicht besucht." Johannes Heymburg de Sweynfurd entered the University of Erfurt in 1409 and Richard Heinberg de Sweyofordia, who is believed to be Gregor's nephew, matriculated at the University of Leipzig in 1441. See Friedrich Beyschlag, "Jung-Sohweinfurt auf hohen Sohulen," *Archiv für Stadt- und Bezirksamt Schweinfurt* 4 (1906): 41, 66.

[23] J. Abet, "Aus der Geschichte der ersten Würzburger Universität unter Bischof Johann von Egloffstein," *Archiv des Historischen Vereins von Unterfranken und Aschaffenburg* 63 (1923): 4; Joseph Aschbach, *Geschichte der Wiener Universität im ersten Jahrhunderte ihres Bestehens,* I (Vienna, 1865, repr. Farnborough, 1967), pp. 599-600.

of the Imperial Chancery in 1442 under Kaspar Schlick (d. 1449). Like other faculties of law in the German Empire at that time, the Faculty of Law of the University of Vienna concentrated on the study of canon law rather than civil law; the candidates in the Faculty were nominally required to attend courses in civil law, but these courses were in fact not given.[24] The doctoral graduates of the Faculty were almost without exception called *Doctores in Decretis* or *Decretorum*.[25] It remains an open question whether Heimburg was only in the Faculty of Arts or entered the Faculty of Law in Vienna.

Little is known about Heimburg's academic career after his matriculation in 1413, except that he obtained the degree of *Doctor in jure canonico* in Padua on February 7, 1430, and that when he took an examination in 1430 for the degree, he was already referred to as *Legum doctor*.[26] In a speech which he made in 1430 to accept the doctorate, Heimburg spoke of many transalpine universities which he had attended.[27] But it is not known which universities besides Vienna he intended. Various attempts to find a clue to this question by studying the matriculation lists of European universities have not been successful. It is possible that before coming to Padua Heimburg, as some have suggested,[28] studied law or other subjects at the University of Würzburg which had been founded in 1402.[29] But since no one was permitted, under the statute of

[24] For further discussion on the University of Vienna during the period of early humanism, see Bauch, *Die Reception;* Grossmann, "Die Frühzeit;" Alphons Lhotsky, *Die Wiener Artistenfakultät 1365-1497* (Graz, 1965); idem, *Aeneas Silvius und Österreich* (Basel and Stuttgart, 1965).

[25] Aschbach, Geschichte, I, pp. 101-104. On the study of civil law in fifteenth-century Germany, see Otto Stobbe, *Geschichte der deutschen Rechtsquellen,* II (Braunschweig, 1864), p. 9; Winfried Trusen, *Anfänge des gelehrten Rechts in Deutschland: Ein Beitrag zur Geschichte der Frührezeption* (Wiesbaden, 1962), pp. 11-33, 106-11.

[26] Arnold Luschin von Ebengreuth, "Quellen zur Geschichte deutschen Rechtshörer in Italien," *Sitzungsberichte der phil.-histor. Klasse der kaiserlichen Akademie der Wissenschaften* [Vienna] 124 (1891): 23; *Acta graduum academicorum Gymnasii Patavini ab anno MCCCCVI ad annum MCCCCL.,* ed. C. Zonta and I. Brotto (Padua, 1922), pp. 166-167.

[27] This speech, *Oratio pro petendis insigniis doctoratus canonici arengata,* is in Cod. lat. mon. 504 ff. 313ᵛ-314 and is printed in Joachimsohn, *Heimburg,* pp. 302-303. This codex was also oopied by Hartmann Sohedel. Cf. Richard Stauber, *Die Schedelsche Bibliothek* (Freiburg im Breisgau, 1908, repr. Nieuwkoop, 1969), p. 32.

[28] [Karl Hagen] in *Braga—Vaterländische Blätter für Kunst und Wissenschaft,* II (Heidelberg, 1839), p. 416; Ullmann, *Reformers,* I, p. 195.

[29] Friedrich A. Reuss, *Johann I. von Egloffstein, Bischof von Würzburg und Herzog zu Franken, Stifter der ersten Hochschule in Würzburg* (Würzburg, 1847), Franz X.

the University of Padua, [30] to obtain the doctorate in either civil or canon law without studying at least six years in Padua, it is probable that Heimburg's legal studies were done in Padua between 1421 and 1428. He then could complete the requirements for the doctorate in canon law in Padua by 1430. The fact that Heimburg spoke in his doctoral speech of studying grammar and philosophy in transalpine universities [31] seems to indicate that his academic career suggested above is probably correct. Prosdocimus de Comitibus, Heinricus de Alano, Paulus de Dotis, and Jacobus de Zocchis de Ferraria, whom Heimburg mentioned as his law professors, all taught in Padua between 1421 and 1430. We may be certain that Heimburg diligently studied classical authors in Padua as he delved in the fields of civil and canon law. He was in this sense not exceptional because a large number of German students who went to Italy to study law were attracted by classical studies. Heimburg may even have been able to listen to the famous humanist Vittorino da Feltre (1373-1446) who held the chair of rhetoric briefly in 1422 in Padua.

 While Heimburg was in Basel, he met many humanists at the council which offered them a good opportunity to search for manuscripts in monasteries and libraries in the North. [32] But contrary to the oft-expressed view by many writers, [33] he was not Aeneas Sylvius's secretary at the council, nor was he especially closely associated with Aeneas. His humanistic interest must have been strengthened as he listened to many speeches and talked with learned men from Italy. But there seems to exist no evidence that Aeneas's direct influence on Heimburg began at this time in Basel.

 We know, however, that when Heimburg became legal advisor to the city of Nuremberg in 1435 as successor to the famous Dr. Conrad Konhofer, [34] he gradually began to gather around him a group of humanists who paved the way

von Wegele, *Geschichte der Universität Wirzburg* (Wirzburg, 1882, repr. Aalen, 1969); Abet, "Aus der Geschichte," pp. 5-18.

[30] Ebengreuth, "Quellen," 23.

[31] Joschimsohn, *Heimburg,* p. 302.

[32] Paul Lehmann, "Konstanz und Basel als Büchermarkte wahrend der grossen Kirchenversammlungen," *Zeitschrift der deutschen Vereins für Buchwesen und Schrifttum* 4 (1921), 6-11, 17-27; reprinted in his *Erforschung des Mittelalters,* I (Stuttgart, 1959), pp. 253-280.

[33] Henricus Pantaleon, *Prosopographiae herorum atque illustrium virorum totius Germaniae,* II (Basel, 1565), p. 413; Melchior Adam, *Vitae Germanorum Jurisconsultorum* (Heidelberg, 1620), p. 2; Ullmann, *Reformers,* I, pp. 195-196; J. F. van Schulte, *Die Geschichte der Quellen und Literatur des canonischen Rechts von Gratian bis auf die Gegenwart,* II (Stuttgart, 1875), p. 372, n. 6.

[34] About this learned churchman, see Martin Weigel, *Dr. Conrad Konhofer (†1452): Ein Beitrag zur Kirchengeschichte Nürnbergs* (Nürnberg, 1928).

for the future development of humanism in the Imperial City. Nuremberg, which had employed learned lawyers as its legal advisors since the fourteenth century [35] and which, with her central location in the German Empire, was the site of imperial diets many times, held a prominent place among the major German cities. [36] Sigismund, King of the Romans, who liked the city, had moved the royal insignia to Nuremberg in 1424, [37] thereby enhancing its prestige. Nuremberg owed its prosperity in no small degree to the conservative rule of patrician families which strengthened their hold on the city government especially after the unsuccessful rebellion of the city's workingmen in 1348-1349 and which ruled the city sternly, if benevolently, in order to maintain political stability. Little attempt was made by the city council, which consisted exclusively of members of these patrician families, to bring in new ideas from outside. The legal advisors, most of whom were non-Nurembergers, could not exceed their advisory rank. The council never permitted them to participate in decision making. In their education and training, Heimburg's predecessors in the fifteenth century had been little affected by humanism. The learned Dr. Konhofer, for example, was essentially a scholastic as is clear from the one hundred and fifty-one manuscripts which he possessed in his library. [38] But in a city which had neither university nor episcopal chancery, the office of legal advisors was probably the only vantage ground from which humanistically inclined lawyers trained in Italy could gradually disseminate the fruits of the new learning.

It is therefore not surprising to note that during his first employment from 1435 to 1440, Heimburg, who was also busy on other missions outside Nuremberg, was unable to do much to promote humanistic studies in this essentially conservative city. But after his return to Nuremberg in 1444 to assume his second term as legal advisor, a small circle of friends of humanistic studies began to gather around him which included Heinrich Leubing (d. 1472), Martin Mair (c. 1420-1480), and Niklas von Wyle (d. 1478). [39] Born in Nordhausen, Leubing studied at the Universities of Leipzig, Erfurt, and Bologna,

[35] See above, n. 8; Stobbe, *Geschichte,* II, p. 59, n. 32; Trusen, *Anfänge,* pp. 222-235.

[36] For a recent treatment of Nuremberg in the fifteenth and sixteenth centuries, see Gerald Strauss, *Nuremberg in the Sixteenth Century* (New York, 1966).

[37] Julia Schnelbögel, "Die Reichskleinodien in Nürnberg 1424-1523," *Mitteilungen des Vereins für Geschichte der Stadt Nürnberg* 51 (1962): 78-159.

[38] H. Petz, "Urkundliche Beiträge zur Gesehichte der Bücherei des Nürnberger Rates, 1429-1538," *Mitteilungen des Vereins für Geschichte des Stadt Nürnberg* 6 (1886): 137-143; Herrmann, *Die Reception,* p. 5.

[39] Herrmann, *Die Reception,* pp. 5-30.

receiving the degree of *Legum doctor* in 1437 from Bologna.[40] After working in Saxony, Mainz, and the Imperial Court, he came to Nuremberg in 1444 as priest of the Church of St. Sebald and also became legal advisor to the city council as Heimburg's colleague. Mair, who was born in Wimpfen, entered the University of Heidelberg in 1438 and received the *Baccalarius in artibus* in 1443.[41] He came to Nuremberg in 1449 as secretary of the council. An admirer of Heimburg, Mair called him *singularis preceptor*.[42] Besides becoming the famous chancellor of Mainz, Mair later obtained the degree of Doctor of civil law from the University of Heidelberg. Probably the most literarily inclined of the three was the Swiss Niklas von Wyle from Bremgarten in the Aargau.[43] He had attended the University of Pavia and came to Nuremberg in 1447 to become secretary of the city council.

Unfortunately, Heimburg's friends did not stay very long in Nuremberg, a city which did not enjoy the reputation of being hospitable to the humanists. Limited as their influence might have been, this group around Heimburg did introduce to this Imperial City the discussion of topics which had been debated by literary men in Italy for some time. The city which delighted in being the host to Regiomontanus (1436-1476) and, briefly, to Conrad Celtis (1459-1508) and which later produced such friends of humanism as Hans Tucher (1428-1491), Hartmann Schedel (1440-1514), and Willibald Pirckheimer (1470-1530) had in Heimburg its earliest supporter of the *studia humanitatis*.[44]

Heimburg's competence as a humanist became clear when he discussed humanistic studies at the Imperial Court in Wiener Neustadt in 1449. Aeneas Sylvius, Bishop of Trieste since 1447, had returned to Wiener Neustadt from his see and was in the audience. After listening to Heimburg's speech Aeneas wrote

---

[40] On Leubing, see Georg A. Will, *Nürnbergisches Gelehrten-Lexicon,* II (Nürnberg, 1756), p. 432; Joachimsohn, *Heimburg,* pp. 108, 129, 195, 251; Herrmann, *Die Reception,* pp. 9, 26; Lieberich, "Die gelehrten Räte," p. 170.

[41] On Mair, see *Allgemeine Deutsche Biographie,* XX (Leipzig, 1884), 113-120; Lieberich, "Die gelehrte Räte," p. 176.

[42] Herrmann, *Die Reception,* p. 11.

[43] On Niklas von Wyle, see Joachimsohn, "Frühhumanismus," pp. 74-126; Bruno Strauss, *Der Übersetzer Nicolaus von Wyle* (Berlin, 1912).

[44] On the term *studia humanitatis,* see Erich König, "Studia humanitatis und verwandte Ausdrücke bei den deutsehen Frühhumanisten," in *Beiträge zur Geschichte der Renaissance und Reformation: Festgabe für J. Schlecht* (Munich, 1917), pp. 202-207; Paul O. Kristeller, *The Classics and Renaissance Thought* (Cambridge, Massachusetts, 1955), pp. 9-12.

him a letter the same day praising him highly.[45] As Cicero brought eloquence from Greece to Italy, wrote Aeneas, so Heimburg will bring it from Italy to Germany.[46] It seems that Aeneas saw in Heimburg the most promising German humanist of the day. This was indeed a remarkable letter because in describing Heimburg's speech and conduct in Rome as head of the Electors' envoys to Pope Eugenius IV in 1446, Aeneas had drawn a highly critical picture of Heimburg stalking about indignantly at night on Monte Giordano with bare head and breast, denouncing the wickedness of the pope and the curia.[47] Critical as Aeneas was of Heimburg the lawyer-politician, he seems to have appreciated the German humanist in him. But Aeneas's warm appreciation of Heimburg's talent turned into bitter criticism as Heimburg became more involved in ecclesiastical and political events.

In some of his speeches, letters, and writings,[48] Heimburg often refers not only to the Bible and Church Fathers, but also to classical writers. In addition to Moses, St. Peter, St. Paul, St. Jerome, St. Augustine, and St. Bernard of Clairvaux, he frequently mentions Socrates, Lactantius, and, of course, Cicero. Other important classical writers and figures whose names Heimburg invoked like other humanists are Homer, Solon, Thales, Zeno, Herodotus, Plato,

---

[45] The letter is printed in Aeneas Silvius Piccolomini, *Opera* (Basel, 1551, repr. Frankfurt am Main, 1967), p. 647; *Der Briefwechsel des Eneas Silvio Piccolomini,* ed. Rudolf Wolkan, Fontes Rerum Austriacarum, II, Abt. Diplomataria et Acta, LXII (Vienna, 1912), pp. 79-81.

[46] *Der Briefwechsel,* pp. 79-80.

[47] Aeneas Silvius Piccolomini, *Historia Rerum Friderici III. Imperatoris,* ed. A.F. Kollár, *Analecta Monumentorum Omnis Aevi Vindobonensia,* II (Vienna, 1761), cols. 123-124.

[48] Besides the speeches at Mantua, which are mentioned in n. 9 above, the following are the speeches and writings of Heimburg in which he refers to classical writers or has citations from them: (1) Speech before the Council of Basel on November 29, 1432, in *Deutsche Reichstagsakten,* X (Göttingen, 1957), 651-656; (2) Speech in 1453 at the Imperial Court, in Aenas Silvius, *Historia,* ed. Kollár, II, 428-431; (3) Letter of March 6,1454, to Johannes Rot, in Cod. Iat. mon. 518 ff. 103ᵛ-107, Cod. Iat. mon. 519 ff. 46 50ᵛ and printed in Joachimsohn, *Heimburg,* pp. 303-310 and Rupprich, *Die Frühzeit,* pp. 275-282, (4) *Appellatio a papa variis modis ad concilium* (1461), in Melchior Goldast, *Monarchia S. Romana Imperii sive Tractatus de Iurisdictione Imperiali seu Regia et Pontificia seu Sacerdotali,* II (Frankfurt, 1614), pp. 1292 [1592]-1595 and Marquard Freher, *Rerum Germanicarum scriptores,* ed. B. G. Struve, II (Strassburg, 1717), pp. 211-214; and (5) *Apologia contra Detractiones et Blasphemias Theodori Laelii Feltrensis Episcopi,* in Goldast, *Monarchia,* II, pp. 1604-1625 and Freher-Struve, *Rerum,* II, pp. 228-255. (4) and (5) are also included in *Jurisconsulti acutissimi . . . Gregorii de Heimberg . . . Scripta nervosa, iuris iustitiaeque plena . . .* (Frankfurt, 1608), which is a collection of his various writings.

Diogenes, Aristotle, Terence, Valerius Maximus, Cato, Sallust, Virgil, Horace, Livy, Seneca, Quintilian, and Plutarch. It was his desire, Heimburg stated, not to swerve from the independence of a Diogenes or a Cato.[49] His famous invective against Cusanus, *Invectiva Gregorii Heimburg utriusque iuris doctoris in reverendissimum Patrem Dominum Nicolaum de Cusa,* itself belongs to the genre of writing which humanists like Petrarch, Boccaccio, Poggio, and Valla used to their advantage.[50] It is also worth noting that like Aeneas and other humanists, who were much interested in geography, Heimburg showed a keen awareness of the importance of geographical knowledge. After discussing the *studia humanitatis* in 1449, for example, Heimburg and Aeneas got involved in a detailed discussion on the origin of the Nile.[51] With regard to his writings, it is to be noted that the *Confutatio primatus papae* is a work written not by Heimburg, but by Matthias Döring, although it was once regarded as one of the most remarkable, sometimes infamous controversial works written with Heimburg's pen.[52]

Heimburg, however, was not inclined merely to cite and imitate ancient writers to adorn his speeches or writings. He used them in his practical way. What he appreciated in the new learning was not mere imitation of classical style and rhetoric, but an ability to express one's own thought and feeling in one's own language. He liked Plutarch's statement that Cicero spoke spontaneously,[53] and was opposed to what he considered the thoughtless and often frivolous attitude of Italian humanists. He would therefore not attempt to transport Italian humanist learning indiscriminately into Germany. For all his admiration and love of classical writers, he did not wish to become their slavish follower. He

---

[49] Goldast, *Monarchia,* II, p. 1593.

[50] The text is in Goldast, *Monarchia,* II, pp. 1626-1631 and Freher-Struve, *Rerum,* II pp. 255-265. On invectives used by humanists, see Voigt, *Die Wiederbelebung,* I, pp. 75, 123 184, 203, 364, II, 150-153, 448-456.

[51] Joachimsohn, *Heimburg,* p. 104; *Der Briefwechsel,* pp. 80-81.

[52] The humanist Matthias Flacius Illyricus (1520-1575) first published the text as *Scriptum contra primatum papae, ante annos 100 compositum . . .* (Magdeburg, 1550). MS. Jones 14 of the Bodleian Library, Oxford contains on ff. 315ᵛ-327 an English translation (*The confutacion of the popes supremacie wrytten by Gregori of Hemburgh*), done probably in 1590. On the authorship of the *Confutatio,* see Bruno Gebhardt, "Die Confutatio primatus papae," *Neues Archiv der Gesellschaft für ältere deutsche Geschichtskunde* 12 (1887): 517-530; P. Albert, "Die Confutatio primatus papae, ihre Quelle und ihr Verfasser," *Historisches Jahrbuch* 11 (1890): 439-490.

[53] It seems clear from the following that Heimburg liked spontaneous speech. Joachimsohn, *Heimburg,* p. 304: ". . . felicissimum autem est, non quidem apium more sparsa oolligere, sed vermium exemplo, quorum ex visceribus sericum prodit, ex se ipso sapere loqui. Quod Ciceronem scisse tradit Plutarcus . . ."

said, as he spoke in Pope Pius II's presence at the Congress of Mantua in 1459, that if his manner of speech was new and different from what the pope was accustomed to at the curia, it was because his was the German way.[54] As his relations with the pope deteriorated, it became increasingly apparent that Heimburg regarded the pope as a paradigm of the superficial imitator of ancient writers.[55] It is perhaps not too far-fetched to see in this conflict between the two, as some have done,[56] a contrast between the Italian and German character, although the real situation was not so simple as to justify the facile analysis.

It seems widely recognized that local circumstances moulded the character of humanism in each country. Humanism in Germany was essentially an outgrowth of humanism in Italy, but it was an intellectual movement among educated persons on a smaller scale than in Italy. It also retained a more traditional and medieval character than the new learning which was pursued by Italian humanists.[57] It was pointed out in 1893 that in Swabia, the Palatinate, and Austria the secular princely courts, the imperial cities, and the universities were the places where humanism first grew, while in Franconia the ecclesiastical princes encouraged the growth of humanism in their courts.[58] This rather simple comparison may no longer be acceptable to recent scholarship. But it did point to the complex nature of the humanist movement in Germany. Heimburg as an early humanist already manifested one of the features of German humanism, that is, to conserve what was native and traditional while accepting from outside the benefits of the new learning. Some humanists in Germany were particularly interested in translating the writings of Italian humanists into German, thereby satisfying not only their thirst for humanist learning, but also their desire to remember their past. Some of Conrad Celtis's works, such as his edition of Roswitha's plays and of the *Ligurinus* of Gunther the Cistercian, and the various translations or *Teutschungen* of Niklas von Wyle may be mentioned as examples of this romantic, nationalistic feature of German humanism. Heimburg himself seems to have consciously emphasized the importance of this approach, when he

---

[54] Joachimsohn, *Heimburg,* p. 105.

[55] Goldast, *Monarchia,* II, p. 1594: "Quod vero me loquacem facit, vir omni pica dicacior, quid dixerim? . . . Fateor quippe me ventositati verborum pro tempore operam dedisee: at non ita ut civilis & Canonicae traditionis praecepta oontempserim: quae ille ne unquam quidem olfecit, nuda verbositate oontentus."

[56] Ullmann, *Reformers,* I, p. 196; Voigt, *Die Wiederbelebung,* II, pp. 285-290.

[57] A classic statement of this point of view is Gerhard Ritter, "Die geschichtliche Bedeutung des deutschen Humanismus," *Historische Zeitechrift* 127 (1923): 393-453.

[58] Max Herrmann, *Albrecht von Eyb und die Frühzeit des deutschen Humanismus* (Berlin, 1893), p. 3.

translated his own Latin work into German.[59] To see in Heimburg a full-fledged nationalist in the modern sense of the term would be premature and exaggerated. But it cannot be denied that Heimburg was affected by the nationalistic consciousness which was growing in Germany at that time.

To understand the position which Heimburg held in the early development of humanism in Germany, it is best to turn to the much discussed letter of Heimburg to his young friend Johannes Rot (c. 1430-1506).[60] It was sent from Nuremberg to Rome on March 6, 1454, in reply to Rot's letter to Heimburg which has been lost. Born in Wemding in Swabia as the son of a shoemaker, the hard-working Rot studied at Italian universities and took the doctorate in canon and civil law at the University of Padua.[61] He is said to have been on friendly terms with humanists like Poggio and Guarino, but we have only evidence of his correspondence with Filelfo.[62] In 1454 Rot was studying rhetoric in Rome under Lorenzo Valla, who was professor of rhetoric there at that time. In the letter to Rot, Heimburg argued that jurisprudence is superior to rhetoric and that Rot should not waste his time studying rhetoric. In his lengthy reply to Heimburg, dated May 16, 1454,[63] Rot strongly defended rhetoric against law and criticized the lawyers for their obscure language. Many humanists since Petrarch and Boccaccio had engaged in a polemic against the lawyers, and Rot's teacher Valla himself wrote in his letter to Candido Decembrio between 1431 and 1433

---

[59] Joachimsohn, *Heimburg,* pp. 197-204. We must note that the vernacular translations of Italian humanist writings were also made outside of Germany. See Kristeller, "European Diffusion," pp. 84-86.

[60] See above, n. 48 (3). Cod. lat. mon. 518 was written in its entirety by Hermann Schedel, while some parts of Cod. lat. mon. 519 were written by his cousin Hartmann Schedel. Hermann used a portion of Heimburg's letter in his own letter to Johannes Ratisbona. See *Hermann Schedels Briefwechsel* (1452-1478), ed. Paul Joachimsohn (Tübingen, 1893), pp. 76-77.

[61] On Johannes Rot (Rott, Roth), see *Allgemeine Deutsche Biographie,* XIV (Leipzig, 1881), 186-188; Max Herrmann, "Ein Brief an Albrecht von Eyb," *Germania—Vierteljahrsschrift für deutsche Alterthumskunde* 33, n.s. 21 (1888): 499-502; Joachimsohn, *Heimburg,* pp. 19, 99-102, 106-107, 112, 158, 170, 251, 274; Herrmann, *Albrecht,* pp. 127-137.

[62] See Joachimsohn, *Heimburg,* p. 106, n. 3.

[63] Joachimsohn, *Heimburg,* pp. 310-316. The text is in Cod. lat. mon. 518 ff. 109-121ᵛ (*Johannis Rot pro defensione retoricae contra jus civile et jurisperiti et oratoris inter se comparatio*) and Cod. lat. mon. 519 ff. 51-64 (*Johannis Rott pro defensione retorice contra jus civile et jurisperiti et oratoris inter se comparatio*). Joachimsohn, *Heimburg,* pp. 310-316, gave excerpts from the letter and Rupprich, *Die Frühzeit,* pp. 282-289, reprinted them. Hermann Schedel used a portion of this letter in his letter to Heinrich Lur. See *Hermann Schedels Briefwechsel,* pp. 157-158.

an incisive attack on lawyers such as Bartolus, Baldus, and Accursius.[64] This exchange of letters between Heimburg and Rot, then, was based on a well established tradition among the humanists.

Besides the difference of their views of humanism, personal factors no doubt played some role in this exchange. Heimburg was by then a strong critic of Aeneas Sylvius, but Rot was desirous of maintaining friendly relations with the future pope, whose help may later have enabled him to obtain a position in the Imperial Chancery. But more important was a battle of principles which was manifested in this literary exchange. Heimburg, who was after all a lawyer, regarded rhetoric as a means to an end. No matter how attractive and interesting studies of classical writers were, they were significant only as a preliminary step toward the study of law, which was to him nothing less than the true philosophy.[65] Jurisprudence was a more serious subject than rhetoric to him. What is notable, however, is that Heimburg fought for jurisprudence in typically humanistic fashion, using many citations from ancient authors. He felt close to classical writers and often cited them. But he had reservations about those who merely copied and repeated the words of ancient writers. Rot, on the other hand, seems to have been taken in by the new learning. In his letter to Albrecht von Eyb, Rot called himself the first champion of humanistic studies in Germany.[66] His answer to Heimburg is more replete than Heimburg's with references to and citations from classical authors, such as Plato, Aristotle, Seneca, Cicero, Virgil, Pliny, Lactantius, Cato, and Solon, as well as his teacher Valla. Both of these men held a doctorate in canon and civil law from an Italian university. But Heimburg was condemned by Aeneas as a heretic, while Rot paved the way under Aeneas's patronage for future advancement in his ecclesiastical career.[67] The contrast was due not so much to their attitude toward

---

[64] For an acoount of this famous debate, see Myron P. Gilmore, *Humanists and Jurists: Six Studies in the Renaissance* (Cambridge, Massachusetts, 1963), pp. 30-32; Guido Kisch, *Gestalten und Probleme aus Humanismus und Jurisprudenz* (Berlin, 1969), pp. 116-124.

[65] In his doctoral speech Heimburg calls the canon law the true philosophy and jurisprudence. Joachimsohn, *Heimburg,* p. 302.

[66] Joachimsohn, *Heimburg,* p. 107, n. 1: "Se fore Germanorum primum, qui artes, que humane intitulantur, amplexus sit." Andreas Bavarus in his letter to Albrecht van Eyb criticized Rot's arrogance. The text of the letter, which is in Cod. lat. mon. 504 f. 2ᵛ (*Andreae Bavari ad Albertum de Eyb epistola de arrogantia Johannis Rottae, qui dicere conatur se esse Germanorum primum, qui artes humanas amplexus sit*), is printed in Herrmann, "Ein Brief," 502-506.

[67] Rot became Bishop of Lavant in 1468 and Bishop of Breslau in 1482. In 1505 he was made Chancellor of the University of Breslau. He was a friend of Rudolf von Rüdesheim, who played an important role in the excommunication of Heimburg. On

humanism as to their personality and other factors. But it does show that there was a variety of views on humanism among those Germans who were affected by the *studia humanitatis*.[68]

All too often Gregor Heimburg has been either severely criticized as a fanatical enemy of the Church and a "child of the devil" or excessively praised as the "Citizen-Luther before the days of Luther." We have instead proposed to examine his development as a humanist and the position which he held in the early growth of humanism in Germany. It would seem that his exposure to the new learning during his study of law in Padua rather than his education in transalpine schools prepared him as one of the earliest humanists in his country. The loss of documents and archival materials concerning his youth and some of the institutions with which he was associated makes it difficult to have a fuller understanding of his life. Furthermore, his writings, which were almost always responses to particular circumstances, must be used with caution. Due attention must be given to the emotional stress under which he often worked and the humanistic rhetoric which he, like others, utilized. But the available evidence shows that his main concern as a student of humanist learning was not mere imitation of ancient writers and Italian humanists, but the rise of a humanism based on local traditions and circumstances.[69]

the later career of Rot, see also Hermann Hoffmann, "Aufzeichnungen des Breslauer Domherrn Stanislau Saner (†1535) über die Bisohöfe Rudolf von Rüdesheim und Johann Roth," *Archiv für schleische Kirchengeschichte* 13 (1955): 82-137.

[68] From the point of view of ecclesiastical advancement, Nicolaus Cusanus, another contemporary German, resembles Rot. Cusanus was also a friend of Pope Pius II whom Heimburg criticized. This is no doubt the reason why Johannes Kymeus, author of the *Des Babst Hercules wider die Deutschen* (Wittenberg, 1538) which criticized Cusanus, praises Heimburg on ff. ii-iii in his book.

[69] I am indebted to the American Philosophical Society for a grant which made possible much of the work for this study. While this article was in press, the following study of Heimburg was brought to my notice: Alfred Wendehorst, "Gregor Heimburg," in *Fränkische Lebensbilder,* ed. Gerhard Pfeiffer, IV (Würzburg, 1971), pp. 112-129.

Duke Sigismund and Gregor Heimburg

The return of Sigismund, Duke of Austria and Count of the Tyrol, to Innsbruck on April 27 or 28, 1446, after gaining independence from the seven year guardianship of his cousin King Friedrich III marked the opening of a new chapter in the history of the Tyrol.[1] Upon the death of his father Friedrich IV ("the Old") on June 24, 1439, the cousin Friedrich ("the Young") had become the eleven-year-old Sigismund's guardian in accordance with the family custom, but then taken Sigismund to Graz in defiance of an agreement between himself and Sigismund's advisors.[2] In Graz, which was Sigismund's birthplace, and after 1443 in Wiener Neustadt the king gave his cousin proper education and training.[3] Friedrich's courts in Graz and Wiener Neustadt were not without cultural amenities, although they were less splendid than other Renaissance courts such as the courts of the Montefeltro family at Urbino or of the Gonzaga family in Mantua. Aeneas Sylvius Piccolomini, who joined the Imperial Chancery early in 1443 after abandoning the Council of Basel in November 1442, took note of the young prince of the Tyrol in Graz and urged him in a letter of December 5, 1443, not to discontinue his humanistic studies. In

I wish to thank the American Philosophical Society for a grant which facilitated the necessary travel and research.

[1] Joseph Chmel, *Geschichte Kaiser Friedrichs IV. und seines Sohnes Maximilian I.,* vol. II (Hamburg, 1843), p. 415; Josef Egger, *Geschichte Tirols von den ältesten Zeiten bis in die Neuzeit,* vol. I (Innsbruck, 1872), p. 544; Karl Moeser u. Fritz Dworschak, *Die große Münzreform unter Erzherzog Sigmund von Tirol* (= Öesterreichisehes Münzu- u. Geldwesen im Mittelalter, vol. 7) (Wien, 1936), p. 10.

[2] Chmel, Geschichte, vol. I (Hamburg, 1840), pp. 414-42; P. Justinian Ladurner, "Ueber Herzog Sigmund's Vormundsehaft 1439-1446", *Archiv f. Gesch. u. Alterthumskunde Tirols,* III (1866): 23-140; Egger, *Geschichte,* vol. I, pp. 533- 35. King Friedrich III had freed himself with difficulty in 1435 from the ten-year guardianship under Friedrich IV, Sigismund's father.

[3] Margarete Ortwein, "Der Innsbrucker Hof zur Zeit Erzherzog Sigmunds des Münzreichen," Unpublished Dissertation, Innsbruck 1936 (TLA Innsbruck, Hs. Nr. 5076), p. 11; Alphons Lhotsky, *Quellenkunde zur mittelalterlichen Geschichte Österreichs* (= MIÖG Erg.-Bd. 19) (Graz/Köln, 1963), p. 430; Berthold Sutter, "Die Residenzen Friedrichs III. in Österreich," in: *Ausstellung—Friedrich III.: Kaiserresidenz Wiener Neustadt* (Wien, [1966]), pp. 140-41. See also Bayer. Staatsbibliothek, München, Cod. germ. mon. 895, f. 254ʳ.

response to Sigismund's request, Aeneas even wrote a model love letter on December 13, 1443, in humanistic style.[4]

It was thanks to the strong pressure exerted by the Tyrolese people on Friedrich III that Sigismund was finally permitted to return to Innsbruck in 1446. If the Tyrolese had not shown their willingness to take the arms to free their ruler, Sigismund might have been forced to remain longer in Wiener Neustadt or Vienna under Friedrich's guardianship.[5] When Sigismund returned to Innsbruck, he was accompanied by four "foreign" advisors, Neuberger, Friedrich Hack, Friedrich von Graben and Jakob Vaist, to whom the administration of the court was entrusted.[6] In 1449 Sigismund married Eleonore, the sixth child of King James I of Scotland.[7] The new palace, called the Mitterhof or Mitterburg, which Sigismund built in Innsbruck, had as its household a rather large number of nobles and servants by contemporary standards.[8] Eleonore, who was inclined to literature and who was friendly with Countess Mechthild of the Palatinate, enlivened in no small degree the cultural atmosphere of Sigismund's court.[9]

---

[4] For the text of these letters, see *Der Briefwechsel des Eneas Silvius Piecolomini*, ed. Rudolf Wolkan, in FRA, II. Abt.: *Diplomataria et acta*, vol. 61 (Wien, 1909), pp. 222-36, 245-47. See also Georg Voigt, *Enea Silvio de' Piccolomini, als Papst Pius der Zweite und sein Zeitalter*, vol. I (Berlin, 1856), pp. 287, 292-93; Lhotsky, *Quellenkunde*, p. 395; Sutter, "Die Residenzen," p. 141.

[5] Albert Jäger, "Der Streit der Tiroler Landschaft mit Kaiser Friedrich III. wegen der Vormundschaft über Herzog Sigismund von Österreich von 1439-1446," *AöG*, vol. 49 (1873): 89-264; Otto Stolz, *Geschichte der Stadt Innsbruck* (Innsbruck, 1959), p. 55. The guardianship was to have lasted only four years according to the agreement. See also Egger, *Geschichte*, vol. I, p. 534; Albert Jäger, *Geschichte der landständischen Verfassung Tirols*, vol. 2, Teil 2 (Innsbruck, 1885), p. 14-15.

[6] Chmel, *Geschichte*, vol. II, p. 415; Egger, *Geschichte*, vol. I, p. 545; Ortwein, "Der Innsbrucker Hof", p. 13.

[7] Chmel, *Geschichte*, vol. II, p. 526; Egger, *Geschichte*, vol. I, pp. 548-49; Moeser u. Dworschak, *Die große Münzreform*, p. 16; Margarete Köfler, "Eleonore von Schottland: Versuch einer Biographic", Unpublished Dissertation, Innsbruck 1968 (TLA Innsbruck Hs. Nr. 5847), pp. 1-7, 14-32; Georg Mutsehlechner, "Nikolaus Cusanus und Eleonore von Schottland", in: *Cusanus-Gedächtnisschrift* (= *Forschungen zur Rechts- u. Kulturgeschichte*, vol. 3, hg. Nikolaus Grass) (Innsbruck/München 1970), p. 251. Cf. *Cod. germ. mon.* 895, f. 254ᵛ. On Eleonore's life and writings, see also *Die deutsche Literatur des Mittelalters*, Verfasserlexikon, vol. I, ed. W. Stammler (Berlin u. Leipzig, 1933), col. 543-47; vol. V ed. K. Langosch (Berlin, 1955), col. 191.

[8] Stolz, *Geschichte*, p. 55.

[9] Karl Kirchlechner, *Aus den Tagen Herzog Sigmunds des Münzreichen und Kaiser Maximilians I.* (Linz, 1884), p. 11; Hans Kramer, *Das Zeitalter des Humanismus in Tirol* [Ewiger Humanismus: Schriften der österr. humanistischen Gesellschaft in

Although the Duke was good-natured, generous and popular among his people, he began to lose control of himself in search of pleasure and merriment especially towards the end of his life. He has been much criticized for his love of display, game and attractive women.[10] But it is probably too much to say that his personal conduct was extraordinarily different from that of many other rulers in his period.

Convinced of the importance of legal advisors, Sigismund began, soon after his return to Innsbruck, to surround himself with advisors, such as Ulrich von Matsch, Wolfgang von Freundsberg, Ludwig von Landsee, Parcival von Annenberg, Heinrich von Morsberg and Oswald Sebner von Reifenstein.[11] The Tyrol, like other regions in Europe, had a long tradition of legal advisors to its rulers. Many able advisors had helped the rulers of the Tyrol in the past with success. Of Sigismund's advisors, a relatively small number resided in the ducal palace in Innsbruck and served the Duke daily. The rest were scattered all over the Duke's lands. Bishop Johann Hinderbach of Trent, Abbot Kaspar Augsburger von St. Georgenberg, Dr. Johann Fuchsmagen from Hall were among the foremost of these advisors.[12] The Gradner brothers, who were Sigismund's

Innsbruck, 13. Heft] (Innsbruck, 1947), p. 7; Lhotsky, *Quellenkunde*, p. 430. On Mechthild, see also Philipp Strauch, *Pfalzgräfin Mechthild in ihren literarischen Beziehungen. Ein Bild aus der schwäbischen Litteraturgeschichte*, d. 15. Jhs. (Tübingen, 1883).

[10] Ludwig Pastor, *Geschichte der Päpste im Zeitalter der Renaissance*, vol. 2. (3rd and 4th ed.: Freiburg i. B., 1904), p. 140; Friedrich Hegi, *Die geächteten Räte des Erzherzog Sigmund von Österreich und ihre Beziehungen zur Sehweiz 1487-1499* (Innsbruck, 1910), p. 2; Moeser u. Dworschak, *Die große Münzreform*, pp. 14-15; Hans Kramer, "Die Grundlinien der Außenpolitik Herzog Sigmunds van Tirol (1427-1496)," *Tiroler Heimat*, vol. 11. (1947): 69.

[11] Egger, *Geschichte*, vol. I, p. 545; Moeser u. Dworschak, *Die große Münzreform*, p. 16; Ortwein, "Der Innsbrucker Hof," pp. 13-14.

[12] Anton Zingerle, *Der Humanismus in Tirol unter Erzherzog Sigmund dem Münzreichen* [Fest-Gruß aus Innsbruck an die XLII. Versammlung deutscher Philologen und Schulmänner in Wien] (Innsbruck, 1843), p. 24. On Johannes Hinderbach, see Zingerle, *Der Humanismus*, pp. 25, 27-31; Viotor v. Hofmann-Wellenhof, "Leben und Sohriften des Doctor Johannes Hinderbach, Bischofs von Trient (1465-1486)," *Zs. d. Ferdinandeums*, 3. Folge, 37. Heft (1893), pp. 203-62; Alfred A. Strnad, "Johannes Hinderbachs Obedienz-Ansprache vor Papst Pius II," *Röm. Histor. Mitteil.*, 10. Heft, 1966/67 (1967), pp. 43-183. For Kaspar Augsburger, see Kirchlechner, *Aus den Tagen*, p. 25; Stammler, *Verfasserlexikon*, vol. II, col. 767 -71; Lhotsky, *Quellenkunde*, p. 436. The following deal with Johann Fuchsmagen (Fusemannus): Zingerle, *Der Humanismus*, p. 25; Sebastian Ruf, "Doctor Johannes Fuchsmagen 1469-1510," *Zs. d. Ferdinandeums für Tirol und Vorarlberg*, 3.

favorite advisors, became so influential that Sigismund was eventually forced to exile them in 1456 upon threat of revolt by the nobility.[13]

One of the most famous events in the history of the Tyrol during Sigismund's reign was no doubt a prolonged feud between him and Cardinal Nicolaus Cusanus as Bishop of Brixen. Although serious efforts were made by both parties to solve the problem, the *cause célèbre* lingered on until Cusanus's death in 1464. Only a brief outline of the complex story can be given here.[14] On March 23, 1450, Pope Nicholas V appointed Cusanus Bishop of Brixen in spite of the fact that the Concordat of Vienna of 1448 provided clearly that bishops were to be elected by their chapters. In fact, after the death of Bishop Johann Röttel of Brixen on February 28, 1450, the Brixen chapter had already on March 14 nominated Leonhard Wiesmayer, one of its members and the chancellor of the Duke, and sent his name to the pope for confirmation. As a reason for his appointment of Cusanus the pope cited the clause of the Vienna Concordat about uncanonical elections, as well as the clause permitting the pope to name a worthier person for an urgent reason.[15] Clearly the pope feared that Duke Sigismund would make further inroads upon the prerogative of the see of Brixen unless a person of great talent was provided to the see to resist the Duke. In retrospect, it is doubtful whether this was a good choice. After the successful legatine tour of Germany and the Low Countries in 1450-1451 to preach the Jubilee indulgence, Cusanus took road to Brixen and entered the episcopal city at

---

Folge, 21. Heft (1877), p. 93-119; Langosch, *Verfasserlexikon,* vol. V, col. 246-47; Lhotsky, *Quellenkunde,* pp. 434-36; Köfler, "Eleonore," p. 191.

[13] Albert Jäger, *Die Fehde der Brüder Vigilius und Bernhard Gradner gegen den Herzog Sigmund von Tirol* [Denkschriften der Wiener Akademie, Phil.-hist. Klasse IX] (1859); Hegi, *Die geächteten Räte,* p. 2; Kramer, "Die Grundlinien," p. 69.

[14] The standard account is Albert Jäger, *Der Streit des Cardinals Nicolaus von Cusa mit dem Herzoge Sigismund von Österreich als Grafen von Tirol* (Innsbruck, 1861 reprinted Frankfurt, 1968). See also Bayer. Staatsbibliothek München, Cod. germ. mon. 975; Albert Jäger, "Regesten und urkundliche Daten über das Verhältniss des Cardinals Nicolaus von Cusa, als Bischof von Brixen, zum Herzoge Sigismund von Öesterreich und zu dem Lande Tirol von 1450 bis 1464," *Archiv f. Kunde österr. Geschichtsquellen,* vol. 4 (1850), pp. 297-329 and vol. 7 (1851), pp. 173-86.

[15] The text of the bull is printed in Carl Mirbt, *Quellen zur Geschichte des Papsttums und des römischen Katholizismus* (4th ed.: Tübingen, 1924), pp. 238-40; Karl Zeumer. *Quellensammlung zur Geschichte der Deutschen Reichsverfassung in Mittelalter und Neuzeit* (= Quellensammlungen zum Staats-, Verwaltungs- u. Völkerrecht, vol. II, pt. 2) (2nd ed.: Tubingen, 1913), pp. 266-68.

Easter in 1452.[16] The zeal which the Bishop tried to end abuses such as simony and concubinage and to enforce the monastic rules astonished and alienated many people in the diocese. Despite resistance and opposition, Cusanus carried out reforms often by threatening excommunication. But his efforts to reform the Benedictine convent of Sonnenburg in the Pustertal were extremely unsuccessful, and this issue further damaged the relationship between him and Sigismund, who felt that as Count of the Tyrol he had jurisdiction over the convent. The obstinacy of the Abbess of the convent, Verena von Stuben, as well as Sigismund's financial troubles, made the affair of Sonnenburg unpleasant and exhausting to all who were concerned. In the early stages of the controversy, Sigismund was helped by his advisors such as Parcival von Annenberg and Hans von Kronmetz. But Lorenz Blumenau, who began to serve Sigismund towards the end of 1457, assumed an increasingly important position among the ranks of the Duke's advisors. Born in Prussia around 1415, Blumenau studied liberal arts at Leipzig and then law at the Universities of Padua and of Bologna, where he was influenced by humanism. Before coming to the Tyrol he served as counsel to the Teutonic Knights from 1446.[17]

After the famous alleged attempt by Duke Sigismund on Cusanus's life at Wilten in May of 1457, Cusanus spent most of his time in the remote, well-protected castle of Andraz, which he called St. Raphaelsburg. His letter to Pope Calixtus III about the incident at Wilten caused much alarm and anger in Rome. In October 1457 the pope laid Sigismund and his followers under an interdict, until Cusanus should have been given freedom and security. In reply, Sigismund sent to the "pope better informed" a strong protest on November 1, 1457 after consultation with his legal advisor.[18] On February 6, 1458, Duke Sigismund issued a protest against the interdict for the second time and declared that he

---

[16] For Cusanus's legatine tour, see Josef Koch, *Nikolaus von Cues und seine Umwelt* [Sitzungsber. d. Heidelberger Akademie d. Wissenschaften, Phil.-hist. Kl., Jg. 1944/48] (Heidelberg, 1948), pp. 116-48; Josef Koch, *Der deutsche Kardinal in deutschen Landen. Die Legationsreise des Nikolaus von Kues (1451/52)* [Kleine Schriften d. Cusanus-Gesellschaft, Heft 5] (Trier, 1964). Cusanus's itinerary between 1452 and 1460 is found in Georg Mutschlechner, "Itinerar des Nikolaus von Kues für den Aufenthalt in Tirol (1452-1460)," Grass, *Cusanus-Gedächtnisschrift,* pp. 525-34.

[17] On Lorenz Blumenau, see Hartmut Boockmann, *Laurentius Blumenau. Fürstlicher Rat-Jurist-Humanist (ca. 1415-1484)* (Göttingen, 1965).

[18] There is much ambiguity about the date of the bull. See Jäger, "Regesten", vol. IV, p. 311; Jäger, *Der Streit,* vol. I, pp. 256-57; Voigt, *Enea,* vol. III (Berlin, 1868), p. 334. Joachimsohn (p. 175, n. 6) believes that the legal advisor was Heimburg.

would not recognize it.[19] After a battle at Enneberg on April 5, 1458, in which some of Cusanus's troops under the command of Gabriel Prack surrounded and slaughtered a band of mercenaries and their leader Jobst von Hornstein hired by the nuns of the convent of Sonnenburg,[20] the relationship between the Bishop and the Duke worsened.

With the election of Aeneas Sylvius as Pope Pius II on August 19, 1458, a new stage in the weary feud began. Since the pope was on terms of friendship with both Cusanus and Sigismund, he hoped to effect a reconciliation between them when he called both men to the Congress of Mantua which began in 1459. Sigismund was received with much pomp and accorded an audience with the pope. In order to ease the tension between the two warring parties, the pope even suspended on January 1, 1460, the interdict which Pope Calixtus III had placed on Sigismund and his followers.[21] But the papal mediation remained unsuccessful, and Sigismund left Mantua on November 29,1459, for Innsbruck.

After the Congress of Mantua, the veteran diplomat Blumenau, together with Hans von Kronmetz, presented on July 14, 1460, a strong appeal to the pope in Rome. The appeal, which was probably written by Blumenau himself, was an attempt to explain the controversy from Sigismund's point of view to a pope "who is to be better informed".[22] When the process against Sigismund began in Siena on August 4, 1460, Blumenau appeared before the pope and pleaded Sigismund's case. Four days later, however, a bull was issued which banned Sigismund and his followers, and the Tyrol was placed under an interdict.[23] Blumenau was imprisoned as a heretic, although he managed later to

[19] Jäger, "Regesten", vol. IV, p. 313; Jäger, *Der Streit,* vol. I, p. 270; Voigt, *Enea,* vol. III, p. 335.

[20] On the battle of Enneberg, see Hermann Hallauer, *Die Schlacht im Enneberg. Neue Quellen zur moralischen Wertung des Nikolaus von Kues* [Kleine Schriften d. Cusanus-Gesellschaft, Heft 9] (Trier 1969).

[21] Jäger, *Der Streit,* vol. I, p. 352; Paul Joachimsohn, *Gregor Heimburg* [Historische Abhandlungen aus dem Münchener Seminar, I. Heft] (Bamberg, 1891), p. 187; Boockmann, *Blumenau,* p. 169.

[22] Jäger, "Regesten," vol. IV, p. 324; Voigt, *Enea,* vol. III, p. 365; Joachimsohn, *Heimburg,* pp. 187-88, Boockmann, *Blumenau,* pp. 171-72.

[23] The bull is printed in Melchior Goldast, *Monarchia S. Romana Imperii . . .,* II (Francofordiae, 1614), pp. 1583-86; Marquard Freher, *Rerum Germanicarum scriptores,* ed. B. G. Struve, Bd. II (Argentorati, 1717), pp.197-202. It is also in Cod. germ. mon. 975, f. 26r-37r; Biblioteca Apostolica Vaticana, Cod. Reg. 478, f. 35r-39r, Cod. Reg. 557, f. 72r-74v. On Cod. Reg. 557, see Rudolf Haubst, *Studien zu Nikolaus von Kues und Johannes Wenck* [Beiträge zur Geschichte d. Philosophie u. Theologie d. Mittelalters, Bd. 38, Heft 1] (Münster i. W., 1955), pp. 22-26.

escape. He continued to serve Sigismund until about 1466, but his role among Sigismund's advisors seems to have lessened after 1460.

The man who replaced Blumenau as Sigismund's chief legal advisor was Gregor Heimburg.[24] Born in Schweinfurt around 1400 as the son of the burgher Hans Heimburg, mayor of Schweinfurt four times, Gregor was probably educated at a Latin school attached to the Church of St. Johannis in Schweinfurt.[25] He matriculated in the Faculty of Arts of the University of Vienna on October 13, 1413, as "pauper".[26] After studying probably at some German universities, he moved to the University of Padua in 1421. He was therefore a contemporary of Cusanus at the university who studied there from 1417 to 1423. An intensive study of canon and Roman law, which he pursued under such famous law professors as Prosdocimus de Comitibus, Heinricus de Alano, Paulus de Dotis and Jacobus de Zocchis de Ferraria,[27] exposed him also to humanistic studies which were then spreading in Italian universities. Heimburg, who was already referred to as *Legum doctor* at the time of his doctoral examination, received the degree of *Doctor in jure canonico* in Padua on February 7, 1430.[28] He then attended the Council of Basel in 1432 as representative of the Archbishop of

---

[24] On Gregor Heimburg in general, see Johann Arnold Ballenstedt, *Vitae Gregorii de Heimburg . . . brevis narratio* (Helmstadii 1737); Clemens Brockhaus, *Gregor von Heimburg* (Leipzig, 1861); Joachimsohn, *Heimburg*.

[25] On the Latin school in Schweinfurt, where the humanists Conrad Celtis and Johann Cuspinian also studied, see V. Völcker, *Geschichte der Studienanstalt Schweinfurt,* vol. I (Schweinfurt, 1882); Karl Ziegler, *Geschichte des humanistischen Gymnasiums in Schweinfurt (1634-1934) und der Lateinischen Schule daselbst* (Schweinfurt, 1934); Friedrich Beyschlag, "Die älteste Geschichte der lateinischen Schule in Schweinfurt (bis 1554)," *Schweinfurter Tagblatt,* Nr. 113, 15. Mai 1905 and Nr. 114, 16. Mai 1905. Joachimsohn, *Heimburg,* p. 2, says: ". . . gab es damals wohl noch keine städtische Schule."

[26] *Die Matrikel der Universität Wien,* vol. I (Graz/Köln, 1956), p. 99; Albin F. Scherhaufer, "Jung-Schweinfurt auf hohen Schulen," *Schweinfurter Heimatblätter,* vol. 26 (1957): 55-56. Joschimsohn, *Heimburg,* p. 2 n. 10, states: "Eine deutsche Universität hat Heimburg, soweit wir sehen, nicht besucht".

[27] Joachimsohn, *Heimburg,* p. 303.

[28] Arnold Luschin v. Ebengreuth, "Quellen zur Geschichte deutscher Rechtshörer in Italien," *Sitzungsberichte d. phil.-hist. Kl. d. kaiserlichen Akademie d. Wissenschaften [Wien],* vol. 124 (1891): 11. Abh., p. 23; *Acta graduum academicorum Gymnasii Patavini ab anno MCCCCVI ad annum MCCCCL,* ed. C. Zonta and I. Brotto (Patavini, 1922), pp. 166-67. It is probable that Heimburg's legal studies were done mostly between 1421 and 1428, and that he then completed the requirements for the doctorate in canon law in 1430.

Mainz,[29] and more or less opposed Cusanus in the dispute about Ulrich of Manderscheid, the Archbishop-elect of Trier.[30] Contrary to the oft-asserted view of many writers, Heimburg was not Aeneas Sylvius's secretary at the council, nor was he especially closely associated with Aeneas.

Thereafter Heimburg became legal advisor to the city of Nürnberg and continued to serve in this capacity almost continuously until 1461, although his services were not confined to Nürnberg during that time.[31] On January 20, 1458,[32] he acquired a position under Duke Albrecht VI of Austria. It was apparently in Albrecht's court in Vienna that Sigismund first met Gregor Heimburg on May 11, 1458.[33] At the Congress of Mantua, Heimburg made three speeches in defense of the Duke of Saxony, Duke Albrecht and Duke Sigismund.[34] He was, however, not serving Duke Sigismund exclusively at that time. To Pope Pius II's great embarrassment, Heimburg alluded in his speech on behalf of Duke Sigismund to the pope's early life by mentioning the love letter

[29] Joachimsohn, *Heimburg,* pp. 18-19. For his speech delivered on November 29, 1432 in Basel, see *Deutsche Reichstagsakten,* vol. X/2 (Göttingen, 1957), pp. 651-56.

[30] On the 1430 episcopal election of Trier, see Erich Meuthen, *Das Trierer Schisma von 1430 auf dem Basler Konzil* [Bücherreihe d. Cusanus-Gesellschaft, vol. 1] (Münster i. W., 1964); Morimichi Watanabe, "The Episcopal Election of 1430 in Trier and Nicholas of Cusa," *Church History,* 34 (1970): 299-316.

[31] Joachimsohn, *Heimburg,* pp. 42-45. His letters of commission issued, respectively, on 4 February 1435, 28 January 1444, 20 December 1450, 20 January 1455 and 19 May 1457 have been preserved at Bayer. Staatsarchiv Nürnberg, 35 neue Laden, Urk. 1575, 1576, 1579, 1677 and 1578.

[32] Joseph Chmel, *Materialien zur österreichischen Geschichte aus Archiven und Bibliotheken,* vol. II (Wien, 1838), pp. 143-44; Jäger, "Regesten," vol. IV, p. 312; Voigt, *Enea,* vol. III, p. 335; Joachimsohn, *Heimburg,* p. 158.

[33] Jäger, "Regesten," vol. IV, p. 315; Jäger, *Der Streit,* vol. I, p. 300; Joachimsohn, *Heimburg,* p. 158.

[34] Heimburg's three speeches in Mantua [(1) October 29, 1449, for Duke Albrecht of Austria; (2) November 12, 1449, for Duke Wilhelm of Saxony; and (3) November 21, 1449, for Duke Sigismund] have been preserved in Bayer. Staatsbibliothek München, Cod. lat. mon. 522, f. 150-63^r [(1), f. 156 - 60^v; (2), f. 150-55; (3), f. 161^v-63^v]. See also Cod. lat. mon. 3786, f. 173^r-74^r for a portion of the speech (1) and Cod. lat. mon. 4016, f. 15^v-18^r and 13^r-15^v for speeches (1) and (2). Cod. Cent. V. App. 15. of the Stadtbibliothek in Nürnberg also contains these three speeches on f. 247-53^v. On the Congress of Mantua, see Voigt, *Enea,* vol. III, pp. 54-110; Giovanni B. Picotti, *La dieta di Mantova e la politica de' Veneziani* [Miscellanea di storia Veneta, Bd. 3, IV] (Venezia 1912).

which the pope had written in 1443 for the Duke, the then ward of King Friedrich III.[35] As the feud between the Duke and the Bishop worsened, the Duke took Heimburg into his service in 1460 on a permanent basis.

The accession of Heimburg to the ranks of Sigismund's advisors seems to have affected the Duke's moves promptly. After the announcement of the ban against Sigismund on August 8, 1460, in Siena, which we referred to above, one of Sigismund's most important appeals to Pope Pius II was issued in Innsbruck on August 13, 1460.[36] There is no doubt that the appeal was authored by Heimburg.[37] This radical appeal to a future pope as well as to a general council placed Heimburg in the forefront of the ducal advisory group. His advice was henceforth eagerly sought by the Duke, who paid him handsomely. It is known that on one occasion the Duke gave Heimburg as a gift a gilded bowl stuffed with ducats.[38]

In assessing Heimburg's role in Sigismund's court in Innsbruck, it is important to note, first of all, that Heimburg was influenced by humanism. As we have seen above, Sigismund became acquainted with Aeneas Sylvius in Graz. It has been asserted that as the youthful Duke's teacher Aeneas had much influence on Sigismund in humanistic studies.[39] Although this view seems unacceptable, it is conceivable that Sigismund received stimulus from the foremost leader of contemporary humanists. After returning to Innsbruck, Sigismund began to encourage humanistic studies whenever possible.[40] It cannot be denied that he himself was not strongly interested in the pursuit of humanistic studies, but he supported them probably because it was something which contemporary rulers were expected to do. A collection of manuscripts in Sigismund's court was increased thanks to his purchases from Augsburg and

[35] Voigt, *Enea,* vol. III, p. 100-101; Joschimsohn, *Heimburg,* p. 204.

[36] The text is in Freher-Struve, *Rerum,* vol. II, p. 203-06. See also Jäger, "Regesten," vol. IV, p. 325; Joachimsohn, *Heimburg,* pp. 188-89.

[37] Joachimsohn, *Heimburg,* p. 188; Boockmann, *Blumenau,* p. 175; Lhotsky, *Quellentunde,* p. 431.

[38] TLA Innsbruck, Raitbuch, vol. I, 1460/61, f. 242[v]. See M. Mayr-Adlwang, "Urkunden und Regesten aus dem k. k. Statthalterei-Archiv in Innsbruck (1364-1490)," *Jb. d. kunsthistor. Sammlungen d. allerhöchsten Kaiserhauses,* vol. XX (1899), p. CLVIII, Nr. 17783; Heinrich Hammer, "Literarische Beziehungen und musikalisches Leben des Hofes Herzog Siegmunds von Tirol," *Zs. d. Ferdinandeums f. Tirol u. Vorarlberg,* 3. Folge, 43. Heft (1899), p. 80.

[39] Hammer, "Literarische Beziehungen," p. 73.

[40] Zingerle, *Der Humanismus,* p. 22; Hammer, "Literarische Beziehungen," p. 72; Lhotsky, *Quellenkunde,* p. 430. Cf. Kramer, *Das Zeitalter,* p. 5.

Ulm.[41] Poets and scholars were welcomed at his court. Perhaps the most famous of the latter group were Johannes Fuchsmagen and Heinrich Stainhöwel.[42] The French-educated Duchess Eleonore was also instrumental in developing an atmosphere conducive to humanistic activities at the court. She seems to have exchanged books frequently with Duke Albrecht of Bavaria to enlighten herself.[43] Her own translation of the French romance, *Ponthus et Sidoine,* into German, done between 1449 and 1456, is one of the examples of her efforts along these lines.[44] As Duchess Regent during her husband's frequent absences from Innsbruck, she seems to have shown sympathy and respect for Cusanus, the learned Bishop of Brixen, despite his struggle against her husband. Of Sigismund's advisors in residence, Blumenau was very much interested in humanistic studies, although he himself left no humanistic writing. He had a large library and sought new manuscripts during his busy career.[45] Since Innsbruck was neither the site of a university nor an episcopal residence, the most advantageous ground from which to develop humanistic studies was no doubt the ducal court of Sigismund. In coming to the court in Innsbruck, therefore, Heimburg could expect a warm welcome from a prince and his followers who understood and sympathized with Heimburg's humanistic interests.

It was the spirit of humanism which influenced Heimburg when he wrote many appeals in defense of Sigismund's cause. His famous apology[46] to Theodore Laelius, Auditor of the Rota and Bishop of Feltre, has many references to classical writers. An exchange of invectives between Cusanus and Heimburg in 1461 shows well that in criticizing each other, these graduates of the University of Padua were using a humanistic form of literary expression which was widely used by humanists at that time.[47] When Heimburg led a ducal

[41] Stammler, *Verfasserlexikon,* vol. I, col. 544; Kramer, *Das Zeitalter,* p. 6.

[42] Stainhöwel translated Boccaccio's *De claris mulieribus* in 1473 for Eleonore. *Stammler Verfasserlexikon,* vol. I, col. 544; Lhotsky, *Quellenkunde,* p. 430.

[43] Kirchlechner, *Aus den Tagen,* p. 17.

[44] Zingerle, *Der Humanismus,* p. 22; Stammler, *Verfasserlexikon,* vol. I, col. 545-47; Lhotsky, *Quellenkunde,* p. 430; Köfler, "Eleonore," pp. 184-88.

[45] His chronicle of the Teutonic Knights in Prussia was not humanistic in orientation although some of his letters show the influence of humanism. Kramer, *Das Zeitalter,* p. 10; Boockmann, *Blumenau,* pp. 208-26.

[46] Freher-Struve, *Rerum,* vol. II, pp. 228-66.

[47] Heimburg's invective against Cusanus is printed in Goldast, *Monarchia,* vol. II, pp. 1626-31; Freher-Struve, *Rerum,* vol. II, p. 266-66. See also Cod. lat. mon. 215, f. 324r-27r; Cod. lat. mon. 3550, f. 369r-78v; Cod. Reg. 557, f. 79r-86v. On the use

delegation to Venice in November 1461 for peace negotiations between the Duke and Cusanus,[48] he came to a republic where considerable humanistic activities had taken place since the middle of the fifteenth century. Received by the Doge Pasquale Malipiero and the Senate on November 27, Heimburg, as spokesman of the ducal delegation, is reported to have made brilliant speeches.[49] Heimburg the humanist rose to the occasion and carried out his task well.

A second factor which we must note in our assessment of Heimburg's role in the ducal court is that while in Sigismund's service, Heimburg championed the cause of conciliarism. The relationship between humanism and conciliarism is not very difficult to establish, as is shown by the presence of humanists at the Councils of Constance and of Basel.[50] Unlike Aeneas Sylvius and Nicolaus Cusanus who had left the conciliar party, Heimburg still clung to conciliarism. The development of conciliarism had certainly had some effect on the Tyrol itself. The role which Sigismund's father Friedrich IV played in the flight of Pope John XXIII from the Council of Constance is well known.[51] Heimburg himself had acquired a first-hand knowledge of the workings of a council when he went to Basel in 1432. It was becoming increasingly popular to appeal to a general council to solve various problems related to ecclesiastical matters. On January 27, 1451, for example, the cathedral chapter of Brixen appealed in Salzburg to a better informed pope or to a general council.[52] This practice was pushed further, until appeals began to be made to a future council.

Pope Pius II was especially concerned about the increased use of the method in the Church. On January 18, 1460, four days after the solemn closing

---

of invectives by humanists, see Georg Voigt, *Die Wiederbelebung des classischen Alterthums oder das erste Jahrhundert des Humanismus* (2nd ed.: Berlin, 1880-81), vol. I, pp. 75, 123, 184, 203, 364, vol. II pp. 150-53, 448-66.

[48] Jäger, *Der Streit*, vol. II, p. 257; Joachimsohn, *Heimburg*, p. 242; [Hans Hörtnagl] "Eine tirolische Gesandtechaft in Venedig," *Innsbrucker Nachrichten*, Samstag, 4. Sept. 1926, Nr. 203, p. 7.

[49] Cod. germ. mon. 975. f. 318r-19r. See Jäger, *Der Streit*, vol. II, pp. 257-69; Joachimsohn, *Heimburg*, pp. 212 n. 4, 240 n. 4, 242.

[50] Paul Lehmann, "Konstanz und Basel als Büchermärkte während der großen Kirchenversammlungen," *Zs. d. deutschen Vereins f. Buchwesen u. Schrifttum*, IV (1921), pp. 6-11, 17-27, reprinted in his *Erforschung des Mittelalters*, vol. I (Stuttgart, 1959), pp. 253-80.

[51] Anselm Sparber, *Kirchengeschichte Tirols* (Innsbruck, 1957), p. 23; idem, *Die Brixner Furstbischöfe im Mittelalter* (Bozen, 1966), p. 126; Alois Leehthaler, *Geschichte Tirols* (Innsbruck, 1970), pp. 69-70, 80.

[52] Jäger, "Regesten," vol. IV, p. 300.

of the Congress of Mantua,[53] he issued the famous bull *Execrabilis* in which he strongly prohibited the practice of appealing from the pope's authority to a general council.[54] Despite the pope's stern warning against any move towards conciliar solutions, Heimburg, who was, as we have seen, the author of Sigismund's strong protest of August 13, 1460,[55] appealed to a future pope as well as to a future general council concerning the Tyrolese affair. This was his first decisive step as Sigismund's advisor. According to Heimburg, the council was already overdue.

On September 9, 1460, shortly after Blumenau's return to Innsbruck from Siena, Sigismund again appealed to a future pope and a future council. The appeal, which was probably drawn up by Heimburg, was sent out to the Archbishop of Salzburg, the Bishop of Freising, the Doge of Venice, the Duke of Milan and other princes.[56] In the meantime, the cathedral chapter of Brixen also appealed on September 2 and 23 from the ill-informed to the better-informed pope.[57] With these appeals to a future pope and a future council, the tone of the feud between Cusanus and the Duke was drastically changed. It was no longer a controversy within the limits approved by the Church, but it went far beyond them. No wonder that Pope Pius II, in his breve of October, 1460, sent to the City Councils of Nürnberg and of Würzburg, condemned and excommunicated Heimburg.[58] The pope also requested the city councils to confiscate Heimburg's property and denounced him as a babbler, an agitator and even as the son of the devil.[59] The excommunication of the Duke and his followers was announced on November 2. Eleven days later the pope ordered the bull of excommunication to be sent out to all spiritual and secular princes. Finally the pope issued a decree that the excommunicated Heimburg be arrested.[60]

[53] The dating of the bull is a matter of controversy. See Voigt, *Enea,* vol. III, pp. 101- 03, Joachimsohn, *Heimburg,* p. 179; Picotti, *La dieta,* pp. 11-12.

[54] For the text, see Mirbt, *Quellen,* pp. 242-43.

[55] See n. 36 above.

[56] Cod. germ. mon. 975, f. 12^{v}-25^{v}. See Jäger, *Der Streit,* vol. II, p. 117; Voigt, *Enea,* vol. III, pp. 380-81; Joachimsohn, *Heimburg,* p. 189.

[57] Jäger, "Regesten," vol. IV, p. 326.

[58] Goldast, *Monarchia,* vol. II, p. 1591; Freher-Struve, *Rerum,* vol. II, pp. 208-10. See also Cod. germ. mon. 975, f. 227^{r}-28^{v}; Cod. Reg. 557, f. 76^{v}; Cod. Cent. V. App. 15., f. 238^{v}-39^{r} On this breve, see Jäger, "Regesten," vol. IV, p. 329; Joachimsohn, *Heimburg,* p.194; Lhotsky, *Quellenbunde,* pp. 431-32.

[59] Voigt, *Enea,* vol. III, pp. 382-83.

[60] Jäger, *Der Streit,* vol. II, p. 148; Voigt, *Enea,* vol. III, p. 383.

In sharp reaction to the condemnation Heimburg issued a new appeal in January 1461 in his own defence. In this appeal, which is perhaps the most widely read of his appeals, Heimburg strongly supported the doctrine of the supremacy of the council over the pope.[61] It is notable that during the same month he represented Sigismund at an assembly at Cheb (Eger), where he gained a promise of support from King George of Podebrady.[62] But the process against Sigismund and his followers as heretics had begun on January 8, 1461,[63] and no doubt Heimburg's position within the Innsbruck court deteriorated as time went by. It was probably because of these changing circumstances that Heimburg began to look for an advisory position elsewhere. On February 22, 1461, he was hired by Diether von Isenburg, the Archbishop-elect of Mainz, who was deeply involved in a feud with the pope over the payment for his pallium.[64] We must note in this connection that Diether's appeal issued at the Diet of Nürnberg on February 23, 1461, which was probably authored by Heimburg, also appealed to a future council.[65] Soon thereafter Heimburg even went to France to find support for the idea of a new council.[66]

---

[61] The Latin text, which is found in Cod. germ. mon. 975, f. 228^v-34^r, is printed in Goldast, *Monarchia,* vol. II, pp. 12 [5] 92-95; Freher-Struve, *Rerum,* vol. II, pp. 211-14. Its German translation, done probably by Heimburg himself, is in Cod. germ. mon. 975, f. 298^r-306^v, as well as in Joachimsohn, *Heimburg,* pp. 197-204. The appeal is also found in the following manuscripts: Univ.-Bibliothek Leipzig, Cod. 1092, f. 33 -36; Stadtarchiv Mainz, Nr. 26, Sammelkasten II, 436; Cod. lat. mon. 215, f. 226^r-28^r; Cod. Cent. V. App. 15, f. 239^r-41^r; Biblioteca Apostolica Vatioana, Cod. Palat. 362, f. 87^v, Cod. Reg. 557, f. 77^r-78^v; Bibliotheca Palat. Vindobonensis, Cod. 3244, f. 1297-32V; Herzogliche Bibliothek Wolfenbuttel, Cod. Wolfenb. 332, f. 16^r-17^v; Universitäts-Bibliothek Würzburg, Cod. M. oh. f. 232^v-33^v. See also Jäger, "Regesten," vol. VII, p. 175; Jäger, *Der Streit,* vol. II, p. 184; Voigt, *Enea,* vol. III, pp. 385-87.

[62] Joachimsohn, *Heimburg,* pp. 208-9; Frederick G. Heymann, *George of Bohemia. King of Heretics* (Princeton, 1965), p. 415.

[63] Goldast, *Monarchia,* vol. II, p. 1579; Jäger, *Der Streit,* vol. II, p. 172; Voigt, *Enea,* vol. II, p. 404.

[64] Joachimsohn, *Heimburg,* p. 109; Boockmann, *Blumenau,* p. 179; Albert Kirnberger, *Diether von Isenberg* (Mainz, 1950), pp. 18-22; Adalbert Erler, *Mittelalterliche Rechtsgutachten our Mainzer Stiftsfehde, 1459-1463* (Wiesbaden, 1964); Alfred A. Strnad, "Neue Quellen zur Mainzer Stiftsfehde (1459-1463)," *Röm. Histor. Mitteil.,* 11 (1969): 222-35.

[65] Joachimsohn, *Heimburg,* pp. 182, 195, 210; Boockmann, *Blumenau,* p. 177.

[66] Joachimsohn, *Heimburg,* pp. 212, 215; Heymann, *George,* p. 416.

The Tyrolese affair dragged on, and the papacy, not Cusanus, began to assume the role of the principal party against the Duke. Since Heimburg's appeal of March 16, 1461,[67] which was issued in Innsbruck on behalf of the Duke, still criticized the pope and supported the conciliar doctrine, Heimburg was once more condemned as a heretic on April 1 and the following day, Maundy Thursday, Sigismund and his followers were again placed under the general ban and excommunication.[68] In reply to another citation against Sigismund issued on February 12, 1462, the Duke published a sharply-worded answer on March 19 towards the end of which Sigismund, no doubt in Heimburg's words, appealed to the apostolic chair, but not to "him who occupied it."[69] We know that Heimburg was still with the Duke at that time and that he helped Sigismund in June 1462 in Innsbruck with a suit concerning his private affairs.[70] But the period of struggle by appeals and pamphlets was coming to a close. With the initiation of mediation attempts on the side of Venice in November 1461 and the arrival of Paolo Morosini on July 10, 1462, at Innsbruck as an arbitrator,[71] a new stage opened in the development of the prolonged controversy.

Duke Sigismund decided to send his second embassy to Venice and named Gregor Heimburg, Lorenz Blumenau and five others as his representatives.[72] As Heimburg's speech in Venice on November 2, 1462, and another speech in 1463 show, he was still not willing to submit to the pope.[73] The Emperor Friedrich III had gained more freedom to concentrate on the Tyrolese affair after settling ruinous internal feuds within the Empire at the peace conference of Prague in

---

[67] Goldast, *Monarchia*, vol. II, pp. 1580- 83; Freher-Struve, *Rerum*, vol. II, pp. 193-97. See Cod. germ. mon. 975, f. 164ʳ-72ʳ; Cod. Reg. 557, f. 70ᵛ-72ʳ; Cod.1092 (Leipzig), f. 42ᵛ-44ᵛ. On the appeal, see Jäger, "Regesten," vol. VII, p. 177; Jäger, *Der Streit*, vol. II, p. 187; Voigt, *Enea*, vol. III, p. 406; Lhotsky, *Quellenkunde*, p. 432.

[68] Freher-Struve, *Rerum*, vol. II, pp. 191-93. See Jäger, "Regesten," vol. VII, p. 177; Jäger, *Der Streit*, vol. II, pp. 198-201; Joachimsohn, *Heimburg*, p. 218; Boockmann, *Blumenau*, p. 179.

[69] Cod. ger. mon. 975, f. 204ʳ-13ᵛ. See also Chmel, *Materialien*, vol. II, pp. 261-64; Jäger, "Regesten," vol. VII, p. 180; Jäger, *Der Streit*, vol. II, pp. 269-71, Voigt, *Enea*, vol. III, p. 414; Joachimsohn, *Heimburg*, p. 241; Boockmann, *Blumenau*, p. 179.

[70] Joachimsohn, *Heimburg*, p. 242 n. 3.

[71] Voigt, *Enea*, vol. III, pp. 414-15; Joachimsohn, *Heimburg*, p. 242.

[72] Jäger, "Regesten," vol. VII, p. 183.

[73] Jäger, "Regesten," vol. VII, p. 183; Jäger, *Der Streit*, vol. II, pp. 374-77; Voigt, *Enea*, vol. II, p. 417 ; Joachimsohn, *Heimburg*, pp. 243-44.

1463. When he interposed in February 1464 to mediate on behalf of his cousin Sigismund, Heimburg's pro-conciliar and anti-papal position became increasingly unacceptable at Sigismund's court. As a result, he seems to have played a far less important role after 1464, although there is evidence that he was on the payroll of the Duke until 1465.[74] With what animosity Heimburg's anti-papal conciliar position was received by Pope Pius II is indicated by the fact that, although Sigismund and his other followers were finally absolved on September 2, 1464, in Wiener Neustadt, Heimburg alone remained condemned even thereafter.[75]

The influence of humanism and the acceptance of conciliarism did not always make a fifteenth-century man as sharp and bitter a critic of the pope as it did Heimburg. In trying to understand Heimburg's relations with Pope Pius II and Duke Sigismund we must, therefore, note as a third factor that Heimburg's personal animosity against Aeneas Sylvius and the Emperor Friedrich III was probably an important reason which prompted him to work I hard for the Duke. Aeneas's defection from the conciliar movement which he supported at the Council of Basel was no doubt one of the reasons why Heimburg harbored a strong antipathy to the pope. For the same reason Heimburg exhibited a great deal of antagonism towards Cusanus. But his disagreement with Aeneas over the nature of humanistic studies seems to have been another factor which contributed to their bitter relationship.

Although influenced by humanism, as we have seen above, Heimburg was critical of Italian humanists who blindly imitated ancient writers. He would study them, but use them in his own fashion without slavishly following their style. He prized the new learning not because it emphasized a mere imitation of classical style and rhetoric, but because it extolled the ability freely to express one's own thought and feelings in one's own words. It was not enough, according to him, to assimilate the style of ancient writers. One must deeply grasp their spirit. He liked Plutarch's statement that Cicero spoke spontaneously,[76] and was opposed to what he considered the thoughtless attitude of some Italian humanists. He would therefore not attempt to transport Italian humanist learning indiscriminately into Germany. Aeneas Sylvius has been

---

[74] TLA Innsbruck, *Raitbuch,* vol. 3, 1463/65, f. 270^r. See also Joachimsohn, *Heimburg,* p. 247; Boockmann, *Blumenau,* p. 185 n. 886.

[75] Voigt, *Enea,* vol. III, p. 421; Joachimsohn, *Heimburg,* pp. 247-48. Heimburg was finally absolved on Maroh 19, 1472 (Joachimsohn, pp. 286-87). On his later years, see Gustav Sommerfeldt, "Aus Doktor Gregor Heimburgs letzten Lebensjahren," *Mitteil. d. Vereins f. Gesch. d. Deutschen in Böhmen,* LXIX (1931): 46-56.

[76] Joachimsohn, *Heimburg,* p. 304. Joachimsohn discusses Heimburg's attitude toward humanism on pp. 3-4, 21, 83, 99-111, 163, 170, 193, 227-31. See also Voigt, *Die Wiederbelebung,* vol. II, pp. 284-90.

called the "apostle of humanism in Germany."[77] But to Heimburg his old humanist acquaintance Aeneas Sylvius was a prime example of the imitators of ancient writers. Heimburg himself said of his own style, as he spoke in Pope Pius II's presence at the Congress of Mantua, that if his manner of speech was new and different from what the pope was accustomed to at the Curia, the reason was that his was the German way.[78] It might be said that his approach to humanistic studies was in a sense a reflection of nascent nationalistic sentiments.

Heimburg's aversion to the Emperor Friedrich III also seems to have driven him to the side of Duke Sigismund. In the Tyrolese affair, the Emperor recognized Cusanus as Bishop of Brixen on March 1, 1451.[79] Having received enormous privileges from Pope Eugenius IV and being on good terms with Pope Pius II, the Emperor was naturally on the papal side. His relationship with Duke Sigismund was never really good since the latter's release from his guardianship in 1446. Heimburg himself asserted later that the whole Tyrolese affair was nothing but a pre-negotiated game by which the Emperor wished to accumulate wealth at the expense of his cousin Sigismund.[80] As has been pointed out by Professor Lhotsky,[81] this is a malicious interpretation of the whole affair. It would seem difficult to deny, however, that Heimburg was very much annoyed by the ineffective leadership which the Emperor provided in the affairs of the Empire. That is why Heimburg was in touch with Dr. Martin Mair, the champion of imperial reform, who tried, among other things, to use the widespread feeling against the Emperor within the Empire to advance his idea of having George of Podebrady elected as King of the Romans. The traditional image of Friedrich III as an indecisive and inactive ruler regarding matters outside his hereditary lands is probably in need of modification.[82] But it appears true that

---

[77] Joachimsohn, *Heimburg,* p. 103. Cf. Paul Joachimsohn, *Geschichtsauffassung und Geschichtsschreibung in Deutschland unter dem Einfluß des Humanismus* (Leipzig, 1910; Aalen, 1968), p. 27.

[78] Joachimsohn, *Heimburg,* p. 105.

[79] Jäger, "Regesten," vol. IV, p. 300.

[80] Joschimsohn, *Heimburg,* pp. 165, 247. Cf. Brigitte Haller, *Kaiser Friedrich III. im Urteil der Zeitgenossen* (Wien, 1965), pp. 77-81.

[81] Lhotsky, *Quellenkunde,* pp. 432-33.

[82] See, for example, Adam Wandruszka, *Das Haus Habsburg. Die Geschichte einer europäischen Dynastie* (Stuttgart, 1956), pp. 87-92; Alphons Lhotsky, "Kaiser Friedrich III. Sein Leben und seine Persönlichkeit," *Ausstellung—Friedrich III.: Kaiserresidenz Wiener Neustadt* (Wien, [1966]): 16-47. Cf. B. Haller, *Kaiser Friedrich*

the Emperor's lack of leadership and his close relationship with the pope were the important reasons for Heimburg's animosity against him. After making acquaintance with Duke Albrecht VI, the Emperor's troublesome and hated brother, and serving him for a while, Heimburg came to the court of the Emperor's former ward. It was not Duke Sigismund but the Emperor Friedrich III whom Heimburg made responsible for his continued condemnation as a heretic after the Duke's absolution in 1464.

As a very famous lawyer of his times, who had been influenced by humanism, Heimburg entered the service of Duke Sigismund who had been engaged in a prolonged feud with Cardinal Cusanus as Bishop of Brixen. The presence of this humanistically trained lawyer almost immediately affected the Duke's moves against Cusanus. Many appeals and protests poured forth from the ducal court which were drawn up by Heimburg. But his strong language and radical conciliar views not only brought upon himself and the Duke condemnations from the pope, but also gradually isolated him within the ducal court as the Duke began to seek reconciliation with the papacy. Conciliarism was under attack, and the papacy was regaining its strength. Despite the changing situation, Heimburg, partly prompted by his personal antagonism against the pope, the emperor and Cusanus, kept his faith in conciliarism. The only course of action open to him after the absolution of Duke Sigismund in 1464 was to move into the service of George of Podebrady, "King of Heretics."[83] Although freed from the influence of Heimburg, Duke Sigismund did not fare well afterwards. On the recommendation of his other "evil" advisors, Sigismund, Archduke of Austria since 1477, started a war against Venice in 1487, which made him so unpopular that he had to be put in the charge of guardians. The arrival of Maximilian I, the Emperor Friedrich III's son, at Innsbruck in 1490 as ruler of the Tyrol opened another new chapter in the history of the Tyrolese people.

III; Brigitte Haller, "Kaiser Friedrich III in literarischen Zeugnissen seiner Zeit und sein Andenken im 16. Jahrhundert," *Ausstellung,* pp. 87-103.

[83] The year 1972 marks the 500th anniversary of Heimburg's death, which occurred in August, 1472 in Dresden. He was buried in the Sophienkirche in Dresden. See C. Gurlitt, *Stadt Dresden* (=Beschreibende Darstellung der älteren Bau- und Kunstdenkmäler des Königreichs Sachsen, Heft 21-23) (Dresden, 1903), p. 96, Sommerfeldt, "Aus Doktor . . . " p. 55. While this article is in the press, the following study of Heimburg was brought to my notice: Alfred Wendehorst, "Gregor Heimburg," *Fränkische Lebensbilder,* ed. Gerhard Pfeiffer, vol. IV (Würzburg, 1971), pp. 112-29.

Imperial Reform in the Mid-Fifteenth Century: Gregor Heimburg and Martin Mair

It is often said that with the end of the Hohenstaufen dynasty the Holy Roman Empire entered a new period in its history which was characterized by its decline and dismemberment. Even before the death of Conrad IV, Emperor Friedrich II's son, in 1254, German ecclesiastical and lay princes had become almost sovereign lords within their domains because of the prerogatives, charters, and concessions granted by Friedrich II (1212-1250). The Statute in Favor of the Princes (*Statutum in favorem principum*) of May 1232[1] had established a legal basis for the future particularistic dismemberment of the Empire. During and after the Interregnum (1256-1273), attempts were made to reform the Empire, but, according to the widely accepted view, the decline of the imperial power after the thirteenth century was unmistakable. We must note in this connection that, instead of telling the story of medieval constitutional problems either from the point of view of the Emperor or from the point of view of the rise of particularist and disruptive elements, recent studies have emphasized the importance of examining such problems in terms of their own times and circumstances. Since the publication of its first volume in 1867 by the Historical Commission in Munich, the *Deutsche Reichstagsakten* have been an important source of information for students of medieval constitutional problems in Germany. Seventeen large volumes in twenty installments have been needed to cover the years 1376-1445. Volume 19, Part I, which deals with the years 1453, and Volume 22, Part I, which takes up the period from 1468 to 1470, were published only in 1969 and 1973 respectively. It is obvious that "discussion of imperial reform cannot go deep"[2] until the pubication of further volumes on the second half of the fifteenth century. The purpose of this article is to examine various attempts, especially in the mid-fifteenth century, to strengthen the weakening Empire by means of imperial reforms and to assess the role which two famous German lawyers, Gregor Heimburg and Martin Mair,

---

[1] The text is in Karl Zeumer, *Quellensammlung zur Geschichte der Deutschen Reichsverfassung,* 2d ed., I (Tübingen, 1913), pp. 55-56.

[2] H.S. Offler, "Aspects of Government in the Late Medieval Empire," in *Europe in the Late Middle Ages,* ed. J.R. Hale et al. (London, 1965), pp. 217-47, esp. 244. On the publication of the *Reichstagsakten* (hereafter *RTA*), see Walter Kammerer, "Zum gegenwärtigen Standort der Reichstagsakten aus Anlass der Herausgabe von Band 17," in *Aus Reichstagen des 15. und 16. Jahrhunderts* (Göttingen, 1958), pp. 9-23.

played in these attempts. In this article we mean by "imperial reform" efforts to reform the constitution of the Empire.

In examining various reform proposals[3] we find that the strengthening of the Diet (*Reichstag*), the establishment of an Imperial Army and the speedy and impartial administration of justice are recurring themes. It is urged in some proposals that the Diet should meet regularly and that there should be an Imperial Army financed by imperial taxation. Other proposals maintain that the administration of justice should be in the hands of a Supreme Court, which should have power to act speedily. The development of leagues, as well as the Public Peace (*Landfriede*), is also a phenomenon which deserves close attention in any study of imperial reform. There were not only leagues among knights and among peasant communities, but also leagues in which towns, knights, princes, and nobles mingled. They all expressed a strong desire for effective political action in the face of disunity and disorder within the Empire.

The earliest comprehensive attempt to restore the power of the Empire dates back to 1254, when Mainz and Worms established a Rhenish League to eliminate disputes between themselves and to restore law and order.[4] But mainly because of a disputed imperial election of 1257, the league itself was split, thereby destroying the first serious attempt at imperial reform. Another important landmark in the history of imperial reform was reached in 1338, a year after the beginning of the Hundred Years' War (1337-1453). On July 16 the first electors' union (*Kurverein*) was organized in Lahnstein, and the next day it was formally established at Rense, laying down firmly the principle that he who is

---

[3] On the *Reichsreform* in general, see Georg von Below, "Die Reichsreform," in *Im Morgenrot der Reformation*, ed. J.V. Pflugk-Harttung (Hersfeld, 1912), pp. 121-62; Erich Molitor, *Die Reichsreformbestrebungen des 15. Jahrhunderts bis zum Tode Kaiser Friedrichs III.* (Breslau, 1921); Eduard Ziehen, *Mittelrhein und Reich im Zeitalter der Reichsreform 1356-1504*, 2 vols. (Frankfurt a.M., 1934); Hans Baron "Imperial Reform and the Habsburgs, 1486-1504: A New Interpretation," *American Historical Review*, 44 (1939), 293-303; Fritz Hartung, *Deutsche Verfassungsgeschichte vom 15. Jahrhundert bis zum Gegenwart*, 8th ed. (Stuttgart, 1950); Erik Hühns, "Theorie und Praxis in der Reichsreformbewegung des 15. Jahrhunderts, Nikolaus von Cues, die Reformatio Sigismundi und Berthold von Henneberg," *Wissenschaftliche Zeitschrift der Humboldt-Universität zu Berlin, Gesellschafts- und Sprachwiss.*, Reihe I (1951/52), pp. 17-34; Friedrich Baethgen "Schisma- und Konzilszeit, Reichsreform und Habsburgs Aufstieg," in *Handbuch der deutschen Geschichte*, ed. Bruno Gebhardt, 8th ed., I (1954), pp. 505-83; Adolf Laufs, "Reichsstädte und Reichsreform," *Zeitschrift der Savigny-Stiftung für Rechtsgeschichte, Germanistische Abteilung* (hereafter *ZRGGA*), 84 (1967): 172-201. Especially on the concept of imperial reform, see Heinz Angermeier, "'Begriff und Inhalt der Reichsreform," *ZRGGA*, 75 (1958): 181-205.

[4] Hans-Peter Scheerer, *Mainz und die Reichsreform* (Diss., Mainz, 1968), pp. 4-6. On the Rhenish League, see Zeumer, *Quellensammlung*, I, pp. 89-94.

elected by a majority of the electors can take the title of a King of the Romans (*rex Romanorum*) and exercise all sovereign rights without need of the consent or confirmation of the Pope.[5] The League of Rense, as it was later called, was an important step forward to the adoption of the Golden Bull of 1356 under Emperor Charles IV (1346-1378).

According to the famous Golden Bull,[6] there were to be seven electors of the Empire, three of them ecclesiastical princes (the archbishops of Mainz, Köln, and Trier) and four lay princes (the king of Bohemia, the duke of Saxony, the margrave of Brandenburg, and the count of the Palatinate). The Bull, which for the first time gave recognition to the seven electors of the Empire who had been the real wielders of power, settled the constitution of the electoral body for the remaining years of the Empire and made the electors virtually independent sovereigns. In the words of one prominent historian, "The Golden Bull fixed and legalized the status quo."[7] Although Article 15 of the Golden Bull forbade leagues and confederations, especially among the cities, without the sanction of the sovereign princes, some leagues were organized in the fourteenth century, such as the Swabian City League of 1376 and 1381, which reflected the desire of the burgher class for a more general representation of the people in public affairs. But these city unions and leagues were concerned not so much with imperial reform as with the relations of the cities to local lords and the king.

In the period after the adoption of the Golden Bull the imperial reform movement remained rather inactive, and no comprehensive reform attempts were made until the beginning of the fifteenth century. Emperor Sigismund's proposal of imperial reform, which he presented at the Imperial Diet of Vienna in 1424,[8] failed because of the opposition of the cities. An attempt to establish an imperial tax system, which was proposed at another Imperial Diet of Frankfurt in 1427, also came to naught.[9] The fundamental problem in both cases was that the Empire lacked a means of enforcing the proposals. Yet it was no longer possible to suppress or break up the reform movement, and it became more intensive and widespread as time passed.

It is undeniably true that the great church councils of the fifteenth century, especially the Council of Constance (1414-1418) and the Council of Basel

---

[5] The notarial instrument is printed in Zeumer, *Quellensammlung*, I, pp. 183-84. Cf. Scheerer, *Mainz*, pp. 7-8.

[6] The text is in Zeumer, *Quellensammlung*, I, pp. 192-214.

[7] Geoffrey Barraclough, *The Origins of Modern Germany*, 2d ed. (Oxford, 1947), p. 317.

[8] *RTA*, 8 (1883), No. 331, pp. 391-92.

[9] *RTA*, 9 (1887), Nos. 75, 76, pp. 90-110. Cf. Zeumer, *Quellensammlung*, I, pp. 237-44.

(1431-1449), gave an impetus to a revitalization of comprehensive imperial reform programs.[10] Many people realized that the problem of imperial reform was closely related to that of church reform: "quia pro reformacione sacri imperii est in multis par racio cum reformacione papatus."[11] Those who were deeply concerned about the state of affairs in the Church were also greatly interested in the problem of comprehensive imperial reform. No wonder that many of the reformers of this period were members of the clergy. The anonymous author of the *Advisamentum sacrorum canonum et doctorum ecclesiae catholicae et electione papae et cardinalium*, etc.,[12] which, among other topics, seriously dealt with imperial reform; Heinrich Toke, canon of Magdeburg, whose tracts *Concepta* of 1430 and *Concilia* of 1442 discussed the reform of imperial institutions;[13] and Nicolaus Cusanus, who presented to the Council of Basel in 1432 one of the most comprehensive reform programs of both Church and Empire, *De concordantia catholica*[14]—these men are good examples of this development. If we add to this list the so-called *Reformatio Sigismundi*, which seems to have been composed in Basel between 1433 and 1439 by a secular

---

[10] Concerning the impact of the conciliar movement on imperial reform, see for example, Hartung *Verfassungsgeschichte,* pp. 13-14, Heinz Angermeier, "Das Reich und der Konziliarismus," *Historische Zeitschrift,* 192 (1961): 529-83; Offler, "Aspects," p. 242, Gunther Hödl, "Zur Reichspolitik des Basler Konzils: Bischof Johannes Schele von Lübeck (1420-1439)," *Mitteilungen des Instituts für Österreichische Geschichtsforschung* (hereafter *MIÖG*), 75 (1967): 46-65; Scheerer, *Mainz,* p. 12.

[11] Quoted in Scheerer, *Mainz,* p. 12. Cf. Laufs, "Reichsstädte," p. 186.

[12] Moliter, *Die Reichsreformbestrebungen,* pp. 46-47, Scheerer, *Mainz,* p. 13.

[13] On Heinrich Toke and his writings, see Rudolf Smend, "Ein Reichsreformprojekt aus dem Schriftenkreise des Basler Konzils," *Neues Archiv der Gesellschaft für ältere deutsche Geschichtskunde,* 32 (1906/07): 746-49; Molitor, *Die Reichsreformbestrebungen,* pp. 50-52, P. Clausen, *Heinrich Toke, ein Beitrag zur Geschichte der Reichs- und Kirchenreform in der Zeit des Basler Konzils* (Diss., Jena, 1939); Paul Lehmann, "Aus dem Rapularius des Heinricus Token," in *Erforschung des Mittelalters,* IV (Stuttgart, 1961), pp. 187-205; Scheerer, *Mainz,* pp. 13-14. H. Loebel, *Die Reformtraktate des Magdeburger Domherrn Heinrich Toke* (Diss., Göttingen, 1949) was not accessible to me.

[14] See Molitor, *Die Reichsreformbestrebungen,* pp. 52-71; Hühns, "Theorie," pp. 22-25; Morimichi Watanabe, *The Political Ideas of Nicholas of Cusa, with Special Reference to his De concordantia catholica* (Geneva, 1963); Paul E. Sigmund, *Nicholas of Cusa and Medieval Political Thought* (Cambridge, Mass., 1963), Johannes Bärmann, "Cusanus und die Reichsreform," *Mitteilungen und Forschungsbeitrage der Cusanus-Gesellschaft* (hereafter *MFCG*), 4 (1964): 74-103, Bernhard Töpfer, "Die Reichsreformvorschläge des Nikolaus von Kues," *Zeitschrift für Geschichtswissenschaft,* 13 (1965): 617-37.

cleric,[15] we have the major reform proposals of the early fifteenth century which deserve our serious consideration. We should note, however, that the practical impact of these proposals has sometimes been overemphasized.

Besides the ecclesiastics who produced literary works influential in the fields of imperial reform and religious ideas, the electors of the Empire came to exert great influence on the imperial reform movement. This new development was manifested in 1436, when the electors in their address to the Emperor demanded a comprehensive reform of the Empire.[16] At the Diet of Eger (Cheb) in July 1437, a further advance towards imperial reform was made by the electors, who announced the establishment of a new general Public Peace, the strengthening of the imperial ban and the regulation of coinage.[17] The reform program of 1438, which was submitted by Elector Otto of the Palatinate on March 10 in Frankfurt, the Public Peace league of March 21, 1438, which was established in Frankfurt by seven electors, and the first Imperial Diet of

---

[15] The text is printed in *Reformation Kaiser Sigmunds,* ed. Karl Beer (Beiheft zu den deutschen Reichstagsakten); (Stuttgart, 1933); *Reformation Kaiser Siegmunds,* ed. Heinrich Koller (Monumenta Germaniae Historica, Staatsschriften des späten Mittelalters, 6); (Stuttgart, 1964). Of the many studies of the *Reformatio Sigismundi,* see, for example, Paul Joachimsohn, "Die Reformation des Kaiser Sigismund," *Historisches Jahrbuch,* 41 (1921): 36-51; Molitor, *Die Reichsreformbestrebungen,* pp. 72-76; Karl Beer, "Zur Entstehungsgeschichte der Reformatio Sigismundi," *MIÖG,* 12. Erg.-Band (1933): 572-675; Karl Beer, "Zur Frage nach dem Verfasser der Reformatio Sigismundi," *MIÖG,* 51 (1937): 161-77; Karl Beer, "Der gegenwärtige Stand der Forschung über die Reformatio Sigismundi," *MIÖG,* 59 (1951): 55-93; Heinrich Koller, 'Eine neue Fassung der Reformatio Sigismundi," *MIÖG,* 60 (1952): 143-54 Thea Buyken, "Der Verfasser der Reformatio Sigismundi," in *Aus Mittelalter und Neuzeit: Festschrift für Gerhard Kallen,* ed. Josef Engel and Hans M. Klinkenberg (Bonn, 1957), pp. 97-116, Heinrich Koller, "Untersuchungen zur Reformatio Sigismundi," *Deutsches Archiv für Erforschung des Mittelalters,* 13 (1957): 482-524; Lothar Graf zu Dohna, *Reformatio Sigismundi: Beiträge zum Verständnis einer Reformschrift des fünfzehnten Jahrhundert* (Göttingen, 1960), Manfred Straube, "Die Reformatio Sigismundi als Ausdruck des revolutionären Bewegungen im 15. Jahrhundert," in *Die frühbürgerliche Revolution in Deutschland,* ed. Gerhard Brendler (Berlin, 1961) pp. 108-15; F.M. Bartos, "Wer ist der Verfasser der Reformation Kaiser Sigmunds?," *Communio Viatorum,* 8 (1965), 123-44; Manfred Straube, "Zur Verfälschung der sogennanten Reformatio Sigismundi durch Lothar Graf zu Dohna," *Wissenschaftliche Zeitschrift der Karl-Marx-Universität Leipzig: Gesellschafts- und Sprachwissenschaftliche,* Reihe, 14 (1965): 419-26, W.D. Wackernagel, "Heinrich von Beinheim an Ecclesiaseical Judge of the 15th Century," in *Essays in Legal History in Honor of Felix Frankfurter,* ed. Morris D. Forkosch (Indianapolis, 1966), pp. 275-88

[16] *RTA,* 12 (1901), No. 31, pp. 52-53.

[17] *RTA,* 12 (1901), No. 75, pp. 126-27.

Nürnberg in July 1438[18] were some of the serious efforts which were made towards imperial reform shortly before or during the brief reign of King Albrecht II from March 18, 1438, to October 27, 1439. According to one historian, the period "marked a first climax in the movement for reform."[19] But there were also adverse developments from the point of view of imperial reform. The electors further strengthened their position by forcing Albrecht in 1438 to sign a "capitulation," which they had authored, in accordance with the ancient practice of requesting political concessions from a new king before his election. The deliberations in the Diet of Nürnberg in July 1438 showed clearly that the electors played a decisive role in the Imperial Diet. The decline of imperial power as a result of the rise of the electors was clear. The electors proposed, for example, that the whole Empire, except Austria and Bohemia, be divided into four circles (*Kreise*), over each of which a prince was to be appointed captain by the king to administer justice in his name in cases of appeal from the ordinary courts. Foreseeing that this plan would place each of the four circles in the hands of one of the greater princes, Albrecht's advisors proposed that there should be six circles rather than four, thus preventing the princes from augmenting their own power as much as they desired.[20] Although the deliberations did not produce any concrete results, they show unmistakably that the king and the electors had different ideas about imperial reform.

It can be said that during the reign of the next ruler, Friedrich III (king 1440-1493; emperor from 1452), no completely new proposals or ideas were introduced to effect imperial reform. The so-called *Reformatio Frederici*[21] of August 14, 1442, which was a Public Peace Law, essentially repeated existing and unchallenged law without offering any new reforms and was far less innovative than the reforms of 1437 and 1438. But there are several factors and events which made the imperial reform movement of the 1450's and 1460's quite different from that in the preceding decades.

---

[18] *RTA*, 13[1] (1925), No. 28, pp. 73-74; No. 102, pp. 156-58.

[19] Offler, "Aspects," p. 243.

[20] Offler, "Aspects," p. 243; Heinrich Koller, "Kaiserliche Politik und die Reformpläne des 15. Jahrhunderts," *Veröffentlichungen des Max-Planck-Instituts für Geschichte*, 36/II (Göttingen, 1972): 61-79, especially p. 76. Koller argues that after the summer of 1439 the war against the Turks became more important to Albrecht II than the reform of the Empire.

[21] The text is in Zeumer, *Quellensammlung*, I, pp. 260-65. See also Molitor, *Die Reichsreformbestrebungen*, pp. 109-10; Hartung, *Verfassungsgeschichte*, p. 5, Offler "Aspects," pp. 238, 244, Laufs, "Reichsstädte," p. 191, Scheerer, *Mainz*, pp. 28-31 Cf. D.G.W. Böhmer, ed., *Kaiser Friedrich's III. Entwurf einer Magna Charta für Deutschland oder die Reformation dieses Kaisers vom Jahr 1441* (Göttingen, 1818).

For twenty-seven years after 1444 Emperor Friedrich III, who was also Duke of Styria (1435-1493) and head of the House of Habsburg, stayed exclusively in his own territories or abroad and did not make an appearance in the "Empire" (*Reich*) in the narrow sense. Secure in his hereditary lands, he is said to have devoted his time and energy to the pursuit of dynastic power (*Hausmacht*). It has been asserted that "interest in the constitutional problem, still real under Sigismund and Albert, flagged until 1486."[22] The eminent British historian Stubbs could write in 1908 that "the reign of Frederick III is the longest and dullest of all German history."[23] Emperor Friedrich III has often been criticized both by his contemporaries and by German historians, who deplore the disintegration of the Empire, for his inaction and lethargy. The stodgy Emperor is said to have moved only when matters related to his hereditary lands were at stake.[24] But many modern historians would not dismiss the age of Friedrich III as the dullest period, nor would they turn their attention only to the negative aspect of his rule. They note, for example, that his policy towards the Church was based on practical, realistic considerations. When King Charles VII of France adopted the Pragmatic Sanction of Bourges in 1438, which became a cornerstone of Gallicanism, the electors of Germany followed the example of the French king in 1439 at the Diet of Mainz by adopting the policy of German neutrality in the struggle between the Pope and the Council of Basel. This policy of neutrality, maintained by Albrecht II during his short reign, was abandoned by Friedrich III, who in 1446 sold, as Gregor Heimburg (c.1400-1472) put it later, his obedience to Rome for 221,000 ducats.[25] The Concordat

[22] Offler, "Aspects," p. 244.

[23] William Stubbs, *Germany in the Later Middle Ages, 1200-1500,* ed. Arthur Hassall (London, 1908), p. 184.

[24] The views which some of Friedrich III's contemporaries had of the Emperor are conveniently collected in Brigitte Haller, *Kaiser Friedrich III. im Urteil der Zeitgenossen* (Wien, 1965). Various attempts to re-evaluate Friedrich III were made by members of the Vienna school in *Ausstellung—Friedrich III.: Kaiserresidenz Wiener Neustadt* (Wien [1966]), pp. 13-230. For a recent, "positive" evaluation of Friedrich and his work, see Walter Zeeden, "Deutschland wahrend der Regierung Kaiser Friedrichs III. (1440-1493)" and "Von der habsburgischen Hausmacht zur habsburgischen Grossmacht: Friedrich III. als Hausmachtpolitiker," in *Handbuch der europäischen Geschichte,* III, ed. Josef Engel (Stuttgart, 1971), pp. 467-79.

[25] Frederick G. Heymann, *George of Bohemia, King of Heretics* (Princeton, 1965), pp. 195, 413. Cf. Heiko Oberman et al., *Defensorium obedientiae apostolicae et alia documenta* (Cambridge, Massachusetts, 1968), pp. 8-9.

of Vienna of 1448,[26] which was negotiated between Pope Nicholas V and
Friedrich III at the Diet of Aschaffenburg, brought about a general settlement of
the Church condition in Germany. It is therefore important to reassess certain
events during his long reign so that we may better understand the nature of
reform proposals made in the mid-fifteenth century.

Two prominent factions existed in the Empire at that time.[27] One of them
consisted of the two princely houses of Wettin and Hohenzollern—the dukes of
Saxony and the margraves of Brandenburg. Its unofficial leader was Margrave
Albrecht Achilles of Ansbach (1414-1486), the younger brother of Elector
Friedrich II of Brandenburg (1440-1470). He had long and successfully posed as
the Emperor's most faithful partisan, defending the Emperor, as we shall see,
against frequent attempts to replace him by a more suitable man. Dr. Peter Knorr
(d. 1478)[28] was his trusted advisor. Opposed to the imperial faction were the
princes of the House of Wittelsbach and the ecclesiastical princes of Bamberg and
Würzburg, with Duke Ludwig der Reiche ("the Rich") of Landshut (1417-1497)
and his cousin, Count Friedrich I der Siegreiche ("the Victorious") of the
Palatinate (1449-1476) serving as their leaders. Criticizing the ineffectiveness of
the Emperor, this faction vehemently demanded imperial reform. The conflict
between the Brandenburg-imperial and the Wittelsbach-reform parties was further
complicated by various important events of the mid-fifteenth century, such as the
fall of Constantinople in 1453, the so-called Mainz *Stiftsfehde* (1459-1463) and
the attempt of some German princes to reform the Empire by elevating King
George of Bohemia (1458-1471) to the Roman kingship. These events show
clearly that some of the electors played an increasingly important role in various
imperial reform programs. If we are to assess the significance of imperial reform
in the mid-fifteenth century, it is necessary first to discuss the Mainz *Stiftsfehde*

---

[26] The text is in Zeumer, *Quellensammlung*, I, pp. 266-68. On the Concordat of
Vienna, see Mandell Creighton, *A History of the Papacy from the Great Schism to the
Sack of Rome*, III (New York, 1897), pp. 106-9; John B. Toews, "Pope Eugenius IV
and the Concordat of Vienna (1448)—An Interpretation," *Church History*, 34 (June
1965): 178-94; John B. Toews, "Formative Forces in the Pontificate of Nicholas V,
1447-1455," *Catholic Historical Review*, 54 (July 1968): 261-84.

[27] The following description of the Hohenzollern-Wittelsbach rivalry is based on
Herta Gallas, *Herzog Ludwig der Reiche von Bayern-Landshut und die
Reichsreformbewegung der Jahre 1459-1467* (Diss., München, 1937), pp. 45-53, 71;
Heymann, *George*, pp. 186-87.

[28] On Dr. Knorr, see Johannes Kist, "Dr. Peter Knorr aus Kulmbach, ein geistlicher
Diplomat des 15. Jahrhundert," *92. Bericht des Historischen Vereins* (1953): 350-64,
Heinz Lieberich, "'Die gelehrten Räte: Staat und Juristen in Baiern in der Frühzeit der
Rezeption," *Zeitschrift für bayerische Landesgeschichte*, 27 (1964): 161; Johannes
Kist, "Peter Knorr," in *Fränkische Lebensbilder*, ed. Gerhard Pfeiffer, II (1968), pp.
159-76.

at some length, and then to relate it to King George's attempts to obtain an imperial crown.

The Mainz *Stiftsfehde* was one of those dreary struggles in which fifteenth-century Germany abounded.[29] On June 18, 1459, the cathedral chapter of Mainz elected by a compromise Diether von Isenburg-Büdingen as Archbishop-Elector of Mainz (1458-1461; 1475-1482), on condition that the league which his predecessor had concluded with Margrave Albrecht Achilles of Ansbach and Count Ulrich V of Württemberg (1433-1480) against Elector Friedrich the Victorious of the Palatinate be renewed. Thus the Mainz *Stiftsfehde* began with strong political overtones. Shortly after the election, an embassy was sent by Diether to obtain papal confirmation from Pope Pius II (1458-1464), who was at that time in Mantua to prepare for a crusade against the Turks. Another important task of the embassy was to ask the Pope to give Diether the archepiscopal pallium. The Pope, unhappy about the presence of only few envoys at the Congress of Mantua and displeased with Diether's failure to appear in person, asked Diether's envoys to pledge that their master would never press for a council or consent to a general assembly of the electoral princes without the Pope's prior permission. These were especially difficult conditions for an Archbishop of Mainz, who, as Germany's first ecclesiastical prince and traditional archchancellor of the Empire, was obliged to call meetings of electors whenever there existed good reason. Diether, angered by Pius's demands and wishing to assert his independence of the Papacy, rejected the conditions. Thanks to the mediation of Diether's friend, Albrecht Achilles, who was in Mantua after December 1459, Pope Pius II softened his stand. After withdrawing his earlier demands and giving confirmation to the election, he told Diether's second em-

---

[29] On the Mainz *Stiftsfehde,* see Ludwig Pastor, *The History of the Popes from the Close of the Middle ages,* ed. Frederick I. Antrobus, III (London, 1894), pp. 164-208; Aloys Schmidt, "Zur Mainzer Stiftsfehde 1462," *Jahrbuch für das Bistum Mainz,* 3 (1948): 89-99; Alois Gerlich, "Die Anfänge des grossen abendländischen Schismas und der Mainzer Bistumsstreit," *Hessisches Jahrbuch für Landesgeschichte,* 6 (1956): 25-76; Adalbert Erler, "Die Mainzer Stiftsfehde 1459-1463 im Spiegel mittelalterlicher Rechtsgutachten," *Sitzungsberichte der wissenschaftlichen Gesellschaft und der Johann Wolfgang Goethe-Universität,* 1/5 (1962): 191-205; Adalbert Erler, *Mittelalterliche Rechtsgutachten zur Mainzer Stiftsfehde 1459-1463* (Wiesbaden, 1964); W.J. Courtenay, "Zur Chronologie der Schriften Gabriel Biels von 1462 und zu seiner Rolle in der Mainzer Stiftsfehde," *Trierer Theologische Zeitschrift,* 74 (1965): 373-76; Oberman, *Defensorium,* esp. pp. 16-41; Alfred A. Strnad, "Neue Quellen zur Mainzer Stiftsfehde (1459-1463)," *Römische Historische Mitteilungen,* 2 (1969): 222-35; Adalbert Erler, "Neue Funde zur Mainzer Stiftsfehde," *Zeitschrift der Savigny-Stiftung für Rechtsgeschichte, Kanonistische Abteilung* (hereafter *ZRGKA*), 89 (1972): 370-86; Dieter Brosius, "Zum Mainzer Bistumsstreit 1459-1463," *Archiv für hessischen Geschichte und Altertumskunde,* N.F., 33 (1975): 111-36. Other famous *Fehden* in Germany around that time were the Soest *Fehde* (1444-1449) and the Münster *Fehde* (1450-1457).

bassy in January 1460 that Diether still had to come to Mantua in person and that he should pay annates, comprising *servitia communia* and *servitia minuta,* which amounted to 11,895 florins 29s. 8d.[30] His envoys were able to pay the amount through a loan from a group of bankers headed by Ambrosius de Spanochiis. When Diether failed to reimburse the amount after an extended period, the sentence of lesser excommunication was pronounced upon him in January 1461.

In the meantime, Diether suffered a military defeat at Pfeddersheim on July 4, 1460, at the hands of Elector Friedrich the Victorious. The two electors quickly formed a twenty-year alliance. The defeat was a turning point in Diether's political career which placed him in a leading position within the anti-imperial and anti-papal party.[31] Although he possessed a pallium, he had not been consecrated. Nor had he been invested by an emperor. He was only an archbishop-elect. Thus under the canon law he, as an excommunicated person, had been deprived of all administrative privileges. But Diether ignored all this and called a meeting of the electors and princes in Nürnberg on February 23, 1461. The legal basis for such a meeting was given as Article 12 of the Golden Bull, which stated that the electors were to assemble every year at Easter for a month. According to ancient custom the Archbishop of Mainz convoked the electoral college. Enraged by Pope Pius's attack, Diether wished to assert his independence of the Papacy and became a strong protagonist of the rights and liberties of the German princes. He came to Nürnberg as spokesman of the electoral opposition to growing papal interference in the Empire.[32] On February

---

[30] Authorities are not in agreement on the amount which Pope Pius II demanded (Erler—20,500 gulden; Menzel—20,650 Rhenish florins, Oberman—20,550 Rhenish gulden; Pastor—20,550 Rhenish florins; Strnad—14,000 Kammer gulden). It is believed that the Pope raised the amount from the usual 10,000 golden in order to defray the cost of a crusade against the Turks which he was organizing. Brosius rejects all of the figures mentioned above on the basis of the documents in the Secret Archives of the Vatican. See Brosius, "Zum Mainzer," pp. 121-23.

[31] Pastor, *History,* III, p. 164; Oberman, *Defensorium,* p. 22; Brosius, "Zum Mainzer," p. 124.

[32] On this controversial Archbishop of Mainz, see Karl Menzel, *Diether von Isenburg, Erzbischof von Mainz, 1459-1463* (Erlangen, 1868); Rudolf Glaser, *Diether von Isenburg-Büdingen, Erzbischof und Kurfürst von Mainz (1459-1463) und die kirchlichen und politischen Reformbestrebungen im 15. Jahrhundert* (Hamburg, 1898) Aloys Schulte, "Zwei Briefe Diether's von Isenburg," *Quellen und Forschungen aus italienischen Archive und Bibliotheken,* 6 (1904): 25-31; Albert Kirnberger, *Diether von Isenburg: Der Gründer der Mainzer Universität* (Mainz, 1950); Ernst Bock "Dieter Graf von Isenburg," in *Neue Deutsche Biographie,* 3 (1957), p. 668, Anton P. Brück, "Dieter von Isenburg," in *Lexikon für Theologie und Kirche,* 2d ed., III (1959), p. 382.

22, 1461, one day before the opening of the Diet in Nurnberg, Diether took into service Dr. Gregor Heimburg, one of the sharpest critics of both Pope and Emperor.[33]

Born around 1400 the son of the burgher Hans Heimburg in Schweinfurt, Gregor entered the University of Vienna on October 3, 1413, and later studied at other "transalpine" universities. Matriculating at the University of Padua probably around 1421, he obtained the degree of *doctor in jure canonico* on February 7, 1430. But the record shows that he had already received the *legum doctor* degree either from another university or from Padua before 1430.[34] The young lawyer then attended the Council of Basel in 1432 as general vicar in ecclesiastical affairs of the Archbishop of Mainz. His service to the city of Nürnberg as legal advisor began in 1435 and continued almost without interruption until 1461, although he worked for many other princes and cities during the same period. On January 20, 1458, he acquired a position under Duke Albrecht VI of Austria, Emperor Friedrich III's brother. It was apparently in Albrecht's court in Vienna that he first met Duke Sigismund of the Tyrol on May 11, 1458.

The following year Heimburg appeared at the Congress of Mantua not only to make speeches on behalf of Duke Friedrich II of Saxony, Duke Albrecht VI of Austria, and Duke Sigismund of the Tyrol, but also to criticize Pope Pius II's crusade program against the Turks. Many appeals and manifestos which were issued by Duke Sigismund during his struggle against Cardinal Nicolaus Cusanus were authored by Heimburg, who was often referred to as Dr.

---

[33] The most thorough discussion of Gregor's life and work is still Paul Joachimsohn, *Gregor Heimburg* (Bamberg, 1891). See also Adolf Bachmann, "Heimburg," in *Allgemeine Deutsche Biographie,* II (1880), pp. 327-30; Alfred Wendehorst, "Gregor Heimburg" *Fränkische Lebensbilder,* IV (1971): 112-29; Morimichi Watanabe, "Humanism in the Tyrol: Aeneas Sylvius, Duke Sigismund and Gregor Heimburg," *Journal of Medieval and Renaissance Studies,* 4 (1974): 177-202; Morimichi Watanabe, "Duke Sigismund and Gregor Heimburg," in *Festschrift Nikolaus Grass zum 60. Geburtstag,* ed. L. Carlen and F. Steinegger, I (Innsbruck, 1974), pp. 559-73; Morimichi Watanabe, "Gregor Heimburg and Early Humanism in Germany," in *Philosophy and Humanism: Renaissance Essays in Honor of Paul O. Kristeller,* ed. Edward P. Mahoney (New York and Leiden, 1976), pp. 406-22.

[34] It is possible that Heimburg received the *legum doctor* degree also from the University of Padua. See Arnold Luschin von Ebengreuth, "Queller zur Geschichte deutschen Rechtshörer in Italien," *Sitzungsberichte der phil.-histor. Klasse der kaiserlichen Akademie der Wissenschaften* (Vienna), 124 (1891): 23; Watanabe, "Gregor Heimburg," pp. 411-13.

Gregorien.[35] In the fall of 1460 Pius II initiated proceedings against Heimburg as the Duke's legal advisor and as author of tracts encouraging opposition to the Apostolic See. Heimburg was excommunicated by name on October 18, 1460. It is no wonder that Heimburg's advice was also sought in 1460 by George of Podebrady, the Hussite King of Bohemia (1458-1471), who also opposed the Papacy. By entering the service of Elector Diether of Mainz in February 1461, Heimburg brought about an anti-papal alliance between Duke Sigismund of the Tyrol and the Archbishop of Mainz.

On February 23, 1461, the day after Heimburg entered Diether's service, the deliberations of the Diet of Nürnberg began. It is not surprising that, advised and supported by the excommunicate Heimburg, Diether, who himself had been excommunicated and who headed the anti-papal opposition, supported Duke Sigismund's cause. Diether proposed in *Appellacio Domini Dytheri AEpisc. Moguntini electi et confirmati . . . in causa Annate*[36] that an appeal be made not to the Pope but to a future general council concerning the annates. The proposal was promptly supported by Elector Friedrich the Victorious of the Palatinate on February 28. Naturally, this ran directly counter to the bull *Execrabilis* of January 18, 1460, in which Pope Pius II strictly prohibited any appeal to future councils.[37] The opponent of the Pope at the Diet of Nürnberg was not just a heretic, but the ranking ecclesiastical prince-elector of the Empire. The author of the *Appellacio,* which Diether presented to the Diet, was no doubt Gregor Heimburg.

What is more important than the *Appellacio* from our point of view is an official declaration adopted at the Diet in which the spirit of the electoral college and of the *Gravamina of the German Nation* was strongly manifested.[38] The

---

[35] It is beyond the scope of this article to discuss in detail the famous conflict between Cardinal Nicolaus Cusanus and Duke Sigismund of the Tyrol over the bishopric of Brixen. See, for example, Albert Jäger, *Der Streit des Cardinals Nicolaus von Cusa mit dem Herzoge Sigmund von Oesterreiah als Grafen von Tirol* (Innsbruck, 1861); Pastor, *History,* III, pp. 178-92, 209-12; Creighton, *History,* III, pp. 235-38, 256-65; Watanabe, "Duke Sigismund."

[36] The text is in Henricus C. Senckenberg, *Selecta iuris et historiarum tum anecdota tum iam edita sed rariora,* IV (Frankfurt a.M., 1738), pp. 392-99; Erler, *Mittelalterliche,* pp. 271-74.

[37] The text and an English translation in Oberman, *Defensorium,* pp. 224-27. See also G.B. Picotti, "La pubblicazione e i primi effetti della 'Execrabilis' di Pio II," *Archivio della R. Società di Storia Patria,* 37 (Rome, 1914): 5-56.

[38] Pastor, *History,* III, pp. 193-96. On the *Gravamina* in general, see Bruno Gebhardt, *Die Gravamina der Deutschen gegen den römischen Hof,* 2d ed. (Breslau, 1895); Anton Störmann, *Die städtischen Gravamina gegen den Klerus am Ausgang des Mittelalters und in der Reformationszeit* (Münster, 1916); Wilhelm Michel, *Das*

declaration *Cum Dei perfecta sint opera*[39] was also, no doubt, inspired by Diether and his advisor Heimburg. A majority of the participants subscribed to the declaration. But Diether's success remained short-lived, because discontent and mistrust soon appeared among the participants, who were preoccupied with their own interests. After the dissolution of the Diet on March 6, a new Diet was called in Frankfurt for May 22, 1461. In the meantime, Heimburg, who, as we have seen, had been excommunicated by the Pope on October 18, 1460, was excluded as a heretic from the communion of the Church. On Maundy Thursday, April 2, 1461, the Pope pronounced the sentence of greater excommunication against Heimburg, as well as against Duke Sigismund and his adherents.

When Rudolf von Rüdesheim (1402-1482)[40] and Francis of Toledo, Pope Pius's nuncios to Germany, negotiated with the German princes in an attempt to pacify their grievances, Emperor Friedrich III forbade the next proposed Diet in Frankfurt, an imperial city. The citizens of Frankfurt sided with the Emperor and refused to receive the princes. In its place an assembly was held in Mainz on June 4, 1461, but was very ill-attended. The only elector present was Diether of Mainz. The two papal nuncios not only succeeded in preventing the excommunicated Heimburg from attending the proceedings, but they defended the Holy See against Diether's attacks with skill and success. The defeat of Diether's party was complete, and the assembly closed without any definite conclusion. Heimburg, who left Maine with a heavy heart, is believed to have gone to France to meet the French king.[41] In the bulls which Pius II published in Tivoli on August 21, 1461, Diether was deposed and Adolf of Nassau was appointed Archbishop of Mainz by a papal provision. With the coming of Adolf to Mainz on November 26, 1461, a fierce conflict broke forth, engulfing the country bordering on the Rhine in war. The Mainz *Stiftsfehde* continued until 1463.[42]

Wiener Konkordat von 1448 und die nachfolgenden Gravamina des Primarklerus des Mainzer Kirchenprovinz (Diss., Heidelberg, 1929).

[39] The text is in Senckenberg, *Selecta,* IV, pp. 360-81. See Erler, *Mittelalterliche,* p. 5.

[40] On Rudolf von Rüdesheim, see Franz Falk, "Rudolf von Rüdesheim," *Der Katholik* 56/II (1876): 428-32; J. Zaun, *Rudolf von Rüdesheim, Fürstbischof von Lavant und Breslau: Ein Lebensbild aus dem 15. Jahrhundert* (Frankfurt a.M., 1881); Hermann Markgraf, "Rudolf von Rüdesheim," in *Allgemeine Deutsche Biographie,* 29 (1889), pp. 529-34; K. Engelbert, "Rudolf Van Rüdesheim," in *Lexikon für Theologie und Kirche,* 2d ed., IX (1964), col. 90.

[41] Cf. Pastor, *History,* III, pp. 133, 197. See below, n. 64. About Rudolf's activities in Mainz, see Zaun, *Rudolf,* pp. 20-25.

[42] Pastor, *History,* III, p. 208; Oberman, *Defensorium,* p. 41; Brosius, "Zum Mainzer," pp. 132-36.

We have so far examined the events of the Mainz *Stiftsfehde* solely from the point of view of German antagonism towards the Papacy. The leading figures in the opposition were Archbishop-Elector Diether of Mainz and Duke Sigismund of the Tyrol, with Gregor Heimburg serving as their advisor. The problem of imperial reform has received little attention in our treatment of their activities. Only when we relate the events surrounding the Mainz *Stiftsfehde* to the attempt of King George of Bohemia to become a King of the Romans are we in a position better to understand the full impact of imperial reform on the political and ecclesiastical state of affairs in the Empire. The man who played an important role in this development is Martin Mair (1400?-1481), a close friend of Gregor Heimburg.

It was the Turkish threat to Christendom and the fall of Constantinople in 1453 which in 1454 resulted in a series of imperial reform proposals. Even Martin Mair, who once worked for the Emperor, was affected by the Emperor's passivity. "It was the lethargy and reserve that Fredrich showed in 1454 at the Regensburg Congress of Princes . . . which, it seems, turned Mair against the Emperor."[43] The utter failure of the Diet of Regensburg in 1454 to reach any decision to organize a crusade against the Turks and especially the Emperor's inability to provide leadership in the whole affair drove many to the reform party. The decade 1454-1464 was filled with schemes and plots. The reform party had begun at a fairly early time to think of other princes or of its members as candidates to replace Emperor Friedrich III. It was suggested that while the Emperor might remain Emperor, his son or some other person of strong character, such as the Duke of Burgundy or Duke Albrecht VI of Austria, could be elected as a King of the Romans without going through the embarrassment of deposing the Emperor. Many were involved in this movement after 1454. Archbishop Jakob von Sirk of Trier (1439-1456), supported by his advisor Dr. Johannes von Lysura (d. 1459),[44] was the moving spirit of the reform party until his death. In addition to Gregor Heimburg, whose antagonism towards the Emperor grew unmistakably from 1453, Martin Mair emerged as one of the most ardent advocates of the idea of imperial reform in the mid-fifteenth century.

---

[43] Heymann, *George,* p. 200.

[44] On Johannes von Lysura, see F.X. Kraus, "Johann von Lieser," in *Allgemeine Deutsche Biographie*, 14 (1881), p. 466; Franz Falk, "Zur Biographie des Johannes von Lysura," *Der Katholik,* 76/II (1896): 437-54; Helmut Weigel, "Kaiser, Kurfürst und Jurist: Friedrich III., Erzbischof Jakob von Trier und Dr. Johannes von Lysura im Vorspiel zum Regensburger Reichstag vom April 1454," in *Aus Reichstagen des 15. und 16. Jahrhundert* (Göttingen, 1958), pp. 80-115.

We know little about Mair's youth.[45] Born in Wimpfen, Franconia, he matriculated at the University of Heidelberg on December 20, 1438, receiving the *baccalareus artium* on July 31, 1443, and the *decretorum licentiatus* on December 17, 1448. After serving as consultant to the city of Schwäbisch Hall in 1448, he became city scribe on February 3, 1449, for the city of Nürnberg. His services to the city continued, as the record shows, until 1479. Mair became an admiring pupil of Heimburg when Mair joined a circle of humanists founded by Heimburg in Nürnberg.

Although his attempt in 1452 to obtain the doctorate from Heidelberg failed, Mair was able to become advisor to Archbishop Jakob von Sirk of Trier in 1454 and Chancellor of Dietrich von Erbach, Archbishop of Mainz (1434-1459), on February 1, 1455. His leanings towards the reform party were by then unmistakable. On July 9, 1459, his close and long relation with Duke Ludwig the Rich of Landshut as advisor and servant began. In this manner Mair gradually strengthened his ties with important members of the reform party. Later in 1459 he became advisor to King George of Bohemia and was able to obtain a licentiate in imperial law from Heidelberg.[46] It was in this year, as we have seen, that the Congress of Mantua opened and the Mainz *Stiftsfehde* began.

If Heimburg's main concern was with the limitation of papal encroachments on the freedom of the Empire, Doctor Martein, as Mair was sometimes called,[47] distinguished himself by the zeal with which he pursued the ideal of imperial reform. As experienced statesman and skilled diplomat, he engaged himself in constant and numerous negotiations with prelates, princes, and other estates of the Empire. From 1454 onward he was on the side of the anti-imperial, reform party, but we find him actually working for Emperor Friedrich

---

[45] There is no adequate study of the life of Martin Mair. See Constantin Höfler, *Über die politische Reformbewegung in Deutschland im XV. Jahrhundert und den Antheil Bayerns an derselben* (München, 1850); Gustav Freiherr von Hasselholdt-Stockheim, *Herzog Albrecht IV. von Bayern und seine Zeit: Archivalischer Beitrag zur deutschen Rechtsgeschichte in der zweiten Hälfte des 15. Jahrhunderts,* I,1 (1459-1465) (Leipzig, 1865), pp. 317-32; Sigmund Riezler, "Martin Mair," in *Allgemeine Deutsche Biographie,* 20 (1884), pp. 113-20; Georg Schrötter, *Dr. Martin Mair: Ein biographischer Beitrag zur Geschichte der politischen und kirchlichen Reformfrage des 15. Jahrhundert* (Diss., München, 1896); Heinz Hürten, "Martin Mair," in *Lexikon für Theologie und Kirche,* 2d ed., VII (1962), col. 117.

[46] Lieberich, "Die gelehrten Räte," p. 176.

[47] Although Mair received his doctorate only in 1465 from the University of Heidelberg, he was apparently addressed before 1465 not only as "Maister Martein Mair," "Meister Martein Mayr," or "Martin Mair, kaiserlichen rechten licentiat," but also as "Dr. Martin Mayr," "doctor dominus Martinus Meyer," or "Doctor utriusque iuris Martinus Mair." Cf. Schrötter, *Dr. Martin Mair,* p. 10 n. 19.

III after 1467.[48] It was the question of whether King George of Bohemia could be elevated to the dignity of a King of the Romans that complicated Mair's efforts to reform the Empire.

King George ascended the throne in March 1458, and the first Congress of Eger was opened in April 1459. It was probably at the Congress that Mair disclosed his comprehensive imperial reform program to King George,[49] who had emerged as the foremost prince in the college of electors. Not only the temporal princes of the reform party, but also the Archbishops of Mainz and Trier wished to recognize and take up friendly relations with the new king. Mair's reform project stipulated that when the King of Bohemia was elected as a King of the Romans by the electors of the Empire, he would be obliged to fulfill the following five requirements:[50] first, establish an ordinary court in order to maintain perpetual peace; second, raise a Christian army against the Turks; third, prohibit the Pope from imposing taxes or calling a council in the Empire without the approval or knowledge of the electors; fourth, confirm and re-enforce the decrees of the Council of Basel, which had been accepted by Germany; and finally, call a parliament of princes in Mainz. Mair exerted great pressure on the sceptical and reluctant George, who was seriously concerned about maintaining good relations with the Emperor, to convince him that the Emperor was by no means disinclined to such an arrangement. He attempted skillfully to use the widespread feeling against the Emperor to promote his project. Fortunately for Mair, the old struggle between the Wittelsbachs and the Hohenzollerns came to a

[48] In 1466 Mair sent a letter of warning to Heimburg against working for the heretical King George. See Riezler, "Mair," p. 117; Joachimsohn, *Heimburg*, p. 262; Heymann, *George*, pp. 418-19. The letter is printed in Joachimsohn, *Heimburg*, pp. 318-24.

[49] Hasselholdt-Stockheim, *Herzog Albrecht IV.*, p. 115; Adolf Bachmann, *Böhmen und seine Nachbarländer unter Georg von Podiebrad (1458-1461) und des Königs Bewegung um die deutsche Krone* (Prag, 1878), pp. 58-59, 65-66; Adolf Bachmann, *Geschichte Böhmens*, II (Gotha, 1905), p. 497; Gallas, *Herzog Ludwig*, p. 89; Heymann, *George*, pp. 201-2; Otakar Odlozilik, *The Hussite King: Bohemia in European Affairs, 1440-1471* (New Brunswick, 1965), pp. 100-102. About the Congresses of Eger, see Karl Siegl, *Eger und das Egerland im Wandel der Zeiten* (Eger, 1931); Heymann, *George*, pp. 189-94.

[50] The "Rathschlag doctor Martin Maier's den konig zw Beheim einem Romischen konig zu machen (1460*)" is printed in Constantin Höfler, *Das kaiserliche Buch des Markgrafen Albrecht Achilles: Vorkurfürstliche Periode 1440-1470* (Bayreuth, 1850), pp. 50-51. See also Franz Palacky, *Urkundliche Beiträge zur Geschichte Böhmens und seiner Nachbarländer im Zeitalter Georg's von Podiebrad 1450-1471* (Fortes Rerum Austriacarum II. Abt., Bd. 20; Wien, 1860), pp. 313-19; Hasselholdt Stockheim, *Herzog Albrecht IV.*, I,1, pp. 119-21, 272-73. Cf. Menzel, *Diether*, pp. 97- 102; Bachmann, *Böhmen*, pp. 258-68; Joachimsohn, *Heimburg*, p. 129; Pastor, *History*, III, p. 176; Heymann, *George*, p. 224; Scheerer, *Mainz*, pp. 38-39.

head when Duke Ludwig of Landshut declared war on Margrave Albrecht Achilles in March 1460. When a sharp conflict between the two veteran warriors resulted in the defeat of Albrecht Achilles, it became clear to King George that he should be closer to the Wittelsbachs than to the Hohenzollerns. Only through the help of the reformist Wittelsbachs could he think of effecting any imperial reform.

By October 1460, King George was convinced of the feasibility of Mair's reform plan. The Emperor, in turn, became increasingly opposed to the King. George's attitudes towards Albrecht Achilles naturally hardened.[51] The first and only prince who accepted this reform plan with enthusiasm was Duke Ludwig of Landshut, who had also been advised by Mair from December 21, 1459. Mair accompanied Duke Ludwig on a visit to Prague in the autumn of 1460 and helped George and Ludwig form a firm alliance on October 8, 1460.[52] As a result, Duke Ludwig decided to work hard to win over all the electoral princes, especially the Archbishops of Mainz and Köln and his cousins, Duke Friedrich the Victorious of the Palatinate, to King George's party. The reformer Mair's efforts were bearing fruit. At the well-attended third Congress of Eger in February 1461, Mair established contact with Heimburg, who was acting as an observer for Duke Sigismund of the Tyrol. Heimburg gained a promise of support for Duke Sigismund from King George. The Bohemian king himself, in turn, seems to have gained the support of several of the leading German princes at the Congress. But Elector Dietrich II of Brandenburg, speaking for the imperial party, pointed out that Eger was not the place for an imperial election, and in view of his opposition the debate ended.[53]

Clearly not all the members of the Congress were in favor of Mair's project. Some princes were secretly reluctant to give such a high honor to the Bohemian king, whose religious views were not acceptable to the Papacy. Heimburg also showed less interest in Mair's project than in combatting papal claims on the Empire. As a result, no formal vote was taken on either Mair's project or on the other issues that had come up at the Congress. Thus the results of the third Congress of Eger were meager.

In the Diet of Nürnberg in February 1461, which soon followed the third Congress of Eger, no attention was given to Mair's plans partly because of King George's absence from the assembly, although his delegates were present in order not to lose contact with his allies. King George had cooperated with Mair for close to two years, but realizing that little good would come of continued

---

[51] Achilles's daughter Ursula had married George's son Heinrich in September 1460. Cf. Siegl, *Eger,* p. 204; Heymann, *George,* p. 193; Odlozilik, *The Hussite King,* p. 114.

[52] Palacky, *Urkundliche,* pp. 232-33. Ludwig and George had begun to conclude agreements already in October 1459.

[53] Heymann, *George,* p. 225.

campaigning for his elevation to a King of the Romans, he gradually began to dissociate himself from Mair. No doubt his pursuit of the Roman kingship had contributed to the deterioration of his relations with the Pope and the Emperor. But one of the most important reasons for the failure of Mair's project was the growing opposition, not of the Emperor himself, but of certain princes of the Empire.

As we have seen, Archbishop Diether of Mainz strongly attacked the Papacy in the same assembly of Nürnberg in 1461 under the guidance of Gregor Heimburg. After his defeat at Pfeddersheim on July 4, 1460, by Duke Friedrich the Victorious, Diether was forced to enter into alliance with the reform party, and became by February 1461 a champion and symbol of the general opposition of the German princes to the influence of the Papacy in Germany. He was no doubt more against Pope than Emperor. But he and Friedrich the Victorious allied themselves on December 3, 1460, to assist King George. Thus was established a coalition of princes against Pope and Emperor. The question whether this common front could ever present a platform from which King George could realize his hopes for the Roman kingship.[54] Dr. Mair, King George's advisor from 1459, was naturally convinced that it could. That is the reason why he negotiated so hard with the Archbishop of Mainz.

The decision to call a parliament and a general council in Frankfort on May 31, 1461, was reached in order to further not only Diether's struggle with Pope Pius II, but also King George's chances for a powerful position as a King of the Romans.[55] Heimburg had become George's advisor in 1460, and there is little doubt that Heimburg and Mair, two former members of a humanist group in Nürnberg, worked together in support of the electors and the Bohemian king.[56] Had their joint work been successful, the imperial reform program drawn

---

[54] Pastor, *History,* III, p. 176, Heymann, *George,* p. 222.

[55] Pastor, *History,* III, pp. 195-97.

[56] Many letters and documents written by Heimburg and Mair in the chancellery of King George have been preserved in two manuscripts (MS XXIII D163 and MS XXIII D172) of the Manuscript Division, National (University) Library (Rukopisy, Státní knihovna), Prague. On these manuscripts, see Constantin Höfler, "Streiflichter auf die böhmische Geschichte," *Archiv für österreichische Geschichtsquellen,* 12 (1854): 320; Palacky, *Urkundliche,* p. xi; Hermann Markgraf, "Die 'Kanzlei' des Königs Georg von Böhmen," *Neues Lausitzische Magazin,* 47 (1870): 214-38, especially p. 216; Joachimsohn, *Heimburg,* pp. 193, 279-81; Rudolf Urbánek, "'Kancelár' krále Jiriho," *Cesky casopis historiky,* 17 (1911): 13-27 [also in *Z husitskeho véku: Vybor historickych úvah a studii* (Prague, 1957) pp. 216-29]; Emma Urbánková, *Rukopisy a vzácné tisky Prazské Universitni Knihovny* (Prague, 1957), p. 42; Odlozilik, *The Hussite King,* p. 314. For the letters of Heimburg and Mair, see, for example, MS XXIII D163 ff. 123-123ᵛ, 127ᵛ-128ᵛ, 169-170ᵛ, 217ᵛ-218ᵛ, 218ᵛ-219ᵛ, 219ᵛ-220ᵛ, 266ᵛ-268ᵛ, 287-287ᵛ, 323ᵛ-324, 341ᵛ-342, 343ᵛ.

up by Mair in 1459 and pursued by King George would have brought about considerable changes within the Empire. Yet the desired common front was never established largely because of the intricate relationship which developed between the Utraquist King George and Archbishop Diether.

It became increasingly necessary for Diether, who was deeply involved in the Mainz *Stiftsfehde* at that time, to demand further proofs of the King's orthodoxy, such as his taking, in public, the communion in one kind. "The more acrimonious the struggle between archbishop and pope became, the more the Archbishop of Mainz had to show that as the leader of a resistance movement against the Curia in the field of imperial and church policy, his orthodoxy was above suspicion."[57] He could no longer be identified with a man suspected of heresy. King George, on the other hand, began to take a more conciliatory position towards the Curia as it became increasingly clear that Mair's reform project was not enthusiastically supported by many German princes. Conflict of interests between Diether and George began to show. King George carefully tried to avoid being associated with Diether and his supporters who criticized the Curia. The failure of the Congress of Eger and of the Diet of Nürnberg in February 1461 to take any action on Mair's project clearly showed George the magnitude of the obstacle separating him from the Roman kingship. Thus by the spring of 1461, King George had reached another turning point in his political career.

Although their friendship was not fully restored, George even began to turn to Emperor Friedrich III for help in 1461.[58] When called upon by the reform party to appear in person before another Diet which was scheduled to meet at Frankfurt on May 22, 1461 the Emperor felt strong enough not to comply with the demand and asked other estates not to attend it. In the end, as we have seen, he was able to forbid the assembly. This did not mean the end of George's influence within the Empire. The influence which he could still exert and the esteem in which he was held were demonstrated when his military and diplomatic intervention compelled the quarreling German princes to make a truce in Prague on December 16, 1461.[59] But his hopes for the Roman kingship were, practically speaking, gone.

In March 1462, Pope Pius II declared to a Czech mission headed by Prokop of Rabstein, King George's Chancellor, and Zdenek Koska of Postupice that he could not accept the obedience of King George until the King eradicated all error from his kingdom, that he forbade the common people to receive

---

[57] Heymann, *George,* p. 223.

[58] See Queen Eleonora's letter of 5 Oct. 1461, to King George in Palacky, *Urkundliche,* p. 251.

[59] Palacky, *Urkundliche,* p. 261; Heymann, *George,* p. 255.

communion in both kinds, and that he revoked the *Compactata* of Prague (1436). In reply King George answered during the great Diet of Prague on August I2, 1462, that he and his family would stake not only their worldly possessions but also their lives for the Chalice.[60] The failure of the Czech mission to Rome in March 1462 to obtain papal recognition of the Compactata and the events during the Diet of Prague clearly marked a turning point in King George's position in European politics. The Pope, who had been first a friendly and then a conditional supporter of George, now became distinctly hostile.[61]

The intensification of the conflict between the Pope and King George after 1462 and the resultant change in the domestic and foreign policy of the King gave birth to a bold plan to establish a universal peace organization which was to ensure the peaceful settlement of conflicts among the states.[62] On August 8, 1461, Antonius Marini of Grenoble, a French master engineer with a wide background, who was in the service of King George from about 1460, had proposed in a letter to the King an alliance of the major Christian powers under the command of the Czech king in order to attack the Turks and to recapture Constantinople. As a result of King George's deteriorating position vis-a-vis the Papacy, Marini's original plan was apparently expanded in the autumn months of 1462 to become a much broader and more grandiose scheme. The new plan to establish a universal peace organization initially in Basel, in which King George was to play a leading role, was drawn up officially in 1463 in the form of a diplomatic instrument entitled *Tractatus pacis toti christianitati fiendae*. It is believed that the authors included not only Marini, but also King George's other advisors, especially Dr. Martin Mair.[63]

---

[60] Creighton, History, III, p. 291; Heymann, *George,* pp. 283-84; Odlozilik, *The Hussite King,* pp. 137-38.

[61] Creighton, *History,* III, pp. 290-92, Heymann, *George,* p. 293.

[62] On the proposal, see Hermann Markgraf, "Über Georgs von Podiebrad Project eines christlichen Furstenbundes," *Historische Zeitschrift,* 21 (1869): 254-304, Hans Pfefermann, *Die Zusammenarbeit der Renaissancepäpste mit den Türken* (Winterthur, 1946), pp. 64-76; Václav Vanecek, "Eine Weltfriedensorganisation nach den Vorschlägen Georgs von Podiebrad und des J.A. Comenius," *Sitzungsberichte der Akademie der Wissensch. zu Berlin,* Klasse für Philosophie, 1962, No. 3 (Berlin, 1963); Václav Vanecek, ed. *The Universal Peace Organization of King George of Bohemia. A Fifteenth-Century Plan for World Peace 1462/1464* (Prague, 1964); Heymann, *George,* pp. 299-315; Václav Vanecek, ed. *Cultus Pacis: Etudes et Documents du "Symposium Pragense Cultus Pacis 1464-1964"* (Prague, 1966).

[63] Vanecek, *The Universal Peace,* pp. 36, 38, 41-42, 44, 64; Heymann, *George,* pp. 300-301, 310; Frantisek Smahel, "The Idea of the Nation in Hussite Bohemia," *Historica,* 17 (1969): 187. The *Tractatus pacis toti christianitati fiendae* has been edited and published by J. Kejr in Vanecek, *The Universal Peace,* pp. 69-78.

The principal purpose of King George's new plan is expressed in the words *cultus pacis,* a cult of peace. In aiming at this high goal, the plan abandoned the idea of a universal medieval empire headed by Emperor and Pope. According to it, the basic units of international relations were independent member states. Members of the plan were to settle all disputes among themselves through an international court of justice, called *parlamentum seu consistorium.* It is notable that the authors wanted not only to exclude the Emperor completely but also to reduce the Pope's influence on the organization drastically. Although mentioned in connection with its finances, the Pope was not expected to become a member of the organization. The authors were also so sensitive to the bull *Execrabilis,* so that a general council was not mentioned. As head of this organization, the authors designated the French king, with whom the Bohemian king wanted to maintain close relations. It is clear that the real purpose of the plan was to answer in a positive way the attack of the Curia against King George. The essentially anti-papal nature of this plan is unmistakable.

Nowhere in Europe was there more criticism of *Execrabilis* than in France, where King Charles VII had adopted the Pragmatic Sanction of Bourges in 1438. As a result, there was in France a great deal of sympathy for the German opposition to the papal power and for the conciliar theory. Although we have insufficient records, we know, as indicated above, that shortly after the failure of the assembly of Mainz in 1461, Heimburg went to France to see King Charles about the possibility of opening a general council against Rome.[64] When Charles VII died on July 22, 1461, his successor Louis XI (1461-1483), because of his deep hatred of his father, rejected his father's policies and initiated negotiations with Pope Pius II, which resulted in the revocation of the Pragmatic Sanction on November 27, 1461. Louis, however, soon became disenchanted with the Pope's policy toward the throne of the kingdom of Naples. Pius II stubbornly supported Alfonso's illegitimate son Ferrante, thereby refusing to recognize Duke René or Duke Jean of Anjou, whom Louis preferred. As a result, the French king nullified the revocation in 1463 and 1464 by a series of royal decrees issued to "defend ourselves against the aggressions of Rome, and for the restoration of the ancient Gallican liberties."[65] Viewed in this light, it is easy to understand why King George made overtures to King Louis in order to bolster his position against the Pope. As in France, it was still popular

[64] Joachimsohn, *Heimburg,* pp. 209, 212, 215; Pastor, *History,* III, pp. 133, 197; Heymann, *George,* pp. 415-16. See n. 41 above.

[65] Pastor, *History,* III, p. 156. See Creighton, *History,* III, pp. 304-5. A diary kept by a member of the 1464 Czech mission to France has been preserved as Jaroslaw, *Diary of an Embassy from King George of Bohemia to King Louis XI of France, in the Year 1464,* trans. A. H. Wratislaw (London, 1871).

in Bohemia to appeal to councils.[66] But Marini's negotiations in France and other countries from 1462 to 1464 to put this plan into effect proved to be in vain, mainly because even King Louis XI was unwilling to accept the essentially anti-papal plan in defiance of the strong opposition of the French prelates.

Curiously enough, Mair proposed in 1463, that is, while King George's peace plan was being developed and negotiated, another project to reform the Empire which also stressed the importance of the Czech king.[67] It is apparent, however, that for some reason the two plans were not well coordinated in detail. Mair's plan of 1463 envisaged a supreme council to include not only King George of Bohemia, Elector Friedrich the Victorious of the Palatinate, Duke Ludwig the Rich of Landshut, and Margrave Albrecht Achilles of Ansbach but also Emperor Friedrich III, who had no role to play in King George's peace plan. It also proposed a permanent salaried supreme court and an imperial tax. These last two proposals were quite ordinary ones that could be found in many previous reform proposals. It is notable that the five ecclesiastical and temporal electors who played an important role up to the middle of the fifteenth century were no longer mentioned as members of the supreme council. In place of them two powerful non-electoral princes were included. In drawing up a new imperial reform proposal, Mair's main concern was clearly how much power princes, whether electoral or non-electoral, could wield in the Empire.

It is obvious from what we have discussed that no study of the imperial reform movement of the fifteenth century and the role which Martin Mair and Gregor Heimburg played in it is adequate unless the relations of the two men are clarified and examined closely. Mair was primarily interested in the problem of imperial reform and devoted his energy to the elevation of King George to the position of a King of the Romans. Heimburg, on the other hand, was apparently more concerned with the growing interference of the Papacy in the Empire than with imperial reform and was deeply involved in the Mainz *Stiftsfehde* as well as with Duke Sigismund's struggle with Cardinal Cusanus. But any serious fifteenth-century reformer of the Empire had to deal with Emperor Friedrich III, who was not only a ruler reluctant to accept any reform projects which would weaken his position within the Empire but also a supporter of the Papacy. The problem of imperial reform simply could not be isolated from that of

[66] Josef Macek, "Le mouvement conciliaire, Louis XI et Georges de Podebrady (en particulier dans la periode 1466-1468)," *Historica*, 15 (Prague, 1968): 5-63; Josef Macek, "Der Konziliarismus in der böhmischen Reformation—besonders in der Politik Georgs von Podiebrad," *Zeitschrift für Kirchengeschichte*, 80 (1969): IV. Folge XVIII, 312-30.

[67] Palacky, *Urkundliche*, pp. 313-19; Molitor, *Die Reichsreformbestrebungen*, p 132; Gallas, *Herzog Ludwig*, p. 136; Scheerer, *Mainz*, pp. 40-41.

ecclesiastical reform. As we have seen, King George's pursuit of the Roman kingship was after all related to the problems arising out of the Mainz *Stiftsfehde*. The imperial reform projects of the mid-fifteenth century, which were mainly promoted by Martin Mair, necessarily assumed religious overtones and resulted in diets, congresses, assemblies and other activities among European princes, both ecclesiastical and temporal.

We must recognize in this connection an important role which lawyers played in the solution of many political and religious problems of the Empire in the mid-fifteenth century.[68] Because only canon law was taught at almost all German universities until the middle of the fifteenth century, many German students, especially from southern and southwestern cities, such as Nürnberg, Ulm, and Eichstätt, began to go to the universities of upper Italy in the thirteenth century to study Roman law, and their number increased rapidly after about 1450. These sons of the nobility, the city patriciate and, increasingly in the fifteenth century and thereafter, the urban bourgeoisie became chancellors, councillors, and advisors of the ecclesiastical and temporal princes or served as secretaries and advocates of large cities after their return to Germany. As a result of the penetration of professional, academic jurisprudence into Germany, Roman law also began to be taught in many German universities after the middle of the fifteenth century. By the end of the century, therefore, was well established in Germany a legal profession which was made up of lawyers who were academically trained either abroad or in German universities.[69]

---

[68] Much progress has been made in recent years in the studies of German lawyers of the late Middle Ages. The old works of Gustav C. Knod, Arnold Luschin von Ebengreuth, Theodor Muther, Emil Seckel, Roderich Stintzing, Otto Stobbe, and Adolf Stölzel are still useful, but they can be supplemented by some recent monographs such as Irmgard Kothe, *Der fürstliche Rat in Württemberg im 15. und 16. Jahrhundert* (Stuttgart, 1938); Franz Wiesacker, "Einfluss des Humanismus auf die Reception: Eine Studie zu Johannes Apels Dialogus," *Zeitschrift für die gesamte Staatswissenschaft,* 100 (1940): 423-56; Winfried Trusen, *Anfänge des gelehrten Rechts in Deutschland: Ein Beitrag zur Geschichte der Frührezeption* (Wiesbaden, 1962); Helmut Coing, "Römisches Recht in Deutschland," *Ius Romanum Medii Aevi,* V,6 (Milan, 1964); Erich Genzmer, "Kleriker als Berufsjuristen im späten Mittelalter," in *Etudes d'histoire du droit canonique dédiées à Gabriel Le Bras,* II (Paris, 1965): 1207-36; Paul Koschaker, *Europa und das römische Recht,* 4th ed. (München, 1966); Helmut Wachauf, *Nürnberger Bürger als Juristen* (Erlangen, 1972); Udo Künzel, *Die Schweinfurter Stadtschreiber und Ratsadvokaten von 1337 bis 1803* (Würzburg, 1974); Karl Heinz Burmeister, *Das Studium des Rechts im Zeitalter des Humanismus im deutschen Rechtsbereich* (Wiesbaden, 1974); Helmut Coing, *Epochen der Rechtsgeschichte in Deutschland,* 3d ed. (München, 1976).

[69] Coing, "Römisches Recht," pp. 13, 47, 54-57, 77-90; Wachauf, *Nürnberger,* p. 66, 69-71; Burmeister, *Das Studium,* pp. 7-13.

Gregor Heimburg, a graduate of the University of Padua, and Martin Mair, a graduate of the University of Heidelberg, were two of the most famous members of the legal profession in fifteenth-century Germany. According to one historian, they belong to "that strange and interesting group of international lawyers who, for a good salary, were willing to serve anyone who might want to employ them, whether Emperor or prince, bishop or city."[70] Dr. Johannes von Lysura, who advised Archbishop Jakob van Sirk of Trier; Dr. Peter Knorr, advisor to Margrave Albrecht Achilles; Dr. Rudolf von Rüdesheim, Pope Pius II's trusted and effective "troubleshooter"; and Dr. Heinrich Leubing (d. 1472),[71] who served, among others, the Archbishop of Mainz, the city of Nürnberg, and Duke Ludwig the Rich of Landshut, were, to name some examples, all lawyers whose activities resembled those of Dr. Heimburg and Dr. Mair. It has been said of Renaissance Florence: "Wherever we look in Florentine public affairs, we find lawyers at work: in diplomacy, in relations with the Republic, in territorial government, in the formation of policy, administration and adjudication, and in the political struggle proper."[72] Studies of fifteenth-century German lawyers who engaged in similar activities have increased in number. But more studies of not only Italian, French, and English lawyers but also their German counterparts are needed if we are to understand the role of the legal profession in early modern Europe.[73]

The fundamental reason for the failure of the imperial reform projects of the mid-fifteenth century was that in an age of the rapid growth of influence of temporal, territorial principalities within the Empire, their interests ran counter to the interests of those ecclesiastical princes who had previously been dominant, such as the archbishops of Mainz, Köln and Trier. In place of the three ecclesiastical elector-princes of the west, temporal princes of the east were exerting greater influence than before. As stated above, some of these rising princes were not even electors of the Empire, but merely territorial princes.[74]

---

[70] Heymann, *George,* p. 199.

[71] On Heinrich Leubing, see Georg A. Will, *Nürnbergisches Gelehrten-Lexicon,* II (Nürnberg, 1756), p. 432; Wilhelm Loose, "Heinrich Leubing; Eine Studie zur Geschichte des fünfzehnten Jahrhundert," *Mitteilungen des Vereins für Geschichte der Stadt Meissen,* I,2 (1883): 34-71; Joachimsohn, *Heimburg,* pp. 79, 108, 129, 195, 251; Arnold Reimann, *Die ältere Pirkheimer* (Leipzig, 1944), pp. 64, 67, 74, 97; Lieberich, "Die gelehrten Räte," pp. 131, 173-74.

[72] Lauro Martines, *Lawyers and Statecraft in Renaissance Florence* (Princeton, 1968), p. 3.

[73] Cf. William J. Bouwsma, "Lawyers in Early Modern Culture," *American Historical Review,* 78 (1973): 303-27.

[74] Baron, "Imperial Reform," pp. 294-95; Offler, "Aspects," pp. 220-21.

The Empire as a whole was at that time little more than a fragmented confederation of hundreds of principalities and autonomous cities. In addition, the traditional notion of a Christian commonwealth (*respublica Christiana*) under Pope and Emperor was becoming very weak. To be sure, religious factors and motives still played a considerable part in European politics. The Hussite King George's hopes for high position were dashed, not by the Emperor himself, but by some powerful temporal electors and princes who were extremely reluctant to range themselves on the side of a king of distinctly Czech origin with doubtful religious credentials. Even King Louis XI of France, who permitted his advisors to commit him to an alliance of friendship with King George in 1464, was unwilling to accept and head an essentially anti-papal peace organization proposed by the Hussite king. But there was no doubt that a process of decomposition of the medieval Christian Empire into territorial states was well under way. Indeed, the Emperor had become by that time "nothing more than one sovereign among many."[75] The inclusion of the Emperor in Mair's imperial reform program of 1463 probably testifies to the fact that Mair recognized the strength of Friedrich III not necessarily as Emperor, but as spokesman of the rising Habsburg power in the east.

In discussing the late Middle Ages in Germany, Heinrich Heimpel, the distinguished medievalist, called it "a period of indeterminateness between the old and the new." "It is," according to him, "precisely this interdetermination, this vacillation between the old and the new, which distinguished the late Middle Ages in Germany."[76] The imperial reform movement of the mid-fifteenth century demonstrated clearly that an age of universal imperial power was almost over, that the rise of territorial states within the Empire was an irreversible development, and that the center of the weakened Empire was shifting from the west to the east. Thus there was no major imperial reform project again until 1486, when Berthold von Henneberg, another Archbishop of Mainz (1484-1504), began serious attempts to reorganize the Empire.[77] It was to be the last major

---

[75] Herman Heimpel, "Characteristics of the Late Middle Ages in Germany," in *Pre-Reformation Germany,* ed. Gerald Strauss (London, 1972), p. 55.

[76] Heimpel, "Characteristics," p. 58. See also pp. 62, 69, 70.

[77] On Berthold von Henneberg and his reform projects, see J.B. Weiss, *Berthold von Henneberg Erzbischof von Mainz (1484-1504): Seine kirchenpolitische und kirchliche Stellung* (Freiburg i.B., 1889); R. Schröder, "Kurmainz unter den Erzbischofen Berthold von Henneberg und Albrecht von Brandenburg als Mittelpunkt der Reichsreformbestrebungen," *ZRGGA,* 18 (1897): 179-82; Karl Bauermeister, "Berthold von Henneberg, Kurfürst und Erzbischof von Mainz (1484-1504)," *Historisches Jahrbuch,* 39 (1918/1919): 731-40; Fritz Hartung, "Berthold von Henneberg, Kurfürst von Mainz," in *Volk und Staat in der deutschen Geschichte* (Leipzig, 1940), pp. 48-66; Fritz Hartung, "Imperial Reform, 1485-1495: Its Course and Its Character," in *Pre-Reformation Germany,* ed. G. Strauss, pp. 73-135.

imperial reform originated in the districts along the Rhine, the old center of German civilization. But mainly because of the opposition of Maximilian I (1493-1519), son of Friedrich III, and of other princes the reform failed. Indeed, it was the ruling princes of the Empire who put an end to the Middle Ages and brought on the modern era.

The author wishes to thank the American Philosophical Society for its support of his research in Europe.

Works of Nicholas of Cusa Cited

Subject Index